"There are many beginning Greek grammars and some few reference grammars, but there are not that many works which help students in the transition from learning paradigms and elementary Greek syntax to reading the Greek of the New Testament. *Going Deeper with New Testament Greek*, authored by three experienced Greek scholars, is such a transitional book that combines intermediate syntax discussion with selected readings in the New Testament. The readings are followed by detailed notes on the grammar, translation, and interpretation of each verse in the selection that will be of immense help to students and will also provide valuable review for pastors and others who want to refresh their knowledge of Greek. This text is a welcome addition to any Greek student's library."

S. M. Baugh, professor of New Testament, Westminster Seminary California

"My college switched to using *Going Deeper with New Testament Greek* for all of our upper-level Greek exegesis courses, and we've never looked back. It is a terrific intermediate grammar for students, fully up on the latest discussions about verbal aspect, perfect tense, and deponency, and yet eminently readable."

Michael F. Bird, academic dean and lecturer in theology, Ridley College, Melbourne, Australia

"Designed for a normal semester, filled with clear examples and helpful readings, *Going Deeper with New Testament Greek* is a classroom-friendly, clear intermediate Greek grammar for those who want to deepen their Greek and their understanding of the New Testament in its original language. So this is a worthy book for worthy but often difficult-to-reach goals."

Darrell L. Bock, senior research professor of New Testament studies and executive director of cultural engagement, Dallas Theological Seminary

"*Going Deeper with New Testament Greek* is certain to become a standard among intermediate Greek grammars. Not only is this grammar readable and grounded in exegesis, but it includes a number of features not normally seen in this category, such as a built-in Greek reader, vocabulary lists, exercises, summary tables, and guides for discourse analysis, textual criticism, and word studies. Informed by the latest research on topics such as verbal aspect and the middle voice, the grammar also incorporates the best of traditional grammatical approaches. *Going Deeper* is up to date, built for the classroom, and aimed at careful exegesis of the Greek New Testament. While I differ on some points, it is my first choice for the classroom."

Constantine R. Campbell, senior vice president of global content and Bible teaching, Our Daily Bread Ministries

"*Going Deeper with New Testament Greek* is the best intermediate Greek textbook I have ever used in more than twenty-five years of teaching Greek, primarily because it was written by and designed for those of us who labor in the classroom. *GDNTG* includes a multitude of resources for teachers and students alike. You will find a well-designed vocabulary section so you won't need to assign a separate vocabulary book. Along with clear and linguistically informed explanations of Greek syntax, the grammar offers plenty of biblical examples and summary charts for material covered in each chapter, along with helpful practice exercises to reinforce the explanations. The textbook also features a built-in Greek reader with selected NT texts for students to translate and reader's notes to guide in interpretation. Unlike many Greek grammars, *GDNTG* is student friendly and thoroughly readable in addition to being nicely formatted. On top of all that, it also comes with plenty of support resources and helps for teachers such as chapter quizzes and answer keys. I strongly recommend it as a one-stop resource for teaching intermediate New Testament Greek."

J. Scott Duvall, professor of New Testament and J. C. and Mae Fuller Chair of Biblical Studies, Ouachita Baptist University

"This well-designed book is highly recommended! It provides a number of unique features not normally included in intermediate Greek grammars (e.g., vocabulary lists, summary charts for each area of syntax, practice sentences that focus on the points covered in each chapter, passages for reading from different portions of the NT, a segment on NT textual criticism). These make the book eminently useful as a textbook for second-year Greek classes in colleges and seminaries. The authors have produced an inviting and highly accessible volume that clearly and accurately sets forth what is needed for students to move from elements of Greek into exegetical study of the NT itself."

Buist M. Fanning, adjunct professor in New Testament studies, Dallas Theological Seminary

"In *Going Deeper with New Testament Greek*, Köstenberger, Merkle, and Plummer have produced a robust, fully integrated, 'teacher's' intermediate grammar. Clearly flowing from years of classroom experience, the book weaves together substantive, up-to-date introductions on Greek syntax, a celebration of the benefits of learning particular aspects of Greek grammar, examples from the New Testament, a variety of active-learning exercises, a built-in reader, and vocabulary. The pedagogical instincts and 'for-the-church' orientation mark the volume as very much in the spirit of the great Greek grammarian A. T. Robertson, to whom the authors offer a tribute. Highly recommended!"

George H. Guthrie, professor of New Testament, Regent College

"Here is a superlative opportunity to sharpen skills for mining gold in the Greek New Testament. The book is a brilliantly conceived, innovative, and authoritative introduction to more advanced New Testament exegesis. Its charts alone are worth the price of the book."

Murray J. Harris, professor emeritus of New Testament exegesis and theology, Trinity Evangelical Divinity School

"After using the same intermediate Greek textbook for more than a decade, making the change to a new textbook was daunting, but I am ecstatic that I did. This textbook is comprehensive in its scope and appropriately thorough in its discussion of each grammatical topic. The vocabulary lists, individual translation exercises, and the built-in reader, which allows the students to use the grammatical tools they have learned to exegete a passage alongside of the textbook's authors, are unique elements that both my students and I enjoyed. As a teacher, I especially appreciated how these master teachers translated their classroom manner, care for students, and passion for the proper interpretation of the

Greek New Testament into a textbook. I give *Going Deeper with New Testament Greek* my highest recommendation!"

Donny R. Mathis II, professor of Christian studies, North Greenville University

"*Going Deeper* provides the teacher and student an intermediate grammar designed for their specific needs. While it can function as a reference grammar, it works best as a book to be read from cover to cover. Its many unique features such as the narrative introductions, vocabulary lists, and biblical texts for reading encourage the student not only to learn but to apply what they have read. I am particularly grateful to see the final chapters on sentence structures, grammatical diagramming, and discourse analysis. When you add in its substantive interaction with Wallace's grammar, it makes *Going Deeper* an excellent intermediate grammar."

William Mounce, president, BiblicalTraining.org

"This grammar's level of detail falls somewhere between Dan Wallace's lengthy grammar (1996) and his abridgment (2000). That is a happy medium for Greek professors who teach intermediate Greek in just one semester. It is student friendly, and it is up to date on Greek verbal aspect and argument diagrams. Highly recommended!"

Andrew David Naselli, associate professor of systematic theology and New Testament, Bethlehem College and Seminary

"*Going Deeper with New Testament Greek* offers an up-to-date option for advancing beyond elementary Greek, taking into account recent developments in Greek voice and the tense/aspect debates. This work differs from most intermediate grammars in that it is designed to be taught through, not just assigned as reading. Each chapter features exercises, vocabulary, graded readings with notes, and much more, making it ideal for second-year courses or for those studying independently."

Steven E. Runge, scholar-in-residence, Logos Bible Software

"Every once in a while you find a book that fills a void. I was fortunate enough to receive an advanced look at this book right before I taught my first intermediate Greek course. Before I saw it, I had surveyed many resources looking for a textbook that combined all the things I wanted to speak about. Unfortunately, I had relegated myself to picking one and then filling in the holes with various articles and supplementary books. But when I received *Going Deeper with New Testament Greek*, I saw that they had accomplished what I had been hoping for. The book was readable, student friendly, and not a reference work. It included practical examples, vocabulary, practice exercises, translation passages, and teacher tools. Most importantly it covers the topics of verbal aspect, text criticism, discourse analysis, word studies, and diagramming on top of the normal Greek function topics. The authors have done the academy and the church a great service, and I highly recommend this textbook. Students will be better at Greek because of it."

Patrick Schreiner, assistant professor of New Testament language and literature, Western Seminary

"In recent years there has been an explosion in the study of Greek syntax, but it is difficult for new students to know the terrain. Köstenberger, Merkle, and Plummer have written a wonderfully clear text that I think will become a standard in the field. The book is a 'one-stop shop' so that everything students need to know in a second-year Greek course is contained here. It seems strange to say that a Greek grammar is a delight to read, but if that can ever be said about a grammar, it applies to this book! Professors and students will profit remarkably from this outstanding work."

Thomas R. Schreiner, James Buchanan Harrison Professor of New Testament Interpretation, professor of biblical theology, and associate dean of the school of theology, The Southern Baptist Theological Seminary

"This remarkable book by Köstenberger, Merkle, and Plummer sets a new standard for intermediate Greek instruction. Each chapter includes clear objectives and summaries, as well as useful illustrations, practice exercises, vocabulary lists, and annotated Greek reading assignments. The authors reflect cutting-edge scholarship on verbal aspect and other matters, and they introduce important topics not typically covered in other Greek textbooks such as textual criticism, lexicography, syntactical and discourse analysis, and continuing with Greek study beyond the classroom. I warmly recommend *Going Deeper with New Testament Greek* as an excellent textbook for students, instructors, and anyone who desires to go deeper with New Testament Greek."

Brian J. Tabb, academic dean and associate professor of biblical studies, Bethlehem College & Seminary, and general editor, *Themelios*

"Professors know the difference between a reference grammar and a teaching grammar. After using a couple of reference grammars in an advanced Greek course, I switched to *Going Deeper* and have been delighted with both its coverage and its pedagogical value. The exercises are superb and students have the opportunity to practice what they are learning in each new chapter. The authors are abreast of linguistic advances in Greek and explain these clearly. The textbook is so clear that I also have used it with success in an online course where I do not have the opportunity to personally explain every nuance. This book already does it well!"

William C. Varner, professor of Greek and Bible, The Master's University

"This volume is a game-changer. Many students take a first-year course in New Testament Greek. But then what? Second-year books are few and vary in quality. Reference grammars are too technical or lengthy for most beginners to use profitably. Enter *Going Deeper*: a thorough but not-too-technical intermediate grammar. With clear organization, wide-ranging coverage, and up-to-date grasp of unfolding discussion in areas like verbal aspect, this volume will be in high demand as a go-to resource for those moving from beginning Greek to the next levels of reading, exegesis, and interpretation. It will, and should, find widespread classroom use."

Robert W. Yarbrough, professor of New Testament, Covenant Theological Seminary

GOING

DEEPER

////////////////////////

WITH NEW
TESTAMENT

GREEK

GOING
DEEPER
WITH NEW TESTAMENT
GREEK

An **Intermediate** Study of the Grammar
and Syntax of the New Testament

Andreas J. **Köstenberger**, Benjamin L. **Merkle**, and Robert L. **Plummer**

B&H
ACADEMIC
NASHVILLE, TENNESSEE

Going Deeper with New Testament Greek, Revised Edition

Copyright © 2020 Andreas J. Köstenberger, Benjamin L. Merkle, and Robert L. Plummer

B&H Academic
Nashville, Tennessee
All rights reserved

ISBN: 978-1-5359-8320-4

Dewey Decimal Classification: 220.6
Subject Heading: BIBLE—CRITICISM \ BIBLE. NEW TESTAMENT \
GREEK LANGUAGE—GRAMMAR

The Greek font used in this work is SymbolGreekTU. SymbolGreekTU is available from www.linguistsoftware.com/lgku.htm.

Greek text taken from Nestle-Aland, Novum Testamentum Graece, 28th Revised Edition, edited by Barbara and Kurt Aland, Johannes Karavidopoulos, Carlo M. Martini, and Bruce M. Metzger in cooperation with the Institute for New Testament Textual Research, Münster/Westphalia, © 2012 Deutsche Bibelgesellschaft, Stuttgart. Used by permission.

Cover images © Gregor Buir/123rf and Achim Prill/123rf.

Printed in the United States of America
2 3 4 5 6 7 8 9 10 SB 25 24 23 22 21 20

CONTENTS

/////////////////

Annotated Readings in the Greek New Testament
Supplemental Table of Contents

PREFACE

/////////////////

In his final letter to his foremost disciple, the apostle Paul made this solemn appeal: "Be diligent to present yourself to God as one approved, a worker who doesn't need to be ashamed, correctly teaching the word of truth" (2 Tim 2:15). The message is clear: Timothy (and, by implication, all teachers of God's Word) must work hard to arrive at a correct interpretation of any given passage of Scripture. Such careful attention to correctly interpreting Scripture was to set Timothy apart from false teachers such as Hymenaeus and Philetus (2 Tim 2:17). Since the NT was written in Greek, and since inerrancy and inspiration extend specifically to the Scriptures in the autographs (original manuscripts), a good working knowledge of NT Greek greatly enhances one's interpretive skill.

In this book, we hope to stir in you a passion, and to provide you with the necessary tools, to "go deeper" in your pursuit of your mastery of NT Greek. You've taken a course or two in elementary Greek, or perhaps taught yourself by using some of the many helpful tools that are available. You've memorized the most common Greek vocabulary, learned the basic forms of the Greek noun, adjective, and verb, studied foundational principles of Greek syntax, and tried your hand at translating NT texts of increasing difficulty. But you know that you've got more to learn. We want to help you take your knowledge of NT Greek to the next level, not as an end in itself but as a means to correctly interpreting and teaching God's Word. So are you ready? Let us take a moment to get oriented, and then we'll be off and running in our quest to "go deeper" with NT Greek.

A GRAMMAR DESIGNED TO BE READ,
NOT MERELY REFERENCED

It seems that the main purpose of the preface of a NT Greek grammar is to justify the writing of yet another grammar. So, in keeping with tradition, here we go. While existing grammars are helpful in many ways and are sure to retain their usefulness, we would like to highlight the unique features of this volume that, we hope, will make it beneficial for both teachers and students.

Ultimately, we wrote this book with college or seminary students in mind. Consequently, our goal was to produce an intermediate Greek text that could be manageably digested when a student reads through the material. For most people, reading a Bible dictionary or encyclopedia is tedious. The same is true with Greek grammars. Greek grammars provide important information, but such books were not designed to be read at length, nor are they particularly user-friendly. In *Going Deeper with New Testament Greek*, we have attempted to present the material in a way that is accessible, and even fun, knowing that most students will be reading the chapters sequentially.

In writing this grammar, the abiding contributions in the history of the study of NT Greek have served as a foundation. In addition to conducting original research, over a dozen standard Greek grammars were consulted. While there is some variety in nomenclature, many grammatical categories (e.g., subjective and objective genitive) are standard. The NT is a comparatively short book, and examples of a given grammatical feature are also limited—especially clear, unambiguous examples. Categories were chosen and examples selected that best describe the dynamics of a given feature of Greek grammar or syntax and that seemed most helpful to students learning intermediate Greek.

NUMBER, SEQUENCE, AND AUTHORSHIP OF CHAPTERS

This book has also been designed with the teacher in mind. For example, it has fifteen chapters because most colleges and seminaries use the semester system that spans about fifteen weeks. Thus, in planning the material, it is easy for the teacher to see that on average one chapter needs to be covered every week (or one chapter every other week if the plan is to cover the book in two semesters). That said, it is certainly up to a teacher's discretion to allot, say, more time to participles and less time to some other feature of NT Greek (perhaps combining some of the cases).

The sequence of the chapters is also intentional. We start with a brief overview of the Greek language and textual criticism because it is helpful to give students at least a minimum of background knowledge with regard to the Greek language and to impress on them the importance of establishing the likely original text (as well as teaching them some skills to decipher the textual apparatus in their GNT). Of course, if in a given class students already have sufficient background in textual criticism (or, for that matter, any other subject), teachers can always opt to skip that particular portion in the book or tell their students to skim the material.

After the introductory chapter on the Greek language and textual criticism, we begin with three chapters on nouns (chaps. 2–4). These chapters are followed by a study of the article and adjectives (chap. 5). The following six chapters then cover various aspects of the Greek verbal system, including an overview of verbs (chap. 6), an introduction to the important, though highly debated, topic of tense-form and verbal aspect (chap. 7), two chapters that cover the various uses of verbs in the indicative mood (chaps. 8–9), the function and use of participles (chap. 10), and then finally infinitives (chap. 11). Various parts of speech, including pronouns, prepositions, conjunctions, adverbs, and particles, are the subjects of chapter 12.

The book concludes with several practical chapters on Greek diagramming and discourse analysis (chap. 13), Greek word studies (chap. 14), and continuing with Greek (chap. 15). The final chapter also includes information on helpful resources, both print and electronic, and finishes with a sampling of encouraging quotes underscoring the great value of keeping up one's knowledge of NT Greek.

While this is a collaborative work, we jointly stand behind the final product.[1] Robert Plummer wrote chapter 1 (The Greek Language & Textual Criticism) as well as chapters 12–15 (Pronouns, Prepositions, etc.; Sentences, Diagramming & Discourse Analysis; Word Studies; and Continuing with Greek); Andreas Köstenberger wrote chapters 2–5 (Nominative, Vocative & Accusative Cases; Genitive Case; Dative Case; The Article & Adjective) and co-authored chapter 7 (Tense & Verbal Aspect) with Benjamin Merkle; and Benjamin Merkle wrote chapter 6 (Verbs: Overview, Subjunctives & Imperatives) and chapters 8–11 (Present, Imperfect & Future Indicatives; Aorist, Perfect & Pluperfect Indicatives; Participles; Infinitives). Ben also compiled the vocabulary lists. The Reading Notes at the end of chapters 1–13 were not necessarily written by the author of a given chapter.

BENEFITS OF GOING DEEPER

Each chapter begins with an example of how knowing the contents of that chapter can guide the student to properly interpret Scripture. In other words, if a student is wondering what will be the "payoff" or benefits of learning the material, the "Going Deeper" section is there to encourage the student to see up front the practical application of grammar and syntax to the exegesis and interpretation of the Bible.

BIBLICAL EXAMPLES

In the content of any given chapter, we provide several biblical examples to illustrate each particular grammatical or syntactical category. Several features concerning these biblical examples are worth noting.

---

[1] While the author of a given chapter wrote a first serious draft, the other two co-authors carefully read each chapter and provided any needed feedback or other input needed to complete the final draft of the chapter. In rare cases, there may not have been complete consensus among the three authors on a given point, in which case the author of a given chapter bears final responsibility for the position taken.

- If a major (i.e., common) category is being discussed and illustrated, then typically five examples will be provided. If the category is less common or is subdivided, then only three (or sometimes two) examples will be given.

- User-friendly formatting allows each example to be quickly recognized.

- Both the Greek words and the English translation of the relevant syntactical forms are highlighted so that they are quickly identifiable.

- Examples are carefully chosen from a wide range of biblical authors whenever possible.

- Although English translations are taken primarily from the CSB, several modern English versions are used (such as the ESV, NASB, NIV, NJKV, and NRSV). This allows the student to see how various English versions translate and interpret selected texts.

PRACTICE SENTENCES

There are very few intermediate grammars that include practice exercises in the grammar itself. Often, if such sentences are available, they are included in a separate volume and thus have to be purchased separately. This volume includes ten carefully chosen practice sentences at the end of every chapter (except for the last two chapters). These exercises allow students to practice the skills they have learned immediately so that they can grow in their skills as NT exegetes.

VOCABULARY LISTS

Typically, in addition to assigning a grammar textbook, a teacher will also need to assign a separate book that provides vocabulary lists (usually listed according to frequency). This text, however, also provides vocabulary for students to memorize at the end of each chapter. Thus, by the end of the textbook, the student will memorize all the words in the NT that occur 15 times or more (a total of 830 words). All of the words that occur 50 times or more (a total of 310 words) are found in the appendix (all students should know these words already since most elementary grammars include these words). The remaining words (occurring 15–49 times = 520 words) are divided up into the first 13 chapters.[2] Each chapter's vocabulary list includes words found in the NT text provided at the end of that chapter as well as additional words from a frequency list (given in descending frequency). Consequently, each chapter contains 40 vocabulary words that must be memorized.[3] The

---

[2] In order to have an equal number of words in every chapter, a few words that occur 14 times were added.

[3] Frequencies were determined in consultation with standard tools such as Warren C. Trenchard, *The Complete Vocabulary Guide to the New Testament*, rev. ed. (Grand Rapids: Zondervan, 1998);

reading sections also include "Vocabulary to Recognize," which lists words that occur fewer than 15 times to aid the students in their translation work. Typically, students are not accountable to memorize words at this level.

BUILT-IN READER

As far as we know, no other intermediate grammar contains a built-in reader.[4] In other words, not only does this textbook include an intermediate-level grammar, practice exercises, and vocabulary lists; it also includes selected NT texts for the student to translate and detailed reading notes to guide the student in interpreting each text. The various texts were carefully selected using at least three criteria: (1) A text must highlight the grammar or syntax discussed in the chapter; (2) a text must be pastorally relevant, theologically foundational, or doctrinally debated; and (3) a text must be around 10–12 verses in length. In addition, a representative text from every NT author has been selected: Matthew (Matt 2:19–23; 6:9–13; 18:10–20), Mark (Mark 1:1–13), Luke (Acts 2:37–47), John (John 2:1–11; 11:30–44), Paul (Rom 3:19–21; 1 Tim 6:11–19; Titus 2:1–10), James (Jas 5:12–20), Peter (1 Pet 5:1–11), the author of Hebrews (Heb 5:11–6:6), and Jude (1–3, 17–25). The reading notes which accompany the Greek texts use various English versions as the illustrative translation for the Greek text (i.e., CSB, ESV, NASB, NIV, NLT). This variation allows students to see the strengths and weaknesses of several English versions.

SUMMARIES

Each chapter includes summary charts for the key material covered in that chapter. These are designed as a helpful review for students and will serve as a study guide as well as a quick reference tool.

TEACHER AIDS

Finally, we have made available various helps for teachers. We realize that it is difficult for a teacher to embrace a new textbook because of the amount of work it takes to incorporate its various elements into a course. Therefore, we have made the following items available for teachers: (1) weekly quizzes; (2) exams (midterm

---

Bruce M. Metzger's *Lexical Aids for Students of New Testament Greek*, 3rd ed. (Grand Rapids: Baker, 1998), John R. Kohlenberger, Edward W. Goodrick, and James A. Swanson, *Greek-English Concordance to the New Testament* (Grand Rapids: Zondervan, 1997) and Andreas J. Köstenberger and Raymond F. Bouchoc, *The Book Study Concordance* (Nashville: B&H Academic, 2003). Frequencies have been adjusted to reflect the NA[28] text.

[4] S. M. Baugh, however, does have a reader with a built-in, highly abbreviated "syntax sketch." *A First John Reader: Intermediate Greek Reading Notes and Grammar* (Phillipsburg, NJ: P&R, 1999).

and final); (3) PowerPoint presentations for each chapter; (4) chapter summaries as a separate document; (5) chapter exercise sentences as a separate document; (6) answer keys for quizzes, exams, and chapter exercise sentences; and (7) automated Moodle quizzes based on the summary charts in each chapter. To access this material, please go to www.deepergreek.com.

ACKNOWLEDGMENTS

A book like this is years in the making and requires the collaboration of many people. First of all, we would like to express our appreciation to one another for the friendship, partnership, and shared love of NT Greek that made working on this volume a joy rather than a chore. Thanks are due to our wives and families for their loyal and sacrificial support of our teaching and writing ministries. We would like to acknowledge a particular debt of gratitude to those who taught us NT Greek: William J. Larkin and D. A. Carson, S. M. Baugh, and Peter "Chip" Denton. We are also grateful to our students, particularly those at Southeastern Baptist Theological Seminary and The Southern Baptist Theological Seminary, for the privilege of working with them and for the lessons they taught us that made us better teachers and communicators of this vital material. Those deserving of special mention are Greg Stiekes, who provided quality research assistance for the chapters on noun cases and the article and adjectives; Dave Phillips, who along with Greg helped with the noun and article charts in the appendix as well as with the subject index for chapters 2–5; and Douglas Wallaker, Jack Brannen, Donnie Hale, and Michael Graham. Thanks are also due to Constantine Campbell, Nicholas Ellis, and Steven Runge, who each in their own way had a shaping impact on the verbal aspect chapter; as well as Mrs. Billie Goodenough, Wes Smith, Paul Lamicela, Kenny Trax, Gregory Wolff, and Samuel Chua who helped with proofreading and formatting this document. We further note that this revised edition contains additional footnotes, not included in the prior edition, that reflect the original and groundbreaking contributions of Daniel B. Wallace to the study of New Testament Greek. Finally, we are grateful for B&H Academic for commissioning this project, for Jim Baird, Chris Cowan, Audrey Greeson, and B&H staff who spent many hours readying the manuscript for publication and will doubtless spend many more marketing and distributing the book.

We are grateful to be able to release this book to teachers and students of NT Greek. The goal of this textbook is to train pastors, missionaries, and Christian laypeople as competent exegetes and interpreters of the Bible. May God graciously help all those who sincerely desire to study the NT in Greek to do so with increasing competence and skill. χάρις ὑμῖν καὶ εἰρήνη πληθυνθείη ("May grace and peace be multiplied to you," 1 Pet 1:2).

A TRIBUTE TO A. T. ROBERTSON

//////////////////

*Perhaps those who pity the grammarian do not know that he finds joy
and is sustained by the conviction that his work is necessary.*

A. T. Robertson[1]

This book is dedicated to the memory of A. T. Robertson. Archibald Thomas Robertson (Nov. 6, 1863–Sept. 24, 1934) was born near Chatham, VA, where he spent the first twelve years of his life before moving to a farm in NC. At the age of twelve (March 1876) he received Christ as his Lord and Savior and was baptized later that year. Four years later, at the age of sixteen, he was licensed to preach. He received his M.A. from Wake For-

est College, Wake Forest, NC (1885) and his Th.M. from The Southern Baptist Theological Seminary, Louisville, KY (1888). Shortly after entering seminary, his Greek professor (and future father-in-law), John Albert Broadus, noticed his linguistic skills, and Robertson soon became his teaching aide. In 1890, Robertson was elected Assistant Professor of New Testament Interpretation. Robertson would teach at Southern for forty-four years until his death in 1934.

As mentioned above, Robertson was the son-in-law of the famous Southern Baptist professor, preacher, and statesman, John Albert Broadus, whose biography Robertson wrote (*Life and Letters of John Albert Broadus*, American Baptist Publication Society, 1901). Robertson is recognized as being a premier NT scholar of his generation, and his work in the Greek NT is in many ways still unsurpassed today. In all, he published forty-five books, most in the field of NT Greek, including

---

[1] A. T. Robertson, *Grammar of the Greek New Testament in the Light of Historical Research,* 4th ed. (Nashville: Broadman, 1934), x.

four NT grammars, fourteen commentaries and studies, six volumes of his *Word Pictures in the New Testament*, eleven histories, and ten NT character studies.[2] His work *A Grammar of the Greek New Testament in the Light of Historical Research* is 1,454 pages long and is still consulted by leading Greek grammarians today. In addition, his *Word Pictures in the New Testament* (which is actually a running commentary that highlights exegetical insights for virtually every verse of the NT) is immensely helpful to this day.

Not only was Robertson a man zealous for Greek, but more importantly, he was passionate about the significant difference that knowing Greek can make for those who preach and teach God's word. Robertson delivered his inaugural address at Southern Seminary entitled "Preaching and Scholarship" on October 3, 1890. This address, though at the beginning of his teaching ministry, demonstrated his commitment to scholarship and his burden for colleges and seminaries to develop capable preachers of the gospel of Jesus Christ. Robertson had a deep passion to equip gospel ministers whose hearts were impassioned and whose minds were enlightened. He vehemently rejected the idea that theological education was a waste of time. He averred, "If theological education will increase your power for Christ, is it not your duty to gain that added power? . . . Never say you are losing time by going to school. You are saving time, buying it up for the future and storing it away. Time used in storing power is not lost."[3] He also rejected the idea that the purpose of the seminary was to make scholars. The question for him was, "Does the college and seminary training tend to make better preachers?" His response:

> If not, it is a failure. The German idea is to make scholars first and preachers incidentally. But ours is to make preachers, and scholars only as a means to that end. We have small need in the pulpit for men that can talk learnedly and obscurely about the tendencies of thought and the trend of philosophy, but do not know how to preach Christ and him crucified. The most essential thing to-day is not to know what German scholars think of the Bible, but to be able to tell men what the Bible says about themselves. And if our system of theological training fails to make preachers, it falls short of the object for which it was established. But if it does meet the object of its creation, it calls for hearty sympathy and support. . . . But my plea is for scholarship that helps men to preach. For after all, the great need of the world is the preaching of the gospel, not saying off a sermon, but preaching that stirs sinful hearts to repentance and godliness.[4]

Robertson also had a heart to train and equip those who could not be formally trained in college or seminary. His work *The Minister and His Greek New Testament* (1923) was designed to help pastors and other church workers begin the study of the Greek NT. In the introduction to his *Word Pictures* he writes,

---

[2] Accessed October 20, 2019, http://archives.sbts.edu/the-history-of-the-sbts/our-professors/ a-t-robertson.

[3] Archibald Thomas Robertson, "Preaching and Scholarship" (Louisville, KY: Baptist Book Concern, 1890), 9–10.

[4] Robertson, "Preaching and Scholarship," 15–16.

The readers of these volumes . . . are expected to be primarily those who know no Greek or comparatively little and yet who are anxious to get fresh help from the study of words and phrases in the New Testament, men who do not have access to the technical book required. . . . The critical student will appreciate the more delicate distinctions in words. But it is a sad fact that many ministers, laymen, and women, who took courses in Greek at college, university, or seminary, have allowed the cares of the world and the deceitfulness of riches to choke off the Greek that they once knew. Some, strangely enough, have done it even in the supposed interest of the very gospel whose vivid message they have thus allowed to grow dim and faint. If some of these vast numbers can have their interest in the Greek New Testament revived, these volumes will be worthwhile. Some may be incited . . . to begin the study of the Greek New Testament. . . . Others who are without a turn for Greek or without any opportunity to start the study will be able to follow the drift of the remarks and be able to use it all to profit in sermons, in Sunday School, or for private edification.[5]

The first edition of Robertson's *Grammar of the Greek New Testament* appeared in 1914. For more than a hundred years, students of the GNT have benefited from his hard work and dedication to scholarship that fuels good preaching. We wish to express our gratitude to God for raising up men like A. T. Robertson who desire to train the next generation of preachers. God greatly used this man—and though Robertson died many years ago, he still speaks through his prolific writings and his exemplary service.

As the authors of this text, we recognize that we stand on the shoulders of giants such as A. T. Robertson and many others like him—men who have gone before us and have made our task much easier. Our hope is that Robertson's desire for capable preachers of God's Word in his generation is facilitated through this volume for yet another generation of students and communicators of God's Word. As you read this Greek grammar, may the Lord fan into flame your love for his Word. And may your ministry be marked by an unquenchable commitment to rightly dividing the Word of truth (2 Tim 2:15).

---

[5] A. T. Robertson, *Word Pictures in the New Testament* (Nashville: Broadman, 1933), viii.

ABBREVIATIONS

////////////////

FREQUENTLY CITED NT GREEK GRAMMARS

BDF

Blass, F., A. Debrunner, and Robert W. Funk. *A Greek Grammar of the New Testament and Other Early Christian Literature*. Chicago: University of Chicago Press, 1961.

Black

Black, David Alan. *It's Still Greek to Me: An Easy-to-Understand Guide to Intermediate Greek*. Grand Rapids: Baker, 1998.

Brooks & Winbery

Brooks, James A. and Carlton L. Winbery. *Syntax of New Testament Greek*. Washington, D.C.: University Press of America, 1979.

Burton

Burton, Ernest De Witt. *Syntax of the Moods and Tenses in New Testament Greek*. 3rd ed. Edinburgh: T&T Clark, 1898.

Dana & Mantey

Dana, H. E. and Julius R. Mantey. *A Manual Grammar of the Greek New Testament*. Toronto: Macmillan, 1927.

Fanning

Fanning, Buist M. *Verbal Aspect in New Testament Greek*. Oxford: Clarendon, 1990.

McKay

McKay, K. L. *A New Syntax of the Verb in New Testament Greek: An Aspectual Approach*. Studies in Biblical Greek 5. New York: Peter Lang, 1994.

Moule

Moule, C. F. D. *An Idiom Book of New Testament Greek*. Cambridge: Cambridge University Press, 1953.

Moulton	Moulton, James Hope. *A Grammar of New Testament Greek*. Vols. 1 & 2. Edinburgh: T&T Clark, 1908, 1919.
Moulton & Turner	Moulton, J. H. and N. Turner. *A Grammar of New Testament Greek. Vols. 3 & 4*. Edinburgh: T&T Clark, 1963, 1976.
NIDNTTE	Silva, Moisés, ed. *New International Dictionary of New Testament Theology and Exegesis*. 5 vols. Grand Rapids: Zondervan, 2014.
Porter, *Idioms*	Porter, Stanley E. *Idioms of the Greek New Testament*. 2nd ed. Sheffield: Sheffield Academic Press, 1994.
Porter, *Verbal Aspect*	Porter, Stanley E. *Verbal Aspect in the Greek of the New Testament, with Reference to Tense and Mood*. Studies in Biblical Greek 1. New York: Peter Lang, 1989.
Robertson	Robertson, A. T. *A Grammar of the Greek New Testament in the Light of Historical Research*. 4th ed. Nashville: Broadman, 1934.
Smyth	Smyth, Herbert Weir. *Greek Grammar*. Cambridge, MA: Harvard University Press, 1956.
Wallace	Wallace, Daniel B. *Greek Grammar Beyond the Basics: An Exegetical Syntax of the New Testament*. Grand Rapids: Zondervan, 1996.
Winer	Winer, George Benedict. *A Grammar of the Idiom of the New Testament*. Andover: Draper, 1892.
Young	Young, Richard A. *Intermediate New Testament Greek: A Linguistic and Exegetical Approach*. Nashville: B&H, 1994.
Zerwick	Zerwick, Maximilian. *Biblical Greek: Illustrated by Examples*. Rome: Scripta Pontificii Instituti Biblici, 1963.

MORPHOLOGICAL ABBREVIATIONS

Tense			Person	
present	pres		first	1st
imperfect	impf		second	2nd
future	fut		third	3rd
aorist	aor		**Gender**	
perfect	per		masculine	masc
pluperfect	pluper		feminine	fem
Voice			neuter	neut
active	act		**Case**	
passive	pass		nominative	nom
middle	mid		genitive	gen
Mood			dative	dat
indicative	ind		accusative	acc
participle	ptc		vocative	voc
subjunctive	sub		**Number**	
imperative	impv		singular	sg
infinitive	inf		plural	pl
optative	opt			

OTHER ABBREVIATIONS

A	Codex Alexandrinus
B	Codex Vaticanus
BBR	*Bulletin for Biblical Research*
BDAG	Bauer, Walter, Frederick Danker, William Arndt, and Wilbur Gingrich, *A Greek-English Lexicon of the New Testament and Other Early Christian Literature*. 3rd ed. Chicago: University of Chicago Press, 2000.
BECNT	Baker Exegetical Commentary on the New Testament
BHGNT	Baylor Handbook on the Greek New Testament
BNTC	Black's New Testament Commentary
BSac	*Bibliotheca Sacra*
CBGM	Coherence-Based Genealogical Method
CEB	Common English Bible
CSB	Christian Standard Bible
DBSJ	*Detroit Baptist Seminary Journal*
EBC	Expositor's Bible Commentary
ECC	Eerdmans Critical Commentary
ECM	*Editio Critica Maior*
EDNT	Balz, H. and G. Schneider. *Exegetical Dictionary of the New Testament*. 3 vols. Grand Rapids: Eerdmans, 1990–93.
EGGNT	Exegetical Guide to the Greek New Testament
ESV	English Standard Version
GNT	Greek New Testament
GTJ	*Grace Theological Journal*
ICC	International Critical Commentary
IGNTP	International Greek New Testament Project
INTF	Institut für neutestamentliche Textforschung
JBL	*Journal of Biblical Literature*
JETS	*Journal of the Evangelical Theological Society*
JSNTSup	Journal for the Study of the New Testament Supplement
KJV	King James Version
LEH	Lust, J., E. Eynikel, and K. Hauspie, eds. *A Greek-English Lexicon of the Septuagint*. Rev. ed. Stuttgart: Deutsche Bibelgesellschaft, 2003.

Louw & Nida	Louw, Johannes P. and Eugene A. Nida. *Greek-English Lexicon of the New Testament Based on Semantic Domains*. 2 vols. New York: United Bible Societies, 1988.
LSJ	Liddell, Henry George and Robert Scott. *A Greek-English Lexicon with a Revised Supplement*, rev. Henry Stuart Jones. Oxford: Clarendon, 1996.
LXX	Septuagint
MS(S)	manuscript(s)
NA	Nestle-Aland
NAC	New American Commentary
NASB	New American Standard Bible
NewDocs	*New Documents Illustrating Early Christianity*. Macquarie University, 1981–present.
NICNT	New International Commentary on the New Testament
NIDNTT	Brown, Colin, ed. *The New International Dictionary of New Testament Theology*. 4 vols. Grand Rapids: Zondervan, 1975–1978.
NIGTC	New International Greek Testament Commentary
NIRV	New International Reader's Version
NIV	New International Version
NKJV	New King James Version
NLT	New Living Translation
NovT	*Novum Testamentum*
NRSV	New Revised Standard Version
NSBT	New Studies in Biblical Theology
NT	New Testament
OT	Old Testament
PIE	Proto Indo-European
PNTC	Pillar New Testament Commentary
RSV	Revised Standard Version
SBG	Studies in Biblical Greek
SBJT	*Southern Baptist Journal of Theology*
SBL	Society of Biblical Literature
TDNT	Kittel, G. and G. Friedrich, eds. *Theological Dictionary of the New Testament*. 10 vols. Trans. and ed. G. W. Bromiley. Grand Rapids: Eerdmans, 1964–76.
TLG	*Thesaurus Linguae Graecae*

TNIV	Today's New International Version
TNTC	Tyndale New Testament Commentary
TrinJ	*Trinity Journal*
TynBul	*Tyndale Bulletin*
UBS	United Bible Society
v., vv.	verse(s)
WBC	Word Biblical Commentary
WTJ	*Westminster Theological Journal*

///////////////

CHAPTER 1

THE GREEK LANGUAGE & TEXTUAL CRITICISM

GOING DEEPER

Matthew lists Jesus's immediate male ancestors as Joseph, Jacob, Matthan, Eleazar, Eliud, and Achim (Matt 1:14–16). Seemingly contradicting Matthew, Luke lists them as Joseph, Heli, Matthat, Levi, Melchi, and Jannai (Luke 3:23–24). Some early Christian scribe (as preserved in the 5th-century Codex Bezae [D]) attempted to harmonize these accounts by inserting the Matthean list of names into Luke's Gospel.[1] The vast majority of Greek manuscripts, however, bear witness to the divergence of names apparently present in the autographs (original manuscripts) of Luke and Matthew. We are reminded that the inspired text is our authority—not some later edited or "corrected" version.

In the late 1400s, Annius of Viterbo popularized the idea that Matthew preserves the genealogy of Joseph while Luke records the genealogy of Mary. Annius's interpretation, however, is based on an unlikely translation of the Greek text in Luke 3:23. A more fitting explanation is provided by Julius Africanus (AD 160–240), an early Christian apologist. Julius, in a letter to Aristides, explains that the Jewish custom of Levirite marriage and the resulting disparity of legal and biological lineage explain the differences between Matthew's and Luke's genealogies.[2]

---

[1] See the textual apparatus for Luke 3:23–31 in Nestle-Aland's 28th edition. If you have a UBS (red) GNT, this variant is not listed in the UBS apparatus because it is certainly not original.

[2] Eusebius, *Ecclesiastical History* 1.7.1–15.

The modern scholar René Laurentin points to the importance of holding to the Gospel authors' original wording rather than forced renderings of the Greek that attempt to prove that Mary was a descendant of David through the Lukan genealogy. Laurentin writes,

> Nothing is truly lost in Mary's not being biologically the daughter of David. The rigor with which the evangelists have avoided this easy solution gives a new indication of their exactitude. They did not invent in order to appease current expectations, as those who came after them did. On the contrary, they accepted the paradoxes which caused the difficulty. This honesty led them to great theological profundity.[3]

If, indeed, Joseph's adoption of Jesus fully legitimizes the Savior's Davidic ancestry, can we not further point out that God's adoption of us as sons and daughters truly grants us eternal access into his Fatherly presence?

CHAPTER OBJECTIVES

The purpose of this chapter is to survey both the history of the Greek language and the discipline of textual criticism. First, we will briefly consider the history of the Greek language and how such knowledge may aid the student of the GNT. Second, we will introduce the discipline of textual criticism—that is, the study of ancient manuscripts and patterns of text transmission with the goal of arriving at the original text (or "earliest attainable text").[4] Finally, we will note recent trends in text criticism.

HISTORY OF THE GREEK LANGUAGE

"Say something for me in Greek!" Most seminary students have probably heard this request from a family member or friend. Such persons, however, look puzzled when the student explains that he is primarily reading Greek of the NT era, not learning *modern* Greek. When students better understand how the Greek language

---

[3] René Laurentin, *The Truth of Christmas, Beyond the Myths: The Gospels of the Infancy of Christ*, trans. Michael J. Wrenn and assoc. (Petersham, MA: St. Bede's Publications, 1986), 345. See also Andreas J. Köstenberger and Alexander Stewart, *The First Days of Jesus: The Story of the Incarnation* (Wheaton: Crossway, 2015).

[4] Eldon Jay Epp represents a more skeptical approach and shuns the term "original text." He writes, "New Testament textual criticism, employing aspects of both science and art, studies the transmission of the New Testament text and the manuscripts that facilitate its transmission, with the unitary goal of establishing the earliest attainable text (which serves as a baseline) and, at the same time, of assessing the textual variants that emerge from the baseline text so as to hear the narratives of early Christian thought and life that inhere in the array of meaningful variants." See "Traditional 'Canons' of New Testament Textual Criticism: Their Value, Validity, and Viability—or Lack Thereof," in *The Textual History of the Greek New Testament: Changing Views in Contemporary Research*, Text-Critical Studies 8, ed. Klaus Wachtel and Michael W. Holmes (Atlanta: SBL, 2011), 127.

of the NT differs from preceding and subsequent forms of the language, they can more easily recognize difficult forms or understand grammatical features that were in transition at the time of the NT. Furthermore, an understanding of the way in which the Greek language evolved will guard against simplistic and erroneous approaches that fail to see the Greek language used in the NT as a snapshot of a changing language.

All languages change over time as they incorporate new influences or alter old forms. Certainly, any modern English speaker can clearly see such changes by reading the King James Version of the Bible (1611) or the plays of William Shakespeare (1564–1616). The Greek language is no exception. To understand the history of the Greek language, we will briefly survey the following historical periods:

FORM OF LANGUAGE	DATES
Proto Indo-European	Prior to 1500 BC
Linear B or Mycenaean	1500–1000 BC
Dialects and Classical Greek	1000–300 BC
Koine Greek	300 BC–AD 330
Byzantine Greek	AD 330–AD 1453
Modern Greek	AD 1453–present

Proto Indo-European

Scholars who study languages classify them according to related families. One such family is the Indo-European family of languages, which includes the sub-families of Greek, Indo-Iranian, Armenian, Albanian, Italic, Celtic, Germanic, and Balto-Slavic.[5] By studying the oldest preserved forms of Indo-European languages and how those languages differ and continued to evolve, scholars are able to reconstruct a preceding, earlier "ancestor language." This common hypothetical ancestor of Indo-European languages is called Proto Indo-European (or PIE, for short), which was used prior to 1500 BC.[6] We have no written records of this early ancestor of the Greek language.[7]

---

[5] See Bruce M. Metzger, *Lexical Aids for Students of New Testament Greek*, rev. ed. (Princeton, NJ: n.p., 1969; repr. 1983), 73.

[6] How far back one can speak of a common Proto-European language is a matter of scholarly conjecture, though possibly it is helpful to think of the PIE period as extending roughly 3000–1500 BC.

[7] In attempting to explain the irregular form of a NT Greek word, scholarly resources occasionally appeal to the "ancestor" form (sometimes the hypothetical PIE form) of the word that was still causing orthographic challenges in the Koine period hundreds of years later. A helpful resource for such morphological explorations is William D. Mounce, *The Morphology of Biblical Greek* (Grand Rapids: Zondervan, 1994).

Linear B

After the Proto Indo-European period but before the Classical period, there was a written precursor to Greek known by scholars as "Linear B." This language is also called Mycenaean, with inscriptions discovered in Mycenae, Crete, and elsewhere. The written alphabet used for Linear B (deciphered by Michael Ventris in 1952) differs from Classical Greek, with each symbol representing a syllable rather than an individual vowel or consonant sound.[8] The relatively recently deciphered inscriptions and clay tablets in Linear B remind the NT Greek student that hundreds of years of changes in the Greek language can be traced through written texts prior to the time of the NT.

This clay tablet with Linear B script, dated to 1450–1375 BC, is Minoan and was found at Knossos, Crete, by Arthur Evans. It records quantities of oil apparently offered to various deities.

Dialects and Classical Greek

Scholars differ as to what to call the next period in the development of the Greek language. A. T. Robertson and Hersey Davis label it the "Age of Dialects" and extend it back to 1000 BC, noting that various regional dialects in Greek coexisted and competed for dominance.[9] These dialects included Aeolic, Doric, Arcado-Cypriot, and Ionic. Homer's epic poems, the *Iliad* and the *Odyssey*, were not written down until roughly 800 BC, so some scholars date the Classical or Dialect period beginning at 800 BC. The various Greek dialects gave way to the political and cultural ascendancy of Athens (and thus the Ionic-Attic dialect) by the fourth

---

[8] According to journalist Margalit Fox, Alice E. Kober, a Classics professor at Brooklyn College, has never received proper recognition for her ground-breaking work that contributed to the deciphering of Linear B. See Margalit Fox, *The Riddle of the Labyrinth: The Quest to Crack an Ancient Code* (New York: Ecco, 2013).

[9] A. T. Robertson and W. Hersey Davis, *A New Short Grammar of the Greek New Testament* (New York: Harper & Brothers, 1933), 8–10.

and fifth centuries BC. These two centuries are viewed as the literary high point of the Classical period in Greek literature.[10]

In previous generations, students often came to seminary having already studied Classical Greek for many years. In fact, several lexicons and reference grammars assume a student's familiarity with differences between Classical and NT Greek. Without any further explanation (and to the dismay of students!), such resources will comment that a form represents the Doric or Aeolic spelling. If students wish to expand their knowledge of Greek back into the Classical period, perhaps the best bridge is still Stephen W. Paine's *Beginning Greek: A Functional Approach* (New York: Oxford University Press, 1961), which includes translation exercises from both Xenophon (fourth century BC) and the NT.

Koine Greek

Several factors contributed to the ongoing evolution of the Greek language into a genuine *lingua franca* (widely used common language) that came to dominate cultural, political, and economic life in Europe and the Near East for centuries. Most significant among these developments were the short-lived but highly successful military conquests of Alexander, son of Phillip II of Macedon. Alexander the Great, as he came to be known, had studied under Aristotle (384–322 BC) and self-consciously sought to bring the culture and language of the Greeks to the lands he subdued. By the year 326 BC, he had conquered much of the known civilized world of his day—from Eastern Europe to India. The Koine (pronounced, "Coy-neigh") period of the Greek language is generally dated to begin after the initial unifying effects of Alexander's conquests (c. 300 BC) and to end with the moving of the capital of the Roman Empire from Rome to Constantinople (AD 330).[11]

During the Koine period, Greek was spoken as a second language by many. Increased trade and travel had a regularizing effect on the language. Consequently, a "common," "widely-spoken" or ordinary dialect emerged. This κοινὴ διάλεκτος (common dialect) is well preserved in innumerable papyri and in the writings of the NT.

Various other terms are sometimes used to refer to Koine Greek with slightly different nuances. These are:

---

[10] The term "Classical Greek" is sometimes applied narrowly to the Attic-Ionic dialect contained in well-known Greek literature of the 4th and 5th centuries BC.

[11] See the next section on "Byzantine Greek."

- *Biblical Greek* – Koine Greek, as preserved specifically in the writings of the OT (LXX) and NT (and OT Apocrypha).

- *New Testament Greek* – Koine Greek, with a focus only on the writings of the NT.

- *Common Greek* – rarely used term; interchangeable with Koine Greek.

- *Vulgar Greek* – "vulgar" in the sense of "ordinary" or broadly-spoken dialect; an even more rarely used term; interchangeable with Koine Greek.

- *Hellenistic Greek* – interchangeable with Koine Greek, though the adjective "Hellenistic" possibly highlights the fact that the ordinary spoken Greek language of this period was widely used as a second language by persons who had adopted Greek language or customs (i.e., "Hellenized" persons).[12] "Hellenistic" is an adjective derived from the Greek adjective meaning "Greek" (Ἑλληνικός).

The Greek of the NT, as an expression of the Koine Greek in the first century AD, is in some sense a picture of an object in motion. The language is in a state of flux, moving toward more explicit expressions and simpler syntactical constructions, as would be expected of a *lingua franca*. Some of the changes we see taking place as the language shifts from Classical to Koine are:

1. Authors regularize the aorist by applying first aorist endings to second aorist verbs. So, for example, one finds εἶπα ("I said," Acts 26:15) alongside εἶπον ("I said," John 16:15).

2. The optative mood is rarely found in Koine Greek. Only sixty-eight uses of the optative are found in the NT, usually in formulaic constructions such as μὴ γένοιτο (NASB, "May it never be," Rom 9:14) or εἴη ("could be," Luke 1:29).

3. Koine authors are prone to use prepositions rather than noun cases alone to communicate relationships more explicitly (e.g., 1 Pet 1:2a, <u>κατὰ</u> πρόγνωσιν θεοῦ πατρὸς <u>ἐν</u> ἁγιασμῷ πνεύματος <u>εἰς</u> ὑπακοὴν καὶ ῥαντισμὸν αἵματος Ἰησοῦ Χριστοῦ; ESV, "<u>according to</u> the foreknowledge of God the Father, <u>in</u> the sanctification of the Spirit, <u>for</u> obedience to Jesus Christ and <u>for</u> sprinkling with his blood").

4. With a simplifying, regularizing trend, -μι verbs sometimes appear with omega verb endings (e.g., Rev 11:9, οὐκ ἀφί<u>ουσιν</u> "they do not permit" [cf. διδό<u>ασιν</u>]).

5. The disappearance of some letters is complete. Digamma (ϝ), formerly appearing after epsilon in the Greek alphabet and pronounced like

---

[12] As Wallace rightly notes (17). Wallace also seeks to clarify the nuances of various terms that are applied to Koine Greek.

English "w," disappears. The letter koppa (ϙ) also disappears.[13] The "memory" of lost letters, however, continues to cause spelling irregularities. καλέω, for example, originally had a digamma at the end of the root and for that reason does not lengthen the contract vowel before a tense formative. Thus, the future of καλέω is καλέσω, not καλήσω.

6. The elaborate hypotactic (subordinated) style of Classical Greek shifts toward parataxis. In paratactic style, an author places assertions side by side rather than in cascades of subordinated clauses. Authors vary in style, but as a general rule, the simpler, paratactic model is more common among Koine writers. For a NT book written almost entirely in paratactic style, see 1 John.

7. Comparative forms are used to express the superlative idea (e.g., Luke 9:48, ὁ μικρότερος, "whoever is least"). The superlative form is commonly elative in sense (e.g., Jas 3:4, ὑπὸ ἐλαχίστου πηδαλίου, "by a very small rudder").[14]

8. Though true of virtually any historical period of any language, during the Koine period words continue to shift in meaning. (This development is called "semantic shift.") During the Classical Greek period, for example, λαλέω meant "to chat" or "to babble."[15] In the NT, however, λαλέω is a general verb for speaking,[16] possibly preferred by authors when the speaker is not being quoted directly.

Other shifts in the Greek language could be noted, but the eight listed above are some of the most common, and any reader of the GNT will soon encounter all the trends listed above. In the first five sentences of the Practice Exercises for this chapter, students will be asked to identify which of the grammatical or orthographic (spelling) shifts above are represented by the underlined words from the GNT.

Byzantine Greek

In AD 330, the capital of the Roman empire moved from Rome to the city of Constantinople (formerly named Byzantium). Thus began a new era for the Greek language. Except in the Holy Roman Empire, Latin was increasingly used for politics, trade, and religion. Byzantine or Medieval Greek maintained continuity with

---

[13] Smyth, 8 (§3). Smyth notes that digamma was written in the Boeotian dialect as late as 200 BC. Digamma and koppa continued to be used in writing numerals.

[14] Though the elative use of the superlative is attested in the Classical period (Smyth, 282 [§1085]), it appears more commonly in the Koine period.

[15] LSJ, 1025–26. Though looked to as a lexicon primarily for classical Greek, LSJ is intended to encompass the Koine.

[16] David Alan Black notes the semantic shift of the verb λαλέω in the Koine period. See *Linguistics for Students of New Testament Greek: A Survey of Basic Concepts and Applications*, 2nd ed. (Grand Rapids: Baker, 1995), 157.

the earlier Koine, but continued to experience syntactical changes and semantic shifts.

Modern Greek

Modern Greek is generally divided into two forms: (1) a literary form, known as Katharevousa or Καθαρεύουσα ("purifying") Greek; and (2) Demotic or Δημοτική ("the people's language").[17] Scholars see a direct evolutionary connection between modern Demotic Greek and its medieval predecessor, while Καθαρεύουσα is viewed as an artificial, contrived form of the language. Compared to many languages, however, Greek has experienced comparatively few changes over the last two thousand years. Most NT Greek students, for example, are able to pick their way through much of a modern Greek Bible. See the chart below that compares the Koine GNT and modern Greek Bible.

KOINE (NT) GREEK	MODERN GREEK BIBLE
Ἐν ἀρχῇ ἦν ὁ λόγος, καὶ ὁ λόγος ἦν πρὸς τὸν θεόν, καὶ θεὸς ἦν ὁ λόγος. (John 1:1)	Ἐν ἀρχῇ ἦτο ὁ Λόγος, καὶ ὁ Λόγος ἦτο παρὰ τῷ Θεῷ, καὶ Θεὸς ἦτο ὁ Λόγος. (John 1:1)

A few NT Greek professors advocate using modern Greek pronunciation because, at points, it seems a more accurate reflection of first-century pronunciation. The vowels omicron and omega, for example, are both pronounced with a long "o" sound (ō) in modern Greek. Both vowels were also apparently pronounced the same way in the Koine period—as evidenced by numerous scribal mistakes where omicron and omega are interchanged (e.g., Rom 5:1, ἔχομεν, "we have"; variant ἔχωμεν, "let us have"). The majority of NT professors, however, currently favor the pronunciation system developed by Erasmus (1466–1536) which employs a distinct vowel sound for each Greek vowel.[18]

TEXTUAL CRITICISM

A History of Text Criticism

Even within the NT itself, we have evidence that the individual NT documents were copied by hand and that these copies circulated among the churches. In Col 4:16, Paul writes, "After this letter has been read at your gathering, have it read

---

[17] Black, *Linguistics for Students of New Testament Greek*, 154.
[18] If a student wishes to learn modern Greek pronunciation, however, resources such as Rosetta Stone software or the Mango Language-learning website (www.mangolanguages.com) have made the task easier. Also, for audio resources developed with commitments to various approaches to pronunciation, see http://www.ntgateway.com/greek-ntgateway/greek-new-testament-texts/. Another helpful resource is BibleMesh, which can be accessed at http://biblemesh.com/course-catalog/biblical-languages.

also in the church of the Laodiceans."[19] Over time, the early church grouped selections of inspired writings and copied them together. By the mid-second century, the four canonical Gospels and Paul's letters were apparently grouped and copied as units. Not much later, the entire NT was grouped and copied as a recognized body of inspired writings. The earliest extant canonical list we have of the NT (the Muratorian Canon) has been dated to AD 190.[20] As early Christians copied, recopied, and copied copies (all by hand), small variations were inevitably introduced into the manuscripts. And, although Church Fathers sometimes speculated about copyist errors or the original reading of manuscripts,[21] it was virtually impossible to codify accurately such discussion until one could reproduce a text without any variation. Thus, after the printing press was introduced to Europe in 1454, possibilities for comparing manuscripts with an unchanging standard arose. At roughly the same time, Europe experienced a revival of interest in classical learning (including the Greek language) and the arrival of the Protestant Reformation (where focus on the meaning of the inspired Scripture necessitated careful argumentation from the text of Scripture in the original languages). The printing press, a revived knowledge of Greek, and a growing interest in the gospel combined to result in the first published printed edition of the GNT by Erasmus in 1516.[22] In producing this text, Erasmus relied on only seven manuscripts, most of poor quality.[23] Today, we have more than 5,000 ancient manuscripts (or partial manuscripts) of the GNT, with the number increasing yearly.[24]

Subsequent generations continued to build on the foundational work of Erasmus in producing "standard" printed versions of the GNT derived from the various ancient manuscripts available to them. Until the mid-nineteenth century, the Byzantine text tradition was assumed as the standard.[25] It was sometimes called the

---

[19] Some scholars have suggested that this "letter from Laodicea" may be Paul's canonical letter to the Ephesians, as the words ἐν Ἐφέσῳ ("in Ephesus," Eph 1:1) are lacking in significant ancient manuscripts.

[20] The Muratorian canon is dated by some scholars as late as the fourth century. For a brief presentation of the views, see Edmon L. Gallagher and John D. Meade, *The Biblical Canon Lists from Early Christianity* (Oxford: Oxford University Press, 2017), 174–83. Certainly, however, Christians distinguished canonical from non-canonical writings prior to the earliest extant canonical lists, as is evidenced within both the NT (e.g., 2 Thess 2:2; 3:17) and the writings of the Apostolic Fathers.

[21] For example, Jerome, Augustine, and Origen. See Bruce M. Metzger and Bart D. Ehrman, *The Text of the New Testament: Its Transmission, Corruption, and Restoration*, 4th ed. (New York: Oxford University Press, 2005), 200.

[22] The Complutensian Polyglot, a printed GNT produced under the direction of Cardinal Ximenes, was apparently completed in 1514 but not formally published until after Erasmus's text.

[23] See Edwin M. Yamauchi, "Erasmus' Contributions to New Testament Scholarship," *Fides et Historia* 19, no.3 (1987): 10–11. Yamauchi writes, "Although Erasmus claimed that he used 'the oldest and most correct copies of the New Testament,' the press of the publisher's deadline forced him to rely on but seven rather late and inferior manuscripts available at Basle" (10).

[24] See the chapter by Jacod Peterson in Elijah Hixson and Peter J. Gurry, eds, *Myths and Mistakes in New Testament Textual Criticism* (Downers Grove: IVP Academic, 2019). Daniel Wallace, director of the Center for the Study of New Testament Manuscripts (CSNTM), regularly reports the discovery of new and significant ancient manuscripts at www.csntm.org.

[25] Scholars also speak of the "Majority text," which means the reading found in the majority of extant NT manuscripts. As the majority of extant NT manuscripts are Byzantine, there is an overlap

textus receptus (received text), so labeled in the preface to a GNT published by the Elzevir brothers in 1633. Over time, principles for adjudicating disputed readings were developed and accepted by the vast majority of scholars.[26] The Byzantine text came to be viewed by many as a later conflation of text traditions and lost its primacy to "eclectic" scholarly editions produced by text critics. Principles that dethroned the Byzantine text and codified the modern discipline of text criticism can be traced to the seminal work of Brian Walton (1600–1661), Johann Bengel (1687–1752), Karl Lachmann (1793–1851), Constantine von Tischendorf (1815–1874), B. F. Westcott (1825–1901), F. J. A. Hort (1828–1892), and others. Principles of text criticism are summarized in the following section.

It should be noted that a small minority of scholars insist that only one "family" of ancient manuscripts (the Byzantine family) preserves the most reliable text of the NT. Yet, even within this Byzantine family of manuscripts, there are numerous minor variations. Modern English-speaking persons who insist on the priority of the Byzantine text family are usually aligned in some way with the "King James Only" movement.[27] They argue that the King James Version (the NT of which is translated from a Byzantine version of the Greek text) is the most reliable because it is based on the best preserved manuscript tradition. The vast majority of Christian scholars, however, believe the evidence points to God preserving his Word through the multiplicity of manuscripts in a variety of text families. God has left us so many manuscripts of such high quality that, even in the places where there are variants in the manuscripts, we can reach a high level of certainty as to what the original text read.[28] God has not seen fit to preserve the autographs (apostolically penned originals) of the NT, but he has preserved *all the words of the autographs* in the many manuscripts that have come down to us.

Students wishing to read an irenic, scholarly argument in favor of Byzantine priority are referred to *The New Testament in the Original Greek: Byzantine Text Form*.[29] This critical edition of the GNT includes not only a carefully constructed critical Byzantine text (based on comparisons of extant NT manuscripts), but also an extensive appendix entitled, "The Case for Byzantine Priority."[30]

---

in the terms. Most Byzantine text readings are considered, by pure mathematical reckoning, as "the Majority text." Of course, because nearly all NT text traditions overlap at roughly 90%, any NT text will be representative of "the Majority text" at most points.

[26] See Eldon Jay Epp's critique of these traditional text-critical principles in "Traditional 'Canons' of New Testament Textual Criticism," 79–127.

[27] For an irenic and cogent refutation of the King James Only position, see James R. White, *The King James Only Controversy: Can You Trust the Modern Translations?*, 2nd ed. (Minneapolis: Bethany House, 2009).

[28] For a recent essay defending the reliability of the GNT, see Daniel B. Wallace, "Has the New Testament Text Been Hopelessly Corrupted?," in *In Defense of the Bible: A Comprehensive Apologetic for the Authority of Scripture*, ed. Steven B. Cowan and Terry L. Wilder (Nashville: B&H, 2013), 139–63.

[29] Maurice A. Robinson and William G. Pierpont, eds., *The New Testament in the Original Greek: Byzantine Textform* (Southborough, MA: Chilton Book Publishing, 2005).

[30] Robinson and Pierpont, *The New Testament in the Original Greek*, 533–86.

Principles of Text Criticism

Traditionally, the discipline of text criticism has sought to determine the original wording of an ancient text for which the autograph has disappeared and for which disputed witnesses exist today. The criteria for determining the original reading of the text can be divided into external and internal criteria. External criteria concern the age, quantity, and provenance (or geographical origin) of the manuscripts consulted. Internal criteria consider how a disputed variant fits within the context of the document (the author's style or the context of his argument). Some prominent modern text critics are known for strongly favoring external or internal criteria, but a reasoned use of all available criteria seems judicious.

The GNT that results from deciding among disputed readings is called an "eclectic" text. The word *eclectic* means "drawn from a variety of sources." In labeling our final product as an "eclectic" text, we are recognizing that there is no ancient manuscript that parallels it word-for-word. While our eclectic GNT overlaps overwhelmingly with the vast majority of all ancient GNT manuscripts, it is, in the end, drawn from a multiplicity of sources, not agreeing at every point with any of them.

External Criteria

1. *Favor the older manuscripts.* With all other things being equal, an older manuscript, being closer in date to the original, is to be preferred. Through paleography (the study of ancient writing), analysis of scribal colophons, and other methods, scholars are able to assign composition dates to ancient manuscripts. Also, external evidence takes into account not only GNT manuscripts, but early versions (translations) and quotations from church fathers. Some scholars discount the Byzantine text completely as a later conflation; others (e.g., KJV-only advocates) prefer the Byzantine text.[31] A balanced approach would lead us to consider individual Byzantine readings insofar as they are witnessed to by early manuscripts and supported by other criteria below.

2. *Favor the reading that is supported by the majority of manuscripts.* This criterion must be qualified by the famous quip, "Manuscripts must be weighed, not counted." For example, if we have fifty medieval Byzantine texts that all rely on the same tenth-century exemplar, then the entire group of manuscripts should be viewed in light of their common origin rather than as fifty independent witnesses.

3. *Favor the reading that is best attested across various families of manuscripts.* Over time, various streams of text transmission developed. Within these streams (traditionally delineated by geographical provenance) flowed manuscripts with similar patterns of variants. So, the disputed reading best represented by a broad swath of transmission

---

[31] This is not to say that all who favor the Byzantine tradition are also KJV-only advocates.

streams (families) is to be preferred.[32] Note the map below depicting the four major text families (Alexandrian, Caesarean, Western, Byzantine).[33]

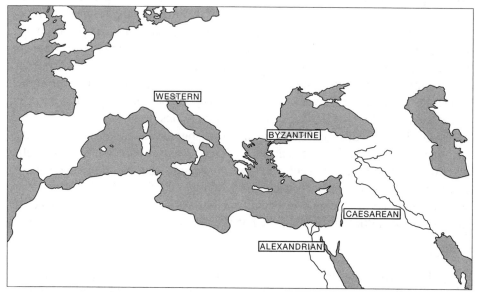

Influential text critic J. K. Elliott asserts that the traditional classification of text families and their use in determining original readings should be rejected as overly-simplistic.[34] Gerd Mink of the Institut für neutestamentliche Textforschung (INTF) in Münster, Germany, has championed a new Coherence-Based Genealogical Method (CBGM). Elliot explains the approach:

> Mink's theory plots the textual flow between manuscripts, declaring the likeliest direction of change and seeing how that trajectory is paralleled elsewhere in the textual tradition. The relevant genealogical connection is seen between the texts and not the palaeographical dating of the manuscripts that happen to bear those texts. There is thus no room for text-types in such a methodology.[35]

---

[32] For an online resource that labels virtually all ancient manuscripts according to their text families, see www.laparola.net/greco/manoscritti.php.

[33] Some scholars contest the legitimacy of the Caesarean text family. David Alan Black writes, "Scholars occasionally refer to a fourth text type—the Caesarean. Found only in the Gospels, this group of manuscripts is often found in company with the Alexandrian or Western text types. Today, however, there is little consensus as to the existence of this group of witnesses. It appears to be the most mixed of any of the groups that can be classified as a text type." See *New Testament Textual Criticism: A Concise Guide* (Grand Rapids: Baker, 1994), 34.

[34] J. K. Elliot, "Recent Trends in Textual Criticism of the New Testament: A New Millennium, a New Beginning?" *Bulletin de l'Académie Belge pour l'Étude des Langues Anciennes et Orientales* 1 (2012): 128–29.

[35] Elliot, "Recent Trends in Textual Criticism of the New Testament," 130. In his review article of the *Editio Critica Maior*, Peter M. Head writes, "The Coherence-Based Genealogical Method is difficult to summarise briefly, and I will not attempt a complete exposition and evaluation here. As a method it attempts, utilizing the complete transcriptions of manuscript witnesses and the power

Though popular resources still present the traditional text-family classifications, scholarly consensus is moving towards seeing the CBGM as rendering the traditional classifications obsolete.

Internal Criteria

1. *Favor the reading that best fits the literary context.* This holds true as a general rule. Of course, sometimes authors of the NT said shocking or unexpected things, so this criterion must not be rigidly applied.

2. *Favor the reading that best corresponds with writings by the same NT author.* Authors have general stylistic patterns and theological motifs. As noted above, however, authors are not always predictable. The use of an amanuensis (ancient secretary) and differing contexts or purposes can explain stylistic variations within the same author's writings.

3. *Favor the reading that best explains the origin of the other variants.* Similar to a detective story, it is sometimes possible to reconstruct a series of mistakes or attempted fixes that all flow from a scribal alteration of the original reading.

4. *Favor the shorter reading.* As texts were often lengthened or clarified, the shorter reading should usually be preferred.

5. *Favor the more difficult reading.* Often the more difficult reading should be favored, as later additions are attempts to "fix" a perceived problem. This criterion cannot be applied in isolation from the other principles mentioned above, but scribes, when not making mistakes of hearing or sight, were prone to smooth out difficulties rather than introduce them.[36]

---

of computer analysis, to deal with the large number of witnesses to the NT text, the problem that these witnesses are related in complex ways involving contamination, and the coincidental emergence of identical readings (specifically for the Catholic Epistles the *ECM* used 164 witnesses and found 3,046 places of textual variation). The CBGM uses textual agreement between transcriptions of manuscripts as a whole to identify specific genealogical relationships (or coherencies) between the texts represented in these manuscripts and the assumed initial text. Beginning with the relatively certain parts of the initial text, using computer analysis, the 'textual flow' at each variant unit can be mapped and preliminary genealogical relationships can be developed." See *"Editio Critica Maior:* An Introduction and Assessment," *TynBul* 61 (2010): 143–44.

[36] See the helpful tool by David Trobisch, *A User's Guide to the Nestle-Aland 28 Greek New Testament*, Text-Critical Studies 9 (Atlanta: SBL, 2013), including the discussion on pp. 22–24.

Common Variations in the GNT

Unintentional Errors

According to one reckoning, 95 percent of textual variants are accidental—the unintentional variations introduced by tired or incompetent scribes.[37] Such variants include the following:[38]

1. *Errors of Sight.* Scribes sometimes copied texts by looking back and forth to a manuscript. By this method, they inevitably made a number of errors of sight. For example, they confused letters that looked similar in appearance, divided words wrongly (the oldest Greek manuscripts of the Bible have no spaces between words), repeated words or sections (i.e., copied the same thing twice), accidentally skipped letters, words, or sections, or changed the order of letters in a word, or words in a sentence. In Codex Vaticanus, for example, at Galatians 1:11, a scribe accidentally wrote τὸ εὐαγγέλιον ("the gospel") three times in succession.

2. *Errors of Hearing.* When scribes copied manuscripts through dictation (i.e., scribes wrote as a manuscript was being read) errors of hearing were made. For example, vowels, diphthongs, or other sounds were misheard, as in Matthew 2:6 in Codex Sinaiticus, where ἐκ σοῦ ("from you") has been wrongly heard and written as ἐξ οὗ ("from whom"). We make similar mistakes in English, for instance, writing "night" when someone says, "knight."

3. *Errors of Writing.* Sometimes scribes introduced errors into texts simply by writing the wrong thing. For example, in Codex Alexandrinus, at John 13:37, a scribe accidentally wrote δύνασαί μοι rather than δύναμαί σοι. Rather than saying to Jesus, "why can't I follow You now," Peter now queries, "why can't you follow me now?"[39]

4. *Errors of Judgment.* Sometimes scribes exercised poor judgment by incorporating marginal glosses (ancient footnotes) into the body of the text or by incorporating similar unintentional corrupting influences. In the fourteenth-century Codex 109, for example, an incompetent scribe has apparently copied continuous lines of text from a manuscript that listed the genealogy of Jesus (Luke 3:23–38) in two columns. The

---

[37] See Arthur G. Patzia, *The Making of the New Testament: Origin, Collection, Text & Canon* (Downers Grove, IL: InterVarsity, 1995), 138.

[38] The material below is from Robert L. Plummer, *40 Questions About Interpreting the Bible* (Grand Rapids: Kregel, 2010), originally derived from Patzia, *Making of the New Testament*, 138–46.

[39] This variant is also possibly an "error of sight" (i.e., the scribe's eyes jumped to the parallel expression in John 13:36). I (Rob) am indebted to Elijah Hixson for pointing out this variant, as well as some other variants mentioned in this section.

resulting genealogy has all the family relations scrambled, even listing God as the son of Aram.[40]

Intentional Errors

The remaining five percent of textual variants resulted from intentional activity on the part of scribes. Such changes included:

1. *Revising Grammar and Spelling.* In an attempt to standardize grammar or spelling, scribes sometimes corrected what they perceived as orthographic or grammatical errors in the text they were copying. For example, though John originally put the nominative case after the preposition ἀπό in Revelation 1:4, later scribes have inserted a genitive form.[41]

2. *Harmonizing Similar Passages.* Scribes had a tendency to harmonize parallel passages and introduce uniformity to stylized expressions. For example, details from the same incident in multiple Gospels might be included when copying any one Gospel. As a professor of Greek, I (Rob) have found it interesting that students sometimes unintentionally insert "Lord" or "Christ" when translating a passage with the name "Jesus." Normally, such students are not intending to promote a "higher Christology"; they are simply conforming their speech to a stylized reference to the Savior. Ancient scribes behaved in a similar way.

3. *Eliminating Apparent Discrepancies and Difficulties.* Scribes sometimes "fixed" what they perceived as a problem in the text. Metzger and Ehrman report that because Origen perceived a geographical difficulty at John 1:28, he changed Βηθανίᾳ ("Bethany") to Βηθαραβᾷ.[42]

4. *Conflating the Text.* Sometimes when a scribe knew of variant readings in the manuscript base from which he was copying, he would simply include both variants within his copy, conflating them. For example, in Acts 20:28, some early manuscripts read τὴν ἐκκλησίαν τοῦ θεοῦ ("the church of God"), while others read τὴν ἐκκλησίαν τοῦ κυρίου ("church of the Lord"). Later manuscripts conflate the readings as τὴν ἐκκλησίαν τοῦ κυρίου καὶ [τοῦ] θεοῦ ("the church of the Lord and God").[43]

5. *Adapting Different Liturgical Traditions.* In a few isolated places, it is possible that church liturgy (i.e., stylized prayers or praises) influenced

---

[40] Metzger and Ehrman, *The Text of the New Testament*, 259.
[41] Metzger and Ehrman, 262.
[42] Metzger and Ehrman, 264.
[43] Metzger and Ehrman, 265.

some textual additions or wording changes (e.g., Matt 6:13, "For yours is the kingdom, and the power, and the glory forever, Amen").

6. *Making Theological or Doctrinal Changes.* Sometimes scribes made theological or doctrinal changes—either omitting something they saw as wrong or making clarifying additions. For example, in Matt 24:36, some manuscripts omit the reference to the Son's ignorance of the day of his return—a passage that is obviously difficult to understand.[44]

Understanding the Textual Apparatuses and Tools

Several affordable or even free GNTs are available in print or digital format. A fundamental question, however, is: What version of the GNT am I reading? Is it the Byzantine text? Is it an eclectic text? If so, which eclectic text?

Any serious student of the GNT must own one (or both) of the two mainstream critical, eclectic texts of the GNT. As more manuscripts have been discovered and more variants recorded—and as both textual decisions and formatting have changed—these critical editions have gone through numerous revisions. The Nestle-Aland *Novum Testamentum Graece* is now in its 28th edition (2013). This version is usually called simply the "Nestle-Aland" and is often abbreviated NA[28]. The superscription ("28" in this case) represents the number of the most recent edition. The United Bible Societies GNT is now in its 5th edition (2014), and is usually called "the UBS." It is abbreviated as UBS[5] and has a red cover, while the Nestle-Aland's cover is usually blue.

Pointing to a scholarly consensus about text-critical methods and the resulting eclectic text, the Nestle-Aland and UBS have published the same eclectic text since UBS[3] (1975) and NA[26] (1979). The two publications differ, however, in punctuation and formatting, as well as in the presentation of textual data. The UBS text (prepared primarily for Bible translators and pastors) aims to list only significant variants that potentially affect translation. At the bottom of the page, significant variants (if any) are listed with extensive textual data. Each disputed text is ranked A, B, C, or D, based on the editorial committee's confidence in deciding the original reading. The preface and introductory section of the UBS text provides a helpful overview of the textual apparatus and should be read in its entirety by intermediate Greek students.

Nestle-Aland differs from the UBS by listing many more variants but providing less textual support for the variants listed. The Nestle-Aland text, aimed at the academic community, provides an especially efficient method for viewing variants—even when those variants are clearly not original and do not affect meaning significantly. Inserted symbols (for example a small, raised circle or square) enable

---

[44] In this text, as in a few other places (e.g., John 4:6), Scripture seems to speak of Jesus from the perspective of his human nature, not intending to deny the omniscience or omnipotence of his divine nature. Others have explained this passage by claiming that prior to his exaltation, Jesus emptied himself of certain divine prerogatives (i.e., the Kenotic theory).

the editors of the NA to include much information about variants in an extremely compact space. Students who own an NA[28] should carefully read the introductory material and learn the "critical signs" that label variations in the text.

Though the free Society of Biblical Literature Greek New Testament (SBLGNT), edited by Michael Holmes, is widely used in digital format by students, modern text critics have raised strident objections against enthroning it as a new *textus receptus*. J. K. Elliott has pointed out that the SBLGNT is an amalgam of four previously printed Greek New Testaments and that it provides no apparatus for variants in ancient manuscripts. The SBLGNT differs from the NA in more than 540 places.[45]

There are three other scholarly NT Greek texts of which the intermediate Greek student should be aware. First, in late 2018, Crossway, in conjunction with the evangelical study center Tyndale House at Cambridge University, released the Tyndale House edition of the Greek New Testament (THGNT). Dirk Jongkind, the lead editor of the work, claims that it is the most accurate Greek New Testament published to date. That is, he claims that, of printed Greek New Testaments, the THGNT is closest in wording to the apostolic autographs. The THGNT is unique in focusing on Greek manuscripts from the first five centuries of transmission and in incorporating recent scholarly insights on scribal habits into the editors' text-critical decisions. Many of the claims of the THGNT are still being debated, and students are referred to the following short book for a more extensive introduction and defense: *An Introduction to the Greek New Testament Produced at Tyndale House*, Cambridge (Crossway, 2019), by Dirk Jongkind. For an extensive video review of the THGNT by Rob Plummer, see: https://vimeo.com/313496503.

Students should also be aware of two other incomplete projects. These are the *Editio Critica Maior* (*ECM*) and the International Greek New Testament Project (IGNTP).[46] The *ECM* is overseen by the Institut für neutestamentliche Textforschung (INTF) in Münster, Germany. The origins of the project date to a call for a more comprehensive text-critical edition of the NT made by Kurt Aland, Jean Duplacy, and Bonifatius Fischer in 1967. So far, only the fascicles for the Catholic Epistles (James–Jude, 1997–2005), a short volume on parallel Gospel pericopes (2011), and the four volumes on the book of Acts (2017) have been published. The goal of the work is to provide a comprehensive look at all significant text variations within the first thousand years of the text's transmission—looking at Greek manuscripts, citations in the Greek Fathers, and significant early versions (translations) where they bear witness to variants in an underlying Greek text.[47]

Peter Williams notes that the *ECM* volume (2nd ed.) of the Catholic Epistles differs from the NA[27] on decisions about the NT text's original wording in only 34

---

[45] J. K Elliott, "Recent Trends," 118. Available online at http://evangelicaltextualcriticism.blogspot.com/2012/03/keith-elliott-on-recent-trends.html. The SBLGNT does provide a minimal apparatus, listing the readings of Bible translations and other critical editions. See http://sblgnt.com/about/.

[46] The IGNTP continues the Critical Greek Testament Project, begun in 1926.

[47] Information in this paragraph was obtained from the Preface and Introduction to the *Editio Critica Maior*.

places, all of which have been incorporated into the new 28th edition of Nestle-Aland.[48] Dirk Jongkind observes that the ECM volumes of Acts differ from the NA[28] at 52 places,[49] all of which will presumably be incorporated into the forthcoming 29th edition of the Nestle-Aland GNT and 6th edition of the United Bible Societies GNT. While intermediate Greek students may use the *ECM* in their campus library, they are unlikely to own it because of (1) the cost, (2) the currently incomplete nature of the project, and (3) the level of detail provided by *ECM*—a detail unnecessary except for the most detailed text-critical study. For example, page 15 of the *ECM* volume covering James features only twelve Greek words from Jas 1:18b–19a. The remainder of the page contains information on textual variants for this small section of text. Such a page is typical of the series.

Another ongoing project of which students should be aware is the International Greek New Testament Project (IGNTP). Beginning in 1948, the IGNTP sought to provide a comprehensive critical edition of the GNT, listing every significant variant in existing ancient manuscripts, quotations, and versions. The IGNTP differs from the ECM in using the *textus receptus*[50] (Byzantine text) as a base text, from which variant readings are noted. This use of the *textus receptus* is simply a scholarly convention, not a normative judgment about the quality of the Byzantine text tradition. The goal of the IGNTP is not to produce a scholarly eclectic text, but simply to provide a comprehensive, accurate recording of NT textual variants. So far, only Luke has been completed (two volumes, published by Oxford University Press in 1984 and 1987). The IGNTP is currently working on the Gospel of John (two volumes already out) in cooperation with the Institut für neutestamentliche Textforschung.[51] In addition to their IGNTP volumes on John, the IGNTP will also produce the *ECM* volume on John. The IGNTP website reports that in 2016, the organization "formally began work on the edition of the Pauline Epistles, which is expected to take around two decades to produce."[52] As Dan Wallace notes, the discipline of text criticism is experiencing a new era of cooperation and collaboration, made easier by digital scanning, the internet, and other evolving technologies. Perhaps your interests have been sparked in this field. If so, receive this challenge from Wallace, which he wrote in 2009:

---

[48] Accessed October 29, 2019, http://marginalia.lareviewofbooks.org/peter-williams-on-the-nestle-aland-novum-testamentum-graece/. Williams notes that the NA[28] text outside of the Catholic Epistles is the same as the NA[27], except for minor changes such as capitalization or formatting. The textual apparatus of the NA[28], however, includes additional and corrected information throughout the entire GNT.

[49] Accessed October 21, 2019, http://evangelicaltextualcriticism.blogspot.com/2018/08/the-text-of-acts-differences-between.html.

[50] Specifically, the chosen *textus receptus* was "published by Clarendon Press, Oxford, in 1873, a reprint of an edition published in 1828 that ultimately is based on the third edition of Stephanus published in 1550." Eckhard J. Schnabel, "Textual Criticism: Recent Developments," in *The Face of New Testament Studies: A Survey of Recent Research*, ed. Scot McKnight and Grant R. Osborne (Grand Rapids: Baker; Leicester: Apollos, 2004), 64.

[51] Two volumes on John have appeared, one with evidence from the papyri (1995) and the other with attestation from the majuscules (2007).

[52] Accessed October 21, 2019, http://www.igntp.org/.

"Collation" is the comparison of a MS [manuscript] to a base text. All the differences, down to the individual letters, are noted. Collation is thus an exact transcription of the MS but done with less effort and less paper. To date, all the MSS [manuscripts] of only one book of the NT have been completely collated. Herman Hoskier took thirty years to collate all MSS for Revelation—a book that has by far fewer MSS than any other NT book.

Complete collations of all NT books are desperately needed. Furthermore, only about 20% of all NT MSS [manuscripts] have published collations and transcriptions. How can we honestly speak about "knowledge of documents" without doing complete collations of them? At present, the work to collate all Greek NT MSS would take about 400 man-years. In short, the harvest is plentiful but the workers are few![53]

Students are encouraged to take a class in NT text criticism to develop deeper knowledge and personal proficiency in the practice of text criticism. Although usually only a small percentage (5 percent?) of students find that they are fascinated by text criticism, perhaps you belong to this select group.

Recent Trends in Text Criticism

In recent years, prominent NT text critics (e.g., Bart Ehrman, Eldon Jay Epp, David Parker) have attempted to redirect the discipline away from determining the original reading of the NT text. Instead, these scholars have called for a study of textual variants as a window into the theological, ecclesiastical, and cultural world in which the documents were copied (and altered). The variants, thus, are a worthy end in themselves. Often this new approach has been combined with an unwarranted skepticism and sensationalistic claims about the wide influence of tendentious scribes.[54]

While not neglecting the worthy study of textual variations in their own right, the long-established discipline of text criticism should lead us to affirm the value and confidence of studying ancient manuscripts of the NT to determine the original reading of the text. In responding to some of the more recent fads in text criticism, Moisés Silva astutely writes:

> In conclusion, I would like to affirm—not only with Hort, but with practically all students of ancient documents—that the recovery of the original text (i.e., the text

---

[53] Daniel B. Wallace, "Challenges in New Testament Textual Criticism for the Twenty-First Century," *JETS* 52 (2009): 97. According to text critic Elijah Hixson, of the 304 extant manuscripts of Revelation, Hoskier only collated 228 (all he had access to at the time). Recently, Tommy Wasserman has collated virtually all known continuous-text manuscripts of Jude. See *The Epistle of Jude: Its Text and Transmission*, Coniectanea Biblica: New Testament Series 43 (Stockholm: Almqvist & Wiksell, 2006). Matt Solomon, a PhD graduate of New Orleans Baptist Theological Seminary, accomplished the same feat for the book of Philemon (private conversation with Elijah Hixson, January 8, 2015).

[54] E.g., Bart D. Ehrman's *Misquoting Jesus: The Story Behind Who Changed the Bible and Why* (New York: HarperCollins, 2005). For a rebuttal of Ehrman's claims, see Andreas Köstenberger, Darrell Bock, and Josh Chatraw, *Truth Matters* (Nashville: B&H, 2014); and the more detailed version by the same authors, *Truth in a Culture of Doubt* (Nashville: B&H, 2014).

in its initial form, prior to the alterations produced in the copying process) remains the primary task of textual criticism. Of course, it is not the only task. The study of early textual variation for its own sake is both a fascinating and a most profitable exercise. And it is also true that we have sometimes been sloppy in our use of the term *original text*. But neither these truths nor the admittedly great difficulties involved in recovering the autographic words can be allowed to dissolve the concept of an original text.[55]

Theological Considerations

Scholars debate what role *a priori* theological commitments should play in academic study. Nevertheless, if Jesus Christ is the climax of God's revelation of himself (as you are likely to affirm if you are reading this text), it seems reasonable to surmise that God would provide an accurate and enduring record of that definitive revelation (cf. John 16:12–15). This logical necessity is furthermore supported by data—lots of it. A massive number of ancient NT manuscripts, their overwhelming similarity, and the ability to arrive at virtual certainty as to the text's original wording through comparative analysis (i.e., text criticism) leads us to affirm God's preservation of his authoritative Word.[56] The words of British paleographer Sir Frederic G. Kenyon nicely summarize the state of NT textual criticism:

> It is reassuring at the end to find that the general result of all these discoveries and all this study is to strengthen the proof of the authenticity of the Scriptures, and our conviction that we have in our hands in substantial integrity, the veritable Word of God.[57]

TEXT CRITICISM: RECOMMENDED WEBSITES	
WEBSITE	CONTENTS
csntm.org	Center for the Study of New Testament Manuscripts. Executive Director, Dan Wallace
nobts.edu/cntts	H. Milton Haggard Center for New Testament Textual Studies, New Orleans Baptist Theological Seminary
ntgateway.com	Website overseen by NT scholar Mark Goodacre; includes helpful section of text criticism links
evangelicaltextualcriticism.blogspot.com	Forum to discuss biblical manuscripts and textual history from an evangelical perspective

---

[55] Moisés Silva, "Response," in *Rethinking New Testament Textual Criticism*, ed. David Alan Black (Grand Rapids: Baker, 2002), 149. For a similar view of recent fads, see Wallace, "Challenges in New Testament Textual Criticism," 79–100.

[56] D. A. Carson notes, "Almost all text critics will acknowledge that 96, even 97 percent, of the Greek New Testament is morally certain. It's just not in dispute." See "Who Is This Jesus? Is He Risen?" a documentary film hosted by D. James Kennedy and Jerry Newcombe (Fort Lauderdale, FL: Coral Ridge Ministries, 2000).

[57] Frederic G. Kenyon, *The Story of the Bible*, 2nd ed. (Grand Rapids: Eerdmans, 1967), 113.

SUMMARY

HISTORY OF THE GREEK LANGUAGE	
FORM OF LANGUAGE	DATES
Proto Indo-European	Prior to 1500 BC
Linear B or Mycenaean	1500–1000 BC
Dialects and Classical Greek	1000–300 BC
Koine Greek	300 BC–AD 330
Byzantine Greek	AD 330–AD 1453
Modern Greek	AD 1453–present

COMMON CHANGES IN GREEK FROM CLASSICAL TO KOINE PERIOD	
CHANGE	EXAMPLE FROM GNT
First aorist endings appear on second aorist verb stems	ἐγὼ δὲ **εἶπα**· τίς εἶ, κύριε; (Acts 26:15). Then I **said**, "Who are You, Lord?" (Acts 26:15).
Less common use of optative mood	ἐμοὶ δὲ **μὴ γένοιτο** καυχᾶσθαι εἰ μὴ ἐν τῷ σταυρῷ τοῦ κυρίου ἡμῶν Ἰησοῦ Χριστοῦ (Gal 6:14). **may it never be** that I should boast, except in the cross of our Lord Jesus Christ (Gal 6:14 NASB).
Increased use of prepositions	εὐλογητὸς ὁ θεὸς καὶ πατὴρ τοῦ κυρίου ἡμῶν Ἰησοῦ Χριστοῦ, ὁ εὐλογήσας ἡμᾶς **ἐν** πάσῃ εὐλογίᾳ πνευματικῇ **ἐν** τοῖς ἐπουρανίοις **ἐν** Χριστῷ (Eph 1:3). Blessed is the God and Father of our Lord Jesus Christ, who has blessed us **with** every spiritual blessing **in** the heavens in Christ (Eph 1:3).
-μι verbs appear with omega verb endings	τὰ πτώματα αὐτῶν οὐκ **ἀφίουσιν** τεθῆναι εἰς μνῆμα (Rev 11:9). They did not **permit** their bodies to be put into a tomb (Rev 11:9).
Disappearance of ϝ and ϟ	**καλέσω** τὸν οὐ λαόν μου λαόν μου καὶ τὴν οὐκ ἠγαπημένην ἠγαπημένην (Rom 9:25). Those who were not my people **I will call** "my people," and her who was not beloved I will call "beloved" (Rom 9:25 ESV).
Greater use of paratactic style	Cf. 1 John and James.
Change in meaning of comparative and superlative forms	μετάγεται ὑπὸ **ἐλαχίστου** πηδαλίου ὅπου ἡ ὁρμὴ τοῦ εὐθύνοντος βούλεται (Jas 3:4). They are guided by a **very small** rudder wherever the will of the pilot directs (Jas 3:4).
Semantic shifts in specific words	σὺ δὲ **λάλει** ἃ πρέπει τῇ ὑγιαινούσῃ διδασκαλίᾳ (Titus 2:1). But as for you, **speak** the things which are fitting for sound doctrine (Titus 2:1 NASB).

TEXT-CRITICAL CRITERIA

EXTERNAL CRITERIA	INTERNAL CRITERIA
Favor the older manuscripts.	Favor the reading that best fits the literary context.
Favor the reading supported by the majority of manuscripts.	Favor the reading that corresponds best with writings by the same author.
Favor the reading best attested across manuscript families.	Favor the reading that best explains the origin of the other variants.
	Favor the shorter reading.
	Favor the more difficult reading.

ERRORS IN THE GNT

UNINTENTIONAL ERRORS

TYPE	EXPLANATION
Errors of sight	Scribe glancing back and forth between manuscripts makes an error.
Errors of hearing	Scribe listening to dictated manuscript makes an error.
Errors of writing	Scribe makes an error in writing that cannot be attributed to a mistake in copying by sight or listening.
Errors of judgment	Scribe wrongly judges what to copy—incorporating a marginal note into the text, for example.

INTENTIONAL ERRORS

TYPE	EXPLANATION
Revision of grammar and spelling	Orthographic or grammatical correction by a scribe.
Harmonization of passages	Deleting or incorporating material so that the passage corresponds with a parallel text (in the Synoptic Gospels, for example).
Elimination of difficulties	Deletion or revision of a perceived error.
Conflation of texts	Scribe incorporates two or more variant readings into his manuscript.
Adaption of liturgical tradition	Addition of liturgical material to text.
Theological or doctrinal change	Scribe omits or adds material to avoid perceived theological difficulty.

CRITICAL EDITIONS OF THE GNT

TEXT	CHARACTERISTICS
United Bible Society, 5th edition (UBS[5])	Eclectic critical text. Notes only significant variants, but provides extensive textual data and an A, B, C, or D ranking. Edition primarily intended for pastors and translators.

CRITICAL EDITIONS OF THE GNT	
Novum Testamentum Graece, 28th edition (Nestle-Aland[28] or NA[28])	Same NT text as UBS, but noting many more variants through a system of symbols incorporated into the text. Fewer textual witnesses provided than in the UBS. Aimed at the academic community.
Editio Critica Maior (*ECM*)	Eclectic critical text of the NT that provides comprehensive manuscript data for the first thousand years of the church. Only the Catholic Epistles, Acts, and a short volume on parallel Gospel pericopes have been completed. Material from *ECM* is gradually being incorporated into Nestle-Aland and UBS.
International Greek New Testament Project (IGNTP)	Using the *textus receptus* as a base, the IGNTP provides nearly exhaustive manuscript evidence for all ancient witnesses. Only the Gospel of Luke has been completed. Two volumes on the Gospel of John (papyri and majuscules) have been published.

PRACTICE EXERCISES

In the first five sentences, label the grammatical or orthographic (spelling) shift in Koine Greek represented by the underlined word(s) in each sentence.

1. καὶ βλέπουσιν ἐκ τῶν λαῶν καὶ φυλῶν καὶ γλωσσῶν καὶ ἐθνῶν τὸ πτῶμα αὐτῶν ἡμέρας τρεῖς καὶ ἥμισυ καὶ τὰ πτώματα αὐτῶν οὐκ <u>ἀφίουσιν</u> τεθῆναι εἰς μνῆμα (Rev 11:9).

2. οἱ δὲ <u>εἶπαν</u> αὐτῷ, ἐν Βηθλέεμ τῆς Ἰουδαίας· οὕτως γὰρ γέγραπται διὰ τοῦ προφήτου (Matt 2:5).

3. ἰδοὺ καὶ τὰ πλοῖα τηλικαῦτα ὄντα καὶ ὑπὸ ἀνέμων σκληρῶν ἐλαυνόμενα, μετάγεται ὑπὸ <u>ἐλαχίστου</u> πηδαλίου ὅπου ἡ ὁρμὴ τοῦ εὐθύνοντος βούλεται (Jas 3:4).

4. τοῦ δὲ Ἰησοῦ γεννηθέντος <u>ἐν</u> Βηθλέεμ τῆς Ἰουδαίας <u>ἐν</u> ἡμέραις Ἡρῴδου τοῦ βασιλέως, ἰδοὺ μάγοι <u>ἀπὸ</u> ἀνατολῶν παρεγένοντο <u>εἰς</u> Ἱεροσόλυμα (Matt 2:1).

5. ὡς καὶ ἐν τῷ Ὡσηὲ λέγει, <u>Καλέσω</u> τὸν οὐ λαόν μου λαόν μου καὶ τὴν οὐκ ἠγαπημένην ἠγαπημένην· (Rom 9:25).

In each of the following five examples, (1) translate the passage both as it stands in the body of the NA²⁸/UBS⁵ and with the selected textual variant in parentheses. (2) In one brief sentence, note the difference in meaning that the variant makes. (3) Record which manuscripts support the variant reading provided in parentheses. (4) Why do you think the editors of your GNT favored the reading that they did? If you have the UBS edition, what letter ranking did the editorial committee assign to their choice? If you have access to Metzger's *Textual Commentary on the Greek New Testament*, check his explanation.

6. Παῦλος ἀπόστολος Χριστοῦ Ἰησοῦ διὰ θελήματος θεοῦ τοῖς ἁγίοις τοῖς οὖσιν [<u>ἐν Ἐφέσῳ</u>] (*variant: omit bracketed words*) καὶ πιστοῖς ἐν Χριστῷ Ἰησοῦ (Eph 1:1).

7. καὶ ταῦτα γράφομεν <u>ἡμεῖς</u> (ὑμῖν), ἵνα ἡ χαρὰ <u>ἡμῶν</u> (ὑμῶν) ᾖ πεπληρωμένη (1 Jn 1:4).

8. αὐτὸς δὲ ὁ κύριος τῆς εἰρήνης δῴη ὑμῖν τὴν εἰρήνην διὰ παντὸς ἐν παντὶ <u>τρόπῳ</u> (τόπῳ) (2 Thess 3:16).

9. δικαιωθέντες οὖν ἐκ πίστεως εἰρήνην <u>ἔχομεν</u> (ἔχωμεν) πρὸς τὸν θεὸν διὰ τοῦ κυρίου ἡμῶν Ἰησοῦ Χριστοῦ (Rom 5:1).

10. ἰδοὺ βάλλω αὐτὴν εἰς <u>κλίνην</u> (φυλακήν) καὶ τοὺς μοιχεύοντας μετ' αὐτῆς εἰς θλῖψιν μεγάλην, ἐὰν μὴ μετανοήσωσιν ἐκ τῶν ἔργων αὐτῆς (Rev 2:22).

VOCABULARY

Vocabulary to Memorize

ἀπαγγέλλω	I announce, proclaim, report (45)
ἀποδίδωμι	I give away, pay, return (48)
ἄρα	so, then, consequently (49)
ἄφεσις, -εως, ἡ	forgiveness (17)
ἄχρι	until (conj. or prep. + gen.) (49)
βάπτισμα, -ατος, τό	baptism (19)
δεύτερος	second (43)
διακονέω	I serve (37)
διέρχομαι	I go through, cross over (43)
ἐκπορεύομαι	I go out, come out (33)
ἐνδύω	I clothe myself, put on, wear (27)
ἐπιγινώσκω	I know, understand, recognize (44)
ἔρημος, ἡ	desert, wilderness (48)
ἑτοιμάζω	I make ready, prepare (40)
ἔτος, -ους, τό	year (49)
εὐδοκέω	I am well pleased, approve (21)
Ἠσαΐας, ὁ	Isaiah (22)
θηρίον, τό	animal, beast (46)
θλῖψις, -εως, ἡ	tribulation, affliction, oppression (45)
θρίξ, τριχός, ἡ	hair (15)
ἱκανός	qualified, able (39)
Ἰορδάνης, -ου, ὁ	the Jordan (15)
ἰσχυρός	strong, mighty, powerful (29)
καθίζω	I cause to sit down, appoint (46)
κρατέω	I grasp, hold (fast), arrest (47)
μετάνοια, ἡ	repentance (22)
ναός, ὁ	temple, sanctuary (45)
ὅμοιος	like, similar (45)
ὀπίσω	after, behind (35)
οὐαί	woe (46)
οὐκέτι	no longer (47)
πειράζω	I tempt, test (38)
ποταμός, ὁ	river (17)
πρό	before, in front of, at (gen) (47)
προσφέρω	I bring to, offer (47)
Σατανᾶς, -ᾶ, ὁ	Satan (36)

σταυρόω	I crucify (46)
τεσσεράκοντα	forty (22)
φυλακή, ἡ	watch, guard, prison (47)
χώρα, ἡ	district, region (28)

Vocabulary to Recognize

ἄγριος	wild (3)
ἀκρίς, ίδος, ἡ	locust (4)
βοάω	I call, shout, cry out (12)
δερμάτινος	(made of) leather (2)
ἐξομολογέω	I confess, admit (10)
εὐθύς	straight (8)
ζώνη, ἡ	belt (8)
Ἰεροσολυμίτης, -ου, ὁ	inhabitant of Jerusalem (2)
ἱμάς, -άντος, ὁ	strap, thong (4)
κάμηλος, ὁ	camel (6)
κατασκευάζω	I make ready, prepare (11)
κύπτω	I bend down (2)
μέλι, -ιτος, τό	honey (4)
Ναζαρέτ, ἡ	Nazareth (12)
ὀσφῦς, -ἡ	waist (8)
περιστερά, ἡ	dove, pigeon (10)
σχίζω	I split, divide, separate, tear apart (11)
τρίβος, ἡ	path (3)
ὑπόδημα, -ατος, τό	sandal (10)

READING THE NEW TESTAMENT

Mark 1:1–13

¹ Ἀρχὴ τοῦ εὐαγγελίου Ἰησοῦ Χριστοῦ [υἱοῦ θεοῦ]. ² Καθὼς γέγραπται ἐν τῷ Ἠσαΐᾳ τῷ προφήτῃ· ἰδοὺ ἀποστέλλω τὸν ἄγγελόν μου πρὸ προσώπου σου, ὃς κατασκευάσει τὴν ὁδόν σου· ³ φωνὴ βοῶντος ἐν τῇ ἐρήμῳ· ἑτοιμάσατε τὴν ὁδὸν κυρίου, εὐθείας ποιεῖτε τὰς τρίβους αὐτοῦ, ⁴ ἐγένετο Ἰωάννης [ὁ] βαπτίζων ἐν τῇ ἐρήμῳ καὶ κηρύσσων βάπτισμα μετανοίας εἰς ἄφεσιν ἁμαρτιῶν. ⁵ καὶ ἐξεπορεύετο πρὸς αὐτὸν πᾶσα ἡ Ἰουδαία χώρα καὶ οἱ Ἱεροσολυμῖται πάντες, καὶ ἐβαπτίζοντο ὑπ᾽ αὐτοῦ ἐν τῷ Ἰορδάνῃ ποταμῷ ἐξομολογούμενοι τὰς ἁμαρτίας αὐτῶν. ⁶ καὶ ἦν ὁ Ἰωάννης ἐνδεδυμένος τρίχας καμήλου καὶ ζώνην δερματίνην περὶ τὴν ὀσφὺν αὐτοῦ καὶ ἐσθίων ἀκρίδας καὶ μέλι ἄγριον. ⁷ Καὶ ἐκήρυσσεν λέγων· ἔρχεται ὁ ἰσχυρότερός μου ὀπίσω μου, οὗ οὐκ εἰμὶ ἱκανὸς κύψας λῦσαι τὸν ἱμάντα τῶν ὑποδημάτων αὐτοῦ. ⁸ ἐγὼ ἐβάπτισα ὑμᾶς ὕδατι, αὐτὸς δὲ βαπτίσει ὑμᾶς ἐν πνεύματι ἁγίῳ. ⁹ Καὶ ἐγένετο ἐν ἐκείναις ταῖς ἡμέραις ἦλθεν Ἰησοῦς ἀπὸ Ναζαρὲτ τῆς Γαλιλαίας καὶ ἐβαπτίσθη εἰς τὸν Ἰορδάνην ὑπὸ Ἰωάννου. ¹⁰ καὶ εὐθὺς ἀναβαίνων ἐκ τοῦ ὕδατος εἶδεν σχιζομένους τοὺς οὐρανοὺς καὶ τὸ πνεῦμα ὡς περιστερὰν καταβαῖνον εἰς αὐτόν· ¹¹ καὶ φωνὴ ἐγένετο ἐκ τῶν οὐρανῶν· σὺ εἶ ὁ υἱός μου ὁ ἀγαπητός, ἐν σοὶ εὐδόκησα. ¹² Καὶ εὐθὺς τὸ πνεῦμα αὐτὸν ἐκβάλλει εἰς τὴν ἔρημον. ¹³ καὶ ἦν ἐν τῇ ἐρήμῳ τεσσεράκοντα ἡμέρας πειραζόμενος ὑπὸ τοῦ σατανᾶ, καὶ ἦν μετὰ τῶν θηρίων, καὶ οἱ ἄγγελοι διηκόνουν αὐτῷ.

Reading Notes[58]

Verse 1

- **Ἀρχὴ τοῦ εὐαγγελίου Ἰησοῦ Χριστοῦ** ("The beginning of the gospel of Jesus Christ") – This is the opening title of Mark's Gospel. ἀρχή is a nominative absolute because it is grammatically unrelated to the rest of the sentence. In addition, ἀρχή is definite even though it is anarthrous since as the initial word in the opening title it is sufficiently specific without the article (cf. Matt 1:1; Rev 1:1).[59] Ἰησοῦ Χριστοῦ is most likely an objective genitive, "the gospel *about* Jesus Christ," or a genitive of content, referring to the written work whose subject or content is Jesus Christ.[60]

- **[υἱοῦ θεοῦ]** ("the Son of God") – As the brackets indicate, υἱοῦ θεοῦ is missing in some key manuscripts, so the editors felt uncertain as to its

---

[58] The English version used in the Reading Notes for this chapter is the CSB.
[59] See Robertson, 781, 793.
[60] So BDF, 90 (§163); Robert H. Stein, *Mark*, BECNT (Grand Rapids: Baker, 2008), 41. Wallace labels Ἰησοῦ Χριστοῦ a "plenary genitive," indicating that this is probably both an objective and subjective genitive (121).

authenticity. The reading Ἰησοῦ Χριστοῦ υἱοῦ θεοῦ is attested by Codex Alexandrinus (A, υἱοῦ τοῦ θεοῦ), Codex Vaticanus (B), Codex Bezae (D), and an ancient correction to Codex Sinaiticus (ℵ¹).[61] The omission of υἱοῦ θεοῦ in certain manuscripts may be due to the similarity in endings of the *nomina sacra* (abbreviations for common words such as "Christ" or "God"), which scribes used in the first few centuries of the church when copying manuscripts.[62] The genitive phrase υἱοῦ θεοῦ, if original, stands in apposition to Ἰησοῦ Χριστοῦ in order to define further the identity of Jesus. In the remainder of his Gospel, Mark does not join the name Jesus with Χριστός but instead always uses Χριστός as a title (e.g., 8:29).

Verse 2

- γέγραπται ("it is written") – Per pass ind 3rd sg γράφω. This could be translated "it stands written" since the focus of the perfect is on the present results of the past action.

- ἐν τῷ Ἠσαΐᾳ τῷ προφήτῃ ("in Isaiah the prophet") – The syntactical function of the phrase τῷ προφήτῃ, a dative of apposition, is to identify Isaiah as a prophet, highlighting the fulfillment of his prophecy in the coming of John the Baptist. Some manuscripts (A W *f13*) read ἐν τοῖς προφήταις which is a clear attempt of a scribe to "fix" the text since the author quotes from Isaiah *and* Malachi. Early Jewish sources conflated texts in this way, so Mark is following the literary conventions of his day. Metzger notes, "The quotation in verses 2 and 3 is composite, the first part being from Mal 3:1 and the second part from Is 40:3. It is easy to see, therefore, why copyists would have altered the words 'in Isaiah the prophet' (a reading found in the earliest representative witnesses of the Alexandrian and Western types of text) to the more comprehensive introductory formula 'in the prophets.'"[63]

- ἰδοὺ ἀποστέλλω τὸν ἄγγελόν μου πρὸ προσώπου σου, ὃς κατασκευάσει τὴν ὁδόν σου ("See, I am sending my messenger ahead of you, he will prepare your way") – This is actually a quotation of Mal 3:1, but in the next verse Mark cites Isa 40:3. Most likely because Isaiah

---

[61] To see the correction added over the original scribe's writing (ℵ*) in Codex Sinaiticus, go to www.codexsinaiticus.org.

[62] Metzger comments, "The absence of υἱοῦ θεοῦ ℵ* Θ 28ᶜ *al* may be due to an oversight in copying, occasioned by the similarity of the endings of the *nomina sacra*. On the other hand, however, there was always a temptation (to which copyists often succumbed) to expand titles and quasi-titles of books. Since the combination of B D W 1ℵ in support of υἱοῦ θεοῦ is extremely strong, it was not thought advisable to omit the words altogether, yet because of the antiquity of the shorter reading and the possibility of scribal expansion, it was decided to enclose the words within square brackets." See Bruce M. Metzger, *A Textual Commentary on the Greek New Testament*, 2nd ed. (New York: UBS, 1994), 62.

[63] Metzger, *Textual Commentary*, 62.

was the major prophet, Mark prefaces this dual citation by saying "As it is written in Isaiah the prophet," not explicitly identifying Malachi as his first source. πρὸ προσώπου σου (literally, "before your face") is a Semitism and may be translated "ahead of You."[64] κατασκευάσει is a fut act ind 3rd sg of κατασκευάζω.

Verse 3

- **φωνὴ βοῶντος ἐν τῇ ἐρήμῳ** ("A voice of one crying out in the wilderness") – This now begins the quote from Isa 40:3. The anarthrous noun φωνή may be translated as either indefinite (CSB) or definite (ESV). In the original context of Isa 40:3, the precise identity of the voice is left unspecified. βοῶντος (pres act ptc masc gen sg βοάω) is a substantival participle ("of the one crying out").

- **ἑτοιμάσατε τὴν ὁδὸν κυρίου, εὐθείας ποιεῖτε τὰς τρίβους αὐτοῦ** ("Prepare the way for the Lord; make His paths straight!") – The quotation includes two imperatives, ἑτοιμάσατε (aor act impv 2nd pl ἑτοιμάζω) and ποιεῖτε (pres act impv 2nd pl ποιέω). The adjective εὐθείας ("straight," at the beginning of the clause for emphasis) is associated with τρίβους.

Verse 4

- **ἐγένετο Ἰωάννης [ὁ] βαπτίζων ἐν τῇ ἐρήμῳ καὶ κηρύσσων** ("John came baptizing in the wilderness and proclaiming") – Some manuscripts do not include the article ὁ, while others do not include the καί. Without the article, βαπτίζων (pres act ptc masc nom sg βαπτίζω) functions as an adverbial participle and is coordinate to κηρύσσων ("baptizing . . . and proclaiming"). With the article, ὁ βαπτίζων functions as a substantival participle ("[John] the one baptizing" or "[John] the Baptist"). A few manuscripts (most notably ℵ) include both the substantival and adverbial use of βαπτίζων in this verse. Perhaps the regular use of ὁ βαπτιστής as a title for John (e.g., Mark 6:25) encouraged the addition of the article with βαπτίζων, so that it functions as a title.[65]

- **βάπτισμα μετανοίας** ("baptism of repentance") – μετανοίας is a descriptive genitive, specifying which kind of baptism John was administering.

- **εἰς ἄφεσιν ἁμαρτιῶν** ("for the forgiveness of sins") – ἁμαρτιῶν is an objective genitive. That is, the sins are not doing the forgiving (which would be subjective genitive), they are being forgiven.

---

[64] So Robertson, 621; Moulton & Turner, 4:16.
[65] See Stein, *Mark*, 52–53.

Verse 5

- **καί** ("and," not translated in CSB) – Mark begins approximately two thirds of his sentences with καί, a distinctly Markan style.

- **ἐξεπορεύετο . . . ἐβαπτίζοντο** ("were going out . . . were baptized") – Impf mid ind 3rd sg ἐκπορεύομαι / impf pass ind 3rd pl βαπτίζω. The two imperfect verbs convey the habitual or repetitive (iterative) nature of people coming to John and being baptized by him. Also notice that the compound subject (πᾶσα ἡ Ἰουδαία χώρα καὶ οἱ Ἰεροσολυμῖται πάντες) has a singular verb (ἐξεπορεύετο), a common feature in Greek. The technical term for this pattern is a Pindaric construction.

- **ἐξομολογούμενοι** ("as they confessed") – Pres mid ptc masc nom pl ἐξομολογέω. A temporal adverbial participle expressing an action that is contemporaneous with ἐβαπτίζοντο ("they were being baptized . . . as they confessed their sins").

Verse 6

- **ἦν . . . ἐνδεδυμένος** ("wore") – This is a periphrastic construction with the imperfect of εἰμί and the perfect participle ἐνδεδυμένος expressing a pluperfect verbal idea ("had been clothed" or perhaps more accurately with an emphasis on the results that existed in the past: "was clothed," i.e., "wore").[66] Since ἐνδύω normally takes a double accusative, τρίχας and ζώνην remain as accusatives after the passive form of ἐνδύω. John's attire characterizes him as a prophet like Elijah (cf. 2 Kgs 1:8; Zech 13:4).

- **ἦν . . . ἐσθίων** ("and ate") – This is another periphrastic construction, in this situation composed of the imperfect of εἰμί and the present participle ἐσθίων expressing an imperfect verbal idea, denoting the customary or habitual nature of John's diet of locusts and wild honey ("was eating"). Note the large number of rare vocabulary words in this verse.

Verse 7

- **ἐκήρυσσεν** ("He proclaimed") – impf act ind 3rd sg κηρύσσω.

- **ὁ ἰσχυρότερός μου** ("someone more powerful than I") – ἰσχυρότερος (nom masc sg) is a comparative adjective of ἰσχυρός ("strong"), followed by the genitive of comparison μου ("than I").

- **οὗ οὐκ εἰμὶ ἱκανὸς κύψας λῦσαι τὸν ἱμάντα τῶν ὑποδημάτων αὐτοῦ** ("I am not worthy to stoop down and untie the strap of His sandals") – The syntax of this sentence is a bit awkward in the original (literally, "Of

---

[66] Wallace, 647–48.

whom I am not worthy having stooped down to loose the strap of His sandals") and is typically smoothed out by the existing English translations. κύψας (aor act ptc masc nom sg κύπτω, "bend down") conveys attendant circumstance (with the aor inf λῦσαι; "to stoop down and untie"; so most translations). The inf λῦσαι clarifies the way in which John considers himself to be unworthy (epexegetical inf). Removing another person's sandal was a menial task similar to footwashing (cf. John 13:14).

Verse 8

- ἐγώ ... αὐτὸς δέ ("I ... but He") – ἐγώ adds emphasis and when juxtaposed with αὐτὸς δέ is used for contrast ("*I* baptized ... but *he* will baptize").

- ὕδατι ... ἐν πνεύματι ἁγίῳ ("with water ... with the Holy Spirit") – Most English translations render these phrases to communicate instrumentality/means (though ὕδατι may be a dative of sphere/space; i.e., "in water").

Verse 9

- Καὶ ἐγένετο ἐν ἐκείναις ταῖς ἡμέραις ("In those days") – Many translations (such as the CSB and the ESV) do not translate the phrase καὶ ἐγένετο, a Semitic construction similar to "and it came to pass" (Judg 19:1; 1 Sam 28:1; cf. Mark 2:15, 23; 4:4).[67] The phrase is often used to introduce a new narrative phrase or a new character (in this case, Jesus) into the story. Notice also the contrast between the many coming to John from Judea and Jerusalem (1:5) and the lone individual coming from Galilee (1:9).

- εἰς τὸν Ἰορδάνην ("in the Jordan") – The preposition εἰς is used where ἐν might be expected (literally, "into the Jordan"; cf. ἐν in Matt 3:6). As reflected throughout Mark, by the time of the NT these two prepositions were used interchangeably.[68]

Verse 10

- καὶ εὐθύς ("As soon as") – A Markan favorite (42 occurrences), εὐθύς (adv, "immediately") may draw attention to a dramatic event (in the present instance, the heavens being torn open and the Spirit descending on Jesus like a dove). See also v. 12.

---

[67] See Moulton & Turner, 4:16.
[68] BDF, 110–11 (§205); Moule, 68; Robertson, 525, 592–93.

- **ἀναβαίνων ... καταβαῖνον** ("He came up . . . descending") – These two participles (pres act ptc masc nom sg ἀναβαίνω and pres act ptc neut acc sg καταβαίνω) are temporal adverbial participles.

- **σχιζομένους** ("torn open") – Pres pass ptc masc acc pl σχίζω. This verb appears only here and at 15:38 in Mark's Gospel, in the latter passage for the tearing apart of the temple veil. In both contexts, the "tearing open" is followed by a declaration of Jesus's identity as the Son of God (1:11; 15:39). There is also a possible allusion to Isa 63:19. The placement of the anarthrous ptc σχιζομένους before τοὺς οὐρανούς forms a chiasm with τὸ πνεῦμα preceding καταβαῖνον.

Verse 11

- **σὺ εἶ ὁ υἱός μου ὁ ἀγαπητός** ("You are my beloved son") – The allusion is to Ps 2:7 LXX (though note the different word order): υἱός μου σὺ εἶ. According to Gundry, "Mark puts σύ, 'you,' in first position to accent the identification of Jesus as God's Son."[69] Moreover, υἱός . . . ἀγαπητός indicates Jesus's special relationship with God, implying that he is his *only* Son.[70]

- **ἐν σοὶ εὐδόκησα** ("with you I am well-pleased.") – εὐδόκησα (aor act ind 1st sg εὐδοκέω), while in the aorist, is certainly present-referring ("with you I am *now* well pleased" not "with you I *was* well pleased" *in the past*), commonly referred to as a gnomic use of the aorist.

Verse 12

- **ἐκβάλλει** ("drove") – This is the first of approximately 150 historical presents in Mark's Gospel, vividly portraying the action of the Spirit driving Jesus into the wilderness to be tempted by the devil (cf. the use of aorist and imperfect forms of [ἀν]άγω in the parallel accounts in Matthew [4:1, ἀνήχθη] and Luke [Luke 4:1, ἤγετο]).

- **εἰς τὴν ἔρημον** ("into the wilderness") – Jesus's sojourn into the wilderness may be reminiscent of the "voice in the wilderness" in v. 3 and John the Baptist's baptizing ministry "in the wilderness" in v. 4 (see also v. 13).

Verse 13

- **ἦν ... πειραζόμενος** ("was . . . being tempted") – The imperfect of εἰμί here could function either in periphrastic construction with the pres

---

[69] Robert H. Gundry, *Mark: A Commentary on His Apology for the Cross* (Grand Rapids: Eerdmans, 1993), 49.

[70] See first numbered definition of ἀγαπητός in BDAG, 7.

pass ptc πειραζόμενος ("was in the wilderness 40 days being tempted"; NASB) or adverbially ("was in the wilderness for 40 days, being tempted"; so CSB, NIV). In the latter case the participle would most likely convey purpose: Jesus was tempted in keeping with God's plan.[71] Mark does not specify *how* Jesus was tempted as do Matthew (Matt 4:1–11) and Luke (4:1–13).

- τεσσεράκοντα ἡμέρας ("40 days") – An accusative of time, Jesus's "40 days" in the wilderness portrays him in contrast to the people of Israel who were tested in the wilderness for 40 *years*, often failing the test.

- διηκόνουν ("were serving him") – Impf act ind 3rd pl διακονέω. The verb διακονέω is in the imperfect tense, here indicating the ongoing service of the angels to Jesus.

---

[71] Wallace notes, "Almost every instance of an adverbial πειράζων in the present tense in the NT that follows the controlling verb suggests purpose" and includes Mark 1:13 (636 n. 60).

/////////////

CHAPTER 2

NOMINATIVE, VOCATIVE & ACCUSATIVE CASES

GOING DEEPER

J ohn's Gospel opens with the majestic words, "In the beginning was the Word, and the Word was with God, and the Word was God. He was with God in the beginning" (John 1:1). "In the beginning" immediately evokes the opening of the Bible in Genesis: "In the beginning God created the heavens and the earth" (Gen 1:1). John wants to tell his readers that his story of Jesus continues the creation story. As Jesus says later in the Gospel, "My Father is still working, and I am working also" (John 5:17). Strikingly, however, John does not say, "In the beginning *God*," but "In the beginning was *the Word*" (ἐν ἀρχῇ ἦν ὁ λόγος).

What is the relationship between God and the Word? The reader does not have to wait long to be told. John immediately explains, "and the Word was *with* God, and the Word *was God*" (καὶ ὁ λόγος ἦν πρὸς τὸν θεόν, καὶ θεὸς ἦν ὁ λόγος). Thus, we find that in John's opening verse, the evangelist says three things about the Word:

1. The Word was in the beginning (ἐν ἀρχῇ ἦν ὁ λόγος).

2. The Word was with God (ὁ λόγος ἦν πρὸς τὸν θεόν).

3. The Word was [himself] God (θεὸς ἦν ὁ λόγος).

Notice that in all three instances, "the Word" (ὁ λόγος) is the grammatical subject of the clause. There is a certain dramatic escalation in John's language here. First, he says that the Word was *in the beginning*. This reminds the reader of the repeated refrain in the creation account: God spoke, and all created things came into being through God's spoken Word. Second, John adds that the Word was in the beginning *with God.*[1] This associates the Word closely with God, the Creator. But what exactly is the nature of this relationship? Third, John asserts, in a striking exclamation point, that the Word *was himself God.* The reader is left to infer that there are two referents of θεός, God (the Father; John 1:14) and the Word (Jesus; John 1:17).[2]

John's striking opening assertion sets up the question of Jesus's identity that will dominate the rest of the entire Gospel, ultimately leading to Jesus's crucifixion: the deity of Christ.[3] In the original historical context, Jesus faces escalating opposition from the Jewish leaders who consider his claim blasphemy (5:17–18; 8:58–59; 10:30–33). Indeed, at Jesus's trial, they tell Pilate the Roman governor, "We have a law, and according to that law He must die, because He made Himself the Son of God" (John 19:7).

In our day, too, there are those who dispute Jesus's claim to deity, not least by challenging the conventional understanding of John 1:1, and here in particular the third phrase, "the Word was God" (θεὸς ἦν ὁ λόγος). In part, the reason for this is that the word order is reversed, with the predicate nominative (θεός) preceding the subject (ὁ λόγος). Is it legitimate to infer from the lack of article in front of θεός that "God" is indefinite and should be rendered "*a* god"? The answer is a firm "no." According to Greek syntax, it is common for a definite nominative predicate noun preceding a finite verb to be without the article. In this way, the subject (articular) is distinguished from the predicate nominative (anarthrous, i.e., without the article), yet without indicating that the latter is indefinite (as in "a god"). Of course, Jesus's deity does not rest on this one verse (see, e.g., John 20:28), but a sufficient knowledge of Greek syntax saves the reader from drawing the wrong conclusion.[4]

CHAPTER OBJECTIVES

The purpose of this and the next two chapters is to cover the various uses of the Greek cases: the nominative, vocative, and accusative (this chapter); the genitive (chap. 3); and the dative (chap. 4). The main benefit you will derive from working through these chapters is that you will be acquainted with all the major categories of usage for each of these cases. Although there is occasional debate on some of the categories, as well as on individual examples, these categories do genuinely capture the essence of the various uses of these cases. Understanding the essence

---

[1] Cf. 1:18, a likely *inclusio*, where the evangelist asserts that Jesus is "at the Father's side."

[2] See also the important textual variant θεός in John 1:18.

[3] For a discussion of the question of Jesus's deity in the context of Jewish monotheism, see Andreas J. Köstenberger and Scott R. Swain, *Father, Son and Spirit: The Trinity and John's Gospel*, NSBT 24 (Downers Grove: InterVarsity, 2007), chap. 1.

[4] Wallace, 266–69. See also the exegetical insight by Wallace in William D. Mounce, *Basics of Biblical Greek: Grammar* (Grand Rapids: Zondervan, 1993), 28–29.

of each category of usage and grasping how the categories differ from one another will increase your ability to interpret the NT more accurately.

THE GREEK CASE SYSTEM

In English, the relationship of a particular substantive (noun or pronoun used in place of a noun) to the rest of a sentence is indicated through word order and prepositions. In Greek, on the other hand, these relationships are indicated by case markers (e.g., 1 John 5:11: ζωὴν αἰώνιον ἔδωκεν ἡμῖν ὁ θεός). In this example, the nominative case ὁ θεός designates the subject; the accusative case ζωὴν αἰώνιον conveys the direct object; and the dative case ἡμῖν specifies the indirect object. Thus, we learn that God (subject) gave eternal life (direct object) to us (indirect object). Because Greek is an inflected language, distinguishing cases by distinctive endings, word order is not needed to mark out a word as the subject, direct object, or indirect object. Rather, word order may convey emphasis, especially when the conventional word order is reversed.

As Brooks & Winbery note, "Case is that aspect of a substantive which indicates its grammatical relationship to the verb and/or other elements in the sentence."[5] In the present volume, we distinguish, as is customary, between five major cases: (1) nominative, (2) genitive, (3) dative, (4) accusative, and (5) vocative.[6] Other, primarily older, grammars employ the eight-case system. Young compares the five-case system and the eight-case system as follows:[7]

FIVE-CASE SYSTEM (FORM)	EIGHT-CASE SYSTEM (FUNCTION)
1. Nominative (Designation)	1. Nominative (Designation)
2. Genitive (Description/Separation)	2. Genitive (Description)
	3. Ablative (Separation)
3. Dative (Interest/Location/Means)	4. Dative (Interest)
	5. Locative (Location)
	6. Instrumental (Means)
4. Accusative (Extension)	7. Accusative (Extension)
5. Vocative (Address)	8. Vocative (Address)

As Robertson notes, the difference between the five-case and the eight-case system essentially consists in whether grammarians take as their point of departure the actual *ending* of the word (form) or the *relationship expressed by* the ending

---

[5] Brooks & Winbery, 2.

[6] The frequency of cases in the NT is as follows: Nominative 30.4%; Genitive 24.6%; Dative 15.3%; Accusative 28.9%; and Vocative 0.8%. Hence the present chapter treats 60% of all case uses in the NT.

[7] Young, 9.

(function).[8] Those using an eight-case system build their system on continuing case distinctions (function) despite the identity of forms in certain cases.[9] Proponents of the five-case system start with distinct forms and proceed to distinguish between different types of usage of identical forms. For example, does τῇ δεξιᾷ τοῦ θεοῦ ὑψωθεὶς in Acts 2:33 mean "exalted *to* the right hand of God" (interest), "exalted *at* the right hand of God" (location), or "exalted *by* the right hand of God" (means)? Both systems have ways of distinguishing between these three major uses of the dative case. But while they arrive at these distinctions by different routes, both systems end up in essentially the same place.[10]

In what follows, we have chosen to follow the five-case system as the simpler and more commonly used way of distinguishing between different case endings. For convenience's sake, we have grouped the nominative, vocative, and accusative together in the present chapter. Separate chapters will be devoted to the genitive and dative, respectively. In each instance, we will discuss the key characteristics of the case in question, followed by the main categories of usage.

NOMINATIVE

The nominative case is used to designate a person or object, normally as the subject.[11] Initially, the nominative was not considered a case, but simply the noun. When the nominative began to be treated as a case, it was still called by the word for noun, nominative, meaning "the naming or noun case."[12] The Greeks called it the naming case because it regularly identifies the main subject of a sentence.[13] Its original use was to help identify the subject of a finite verb, and this remains its most common function.[14] The nominative occurs more often in the NT than any other case.[15]

In Greek, the verb expresses the subject as part of the verb form. For example, λέγει means "he, she, or it says." In the third person singular, in particular, the meaning of the ending by itself is inconclusive, and "it was often felt necessary

---

[8] Robertson, 447. See Wallace who comments, "[T]he basic difference between the two is a question of *definition*. The eight-case system defines case in terms of *function*, while the five-case system defines case in terms of *form*" (32). Wallace also notes that most today use the five-case system; those who used the eight-case system in the past (in part owing to the history of the language), include Robertson, Dana & Mantey, and Brooks & Winbery.

[9] However, while the five-case system is based strictly on *form*, one cannot equally say that the eight-case system is based strictly on *function*, for if that were true, as Wallace points out, "then there should be over *one hundred* cases in Greek" (34). Therefore, it is more accurate to say that while the five-case system is strictly a matter of form, the eight-case system is a matter of both form *and* function.

[10] See Robertson, 448 for the example.

[11] Porter, *Idioms*, 83; Brooks & Winbery, 3.

[12] Robertson, 456.

[13] Wallace, 37; Robertson, 456.

[14] Dana & Mantey, 68–69; Wallace, 38.

[15] Wallace, 37.

to 'name' the subject more definitely, so a noun was used."[16] The nominative is therefore "more than the case of the subject; it is the case of specific *designation*, and is in appositional relationship."[17] For the nominative, it seems best to distinguish between major uses (subject, predicate nominative, apposition) and other uses (nominative of address, nominative of appellation, nominative absolute, and hanging nominative).

MAJOR USES OF THE NOMINATIVE	Subject
	Predicate Nominative
	Apposition
OTHER USES OF THE NOMINATIVE	Address
	Appellation
	Absolute
	Hanging Nominative

Major Uses

The major uses of the nominative involve a grammatical construction in which the nominative case is dependent on the rest of the sentence.[18] They are subject, predicate nominative, and apposition.

Subject

The nominative is frequently "the grammatical subject of a clause."[19] Most commonly, the noun in the nominative case is the subject of a finite verb. Normally, the verb is explicitly stated, though at times it is merely implied (most frequently, a form of εἰμί). The nominative can be the subject of active, passive, or middle verbs. If active, the subject performs an action. If passive, the subject is being acted upon by an agent. If middle, the subject acts upon itself or on its own behalf, or emphasis is put on the subject.[20] The subject can be a noun (with or without the article and/or an adjective), a pronoun, or even a whole noun phrase (such as a relative clause).

- τότε παραγίνεται ὁ Ἰησοῦς ἀπὸ τῆς Γαλιλαίας (Matt 3:13)

  Then **Jesus** arrived from Galilee (NASB)

  Jesus is the subject of the main verb, παραγίνεται.

---

[16] Black, 46.

[17] Dana & Mantey, 68–69. For this reason, Dana & Mantey include the use of the subject under the rubric of the nominative of apposition (69).

[18] Among the major grammars, Wallace alone makes the distinction between grammatically dependent and independent uses of the nominative (49).

[19] Porter, *Idioms*, 84.

[20] Wallace, 38.

- Ἰωάννης μαρτυρεῖ περὶ αὐτοῦ καὶ κέκραγεν λέγων (John 1:15)

  John testified about Him and cried out, saying (NASB)

  In this case, John is the subject of both finite verbs, as well as the participle.

- ἀνήρ ἐστιν κεφαλὴ τῆς γυναικός (Eph 5:23)

  the **husband** is the head of the wife

  Note that ἀνήρ is the subject while κεφαλή is the predicate nominative. Both nouns lack the article, so word order helps distinguish between subject and predicate nominative.

- ἵνα παρακληθῶσιν **αἱ καρδίαι** αὐτῶν συμβιβασθέντες ἐν ἀγάπῃ (Col 2:2)

  that their **hearts** may be encouraged, having been knit together in love (NASB)

  Here αἱ καρδίαι is the subject of a finite verb in a dependent clause, as well as the subject of the adverbial participle συμβιβασθέντες.

- καὶ ἄλλος **ἄγγελος** ἦλθεν καὶ ἐστάθη ἐπὶ τοῦ θυσιαστηρίου (Rev 8:3)

  Another **angel** . . . came and stood at the altar

  The subject, "angel," is further modified by the adjective ἄλλος.

Predicate Nominative

Sometimes, there are two nominatives in a sentence: a subject nominative and a predicate nominative. In these instances, the predicate nominative provides further information about the subject. At times, the subject and the predicate nominative are virtually equivalent. More commonly, however, the predicate nominative describes a larger category of which the subject is a subset.[21] In this regard, the predicate nominative is not dissimilar to an apposition.[22] Grammatically, the predicate nominative serves as the complement (or completive) of a copulative verb (expressing a state of being rather than an action), that is, a linking verb such as εἰμί, γίνομαι, or ὑπάρχω (e.g., "I am **the door**," ἐγώ εἰμι **ἡ θύρα**).[23]

Since sentences with a predicate nominative have two nominatives in a sentence—the subject nominative and the predicate nominative—the question arises

---

[21] See Wallace, 40–42 for a discussion of the two categories.

[22] See Robertson, 457; cf. BDF, 80 (§145). See the following category.

[23] Robertson (457) adds καλεῖσθαι (e.g., Luke 2:21; 19:2; Jas 2:23). Brooks & Winbery disagree and treat καλεῖσθαι under appellation (4–5). Note also that at times in the GNT the predicate nominative is substituted by the preposition εἰς plus an accusative noun. There is some discussion as to whether this construction reflects Semitic influence (see the discussion in Robertson, 458). The construction is found in places where a given NT writer cites the OT (LXX), as in Mark 10:8: "and the two will become **one flesh**" (καὶ ἔσονται οἱ δύο **εἰς σάρκα μίαν** = Gen 2:24 LXX).

how one can distinguish the predicate nominative from the subject. Wallace supplies the following helpful guidelines:[24]

1. The subject is the *pronoun*, whether made explicit or implied in the finite verb: ὑμεῖς ἐστε τὸ φῶς τοῦ κόσμου ("**You** are the light of the world"; Matt 5:14).

2. The subject will have the *article*: τὸ **φορτίον** μου ἐλαφρόν ἐστιν ("My **burden** is light"; Matt 11:30); θεὸς ἦν ὁ λόγος ("**the Word** was God"; John 1:1);

3. The subject may be a *proper name*: ἦν δὲ **Καϊάφας** ὁ συμβουλεύσας τοῖς Ἰουδαίοις ("Now **Caiaphas** was the one who had advised the Jews"; John 18:14).

There are, however, times when the above guidelines by themselves are not conclusive. In such instances, the following order of priority, or "pecking order" can be established.[25] First, the *pronoun* is to be given priority: "**He** [lit., this one] is the Son of God" (οὗτός ἐστιν ὁ υἱὸς τοῦ θεοῦ; Acts 9:20; see also Matt 11:14; 1 John 5:9). Second, in adjudicating between articular nouns and proper names, *word order* may be determinative: "My **Father** is the gardener " (ὁ **πατήρ** μου ὁ γεωργός ἐστιν; John 15:1; see also Matt 6:22; 13:55; John 8:39; 1 John 2:7).

- ὁ λόγος **σὰρξ** ἐγένετο (John 1:14)

  the Word became **flesh**

      The subject has the article.

- Ἰησοῦς ἐστιν ὁ **χριστὸς** ὁ **υἱὸς** τοῦ θεοῦ (John 20:31)

  Jesus is **the Christ, the Son** of God (NASB)

      The proper name, Jesus, indicates the subject.[26]

- αὐτὸς γάρ ἐστιν ἡ **εἰρήνη** ἡμῶν (Eph 2:14)

  For He is our **peace**

      In cases where a pronoun and an articular noun are present, the pronoun will be the subject.

---

[24] Wallace, 42–45. Wallace follows, with some modifications, the work of McGaughy, *Toward a Descriptive Analysis of Εἶναι as a Linking Verb in the Greek New Testament*, Dissertation Series, 6 (SBL: 1972). See also Young, 64–66 for an additional helpful discussion on determining the subject and predicate nominate.

[25] See Wallace, 44–46. Apparently Wallace was the first to refer to this ordered list as a "pecking order."

[26] But note that D. A. Carson contends that the sentence should rather be rendered, "the Messiah, the Son of God, is Jesus." See "The Purpose of the Fourth Gospel: John 20:30–31 Reconsidered," *JBL* 108 (1987): 639–51; idem, "Syntactical and Text-Critical Observations on John 20:30–31: One More Round on the Purpose of the Fourth Gospel," *JBL* 124 (2005): 693–714.

- γίνεσθε δὲ **ποιηταὶ** λόγου καὶ μὴ μόνον **ἀκροαταί** (Jas 1:22)

  But be **doers** of the word and not **hearers** only

  > The subject is implied in the verb γίνεσθε (i.e., "*you* be . . .").

- ὁ θεὸς **ἀγάπη** ἐστίν (1 John 4:8)

  God is **love**

  > The articular noun is the subject. Note that subject and predicate nominative are not
  > reversible: God is love, but love is not God.

Apposition

Two nominative substantives can stand in apposition to each other. When this
takes place, the first nominative is the subject and the second further explains or
identifies the subject.[27] This can be done by clarification, description, or identification. Wallace concisely and accurately notes that an appositional relationship
includes the following four features: "(1) two adjacent substantives (2) in the same
case, (3) which refer to the same person or thing, (4) and have the same syntactical
relationship to the rest of the clause."[28]

- τίς δύναται ἀφιέναι ἁμαρτίας εἰ μὴ εἷς **ὁ θεός**; (Mark 2:7)

  Who can forgive sins but **God** alone?

  > In the Greek, "God," ὁ θεός, stands in apposition to "one" (εἷς).

- οὐκ εἰμὶ ὥσπερ οἱ λοιποὶ τῶν ἀνθρώπων, **ἅρπαγες, ἄδικοι, μοιχοί**
  (Luke 18:11)

  I'm not like other people—**greedy, unrighteous, adulterers**

  > The list of nominatives are all in apposition to οἱ λοιποὶ and includes two adjectives
  > and a noun, all of which are plural to agree with "the rest."

- Ἀνδρέας **ὁ ἀδελφὸς** Σίμωνος Πέτρου (John 1:40)

  Andrew, Simon Peter's **brother**

- ἦν δὲ ἐγγὺς τὸ πάσχα, **ἡ ἑορτὴ** τῶν Ἰουδαίων (John 6:4)

  Now the Passover, **the feast** of the Jews, was near (NASB)

  > The Passover is further defined as "the feast of the Jews." In this case the nominative
  > in apposition is a different gender than the first substantive, but they still refer to the
  > same thing.

---

[27] Apposition is found in other cases as well, but here we are treating only the nominative.
[28] Wallace, 48.

- Παῦλος **δοῦλος** Χριστοῦ Ἰησοῦ (Rom 1:1)

  Paul, a **servant** of Christ Jesus

  > As in all of his letters, Paul further identifies himself, in the present instance as a servant or slave of Jesus Christ.

Other Uses

Other uses of the nominative involve a construction in which the nominative is grammatically independent from the rest of the sentence. These include the nominative of address, the nominative of appellation, the nominative absolute, and the hanging nominative.

Address

Occasionally in the NT, a nominative is used in the place of a vocative in direct address.[29] This use is in keeping with the nature of the nominative as a "naming" case.[30] Blass observes that there is "a tendency for the nominative to usurp the place of the vocative," even as far back as Homer.[31] Examples include a majority of articular uses and a few anarthrous instances (with or without ὦ).

- ἐλέησον ἡμᾶς, **υἱὸς** Δαυίδ (Matt 9:27)

  Have mercy on us, **Son** of David (cf. 15:22)

- ἀββα **ὁ πατήρ**, πάντα δυνατά σοι (Mark 14:36)

  Abba! **Father**! All things are possible for you

  > Here "Father" is in the nominative, while "Abba" is in the vocative.

- **οἱ ἄνδρες**, ἀγαπᾶτε τὰς γυναῖκας (Eph 5:25)

  Husbands, love your wives

- ὁ θρόνος σου **ὁ θεὸς** εἰς τὸν αἰῶνα τοῦ αἰῶνος (Heb 1:8)

  Your throne, **O God**, is forever and ever (ESV)

  > The finite verb "is" is implied.[32]

---

[29] Young, 12, identifies approximately 60 such uses.

[30] Wallace, 56; see the introduction above. Robertson, 461, followed by Dana & Mantey, 72, denies that this is a legitimate category.

[31] BDF, 81 (§147). Similarly, Moule notes, "Although the true Vocative is found . . . it is being supplanted by the Nominative," citing Luke 8:54; Mark 5:41; Luke 18:11; and Heb 1:8 (*Idiom Book*, 31–32). Zerwick notes that the fact that the nominative and vocative are sometimes identical in form accounts for the tendency to eliminate the distinction (*Biblical Greek*, 11).

[32] For more examples of the nominative of address, see Matt 16:17; Mark 5:8; 9:19; Luke 9:41; 24:25; John 17:25; 19:3; Acts 13:10; 18:14; 27:21; Rom 1:13; Gal 3:1; Eph 5:22; 6:1; Rev 15:3. See also Robertson, 461; BDF, 81–82 (§147).

- εὐφραίνου ἐπ' αὐτῇ, οὐρανὲ καὶ **οἱ ἅγιοι** καὶ **οἱ ἀπόστολοι** καὶ **οἱ προφῆται** (Rev 18:20)

  Rejoice over her, O heaven, and you **saints** and **apostles** and **prophets** (NASB)

Appellation

The nominative of appellation features a title as though it were a proper name.[33] Blass calls this the "[n]ominative used to introduce names."[34] As Dana & Mantey observe, "Since the nominative is by nature the naming-case, it is not strange that there should be a tendency to put proper names in this case irrespective of contextual relations."[35] The key to identifying the nominative of appellation in the NT is that the nominative is used as a proper name when the word used would normally be in another case.[36] The nominative of appellation "usually occurs after verbs of naming and calling, such as the passive voice of λέγω and καλέω."[37]

- καὶ ἐκλήθη τὸ ὄνομα αὐτοῦ **Ἰησοῦς** (Luke 2:21)

  His name was then called **Jesus** (NASB)

  > This is an example of καλέω in the passive followed by the nominative, rather than an accusative as expected.

- ὑμεῖς φωνεῖτέ με· **ὁ διδάσκαλος**, καί· **ὁ κύριος** (John 13:13)

  You call me **Teacher** and **Lord**

  > Here one would expect "teacher" and "lord" to be in the accusative case as objects of the verb and in agreement with με, but they are in the nominative instead.

- οὐκ ἠρνήσω τὴν πίστιν μου καὶ ἐν ταῖς ἡμέραις Ἀντιπᾶς **ὁ μάρτυς** μου ὁ πιστός μου (Rev 2:13)

  And you . . . did not deny your faith in Me, even in the days of Antipas, my faithful **witness**

  > While "Antipas" is in the genitive, the appellation "my faithful witness" is in the nominative.

Absolute

As is the case with all the special uses of the nominative, the noun in the nominative case is grammatically independent ("absolute") from the remainder of the sentence.[38] In this sense, *all* the special uses of the nominative—not merely the

---

[33] Wallace, 61.
[34] BDF, 79 (§143).
[35] Dana & Mantey, 69.
[36] Wallace groups this use of the nominative under the rubric "Nominatives in Place of Oblique Cases" and notes that such uses are rare, occurring mostly in Revelation (61).
[37] Young, 13.
[38] Wallace, 49.

nominative absolute—are instances of an "independent nominative," though some use this designation interchangeably with "nominative absolute."[39] Others do not distinguish between the nominative absolute and the hanging nominative.[40] The difference between these two uses of the nominative, however, is that the nominative absolute, unlike the hanging nominative, occurs "in introductory material (such as titles, headings, salutations, and addresses), which are not to be construed as sentences."[41]

- ἀρχὴ τοῦ εὐαγγελίου Ἰησοῦ Χριστοῦ (Mark 1:1)

  The beginning of the gospel of Jesus Christ

- χάρις ἔλεος εἰρήνη ἀπὸ θεοῦ πατρὸς καὶ Χριστοῦ Ἰησοῦ τοῦ κυρίου ἡμῶν (1 Tim 1:2)

  Grace, **mercy** and **peace** from God the Father and Christ Jesus our Lord

  This is an opening salutation from Paul to Timothy.[42]

- Παῦλος δοῦλος θεοῦ (Titus 1:1)

  Paul, a servant of God

- Συμεὼν Πέτρος δοῦλος καὶ ἀπόστολος Ἰησοῦ Χριστοῦ (2 Peter 1:1)

  Simon Peter, a servant and an apostle of Jesus Christ

  "Simon Peter" is a nominative absolute while "a servant" and "an apostle," as mentioned above, are in apposition, further specifying Peter's identity.

- ἀποκάλυψις Ἰησοῦ Χριστοῦ (Rev 1:1)

  The **revelation** of Jesus Christ

Hanging Nominative

Finally, the hanging nominative (also called "pendent" or "suspended nominative"[43] or *nominativus pendens*) "is *the logical rather than syntactical subject* at the beginning of a sentence, followed by a sentence in which this subject is now replaced by a pronoun in the case required by the syntax."[44] It is different from the nominative absolute in that it is connected to the rest of the sentence. Yet unlike

---

[39] See Young, 14; Brooks & Winbery, 5–6.

[40] So Robertson, 459; Black, 47.

[41] Wallace, 49, with reference to Funk (the entire phrase is italicized in Wallace). Young treats exclamations, "cleft constructions" (i.e., hanging nominatives), and proverbial sayings under the category "Nominative Absolute" (14–15). Similarly, Brooks & Winbery, 6–7.

[42] For other NT salutations, see Rom 1:7; 1 Cor 1:3; 2 Cor 1:2; Gal 1:3; Eph 1:2; Phil 1:2; Col 1:2; 1 Thess 1:1; 2 Thess 1:2; 2 Tim 1:2; Titus 1:4; Phlm 3.

[43] Robertson, 459.

[44] Wallace, 51 (emphasis original). Similarly, Zerwick begins his treatment of the nominative with the pendent nominative (*Biblical Greek*, 9 [§14]).

the major uses (subject, predicate nominative, apposition), it is grammatically in-dependent from the remainder of the sentence. More specifically, one discerns a grammatical shift between the pendent nominative and the rest of the sentence that can be explained by logic rather than syntax. The following examples will illus-trate this apparent incongruity.

- τὸ δὲ καλὸν **σπέρμα** οὗτοί εἰσιν οἱ υἱοὶ τῆς βασιλείας (Matt 13:38)

  and the good **seed**—these are the children of the kingdom

  > "The good seed" is grammatically independent from the rest of the sentence, which the CSB indicates with an em-dash.

- **ταῦτα** ἃ θεωρεῖτε ἐλεύσονται ἡμέραι ἐν αἷς οὐκ ἀφεθήσεται λίθος ἐπὶ λίθῳ (Luke 21:6)

  These things that you see—the days will come when not one stone will be left on another

  > The CSB helpfully indicates the break in syntax with an em-dash.

- ἢ **ἐκεῖνοι οἱ δεκαοκτὼ** ἐφ᾽ οὓς ἔπεσεν ὁ πύργος ἐν τῷ Σιλωὰμ καὶ ἀπέκτεινεν αὐτούς, δοκεῖτε . . . . (Luke 13:4)

  Or **those eighteen** that the tower in Siloam fell on and killed—do you think . . . .

  > The CSB uses an em-dash to separate the pendent nominative, "those eighteen," from the rest of the sentence.

- **ὑμεῖς** ὃ ἠκούσατε ἀπ᾽ ἀρχῆς, ἐν ὑμῖν μενέτω (1 John 2:24)

  Let what **you** heard from the beginning abide in you (ESV)

  > Literally, the Greek reads, "**You**, what you have heard from the beginning, let it abide [or remain] in you."

- **ὁ νικῶν** ποιήσω αὐτὸν στῦλον ἐν τῷ ναῷ τοῦ θεοῦ μου (Rev 3:12)

  The one who conquers, I will make him a pillar in the temple of my God (ESV)

  > The ESV translation helpfully brings out the presence of a pendent nominative in this passage by inserting a comma between "The one who conquers" and the rest of the sentence.[45]

Some grammarians explain the effect of the hanging nominative with either em-phasis or emotion.[46] This is of some value, but such explanations need to be sup-plemented by an understanding of the function of the hanging nominative in the

---

[45] For more examples of the hanging nominative, see Matt 12:36; John 1:12; 7:38; Rev 2:26; 3:21.

[46] See, e.g., Wallace, 52; Young, 15; and Porter, *Idioms*, 85–86. See Steven E. Runge, *Discourse Grammar of the New Testament: A Practical Introduction for Teaching and Exegesis* (Peabody, MA: Hendrickson, 2010), 287, and his entire chapter 14 on Left-Dislocations.

larger discourse context. Runge characterizes constructions such as the hanging nominative as "left-dislocations" that serve the purpose of announcing a topic or shifting contexts.[47] Hanging nominatives draw additional attention to the topic or subject that is being introduced.[48]

VOCATIVE

The vocative (from Latin *vocare*, "to call") usually occurs at the beginning of a sentence and indicates the person or group that is being addressed by a particular statement or command. There is some question as to whether the vocative technically qualifies as a separate case, although those who deny it is a case concede it must be treated like one.[49] However, it is best to treat the vocative as a discrete case for two reasons. First, it is sufficiently distinct in certain forms, in particular the second and third declension singular. Second, while grammatically independent, it does have an important function in discourse, indicating the intended audience or recharacterizing them.[50] The vocative, as mentioned, essentially conveys direct address, whether with or without the article or with the inflectional particle ὦ.[51]

USES OF THE VOCATIVE	Direct Address

Direct Address

The most common use of the vocative in the NT involves the use of a substantive without the article to identify the person or thing that is being addressed.[52]

---

[47] Runge, *Discourse Grammar*, 290, with reference to Knud Lambrecht, *Information Structure and Sentence Form: Topic, Focus, and the Mental Representations of Discourse Referents*, CSL 71 (Cambridge: Cambridge University Press, 1996), 176.

[48] See the helpful summary in Runge, *Discourse Grammar*, 312.

[49] Robertson, 461; Dana & Mantey, 72.

[50] Wallace, 66–67; Brooks & Winberry, 64; Mounce, *Morphology of Biblical Greek*, 167 (see chap. 1, n. 7); Runge, *Discourse Grammar*, 117–22, 349–55.

[51] In 17 instances in the NT, the inflectional particle ὦ is used in conjunction with the vocative (Matt 15:28; 17:17 // Mark 9:19 // Luke 9:41; 24:25; Acts 1:1; 13:10; 18:14; 27:21; Rom 2:1, 3; 9:20; 11:33; Gal 3:1; 1 Tim 6:11, 20; Jas 2:20), though it is debated whether or not this indicates special emphasis or emotion. It seems best to infer or confirm any such emphatic or emotional content from the context. In addition, the vocative occurs occasionally in apposition to another vocative (Matt 15:22; Luke 4:34; 17:13). Some grammars classify the use of the vocative singularly as direct address. For example, Dana & Mantey comment, "The vocative has but a single use, and that is as the case of direct address" (71). Similarly, Black states, "The vocative is simply used for direct address" (*Still Greek*, 47). Wallace distinguishes between simple and emphatic (or emotional) address, also making reference to a "vocative of exclamation" (though he acknowledges that it is only rarely used and all its instances are disputed; 68–70). However, it is best to limit oneself to observable grammatical categories and to leave interpretive issues to contextual exegesis.

[52] Occasionally, the noun is modified by an adjective in the vocative, whether with or without ὦ (Mark 9:19 [ὦ γενεὰ ἄπιστος]; John 17:25 [πάτερ δίκαιε]; Phil 4:3 [σύζυγε γνήσιε]; Jas 2:20 [ὦ ἄνθρωπε κενέ]).

- **κύριε**, ἐὰν θέλῃς δύνασαί με καθαρίσαι (Matt 8:2)

  Lord, if you are willing, you can make me clean

- **διδάσκαλε**, ἤνεγκα τὸν υἱόν μου πρὸς σέ (Mark 9:17)

  Teacher, I brought my son to you

- **Λάζαρε**, δεῦρο ἔξω (John 11:43)

  Lazarus, come out!

  > In this case, the noun in the vocative is a proper name, Lazarus.

- ἀναστάς, **Πέτρε**, θῦσον καὶ φάγε (Acts 10:13)

  Get up, **Peter**; kill and eat!

- σὺ δέ, **ὦ ἄνθρωπε** θεοῦ, ταῦτα φεῦγε (1 Tim 6:11)

  But as for you, **O man** of God, flee these things (ESV)

ACCUSATIVE

The accusative case is the case of *limitation* or *extension*, delimiting the action of a verb. The accusative "measures an idea as to its content, scope, [or] direction."[53] You may visualize the function of the accusative as indicating "the point toward which something is proceeding" or "the space traversed in such motion or direction."[54] The most frequent idea conveyed by the use of the accusative thus essentially encompasses three elements: the end, direction, or extent of an action.[55] In each case, the accusative limits the action. For example, Matthew 22:24 contains the clause, "his brother is to marry his wife" (ἐπιγαμβρεύσει ὁ ἀδελφὸς αὐτοῦ τὴν γυναῖκα αὐτοῦ). The phrase "his brother is to marry" is completely open-ended, but "his brother is to marry *his wife*" puts a clear limit on the verbal action.

According to Dana & Mantey, the accusative is "probably the oldest" and "certainly the most widely used of all the Greek cases. Its function is more general than that of any other case."[56] There are two main types of usage of the accusative: (1) substantival, and (2) adverbial.[57]

---

[53] Robertson, 468.

[54] Dana & Mantey, 91, citing William Webster, *Syntax and Synonyms of the Greek Testament* (London: Rivingtons, 1864), 63.

[55] Dana & Mantey, 91–92.

[56] Dana & Mantey, 91.

[57] The term "adverbial accusative" is common among modern Greek grammars, going back at least as far as Robertson in 1919. The term "substantival accusative," however, is a category unique to Wallace, and it appears he is the first major grammarian to organize the uses of the accusative in these two groups (179).

		Direct Object
SUBSTANTIVAL USES OF THE ACCUSATIVE		Cognate Accusative
		Double Accusative
		Subject of Infinitive
		Apposition
ADVERBIAL USES OF THE ACCUSATIVE		Measure
		Manner
		Respect

Substantival Uses of the Accusative

The substantival uses of the accusative include the accusative direct object, the cognate accusative, the double accusative, the accusative subject of the infinitive, and the accusative in simple apposition.

Direct Object

The most common use of the accusative is as the direct object of a transitive verb. As the direct object, the accusative is the recipient of the action and thus limits the scope of the action of the verb. The use of the accusative direct object is so common that the interpreter should routinely approach an accusative with the assumption that it indicates the direct object.[58] One may also conceive of the accusative direct object in terms of certain (transitive) verbs taking the accusative, such as causative verbs (causing an action to be performed on a given object) or verbs of emotion.[59]

- καὶ οὐκ ἐγίνωσκεν **αὐτὴν** ἕως οὗ ἔτεκεν **υἱόν** (Matt 1:25)

  but did not have sexual relations with **her** until she gave birth to **a son**

  Joseph had no sexual relations with *Mary*, his fiancée, until she gave birth specifically to a *son*.

- καὶ ἀπέστειλεν πρὸς τοὺς γεωργοὺς τῷ καιρῷ **δοῦλον** (Mark 12:2)

  At the *harvest* time he sent **a slave** to the vine-growers (NASB)

  In the parable of the wicked tenants, the owner of the vineyard specifically sent a *slave* (later, he would send his own *son*).

---

[58] Wallace, 179.

[59] See BDF, 82 (§148); Robertson, 471–77. As Robertson observes, however, transitive verbs do not always take the accusative, and some verbs can function as either transitive or intransitive. It is also important to remember that verbs may be transitive in Greek but intransitive in English or vice versa.

- οὕτως γὰρ ἠγάπησεν ὁ θεὸς **τὸν κόσμον**, ὥστε **τὸν υἱὸν** τὸν μονογενῆ ἔδωκεν (John 3:16)

  For God so loved **the world**, that he gave his only **Son** (ESV)

  > God specifically loved the *world*—the world he had made, and here specifically *people* who had fallen into sin—so that he gave, specifically his one and only *Son*, as a sacrifice for our sins.

- οἱ ἄνδρες, ἀγαπᾶτε **τὰς γυναῖκας** (Eph 5:25)

  Husbands, love your **wives**

  > Husbands are called upon specifically to love their *wives* ("your" is inferred from the context).

- κήρυξον **τὸν λόγον** (2 Tim 4:2)

  preach **the word** (ESV)

  > Paul wants Timothy to be diligent to proclaim the Christian *message*.

Cognate Accusative

The cognate accusative of the direct object is aligned with the verb either with regard to the root of the word or with regard to the idea conveyed. The choice of a cognate for the accusative does not necessarily indicate any emphasis, unless another word is modifying it attributively, as in Matthew 2:10, in the examples below.[60] It usually functions as the direct object of the verb.

- ἰδόντες δὲ τὸν ἀστέρα <u>ἐχάρησαν</u> **χαρὰν** μεγάλην σφόδρα (Matt 2:10)

  When they saw the star, they <u>rejoiced</u> exceedingly with great **joy** (NASB)

  > The CSB here uses an idiomatic translation, "were overwhelmed with joy," to improve upon the literal, "they rejoiced with very great joy."

- <u>φορτίζετε</u> τοὺς ἀνθρώπους **φορτία** δυσβάστακτα (Luke 11:46)

  You <u>load</u> people with **burdens** that are hard to carry

  > The Greek could also be translated, "You burden people with burdens that are hard to bear."

- τίς <u>ποιμαίνει</u> **ποίμνην** (1 Cor 9:7)

  who <u>shepherds</u> a **flock**

- ἵνα <u>στρατεύῃ</u> ἐν αὐταῖς τὴν καλὴν **στρατείαν** (1 Tim 1:18)

  that by them you <u>fight</u> the good **fight** (NASB)

---

[60] BDF, 84–85 (§153).

- ἐάν τις ἴδῃ τὸν ἀδελφὸν αὐτοῦ <u>ἁμαρτάνοντα</u> **ἁμαρτίαν** μὴ πρὸς θάνατον (1 John 5:16)

  If anyone sees a fellow believer <u>committing</u> **a sin** that doesn't lead to death

Double Accusative

In certain contexts, a given verb may require more than one object to complete the meaning. These verbs take either (1) a personal and impersonal object or (2) a direct and predicate object.[61] Wallace has noted that in cases where two accusatives denote a person and an impersonal object, the nearer object is the thing, while the more remote object is the person.[62] A simple example comes from 1 Cor 3:2: "I gave **you** <u>milk</u>" (<u>γάλα</u> **ὑμᾶς** ἐπότισα), whereby "you" (**ὑμᾶς**) is the personal accusative and "milk" (<u>γάλα</u>) the impersonal accusative.

- <u>ὃν</u> αἰτήσει ὁ υἱὸς αὐτοῦ **ἄρτον** (Matt 7:9)

  if his son asks <u>him</u> for **bread** (ESV)

- καὶ ἐν ἐκείνῃ τῇ ἡμέρᾳ <u>ἐμὲ</u> οὐκ ἐρωτήσετε **οὐδέν** (John 16:23)

  In that day you will not ask <u>me</u> **anything**

- πάλιν χρείαν ἔχετε τοῦ διδάσκειν <u>ὑμᾶς</u> τινὰ **τὰ στοιχεῖα** τῆς ἀρχῆς τῶν λογίων τοῦ θεοῦ (Heb 5:12)

  you need someone to teach <u>you</u> **the basic principles** of God's revelation again

In the second type of pattern, the first accusative is the verbal object while the second accusative serves as the predicate complement. Matthew 4:19 may serve as an example: "Follow Me, and I will make <u>you</u> **fishers** of men" (NASB; δεῦτε ὀπίσω μου, καὶ ποιήσω <u>ὑμᾶς</u> **ἁλιεῖς** ἀνθρώπων), in which case "fishers of men" further specifies what Jesus makes his disciples. Certain verbs commonly take the double accusative (in either pattern), such as verbs of asking or inquiring (e.g., αἰτέω), verbs of dressing or undressing (e.g., περιβάλλω), and a number of causative verbs (e.g., ποτίζω).

- ὁ υἱὸς τοῦ ἀνθρώπου οὐκ ἦλθεν διακονηθῆναι ἀλλὰ διακονῆσαι καὶ δοῦναι <u>τὴν ψυχὴν</u> αὐτοῦ **λύτρον** ἀντὶ πολλῶν (Matt 20:28)

  the Son of Man came not to be served but to serve, and to give <u>his life</u> as **a ransom** for many (ESV)

---

[61] So Dana & Mantey, 94, and most grammars.

[62] Wallace, 181. He goes on to say, "[T]he person is the object *affected*, while the thing is the object *effected*" (Wallace, 181). He also observes that whereas the normal expectation would be for a verb to take a dative of person as the indirect object and an accusative of thing as the direct object, some verbs take two accusatives instead (Wallace, 181).

- μὴ ποιεῖτε <u>τὸν οἶκον</u> τοῦ πατρός μου **οἶκον** ἐμπορίου (John 2:16)

  do not make my Father's <u>house</u> **a house** of trade (ESV)

- ὁ δοὺς <u>ἑαυτὸν</u> **ἀντίλυτρον** ὑπὲρ πάντων (1 Tim 2:6)

  who gave <u>himself as</u> **a ransom** for all

Subject of Infinitive

At times, the accusative functions as the subject of an infinitive although strictly speaking, the infinitive cannot have its own subject.[63] In such cases, the accusative indicates the agent who performs the action conveyed by the infinitive.[64] So in Matthew 14:22, we read that Jesus "made the disciples get into the boat" (ἠνάγκασεν τοὺς μαθητὰς ἐμβῆναι εἰς τὸ πλοῖον). The direct object of the verb is "the disciples" (τοὺς μαθητάς), which also functions as the subject of the infinitive "get into" (ἐμβῆναι).

- ὅτι λέγετε ἐν Βεελζεβοὺλ ἐκβάλλειν **με** τὰ δαιμόνια (Luke 11:18)

  For you say **I** drive out demons by Beelzebul

  > "I" functions as the subject of "cast out."

- πρὸ τοῦ σε **Φίλιππον** φωνῆσαι ὄντα ὑπὸ τὴν συκῆν εἶδόν σε (John 1:48)

  Before **Philip** called you, when you were under the fig tree, I saw you

  > Grammatically, an alternative translation would be "Before **you** (σε) called Philip," though contextually this rendering is not likely.

- καθώς ἐστιν δίκαιον ἐμοὶ τοῦτο φρονεῖν ὑπὲρ πάντων ὑμῶν διὰ τὸ ἔχειν **με** ἐν τῇ καρδίᾳ ὑμᾶς (Phil 1:7)

  It is right for me to think this way about you all, because **I** hold you in my heart (ESV)

  > Again, the alternative would be "because **you** hold me in [your] heart."

- καὶ γὰρ ὀφείλοντες εἶναι διδάσκαλοι διὰ τὸν χρόνον, πάλιν χρείαν ἔχετε τοῦ διδάσκειν ὑμᾶς **τινὰ** τὰ στοιχεῖα τῆς ἀρχῆς τῶν λογίων τοῦ θεοῦ (Heb 5:12)

  Although by this time you ought to be teachers, you need **someone** to teach you the basic principles of God's revelation again.

  > "Someone" (τινά), though in the accusative, is the implied subject of "to teach" (διδάσκειν).

---

[63] This is because the infinitive is not a finite verb. For a detailed discussion, see James L. Boyer, "The Classification of Infinitives: A Statistical Study," *GTJ* 6 (1985): 18–20; Robertson, 1082–85.

[64] See Robertson, 490. Some view this use of the accusative as an accusative of <u>respect</u> or <u>general reference</u> (e.g., Young, 18; see further the discussion below).

- εἰς τὸ μὴ ἐγκόπτεσθαι **τὰς προσευχὰς** ὑμῶν (1 Pet 3:7)

  so that your **prayers** will not be hindered

  "Your prayers" serves as the subject for the passive infinitive ἐγκόπτεσθαι.

Apposition

Similar to other cases, the accusative can be used in apposition to a second substantive in the accusative. Typically, the two accusatives occur one after the other, both referring to the same person or thing, with the second accusative further specifying the first accusative.[65] It is often helpful to insert the word "namely" before the second substantive to help determine whether placing the words in apposition to each other makes sense. For example, in 1 John 2:1, listed below, the relationship between "advocate" and "Jesus Christ" can be brought out by saying "We have an advocate with the Father, *namely* Jesus Christ the righteous." In such instances, the "first accusative substantive can belong to *any* accusative category," and the second accusative serves to clarify the first.[66]

- ἡγούμενος . . . ποιμανεῖ τὸν λαόν μου **τὸν Ἰσραήλ** (Matt 2:6)

  a ruler . . . will shepherd my people **Israel**

- καὶ ἐπὶ πῶλον **υἱὸν** ὑποζυγίου (Matt 21:5)

  and on a colt, **the foal** of a donkey

- ἐξελέξαντο Στέφανον, **ἄνδρα** πλήρης πίστεως (Acts 6:5)

  So they chose Stephen, **a man** full of faith

- ἀναγκαῖον δὲ ἡγησάμην Ἐπαφρόδιτον **τὸν ἀδελφὸν** καὶ **συνεργὸν** καὶ **συστρατιώτην** μου (Phil 2:25)

  But I considered it necessary to send you Epaphroditus—my **brother**, **co-worker**, and **fellow soldier**

- παράκλητον ἔχομεν πρὸς τὸν πατέρα, **Ἰησοῦν χριστὸν** δίκαιον (1 John 2:1)

  we have an Advocate with the Father, **Jesus Christ** the righteous (NASB)

  Notice here that nouns in apposition do not need to be next to each other in Greek. It is the use of the case that helps identify how they are functioning and their relationship to each other. In the present instance, the apposition (Ἰησοῦν χριστόν, "Jesus Christ") is several words removed from the initial object (παράκλητον, "Advocate").

---

[65] Wallace, 198–99.
[66] Wallace, 199.

Adverbial Uses of the Accusative

In this type of usage, the accusative functions in essence like an adverb in that it specifies manner, measure (time or space), or another aspect entailed by a given action. In fact, a number of words (quite frequently neuter adjectives as in the first example below) were employed with such frequency in an adverbial sense in the accusative that for all practical purposes they became adverbs (e.g., μᾶλλον, πρότερον, πλεῖστον).[67] As Brooks & Winbery note, "The adverbial accusative modifies a verb rather than serving as its object."[68] We will highlight three different uses of the adverbial accusative: (1) measure, (2) manner, and (3) respect.[69]

Measure

The accusative of measure indicates the extent of the action conveyed by a given verb, indicating either how long (which is the more common use) or how far the action took place.[70]

- καὶ προσελθὼν **μικρόν**, ἔπεσεν ἐπὶ πρόσωπον αὐτοῦ (Matt 26:39)

  And going **a little farther** he fell on his face (ESV)

- καὶ αὐτὸς ἀπεσπάσθη ἀπ᾿ αὐτῶν ὡσεὶ λίθου **βολήν** (Luke 22:41)

  Then he withdrew from them about a stone's **throw**

- καὶ ἐν ταῖς οὐραῖς αὐτῶν ἡ ἐξουσία αὐτῶν ἀδικῆσαι τοὺς ἀνθρώπους **μῆνας** πέντε (Rev 9:10)

  so that with their tails they had the power to harm people for five **months**

Manner

An accusative of manner indicates how a given action takes place. It functions similarly to an adverb in that it further qualifies the action of a verb.[71]

- ὕπαγε **πρῶτον** διαλλάγηθι τῷ ἀδελφῷ σου (Matt 5:24)

  First go and be reconciled with your brother or sister

---

[67] Dana & Mantey, 93.

[68] Brooks & Winbery, 52.

[69] Other, less frequent, categories include: (1) the accusative used in oaths (Mark 5:7; Acts 19:13; Jas 5:12); (2) the accusative absolute (Acts 26:3; 1 Cor 16:6; Eph 1:17–18); (3) the predicate accusative (Luke 4:41; John 2:9; Acts 9:11); and (4) the accusative with passive verbs (Mark 1:6; 1 Cor 12:13; Heb 6:9). In addition, certain prepositions take the accusative, such as εἰς ("into"), διά ("on account of"), κατά ("according to"), μετά ("after"), παρά ("alongside of"), πρός ("to, towards, with"), and ὑπό ("under"). See Murray J. Harris, *Prepositions and Theology in the Greek New Testament: An Essential Reference Resource for Exegesis* (Grand Rapids: Zondervan, 2012).

[70] Brooks & Winbery, 52; BDF 88 (§161).

[71] Brooks & Winbery, 55; Young, 19.

- δικαιούμενοι **δωρεὰν** τῇ αὐτοῦ χάριτι (Rom 3:24)

  They are justified **freely** by his grace

- ἀσπάζεται ὑμᾶς ἐν κυρίῳ **πολλὰ** Ἀκύλας καὶ Πρίσκα (1 Cor 16:19)

  Aquila and Priscilla send you greetings **warmly** [lit., "many"; cf. KJV: "much"] in the Lord

Respect

As previously stated, at its core, the accusative case is the case of *limitation*, delimiting the *extent* of the action of a given verb in some way. The accusative of respect limits the action of the verb by indicating what the verb relates to.[72] Wallace supplies the following helpful guidelines for identifying this construction: if you can supply the words "with reference to" or "concerning," you may have this kind of construction. He also notes that this use is rather uncommon in the NT.[73] The accusative of respect may be used with or without a preposition.[74]

- ἐδικαίωσαν τὸν θεὸν βαπτισθέντες **τὸ βάπτισμα** Ἰωάννου (Luke 7:29)

  they acknowledged God's justice, having been baptized **with the baptism** of John (NASB)

  > The NASB supplies the word "with" to indicate that it was with respect to John's baptism that they were baptized.

- ἀκούσαντες δὲ κατενύγησαν **τὴν καρδίαν** (Acts 2:37)

  When they heard this, they were pierced **to the heart**

  > The sense of Luke's statement is, "they were pierced *with reference to* the heart."

- ἀλλὰ καθὼς δεδοκιμάσμεθα ὑπὸ τοῦ θεοῦ πιστευθῆναι **τὸ εὐαγγέλιον** (1 Thess 2:4)

  Instead, just as we have been approved by God to be entrusted with **the gospel**

  > Here, the verb πιστευθῆναι, a passive form, has the sense "to be entrusted with" followed by the accusative noun εὐαγγέλιον.

---

[72] Brooks & Winbery, 55.

[73] Wallace, 203.

[74] See Brooks & Winbery who supply the following examples: (1) without preposition: Mark 14:72; 1 Cor 9:25; Eph 4:15; Heb 2:17; 5:12; 1 Pet 1:12; (2) with prepositions: εἰς – Rom 15:2; 16:19; κατά – Rom 4:4; 1 Cor 15:3; περί – Luke 10:40; Phil 2:23; πρός – Luke 12:41; 2 Cor 5:10 (56–57).

SUMMARY

MAJOR USES OF THE NOMINATIVE		
SUBJECT	The subject of a finite verb.	Ἰωάννης μαρτυρεῖ περὶ αὐτοῦ ("**John** testified about Him"; John 1:15 NASB).
PREDICATE NOMINATIVE	Provides further information about the subject as a complement of a copulative verb (expressing a state of being).	ὁ λόγος **σὰρξ** ἐγένετο ("the Word became **flesh**"; John 1:14).
APPOSITION	Further explains the subject by clarification, description, or identification.	Παῦλος **δοῦλος** Χριστοῦ Ἰησοῦ ("Paul, a **servant** of Christ Jesus"; Rom 1:1).
OTHER USES OF THE NOMINATIVE		
ADDRESS	Used in the place of a vocative in direct address.	οἱ **ἄνδρες**, ἀγαπᾶτε τὰς γυναῖκας ("**Husbands**, love your wives"; Eph 5:25).
APPELLATION	Used in conjunction with an address or title where a case other than the nominative would be expected.	ὑμεῖς φωνεῖτέ με Ὁ **διδάσκαλος** ("You call me **Teacher**"; John 13:13).
ABSOLUTE	Grammatically independent use of the nominative in introductory material (such as titles, headings, salutations, or addresses).	**Παῦλος** δοῦλος θεοῦ ("**Paul**, a servant of God"; Titus 1:1).
HANGING NOMINATIVE	The logical rather than syntactical subject at the beginning of a sentence.	ὁ **νικῶν** ποιήσω αὐτὸν στῦλον ἐν τῷ ναῷ τοῦ θεοῦ μου ("**The one who conquers**, I will make him a pillar in the temple of my God"; Rev 3:12 ESV).

USES OF THE VOCATIVE		
DIRECT ADDRESS	The use of the articular or non-articular vocative to designate the person or thing being addressed.	**Λάζαρε**, δεῦρο ἔξω ("**Lazarus**, come out!"; John 11:43).

SUBSTANTIVAL USES OF THE ACCUSATIVE		
DIRECT OBJECT	Serves as the recipient of the action.	οὕτως γὰρ ἠγάπησεν ὁ θεὸς **τὸν κόσμον** ("For God so loved **the world**"; John 3:16 ESV).
COGNATE ACCUSATIVE	Aligned with the verb either with regard to the lexical root or the idea conveyed.	ἵνα **στρατεύῃ** ἐν αὐταῖς τὴν καλὴν **στρατείαν** ("that by them you <u>fight</u> the good **fight**"; 1 Tim 1:18 NASB).

SUBSTANTIVAL USES OF THE ACCUSATIVE		
DOUBLE ACCUSATIVE	A verb requires more than one accusative object to complete the thought, taking either (1) a personal and impersonal object or (2) a direct and predicate object.	(1) ὃν αἰτήσει ὁ υἱὸς αὐτοῦ **ἄρτον** ("if his son asks <u>him</u> for **bread**"; Matt 7:9 ESV). (2) ὁ δοὺς <u>ἑαυτὸν</u> **ἀντίλυτρον** ὑπὲρ πάντων ("who gave <u>himself</u> as **a ransom** for all"; 1 Tim 2:6).
SUBJECT OF INFINITIVE	Functions as the subject of an infinitive, indicating the agent performing the action conveyed by the infinitive.	πρὸ τοῦ σε **Φίλιππον** φωνῆσαι . . . εἶδόν σε ("Before **Philip** called you . . . I saw you"; John 1:48).
APPOSITION	Two accusatives are juxtaposed, both referring to the same person or thing, with the second accusative further specifying the first accusative.	καὶ ἐπὶ πῶλον **υἱὸν** ὑποζυγίου ("and on a colt, **the foal** of a donkey"; Matt 21:5).
ADVERBIAL USES OF THE ACCUSATIVE		
MEASURE	Functions in essence like an adverb in that it specifies measure (time or space).	καὶ προσελθὼν **μικρόν**, ἔπεσεν ἐπὶ πρόσωπον αὐτοῦ ("And going **a little farther** he fell on his face"; Matt 26:39 ESV).
MANNER	Functions in essence like an adverb in that it specifies manner.	δικαιούμενοι **δωρεὰν** τῇ αὐτοῦ χάριτι ("They are justified **freely** by His grace"; Rom 3:24).
RESPECT	Restricts the reference of the verbal action, indicating in what regard an action is represented as true.	κατενύγησαν **τὴν καρδίαν** ("they were pierced **to the heart**"; Acts 2:37).

PRACTICE EXERCISES

In each of the following examples, (1) identify the case of each underlined noun and (2) determine the specific use of the noun based on its case.

1. <u>Παῦλος</u> <u>ἀπόστολος</u> Χριστοῦ Ἰησοῦ διὰ θελήματος θεοῦ καὶ <u>Τιμόθεος</u> ὁ <u>ἀδελφός</u> (2 Cor 1:1).

2. <u>ἄνθρωπε</u>, τίς <u>με</u> κατέστησεν <u>κριτὴν</u> ἢ <u>μεριστὴν</u> ἐφ' ὑμᾶς; (Luke 12:14).

3. Ἰησοῦς οὖν ἰδὼν τὴν <u>μητέρα</u> καὶ τὸν <u>μαθητὴν</u> παρεστῶτα ὃν ἠγάπα, λέγει τῇ μητρί· <u>γύναι</u>, ἴδε ὁ <u>υἱός</u> σου (John 19:26).

4. μὴ πολλοὶ <u>διδάσκαλοι</u> γίνεσθε, <u>ἀδελφοί</u> μου, εἰδότες ὅτι μεῖζον <u>κρίμα</u> λημψόμεθα (Jas 3:1).

5. οὐκ ἔσχηκα ἄνεσιν τῷ πνεύματί μου τῷ μὴ εὑρεῖν <u>με</u> <u>Τίτον</u> τὸν <u>ἀδελφόν</u> μου (2 Cor 2:13).

6. <u>δωρεὰν</u> ἐλάβετε, <u>δωρεὰν</u> δότε (Matt 10:8).

7. <u>Συμεὼν Πέτρος δοῦλος</u> καὶ <u>ἀπόστολος</u> Ἰησοῦ Χριστοῦ (2 Pet 1:1).

8. ἐνορκίζω <u>ὑμᾶς</u> τὸν <u>κύριον</u> ἀναγνωσθῆναι τὴν <u>ἐπιστολὴν</u> πᾶσιν τοῖς ἀδελφοῖς (1 Thess 5:27).

9. <u>ὁ νικῶν</u> ποιήσω <u>αὐτὸν</u> <u>στῦλον</u> ἐν τῷ ναῷ τοῦ θεοῦ μου (Rev 3:12).

10. καὶ ἰδοὺ ἐγὼ μεθ᾽ ὑμῶν εἰμι πάσας τὰς <u>ἡμέρας</u> ἕως τῆς συντελείας τοῦ αἰῶνος (Matt 28:20).

VOCABULARY

Vocabulary to Memorize

ἁμαρτάνω	I sin (43)
ἄξιος	worthy, fit, deserving (41)
ἅπτω	I touch, take hold of (39)
ἄρχων, -οντος, ὁ	ruler, authority, judge (37)
βούλομαι	I wish, want, desire (37)
δέω	I bind, tie (43)
ἐγγίζω	I draw near, approach (42)
ἑκατόν	one hundred (17)
ἐκεῖθεν	from there (37)
ἐλέγχω	I reprove, correct (17)
ἐμαυτοῦ	(of) myself (37)
ἔμπροσθεν	in front of, before (48)
ἐπιτίθημι	I lay upon, put upon (39)
ἐργάζομαι	I work, do, perform (41)
εὐλογέω	I bless, praise (42)
θαυμάζω	I marvel, am amazed, wonder (43)
θεραπεύω	I heal, restore, serve (43)
θύρα, ἡ	door, gate, entrance (39)
καινός	new, unused (42)
καλῶς	well (37)
καυχάομαι	I boast, glory (37)
κερδαίνω	I gain (17)
λύω	I loose (42)
μαρτυρία, ἡ	testimony, witness (37)
μάρτυς, ὁ	witness (35)
μικρός	small, short (46)
οἰκοδομέω	I build (up), erect, edify (40)
οὗ	where (25)
παραλαμβάνω	I take (to myself), take with/along (49)
παρίστημι	I place beside, present (41)
πέντε	five (38)
περισσεύω	I exceed, overflow, abound (39)
πλανάω	I go astray, be misled, wander about aimlessly (39)
πράσσω	I do, accomplish, practice (39)
πρόβατον, τό	sheep (39)
σπέρμα, -ατος, τό	seed, descendants, children (43)

τέλος, -ους, τό	end, goal (40)
τελώνης, -ου, ὁ	tax-collector (21)
τέσσαρες	four (41)
ὥσπερ	(just) as, so (36)

Vocabulary to Recognize

ἐθνικός	unbelieving, worldly (4)
ἐνενήκοντα	ninety (4)
ἐννέα	nine (5)
καταφρονέω	I look down on, despise, scorn (9)
μεταξύ	between (9)
παρακούω	I refuse to listen to, disobey (3)
πρᾶγμα, -ατος, τό	thing, matter, affair (11)
συμφωνέω	I am of one mind, agree (6)

READING THE NEW TESTAMENT

Matthew 18:10–20

¹⁰ Ὁρᾶτε μὴ καταφρονήσητε ἑνὸς τῶν μικρῶν τούτων· λέγω γὰρ ὑμῖν ὅτι οἱ ἄγγελοι αὐτῶν ἐν οὐρανοῖς διὰ παντὸς βλέπουσι τὸ πρόσωπον τοῦ πατρός μου τοῦ ἐν οὐρανοῖς. ¹¹ [See discussion of text-critical issue below] ¹² Τί ὑμῖν δοκεῖ; ἐὰν γένηταί τινι ἀνθρώπῳ ἑκατὸν πρόβατα καὶ πλανηθῇ ἓν ἐξ αὐτῶν, οὐχὶ ἀφήσει τὰ ἐνενήκοντα ἐννέα ἐπὶ τὰ ὄρη καὶ πορευθεὶς ζητεῖ τὸ πλανώμενον; ¹³ καὶ ἐὰν γένηται εὑρεῖν αὐτό, ἀμὴν λέγω ὑμῖν ὅτι χαίρει ἐπ᾽ αὐτῷ μᾶλλον ἢ ἐπὶ τοῖς ἐνενήκοντα ἐννέα τοῖς μὴ πεπλανημένοις. ¹⁴ οὕτως οὐκ ἔστιν θέλημα ἔμπροσθεν τοῦ πατρὸς ὑμῶν τοῦ ἐν οὐρανοῖς ἵνα ἀπόληται ἓν τῶν μικρῶν τούτων. ¹⁵ Ἐὰν δὲ ἁμαρτήσῃ [εἰς σὲ] ὁ ἀδελφός σου, ὕπαγε ἔλεγξον αὐτὸν μεταξὺ σοῦ καὶ αὐτοῦ μόνου. ἐάν σου ἀκούσῃ, ἐκέρδησας τὸν ἀδελφόν σου· ¹⁶ ἐὰν δὲ μὴ ἀκούσῃ, παράλαβε μετὰ σοῦ ἔτι ἕνα ἢ δύο, ἵνα ἐπὶ στόματος δύο μαρτύρων ἢ τριῶν σταθῇ πᾶν ῥῆμα· ¹⁷ ἐὰν δὲ παρακούσῃ αὐτῶν, εἰπὲ τῇ ἐκκλησίᾳ· ἐὰν δὲ καὶ τῆς ἐκκλησίας παρακούσῃ, ἔστω σοι ὥσπερ ὁ ἐθνικὸς καὶ ὁ τελώνης. ¹⁸ Ἀμὴν λέγω ὑμῖν· ὅσα ἐὰν δήσητε ἐπὶ τῆς γῆς ἔσται δεδεμένα ἐν οὐρανῷ, καὶ ὅσα ἐὰν λύσητε ἐπὶ τῆς γῆς ἔσται λελυμένα ἐν οὐρανῷ. ¹⁹ Πάλιν [ἀμὴν] λέγω ὑμῖν ὅτι ἐὰν δύο συμφωνήσωσιν ἐξ ὑμῶν ἐπὶ τῆς γῆς περὶ παντὸς πράγματος οὗ ἐὰν αἰτήσωνται, γενήσεται αὐτοῖς παρὰ τοῦ πατρός μου τοῦ ἐν οὐρανοῖς. ²⁰ οὗ γάρ εἰσιν δύο ἢ τρεῖς συνηγμένοι εἰς τὸ ἐμὸν ὄνομα, ἐκεῖ εἰμι ἐν μέσῳ αὐτῶν.

Reading Notes[75]

Verse 10

- Ὁρᾶτε ("see") – Pres act imp 2nd pl ὁράω. This word functions rhetorically to draw attention to the following command (μὴ καταφρονήσητε). We find similar constructions with ὁρᾶτε in Matt 9:30; 16:6; and 24:6.

- μὴ καταφρονήσητε ("do not despise") – Aor act sub 2nd pl καταφρονέω. Here we have an example of the negated aorist subjunctive used as an imperative—the prohibitory subjunctive (i.e., the subjunctive used to prohibit something). It is important to note the distinction here between form (subjunctive) and function (imperative). When morphologically tagging (labeling) such forms for a digital text, scholars must decide whether to label the words according to form or function. Students should be aware that such prior tagging decisions will influence search results of digital Greek texts.

---

[75] The English version used in the Reading Notes for this chapter is the ESV.

- **ἑνὸς τῶν μικρῶν τούτων** ("one of these little ones") – τῶν μικρῶν is an example of the partitive genitive—"the whole" of which something else is a part (see also v. 15 and ἐξ ὑμῶν in v. 19). That is, there is a group of little ones (the whole) and Jesus refers to one of them (the part). ἑνός is a genitive direct object following the verb καταφρονέω ("despise").

- **λέγω γὰρ ὑμῖν ὅτι** ("For I tell you that") – γάρ is called a post-positive particle, i.e., a little word (particle) that almost always comes second (post-positive) in a phrase. Here γάρ functions to introduce an explanatory subordinate clause. That is, the subordinate clause introduced by γάρ explains why Jesus's disciples should not look down on "one of these little ones." ὅτι introduces the content of Jesus's discourse following the verb of speaking (λέγω). Depending on context, ὅτι can also introduce causal clauses, and in such cases it is usually translated "for" or "because" in English.

- **οἱ ἄγγελοι αὐτῶν ἐν οὐρανοῖς διὰ παντός** ("in heaven their angels always see") – αὐτῶν is a genitive of relationship, or possibly genitive of possession (in a broad metaphorical sense).[76] Note the plural οὐρανοῖς (literally, "heavens") mirroring the Semitic plural שָׁמַיִם (heavens). The prepositional phrase διὰ παντός (literally, "through all [circumstances]"), like ἐν οὐρανοῖς, also is an adverbial modifier of the verb βλέπουσι, describing when this seeing occurs, i.e., "always."

- **βλέπουσι τὸ πρόσωπον τοῦ πατρός μου τοῦ ἐν οὐρανοῖς** ("see the face of my Father who is in heaven") – βλέπουσι is a pres act ind 3rd pl of βλέπω. Obviously, the reference to God's "face" is an anthropomorphism—the use of human attributes to describe God which is not to be taken literally. The article τοῦ substantizes the prepositional phrase ἐν οὐρανοῖς, turning it into an adjectival modifier of τοῦ πατρός μου (see also vv. 14, 19).

Verse 11

- The NA²⁸ and UBS⁵ do not include any text after v. 11, judging the additional words in some manuscript traditions to be a later addition to Matthew's original writing. The Byzantine text tradition, reflected in the KJV translation, records these words for v. 11: ἦλθεν γὰρ ὁ υἱὸς τοῦ ἀνθρώπου

---

[76] D. A. Carson argues, "It is true that angels are sent to minster to those who will inherit salvation (Heb 1:14). But nowhere in Scripture or Jewish tradition of the NT period is there any suggestion that there is one angel for one person. . . . The most likely explanation is the one Warfield (*Selected Shorter Writings*, 1:253–66) defends. The 'angels' of the 'little ones' are their spirits after death, and they always see the heavenly Father's face. Do not despise these little ones, Jesus says, for their destiny is the unshielded glory of the Father's presence." See "Matthew," in *Matthew–Mark*, EBC 9, rev. ed. (Grand Rapids: Zondervan, 2010), 454. The most natural reading of the text, however, seems to favor some type of angelic guardians in heaven.

σῶσαι τὸ ἀπολωλός ("For the Son of Man is come to save that which was lost"). As the additional words are missing from the best and earliest manuscripts (external evidence), and we detect a harmonizing scribal tendency with Luke 19:10 (internal reasoning), we have good grounds for concluding that Matthew did not write these words at this point in his Gospel. Modern Bible translations have good reasons for not including a "verse 11." Metzger writes, "There can be little doubt that the words ἦλθεν γὰρ ὁ υἱὸς τοῦ ἀνθρώπου (ζητῆσαι καὶ) σῶσαι τὸ ἀπολωλός are spurious here, being absent from the earliest witnesses representing several textual types (Alexandrian, Egyptian, Antiochian), and manifestly borrowed by copyists from Lk 19.10. The reason for the interpolation was apparently to provide a connection between ver. 10 and verses 12–14."[77] In reality, modern Bible translation committees are not removing a part of the inspired text; they are removing an addition to the inspired text made by a later scribe.

Verse 12

- **Τί ὑμῖν δοκεῖ;** ("What do you think?") – Literally, "What does it seem to you?" δοκεῖ is the pres act ind 3rd sg of δοκέω. ὑμῖν is a dative of reference or respect, i.e., how does it seem from the reference point of the "you" (the disciples)? (see also σοι in v. 17).

- **ἐὰν γένηταί τινι ἀνθρώπῳ ἑκατὸν πρόβατα** ("If a man has a hundred sheep")" – Literally, "If there is [belonging] to a certain man a hundred sheep." ἐάν introduces the protasis ("if" clause) of a 3rd class conditional sentence—presenting a hypothetical reality for the hearers' consideration. γένηται is aor mid sub 3rd sg of γίνομαι, with the implied impersonal subject, translated "there is" or "it is." ἀνθρώπῳ is a dative of possession.

- **καὶ πλανηθῇ ἓν ἐξ αὐτῶν** ("and one of them has gone astray") – πλανηθῇ is an aor pass sub 3rd sg of πλανάω. The prepositional phrase ἐξ αὐτῶν functions as a partitive. Note the rough breathing mark over ἕν distinguishing it as the neut sg cardinal number "one." The preposition ἐν has a smooth breathing mark and lacks an accent.

- **οὐχὶ ἀφήσει τὰ ἐνενήκοντα ἐννέα ἐπὶ τὰ ὄρη** ("does he not leave the ninety-nine on the mountains") – οὐχί begins a rhetorical question. Such questions marked with some variation of οὐ ("no," "not," here οὐχί being more emphatic) usually imply a positive answer (i.e., "Yes! Why yes, of course he will do that!"). ἀφήσει is fut act ind 3rd sg of ἀφίημι, a deliberative future.

- **καὶ πορευθεὶς ζητεῖ τὸ πλανώμενον;** ("and go in search of the one that went astray?") – πορευθείς (aor pass ptc masc nom sg πορεύομαι), a

---

[77] Metzger, *Textual Commentary*, 36.

participle of attendant circumstances, here translated as another indicative verb. ζητεῖ is a pres act ind 3rd sg of the contract verb ζητέω. Note the circumflex over the final diphthong, marking the contraction of vowels (ζητέ + ει = ζητεῖ). τὸ πλανώμενον (pres pass ptc neut acc sg πλανάω) is a substantival participle functioning as the direct object of ζητεῖ.

Verse 13

- **καὶ ἐὰν γένηται εὑρεῖν αὐτό** ("And if he finds it") – Literally, "And if it should happen that he finds it." This periphrastic construction possibly reflects Semitic influence (cf. Luke 11:27). εὑρεῖν is aor act inf of εὑρίσκω and has an implied subject accusative αὐτόν.

- **ἀμὴν λέγω ὑμῖν ὅτι** ("truly, I say to you") – ὅτι functions to introduce the content of Jesus's following pronouncement.

- **χαίρει ἐπ' αὐτῷ** ("he rejoices over it") – Pres act ind 3rd sg χαίρω. Following verbs that express emotions or opinions, ἐπί sometimes functions causally—as here.[78] αὐτῷ is dative because of the preposition ἐπί, which is frequently followed by a dative object.

- **μᾶλλον ἢ ἐπὶ τοῖς ἐνενήκοντα ἐννέα** ("more than over the ninety-nine") – The construction μᾶλλον ἤ ("more than") is used to communicate comparison between two things. Though ἐνενήκοντα ἐννέα ("ninety-nine") is an indeclinable cardinal number, the article τοῖς makes its dative function clear.

- **τοῖς μὴ πεπλανημένοις** ("that never went astray") – Per pass ptc neut dat pl πλανάω. The dative participle, whose case is governed by ἐπί, is substantival. As expected, the non-indicative form is negated by μή.

Verse 14

- **οὕτως οὐκ ἔστιν θέλημα** ("So it is not the will") – Pres ind 3rd sg εἰμί, which has an implied impersonal subject ("it"). θέλημα functions as the predicate nominative and lacks the article, though the following prepositional phrase clearly imbues the noun with a definite sense.

- **ἔμπροσθεν τοῦ πατρὸς ὑμῶν τοῦ ἐν οὐρανοῖς** ("of my Father who is in heaven") – Notice that the ESV chooses to follow the reading that includes μου (B F H *f13*) instead of ὑμῶν (א Dc L W *f1 Byz*). Most commentators note the Semitic style of this whole phrase. BDAG, citing this use of ἔμπροσθεν, classifies it "as a reverential way of expressing oneself, when one is speaking of an eminent pers[on] and esp. of God, not to connect the

---

[78] BDAG, 365, definition 6c; see also Jas 5:1.

subject directly with what happens, but to say that it took place 'before someone.'"[79]

- ἵνα ἀπόληται ἓν τῶν μικρῶν τούτων ("that one of these little ones should perish") – ἵνα introduces a content clause—giving us the content of the Father's will. ἀπόληται is an aor mid sub 3rd sg of ἀπόλλυμι.

Verse 15

- Ἐὰν δὲ ἁμαρτήσῃ [εἰς σὲ] ὁ ἀδελφός σου ("If your brother sins against you") – δέ is a post-positive particle. While the exact function of δέ is debated, it is rendered with a wide variety of English glosses—or sometimes, it is untranslated (as above). Greek authors seem to prefer δέ as a transitional word when there is "change" or "difference" introduced into the flow of thought. Here, the speaker (Jesus) transitions from parable to explicit communal injunction. εἰς σέ is in brackets because of the textual debate about its inclusion. The editors of UBS[5] gave the variant a "C" rating (indicating that the UBS committee "had difficulty in deciding which variant to place in the text").[80] Students will note in the textual apparatus that two early codices (ℵ, Sinaiticus, and B, Vaticanus) lack the variant.[81] Regardless of whether the variant was present or not in the original manuscript, the sense of the passage is largely unchanged. ὁ ἀδελφός σου refers to an outwardly visible member of the Christian community. As v. 17 will imply, depending on the brother's response to rebuke, he may be a "false brother."

- ὕπαγε ἔλεγξον αὐτόν ("go and tell him his fault") – Pres act impv 2nd sg ὑπάγω. Though the present imperative frequently commands a regular or repeated activity, the context here clearly points to a discrete occasion. Verbs of motion prefer the present tense-form even for a command for a specific occasion. ἔλεγξον is aor act impv 2nd sg of ἐλέγχω. The word "and" is supplied in English translation for smoothness of style; in the original Greek, there is no conjunction between the two commands.

- μεταξὺ σοῦ καὶ αὐτοῦ μόνου ("between you and him alone") – The preposition μεταξύ is followed by genitive object—here a compound genitive (σοῦ καὶ αὐτοῦ). About addressing an offense privately, A. T.

---

[79] BDAG, 325, definition 1.b.δ.

[80] Metzger notes, "It is possible that the words εἰς σέ are an early interpolation into the original text, perhaps derived by copyists from the use of εἰς ἐμέ in ver. 21. On the other hand, it is also possible to regard their omission as either deliberate (in order to render the passage applicable to sin in general) or accidental (for in later Greek the pronunciation of η, ῃ, and ει was similar)" (*Textual Commentary*, 36).

[81] You can go to www.codexsinaiticus.org to view the ancient codex for yourself.

Robertson remarks, "Such private reproof is hard to do, but it is the way of Christ."[82]

- **ἐάν σου ἀκούσῃ** ("If he listens to you") – ἐάν begins another third class conditional clause. ἀκούσῃ is aor act sub 3rd sg of ἀκούω. The verb ἀκούω often takes a genitive object, as here (σου).

- **ἐκέρδησας τὸν ἀδελφόν σου** ("you have gained your brother") – Aor act ind 2nd sg κερδαίνω. The direct object of the verb is the masc acc sg τὸν ἀδελφόν, with the article as expected when modified by a genitive personal pronoun.

Verse 16

- **ἐὰν δὲ μὴ ἀκούσῃ** ("But if he does not listen") – Aor act sub 3rd sg ἀκούω. While ἀκούω can refer simply to the physiological reality of hearing sound(s), in this verse, ἀκούω clearly has connotations of hearing *favorably*.

- **παράλαβε μετὰ σοῦ ἔτι ἕνα ἢ δύο** ("take one or two others along with you") – Aor act impv 2nd sg παραλαμβάνω. Note that present imperative endings are normally used with 2nd aorist forms, as here (παράλαβε).

- **ἵνα ἐπὶ στόματος δύο μαρτύρων ἢ τριῶν σταθῇ πᾶν ῥῆμα** ("that every charge may be established by the evidence of two or three witnesses") – ἵνα introduces a purpose clause followed by the aor pass sub 3rd sg of ἵστημι. Matthew's use of στόμα here is an example of metonymy where "mouth" figuratively stands in for the utterance of the mouth (i.e., testimony). While introductory Greek students usually learn "word" as the only definition for ῥῆμα, Louw & Nida list these two additional semantic fields for ῥῆμα: statement (§33.98) and event (§13.115). Which meaning seems to be intended in Matthew 18:16?

Verse 17

- **ἐὰν δὲ παρακούσῃ αὐτῶν** ("If he refuses to listen to them") – παρακούσῃ is an aor act sub 3rd sg of παρακούω. This verb is regularly followed by a genitive direct object, as here (αὐτῶν; cf. τῆς ἐκκλησίας later in this verse).

- **εἰπὲ τῇ ἐκκλησίᾳ** ("tell it to the church") – Aor act impv 2nd sg λέγω. τῇ ἐκκλησίᾳ is a dative of indirect object. This is only one of two verses in the Gospels where the word ἐκκλησία occurs (see also Matt 16:18). Some liberal scholars question whether Jesus envisaged an ongoing community

---

[82] A. T. Robertson, *Word Pictures in the New Testament*, vol. 1 (Nashville: B&H, 1930; reprint), 148.

with leadership and boundaries of the type described here. Thus, some-times Jesus's instructions here are classified as a later ecclesiastical in-terpolation. Nevertheless, if Jesus truly was one of the greatest teachers and leaders in history, even from a purely non-supernatural perspective, it seems likely that he would envision the forthcoming needs of his bur-geoning group of followers. Though the word ἐκκλησία might not occur elsewhere in the Gospels, the concept of a defined community of Jesus's followers is often found.[83]

- ἐὰν δὲ καὶ τῆς ἐκκλησίας παρακούσῃ ("And if he refuses to listen even to the church") – καί is either ascensive ("even," as in the ESV translation above) or connective ("and"). Only context can determine its function.

- ἔστω σοι ὥσπερ ὁ ἐθνικὸς καὶ ὁ τελώνης ("let him be to you as a Gentile and a tax collector") – ἔστω is a pres impv 3rd sg of εἰμί. The third singular imperative in Greek is frequently translated as "let him . . . ." Stu-dents must understand that "let him . . ." is not a statement of permission, but a command. It could be translated "he must/should . . . ." ὁ ἐθνικός and ὁ τελώνης both have the article because they stand for the generic category or class of tax collectors and unbelievers (literally, as in the ESV: "Gentile"). In English, we usually communicate that a noun represents a generic category with an indefinite article ("a" or "an") or by employ-ing the plural of the noun (i.e., "treat him like you treat *Gentiles* and tax *collectors*").

Verse 18

- Ἀμὴν λέγω ὑμῖν ("Truly, I say to you") – This pleonastic (redundant) phrase is left out of some dynamically-equivalent translations. The phrase functions rhetorically to emphasize the following pronouncement.

- ὅσα ἐὰν δήσητε ἐπὶ τῆς γῆς ἔσται δεδεμένα ἐν οὐρανῷ ("whatever you bind on earth shall be bound in heaven") – The correlative pronoun (ὅσα; lexical form: ὅσος) with the indefinite particle ἄν (or ἐάν) is trans-lated as an indefinite relative clause (i.e., "whatever . . ."). δήσητε is aor act sub 2nd pl of δέω. The prepositional phrase ἐπὶ τῆς γῆς is translated "on earth" (i.e., in this visible and tangible realm of local church life). ἔσται is the fut mid 3rd sg of εἰμί. δεδεμένα is per pass ptc neut nom pl of δέω. Grammarians debate how to translate the future of εἰμί + per pass ptc, a relatively rare perfect periphrastic participle.[84] The two main options are (1) "will or shall be bound" (ESV, NIV) or (2) "will have

---

[83] See Benjamin L. Merkle, "The Meaning of Ἐκκλησία in Matthew 16:18 and 18:17," *BSac* 167 (2010): 281–91.

[84] Fanning states that there are only six such constructions in the NT, including the present usage (Fanning, *Verbal Aspect*, 322–23): Matt 16:19 (twice); 18:18 (twice); Luke 12:52–53a; Heb 2:13.

been bound" (CSB).[85] The "binding" and "loosing" in these passages refers to the church's temporal pronouncement of who is forgiven by God ("loosed" from sins), distinguished from those who are outside of his favor (still "bound" by sins).[86]

- **καὶ ὅσα ἐὰν λύσητε ἐπὶ τῆς γῆς ἔσται λελυμένα ἐν οὐρανῷ** ("and whatever you loose on earth shall be loosed in heaven") – λύσητε is the aor act sub 2nd pl of λύω. λελυμένα is the per pass ptc neut nom pl of λύω.

Verse 19

- **Πάλιν [ἀμὴν] λέγω ὑμῖν ὅτι** ("Again I say to you") – ἀμήν is put in brackets by the editors of the GNT because there is significant debate as to whether Matthew included the word in his original composition or whether it was added by later scribes. If the word was added by later scribes, it was likely an inadvertent harmonization with a common phrase spoken by Jesus in the Gospels. Note the textual apparatus in your UBS or Nestle-Aland GNT.

- **ἐὰν δύο συμφωνήσωσιν ἐξ ὑμῶν ἐπὶ τῆς γῆς περὶ παντὸς πράγματος οὗ ἐὰν αἰτήσωνται** ("if two of you agree on earth about anything they ask") – συμφωνήσωσιν is an aor act sub 3rd pl of συμφωνέω. Jesus often speaks hyperbolically (περὶ παντὸς πράγματος), but underlying his invitation to prayer about *any matter* are unstated qualifications—the main one being that the prayer is in accord with the Father's will (1 John 5:14). Certainly, Jesus is not promising that a sinful request will be granted as long as two Christians agree. The relative pronoun οὗ + the indefinite particle ἄν (or ἐάν in this case) introduces an indefinite relative clause. αἰτήσωνται is aor mid sub 3rd pl of αἰτέω. Verbs of asking/requesting often appear in the middle voice in Greek.

- **γενήσεται αὐτοῖς παρὰ τοῦ πατρός μου τοῦ ἐν οὐρανοῖς** ("it will be done for them by my Father in heaven") – Literally, "it will come about for them from my Father in the heavens." γενήσεται fut mid ind 3rd sg γίνομαι. αὐτοῖς is a dative of personal interest (advantage).

Verse 20

- **οὗ γάρ εἰσιν δύο ἢ τρεῖς συνηγμένοι** ("For where two or three are gathered") – οὗ, though in form a genitive relative pronoun, functions as

---

[85] For a discussion of this construction with reference to Matt 16:19, 18:18, and John 20:23, see Carson, "Matthew," 421–26. Carson's discussion supports the CSB rendering ("will have been bound"). If Carson and the CSB are correct, the meaning of the text is that as the church faithfully announces God's salvation and warns those who reject God's grace, the church's temporal pronouncements reflect God's prior divine decree.

[86] See Craig L. Blomberg, *Matthew*, NAC (Nashville: Broadman, 1992), 280.

an adverbial particle of place ("where"). The participle συνηγμένοι (per pass ptc masc nom pl συνάγω) completes the verbal idea as a periphrastic participle. While this verse is often cited with regard to small group prayer, it should be noted that the larger context of the passage is about church discipline. That is, the prayer in v. 19 is most naturally understood as dealing with the straying brother. One might paraphrase Jesus's words: "As you are led by my Spirit in dealing with a straying brother or sister, don't be discouraged or afraid, my authoritative and comforting presence is there. You are not acting alone, but under and with my authority."

- εἰς τὸ ἐμὸν ὄνομα ("in my name") – ἐμόν is a pronominal adjective meaning "my" (lexical form: ἐμός). The pronominal adjective is rarer than the genitive personal pronoun and possibly more emphatic (e.g., "in my own name").

- ἐκεῖ εἰμι ἐν μέσῳ αὐτῶν ("there am I among them") – Literally, "there I am in their midst." αὐτῶν is probably best labeled a genitive of possession (metaphorical).

/////////////////

CHAPTER 3

GENITIVE CASE

GOING DEEPER

Christmas cards frequently proclaim, and Christmas carols echo, the well-known angelic pronouncement at Jesus's birth of "peace on earth, good will toward men."[1] Or do they? A closer look at the actual passage in Luke 2:14 proves both intriguing and illuminating. In context, Luke opens his narrative of the birth of Jesus Christ with reference to the Roman emperor Caesar Augustus (31/27 BC–AD 14) who presided over the "Golden Age" of Rome and was widely heralded for having ushered in the period of *Pax Romana*, the "Roman peace." Jesus was born during the reign of Augustus, the Roman "Prince of peace." In keeping with Isaiah's prophecy, Jesus, too, came as the "Prince of peace," and yet, the peace he came to bring was of an entirely different kind.[2] Jesus's peace was not coercive, backed up by Roman military might; it was an otherworldly, supernatural peace—peace with God—that no human power can procure and no amount of money can buy.

In God's providence, the census ordered by Caesar Augustus brought Joseph, Jesus's adoptive father, and Jesus's mother Mary from Nazareth where they lived to Joseph's ancestral home of Bethlehem, the town of David. According to Micah's prophecy, this was the city where the Messiah was to be born.[3] In the tradition of David, the shepherd-king, it was there—in Bethlehem—that Mary gave birth to

---

[1] An example is "It Came Upon a Midnight Clear," written by the Unitarian minister Edmund Sears.

[2] Cf. Isa 9:6. See also John 14:27: "Peace I leave with you. My peace I give to you. I do not give to you as the world gives."

[3] Cf. Mic 5:2, cited in Matt 2:6.

Jesus. Local shepherds became the bewildered recipients of an angelic visitation pronouncing good news: "Today in the town of David a Savior has been born to you; he is the Messiah, the Lord. This will be a sign to you: You will find a baby wrapped in cloths and lying in a manger" (Luke 2:11–12 NIV).

At this announcement, a contingent of angels appeared, praising God and saying, "Glory to God in the highest heaven, and on earth peace to *those on whom his favor rests*" (NIV; δόξα ἐν ὑψίστοις θεῷ καὶ ἐπὶ γῆς εἰρήνη ἐν ἀνθρώποις εὐδοκίας). Grammatically speaking, the subject of the first clause is δόξα ("Glory") and the subject of the second clause is εἰρήνη ("peace"). The contrasting locations are ἐν ὑψίστοις ("in the highest") and ἐπὶ γῆς ("on earth"), and the respective recipients θεῷ ("God") and ἀνθρώποις εὐδοκίας ("those [lit., the men/people] on whom his favor rests"). Most modern English translations render the noun εὐδοκίας (literally, "of good pleasure") as denoting an attribute of the recipients of peace rather than as a second subject on par with "peace."[4] Are those Christmas cards and carols that proclaim "peace on earth, good will toward men," wrong then? Let's take a look.

First of all, there is a text-critical issue.[5] Does the original text of Luke 2:14 read εὐδοκίας ("of good pleasure," genitive case) or εὐδοκία ("good will," nominative case)? In Greek, the difference is only a single letter, a final sigma (ς). A look at the oldest and most reliable manuscripts makes clear that all three major codices—Sinaiticus (א), Alexandrinus (A), and Vaticanus (B)—point to εὐδοκίας as the original wording. Interestingly, in both Sinaiticus and Vaticanus, later correctors erased the final sigma in order to change the harder genitive to the easier nominative reading which subsequently found its way into many Byzantine manuscripts and writings by the Church Fathers.[6] Later still, the King James Version based its rendering of Luke 2:14 on this textual tradition, issuing in the translation, "on earth peace, good will toward men." And many Christmas cards and carols followed suit!

But, you may ask, what difference does it make whether "good will" is in the nominative or genitive case in the present passage? Is there an actual difference in meaning between these two renderings? In fact, there is. The traditional English translation "peace on earth, good will toward men" pronounces peace and good will toward *all* people, that is, humanity at large. While at some level this is doubtless true with regard to Christ's birth (see the reference to "great joy for all the people" in Luke 2:10), the angels' pronouncement is almost certainly restricted more specifically to "those on whom God's favor rests," that is, "the people of God's good pleasure."[7] And how does one become the recipient of God's good pleasure? In short: by putting their faith in Jesus the Messiah.

---

[4] ESV: "on earth peace among those with whom he is pleased"; CSB: "and peace on earth to people he favors" (footnote: Or *earth to men of good will*).

[5] See Metzger, *Textual Commentary*, 111.

[6] See Metzger, *Textual Commentary*, 111.

[7] Interestingly, the Dead Sea Scrolls attest to the fact that this was a common Semitic phrase. Metzger mentions 1QH 4.32–33; 11.9 ("the sons of his [God's] good pleasure"); and 8.6 ("the elect

At his baptism, and again at the transfiguration, Jesus himself was uniquely declared to be God's beloved Son with whom God was well pleased.[8] Now, through Jesus's human birth and ultimately through his sacrificial cross-death on our behalf, peace with God is available to those who become recipients of divine favor through faith in God's beloved Son. *This* is the "good news" the angels proclaimed at Christ's birth, and this is the gospel we are called to proclaim to others in our day. Thus, knowledge of textual criticism and Greek grammar, along with careful study of the context of Luke 2:14, reap rich dividends in theological understanding. The angels rejoice and praise God for working out his salvation in and through the birth of the Messiah. And "the people in whom God draws near through Jesus will experience the harmony and benefits that God bestows on his own."[9]

CHAPTER OBJECTIVES

The purpose of this chapter is to cover the various uses of the Greek case called the genitive. The main benefit you will derive from working through this chapter is that you will be acquainted with all the major categories of usage for the genitive. Although scholars debate the specific nomenclature of some of these categories, as well as individual examples, they genuinely capture the essence of the various uses of the genitive case. Understanding the essence of each category and grasping how they differ from one another will make an important contribution toward helping you interpret the NT more accurately.

INTRODUCTION TO THE GENITIVE CASE

The genitive is the case of *description* or *quality* and in some cases *separation*.[10] Whereas the accusative case limits verbs, the genitive limits *nouns*. The function of the genitive is similar to that of an *adjective* or *adverb*, denoting the quality of a

---

of his [God's] good pleasure") (*Textual Commentary*, 111). See also Darrell L. Bock, *Luke 1:1–9:50*, BECNT (Grand Rapids: Baker, 1994), 220.

[8] Note that while the noun εὐδοκία is rare in the biblical Gospels (elsewhere only in Matt 11:26 // Luke 10:21), the verb εὐδοκέω is found in the Synoptic accounts of Jesus's baptism (Matt 3:17 // Mark 1:11 // Luke 3:22) and Transfiguration (Matt 17:5). Luke 12:32 also includes reference to Jesus's saying that it was the Father's "good pleasure" to give his followers the kingdom.

[9] Bock, *Luke 1:1–9:50*, 221. See also his discussion of the contemporary implications of this passage on pp. 400–401; and the exegetical insight by Verlyn Verbrugge in Mounce, *Basics of Biblical Greek*, 45 (see chap. 2, n. 4). For a study of the NT birth narratives as well as the Johannine prologue, see Köstenberger and Stewart, *The First Days of Jesus* (see chap. 1, n. 3).

[10] Young, 23. Wallace speaks of "qualification (or limitation as to kind) and (occasionally) separation" (77). Black calls the genitive "the describing case" (*Still Greek*, 48); Robertson speaks of the "specifying" case (493). Porter maintains that "the essential semantic feature of the genitive case is restriction" (*Idioms*, 83); Brooks & Winbery, 92. Similarly, Dana & Mantey describe the basic function of the genitive as being "to set more definitely the limits of an idea as to its class or kind" (72). Grammars using the 8-case system subsume instances where the genitive conveys the notion of separation under the "ablative case" (e.g., Brooks & Winbery, 21–31).

given person or thing.[11] The phrase "Father **of our Lord Jesus Christ**" (πατὴρ τοῦ κυρίου ἡμῶν Ἰησοῦ Χριστοῦ) in Eph 1:3, for example, both limits the scope of the word "Father" and specifies that God is the Father "of our Lord Jesus Christ." In most cases, the English translation will include the word "of." This at times may lead to ambiguity, such as when speaking of "the revelation of Christ," which may alternatively refer to Christ revealing *himself* to others (subjective genitive) or a biblical writer's teaching *about* Christ (objective genitive).[12] In terms of word order, the genitive normally *follows* the noun it qualifies but *precedes* it when the reference denotes emphasis or contrast.[13]

Another interesting feature of NT instances of the genitive is that genitives tend to string together, especially in Paul's writings (genitive chains or concatenative genitives). In such cases, each genitive further qualifies the genitive that precedes it. Blass, Debrunner, and Funk speak of "a quite cumbersome accumulation of genitives" at some occasions in which "the governing genitive must always precede the dependent genitive."[14] Second Corinthians 4:4 may serve as an example: "the light **of the gospel of the glory of Christ**" (τὸν φωτισμὸν **τοῦ εὐαγγελίου τῆς δόξης τοῦ Χριστοῦ**). In this case, the noun "the light" (τὸν φωτισμόν) is described as proceeding from "the gospel" (τοῦ εὐαγγελίου; first genitive), which is further described as having as its content "the glory" (τῆς δόξης; second genitive) specifically "of Christ" (τοῦ Χριστοῦ; third genitive).[15]

The uses of the genitive can be broken down into three major categories: adjectival, verbal, and adverbial. In addition, genitives may be used in other ways, such as genitives of apposition or genitive direct objects.[16] Some grammarians (such as Moule) are minimalists, trying to reduce the categories to as few as possible, fearing that too many categories may only confuse the student. Others (such as Wallace) try to bring out as many variations in the NT use of genitives as possible. In this chapter, we will try to steer a middle course. The proliferation of categories for the genitive can indeed be bewildering. Students are encouraged to start by asking themselves if a given instance of the genitive is adjectival, verbal, or adverbial and then try to determine the specific use of the genitive within those three categories.

---

[11] See, e.g., Brooks & Winbery: "the genitive functions very much like an adjective" (8). Black says the genitive "is basically adjectival in function" but "is more emphatic than the adjective" (*Still Greek*, 48). Similarly, Dana & Mantey state that it is "more emphatic than that of the adjective" (73).

[12] See Wallace, who speaks of the "elasticity" of the genitive which includes antithetical possibilities (74–75).

[13] Robertson cites Acts 14:1 as an example of emphasis: "a great number **of both Jews and Greeks** believed" (πιστεῦσαι Ἰουδαίων τε καὶ Ἑλλήνων πολὺ πλῆθος) and Phil 2:25 as an example of contrast: "<u>my</u> brother, co-worker, and fellow soldier, as well as **your** messenger and minister to my need" (τὸν ἀδελφὸν καὶ συνεργὸν καὶ συστρατιώτην <u>μου</u>, **ὑμῶν** δὲ ἀπόστολον καὶ λειτουργὸν τῆς χρείας μου) (502).

[14] BDF, 93 (§168).

[15] Cf. Zerwick, 18 (§47). Robertson uses the example of 1 Thess 1:3, where 21 of the 27 words are genitives, and 3 of the words that are not genitives are καί (503).

[16] See especially Young, 38–41, who labels these as "genitives functioning as noun phrases."

They may want to use the summary charts in the back and then go to the more detailed description of each individual category below.

ADJECTIVAL USES OF THE GENITIVE	Description
	Attributive
	Possession
	Relationship
	Source
	Material or Content
	Partitive
VERBAL USES OF THE GENITIVE	Subjective
	Objective
ADVERBIAL USES OF THE GENITIVE	Time or Place
	Separation
	Means or Agency
	Comparison
	Price
OTHER USES	Apposition
	Direct Object

ADJECTIVAL USE

As mentioned, the genitive is the case of *description* or *quality*. In this regard, it is similar in function to the adjective, which likewise provides a further description of a noun by assigning it a given quality (e.g., "the *good* shepherd"). For this reason the (1) genitive of description (discussed first below) represents virtually the quintessential type of usage of the genitive. While the nomenclature varies in the standard grammars, most grammarians also discuss (2) the attributive genitive; (3) the genitive of possession; (4) the genitive of relationship; (5) the genitive of source; (6) the genitive of material or content; and (7) the partitive genitive.[17]

Description

The genitive of description further limits or defines its head noun in some way that is not better described by other common genitival uses. As Wallace rightly notes, this is a catch-all category, because all genitives are in essence descriptive.[18] The remaining adjectival uses of the genitive discussed below are more nuanced

---

[17] See the Genitive Case Categories chart in Appendix 2.
[18] Wallace, 79. Similarly, Dana & Mantey, 75.

instances of this broad category. Genitive of description, then, is the last-choice category when none of the more specific categories seem to fit.[19]

- ἀνεκτότερον ἔσται γῇ Σοδόμων καὶ Γομόρρων ἐν ἡμέρᾳ **κρίσεως** (Matt 10:15)

  It will be more tolerable on the day **of judgment** for the land of Sodom and Gomorrah

  > The genitive offers a further description of the day that Jesus is speaking about.

- ἐγένετο Ἰωάννης . . . κηρύσσων βάπτισμα **μετανοίας** (Mark 1:4)

  John came . . . proclaiming a baptism **of repentance**

  > John's baptism expresses repentance or is accompanied by repentance. Note, the noun βάπτισμα is further limited or described by the genitive μετανοίας, but none of the other major genitival categories expresses precisely the biblical author's specific nuance (which is determined by a careful contextual reading).

- ἐγώ εἰμι ἡ θύρα **τῶν προβάτων** (John 10:7)

  I am the **gate for the sheep**

- θησαυρίζεις σεαυτῷ ὀργὴν ἐν ἡμέρᾳ **ὀργῆς** (Rom 2:5)

  you are storing up wrath for yourself in the day **of wrath**

  > The day of wrath is described as a day characterized by God's wrath upon humanity's sin.

- ἐν ἡμέρᾳ **σωτηρίας** (2 Cor 6:2)

  in the day **of salvation**

  > That future day is here described as a day *of salvation* for believers.[20]

Attributive

The attributive genitive is also called the "Hebrew genitive," or "genitive of quality."[21] It denotes an attribute of the head term, conveying an emphatic adjectival idea.[22] This use of the genitive is common in Hebrew where a construct chain is used to describe an adjectival relationship. For example, Gen 37:3 refers to a "robe of many colors." The Hebrew is a simple construct relationship (כְּתֹנֶת פַּסִּים), which means a "many colored robe." In fact, the LXX treats this phrase, and many like it, as a simple adjectival relationship (χιτῶνα ποικίλον). If you can take the genitival modifier and place it in adjectival form in front of the head noun in your

---

[19] So rightly Young, 23.

[20] For more examples of the genitive of description, see Matt 13:18; 24:37; Rom 6:6; Eph 2:2; Col 1:22; 1 Thess 5:5; Rev 9:1.

[21] See Zerwick, 14; and BDF, 91 respectively.

[22] Young, 24; Wallace, 86.

English translation (and that construction conveys the biblical author's meaning), then the genitive is rightly labeled as an attributive genitive.[23]

- ἑαυτοῖς ποιήσατε φίλους ἐκ τοῦ μαμωνᾶ **τῆς ἀδικίας** (Luke 16:9)

  make friends for yourselves by means of **the unrighteous** wealth (ESV)

  Literally, the phrase reads "wealth of unrighteousness," denoting a quality or attribute of money.

- πορεύου, ὅτι σκεῦος **ἐκλογῆς** ἐστίν μοι οὗτος (Acts 9:15)

  Go, for this man is my **chosen** instrument

  Literally, the phrase reads "instrument of choice."

- οἷς ἠθέλησεν ὁ θεὸς γνωρίσαι τί τὸ πλοῦτος **τῆς δόξης** (Col 1:27)

  God wanted to make known among the Gentiles **the glorious** wealth

  Literally, the phrase reads, "the riches of the glory."

- φέρων τε τὰ πάντα τῷ ῥήματι **τῆς δυνάμεως** αὐτοῦ (Heb 1:3)

  sustaining all things by his **powerful** word

  Literally, the phrase reads "by the word of his power." Again, "his" (αὐτοῦ) is a possessive genitive.

- ἐλέγξαι πᾶσαν ψυχὴν περὶ πάντων τῶν ἔργων **ἀσεβείας** αὐτῶν (Jude 15)

  to convict all the ungodly concerning all the **ungodly** acts

  Literally, the phrase reads "their works of ungodliness."[24]

Possession

The genitive of possession identifies ownership with regard to the noun it modifies. For a genitive relationship to be considered possessive, the head noun must be something that can be owned, and therefore will not normally refer to concepts. In many cases, this involves the use of a possessive pronoun.[25]

---

[23] Wallace, 87.

[24] For more examples of the attributive genitive, see Luke 18:6; Rom 6:6; 8:21; 11:8; Gal 6:1; Heb 7:2. Wallace distinguishes the *attributive* genitive from the *attributed* genitive (citing Rom 6:4; Phil 1:22; 3:8; 1 Pet 1:7 as examples of the latter; 89–90; see also Rom 1:25; Eph 1:17–18; Jas 3:9). The two types of use are identical in structure, but in the case of the attributed adjective, "the head noun, rather than the genitive [itself], is functioning (in sense) as an attributive adjective" (89; sometimes called a "reverse adjectival genitive"). For example, in Rom 6:4 καινότητι ζωῆς means "newness of life" (attributed) and not "living newness" (attributive).

[25] Young, 25; Wallace, 82.

- **ἡμῶν** ἔσται ἡ κληρονομία (Mark 12:7)

  the inheritance will be **ours**

  > The word order (genitive pronoun preceding the noun) may indicate emphasis.

- ἐμβὰς δὲ εἰς ἓν τῶν πλοίων, ὃ ἦν **Σίμωνος** (Luke 5:3)

  He got into one of the boats, which **belonged to Simon**

  > Simon was the owner of the boat.

- καὶ εἰσελθόντες εἰς τὸν οἶκον **Φιλίππου** (Acts 21:8)

  we entered the house **of Philip**

  > The house was owned by Philip.

- πάντα γὰρ **ὑμῶν** ἐστιν (1 Cor 3:21)

  for everything is **yours**

- ἔπειτα οἱ **τοῦ Χριστοῦ** ἐν τῇ παρουσίᾳ αὐτοῦ (1 Cor 15:23)

  after that those who are **Christ's** at His coming (NASB)

  > The genitive designates those who belong to Christ at the second coming.

Relationship

The genitive of relationship normally denotes a family relationship, whether a person's parent or spouse or some other kinship relationship. The word indicating the relationship is often (but not always) omitted but can easily be inferred from the context.[26] At times reference is made to the family in a general sense.[27]

- Ἰάκωβον τὸν **τοῦ Ζεβεδαίου** (Matt 4:21)

  James the *son* **of Zebedee** (NASB)

  > The Greek reads literally, "James the of Zebedee" (note that "son" is appropriately italicized in the NASB); "son" is easily inferred.

- Μαρία ἡ **Ἰωσῆτος** (Mark 15:47)

  Mary the mother **of Joses**

  > "Mother" must be implied from the context.

---

[26] Dana & Mantey, 76–77.
[27] Robertson, 502.

- ἐγένετο ῥῆμα θεοῦ ἐπὶ Ἰωάννην τὸν **Ζαχαρίου** υἱὸν (Luke 3:2)

God's word came to John the son **of Zechariah**

> In this case, "son" is made explicit; the word order is article–genitive–noun in the accusative.

- ἐδηλώθη γάρ μοι περὶ ὑμῶν, ἀδελφοί μου, ὑπὸ **τῶν Χλόης** (1 Cor 1:11)

For it has been reported about you to me, my brothers and sisters, by **members of Chloe's household**

> Literally, the expression simply reads, "by [those] of Chloe." One may reasonably infer that this constitutes a general reference to Chloe's household.

- ἀδελφὸς δὲ Ἰακώβου (Jude 1)

a brother **of James**

> The relationship is made clear by supplying "brother."[28]

Source

The genitive of source indicates the origin of the head noun (note the translation "from" rather than "of"). Brooks & Winbery note that there will be times where a distinction between the genitive of source and the subjective genitive will be hard to make, since what a person produces (subjective genitive) has its origin in that person (genitive of source). The way to distinguish between the two is by keeping in mind that the subjective genitive is normally used with nouns conveying action.[29] For example, the reference to "the **Father's** promise" (τὴν ἐπαγγελίαν **τοῦ πατρός**) in Acts 1:4 may at first appear to be a genitive of source, since the promise comes *from* the Father. But ἐπαγγελίαν is a noun of action, so this is probably an instance of a subjective genitive.[30]

- ἀγνοοῦντες γὰρ τὴν **τοῦ θεοῦ** δικαιοσύνην (Rom 10:3)

Since they are ignorant of the righteousness **of God**

- ἵνα διὰ τῆς ὑπομονῆς καὶ διὰ τῆς παρακλήσεως **τῶν γραφῶν** τὴν ἐλπίδα ἔχωμεν (Rom 15:4)

so that we may have hope through endurance and through the encouragement **from the Scriptures**

- ἵνα ἡ ὑπερβολὴ τῆς δυνάμεως ᾖ **τοῦ θεοῦ** καὶ μὴ ἐξ ἡμῶν (2 Cor 4:7)

so that this extraordinary power may be **from God** and not from us

---

[28] For more examples of the genitive of relationship, see Mark 3:17; 5:35; Luke 6:16; 24:10; John 6:71; 19:25; 21:25; Acts 1:13; 13:22; Gal 5:24.

[29] Brooks & Winbery, 23.

[30] We owe this example to Brooks & Winbery (23).

- καὶ ἡ εἰρήνη **τοῦ θεοῦ** ἡ ὑπερέχουσα πάντα νοῦν φρουρήσει τὰς καρδίας ὑμῶν (Phil 4:7)

  And the peace **of God**, which surpasses all understanding, will guard your hearts[31]

- πᾶσα προφητεία γραφῆς **ἰδίας ἐπιλύσεως** οὐ γίνεται (2 Pet 1:20)

  No prophecy of Scripture comes **from someone's own interpretation** (ESV)[32]

Material or Content

The genitive of material indicates the material of which the head term is made. Wallace notes that this use is rather rare in the NT, because this idea is normally conveyed by ἐκ + the genitive.[33] The genitive of content is similar, but describes the material that is *contained in* the head term. The genitive of content does not apply only to physical content, as in "a cup of water" (see Mark 9:41 below). It can also refer to "communicative content," as in "the message of the cross" (see 1 Cor 1:18 below).[34]

Material

- οὐδεὶς δὲ ἐπιβάλλει ἐπίβλημα **ῥάκους** ἀγνάφου (Matt 9:16)

  But no one puts a patch **of** unshrunk **cloth** (NASB)

  > This genitive of material indicates that the patch was made of cloth.

- ἡ οὖν Μαριὰμ λαβοῦσα λίτραν μύρου **νάρδου πιστικῆς** πολυτίμου (John 12:3)

  Mary therefore took a pound of very costly perfume **of pure nard** (NASB)

- γόμον **χρυσοῦ** καὶ **ἀργύρου** καὶ **λίθου** τιμίου καὶ **μαργαριτῶν** (Rev 18:12)

  cargo **of gold**, **silver**, **jewels** , and **pearls**

---

[31] Wallace labels this a genitive of production (104–6). He acknowledges the similarity of the former with the genitive of source but contends that the genitive of production/producer indicates more active involvement on the part of the term in the genitive (compare "angel from heaven," where heaven is simply the angel's point of origin or departure, and "peace of God" which implies a more active role on the part of God in bringing about this peace; 105). Possible instances of the genitive of production/producer are Rom 4:11; Gal 5:22; Eph 4:3; and 1 Thess 1:3. Possible instances of the genitive of product are Rom 15:13, 33; and 16:20 (see also Rom 15:5; 1 Cor 14:33; 2 Cor 13:11; Phil 4:9; and Heb 1:9).

[32] For more examples of the genitive of source, see Rom 15:18, 22; 2 Cor 11:26; and Rev 9:11.

[33] Wallace, 91.

[34] Young, 27.

Content

The genitive of content, whether literally or figuratively, indicates the content of an object or abstract noun.

- ὃς γὰρ ἂν ποτίσῃ ὑμᾶς ποτήριον **ὕδατος** (Mark 9:41)

  And whoever gives you a cup **of water**

    This genitive of content indicates that the cup was filled with water.

- κομίσασα ἀλάβαστρον **μύρου** (Luke 7:37)

  She brought an alabaster jar **of perfume**

    The genitive indicates that the jar was full of perfume.

- ὁ λόγος γὰρ ὁ **τοῦ σταυροῦ** τοῖς μὲν ἀπολλυμένοις μωρία ἐστίν (1 Cor 1:18)

  For the word **of the cross** is foolishness to those who are perishing

    This is an example of what Young calls a genitive of content containing "communicative content" (i.e., a figurative use).[35]

Partitive Genitive

The partitive genitive can be slightly challenging to understand.[36] The head substantive in the phrase represents a "part" of some whole. The whole is described by the genitive. For example, in the phrase τινες τῆς κουστωδίας ("some of the guards," Matt 28:11), the genitive phrase τῆς κουστωδίας indicates the whole, the guards, while the head substantive τινες indicates the *part* of the whole, *some* of the guards. The head noun will be a number, percentage, or adjective describing the whole, such as "some." At times the partitive genitive occurs in conjunction with the preposition ἀπό or ἐκ and is articular.

- ἦσαν δέ τινες **τῶν γραμματέων** ἐκεῖ καθήμενοι (Mark 2:6)

  But some **of the scribes** were sitting there

    The large group is the scribes; "some" denotes a portion of the whole.

- ἐμβὰς δὲ εἰς ἓν **τῶν πλοίων** (Luke 5:3)

  He got into one **of the boats**

    There were several boats; "one of the boats" again denotes a part of the whole.

---

[35] For more examples of the genitive of content, see Matt 24:14; Mark 14:13; Rom 11:33; Col 2:3, 9; Rev 18:12. Young distinguishes between spatial and communicative content (27).

[36] Wallace makes a good case for calling this category "wholative" (84, n. 34), but we use "partitive" here because it reflects standard usage.

- εἰς τὸ εἶναι ἡμᾶς ἀπαρχήν τινα **τῶν** αὐτοῦ **κτισμάτων** (Jas 1:18)

  so that we would be a kind of firstfruits **of his creatures**

  > The firstfruits are a portion of all of God's creatures. "His" (αὐτοῦ) is a genitive of possession.

- καὶ τὸ τρίτον **τῆς γῆς** κατεκάη καὶ τὸ τρίτον **τῶν δένδρων** κατεκάη (Rev 8:7)

  So a third **of the earth** was burned up, a third **of the trees** were burned up

  > In John's vision, not the entirety of the earth and of the trees was burned up but only a third each.

- ἵνα ἀποκτείνωσιν τὸ τρίτον **τῶν ἀνθρώπων** (Rev 9:15)

  so that they might kill a third **of mankind** (NASB)[37]

VERBAL USE

The verbal use of the genitive occurs when the genitive is related to a head noun that communicates an action and could be "transformed" into a verb.[38] We may distinguish (1) the subjective genitive and (2) the objective genitive.[39] This distinction has recently been the subject of considerable scholarly debate with regard to the question as to whether the Pauline phrase πίστις Χριστοῦ is best translated as "faith in Christ" (objective genitive) or as "the faithfulness of Christ" (subjective genitive).[40]

---

[37] For more examples of the partitive genitive, see Matt 6:29; 15:24; 21:11; Mark 2:16; 6:23; Luke 1:26; 4:29; 8:44; 11:18; 16:24; 18:11; 19:8; John 2:1; Acts 7:52; Rom 11:17; 15:26; 16:5; 1 Tim 1:20; 1 Pet 5:9; Jude 13; Rev 5:11.

[38] Both Young and Wallace place subjective and objective genitives into a separate category. Young calls these "Genitives Functioning in Deep Structure Event Clauses," because the head noun and genitive can be thought of as reflecting an underlying clause made up of a subject and verb (29). While Young's discussion is useful, Wallace's nomenclature, "Verbal Genitive," is more helpful. He notes that the primary advantage of this is due to the importance of these genitives, as well as the challenge of properly understanding them (112).

[39] In addition, some grammars also discuss the plenary genitive, in which the genitive appears to be *both* subjective *and* objective (e.g., Wallace, 119; cf. Zerwick 12–14, [§§36–39]; examples cited include Mark 1:1, 14; John 5:42; Rom 1:1; 5:5; 15:16; 2 Cor 5:14; 1 Thess 2:2, 8–9; 2 Thess 3:5; Rev 1:1).

[40] E.g., Rom 3:22; Gal 2:16; 3:22; Phil 3:9. See the excellent survey in Matthew C. Easter, "The *Pistis Christou* Debate: Main Arguments and Responses in Summary," *Currents in Biblical Research* 9 (2010): 33–47. See also the essays in M. F. Bird and P. M. Sprinkle, eds., *The Faith of Jesus Christ: Exegetical, Biblical, and Theological Studies* (Milton Keynes, UK: Paternoster, 2009). While traditionally the objective genitive (also called the "anthropological reading"; defended, e.g., by Thomas R. Schreiner, *Romans*, 2nd ed. BECNT [Grand Rapids: Baker, 2018], 189–94) was largely favored, the subjective genitive (also called "the Christological reading"; e.g., Richard Hays, *The Faith of Jesus Christ: The Narrative Substructure of Galatians 3:1–4* [Grand Rapids: Eerdmans, 2002]) has gained currency.

Subjective Genitive

When a genitive noun is attached to a head noun having an inherent verbal quality (e.g., love, anger, desire), then the genitive often functions as the subject of that verbal idea. For example, if the expression "love of God" could be rearranged to "God loves x" and maintain accurately the author's intent, then "of God" is a subjective genitive. One of many examples in the NT can be found in 2 Cor 5:14, which states, "For the love **of Christ** controls us" (NASB; ἡ γὰρ ἀγάπη **τοῦ Χριστοῦ** συνέχει ἡμᾶς).[41] The head noun ἀγάπη has an inherent verbal quality, and we are thus predisposed to read the genitive attached to it as a subjective or objective genitive.[42] Context makes clear that Paul is speaking about Christ's love for his people, so τοῦ Χριστοῦ would be the subject of the verbal idea "love"—a subjective genitive. Whether a given genitive is a subjective or objective genitive (or some other kind of genitive) can be inferred only from the context.

- ἡ πίστις **σου** σέσωκέν σε (Luke 18:42)

  Your faith has saved you

  The person Jesus healed exercised faith.

- ἐν τῇ ὑπομονῇ **ὑμῶν** κτήσασθε τὰς ψυχὰς ὑμῶν (Luke 21:19)

  By **your** endurance gain your lives

  Jesus is calling on his hearers to endure.

- αὕτη ἐστὶν ἡ μαρτυρία **τοῦ Ἰωάννου** (John 1:19)

  This was **John's** testimony

  John the Baptist testified.

- τίς ἡμᾶς χωρίσει ἀπὸ τῆς ἀγάπης **τοῦ Χριστοῦ** (Rom 8:35)

  Who can separate us from the love **of Christ**?

  Paul is not speaking of *our* love *for Christ* (which would be an objective genitive; see below), but *Christ's* love *for us*.

- ἐν τούτῳ ἐφανερώθη ἡ ἀγάπη **τοῦ θεοῦ** ἐν ἡμῖν (1 John 4:9)

  God's love was revealed among us in this way

  John is writing about God demonstrating *his* love for *us*, not the love *we* exercised toward *him*.

---

[41] Conversely, there are times when a NT writer speaks of believers' love *for God* (e.g., 1 John 2:5; 5:3).

[42] See below for objective genitive.

Objective Genitive

When a genitive noun is attached to a head noun having an inherent verbal quality (e.g., love, anger, desire), then the genitive often functions as the object of that verbal idea. If the expression "love of God" could be rearranged to "x loves God" and maintain accurately the author's intent, then "of God" is an objective genitive. "x" in the example stands for the subject implied in the literary context (e.g., he, she, they, I, etc.). To state the same idea slightly differently, the objective genitive *receives* the action, serving as the object to the verbal idea implied in the noun it modifies.

A great verse to illustrate the distinction between the subjective and the objective genitive is Acts 9:31 (ESV): "So the church . . . had peace and was being built up. And walking in the fear **of the Lord** [objective genitive] and in the comfort **of the Holy Spirit** [subjective genitive], increased in numbers" (ἡ μὲν οὖν ἐκκλησία . . . εἶχεν εἰρήνην οἰκοδομουμένη, καὶ πορευομένη τῷ φόβῳ **τοῦ κυρίου** καὶ τῇ παρακλήσει **τοῦ ἁγίου πνεύματος** ἐπληθύνετο). The church feared the Lord (objective genitive), and the Holy Spirit encouraged believers (subjective genitive).

- ἡ δὲ **τοῦ πνεύματος** βλασφημία οὐκ ἀφεθήσεται (Matt 12:31)

  but the blasphemy **against the Spirit** will not be forgiven

  The Holy Spirit becomes the object of blasphemy.

- ἔχετε πίστιν **θεοῦ** (Mark 11:22)

  Have faith **in God**

  Robertson comments, "we rightly translate [this phrase] 'have faith in God,' though the genitive does not mean 'in,' but only the God kind of faith."[43]

- διὰ τὸν φόβον **τῶν Ἰουδαίων** (John 7:13)

  for fear **of the Jews** (ESV)

- μαρτυρῶ γὰρ αὐτοῖς ὅτι ζῆλον **θεοῦ** ἔχουσιν (Rom 10:2)

  I can testify about them that they have zeal **for God**

  God serves as the object of zeal.

- καθὼς τὸ μαρτύριον **τοῦ Χριστοῦ** ἐβεβαιώθη ἐν ὑμῖν (1 Cor 1:6)

  In this way, the testimony **about Christ** was confirmed among you

  Christ was not doing the testifying (which would be subjective genitive); rather, he was the object of the church's proclamation.

---

[43] Robertson, 500.

ADVERBIAL USE

In many instances, the genitive is similar in function to an adverb. We may distinguish between: (1) the genitive of time or place; (2) the genitive of separation; (3) the genitive of means or agency; (4) the genitive of comparison; and (5) the genitive of price.

Time or Place

The genitive of time or place indicates the location in time or space where an action occurs. The focus is on kind or quality, and reference may be made to both "position in space (i.e., in, at, on, under) and extension through space (i.e., toward, from)."[44] In the NT, time is indicated by as many as three cases: the genitive, the dative, and the accusative. In general, kind of time (or time during which) is indicated by the genitive; point in time (answering the question "When?") by the dative; and extension of time (answering the question "How long?") by the accusative.[45]

Time

- Τῇ δὲ μιᾷ τῶν σαββάτων **ὄρθρου βαθέως** (Luke 24:1)

  But on the first day of the week, **very early in the morning**

- ὁ ἐλθὼν πρὸς αὐτὸν **νυκτὸς** τὸ πρῶτον (John 19:39)

  who had previously come to him **at night**

- πορεύσεται πρὸς αὐτὸν **μεσονυκτίου** (Luke 11:5)

  he goes to him **at midnight**[46]

Place

- μετὰ δὲ τὴν μετοικεσίαν **Βαβυλῶνος** (Matt 1:12)

  After the exile **to Babylon** (NIV)

  > Note the translation "to Babylon" (rather than "of Babylon"). Alternatively, this could also be classified as a Hebrew genitive, designating the Babylonian exile (as opposed to, e.g., the Assyrian exile).

- **ἐκείνης** ἤμελλεν διέρχεσθαι (Luke 19:4)

  He was about to pass **that way**

---

[44] Young, 34.
[45] Wallace, 123.
[46] For more examples of the genitive of time, see Matt 25:6; Mark 5:5; 11:13; 13:18, 35; 16:1; Luke 17:4; 18:12; Acts 26:13; Jude 6; Rev 2:10; 4:8.

- καὶ θεωρεῖτε καὶ ἀκούετε ὅτι οὐ μόνον Ἐφέσου (Acts 19:26)

  You see and hear that not only **in Ephesus**[47]

Separation[48]

The genitive of separation indicates motion away from or distance, whether literally or figuratively. It is called the genitive of disassociation in older grammars, and an English translation of a genitive of separation usually is prefixed by the addition of the words "from," "away from," or "apart from."[49] The genitive marks the place from which distance or separation is being measured. Often this use is found in conjunction with verbs containing the prepositional prefix ἀπό.[50]

- τὸ καινὸν **τοῦ παλαιοῦ** (Mark 2:21)

  the new **from the old** (ESV)

- ἐκώλυσεν αὐτοὺς **τοῦ βουλήματος** (Acts 27:43)

  kept them **from their intention** (NASB)

- ἀποστήσονταί τινες **τῆς πίστεως** (1 Tim 4:1)

  some will depart **from the faith**[51]

- ἀπέχεσθαι **τῶν σαρκικῶν ἐπιθυμιῶν** (1 Pet 2:11)

  to abstain **from** sinful **desires**

- τῶν διὰ τὴν ἕξιν τὰ αἰσθητήρια γεγυμνασμένα ἐχόντων πρὸς διάκρισιν **καλοῦ** τε καὶ **κακοῦ** (Heb 5:14)

  for those whose senses have been trained to distinguish **between good** and **evil**[52]

---

[47] For more examples of the genitive of place, see Luke 5:19; 16:24; 1 Cor 4:5; 1 Pet 1:1; 3:4.

[48] This category is also labeled the "ablatival genitive" (so Wallace) or "genitive of disassociation" (so Young).

[49] Wallace, 108.

[50] In examples where ἀπό is used as a verbal prefix, the genitive as still dependent on the preposition.

[51] Note that this example is disputed. Some take this as a partitive genitive, "some from the faith will depart."

[52] For more examples of the genitive of separation, see Matt 10:14; Luke 2:37; Acts 15:29; 27:43; Rom 1:4; 10:12; 1 Cor 9:21; 15:41; Gal 5:7; Eph 2:12; Heb 13:7; 1 Pet 3:21; 4:1; 2 Pet 1:14; Rev 8:5; 21:2.

Means or Agency

Means

The genitive of means conveys the *impersonal* means or instrument by which a given action is carried out. This type of genitive is translated with "by" rather than "of."

- ἀλλ' ἐπιστεῖλαι αὐτοῖς τοῦ ἀπέχεσθαι τῶν ἀλισγημάτων **τῶν εἰδώλων** (Acts 15:20)

  but instead we should write to them to abstain from things polluted **by idols**

- ἃ καὶ λαλοῦμεν οὐκ ἐν διδακτοῖς **ἀνθρωπίνης σοφίας** λόγοις (1 Cor 2:13)

  We also speak these things not in words taught **by human wisdom**

- ὁ γὰρ θεὸς ἀπείραστός ἐστιν **κακῶν** (Jas 1:13)

  since God is not tempted **by evil**[53]

Agency

The genitive of agency communicates the personal means or instrument by which an action is carried out. Like the genitive of means, this type of genitive is translated with "by" rather than "of."

- ἐν γεννητοῖς **γυναικῶν** (Matt 11:11)

  Among those born **of women**

  The reference is to those born *by* women.

- δεῦτε, οἱ εὐλογημένοι **τοῦ πατρός μου** (Matt 25:34)

  Come, you who are blessed **by my Father**

- ἱκανὸς δὲ κλαυθμὸς ἐγένετο **πάντων** (Acts 20:37)

  There were many tears shed **by everyone**[54]

---

[53] For more examples of the genitive of means, see Acts 1:18; Rom 4:11; Phil 2:8.

[54] For more examples of the genitive of agency, see John 6:45; 18:16; Rom 1:6–7; 8:33; 1 Cor 2:13.

Comparison

At times the genitive is used to denote comparison (in which case the appropriate translation is "than").[55] In such instances, the basis or standard on which the comparison is made is put in the genitive case. The genitive of comparison is regularly used in conjunction with a comparative adjective (e.g., μείζων).

- ὁ δὲ ὀπίσω μου ἐρχόμενος ἰσχυρότερός **μού** ἐστιν (Matt 3:11)

  But after me comes one who is more powerful **than I** (NIV)

- ἐὰν μὴ περισσεύσῃ ὑμῶν ἡ δικαιοσύνη πλεῖον **τῶν γραμματέων** καὶ **Φαρισαίων** (Matt 5:20)

  unless your righteousness surpasses **that of the scribes** and **Pharisees**

  > Literally, the phrase reads, "unless your righteousness abounds more than that of the scribes and Pharisees" (note also the emphatic position of "your" [ὑμῶν], a possessive genitive).

- ἡ γὰρ ψυχὴ πλεῖόν ἐστιν **τῆς τροφῆς** καὶ τὸ σῶμα **τοῦ ἐνδύματος** (Luke 12:23)

  For life is more **than food** and the body more **than clothing**

- Ἐγὼ δὲ ἔχω τὴν μαρτυρίαν μείζω **τοῦ Ἰωάννου** (John 5:36)

  But I have a greater testimony **than John's**

- μείζων ἐστὶν ὁ θεὸς **τῆς καρδίας** ἡμῶν (1 John 3:20)

  God is greater **than** our **heart** (ESV)[56]

Price

The genitive of price indicates the price or the value that attaches to a given item. Some grammars list this under "genitive of measure."[57]

- οὐχὶ δύο στρουθία **ἀσσαρίου** πωλεῖται; (Matt 10:29)

  Are not two sparrows sold **for a penny**? (ESV)

- προσηνέχθη αὐτῷ εἷς ὀφειλέτης **μυρίων ταλάντων** (Matt 18:24)

  one who owed **ten thousand talents** was brought before him

---

[55] Alternatively, the particle "than" (ἤ) is used: "He rejoices over that sheep more **than** over the ninety-nine that did not go astray" (χαίρει ἐπ᾽ αὐτῷ μᾶλλον ἤ ἐπὶ τοῖς ἐνενήκοντα ἐννέα τοῖς μὴ πεπλανημένοις; Matt 18:13).

[56] For more examples of the genitive of comparison, see Matt 5:37; 6:25; 10:31; 11:11; 12:33; Mark 1:7; John 13:16; 14:28; 20:4; 1 Cor 1:25; Heb 7:26; 1 Pet 1:7.

[57] Smyth, 318; Brooks & Winbery, 11–12.

- οὐχὶ **δηναρίου** συνεφώνησάς μοι; (Matt 20:13)

  Didn't you agree with me **on a denarius**?

- ἠγοράσθητε γὰρ **τιμῆς** (1 Cor 6:20)

  For you have been bought **with a price** (NASB)

- χοῖνιξ σίτου **δηναρίου**, καὶ τρεῖς χοίνικες κριθῶν **δηναρίου** (Rev 6:6)

  A quart of wheat **for a denarius**, and three quarts of barley **for a denarius**[58]

OTHER USES

There are several other uses of the genitive that do not easily fit into the classification scheme (adjectival, verbal, or adverbial) above. Many of these are infrequent in the NT and have been dealt with briefly in relevant footnotes attached to more significant uses above. The most important other uses of the genitive in the NT are the genitive of apposition and the genitive of direct object.[59]

Apposition

It is possible to distinguish two types of genitive appositional constructions. The genitive in *simple apposition* provides an alternate name for a given noun in the genitive. Both the head term in the genitive and the genitive of apposition thus refer to the same person or object, though they describe it in different ways.[60] In

---

[58] For more examples of the genitive of price, see Matt 16:26; 20:2; 26:9; Mark 6:37; 14:5; Luke 12:6; John 12:5; Acts 5:8; 22:28; 1 Cor 7:23; Heb 12:16; Jude 11.

[59] Other genitive uses not referenced above include: (1) the genitive of advantage (indicating the person or thing on behalf of whom or which something is done, similar to the dative of advantage, translated with "for"; e.g., Acts 4:9; Col 4:3; Brooks & Winbery, 18); (2) the genitive of destination, direction, or purpose (translated with "for"; e.g., Matt 10:5; John 5:29; Rom 8:36; Gal 2:7; Col 1:24; 4:3; Wallace, 100–101; cf. BDF, 92 [§166]; Young, 37); (3) the genitive of reason (e.g., Phlm 1, 13; Jas 1:17; Young, 37); and (4) the genitive of subordination (indicating that which is subordinated to the dominion of a head noun, translated with "over"; e.g., Matt 9:34; Mark 15:32; John 12:31; Acts 4:26; 2 Cor 4:4; Rev 1:5; 15:3; Wallace, 103). Other categories, such as the genitive of attendant circumstance (Brooks & Winbery, 19) or the genitive of oaths (Brooks & Winbery, 20), involve the use of a preposition. Others, such as the genitive of association, are found in conjunction with a verbal prefix (such as σύν; Wallace, 128). Yet, other categories may be doubtful, such as the genitive of reference (limiting the frame of reference of a head term), since most of the examples given in the literature can be fitted into other, more standard categories. For example, Brooks & Winbery cite John 1:14, "full of grace and truth" (πλήρης **χάριτος** καὶ **ἀληθείας**), which could also be genitive of content; Wallace and Dana & Mantey cite Heb 3:12, "an evil heart of unbelief" (καρδία πονηρὰ **ἀπιστίας**), which may be an attributive genitive (other examples given are Matt 3:8; 21:21; 23:28; Col 1:10, 15; Heb 5:13; Jas 1:13; 3:8). The genitive absolute will be treated in the chapter on participles below.

[60] See Wallace, 95–96 for a helpful discussion of the differences between the two kinds of appositional genitives.

translating the genitive in simple apposition, the word "of" will usually not be used in translation.

Simple Apposition

- τότε ἐπληρώθη τὸ ῥηθὲν διὰ Ἰερεμίου **τοῦ προφήτου** (Matt 2:17)

  Then what was spoken through Jeremiah **the prophet**

  Jeremiah is identified as "the prophet."

- καὶ σὺ μετὰ τοῦ Ναζαρηνοῦ ἦσθα **τοῦ Ἰησοῦ** (Mark 14:67)

  You also were with the Nazarene, **Jesus** (ESV)

  The Nazarene is identified as Jesus.

- ἐν δικαιοσύνῃ τοῦ θεοῦ ἡμῶν καὶ σωτῆρος **Ἰησοῦ Χριστοῦ** (2 Pet 1:1)

  through the righteousness of our God and Savior **Jesus Christ**

  In a momentous affirmation of his deity, "our God and Savior" is identified as Jesus Christ.[61]

The *epexegetical* genitive provides a clarifying or explanatory identifier of the head noun, which may be *in any case* (determined by its own grammatical function in the sentence). In translation, the phrase "namely," "which is," or "that is," is often used.

Epexegetical

- ἐκεῖνος δὲ ἔλεγεν περὶ τοῦ ναοῦ **τοῦ σώματος** αὐτοῦ (John 2:21)

  But he was speaking about the temple **of** his **body** (ESV)

  The evangelist refers to the temple *which is* Jesus's body.

- καὶ λήμψεσθε τὴν δωρεὰν **τοῦ ἁγίου πνεύματος** (Acts 2:38)

  you will receive the gift **of the Holy Spirit**

  Peter here speaks of the gift, *namely* the Holy Spirit.

- θεός, ὁ δοὺς ἡμῖν τὸν ἀρραβῶνα **τοῦ πνεύματος** (2 Cor 5:5)

  God, who gave us **the Spirit** as a downpayment

  Paul refers to the downpayment, *which is* the Spirit.[62]

---

[61] For more examples of the simple appositional genitive, see Matt 12:17; 24:15; Mark 6:17; 11:10; Luke 3:4; Rom 9:10; 2 Cor 11:32; Titus 2:13; 3:6.

[62] For more examples of the genitive of apposition, see Luke 2:41; 22:1; John 11:13; 13:1; Acts 2:33, 38; 2 Cor 1:22; 5:1; Eph 1:14; 2:15; 1 Thess 5:8; 2 Pet 2:6; Rev 1:3; 2:10; 14:10.

Direct Object

The genitive routinely occurs after certain verbs. Normally, the direct object of a verb occurs in the accusative case, but some verbs take their direct object in the genitive case. Such verbs can be grouped into five major categories: (1) verbs of sensation (ἀκούω, ἅπτω, γεύομαι, κρατέω), (2) verbs of emotion or volition (ἐπιθυμέω, ἐπιλανθάνομαι, μιμνήσκομαι, μνημονεύω, τυγχάνω), (3) verbs of sharing (κοινωνέω, μεταλαμβάνω, μετέχω), (4) verbs of ruling (ἄρχω, βασιλεύω, κυριεύω), and (5) verbs of separation (ἀφίστημι, ὑστερέω, φείδομαι).[63]

- μή τινος ὑστερήσατε (Luke 22:35)

  you did not <u>lack</u> **anything**, did you? (NASB)

- οἱ νεκροὶ <u>ἀκούσουσιν</u> **τῆς φωνῆς** τοῦ υἱοῦ τοῦ θεοῦ (John 5:25)

  the dead will <u>hear</u> **the voice** of the Son of God

- **ἀργυρίου ἢ χρυσίου ἢ ἱματισμοῦ** οὐδενὸς <u>ἐπεθύμησα</u> (Acts 20:33)

  I have not <u>coveted</u> anyone's **silver** or **gold** or **clothing**

- ἁμαρτία γὰρ **ὑμῶν** οὐ <u>κυριεύσει</u> (Rom 6:14)

  For sin will not <u>rule over</u> **you**

- οὐ δύνασθε **τραπέζης** κυρίου <u>μετέχειν</u> καὶ **τραπέζης** δαιμονίων (1 Cor 10:21)

  You cannot <u>share</u> in the Lord's **table** and the **table** of demons[64]

---

[63] See Wallace who lists 10 individual categories: (1) verbs of sharing or partaking and verbs with a partitive genitive idea, (2) verbs meaning "touch" or "take hold of," (3) verbs meaning "strive after, desire" or "reach, obtain," (4) verbs meaning "fill, be full of" [conventionally identified under the rubric genitive of content], (5) verbs of perception, (6) verbs related to smell, (7) verbs meaning "remember" or "forget," (8) verbs of emotion, (9) verbs meaning "rule, govern" or "surpass"; (10) verbs of accusing (131; see BDF, 93–96 [§§169–78]). For similar categories, see Black, 50; Young, 40–41; and Robertson, 507–12 (with separate treatments of the genitive and the ablative).

[64] In addition, a considerable number of genitives occur after various other parts of speech, such as adjectives (e.g., Matt 26:66), adverbs (e.g., Phil 1:27), and prepositions (e.g., John 1:3). Certain adjectives, such as ἄξιος ("worthy"), as well as certain adverbs, typically take the genitive. Several common prepositions (such as ἀπό, ἐκ, or χωρίς) take the genitive, as do 40 of the 42 "improper prepositions" (such as ἄχρι[ς], ἔμπροσθεν, or πλησίον) found in the NT. See Harris, *Prepositions and Theology*, 239–51 (see chap. 2, n. 69). See further chapter 12 on prepositions.

SUMMARY

ADJECTIVAL USES OF THE GENITIVE		
DESCRIPTION	Further limits or describes the head noun, but other common genitival categories do not capture the specific nuance.	βάπτισμα **μετανοίας** ("a baptism **of repentance**"; Mark 1:4).
ATTRIBUTIVE	Denotes an attribute or innate quality of the head term, conveying an emphatic adjectival idea.	τῷ ῥήματι **τῆς δυνάμεως** αὐτοῦ ("by his **powerful** word"; Heb 1:3).
POSSESSION	Identifies ownership with regard to the noun it modifies, often employing the use of a possessive pronoun.	καὶ εἰσελθόντες εἰς τὸν οἶκον **Φιλίππου** ("we entered the house **of Philip**"; Acts 21:8).
RELATIONSHIP	Denotes a family relationship such as a person's parent or spouse. The word indicating the relationship is often omitted and must be inferred.	Ἰάκωβον τὸν **τοῦ Ζεβεδαίου** ("James the son **of Zebedee**"; Matt 4:21).
SOURCE	Indicates the origin of the head noun ("from").	τὴν **τοῦ θεοῦ** δικαιοσύνην ("the righteousness **of God**"; Rom 10:3).
MATERIAL OR CONTENT	Indicates the material of which the head term is made or specifies the content of an object or abstract noun.	**Material:** γόμον **χρυσοῦ** ("cargo **of gold**"; Rev 18:12). **Content:** ποτήριον **ὕδατος** ("a cup **of water**"; Mark 9:41).
PARTITIVE	Whether by itself or in conjunction with the preposition ἀπό or ἐκ, the articular noun in the genitive denotes the whole of which the head noun is a part.	ἓν **τῶν πλοίων** ("one **of the boats**"; Luke 5:3).
VERBAL USES OF THE GENITIVE		
SUBJECTIVE	Functions semantically as the subject of the verbal idea implied in the head noun, producing the action.	τίς ἡμᾶς χωρίσει ἀπὸ τῆς ἀγάπης **τοῦ Χριστοῦ**; ("Who can separate us from the love **of Christ**?"; Rom 8:35).
OBJECTIVE	Functions semantically as the direct object of the verbal idea implicit in the head noun, receiving the action.	ἔχετε πίστιν **θεοῦ** ("Have faith **in God**"; Mark 11:22).

ADVERBIAL USES OF THE GENITIVE		
TIME OR PLACE	Indicates the location in time or space where an action occurs. The focus is on kind or quality.	*Time:* ὁ ἐλθὼν πρὸς αὐτὸν **νυκτὸς** τὸ πρῶτον ("who had previously come to him **at night**"; John 19:39).
		Place: μετὰ δὲ τὴν μετοικεσίαν **Βαβυλῶνος** ("After the exile **to Babylon**"; Matt 1:12 NIV).
SEPARATION	Indicates motion away from or distance, whether literally or figuratively ("from").	ἀποστήσονταί τινες **τῆς πίστεως** ("some will depart **from the faith**"; 1 Tim 4:1).
MEANS OR AGENCY	Conveys the impersonal means or personal agent by which a given action is carried out ("by").	*Means:* ὁ γὰρ θεὸς ἀπείραστός ἐστιν **κακῶν** ("Since God is not tempted **by evil**"; Jas 1:13).
		Agency: δεῦτε, οἱ εὐλογημένοι **τοῦ πατρός μου** ("Come, you who are blessed **by my Father**"; Matt 25:34).
COMPARISON	Used to denote comparison in conjunction with a comparative adjective ("than").	μείζων ἐστὶν ὁ θεὸς **τῆς καρδίας** ἡμῶν ("God is greater **than** our **heart**"; 1 John 3:20).
PRICE	Indicates the price that is paid or the value that attaches to a given item.	ἠγοράσθητε . . . **τιμῆς** ("you have been bought **with a price**"; 1 Cor 6:20 NASB).
OTHER USES OF THE GENITIVE		
APPOSITION	The genitive of apposition provides an alternate designation (simple) of a genitive head noun or provides an explanatory (epexegetical) restatement of a head noun in any case.	*Simple:* διὰ Ἰερεμίου **τοῦ προφήτου** ("through Jeremiah **the prophet**"; Matt 2:17).
		Epexegetical: τὴν δωρεὰν **τοῦ ἁγίου πνεύματος** ("the gift **of the Holy Spirit**"; Acts 2:38).
DIRECT OBJECT	Verbs of sensation, emotion or volition, sharing, ruling, or separation take their direct object in the genitive case (instead of the accusative case).	μή **τινος** ὑστερήσατε ("you did not lack **anything**, did you?"; Luke 22:35 (NASB).

PRACTICE EXERCISES

In each of the following examples, determine the specific use of the genitive case based on the categories provided in this chapter.

1. ὁ δὲ μικρότερος ἐν τῇ βασιλείᾳ <u>τῶν οὐρανῶν</u> μείζων <u>αὐτοῦ</u> ἐστιν (Matt 11:11).

2. ἐμβὰς δὲ εἰς ἓν <u>τῶν πλοίων</u>, ὃ ἦν <u>Σίμωνος</u>, ἠρώτησεν αὐτόν (Luke 5:3).

3. μνημονεύετε <u>τῆς γυναικὸς</u> Λώτ (Luke 17:32).

4. καὶ Σίμων ὁ ζηλωτὴς καὶ Ἰούδας <u>Ἰακώβου</u> (Acts 1:13).

5. τήν τε ἐπαγγελίαν <u>τοῦ πνεύματος</u> <u>τοῦ ἁγίου</u> λαβὼν παρὰ <u>τοῦ πατρός</u>, ἐξέχεεν τοῦτο (Acts 2:33).

6. καθὼς τὸ μαρτύριον <u>τοῦ Χριστοῦ</u> ἐβεβαιώθη ἐν ὑμῖν (1 Cor 1:6).

7. προσδεχόμενοι τὴν μακαρίαν ἐλπίδα καὶ ἐπιφάνειαν <u>τῆς δόξης</u> <u>τοῦ μεγάλου</u> <u>θεοῦ</u> καὶ σωτῆρος ἡμῶν <u>Ἰησοῦ Χριστοῦ</u> (Titus 2:13).

8. οὕτως ἔσται ἡ παρουσία <u>τοῦ υἱοῦ</u> <u>τοῦ ἀνθρώπου</u> (Matt 24:27).

9. ὅτι ὁ παθὼν σαρκὶ πέπαυται <u>ἁμαρτίας</u> (1 Pet 4:1).

10. οὐ δικαιοῦται ἄνθρωπος ἐξ ἔργων <u>νόμου</u> ἐὰν μὴ διὰ πίστεως <u>Ἰησοῦ Χριστοῦ</u> (Gal 2:16).

VOCABULARY

Vocabulary to Memorize

ἀγρός, ὁ	field, country (36)
ἀκάθαρτος	unclean, impure (32)
ἀκροβυστία, ἡ	uncircumcision (20)
ἀναγινώσκω	I read (aloud) (32)
ἄνεμος, ὁ	wind (31)
ἀρνέομαι	I deny, reject (33)
βιβλίον, τό	book, scroll (34)
διαθήκη, ἡ	covenant, decree, last will and testament (33)
διακονία, ἡ	service, office, ministry, deacon (34)
δικαιόω	I justify, vindicate (39)
διότι	for, because, therefore (23)
δυνατός	powerful, strong, mighty, able (32)
ἐγγύς	near, close to (31)
ἔξεστιν	it is lawful, permitted (31)
ἐπίγνωσις, -εως, ἡ	knowledge, recognition (20)
εὐθέως	immediately (36)
ἐχθρός	hostile, hated (32)
ἥλιος, ὁ	sun (32)
ἱερεύς, -εως, ὁ	priest (31)
καθαρίζω	I cleanse, purify (31)
καταργέω	I cancel, nullify, make void (27)
λογίζομαι	I account, reckon, conclude (40)
μέλος, -ους, τό	member, part, limb (34)
ναί	yes, certainly, indeed (33)
νυνί	now (20)
ὀργή, ἡ	anger, wrath, punishment (36)
οὖς, ὠτός, τό	ear, hearing (36)
παραγίνομαι	I come, arrive, appear (37)
παρρησία, ἡ	confidence, boldness (31)
περιτομή, ἡ	circumcision (36)
πλήν	yet, however, but (31)
ποῖος	of what kind? (33)
ποτήριον, τό	cup (31)
ποῦ	where? (48)
πτωχός	poor (34)
ὑποστρέφω	I turn back, return (35)

ὑστερέω	I fall short of, lack (16)
φανερόω	I reveal, make manifest, show (49)
Φίλιππος, ὁ	Philip (36)
χωρίς	without, apart from (41)

Vocabulary to Recognize

ἁμάρτημα, -ατος, τό	sin, transgression (4)
ἀνοχή, ἡ	forbearance, tolerance (2)
ἀπολύτρωσις, -εως, ἡ	redemption, release, deliverance (10)
διαστολή, ἡ	distinction, difference (3)
δωρεάν	freely, as a gift, without payment (9)
εἴπερ	if indeed, if perhaps (6)
ἐκκλείω	I exclude, shut out (2)
ἔνδειξις, ἡ	demonstration, proof (4)
ἱλαστήριον, τό	propitiation (2)
καύχησις, ἡ	boasting (11)
πάρεσις, ἡ	passing over (1)
προγίνομαι	it happens before, be done before (1)
προτίθημι	I present, put forward, display publicly (3)
ὑπόδικος	answerable, accountable (1)
φράσσω	I shut, close (3)

READING THE NEW TESTAMENT

Romans 3:19–31

¹⁹ Οἴδαμεν δὲ ὅτι ὅσα ὁ νόμος λέγει τοῖς ἐν τῷ νόμῳ λαλεῖ, ἵνα πᾶν στόμα φραγῇ καὶ ὑπόδικος γένηται πᾶς ὁ κόσμος τῷ θεῷ· ²⁰ διότι ἐξ ἔργων νόμου οὐ δικαιωθήσεται πᾶσα σὰρξ ἐνώπιον αὐτοῦ, διὰ γὰρ νόμου ἐπίγνωσις ἁμαρτίας. ²¹ Νυνὶ δὲ χωρὶς νόμου δικαιοσύνη θεοῦ πεφανέρωται μαρτυρουμένη ὑπὸ τοῦ νόμου καὶ τῶν προφητῶν, ²² δικαιοσύνη δὲ θεοῦ διὰ πίστεως Ἰησοῦ Χριστοῦ εἰς πάντας τοὺς πιστεύοντας. οὐ γάρ ἐστιν διαστολή, ²³ πάντες γὰρ ἥμαρτον καὶ ὑστεροῦνται τῆς δόξης τοῦ θεοῦ ²⁴ δικαιούμενοι δωρεὰν τῇ αὐτοῦ χάριτι διὰ τῆς ἀπολυτρώσεως τῆς ἐν Χριστῷ Ἰησοῦ· ²⁵ ὃν προέθετο ὁ θεὸς ἱλαστήριον διὰ [τῆς] πίστεως ἐν τῷ αὐτοῦ αἵματι εἰς ἔνδειξιν τῆς δικαιοσύνης αὐτοῦ διὰ τὴν πάρεσιν τῶν προγεγονότων ἁμαρτημάτων ²⁶ ἐν τῇ ἀνοχῇ τοῦ θεοῦ, πρὸς τὴν ἔνδειξιν τῆς δικαιοσύνης αὐτοῦ ἐν τῷ νῦν καιρῷ, εἰς τὸ εἶναι αὐτὸν δίκαιον καὶ δικαιοῦντα τὸν ἐκ πίστεως Ἰησοῦ. ²⁷ Ποῦ οὖν ἡ καύχησις; ἐξεκλείσθη. διὰ ποίου νόμου; τῶν ἔργων; οὐχί, ἀλλὰ διὰ νόμου πίστεως. ²⁸ λογιζόμεθα γὰρ δικαιοῦσθαι πίστει ἄνθρωπον χωρὶς ἔργων νόμου. ²⁹ ἢ Ἰουδαίων ὁ θεὸς μόνον; οὐχὶ καὶ ἐθνῶν; ναὶ καὶ ἐθνῶν, ³⁰ εἴπερ εἷς ὁ θεὸς ὃς δικαιώσει περιτομὴν ἐκ πίστεως καὶ ἀκροβυστίαν διὰ τῆς πίστεως. ³¹ νόμον οὖν καταργοῦμεν διὰ τῆς πίστεως; μὴ γένοιτο· ἀλλὰ νόμον ἱστάνομεν.

Reading Notes[65]

Verse 19

- **λέγει . . . λαλεῖ** ("[it] says . . . [it] speaks") – Although these words are similar in meaning and often used interchangeably, "Paul may intend a difference here, with λέγω emphasizing more the content of what is said and λαλέω the act of speaking itself."[66]

- **τοῖς ἐν τῷ νόμῳ** ("to those who are subject to the law") – The dative plural article (τοῖς) functions as a substantizer, turning the prepositional phrase into a virtual noun. Notice that Paul says they (i.e., the Jews) were literally "in the law," meaning in the sphere of the law. This is different than what Paul has in mind when he states that some are "under law" (ὑπὸ νόμον; Rom 6:14). The former involves living under the Law of Moses and the OT whereas the latter is an antithesis to living "under grace." This phrase functions as the indirect object of the verb λαλεῖ.

---

[65] The English version used in the Reading Notes for this chapter is the CSB.
[66] Douglas Moo, *The Letter to the Romans*, 2nd ed. NICNT (Grand Rapids: Eerdmans, 2018), 213 n609.

- ἵνα πᾶν στόμα φραγῇ καὶ ὑπόδικος γένηται πᾶς ὁ κόσμος ("so that every mouth may be shut and the whole world may become subject") – ἵνα normally communicates purpose (and only sometimes result) but because here the result is also certain, it includes both ideas.[67] ἵνα is followed by two subjunctive verbs: φραγῇ (aor pass sub 3rd sg φράσσω) and γένηται (aor mid sub 3rd sg γίνομαι).

- τῷ θεῷ ("to God's judgment") – Literally, "to God." This is either a dative of respect meaning that the whole world will be held accountable specifically to God's judgment or a locative dative meaning that the whole world will be accountable *before* God.

Verse 20

- διότι ("For") – This conjunction can be translated "therefore" but here it has a causal meaning and so it is best to translate it as "because" or "for." That is, this verse gives the reason for v. 19 (why every mouth is stopped and why the whole world is condemned).

- ἐξ ἔργων ("by the works") – ἔργων is in the genitive case because of the preposition ἐξ (from ἐκ). There are other examples in the passage where a noun or pronoun is found in the genitive case because it is the object of a preposition: ἐνώπιον αὐτοῦ (v. 20), διὰ . . . νόμου (v. 20), χωρὶς νόμου (v. 21), ὑπὸ τοῦ νόμου (v. 21), ὑπό . . . τῶν προφητῶν (v. 21), διὰ πίστεως (v. 22), διὰ τῆς ἀπολυτρώσεως (v. 24), διὰ [τῆς] πίστεως (vv. 25, 30, 31), ἐκ πίστεως (vv. 26, 29), διὰ νόμου (v. 27 [x2]), and χωρὶς ἔργων (v. 28).

- ἐξ ἔργων νόμου ("by the works of the law") – The genitive νόμου could be taken as an objective genitive ("works that fulfill the law") or as a subjective genitive ("works that the law requires" or "works produced by the law"). In the end, there does not seem to be much of a distinction. Most interpreters understand "works of the law" to be "doing what the law requires" or "all the works demanded by the law."[68] The New Perspective on Paul, however, maintains that this is a way of describing those tenets of the law (particularly circumcision, Sabbath observance, and food laws) that keep the Gentiles outside Judaism.[69]

- δικαιωθήσεται ("will be justified") – Fut pass ind 3rd sg δικαιόω. This is an example of a divine passive since it is God who is the agent who justifies.

---

[67] So Wallace, 473–74.

[68] Moo, *Romans*, 216; Schreiner, *Romans*, 180, respectively.

[69] So James G. D. Dunn, *Romans 1–8*, WBC (Dallas: Word, 1988), 158–59; N. T. Wright, *Justification: God's Plan and Paul's Vision* (Downers Grove, IL: IVP Academic, 2009), 116–17.

- **πᾶσα σὰρξ ἐνώπιον αὐτοῦ** ("no one [lit. "all flesh"] . . . in his sight") –
The word σάρξ has a wide semantic range. It can mean (1) human being
(1 Cor 1:19; Gal 2:16), (2) physical body (1 Cor 15:39; Phil 1:22; Col
1:24), (3) physical descent (Rom 1:3; 4:1; 9:3, 5), and (4) sinful nature
(Rom 7:5; 8:9; 13:14; Gal 5:19). Here it clearly refers to human beings (so
ESV, NIV).

- **ἐπίγνωσις ἁμαρτίας** ("the knowledge of sin") – This is probably an
objective genitive ("knowledge about sin"). Moo comments that "what
is meant is that the law gives to people an understanding of 'sin' (singular) as a power that holds everyone in bondage and brings guilt and
condemnation."[70]

Verse 21

- **Νυνὶ δέ** ("But now") – This marks a logical and temporal transition in the
epistle. After declaring that both Gentiles (chap. 1) and Jews (chap. 2)—
indeed all, both Jews and Gentiles (chap. 3)—have sinned and are under
God's wrath, Paul now turns to offer the good news of the gospel. The
paragraph of Rom 3:21–26 has been viewed by many as the most important text in the entire Bible. For example, Luther described it as "the chief
point, and the very central place of the Epistle, and of the whole Bible."[71]
C. E. B. Cranfield calls these verses "the centre and heart" of Romans.[72]
Martyn Lloyd-Jones likewise affirms that this text "is the acropolis of the
Bible and of the Christian faith."[73] Leon Morris describes it as "possibly
the most important single paragraph ever written."[74] Finally, John Piper
comments that Romans 3:21–26 "is the Mount Everest of the Bible. . . .
There are great sentences in the Bible, and great paragraphs and great
revelations, but it doesn't get any greater than this paragraph in Romans
3:21–26."[75]

- **χωρὶς νόμου . . . ὑπὸ τοῦ νόμου καὶ τῶν προφητῶν** ("apart from the
law . . . by the Law and the Prophets") – It is clear from the context that
the two instances of the term νόμος do not reflect the same usage. The
first instance probably refers to the Mosaic covenant whereas the second
is more narrow, referring to the Torah or the Pentateuch. Some claim that

---

[70] Moo, *Romans*, 220.
[71] Margin of the Luther Bible, on 3:23ff.
[72] C. E. B. Cranfeld, *Romans: A Shorter Commentary* (Grand Rapids: Eerdmans, 1985), 68.
[73] D. M. Lloyd-Jones, *Romans: An Exposition of Chapters 3.20–4.25, Atonement and Justification*
(Grand Rapids: Zondervan, 1971), 65.
[74] Leon Morris, *The Epistle to the Romans* (Grand Rapids: Eerdmans, 1988), 173.
[75] John Piper, "The Demonstration of God's Righteousness, Part 3," preached May 23, 1999.

the same word cannot have two different meanings in the same context. This verse, however, shows such simplistic linguistic claims are invalid.[76]

- **δικαιοσύνη θεοῦ** ("righteousness of God") – The genitive θεοῦ can be interpreted as (1) a possessive genitive ("a righteousness belonging to God" or "God's own righteousness"), (2) a genitive of source ("righteousness from God"), (3) an objective genitive ("righteousness that is valid before God"), or (4) a subjective genitive ("righteousness that is being shown by God" or "God's saving power"). Option 2 is probably best but some scholars argue that option 4 is also possible (usually taken in addition to, and not instead of, 2).[77] This phrase occurs four times in this passage (vv. 21, 22, 25, 26).

- **πεφανέρωται** ("been revealed") – Per pass ind 3rd sg φανερόω.

- **μαρτυρουμένη** ("attested") – Pres pass ptc fem nom sg μαρτυρέω. This is most likely a concessive participle which implies that the action of the main verb is true (i.e., apart from the law God's righteousness is revealed), in spite of the action of the participle (*though* it is attested by the Law and the Prophets).

Verse 22

- **διὰ πίστεως Ἰησοῦ Χριστοῦ** ("through faith in Jesus Christ") – Although there is considerable debate, Ἰησοῦ Χριστοῦ is probably an objective genitive (faith in Christ) and not a subjective genitive (the faithfulness of Christ).[78] Moo maintains that the most decisive point is the comparison between the noun plus genitive construction (as found here in Rom 3:22) with the cognate verb (i.e., πιστεύω). He summarizes the "faith" language in Paul: "Paul often makes believers the subject of the verb 'believe' (*pisteuō*), but he never clearly makes Christ the subject of the verb. In Paul, Christians 'believe'; but Christ does not (at the linguistic level, of course)."[79]

---

[76] Murray aptly notes, "We have here an instructive example of the ease with which the apostle can turn from one denotation of the word 'law' to another. The righteousness that is unreservedly without law in one sense of the word 'law' is, nevertheless, witnessed to and therefore proclaimed by the law in another sense of that term. Law in one sense pronounces the opposite of justification, the law in another sense preaches justification. This illustrates the necessity in each case of determining the precise sense in which the term 'law' is used by the apostle and we must not suppose that the term has always the same denotation and connotation. Exposition has suffered from failure to recognize this variation. Here the variation is exemplified in two consecutive clauses." See John Murray, *The Epistle to the Romans*, NICNT (Grand Rapids: Eerdmans, 1959), 1:110.

[77] So Moo, *Romans*, 77–82; Schreiner, *Romans*, 67–82.

[78] So Moo, *Romans*, 244–46; Schreiner, *Romans*, 189–94; Dunn, *Romans*, 166; Murray, *Romans*, 110–11. Wallace argues that the grammatical arguments slightly favor the subjective genitive (Wallace, 114–16).

[79] Moo, *Romans*, 245.

- **τοὺς πιστεύοντας** ("who believe") – Pres act ptc masc acc pl πιστεύω (substantival ptc).

Verse 23

- **ἥμαρτον** ("have sinned") – Aor act ind 3rd pl ἁμαρτάνω. This usage of the aorist demonstrates that the aorist does not necessarily communicate a once-for-all action (that must be determined by the context, not by the tense-form). Rather, this usage can be described as a constative or summary aorist which, like a snap-shot, presents the sins of people throughout history in a single moment.[80]

- **ὑστεροῦνται** ("fall short of") – Pres pass ind 3rd pl ὑστερέω.[81] The shift in tense might stress that whereas all people sinned in the past, all (even believers) presently lack the glory of God. Another interpretation is that this is simply a gnomic use of the present, which signifies that everyone in every place at every time falls short of God's glory.[82]

- **τῆς δόξης τοῦ θεοῦ** ("the glory of God") – τῆς δόξης is in the genitive case because the ὑστερέω takes its direct object in the genitive instead of the accusative.[83] The second genitive, τοῦ θεοῦ, is a genitive of possession ("God's glory").

Verse 24

- **δικαιούμενοι δωρεάν** ("they are justified freely") – Pres pass ptc masc nom pl δικαιόω. The subject of this adverbial participle is probably πάντες ("all") in v. 23.[84] δωρεάν ("freely" or "as a gift") is an adverbial accusative of manner.

- **τῇ αὐτοῦ χάριτι** ("by his grace") – τῇ χάριτι is a dative of means (they are justified by means of God's grace). Notice that the possessive pronoun is sandwiched in between the article and the noun (see also the similar construction in v. 25: ἐν τῷ <u>αὐτοῦ</u> αἵματι).

---

[80] "In Rom. 3:23, ἥμαρτον is evidently intended to sum up the aggregate of the evil deeds of men, of which the apostle has been speaking in the preceding paragraphs (1:18–3:20). It is therefore a collective historical Aorist" (Burton, 28).

[81] In the passive voice, the verb ὑστερέω means "lack, be lacking, go without, come short of w. gen. of the thing" (BDAG, 1044).

[82] Schreiner, *Romans*, 194.

[83] It is possible to think that the genitive is functioning in a "normal" manner because it is translated as "of the glory." But this is to confuse the verb and the object. The verb ὑστερέω means "to fall short of [something]" (notice that the "of" is part of the verb). One way to solve this issue is to substitute a different gloss for the verb. For example, "For all have sinned and *lack* the glory of God." With this rendering, it is easy to see that "the glory" is the direct object of the verb.

[84] See Moo, *Romans*, 248. Moo rightly notes that in its connection with "being justified," the word πάντες "indicates not universality ('everybody') but lack of particularity ('anybody')."

- **διὰ τῆς ἀπολυτρώσεως τῆς ἐν Χριστῷ Ἰησοῦ** ("through the redemption that is in Christ Jesus") – The second phrase (τῆς ἐν Χριστῷ Ἰησοῦ) modifies τῆς ἀπολυτρώσεως, which is indicated by the repetition of the article. The article then functions as a substantiver, turning the prepositional phrase into an adjective ("the in-Christ-Jesus redemption").

Verses 25–26

- **ὅν** ("him") – This is a relative pronoun (masc acc sg) literally meaning "whom" (i.e., Jesus Christ).

- **προέθετο** ("[God] presented") – Aor mid ind 3rd sg προτίθημι. This verb is the main verb for this and the next verse which include nine prepositional phrases.

- **ἱλαστήριον** ("the mercy seat") – This word refers to the place where God's wrath is appeased and grammatically it is a double accusative (the other accusative being ὅν). ἱλαστήριον only occurs here and in Heb 9:5 but ἱλασμός ("appeasement necessitated by sin")[85] occurs in 1 John 2:2 and 4:10 and the verb ἱλάσκομαι occurs in Luke 18:13 and Heb 2:17.

- **διὰ [τῆς] πίστεως ἐν τῷ αὐτοῦ αἵματι** ("by his blood, through faith") – The prepositional phrase ἐν τῷ αὐτοῦ αἵματι most likely communicates means and modifies ἱλαστήριον and not διὰ [τῆς] πίστεως. In other words, "'In his blood' singles out Christ's blood as the means by which God's wrath is propitiated."[86] The article τῆς is put in brackets because there is doubt as to whether it is original. Metzger comments, "On the one hand, the article may have been added by copyists who wished to point back to διὰ πίστεως Ἰησοῦ Χριστοῦ in ver. 22. On the other hand, later in the chapter when Paul uses πίστις absolutely (i.e., without a modifier), διά is followed by the article (cf. verses 30 and 31)."[87]

- **εἰς ἔνδειξιν τῆς δικαιοσύνης αὐτοῦ** ("to demonstrate his righteousness") – Verses 25 and 26 offer three purpose clauses, the first being introduced by the preposition εἰς (v. 25), the second with πρός (v. 26) and the third with εἰς τό + an infinitive (v. 26). The CSB correctly interprets the genitive construction τῆς δικαιοσύνης αὐτοῦ as an objective genitive (literally, "for a demonstration of his righteousness" = "in order to demonstrate his righteousness").

- **διὰ τὴν πάρεσιν τῶν προγεγονότων ἁμαρτημάτων** ("because . . . [he] passed over the sins previously committed") – Literally, "because of the passing over of the previously committed sins." The participle

---

[85] BDAG, 474.
[86] Moo, *Romans*, 258.
[87] Metzger, *Textual Commentary*, 449.

προγεγονότων (per act ptc neut gen pl προγίνομαι) is used attributively, modifying ἁμαρτημάτων ("the previously committed sins"). ἁμαρτημάτων is best taken as an objective genitive ("he passed over sins").

- ἐν τῇ ἀνοχῇ τοῦ θεοῦ ("in [God's] restraint") – The verse break at the beginning of this prepositional phrase obscures the connection with the preceding phrase indicating that God previously passed over sins ("because *in His restraint* God passed over . . ."). The genitive θεοῦ is possessive ("God's restraint") or more likely is a subjective genitive ("God is restraining").

- εἰς τὸ εἶναι αὐτὸν δίκαιον ("so that he would be just") – As mentioned above, εἰς τό + an infinitive (εἶναι, pres act inf εἰμί) communicates purpose. Also remember that the subject of the infinitive is in the accusative case (αὐτόν = "he").

- καὶ δικαιοῦντα τὸν ἐκ πίστεως Ἰησοῦ ("and justify the one who has faith in Jesus") – Although καί could be translated as "and" it is also possible to take it concessively ("even").[88] That is, in order that God might be just *even in* justifying the one who has faith in Jesus. The article τόν functions as a substantizer, turning the prepositional phrase ἐκ πίστεως Ἰησοῦ into a virtual noun.

Verse 27

- Ποῦ οὖν ἡ καύχησις; ("Where then is boasting?") – Notice that the Greek has no verb and so one must be supplied in English ("is").

- ἐξεκλείσθη ("It is excluded") – Aor pass ind 3rd sg ἐκκλείω.

- διὰ ποίου νόμου ("By what kind of law?") – There is debate as to whether νόμος refers to the Torah or OT or whether it means "principle" or "rule."

- τῶν ἔργων; ("By one of works?") – The words διὰ νόμου need to be supplied from the previous sentence ("*by a law* of works?").

- ἀλλὰ διὰ νόμου πίστεως ("No, on the contrary, by a law of faith") – The genitive πίστεως is probably a descriptive genitive ("faith-law") or a genitive of apposition ("a law, that is, faith").[89]

Verse 28

- λογιζόμεθα ("we conclude") – Pres mid ind 1st pl λογίζομαι. The first person plural ("we") is probably an editorial "we" (epistolary plural).

---

[88] So Moo, *Romans*, 262. He comments, "Paul's point is that God can maintain his righteous character . . . even while he acts to justify sinful people . . . because Christ, in his propitiatory sacrifice, provides full satisfaction of the demands of God's impartial, invariable justice" (262–63).

[89] Robertson takes νόμου πίστεως as appositional (498).

- **δικαιοῦσθαι** ("is justified") – Pres pass inf δικαιόω. This is an example of a divine passive. God justifies a person by faith.

- **πίστει** ("by faith") – Dative of means.

- **ἄνθρωπον** ("a person") – The subject of the verb δικαιοῦσθαι, because an infinitive takes its subject in the accusative case.

Verse 29

- **ἢ Ἰουδαίων ὁ θεὸς μόνον;** ("Or is God the God of the Jews only?") – The genitive Ἰουδαίων is probably best categorized as a genitive of possession ("God belonging to the Jews"). Again notice that the verb must be supplied ("is").

- **οὐχί** ("not") – The particle οὐχί (or οὐκ or οὐ) occurs with the indicative mood and when used with a question anticipates an affirmative answer.

Verse 30

- **δικαιώσει** ("will justify") – Fut act ind 3rd sg δικαιόω.

- **ἐκ πίστεως καί . . . διὰ τῆς πίστεως** ("by faith and . . . through faith") – The difference in prepositions (ἐκ versus διά) is probably just stylistic, presumably to add variety to the statement, and not of any interpretive value. The same is true for πίστει in v. 28.

Verse 31

- **καταργοῦμεν** ("Do we . . . nullify ") – Pres act ind 1st pl καταργέω.

- **μὴ γένοιτο** ("Absolutely not") – Aor mid opt 3rd sg γίνομαι. This use of the optative expresses very emphatically that nothing could be further from the truth. This phrase is used 15 times in the NT, and 14 of those occurrences are used by Paul (including 10 occurrences in Romans).

- **ἱστάνομεν** ("we uphold") – Pres act ind 1st pl ἵστημι.

////////////////

CHAPTER 4

DATIVE CASE

GOING DEEPER

In his second epistle, the apostle Peter encourages his readers with these stirring words: "His divine power has given us everything required for life and godliness, through the knowledge of him who called us **by his own glory and goodness**" (ὡς πάντα ἡμῖν τῆς θείας δυνάμεως αὐτοῦ τὰ πρὸς ζωὴν καὶ εὐσέβειαν δεδωρημένης διὰ τῆς ἐπιγνώσεως τοῦ καλέσαντος ἡμᾶς **ἰδίᾳ δόξῃ καὶ ἀρετῇ**; 2 Pet 1:3). As we pursue a godly life, we can be assured that our powerful God has already supplied us with everything we need—through our personal relationship with Jesus Christ! This is an amazing thought. Rather than saving us only to let us struggle on our own in living the Christian life, God has supplied us—in Christ!— with all the resources we need to cultivate godliness.

That much is clear. But as a closer look reveals, the phrase "by His own glory and goodness" is not quite as clear as it may appear at first. Consulting some of the major English translations, we find the following:

- NIV: "by his own glory and goodness"
- NASB: "by His own glory and excellence"
- ESV: "to (or by) his own glory and excellence (or virtue)"
- NLT: "by means of his marvelous glory and excellence"
- CSB: "by his own glory and goodness"
- NKJV: "by glory and virtue"

- NRSV: "by (or through) his own glory and goodness"[1]

While most translations seem to construe the dative ἰδίᾳ δόξῃ καὶ ἀρετῇ as conveying means (made explicit by the NLT: "*by means of* his marvelous glory and excellence"), at least one translation, the ESV, reads "*to* his own glory and excellence" (though supplying the alternative, "by," in a footnote). This would express Peter's message a bit differently: rather than God calling us *by his own* glory and excellence (focusing on glory and excellence as a divine attribute to be emulated by believers), he would call us *to* his glory and excellence (direction), though his calling would presumably still be grounded in God's glory and excellence.[2] How, then, are we to interpret this passage? What do the commentaries say?

Richard Bauckham writes, "The dative can hardly give the sense 'called to' (which would require εἰς and the accusative, as in 1 Pet 5:10), but should be taken as instrumental."[3] Thomas Schreiner, with reference to Bauckham, essentially concurs, though he cites 2 Tim 1:9 as an example of a passage where the dative in conjunction with a passive form of the verb καλέω ("call") can be translated as "called to."[4] Gene Green observes, "Peter's statement appears to be that God calls his people '*to* his own glory and virtue'" (adducing the possible parallels 1 Thess 2:12 and 2 Thess 2:14). However, he points out that the expression ἰδίᾳ δόξῃ καὶ ἀρετῇ, "in accordance with his own glory and virtue," "echoes ancient honorific decrees" and thus "'points to the instrumental cause of the invitation,' and the dative should be understood as instrumental: 'in keeping with (in view of) his own reputation and arete.'"[5]

It appears, therefore, that most commentators and translations favor the view that ἰδίᾳ δόξῃ καὶ ἀρετῇ represents an instrumental dative (conveying the *means* by which God called us): God called us "by his own glory and excellence." What is more, as mentioned, Peter affirms that we have access to this divine glory and excellence through our personal relationship with ("knowledge of") the Lord Jesus Christ. Building on this affirmation, Peter then exhorts his readers: "For this very reason, make every effort to supplement your faith with virtue [here is our word ἀρετή again], and virtue [the third use of ἀρετή] with knowledge" (2 Pet 1:5 ESV).

In this remarkable passage, then, grace is free, but it is not cheap. Rather, it is presented as conveying an obligation, a duty to supplement our faith with a series

---

[1] Note in this regard the variant διὰ δόξης καὶ ἀρετῆς in 𝔓⁷², B, and several Byzantine manuscripts. However, as Metzger rightly notes, most likely scribes mistook ἰδίᾳ (a common word in 2 Peter) for διά (see Metzger, *Textual Commentary*, 629).

[2] In addition, there seems to be a certain amount of variation in the way in which modern English translations translate the rare term ἀρετή, whether as "goodness" (CSB, NIV, NRSV), "excellence" (NASB, ESV, NLT), or "virtue" (NKJV, ESV footnote). Interestingly, the ESV translates the term as "excellence" in v. 3 but as "virtue" (twice) in v. 5! Note that the term occurs elsewhere in the NT only in Phil 4:8 and 1 Pet 2:9 (there in the plural, alluding to Isa 43:20).

[3] Richard J. Bauckham, *Jude, 2 Peter*, WBC 50 (Waco, TX: Word, 1983), 178.

[4] Thomas R. Schreiner, *1, 2 Peter, Jude*, NAC 37 (Nashville: B&H, 2003), 292 n. 16.

[5] Gene L. Green, *Jude and 2 Peter*, BECNT (Grand Rapids: Baker, 2008), 183–84, citing F. W. Danker, *Benefactor: Epigraphic Study of a Graeco-Roman and New Testament Semantic Field* (St. Louis: Clayton, 1982), 457–58.

of Christian virtues such as self-control, steadfastness, and brotherly love (2 Pet 1:5–7). In this way, Peter maintains, believers will "confirm [their] calling and election" and be rendered neither ineffective nor unfruitful in their Christian lives and ministry (2 Pet 1:10 and 8, respectively). Salvation may be by faith alone (the Reformation principle of *sola fide*)—but, as the adage goes, faith is never alone; it must be supplemented by an active pursuit of Christian virtues and a variety of good works (see Jas 2:14–26; Eph 2:8–10). In the end, therefore, Peter affirms that we are both called *by* God's glory and excellence and *to* a vigorous pursuit of excellence consisting in a series of godly attributes.[6]

CHAPTER OBJECTIVES

The purpose of this chapter is to cover the various uses of the Greek dative case. The main benefit you will derive from working through this chapter is that you will be acquainted with all the major categories of usage for the dative (and some minor ones). Although scholars debate the specific nomenclature of some of these categories, as well as individual examples, these categories and subcategories genuinely capture the essence of the various uses of the dative case. Understanding the characteristic of each category and grasping how these types of usage differ from one another will go a long way toward helping you interpret the NT more accurately.

INTRODUCTION TO THE DATIVE CASE

The dative limits the action of the verb, or the significance of the noun or adjective, in one of three ways: (1) by indicating the *person* involved (pure dative), (2) by denoting the *location* of the action (locative dative), or (3) by supplying the *means* by which an action is accomplished (instrumental dative). Those favoring an 8-case system (such as Robertson) classify the above uses of the dative as three separate case categories (i.e., the true dative case, the locative case, and the instrumental case); those operating with a 5-case system treat these types of usage as three subcategories of the dative case (pure dative, locative dative, and instrumental dative).

The true dative is the case of personal interest and is most commonly applied to persons, though it can also relate to things. Frequently, the dative of personal interest is used in conjunction with an accusative indicating the direct object of a given action. For example, Matt 5:40 states, "let **him** have your coat" (ἄφες **αὐτῷ** καὶ τὸ ἱμάτιον), where αὐτῷ is in the dative (indirect object) while τὸ ἱμάτιον is in the accusative (direct object). While the dative of indirect object constitutes the most

---

[6] For a book-length treatment, see Andreas J. Köstenberger, *Excellence: The Character of God and the Pursuit of Scholarly Virtue* (Wheaton, IL: Crossway, 2011).

common use of the pure dative, other types of usage such as the dative of personal interest (whether of advantage or disadvantage), the dative of reference or respect, and the dative of possession can be observed as well.

The locative use of the dative is fairly straightforward and can be subdivided into: the dative of (1) place (literal use), (2) sphere (figurative use), or (3) time (temporal location). Among the various subcategories of the instrumental dative are the datives of: (1) means, (2) manner, (3) agency, and (4) association. Finally, there are several other uses such as: (1) the dative of cause, (2) the cognate dative, (3) the dative of simple apposition, and (4) the dative of direct object (following certain verbs).

PURE DATIVE	Indirect Object
	Personal Interest
	Reference or Respect
	Possession
LOCATIVE DATIVE	Place
	Sphere
	Time
INSTRUMENTAL DATIVE	Means
	Manner
	Agency
	Association
OTHER USES	Cause
	Cognate Dative
	Apposition
	Direct Object

On the whole, the dative case is easier to categorize than the genitive, which, as we have seen, displays considerable variety in the way in which it is used in the NT. The best course of action, similar to the other cases, is to determine whether a given instance of the dative case falls into the category of pure dative, locative, or instrumental dative and then to pinpoint the precise subcategory.

PURE DATIVE

As Robertson observes, the main idea of the pure dative is "personal interest. . . . The accusative, genitive and dative are all cases of inner relations, but the dative has a distinctive personal touch not true of the others."[7] The pure dative, therefore,

---

[7] Robertson, 536.

indicates "the person *to* or *for* whom something is done,"[8] denoting "the person who is interested in or affected by the action."[9] When applied to things, the idea usually becomes that of respect or reference. The pure dative can be subdivided into the dative of: (1) indirect object, (2) personal interest (whether dative of advantage or disadvantage), (3) reference or respect, and (4) possession.

Indirect Object

Very commonly, as mentioned, verbs take an accusative direct object as well as a dative indirect object.

- καὶ ἐλάλησεν **αὐτοῖς** πολλὰ ἐν παραβολαῖς (Matt 13:3)

  Then he told **them** many things in parables

  > The people in the crowd were blessed to be the recipients of many parables told by Jesus.

- δὸς δόξαν **τῷ θεῷ** (John 9:24)

  Give glory **to God**

  > The command has "glory" as its direct object and "God" as its indirect object, the one who is the recipient of the action.

- καὶ ἐλάλησαν **αὐτῷ** τὸν λόγον τοῦ κυρίου (Acts 16:32)

  Then they spoke the word of the Lord **to him**

- ταύτην τὴν παραγγελίαν παρατίθεμαί **σοι**, τέκνον Τιμόθεε (1 Tim 1:18)

  This charge I entrust **to you**, Timothy, my child (ESV)

  > Paul entrusts "this charge" (the direct object) "to Timothy" (the indirect object).

- ὥστε καὶ οἱ πάσχοντες κατὰ τὸ θέλημα τοῦ θεοῦ **πιστῷ κτίστῃ** παρατιθέσθωσαν τὰς ψυχὰς αὐτῶν ἐν ἀγαθοποιΐα (1 Pet 4:19)

  So then, let those who suffer according to God's will entrust themselves **to a faithful Creator** while doing what is good

  > Again, the dative is personal, denoting a trust relationship between the sufferer and God, the "faithful Creator."[10]

---

[8] Black, 52.

[9] Smyth, 338.

[10] For more examples of the dative of indirect object, see Matt 5:40; 7:6; 13:13; 18:26; Mark 10:13; 14:44; John 1:43; 10:28; Acts 13:22; 2 Cor 5:9, 11; Jas 2:16; and Rev 16:6. In addition, Wallace discusses a "dative of destination," a rare type of usage that describes "a transfer of something from one place to another," with the dative indicating the final destination of the action conveyed by the verb (Wallace, 147; e.g., Matt 21:5; Luke 15:25; Heb 12:22); and a "dative of recipient" that appears in verbless constructions such as in titles or salutations (Wallace, 148; e.g., Acts 23:26; Phil 1:1; 1 Pet 3:15).

Personal Interest

The dative of interest denotes the person interested in (positively or negatively) the verbal action.[11] That is, the dative of interest conveys either advantage or disadvantage. Many grammarians point out that the dative of interest is only a specialized use of the dative of indirect object. As Brooks & Winbery put it, "All datives of advantage or disadvantage are in fact indirect objects, and all indirect objects to a greater or lesser degree express advantage or disadvantage."[12] As Porter rightly notes, the designation "dative of advantage or disadvantage" "combines syntactical and contextual designations," that is, it must be inferred from the context in which a given instance of the dative case occurs.[13]

Advantage

The dative of advantage is normally used with the word "for," indicating that the action is meant to benefit the recipient. It expresses a favorable personal relation.[14]

- μὴ θησαυρίζετε **ὑμῖν** θησαυροὺς ἐπὶ τῆς γῆς (Matt 6:19)

  Don't store up **for yourselves** treasures on earth

- καὶ ὑπὲρ πάντων ἀπέθανεν ἵνα οἱ ζῶντες μηκέτι **ἑαυτοῖς** ζῶσιν ἀλλὰ **τῷ** ὑπὲρ αὐτῶν **ἀποθανόντι** καὶ **ἐγερθέντι** (2 Cor 5:15)

  And he died for all so that those who live should no longer live **for themselves**, but **for the one who died** for them and **[for the one who] was raised**

- ἡτοιμασμένην ὡς νύμφην κεκοσμημένην **τῷ ἀνδρὶ** αὐτῆς (Rev 21:2)

  prepared like a bride adorned **for** her **husband**[15]

Disadvantage

The dative of disadvantage is a subset of the dative of personal interest and the obverse of the dative of advantage, indicating the person to whose detriment a given action has occurred, is occurring, or will occur. As such, it is best translated with "against."

---

[11] Wallace, 142, notes that the dative of interest will on rare occasions refer to a thing.

[12] Brooks & Winbery, 33 (see also Dana & Mantey, 84; Robertson, 538). Young does not treat advantage or disadvantage as separate categories at all but instead includes "benefaction" and "opposition" as subcategories of indirect object, along with "experience" (43).

[13] Porter, *Idioms*, 98.

[14] Robertson, 538.

[15] For more examples of the dative of advantage, see Mark 10:51; John 16:7; Rom 14:6; 6:13; 9:19; 2 Cor 5:13; Eph 5:19; Rev 13:2.

- ὥστε μαρτυρεῖτε **ἑαυτοῖς** ὅτι υἱοί ἐστε τῶν φονευσάντων τοὺς προφήτας (Matt 23:31)

  So you testify **against yourselves** that you are descendants of those who murdered the prophets

- ἡ δὲ Ἡρῳδιὰς ἐνεῖχεν **αὐτῷ** (Mark 6:19)

  So Herodias held a grudge **against him**

- ὁ χρυσὸς ὑμῶν καὶ ὁ ἄργυρος κατίωται, καὶ ὁ ἰὸς αὐτῶν εἰς μαρτύριον **ὑμῖν** ἔσται (Jas 5:3)

  Your gold and silver are corroded, and their corrosion will be a witness **against you**[16]

Reference or Respect

The dative of reference provides a limitation, setting concrete boundaries for a given relationship. It can be used with a main or copulative (i.e., linking) verb or an adjective.[17] This type of usage of the dative case could also be called "dative of respect," "frame of reference dative," "limiting dative," "qualifying dative," or "contextualizing dative."[18]

- οἱ κατεσθίοντες τὰς οἰκίας τῶν χηρῶν καὶ **προφάσει** μακρὰ προσευχόμενοι (Mark 12:40)

  They devour widows' houses and say long prayers **just for show**

- πάντα τὰ γεγραμμένα διὰ τῶν προφητῶν **τῷ υἱῷ** τοῦ ἀνθρώπου (Luke 18:31)

  Everything that is written **about the Son** of Man by the prophets will be accomplished (ESV)

---

[16] For more examples of the dative of disadvantage, see Luke 10:11; Rom 10:2; 11:9; 1 Cor 4:4; 11:29; Phil 1:28; Heb 6:6; Rev 2:5.

[17] Grammarians are sometimes divided on the idea of respect and sphere (on which see below). For example, 1 Cor 14:20, "Brothers and sisters, don't be childish **in your thinking**, but be infants in regard to evil and adult **in your thinking**" (ἀδελφοί, μὴ παιδία γίνεσθε **ταῖς φρεσὶν** ἀλλὰ τῇ κακίᾳ νηπιάζετε, **ταῖς** δὲ **φρεσὶν** τέλειοι γίνεσθε) could be taken as indicating "with *respect* to your thinking" or "in the *sphere* of your thinking," though the former seems more probable.

[18] Wallace, 145.

- ὃ γὰρ ἀπέθανεν, **τῇ ἁμαρτίᾳ** ἀπέθανεν ἐφάπαξ· ὃ δὲ ζῇ, ζῇ **τῷ θεῷ** (Rom 6:10)

  For the death he died, he died **to sin** [i.e., *with reference to* sin] once for all time; but the life he lives, he lives **to God**

    This kind of language pervades Paul's discussion in Romans 6 (e.g., v. 2: "How can we who died **to sin** still live in it?" [οἵτινες ἀπεθάνομεν **τῇ ἁμαρτίᾳ**, πῶς ἔτι ζήσομεν ἐν αὐτῇ;]).

- πάντα **μοι** ἔξεστιν (1 Cor 6:12)

  Everything is permissible **for me**

- εἰ δὲ καὶ ἰδιώτης **τῷ λόγῳ** (2 Cor 11:6)

  Even if I am untrained **in public speaking**[19]

Possession

The dative of possession (which can be translated with "belonging to") represents a unique construction in which the dative *possesses* the *subject* of an equative verb (such as εἰμί, γίνομαι, ὑπάρχω, focusing on a state of being), whether the subject is a person, thing, idea, or quality.[20] Dana & Mantey describe the dative of possession as "personal interest particularized to the point of ownership."[21] The dative of possession is roughly akin to the genitive of possession, except that generally the genitive of possession emphasizes the *person* who possesses while the dative of possession is used to stress the *object* being possessed.[22]

- τί **σοι** ὄνομά ἐστιν (Luke 8:30)

  What is **your** name?

    The question could more literally be rendered, "What name is to you?"

- **οἷς** οὐκ ἔστιν ταμεῖον οὐδὲ ἀποθήκη (Luke 12:24)

  they don't have a storeroom or a barn

    The Greek reads more literally, "**To them** there is not a storeroom or a barn."

---

[19] For more examples of the dative of reference or respect, see Matt 5:8; 6:25; 18:2; Acts 14:22; 21:21; Rom 4:20; 5:19; 6:2, 11; 8:12; 14:4; 1 Cor 2:14; 6:12; 14:20; 2 Cor 5:13; Eph 6:12; Phil 2:7; Titus 2:2; Heb 5:11; Jas 2:5; 1 Pet 4:6; 2 Pet 3:18. Wallace also isolates what he calls an "ethical dative or dative of feeling," a rare usage which is really a subset of the dative of reference indicating a person's feelings or viewpoint (146–47; possible examples include Acts 7:20; 1 Cor 9:2; 2 Cor 10:4; Phil 1:21; 2 Pet 3:14). Winer calls this the "dative of opinion or decision" (212).

[20] Wallace, 149–50; see Black, 52.

[21] Dana & Mantey, 85.

[22] BDF, 102 (§189).

- ἔστιν δὲ συνήθεια **ὑμῖν** (John 18:39)

You have a custom

> Literally, the Greek reads, "There is a custom **to/for you**."

- **ὑμῖν** γάρ ἐστιν ἡ ἐπαγγελία καὶ **τοῖς τέκνοις** ὑμῶν (Acts 2:39)

For the promise is **for you** and **for** your **children**

> The promise of the Messiah's coming belongs to Israel and her descendants (and to all who are far off).

- **ᾧ** ἐστιν ἡ δόξα καὶ τὸ κράτος εἰς τοὺς αἰῶνας τῶν αἰώνων, ἀμήν (1 Pet 4:11)

To him be the glory and the power forever and ever[23]

LOCATIVE DATIVE

The locative dative case is always "in."[24] It indicates the position of a noun in, on, among, at, or by a given location.[25] The location may be literal/spatial (the "dative of place"), figurative/metaphorical (the "dative of sphere"), or temporal (the "dative of time").[26] Some conflate the dative of place and the dative of sphere into one single category, variously called "dative of place" or "dative of space."[27] As mentioned, some examples adduced as "dative of sphere" more properly belong to the rubric "dative of reference."[28]

---

[23] For more examples of the dative of possession, see Matt 18:12; 19:27; Mark 2:18; Luke 1:14; 2:7; 4:16; 9:38; 21:4; John 1:6; Acts 2:43; 8:21; 21:23; Rom 7:3; 2 Pet 1:8. In addition, Young isolates what he calls the "dative of relationship" because in English we do not normally speak of "owning" or "possessing" a person (e.g., Luke 9:38; John 13:35; Acts 19:31); as well as the "dative of identification" in the case of personal names because we do not usually think of people "owning" their names (e.g., Mark 5:22; John 1:6; see Matt 1:21; 53; Young, 53–54). However, it is best to treat these uses as instances of the dative of possession while duly noting Young's cautions.

[24] At times, writing a Greek textbook is a dry affair, so please forgive us for this feeble attempt at a pun. Note that Robertson calls the locative "the *in* case" (520), though with no hint of a deliberate word play.

[25] Dana & Mantey, 86. They write, "[W]e may define the locative as the case of *position*" (87).

[26] In addition, Robertson identifies a "locative with verbs" (e.g., Acts 21:21; 2 Cor 7:11; Eph 4:18; Jas 1:2; Robertson, 523–24).

[27] E.g., Wallace, 153; Robertson, 521; Young, 48.

[28] Young, 48. See also Wallace, who notes this tension and suggests the rule of thumb that in the dative of *reference*, "the word to which the dative stands related [is] detached or *separated* somehow from the dative" (e.g., Rom 6:2) while the dative of *sphere* "views the word to which the dative stands related as *incorporated* within the realm of the dative" (e.g., Eph 2:1; Wallace, 154).

Place

The dative of place pinpoints the literal physical location of a substantive in the dative case.[29] In English, the translation must be chosen in keeping with the appropriate preposition, whether "in," "on," "among," "at," "to," or "by."

- καὶ εὐθέως δραμὼν εἷς ἐξ αὐτῶν καὶ λαβὼν σπόγγον πλήσας τε ὄξους καὶ περιθεὶς **καλάμῳ** ἐπότιζεν αὐτόν (Matt 27:48)

  Immediately one of them ran and got a sponge, filled it with sour wine, put it **on a stick**, and offered him a drink

  > The sense here is not "to or for a stick" or "by means of a stick," but "on a stick," denoting physical location.

- περιβλεψάμενος τοὺς περὶ αὐτὸν **κύκλῳ** καθημένους (Mark 3:34)

  looking at those sitting **in a circle** around him

  > Again, the reference is plainly to the physical arrangement of those seated in a circle around Jesus.

- καὶ οἱ στρατιῶται πλέξαντες στέφανον ἐξ ἀκανθῶν ἐπέθηκαν αὐτοῦ **τῇ κεφαλῇ** (John 19:2)

  The soldiers also twisted together a crown of thorns, put it **on** his **head**

  > The soldiers put the crown of thorns on Jesus's (literal) head.

- τοῦτον ὁ θεὸς ἀρχηγὸν καὶ σωτῆρα ὕψωσεν **τῇ δεξιᾷ** αὐτοῦ (Acts 5:31)

  God exalted this man **to** his **right hand** as ruler and Savior

- οἱ **τῷ θυσιαστηρίῳ** παρεδρεύοντες (1 Cor 9:13)

  those who serve **at the altar** (ESV)

  > "At the altar" denotes the location where those performing the temple services were serving.[30]

Sphere

The dative of sphere identifies the figurative or metaphorical location (i.e., the sphere) of a noun in the dative case.[31] The boundaries established are "logical rather than spatial or temporal, confining one idea within the bounds of another,

---

[29] Young, 48.

[30] For more examples of the dative of place, see Luke 10:30; 21:26; John 14:16; Acts 2:33; 9:3; 1 Cor 9:13; 2 Cor 3:7; Col 2:14; Heb 9:24.

[31] Brooks & Winbery call the dative of sphere "a metaphorical use of the locative in figurative expressions," the location being "in a logical sphere rather than in space or time" (40).

thus indicating the sphere within which the former idea is to be applied."[32] As mentioned, some grammarians subsume this use under "dative of place."

- ἀναστενάξας **τῷ πνεύματι** αὐτοῦ (Mark 8:12)

  sighing deeply **in** his **spirit**

- ἐσκοτωμένοι **τῇ διανοίᾳ** ὄντες (Eph 4:18)

  They are darkened **in their understanding**[33]

- καὶ Μωϋσῆς μὲν πιστὸς ἐν **ὅλῳ τῷ οἴκῳ** αὐτοῦ (Heb 3:5)

  Moses was faithful as a servant **in all** God's **household**

- ἀεὶ πλανῶνται **τῇ καρδίᾳ** (Heb 3:10)

  They always go astray **in** their **heart** (ESV)

- ἵνα ὑμᾶς προσαγάγῃ τῷ θεῷ, θανατωθεὶς μὲν **σαρκὶ** ζῳοποιηθεὶς δὲ **πνεύματι** (1 Pet 3:18)

  that he might bring us to God, being put to death **in the flesh** but made alive **in the spirit**[34]

Time

The dative of time denotes when an action occurred. While typically the genitive of time expresses the *kind* of time or *time during which*, and the accusative of time indicates the *extent* of time, the dative of time typically denotes the *point* in time at which a particular event is taking place.[35] The three uses can be illustrated by Luke 23:56b–24:1a: "And they rested **on the Sabbath** [accusative, duration of time] according to the commandment. **On the first day** [dative, locative of time] of the week, **very early** [genitive, kind of time] in the morning, they came to the tomb" (καὶ τὸ μὲν **σάββατον** ἡσύχασαν κατὰ τὴν ἐντολήν. τῇ δὲ **μιᾷ** τῶν σαββάτων **ὄρθρου βαθέως** ἐπὶ τὸ μνῆμα ἦλθον).[36]

---

[32] Dana & Mantey, 87.

[33] Alternatively, this could be understood as a dative of respect.

[34] Although note that there is a considerable amount of discussion in the scholarly literature on how to interpret these two datives. For more examples of the dative of sphere, see Matt 5:3, 8; Acts 14:16; 18:5; 21:21; Rom 4:19; Eph 2:1; Heb 12:22; 1 Pet 4:1; Jude 11. In addition, some grammarians (e.g., Wallace, 157; Winer, 215) identify a "dative of rule" indicating the standard according to which something conforms (e.g., Acts 14:16; 15:1; Gal 6:16; 1 Pet 2:21), though some of these examples may be subsumed under the dative of sphere or classified in other ways.

[35] Wallace, 156. Some grammarians separate the dative of time, indicating the *point* in time, from the dative of measure, indicating the *length* of time (see Robertson, 527–28). However, both instances can be considered under the dative of time.

[36] We owe this example to Robertson, 522.

- ἐπορεύθη ὁ Ἰησοῦς **τοῖς σάββασιν** διὰ τῶν σπορίμων (Matt 12:1)

  Jesus passed through the grainfields **on the Sabbath**

  <small>The dative indicates the point in time at which Jesus passed through the grainfields.</small>

- καὶ **αὐτῇ τῇ ὥρᾳ** ἐπιστᾶσα ἀνθωμολογεῖτο τῷ θεῷ (Luke 2:38)

  At that very moment, she came up and began to thank God

- καὶ **τῇ ἡμέρᾳ τῇ τρίτῃ** γάμος ἐγένετο ἐν Κανὰ τῆς Γαλιλαίας (John 2:1)

  On the third day a wedding took place in Cana of Galilee

- **τῇ νυκτὶ ἐκείνῃ** ἦν ὁ Πέτρος κοιμώμενος (Acts 12:6)

  on that very night, Peter . . . was sleeping

- καὶ ἔπεσαν **μιᾷ ἡμέρᾳ** εἴκοσι τρεῖς χιλιάδες (1 Cor 10:8)

  and **in a single day** twenty-three thousand people died

  <small>The dative indicates a point in time.[37]</small>

INSTRUMENTAL DATIVE

The instrumental use of the dative is a fairly broad category that indicates how an action is carried out. The term in the instrumental dative indicates that *by* which or *with* which a given action is completed.[38] The instrumental dative can be subdivided into the following types of usage: (1) means, (2) manner, (3) agency, and (4) association.

Means

This particular use of the dative case indicates the means or instrument by which a person intentionally accomplishes a given purpose or end.[39] Brooks & Winbery call this "the most common, the simplest, the most obvious use of the [instrumental] case."[40] In English translation, the dative of means may be conveyed by adding "by," "by means of," or "with." In contrast to the dative of (personal) agency, the dative of means is always *impersonal*.[41]

---

[37] For more examples of the dative of time, see Matt 14:25; 24:20, 42; Mark 12:2; 14:12, 30; Luke 2:41; 9:37; 13:14, 16; 20:10; 24:1; John 2:20; 20:19; Acts 12:6; 13:20; 23:11; Rom 16:25; 2 Cor 6:2.

[38] Brooks & Winbery, 42.

[39] Young, 49.

[40] Brooks & Winbery, 42.

[41] Brooks & Winbery, 42.

- ὥσπερ οὖν συλλέγεται τὰ ζιζάνια καὶ **πυρὶ** [κατα] καίεται (Matt 13:40)

  Just as the weeds are gathered and burned **with fire** (ESV)

- ἦν κράζων καὶ κατακόπτων ἑαυτὸν **λίθοις** (Mark 5:5)

  he was always crying out . . . cutting himself **with stones**

- **τοῖς δάκρυσιν** ἤρξατο βρέχειν τοὺς πόδας αὐτοῦ καὶ **ταῖς θριξὶν** τῆς κεφαλῆς αὐτῆς ἐξέμασσεν (Luke 7:38)[42]

  She began to wet his feet **with her tears** and wiped them **with the hair** of her head (ESV)

- ἀνεῖλεν δὲ Ἰάκωβον τὸν ἀδελφὸν Ἰωάννου **μαχαίρῃ** (Acts 12:2)

  and he executed James, John's brother, **with the sword**

- πεπληρωμένους **πάσῃ ἀδικίᾳ πονηρίᾳ πλεονεξίᾳ κακίᾳ** (Rom 1:29)[43]

  They are filled **with all unrighteousness, evil, greed, and wickedness**[44]

Manner

The dative of manner expresses the mode or manner in which an action is carried out and can be translated into English with the preposition "with" or "in" answering the question, "How?" In many instances, as several of the examples below demonstrate, the dative in English translation can simply be turned into an adverb.[45]

- καὶ συνεβουλεύσαντο ἵνα τὸν Ἰησοῦν **δόλῳ** (Matt 26:4)

  and they conspired to arrest Jesus **in a treacherous way**

- **παρρησίᾳ** τὸν λόγον ἐλάλει (Mark 8:32)

  He spoke **openly** about this

---

[42] Wallace classifies at least one of these datives as a "dative of material." This is a category unique to Wallace. He says it occurs only rarely and is to be distinguished from the dative of means in that the dative of material is not a tool (Wallace, 169–70). However, all the examples Wallace gives can just as easily be understood as datives of means, and we have therefore decided not to further divide this category.

[43] Robertson, 533, labels this as a dative of means. Wallace places this usage, and the two uses of πληρόω with the dative found in the NT (Luke 2:40; 2 Cor 7:4), in another unique category, the "dative of content" (Wallace, 170–71). However, these uses can plausibly be understood as examples of the dative of means rather than a separate subcategory.

[44] For more examples of the dative of means, see Matt 8:16; 13:15; Mark 5:4; 6:13; 9:49; Luke 6:1; John 11:2; Rom 3:28; 14:15; 15:18; Gal 2:13; Eph 2:8.

[45] Young, 50.

- ἐχάρη καὶ παρεκάλει πάντας **τῇ προθέσει** τῆς καρδίας προσμένειν τῷ κυρίῳ (Acts 11:23)

  he was glad and encouraged all of them to remain true to the Lord **with devoted** hearts

- εἰ ἐγὼ **χάριτι** μετέχω (1 Cor 10:30)

  If I partake **with thankfulness** (ESV)

- ἡμεῖς δὲ πάντες **ἀνακεκαλυμμένῳ προσώπῳ** τὴν δόξαν κυρίου κατοπτριζόμενοι τὴν αὐτὴν εἰκόνα (2 Cor 3:18)

  We all, **with unveiled faces**, are looking as in a mirror at the glory of the Lord[46]

Agency

The dative of agency denotes the person who carries out the action of the verb. As a result, the dative will always be a *personal* agent, which contrasts with the dative of means, where the dative is always *impersonal*. The verbs involved will typically be passive. The dative of agency is not common, as agency is normally expressed by the preposition ὑπό followed by the genitive.[47]

- προσέχετε δὲ τὴν δικαιοσύνην ὑμῶν μὴ ποιεῖν ἔμπροσθεν τῶν ἀνθρώπων πρὸς τὸ θεαθῆναι **αὐτοῖς** (Matt 6:1)

  Be careful not to practice your righteousness in front of others, to be seen **by them** (see Matt 23:5)

- οὐδὲν ἄξιον θανάτου ἐστὶν πεπραγμένον **αὐτῷ** (Luke 23:15)

  nothing deserving death has been done **by him** (ESV)[48]

---

[46] For more examples of the dative of manner, see Mark 14:65; Luke 22:15; John 7:13; Acts 11:23; 16:37; 1 Cor 11:5; 2 Cor 7:4; Eph 2:3; Phil 1:18; Heb 2:7; Rev 5:12; 18:21.

[47] Young, 50; Dana & Mantey, 91; Brooks & Winbery 48. Wallace has an extended discussion of the dative of agency and takes a more restrictive view than presented here. According to Wallace, the dative of agency can be identified through four criteria: (1) the dative must be *personal*; (2) the person indicated by the dative must carry out the action of the verb *deliberately*; (3) the construction will use a *perfect* passive verb; and, as a "rule of thumb," (4) the agent could be the *subject* of the verb were the sentence reworded using an active verb (Wallace, 164–65; emphasis added). As a result, Wallace disqualifies examples such as 1 Tim 3:16 because he views the action of seeing in this verse as not deliberate (his criterion 2) and because the verb tense-form is aorist, not perfect (his criterion 3). However, there does not seem to be any need to be as restrictive in limiting the dative of agency, because personal agency is involved in this broader set of examples and there is no good reason to exclude activities such as seeing as insufficiently deliberate.

[48] Several grammarians consider this to be the clearest or even only NT example (Zerwick, 21 [§59]; BDF, 102 [§191]; Robertson, 542). See also Porter, *Idioms*, 98–99, who groups instrument, agent, cause, means or manner together and comments, "Many grammarians separate these categories, but it is in fact difficult to establish a specific difference in most instances."

- νομοδιδάσκαλος τίμιος **παντὶ τῷ λαῷ** (Acts 5:34)

  a teacher of the Law, respected **by all the people** (NASB)

- εἰ δὲ **πνεύματι** ἄγεσθε (Gal 5:18)

  But if you are led **by the Spirit**

- ὤφθη **ἀγγέλοις** (1 Tim 3:16)

  seen **by angels**[49]

Association

The dative of association indicates people or things that are connected with the subject of the verb as the action is carried out. Admittedly, the connection between the overall category of "instrumental dative" and the notion of personal association is not always readily apparent, but the dative of association fits the category of "instrumental dative" better than the other main categories of the "pure dative" and the "locative dative."[50] Perhaps, as Brooks & Winbery suggest, we may think of the second party furnishing "the means by which association takes place."[51] In such constructions, there is often a compound verb with the prepositional prefix σύν (translated "with"; see examples 1, 2, 3, and 5 below).

- καὶ οὐκ ἠδύναντο <u>συν</u>τυχεῖν **αὐτῷ** διὰ τὸν ὄχλον (Luke 8:19)

  but they could not meet **with him** because of the crowd

  > In this case, the verbal prefix σύν governs the use of the dative.

- καὶ ὄφελόν γε ἐβασιλεύσατε, ἵνα καὶ ἡμεῖς **ὑμῖν** <u>συμ</u>βασιλεύσωμεν (1 Cor 4:8)

  and I wish you did reign, so that we could also reign **with you**!

- ἐὰν δὲ καὶ χωρισθῇ, μενέτω ἄγαμος ἢ **τῷ ἀνδρὶ** καταλλαγήτω (1 Cor 7:11)

  But if she does leave, she must remain unmarried or be reconciled **to her husband**

- <u>συν</u>ταφέντες **αὐτῷ** ἐν τῷ βαπτισμῷ (Col 2:12)

  Having been buried **with him** in baptism (ESV)

---

[49] For more possible examples of the dative of agency, see John 18:15; Rom 8:14; 14:18; Jas 3:7; 2 Pet 3:14; Jude 1.

[50] Wallace, 159.

[51] Brooks & Winbery, 47.

- ἀλλ' οὐκ ὠφέλησεν ὁ λόγος τῆς ἀκοῆς ἐκείνους μὴ <u>συγκεκερασμένους</u> τῇ πίστει **τοῖς ἀκούσασιν** (Heb 4:2)

  but the message they heard did not benefit them, since they were not united **with those who heard it** in faith[52]

OTHER USES

There are several other uses of the dative that do not easily fit into the classification scheme above. Many of these are infrequent in the NT and have been dealt with briefly in relevant footnotes attached to more significant uses above. The most important other uses of the dative in the NT are (1) the dative of cause, (2) the cognate dative, (3) the dative in simple apposition, and (4) the dative of direct object.

Cause

The dative of cause indicates the grounds or reason of the action of a given verb.[53] Robertson says it indicates "motive" or "occasion."[54] Brooks & Winbery simply note that the dative of cause "indicates what caused the action of the verb to be performed."[55] Wallace draws a helpful distinction between the datives of means and cause: the dative of *means* indicates *how* an action is performed whereas the dative of *cause* indicates the *basis* for an action.[56]

- ἐγὼ δὲ **λιμῷ** ὧδε ἀπόλλυμαι (Luke 15:17)

  here I am dying **[because] of hunger!**[57]

- τινὲς δὲ **τῇ συνηθείᾳ** ἕως ἄρτι τοῦ εἰδώλου ὡς εἰδωλόθυτον ἐσθίουσιν (1 Cor 8:7)

  but some, **being accustomed** to the idol until now, eat *food* as if it were sacrificed to an idol (NASB)

  > The idea is that they eat this way *because of* their accustomation to idols.

- μή πως **τῇ περισσοτέρᾳ λύπῃ καταποθῇ** ὁ τοιοῦτος (2 Cor 2:7)

  Otherwise, he may be overwhelmed **by excessive grief**

---

[52] For more examples of the dative of association, see Mark 9:4; Luke 14:25; 15:2, 9; 23:51; 24:4, 15; John 4:9; 6:22; Acts 1:21; Rom 11:2; 1 Cor 5:9; 2 Cor 6:14; Eph 2:5; Col 3:1; 2 Thess 3:14; Heb 11:25, 31; Jas 2:22.

[53] Young calls this a "dative of reason" (52).

[54] Robertson, 532. Brooks & Winbery observe that "[t]he reference may be to an *external* cause and thus an occasion or to an *internal* cause and thus a motive" (43; emphasis added).

[55] Brooks & Winbery, 43.

[56] Wallace, 167.

[57] Note the freer, more idiomatic rendering in the NIV: "And here I am starving to death!"

- μόνον ἵνα **τῷ σταυρῷ** τοῦ Χριστοῦ μὴ διώκωνται (Gal 6:12)

  but only to avoid being persecuted **for the cross** of Christ

- καὶ ἀπαλλάξῃ τούτους, ὅσοι **φόβῳ** θανάτου διὰ παντὸς τοῦ ζῆν ἔνοχοι ἦσαν δουλείας (Heb 2:15)

  and free those who were held in slavery all their lives **by the fear** of death[58]

Cognate Dative

The cognate dative is aligned with the verb either with regard to the root of the word or with regard to the idea conveyed.[59] The cognate dative is sometimes called the "Hebraic" dative because of its affinity with the similar construction in the Hebrew OT.[60] In English, it is often most appropriate to translate the cognate dative with an intensifying adjective (such as "utterly," "fervently," or "earnestly"; see below; cognate verbs are underlined).

- ὁ κακολογῶν πατέρα ἢ μητέρα **θανάτῳ** <u>τελευτάτω</u> (Matt 15:4)

  Whoever reviles father or mother <u>must</u> **surely** <u>die</u> (ESV)

- <u>ἐξέστησαν</u> **ἐκστάσει μεγάλῃ** (Mark 5:42)

  <u>they were</u> **utterly** <u>astounded</u>

  Literally, "they were astonished with great astonishment."

- ὁ δὲ φίλος τοῦ νυμφίου ὁ ἑστηκὼς καὶ ἀκούων αὐτοῦ **χαρᾷ** <u>χαίρει</u> (John 3:29)

  But the groom's friend, who stands by and listens for him, <u>rejoices</u> **greatly**

- **παραγγελίᾳ** <u>παρηγγείλαμεν</u> ὑμῖν μὴ διδάσκειν ἐπὶ τῷ ὀνόματι τούτῳ (Acts 5:28)

  <u>We</u> **strictly** <u>charged</u> you not to teach in this name (ESV)

  The ESV highlights the force of the cognate dative by translating the phrase as "strictly charged," emphasizing the verbal action.

---

[58] For more examples of the dative of cause, see Rom 4:20; 11:20, 30–32; Phil 1:14; 2 Thess 2:12; 1 Pet 4:12.

[59] Wallace helpfully highlights both the lexical and the conceptual subgroups of the cognate dative and offers specific examples of each (168–69).

[60] E.g., Gen 2:17: "for on the day you eat from it, **you will certainly die**" (LXX: ᾗ δ' ἂν ἡμέρᾳ φάγητε ἀπ' αὐτοῦ, **θανάτῳ ἀποθανεῖσθε**). See Robertson, 531; Zerwick, 21 (§62).

- ἀναθέματι <u>ἀνεθεματίσαμεν</u> ἑαυτοὺς (Acts 23:14)

  <u>We have</u> **strictly** <u>bound</u> ourselves (ESV)[61]

Apposition

Like simple apposition in the other cases, the dative in simple apposition provides an alternate name for a given substantive in the dative. In such instances, the second dative makes the first dative more specific by further identifying it. This usage is a function of the syntax rather than a function of the dative case itself.

- οὐκ ἐκβάλλει τὰ δαιμόνια εἰ μὴ ἐν τῷ Βεελζεβοὺλ **ἄρχοντι** τῶν δαιμονίων (Matt 12:24)

  This man drives out demons only by Beelzebul, **the ruler** of the demons

  "The ruler of demons" stands in simple apposition to "Beelzebul."

- πλησίον τοῦ χωρίου ὃ ἔδωκεν Ἰακὼβ Ἰωσὴφ **[τῷ] υἱῷ αὐτου** (John 4:5)

  near the property that Jacob had given **his son** Joseph

  "His son" is in apposition to "Joseph."

- ἐγένετο δὲ ἡμέρας ἱκανὰς μεῖναι ἐν Ἰόππῃ παρά τινι Σίμωνι **βυρσεῖ** (Acts 9:43)

  And Peter stayed for some time in Joppa with Simon, **a leather tanner**

  "A leather tanner" is in apposition to "Simon."

- εὐχαριστοῦμεν τῷ θεῷ **πατρὶ** τοῦ κυρίου ἡμῶν Ἰησοῦ Χριστοῦ πάντοτε (Col 1:3)

  We always thank God, **the Father** of our Lord Jesus Christ

  "The Father" provides a simple apposition to "God."

- μόνῳ θεῷ **σωτῆρι** ἡμῶν (Jude 25)

  to the only God, our **Savior**

  "Our Savior" is in simple apposition to "God."[62]

---

[61] For more examples of explicit (linguistic) cognate datives, see Matt 13:14; Mark 1:25; Luke 22:15; Acts 2:7. For more examples of conceptual cognates, see 1 Peter 1:8; Rev 5:2, 11–12; 7:10; 8:13; 10:3; 14:7, 9 (Wallace, 135).

[62] For more examples of the dative in simple apposition, see Matt 27:2; Mark 1:2; Luke 11:15; Acts 5:1; 10:6; 11:5; Rom 6:23; Col 1:17; 1 Thess 1:1; Heb 12:22; Rev 11:18. A similar construction is the predicate dative, which involves instances where a substantive in the dative makes an assertion about another substantive in the dative similar to a predicate nominative (e.g., Acts 16:21: "it is not legal for us as **Romans**" [οὐκ ἔξεστιν ἡμῖν . . . **Ῥωμαίοις** οὖσιν]; see also Gal 4:8).

Direct Object

The dative commonly occurs after certain verbs. Normally, the direct object of a verb occurs in the accusative case, but some verbs take their direct object in the dative case. Such verbs can be grouped into the following categories: trusting (πιστεύω); obeying (ὑπακούω, ἀπειθέω); serving (διακονέω, δουλεύω); worshiping (προσκυνέω, λατρεύω); thanksgiving (εὐχαριστέω); and following (ἀκολουθέω).[63]

- οἱ δὲ εὐθέως ἀφέντες τὰ δίκτυα <u>ἠκολούθησαν</u> **αὐτῷ** (Matt 4:20)

  Immediately, they left their nets and <u>followed</u> **him**

- ὁ ἄνεμος καὶ ἡ θάλασσα <u>ὑπακούει</u> **αὐτῷ** (Mark 4:41)

  the wind and the sea <u>obey</u> **him**

- Ἄρα οὖν αὐτὸς ἐγὼ τῷ μὲν νοῒ <u>δουλεύω</u> **νόμῳ** θεοῦ τῇ δὲ σαρκὶ **νόμῳ** ἁμαρτίας (Rom 7:25)

  So then, with my mind I myself am <u>serving</u> **the law** of God with my mind, but with my flesh [I <u>serve</u>] **the law** of sin[64]

- Ἀβραὰμ <u>ἐπίστευσεν</u> **τῷ θεῷ** (Gal 3:6)

  Abraham <u>believed</u> **God** (ESV)

- <u>εὐχαριστοῦμεν</u> **τῷ θεῷ** . . . πάντοτε (Col 1:3)

  We always <u>thank</u> **God**

---

[63] Wallace, 171–72.

[64] Datives also occur after some prepositions, such as ἐν, ἐπί, παρά, and σύν (see, e.g., Luke 12:44; Rom 2:13; Col 1:16). This will be treated in more detail in chapter 12; see also Harris, *Prepositions and Theology* (see chap. 2, n. 69). Datives after certain nouns or adjectives are comparatively rare in the NT. An example of a dative after a noun is Matt 8:34: "At that, the whole town went out to meet **Jesus**" (καὶ ἰδοὺ πᾶσα ἡ πόλις ἐξῆλθεν εἰς <u>ὑπάντησιν</u> **τῷ Ἰησοῦ**). Literally, the Greek reads, "they went out unto a <u>meeting</u> [noun] **with Jesus**" (i.e., the verb takes a dative of association). An example of a dative following an adjective is Matt 13:31: "The kingdom of heaven is <u>like</u> a mustard **seed**" (<u>ὁμοία</u> ἐστὶν ἡ βασιλεία τῶν οὐρανῶν **κόκκῳ** σινάπεως).

SUMMARY

PURE DATIVE		
INDIRECT OBJECT	Indicates the one for whom or in whose interest an act is performed.	δὸς δόξαν τῷ θεῷ ("Give glory **to God**"; John 9:24).
PERSONAL INTEREST (ADVANTAGE OR DISADVANTAGE)	Denotes the person (or rarely, the thing) to whose benefit or detriment a verbal action occurs.	*Advantage:* ὡς νύμφην κεκοσμημένην τῷ ἀνδρὶ αὐτῆς ("like a bride adorned **for** her **husband**"; Rev 21:2).
		Disadvantage: ἡ δὲ Ἡρῳδιὰς ἐνεῖχεν αὐτῷ ("So Herodias held a grudge **against him**"; Mark 6:19).
REFERENCE OR RESPECT	Limits the extent to which something is presented as true, qualifying a statement that would otherwise not be true.	τῇ ἁμαρτίᾳ ἀπέθανεν ἐφάπαξ ("he died **to sin** once for all"; Rom 6:10).
POSSESSION	Unique construction in which the dative possesses the subject of an equative verb (such as εἰμι or γίνομαι).	ὑμῖν γάρ ἐστιν ἡ ἐπαγγελία ("For the promise is **for you**"; Acts 2:39).
LOCATIVE DATIVE		
PLACE	Pinpoints the literal physical location of a noun in the dative case.	τοὺς περὶ αὐτὸν κύκλῳ καθημένους ("those sitting **in a circle** around him"; Mark 3:34).
SPHERE	Identifies the figurative or metaphorical location (i.e., sphere or realm) of a noun in the dative case.	ἀναστενάξας τῷ πνεύματι αὐτοῦ ("sighing deeply **in** his **spirit**"; Mark 8:12).
TIME	Indicates the point in time (location in time) at which the action of a verb is accomplished.	καὶ τῇ ἡμέρᾳ τῇ τρίτῃ γάμος ἐγένετο ("**On the third day**, a wedding took place"; John 2:1).
INSTRUMENTAL DATIVE		
MEANS	Denotes the impersonal means by which the action of a given verb is accomplished.	κατακόπτων ἑαυτὸν λίθοις ("cutting himself **with stones**"; Mark 5:5).
MANNER	Denotes the manner in which the action of a given verb is accomplished.	παρρησίᾳ τὸν λόγον ἐλάλει ("He spoke **openly** about this"; Mark 8:32).
AGENCY	Denotes the personal agency by which the action of a given verb is accomplished.	εἰ δὲ πνεύματι ἄγεσθε ("But if you are led **by the Spirit**"; Gal 5:18).
ASSOCIATION	Denotes the person or thing with which a person is associated or by which a person is accompanied.	συνταφέντες αὐτῷ ἐν τῷ βαπτισμῷ ("Having been buried **with him** in baptism"; Col 2:12 ESV).

		OTHER USES	
CAUSE	Indicates the basis or reason of the action of a given verb, whether external (occasion) or internal (motivation).	ἐγὼ δὲ **λιμῷ** ὧδε ἀπόλλυμαι ("here I am dying **[because] of hunger!**"; Luke 15:17).
COGNATE DATIVE	Use of a dative noun that is a cognate (of the same stem) to the verb it modifies either formally or conceptually.	<u>ἐξέστησαν</u> **ἐκστάσει μεγάλῃ** ("<u>they were</u> **utterly** <u>astounded</u>"; Mark 5:42).
APPOSITION	Two related substantives refer to the same person or thing.	ἐν τῷ Βεελζεβοὺλ **ἄρχοντι** τῶν δαιμονίων ("by Beelzebul, **the ruler** of the demons"; Matt 12:24).
DIRECT OBJECT	The dative occurs after certain verbs of trusting, obeying, serving, worshiping, thanksgiving, or following and functions as the direct object.	εὐχαριστοῦμεν **τῷ θεῷ** . . . πάντοτε ("We always thank **God**"; Col 1:3).

PRACTICE EXERCISES

In each of the following examples, determine the specific use of the dative case based on the categories provided in this chapter.

1. ἡ δὲ ἐλθοῦσα προσεκύνει <u>αὐτῷ</u> λέγουσα, Κύριε, βοήθει <u>μοι</u> (Matt 15:25).

2. καὶ εὐθὺς ἐπιγνοὺς ὁ Ἰησοῦς <u>τῷ πνεύματι</u> αὐτοῦ (Mark 2:8).

3. ὁ γὰρ ἐσθίων καὶ πίνων κρίμα <u>ἑαυτῷ</u> ἐσθίει καὶ πίνει (1 Cor 11:29).

4. ἐγὼ . . . <u>ὕδατι</u> βαπτίζω ὑμᾶς (Luke 3:16).

5. τί ποιεῖτε ὃ οὐκ ἔξεστιν <u>τοῖς σάββασιν</u>; (Luke 6:2).

6. ἔρχεται ὥρα ὅτε οὐκέτι ἐν παροιμίαις λαλήσω ὑμῖν, ἀλλὰ <u>παρρησίᾳ</u> περὶ τοῦ πατρὸς ἀπαγγελῶ ὑμῖν (John 16:25).

7. ἠκολούθει δὲ <u>τῷ Ἰησοῦ</u> Σίμων Πέτρος καὶ ἄλλος μαθητής. ὁ δὲ μαθητὴς ἐκεῖνος . . . συνεισῆλθεν <u>τῷ Ἰησοῦ</u> εἰς τὴν αὐλὴν τοῦ ἀρχιερέως (John 18:15).

8. ὥσπερ γὰρ ὑμεῖς ποτε ἠπειθήσατε <u>τῷ θεῷ</u>, νῦν δὲ ἠλεήθητε <u>τῇ</u> τούτων <u>ἀπειθείᾳ</u> (Rom 11:30).

9. καὶ καθὼς θέλετε ἵνα ποιῶσιν <u>ὑμῖν</u> οἱ ἄνθρωποι ποιεῖτε <u>αὐτοῖς</u> ὁμοίως (Luke 6:31).

10. καὶ ὄντας ἡμᾶς νεκροὺς <u>τοῖς παραπτώμασιν</u> συνεζωοποίησεν <u>τῷ Χριστῷ</u>, <u>χάριτί</u> ἐστε σεσῳσμένοι (Eph 2:5).

VOCABULARY

Vocabulary to Memorize

ἀγοράζω	I buy, purchase (30)
ἀδικέω	I do wrong, treat unjustly (28)
ἀληθινός	true, real, genuine (28)
ἀνάγκη, ἡ	necessity, pressure (17)
ἅπαξ	once and for all (14)
ἀρνίον, τό	lamb, sheep (30)
ἁρπάζω	I grasp, snatch, seize (14)
Βαρναβᾶς, ὁ	Barnabas (28)
γαμέω	I marry (28)
γνῶσις, -εως, ἡ	knowledge (29)
διακρίνω	I discriminate, judge, doubt (19)
ἐλεέω	I have mercy on (29)
ἔλεος, -ους, τό	mercy, compassion (27)
ἐπιθυμία, ἡ	lust, craving, desire (39)
ἐπικαλέω	I call (upon), name (30)
ἐπιτιμάω	I rebuke, reprove, warn (29)
ἡγέομαι	I lead, think, consider (28)
θυγάτηρ, -τρός, ἡ	daughter, girl (28)
θυσία, ἡ	sacrifice, offering (28)
Ἰάκωβος, ὁ	James (42)
ἴδε	look, see, behold (29)
Ἰούδας, ὁ	Jude, Judah, Judas (44)
Καῖσαρ, -αρος, ὁ	Caesar, emperor (29)
μάχαιρα, ἡ	sword (29)
μιμνήσκομαι	I remember, recollect (23)
μισέω	I hate, detest (40)
μισθός, ὁ	pay, wages, reward (29)
παράκλησις, -εως, ἡ	encouragement, comfort (29)
παρέρχομαι	I pass by, neglect, disobey (29)
πάσχα, τό	Passover (29)
ποτέ	once, formerly, ever (29)
σκανδαλίζω	I cause to stumble (29)
σκότος, -ους, τό	darkness (31)
συνείδησις, -εως, ἡ	conscience (30)
σωτήρ, -ῆρος, ἡ	savior, deliverer (24)
σωτηρία, ἡ	salvation, deliverance (46)

φίλος	beloved, friend (29)
φόβος, ὁ	fear, reverence, respect (47)
φυλάσσω	I guard, protect (31)
φυλή, ἡ	tribe, nation, people (31)

Vocabulary to Recognize

ἀγαλλίασις, ἡ	exultation (5)
ἄμωμος	blameless (8)
ἀποδιορίζω	I divide, separate (1)
ἄπταιστος	without stumbling (1)
ἀσέβεια, ἡ	impiety (6)
ἐλεάω	I have mercy on (3)
ἐμπαίκτης, -ου, ὁ	mocker (2)
ἐπαγωνίζομαι	I contend (1)
ἐποικοδομέω	I edify, build up/on (7)
κατενώπιον	opposite, in the presence of (3)
κλητός	called, invited (10)
κοινός	communal, common (14)
κράτος, τό	power, rule (12)
μεγαλωσύνη, ἡ	majesty (3)
πληθύνω	I multiply, grow, increase (12)
προλέγω	I foretell, proclaim beforehand (12)
προσδέχομαι	I wait for (14)
σπιλόω	I stain, defile (2)
σπουδή, ἡ	eagerness, earnestness, diligence (12)
χιτών, -ῶνος, ὁ	garment, shirt (11)
ψυχικός	natural, unspiritual, worldly (6)

READING THE NEW TESTAMENT

Jude 1–3, 17–25

¹Ἰούδας Ἰησοῦ Χριστοῦ δοῦλος, ἀδελφὸς δὲ Ἰακώβου, τοῖς ἐν θεῷ πατρὶ ἠγαπημένοις καὶ Ἰησοῦ Χριστῷ τετηρημένοις κλητοῖς· ²ἔλεος ὑμῖν καὶ εἰρήνη καὶ ἀγάπη πληθυνθείη. ³Ἀγαπητοί, πᾶσαν σπουδὴν ποιούμενος γράφειν ὑμῖν περὶ τῆς κοινῆς ἡμῶν σωτηρίας ἀνάγκην ἔσχον γράψαι ὑμῖν παρακαλῶν ἐπαγωνίζεσθαι τῇ ἅπαξ παραδοθείσῃ τοῖς ἁγίοις πίστει. . . . ¹⁷Ὑμεῖς δέ, ἀγαπητοί, μνήσθητε τῶν ῥημάτων τῶν προειρημένων ὑπὸ τῶν ἀποστόλων τοῦ κυρίου ἡμῶν Ἰησοῦ Χριστοῦ ¹⁸ὅτι ἔλεγον ὑμῖν ἐπʼ ἐσχάτου χρόνου ἔσονται ἐμπαῖκται κατὰ τὰς ἑαυτῶν ἐπιθυμίας πορευόμενοι τῶν ἀσεβειῶν. ¹⁹Οὗτοί εἰσιν οἱ ἀποδιορίζοντες, ψυχικοί, πνεῦμα μὴ ἔχοντες. ²⁰ὑμεῖς δέ, ἀγαπητοί, ἐποικοδομοῦντες ἑαυτοὺς τῇ ἁγιωτάτῃ ὑμῶν πίστει, ἐν πνεύματι ἁγίῳ προσευχόμενοι, ²¹ἑαυτοὺς ἐν ἀγάπῃ θεοῦ τηρήσατε προσδεχόμενοι τὸ ἔλεος τοῦ κυρίου ἡμῶν Ἰησοῦ Χριστοῦ εἰς ζωὴν αἰώνιον. ²²καὶ οὓς μὲν ἐλεᾶτε διακρινομένους, ²³οὓς δὲ σῴζετε ἐκ πυρὸς ἁρπάζοντες, οὓς δὲ ἐλεᾶτε ἐν φόβῳ μισοῦντες καὶ τὸν ἀπὸ τῆς σαρκὸς ἐσπιλωμένον χιτῶνα. ²⁴Τῷ δὲ δυναμένῳ φυλάξαι ὑμᾶς ἀπταίστους καὶ στῆσαι κατενώπιον τῆς δόξης αὐτοῦ ἀμώμους ἐν ἀγαλλιάσει, ²⁵μόνῳ θεῷ σωτῆρι ἡμῶν διὰ Ἰησοῦ Χριστοῦ τοῦ κυρίου ἡμῶν δόξα μεγαλωσύνη κράτος καὶ ἐξουσία πρὸ παντὸς τοῦ αἰῶνος καὶ νῦν καὶ εἰς πάντας τοὺς αἰῶνας, ἀμήν.

Reading Notes[65]

Verse 1

- **Ἰούδας Ἰησοῦ Χριστοῦ δοῦλος, ἀδελφὸς δὲ Ἰακώβου** ("Jude, a bond-servant of Jesus Christ, and brother of James") – Ἰούδας is a nominative absolute (identifying the author of the letter) followed by two nominatives in apposition, δοῦλος, and ἀδελφός. If we are correct to identify this Jude as the son of Mary and Joseph (Matt 13:55; Mark 6:3), it is noteworthy that he describes himself as a bond-servant to his half-brother, Jesus.[66]

- **τοῖς ἐν θεῷ πατρὶ ἠγαπημένοις καὶ Ἰησοῦ Χριστῷ τετηρημένοις κλητοῖς** ("To those who are the called, beloved in God the Father, and kept for Jesus Christ") – τοῖς . . . κλητοῖς ("To those who are the called"), a masc dat pl adjective (substantive) functioning as the dative of indirect

---

[65] The English version used in the Reading Notes for this chapter is the NASB.

[66] Michael Green writes, "We can learn a good deal about a man by listening to what he has to say about himself." *2 Peter and Jude*, TNTC 18 (Leicester: InterVarsity; Grand Rapids: Eerdmans, 1987; repr. 1999), 167.

object, identifying the recipients of Jude's letter.[67] ἠγαπημένοις and τετηρημένοις (per pass ptc masc dat pl ἀγαπάω and τηρέω) can either be understood as attributive, modifying κλητοῖς, or as substantive, in apposition to κλητοῖς. Ἰησοῦ Χριστῷ is a dative of agency ("by Jesus Christ," CEB) or possibly advantage ("for Jesus Christ," NASB).[68] Reminder: the proper name "Jesus" (Ἰησοῦς) is irregular so both the genitive and dative forms are spelled the same. The prepositional phrase ἐν θεῷ πατρί ("in God the Father") also functions to communicate agency (in the sense of "by"). πατρί is in apposition to θεῷ, further clarifying or defining who God is.

Verse 2

- **πληθυνθείη** ("May . . . be multiplied") – Aor pass opt 3rd sg πληθύνω. See 1 Peter 1:2 and 2 Peter 1:2 for nearly identical voluntative uses of the optative. The use of a singular verb (πληθυνθείη) with a compound subject (ἔλεος ὑμῖν καὶ εἰρήνη καὶ ἀγάπη) is fairly common in Greek.

Verse 3

- **πᾶσαν σπουδὴν ποιούμενος γράφειν ὑμῖν** ("while I was making every effort to write you") – Literally, "[although] making all haste to write to you." ποιούμενος (pres mid ptc masc nom sg ποιέω) functions concessively (add "although" in English), though the NASB renders the participle temporally ("while").[69] γράφειν (pres act inf γράφω) is a purpose infinitive. The phrase πᾶσαν σπουδὴν ποιούμενος is essentially a strengthened form of the participle for σπουδάζω ("hasten, endeavor") which is sometimes followed by a purpose infinitive (e.g., Eph 4:3, σπουδάζοντες τηρεῖν). ὑμῖν is a dative of indirect object.

- **ἀνάγκην ἔσχον γράψαι ὑμῖν** ("I felt the necessity to write to you") – Literally, "I had necessity to write to you." ἔσχον is an aor act ind 1st sg of ἔχω.[70] The true root (*σεχ) of the verb ἔχω is visible in the aorist form—in this case with "zero vowel gradation" (i.e., the vowel in the root has dropped out). γράψαι (aor act inf γράφω) is an explanatory infinitive, clarifying what sort of necessity (ἀνάγκην) Jude felt (i.e., a necessity to write). The aorist tense usually presents as action as a whole, without

---

[67] Wallace creates a subcategory for dative of indirect objects used in verbless constructions—normally in the introduction of letters. He calls this the "dative of recipient" (148).

[68] Richard Bauckham labels Ἰησοῦ Χριστῷ as a dative of advantage, "for Jesus Christ." He writes, "The meaning 'by Jesus Christ' is unlikely since God should be the agent implied in both ἠγαπημένοις and τετηρημένοις, 'kept,' and the dative of agent is rare in the NT" (Bauckham, *Jude, 2 Peter*, 19).

[69] See the discussion in Schreiner, *1, 2 Peter, Jude*, NAC, 433–34.

[70] Bauckham labels ἔσχον as an epistolary aorist (*Jude, 2 Peter*, 28).

further comment or emphasis on progression or completion. This normal sense seems to fit the context here. ὑμῖν is a dative of indirect object.

- **παρακαλῶν ἐπαγωνίζεσθαι** ("appealing that you contend") – παρακαλῶν is a pres act ptc masc nom sg of παρακαλέω. The participle here functions to express purpose (Jude writes for the purpose of appealing/exhorting). The content of that appeal is given in the infinitive of indirect discourse, ἐπαγωνίζεσθαι (pres mid inf ἐπαγωνίζομαι).

- **τῇ ἅπαξ παραδοθείσῃ τοῖς ἁγίοις πίστει** ("for the faith which was once for all handed down to the saints") – τῇ . . . πίστει ("for the faith") is dative of advantage.[71] παραδοθείσῃ (aor pass ptc fem dat sg παραδίδωμι) modifies πίστει as an attributive participle. τοῖς ἁγίοις is a dative of indirect object.

Verse 17

- **μνήσθητε τῶν ῥημάτων τῶν προειρημένων** ("remember the words that were spoken beforehand") – μνήσθητε is an aor pass impv 2nd pl of μιμνήσκομαι. The aorist imperative is often used to command a specific occurrence. In looking at broader NT patterns for the word μιμνήσκομαι, we note that of 23 occurrences, 18 forms are aorist, 2 are perfect, 2 are present,[72] and 1 is future. Thus, we should not read too much into Jude's selection of the aorist tense, as it was likely the default tense for μιμνήσκομαι in his day. προειρημένων (per pass ptc neut gen pl προλέγω or, as listed by 2nd aor form in BDAG, προεῖπον) functions as an attributive participle modifying τῶν ῥημάτων.

Verse 18

- **ὅτι ἔλεγον ὑμῖν** ("they were saying to you") – ἔλεγον is an impf act ind 3rd pl of λέγω. ὑμῖν is a dative of indirect object. Most English translations do not translate ὅτι because it is understood as introducing direct discourse, represented by quotation marks (". . .") in English.

- **ἐπ᾽ ἐσχάτου χρόνου ἔσονται ἐμπαῖκται** ("In the last time there will be mockers") – ἐπί is used here as "a marker of temporal associations" (translated "in the time of, at, on, for").[73] This is not a common use of ἐπί (entry 18 in BDAG) and reminds us that prepositions are fluid in meaning and consideration of context is always important for proper translation. ἔσονται is a fut mid ind 3rd pl of εἰμί. ἐμπαῖκται should be understood

---

71 So Robertson, *Word Pictures*, 186 and Bauckham, *Jude, 2 Peter*, 31.
72 Furthermore, one of the present forms (Heb 2:6) is a quote from the LXX (Ps 8:5).
73 BDAG, 367.

as the subject of ἔσονται (more literally, "In the end time, mockers will be . . .").

- **κατὰ τὰς ἑαυτῶν ἐπιθυμίας πορευόμενοι τῶν ἀσεβειῶν** ("following after their own ungodly lusts") – πορευόμενοι (pres mid ptc nom masc pl πορεύομαι) functions as a periphrastic participle (i.e., a participle used in conjunction with a form of εἰμί). ἐπιθυμίας . . . τῶν ἀσεβειῶν is translated literally "lusts of ungodliness." τῶν ἀσεβειῶν represents the common attributive function of the genitive.[74]

Verse 19

- **Οὗτοί εἰσιν οἱ ἀποδιορίζοντες, ψυχικοί, πνεῦμα μὴ ἔχοντες** ("These are the ones who cause divisions, worldly-minded, devoid of the Spirit") – εἰσιν is a pres ind 3rd pl of εἰμί. Reminder: the copulative verb (here εἰσιν) takes a predicate nominative (οἱ ἀποδιορίζοντες), not a direct object in the accusative. ἀποδιορίζοντες (pres act ptc masc nom pl ἀποδιορίζω) functions as a substantival participle. ψυχικοί is literally translated "natural" or "worldly" (the opposite of "spiritual"). BDAG defines ψυχικός as "pert[aining] to the life of the natural world and whatever belongs to it, in contrast to the realm of experience whose central characteristic is πνεῦμα, *natural, unspiritual, worldly*."[75] ἔχοντες (pres act ptc masc nom pl ἔχω) is an anarthrous substantival participle in apposition to the previous two descriptions of the false teachers. Jude labels his opponents as divisive, worldly, and unspiritual.

Verse 20

- **ἐποικοδομοῦντες ἑαυτοὺς τῇ ἁγιωτάτῃ ὑμῶν πίστει** ("building yourselves up on your most holy faith") – ἐποικοδομοῦντες (pres act ptc masc nom pl ἐποικοδομέω) communicates means, rendered so more explicitly in the NIV: "by building." In other words, it is *by* building themselves up and *by* praying that the Christians will obey the command to keep themselves in the love of God.[76] ἁγιωτάτῃ is the superlative form (fem dat sg)

---

[74] Noting the plural form of ἀσέβεια that Jude employs, Bauckham suggests that ἀσεβειῶν could be an objective genitive, "desires for ungodly deeds" (*Jude, 2 Peter*, 103).

[75] BDAG, 1100. Concerning ψυχικός, John Calvin writes, "The word *sensual*, or animal, stands opposed to spiritual, or to the renovation of grace; and hence it means the vicious or corrupt, such as men are when not regenerated. For in that degenerated nature which we derive from Adam, there is nothing but what is gross and earthly; so that no part of us aspires to God, until we are renewed by his Spirit." See *Commentaries on the Catholic Epistles*, trans. and ed. John Owen (repr.; Grand Rapids: Baker, n.d.), 445.

[76] The three participles in vv. 20 and 21 (ἐποικοδομοῦντες, προσευχόμενοι, προσδεχόμενοι), regardless of how we label them, carry an imperative sense. Possibly they are participles of attendant circumstance and should be translated as imperatives (so NRSV).

of ἅγιος (thus, the translation "most holy"). Superlative adjectives often have an elative sense ("very") in the Koine period, and though all English translations follow Tyndale's wording ("most holy faith"), the elative sense is surely correct.[77] Jude is not comparing faith traditions based on their varying levels of holiness (i.e., holy faith, more holy faith, and most holy faith). Instead, Jude is emphasizing how blazingly pure this divine revelation (i.e., the Christian faith) is.[78] Such holiness/purity is in sharp distinction from the licentiousness of the wicked teachers attacked by Jude (vv. 8, 12–16).[79] The dative phrase τῇ ἁγιωτάτῃ . . . πίστει, a function of the verbal prefix ἐπί, gives the foundation upon which Christians are to build, or, as Bauckham translates, "Build yourselves up on the foundation of your most holy faith."[80]

- ἐν πνεύματι ἁγίῳ προσευχόμενοι ("praying in the Holy Spirit") – προσευχόμενοι (pres mid ptc masc nom pl προσεύχομαι), alongside ἐποικοδομοῦντες ("build"), is best understood as a participle of means (see above). Christians are expected to pray ἐν πνεύματι ἁγίῳ (in the Holy Spirit). This prepositional phrase communicates agency. That is, the Christian should pray by means of the Spirit's enabling and leading. In a chapter on the use of the dative, it is good to remember that many nouns are in the dative case simply because of their governing prepositions, as here. (The preposition ἐν must be followed by the dative case; anything else is a grammatical mistake.)

Verse 21

- ἑαυτοὺς ἐν ἀγάπῃ θεοῦ τηρήσατε ("keep yourselves in the love of God") – τηρήσατε is an aor act impv 2nd pl of τηρέω. The prepositional phrase ἐν ἀγάπῃ θεοῦ ("in the love of God") functions spherically, in a metaphorical sense. Christians are commanded to keep themselves in the realm or sphere where God's fatherly love rests undisturbed upon them. θεοῦ is likely a subjective genitive (i.e., the love which God has for his people).[81] Robertson notes that in v. 1, the recipients of Jude's letter are described as Ἰησοῦ Χριστῷ τετηρημένοις ("kept by Jesus Christ"), but

---

[77] So BDF, 32–33 (§60).

[78] Paul Gardner writes, "We must note that the faith is 'most holy,' that is, it is set apart, it is from God himself. It is not therefore a subjective personal faith that Jude is talking of here. Rather, he is calling them back to that which is revealed, the 'given-ness' of Christianity." *1 & 2 Peter & Jude: Christian Living in an Age of Suffering*, Focus on the Bible Series (Scotland, UK: Christian Focus, 2013), 376.

[79] Bauckham, *Jude, 2 Peter*, 113.

[80] Bauckham, *Jude, 2 Peter*, 112–13. See also BDAG, ἐποικοδομέω, 387.

[81] Wallace lists ἀγάπη θεοῦ in Jude 21 as a genitive construction for which it is difficult to decide between objective and subjective genitive (121 n. 136).

here they are commanded to keep *themselves*. "Human responsibility and divine sovereignty are presented side by side."[82]

- **προσδεχόμενοι τὸ ἔλεος τοῦ κυρίου ἡμῶν Ἰησοῦ Χριστοῦ εἰς ζωὴν αἰώνιον** ("waiting anxiously for the mercy of our Lord Jesus Christ to eternal life") – προσδεχόμενοι (pres mid ptc masc nom pl προσδέχομαι) is best rendered as a contemporaneous temporal clause (so NIV: "as you wait").[83] The phrase τὸ ἔλεος τοῦ κυρίου ἡμῶν Ἰησοῦ Χριστοῦ ("the mercy of our Lord Jesus Christ") refers to Christ's second coming, when the believer will experience fully God's undeserved mercy, resulting in eternal life (εἰς ζωὴν αἰώνιον). The preposition εἰς functions here to communicate result. The appearance of God's mercy at Christ's return ushers us into (results in) eternal life.

Verse 22

- **καὶ οὓς μὲν ἐλεᾶτε διακρινομένους** ("And have mercy on some, who are doubting") – ἐλεᾶτε is a pres act impv 2nd pl of ἐλεάω ("have mercy on"). διακρινομένους (pres mid ptc masc acc pl διακρίνω) functions as a substantival participle ("[those] who are doubting"). The particle μέν introduces an idea that is contrasted with two other ideas, both introduced by δέ in v. 23. This is the classic μέν . . . δέ construction ("on the one hand . . . on the other hand").[84] Jude instructs us here that the appropriate response to another's doubt is mercy—compassionate and practical concern.

Verse 23

- **οὓς δὲ σῴζετε ἐκ πυρὸς ἁρπάζοντες** ("save others, snatching them out of the fire") – σῴζετε is a pres act impv 2nd pl of σῴζω. Many English versions rightly translate ἁρπάζοντες (pres act ptc masc nom pl ἁρπάζω) as communicating means ("by"; so CSB, ESV, NIV). The prepositional phrase ἐκ πυρός ("from the fire") communicates separation ("from," "away from"). Jude pictures needy persons so in danger of God's imminent judgment that it is as if they are already standing in the fires of hell. They are proleptically pictured as in the fires of Gehenna (see Amos 4:11; Zech 3:2; Matt 5:22; 18:8).

- **οὓς δὲ ἐλεᾶτε ἐν φόβῳ** ("on some have mercy with fear") – ἐλεᾶτε is a pres act impv 2nd pl of ἐλεάω. The prepositional phrase ἐν φόβῳ ("with fear") communicates the manner in which believers are to show mercy.

---

[82] Robertson, *Word Pictures*, 194–95.

[83] Or possibly a participle of attendant circumstances (translated imperativally), as in the NRSV.

[84] BDF questions whether this structure (οὓς μέν . . . οὓς δέ) is an example of relative clauses with a main clause missing (255 [§482]). Thus, BDF labels this section of Jude as a debated example of aposiopesis ("a breaking-off of speech due to strong emotion or modesty").

That is, they are to rescue sinners with a godly trepidation as they reflect on the personal danger to their spiritual lives by coming in such close contact with deceitful and ensnaring wickedness.

- **μισοῦντες καὶ τὸν ἀπὸ τῆς σαρκός ἐσπιλωμένον χιτῶνα** ("hating even the garment polluted by the flesh") – Jude continues with a participle of manner (μισοῦντες, pres act ptc masc nom pl μισέω) further elaborating on the way in which mercy is to be shown—not in vapid sentimentalism, but in a loving compassion inseparable from the holy hatred of sin. ἐσπιλωμένον (per pass ptc masc acc sg σπιλόω) functions attributively, modifying χιτῶνα. The prepositional phrase ἀπὸ τῆς σαρκός ("by the flesh") functions to communicate means, that is, garments metaphorically stained *by* the fallen sinful person wearing them who has indulged his or her base desires.

Verse 24

- **Τῷ δὲ δυναμένῳ φυλάξαι ὑμᾶς ἀπταίστους** ("Now to Him who is able to keep you from stumbling") – Literally, "to protect/guard you [as] non-stumbling ones." Τῷ . . . δυναμένῳ is a substantival participle (pres mid ptc masc dat sg δύναμαι) functioning as a dative of indirect object. The following verse (v. 25) expresses the praise and adoration to be given "to Him who is able," i.e., to God. φυλάξαι (aor act inf φυλάσσω) is a complementary infinitive, taking a double accusative—ὑμᾶς (the direct object) and ἀπταίστους (the predicate object or complement).

- **καὶ στῆσαι κατενώπιον τῆς δόξης αὐτοῦ ἀμώμους ἐν ἀγαλλιάσει** ("and to make you stand in the presence of His glory blameless with great joy") – στῆσαι (aor act inf ἵστημι) is the second complementary infinitive in v. 24. (Both complementary infinitives are grammatically dependent on the substantival participle, δυναμένῳ, "to Him who is able"). ἀμώμους ("blameless") is the predicate object (complement) in another double accusative construction (see above). There is an ellipsis of ὑμᾶς as the direct object of στῆσαι. The prepositional phrase ἐν ἀγαλλιάσει ("with/in great joy) communicates the manner in which God's people stand before him (i.e., joyfully).

Verse 25

- **μόνῳ θεῷ σωτῆρι ἡμῶν διὰ Ἰησοῦ Χριστοῦ τοῦ κυρίου ἡμῶν** ("to the only God our Savior, through Jesus Christ our Lord") – μόνῳ θεῷ ("the only God") and σωτῆρι ("Savior") are datives in apposition to δυναμένῳ ("to Him who is able"). τοῦ κυρίου is a genitive in apposition to Ἰησοῦ Χριστοῦ.

- δόξα μεγαλωσύνη κράτος καὶ ἐξουσία πρὸ παντὸς τοῦ αἰῶνος καὶ νῦν καὶ εἰς πάντας τοὺς αἰῶνας, ἀμήν (*"be* glory, majesty, dominion and authority, before all time and now and forever. Amen.") – There is an ellipsis of the verb εἴη ("be" pres act opt 3rd sg εἰμί) or some similar verb.

//////////////

CHAPTER 5

THE ARTICLE & ADJECTIVE

GOING DEEPER

A few years ago, my family and I (Andreas) visited Westminster Abbey, the venerable cathedral that over the centuries has witnessed a large number of historic events. The Abbey has served as the coronation church since 1066 and is the final resting place of seventeen monarchs and of many other significant people in England's history. Toward the end of our visit, I noticed one of the less conspicuous burial places in the Abbey: a plaque bearing the name of Granville Sharp (1735–1813). In the larger world, Sharp is primarily known for his work opposing the slave trade; in fact, he was one of the first to campaign for its abolition. In scholarly circles, however, his fame rests on having formulated what has come to be known as the "Granville Sharp Rule."

In short, this rule asserts that if two or more singular substantives (except for personal names) are governed by a single article, the second and any subsequent substantives relate to or further describe the first. The major significance of Sharp's Rule pertains to several important christological passages in the NT which, if Sharp's Rule is valid, affirm the deity of Jesus. Thus, in Titus 2:13, Paul writes, "while we wait for the blessed hope and appearing of the glory of *our great God and Savior*, Jesus Christ" (προσδεχόμενοι τὴν μακαρίαν ἐλπίδα καὶ ἐπιφάνειαν τῆς δόξης **τοῦ μεγάλου θεοῦ καὶ σωτῆρος ἡμῶν** Ἰησοῦ Χριστοῦ). Over the centuries, there has been considerable discussion as to what Sharp's Rule is and whether or not it supports the above-cited identification of Jesus Christ as God.

J. Christopher Edwards, for example, has argued that "Jesus Christ" stands in apposition, not to "our great God and Savior," but to *the glory* of our great God and Savior," affirming that Jesus is the *glory* of God but not necessarily God himself.[1] However, Murray Harris, in a concise but compelling response, defended the traditional view, citing several major problems with Edwards's view.[2] Harris notes that it is highly unlikely that "Jesus Christ" affirms the entire phrase "the glory of our great God and Savior" rather than the more immediate antecedents, "great God and Savior." He also points out that while the title "Savior" is applied to Jesus elsewhere in the Letters to Timothy and Titus (2 Tim 1:10; Titus 1:4; 3:6), the title "glory of God" is not. Also, Harris notes that almost all grammarians and lexicographers, as well as many commentators on Titus and the majority of modern English translations, support the traditional rendering of Titus 2:13.

The deity of Jesus does not rest solely on the Granville Sharp Rule and the passages to which it may apply. For example, in John 20:28 Thomas is shown to worship Jesus with the words, "My Lord and my God!" There can be no question that the referent of "Lord" and "God" in this passage is Jesus. In fact, the passage seems to form an *inclusio* in John's Gospel together with the initial affirmations of Jesus's deity in 1:1 and 1:18. Other NT passages likewise affirm Jesus's deity both explicitly and implicitly.[3] This is not the place to make a sustained argument for the traditional understanding of Titus 2:13 or other similar passages, nor is this necessary, because such a case has already been ably presented.[4] Suffice it to say that not a little weight may rest on a mere article (or lack thereof) in the NT. Let this be your encouragement, therefore, at the beginning of this chapter, to make every effort to arrive at an accurate understanding of the Greek article as well as the Greek adjective.

CHAPTER OBJECTIVES

The purpose of this chapter is to cover the various uses of the Greek article and adjective. Both the article and the adjective sustain a close relationship with the noun which was treated in chapters 2–4. The main benefit you will derive from working through this chapter is that you will become acquainted with all the major categories of usage for the article and the adjective (and some minor ones). Understanding the essence of each category and grasping how these types of usage differ from one another will help you interpret the NT more accurately.

---

[1] J. Christopher Edwards, "The Christology of Titus 2:13 and 1 Timothy 2:5," *TynBul* 62 (2011): 143–47. Edwards makes his case primarily on the basis of the supposed similarity between Titus 2:13 and 1 Tim 2:5 and their shared OT background.

[2] Murray J. Harris, "A Brief Response to 'The Christology of Titus 2:13 and 1 Tim. 2:5' by J. Christopher Edwards," *TynBul* 62 (2011): 149–50.

[3] See, e.g., John 5:17–18; 10:30–33; Rom 9:5; Phil 2:5–8; Heb 1:8.

[4] See esp. Murray J. Harris, *Jesus as God: The New Testament Use of Theos in Reference to Jesus* (Grand Rapids: Baker, 1992; repr. Eugene, OR: Wipf & Stock, 2008), 173–85. See also the work by Wallace mentioned in the further discussion of the Granville Sharp Rule below and the interchange on Granville Sharp's Rule between Stanley E. Porter and Daniel B. Wallace in *JETS* 56 (2013): 79–106.

THE ARTICLE

Introduction to the Article

The article is used more than any other word in the NT—almost 20,000 times or one out of every seven words. Ironically, however, the article is also among the most misunderstood features of NT Greek, and there are still areas pertaining to the use of the article that require further research. Nevertheless, the presence or absence of the article is often significant for interpretation. As Wallace notes, the use of the article is "the crucial element to unlocking the meaning of scores of passages in the NT . . . there is no more important aspect of Greek grammar than the article to help shape our understanding of the thought and theology of the NT writers."[5]

The origin of the article can be traced back to the demonstrative pronoun: "That is, its original force was to *point out* something. It has largely kept the force of drawing attention to something."[6] Yet, contrary to popular misconceptions, the article's function is *not primarily to make something definite*,[7] although the article is used for that purpose. In fact, there are multiple ways in which a noun in Greek can be definite apart from the article, so that when the article is used when it need not be, it must be for some other purpose. The basic functions of the article are at least three:[8]

1. The most common aspect of the article is its ability to *conceptualize*, that is, it transforms a word or phrase into a concept. Adjectives, prepositional phrases, various verb forms such as present or past participles, and several other types of words can all be used substantively.

2. The article is regularly used to *identify*, that is, it distinguishes a particular substantive, pointing it out and separating it in some way. In so doing, the article distinguishes: (1) individuals from other individuals, (2) classes from other classes, and (3) qualities from other qualities.[9]

3. At times, the Greek article is also used to make a substantive *definite*. As mentioned, this does not mean that the article's basic function is to make a word definite; it does mean, however, that when an article *is* used, the term it modifies will necessarily be definite. This point bears elaborating on, as it may be confusing. A substantive with the article is always definite; however, the substantive can be definite without

---

[5] Wallace, 208.

[6] Wallace, 208, emphasis original.

[7] Cf. Porter: "The presence or absence of the article does not make a substantive definite or indefinite" (*Idioms*, 103). Contrary to Young, 55.

[8] See the discussion and use of these three categories in Wallace, 209–10 including Chart 17, "The Basic Forces of the Article."

[9] Robertson, 756–58.

the article as well. As a result, while substantives with the article are always definite, this is not the only or primary function of the article.

To summarize, the article *conceptualizes*, *identifies*, and *definitizes*.[10] However, care must be taken in interpreting the significance of the presence or absence of the article in a given instance.[11] The following schema may serve as the starting point for the most common article usage:[12]

SUBSTANTIVE	USE 1	USE 2
ARTICULAR	(a) Particular	(c) Generic
ANARTHROUS	(b) Non-particular	(d) Definite

When the article is used, the substantive may refer to a particular item or represent a category of items; when the article is not used, the substantive may refer to the non-particular (indefinite or qualitative) character of an item or to an individual item. Yet, as Porter cautions, "Matters of particularity and individuality are established not on the basis of whether the article is present, but on the basis of the wider context."[13] Robertson agrees: "It would have been very easy if the absence of the article in Greek always meant that the noun was indefinite, but . . . this is not the case. The anarthrous noun may *per se* be either definite or indefinite."[14]

In seeking to assign the use of the article to one of the following categories or subcategories, it will be important to keep in mind that the function of the article in a particular instance may encompass multiple categories. It will therefore be best to start by finding the most appropriate category and then looking to see if there are other categories that may be appropriate as well. In this regard, as mentioned, context will be an indispensable guide. The broad categories treated below are as follows: (1) the article with substantives, (2) the article functioning as a pronoun, (3) the absence of the article, and (4) special rules.[15]

---

[10] These terms are Wallace's; see Wallace, 210.

[11] For example, the article often serves to mark the syntactical function of a word or phrase, in which case it may not serve any of these three purposes. For example, the article can make a word or phrase an attributive modifier, help distinguish the subject from a predicate nominative, or identify the case of indeclinable nouns. For a detailed list of these functions, see Wallace, 238–43.

[12] Porter, *Idioms*, 104.

[13] Porter, *Idioms*, 104.

[14] Robertson, 796.

[15] Wallace (1996) makes a significant contribution to this area which has furthered our understanding of the Greek article. We will be following, with some adjustments, his clear and pedagogically effective approach. Our abbreviated discussion of this issue will be completed in the following 12 pages. Wallace, on the other hand, meticulously surveys the Greek article in 83 pages, and curious students are referred there for a fuller treatment of these matters.

WITH SUBSTANTIVES	Particular	Identification
		Par Excellence
		Monadic
		With Abstract Nouns
		Previous Reference
	Generic	
AS A PRONOUN	As Personal Pronoun	
	As Relative Pronoun	
	As Possessive Pronoun	
	As Demonstrative Pronoun	
	As Alternate Pronoun	
ABSENCE OF ARTICLE	Non-particular	Indefinite
		Qualitative
	Definite	
SPECIAL RULES	Granville Sharp Rule	
	Colwell's Rule	
	Apollonius's Canon	

The Article with Substantives

The article with substantives lies at the core of the NT use of the article. In such instances, the article particularizes a substantive or uses it generically. "The individualizing article particularizes, distinguishing otherwise similar objects; the generic (or categorical) article is used to distinguish one category of individuals from another."[16] It is essential to remember that the article can function with not just nouns, but virtually any part of speech. In other words, the article can take almost any non-substantive and make it function like a substantive. This includes adverbs, adjectives, participles, infinitives, prepositional phrases, particles, even entire clauses, statements, or quotations. As mentioned in the introduction, the role of the article in such instances is to conceptualize.

The Particularizing Article

The particularizing article serves to "identify or denote persons or things and to distinguish them from all others."[17] This is the article's basic function. The most important subcategories of the individualizing article include the following: (1) identification, (2) *par excellence*, (3) monadic (one-of-a-kind), (4) with abstract

---

[16] Wallace, 216.
[17] Brooks & Winbery, 73.

nouns, and (5) previous reference (anaphoric). The following examples illustrate these various instances of the individualizing article:[18]

1. *Identification:* ποῦ ἐστιν ὁ τεχθεὶς βασιλεὺς τῶν Ἰουδαίων ("Where is **he** who has been born King of the Jews?"; Matt 2:2). The article is used to identify the particular king of Jews, the one just born. This type of usage is frequently used to distinguish one individual or object from another.

2. *Par excellence:*[19] ὁ προφήτης εἶ σύ ("Are you **the** Prophet?"; John 1:21). The article identifies one who is in a class by himself. There were other prophets, but there was only one individual who qualified as "the Prophet" *par excellence* envisaged by Moses (cf. Deut 18:15, 18).

3. *Monadic ("one-of-a-kind"):* οὕτως γὰρ ἠγάπησεν ὁ θεὸς τὸν κόσμον, ὥστε **τὸν** υἱὸν **τὸν** μονογενῆ ἔδωκεν ("For God so loved the world, that he gave **his** only Son"; John 3:16 ESV). There is only one unique Son of God. The adjectival phrase highlights that this is not one son among many, but the one-of-a-kind son.[20]

4. *With abstract nouns:* ἡ σωτηρία ἐκ τῶν Ἰουδαίων ἐστίν ("salvation is from the Jews"; John 4:22). "Salvation" (σωτηρία) is an abstract noun. In such (common) instances where a Greek article is used in conjunction with an abstract noun, no article should be used in English translation.

5. *Previous reference (anaphoric):* πόθεν οὖν ἔχεις **τὸ** ὕδωρ τὸ ζῶν ("So where do You get **that** 'living water'?"; John 4:11 ESV). The article is pointing back to a substantive that was previously mentioned (note the translation with the demonstrative "that"). This includes individuals who were previously mentioned in a narrative.[21]

---

[18] For a more detailed listing of sub-categories of the individualizing article, along with examples, see Wallace, 216–27.

[19] Wallace, 222–23; BDF §263.

[20] "A substantive is monadic when it is the only such thing there is" (Brooks & Winbery, 73). As Wallace explains, the article *par excellence* points to an *extreme* class, while the monadic article points to a *unique* class. So "*the* Christ" is monadic, for there is only one Messiah, but "*the* Lord" is *par excellence* because there are many lords (223–24). Wallace elaborates, "When the articular substantive has an adjunct (such as an adjective or gen phrase), the entire expression often suggests a monadic notion. If no modifier is used, the article is typically *par excellence*" (224). Thus in Mark 9:47, "**the** kingdom of God" (ἡ βασιλεία τοῦ θεοῦ) is monadic, while in Matt 9:35, "**the** kingdom" (ἡ βασιλεία) is *par excellence*. Similarly, in this example, "God" is likely *par excellence*, since there are many "gods" (1 Cor 8:5), yet "world" is monadic, since there is only one world.

[21] In such instances, normally no article is used with the proper name when an individual is first introduced, while in subsequent references the anaphoric article is used to point backward to that individual. See, e.g., Acts 8:1: "**Saul** agreed with putting him to death" (Σαῦλος δὲ ἦν συνευδοκῶν τῇ ἀναιρέσει αὐτοῦ); and 9:1: "Now, **Saul** was still breathing threats and murder against the disciples of the Lord" (ὁ δὲ Σαῦλος ἔτι ἐμπνέων ἀπειλῆς καὶ φόνου εἰς τοὺς μαθητὰς τοῦ κυρίου); or Acts 10:1: "There was a man in Caesarea named **Cornelius**" (ἀνὴρ δέ τις ἐν Καισαρείᾳ ὀνόματι

The Generic Article

The generic use of the article is less frequent than the individualizing article, but it still occurs hundreds of times in the NT. As Wallace notes, "While the individualizing article distinguishes or identifies a particular object belonging to a larger class, the generic article distinguishes one class from another," that is, "[i]t categorizes rather than particularizes."[22] For example, a generic use of ὁ ἄνθρωπος would be "human as a class" or "humankind," with the article serving to distinguish this class from other classes such as the animal kingdom or the realm of angels (e.g., "the man on the street"). The generic article is often found in statements of universal principles (see examples below). It may at first seem that in instances where the generic article is used, the substantive is not definite, since the word "the" in English is not always included in the translation. This is not the case, however. The generic article is used to speak of a definite *class* in distinction from other classes, rather than a definite *individual* in distinction from other individuals. In English, the article is normally not used to indicate this distinction.[23]

- προσέχετε ἀπὸ **τῶν** ψευδοπροφητῶν (Matt 7:15 ESV)

  Beware of false prophets

  > Jesus does not have specific false prophets in mind but rather is warning about this particular class of people, false as opposed to true prophets.

- ἵνα πᾶς **ὁ** πιστεύων εἰς αὐτὸν μὴ ἀπόληται ἀλλ᾽ ἔχῃ ζωὴν αἰώνιον. (John 3:16)

  so that everyone **who** believes in him will not perish but have eternal life.

  > This is a statement speaking of people in general.

- δεῖ οὖν **τὸν** ἐπίσκοπον ἀνεπίλημπτον εἶναι (1 Tim 3:2)

  An overseer, therefore, must be above reproach

  > The generic article here indicates a representative from a particular class. Paul is saying that an overseer, as a specific class of office, must be above reproach. The plural can therefore be translated with "as a class" and the singular with "as a representative of a class."

The Article Functioning as a Pronoun

While the article is not a pronoun as such, as mentioned above, it traces its origin back to the pronoun and in certain situations may function like a pronoun. Specifically, it may function as a (1) personal pronoun, (2) relative pronoun, (3) possessive

---

Κορνήλιος); and 10:17: "the men who had been sent by **Cornelius** . . . stood at the gate" (οἱ ἄνδρες οἱ ἀπεσταλμένοι ὑπὸ **τοῦ Κορνηλίου** . . . ἐπέστησαν ἐπὶ τὸν πυλῶνα). See Black, 78.

[22] Wallace, 227.

[23] Basil L. Gildersleeve, *Syntax of Classical Greek from Homer to Demosthenes* (New York: American Book Company, 1900), 2:255; Robertson, 757–58; Wallace, 227–28.

pronoun, (4) demonstrative pronoun, or (5) alternate pronoun (this use is rare). The following examples will serve to illustrate the range of options.

1. ***Personal pronoun:*** οἱ δὲ εἶπαν αὐτῷ ("**They** told him"; Matt 2:5).

2. ***Relative pronoun:*** δοξάσωσιν τὸν πατέρα ὑμῶν **τὸν** ἐν τοῖς οὐρανοῖς ("give glory to your Father **who is** in heaven"; Matt 5:16 ESV).

3. ***Possessive pronoun:*** ὁ δὲ διεῖλεν αὐτοῖς **τὸν** βίον ("And he divided **his** property between them"; Luke 15:12 ESV). This is a relatively common use of the article in the New Testament.

4. ***Demonstrative pronoun:*** οἱ δὲ ἐν τῷ πλοίῳ προσεκύνησαν αὐτῷ ("Then **those** in the boat worshiped him"; Matt 14:33).

5. ***Alternate pronoun:*** καὶ αὐτὸς ἔδωκεν **τοὺς** μὲν ἀποστόλους, **τοὺς** δὲ προφήτας, **τοὺς** δὲ εὐαγγελιστάς, **τοὺς** δὲ ποιμένας καὶ διδασκάλους ("And He gave **some** *as* apostles, and **some** *as* prophets, and **some** *as* evangelists, and **some** *as* pastors and teachers"; Eph 4:11 NASB).

The Absence of the Article

As noted earlier, the primary function of the article is not to make a substantive definite. Similarly, the *absence* of the article does not necessarily mean that a substantive is *indefinite*. If there is no article, the noun may still be definite (though it may not be), depending on syntactical and contextual indicators. There are essentially three possibilities when the article is absent: (1) indefinite substantive, (2) qualitative substantive, or (3) definite substantive.[24]

In the first instance, that of an *indefinite* substantive, the noun is indefinite when it does not refer to a particular object but merely speaks of it as a class.[25] Mark 3:9 may serve as an example: "Then he told his disciples to have **a small boat** ready for him" (καὶ εἶπεν τοῖς μαθηταῖς αὐτοῦ ἵνα **πλοιάριον** προσκαρτερῇ αὐτῷ). Nothing is mentioned to single this boat out specifically from any others.

In the second type of use, that of a *qualitative* substantive, the focus is on what *kind* of object it is. As mentioned, the absence of the article may indicate focus on the *quality*, rather than *particularity*, of a given substantive.[26] The qualitative (anarthrous, i.e., article-less) use is like the articular generic noun in that it focuses on traits characteristic of a certain *kind* or *class*. However, whereas the generic noun can refer to a group, the qualitative use most often refers to a single

---

[24] Wallace, 243.

[25] Young, 68.

[26] Porter, *Idioms*, 105. See also Young, who comments, "When the author wants to focus on the quality, character, nature, or class of the noun, he will omit the article" (68). Likewise, Zerwick notes, "The omission of the article shows that the speaker regards the person or thing not so much as this or that person or thing, but rather as *such* a person or thing, i.e., regards not the individual but rather its nature or quality" (*Biblical Greek*, 55).

individual.[27] For example, consider John 1:14, which says that Jesus was "full of **grace** and **truth**" (πλήρης **χάριτος** καὶ **ἀληθείας**). The absence of the article indicates a focus on Jesus's quality or essence.

The third possibility when the article is absent is that of a *definite* substantive. In such cases, emphasis is placed on individual identity, and the substantive is particularized or specified even though it lacks the article.[28] When the substantive lacks the article, context is the only way to determine whether the author intends the reference to be definite or not. The most important and common instances where anarthrous nouns are definite are: (1) proper names, (2) prepositional objects, (3) predicate nominatives, and (4) abstract nouns.[29]

1. *Proper name:* **Παῦλος** καὶ **Σιλᾶς** προσευχόμενοι ὕμνουν τὸν θεόν ("**Paul** and **Silas** were praying and singing hymns to God"; Acts 16:25). Proper names are regularly, though not always, anarthrous.[30]

2. *Prepositional object:* χαίρετε ἐν **κυρίῳ** πάντοτε ("Rejoice in **the Lord** always"; Phil 4:4). The preposition ἐν helps render κυρίῳ definite apart from the article.

3. *Predicate nominative:* εἶπεν γὰρ ὅτι θεοῦ εἰμι **υἱός** ("For he said, 'I am **the Son** of God.'"; Matt 27:43 ESV). In context, it is clear that the charge was that Jesus claimed to be "the" (not merely "a") Son of God.

4. *Abstract noun:* ἡμεῖς δὲ ἡμέρας ὄντες νήφωμεν ἐνδυσάμενοι . . . περικεφαλαίαν **ἐλπίδα** σωτηρίας ("But since we belong to the day, let us be sober, having put on . . . for a helmet **the hope** of salvation"; 1 Thess 5:8 ESV). The noun ἐλπίδα is anarthrous but not indefinite.

Special Rules

There are three special rules pertaining to the use of the Greek article that need to be discussed to round out the treatment above: (1) the Granville Sharp Rule, (2) Colwell's Rule, and (3) Apollonius's Canon.

Granville Sharp Rule

The Granville Sharp Rule describes the relationship between a series of substantives joined by καί and governed by a single article. Sharp presented the rule as follows:

---

[27] Wallace, 244.

[28] See Porter, *Idioms*, 105; Wallace, 245.

[29] For additional examples of categories when anarthrous nouns can be definite, see Wallace, 245–54.

[30] For extended discussions of the use of the article with proper names, see Robertson, 759–61; BDF 135–36 (§260). In short, proper names do not require the article and do not usually take the article in the NT, but they may be articular to indicate a particular type of identification, such as previous reference. For example, in Acts 9:1 the reference to Saul is articular, pointing back to the anarthrous references to Saul in Acts 7:58; 8:1, 3.

When the copulative καὶ connects two nouns of the same case, [viz. nouns (either substantive or adjective, or participles) of personal description respecting office, dignity, affinity, or connection, and attributes, properties, or qualities, good or ill,] if the article ὁ, or any of its cases, precedes the first of the said nouns or participles, and is not repeated before the second noun or participle, the latter always relates to the same person that is expressed or described by the first noun or participle: *i.e., it denotes a further description of the first-named person. . . .*[31]

The rule has three important qualifications that must be met for each substantive: they must be (1) singular, (2) personal,[32] and (3) non-proper.[33] To simplify, Sharp's rule states that when a single article governs two singular, personal, non-proper substantives of the same case that are joined by καὶ, they refer to the same person. For example, in 2 Peter 1:11, "For in this way, entry into the eternal kingdom of **our Lord and Savior** Jesus Christ will be richly provided to you" (οὕτως γὰρ πλουσίως ἐπιχορηγηθήσεται ὑμῖν ἡ εἴσοδος εἰς τὴν αἰώνιον βασιλείαν **τοῦ κυρίου ἡμῶν καὶ σωτῆρος** Ἰησοῦ Χριστοῦ), the singular article τοῦ governs κυρίου and σωτῆρος, both of which are singular, personal, and non-proper nouns. They together therefore modify Ἰησοῦ Χριστοῦ, indicating that Jesus is Lord and Savior.

Conversely, the following example from John 7:45 does not qualify, because the nouns are in the plural and also because they involve proper names: "Then the officers came to **the chief priests and Pharisees**" (ESV) (ἦλθον οὖν οἱ ὑπηρέται πρὸς **τοὺς ἀρχιερεῖς καὶ Φαρισαίους**). Neither does the following example from Matt 17:1 constitute an instance of the Granville Sharp Rule because, again, it involves proper names: "Jesus took **Peter, James, and** his brother **John**" (παραλαμβάνει ὁ Ἰησοῦς **τὸν Πέτρον καὶ Ἰάκωβον καὶ Ἰωάννην** τὸν ἀδελφὸν αὐτοῦ). Otherwise, Peter, James, and John would be the same person![34]

By contrast, in other passages such as Acts 26:30, the different persons or groups mentioned all have the article: "So **the** king, **the** governor, Bernice, and those sitting with them got up" (ἀνέστη τε ὁ βασιλεὺς καὶ ὁ ἡγεμὼν ἥ τε Βερνίκη καὶ οἱ συγκαθήμενοι αὐτοῖς). Here the king and the governor, as well as of course Bernice and those sitting with them, are separate people, so they all have the article. While Bernice is a proper name and "those sitting with them" is plural, "the king" and "the governor" both are nouns in the singular (not proper names), but the presence of the article preceding both nouns keeps them separate.

---

[31] Granville Sharp, *Remarks on the Uses of the Definite Article in the Greek Text of the New Testament, Containing Many New Proofs of the Divinity of Christ, from Passages which Are Wrongly Translated in the Common English Version,* 3rd ed. (London: C. and W. Galabin, 1803), 3 (emphasis original).

[32] That is, they must refer to individuals.

[33] Wallace, 271–72.

[34] This does not mean that the single article governing the nouns is not important. Wallace includes a detailed discussion of how the Granville Sharp construction impacts the interpretation of passages where these criteria are not met (277–90).

The two most significant NT passages are Titus 2:13: "while we wait for the blessed hope and appearing of the glory of <u>our great God and Savior</u>, Jesus Christ" (προσδεχόμενοι τὴν μακαρίαν ἐλπίδα καὶ ἐπιφάνειαν τῆς δόξης <u>τοῦ μεγάλου θεοῦ καὶ σωτῆρος ἡμῶν</u> Ἰησοῦ Χριστοῦ) and 2 Pet 1:1: "through the righteousness of our God and Savior Jesus Christ" (ἐν δικαιοσύνῃ <u>τοῦ θεοῦ ἡμῶν καὶ σωτῆρος</u> Ἰησοῦ Χριστοῦ). In both passages, one written by Paul, the other by Peter, there is one article followed by a singular, personal, non-proper noun, καί, and a second singular, personal, non-proper noun, plus the phrase "Jesus Christ" in apposition. We have already discussed Titus 2:13 in the introduction above.

Colwell's Rule

According to Colwell's Rule, a definite predicate nominative does not usually take the article when preceding the copula (linking verb).[35] For example, John 1:1 reads, "In the beginning was the Word, and the Word was with God, and **the Word was God**" (ἐν ἀρχῇ ἦν ὁ λόγος, καὶ ὁ λόγος ἦν πρὸς τὸν θεόν, καὶ **θεὸς ἦν ὁ λόγος**). In this passage, the anarthrous predicate nominative θεός precedes the copula ἦν. In context, this means neither that the Word and God are equated nor that the Word is "a" god (indefinite) but that the Word is essentially (quality) God.

In Matt 27:42, we read, "He is **the King** of Israel" (βασιλεὺς Ἰσραήλ ἐστιν). The subject "he" is implicit in the verb ἐστιν, and the preceding predicate nominative βασιλεύς lacks the article while being definite as indicated by the context. Similarly, Heb 9:15 refers to Jesus, saying, "He is **the mediator** of a new covenant" (διαθήκης καινῆς **μεσίτης** ἐστίν). The predicate nominative μεσίτης precedes the copula and is definite by context. Fitting Colwell's rule, it is also anarthrous. On the other hand, in Mark 6:3, "Isn't this the **carpenter**?" (οὐχ οὗτός ἐστιν ὁ **τέκτων**;), the predicate nominative (not preceding the copula) has the article, but the demonstrative pronoun is the subject.

A final instructive set of examples comes from John 8:12 and 9:5. Both passages are virtually identical in content, identifying Jesus as "the light of the world," but in the former passage, the wording is ἐγώ εἰμι τὸ φῶς τοῦ κόσμου, while in the latter passage it is φῶς εἰμι τοῦ κόσμου. This comparison shows that, as in John 9:5, a definite predicate nominative does not usually take the article when *preceding* the linking verb (Colwell's Rule), though when it *follows* the linking verb, it usually does (cf. John 8:12).

Apollonius's Canon

According to Apollonius's Canon (named after Apollonius Dyscolus, a second-century Greek grammarian), when two nouns are in a genitive construction, both the head noun and the noun in the genitive case either have or lack the article. There is little discernible difference between these two constructions, and the article carries little semantic weight since the expression can be definite even when

---

[35] See E. C. Colwell, "A Definite Rule for the Use of the Article in the Greek New Testament," *JBL* 52 (1933): 12–21. Colwell demonstrated that a definite predicate nominative preceding the copula occurs without the article about 87 percent of the time. See the discussion in Wallace, 256–70.

articles are lacking. For example, "the Word of God" would most likely be expressed as either ὁ λόγος τοῦ θεοῦ (John 10:35) or λόγος θεοῦ (1 Pet 1:23)—both of which mean "the Word of God" with little discernible difference—but not λόγος τοῦ θεοῦ or ὁ λόγος θεοῦ. However, while Apollonius's Canon generally holds true, it is not without exceptions.[36]

The corollary to this rule (Apollonius's Corollary) is that when both nouns lack the article, they normally share the same semantic force.[37] In other words, if both nouns lack the article and it can be determined that one of them is definite, it follows that the other—and thus the entire expression—is definite as well. For example, in Matt 12:42, "**The** queen of **the** South will rise up" (ESV) (βασίλισσα νότου ἐγερθήσεται), "**the**" is the proper way to construe the head noun, since the reference to the "south" is definite, referring to the land of Sheba (see 1 Kgs 10:1; 2 Chr 9:1) and therefore the entire phrase is definite as well. In Luke 4:18, "The Spirit of the Lord is on me" (πνεῦμα κυρίου ἐπ' ἐμέ), likewise, the proper rendering is "**the** Spirit of **the** Lord," not "*a* spirit of *a* Lord." Finally, in 2 Cor 6:2, "now is the day of salvation" (ἰδοὺ νῦν ἡμέρα σωτηρίας), reference is made to "**the** day of salvation," not "*a* day of *a* salvation."

THE ADJECTIVE

Introduction to the Adjective

The word "adjective" comes from a Latin word meaning "to add something." The main function of the adjective is that of qualifying the noun or substantive to which it is related by distinguishing it from other nouns or by further describing it.[38] As such, the adjective agrees with the term it modifies in gender, case, and number. Watching for this agreement is important and can help prevent us from misconstruing the syntax of a given passage of Scripture. Consider, for example, the KJV translation of Matt 26:27, narrating the institution of the Lord's Supper: "Drink ye **all** of it" (πίετε ἐξ αὐτοῦ **πάντες**), which could be taken to mean, "Drink the entire contents of the *cup*." However, because the adjective "all" (πάντες) is nominative masculine plural, it must be referring to Jesus's *disciples* (all of whom are supposed to drink from the communal cup), not the cup ("it" [αὐτοῦ], which is in the genitive singular).[39]

In terms of the history of the Greek language, there is evidence to suggest that nouns and adjectives share a common origin, which would explain similarities

---

[36] S. D. Hull, "Exceptions to Apollonius' Canon in the New Testament: A Grammatical Study," *TrinJ* 7 (1986): 3–16.

[37] David W. Hedges, "Apollonius' Canon and Anarthrous Constructions in Pauline Literature: An Hypothesis" (M.Div. thesis, Grace Theological Seminary, 1983).

[38] Interestingly, the Greek language treats numbers as adjectives as well in that they describe a noun in terms of its quantity. See BDF, 34–35 (§63); Black, 63; and especially Robertson, 671–75.

[39] The example is from Young, 80.

between them in terms of declension. While there are certain affinities between the adjective and the genitive case in that both are used to describe a given noun, historically, it appears that the use of the adjective grew out of the substantive use and is not simply a variation of the genitive.[40] An example of a phrase where a noun functions adjectivally in the NT is the description of God as "Lord Almighty" (κύριος παντοκράτωρ), where the noun "Almighty" is used like an adjective. This is similar to English usage, where an expression such as "church member" uses the word "church" in a quasi-adjectival manner.

In this section, we will present the major uses of the adjective in the NT in two basic categories: (1) the general use of the adjective, whether (a) predicate, (b) attributive, (c) substantival, or (d) adverbial; and (2) the use of the adjective to show kind/degree, which includes adjectives that are (a) positive, (b) comparative, (c) superlative, and (d) elative, plus (e) special cases or irregularities. When we get to those irregularities—such as the use of the positive for the comparative or the superlative, or the use of the comparative for the superlative—you may ask yourself why Greek speakers and writers could not just simply stick to their own rules. Remember, though, that popular usage has its own logic, and in any case it is ultimately pointless to argue or whine about Greek usage—it is much better (and efficient!) to accept what we actually find in the pages of the NT and not try to understand the thinking behind a given phenomenon. What is more, Greek was a living language, and its rules changed over time, just like any language. After all, at times we like to bend the rules in English, too, such as if a son says to his father that he is the "bestest" father in the world. While such use of the superlative is technically incorrect, we certainly know what is meant.

General Use of the Adjective

The general use of the Greek adjective falls into the following four major categories: (1) predicate (modifying a copulative or "being" verb), (2) attributive (this is the function we typically associate with an adjective), (3) substantival (functioning as a noun), and (4) adverbial (used like an adverb). While the third and fourth categories are fairly straightforward, it is not as easy to distinguish between attributive and predicate adjectives, at least in certain contexts. This is the case especially since the adjective may or may not have the article and since in some predicate constructions the verb is omitted and merely implicit. The following chart lays out the options:[41]

---

[40] Robertson, 650–51.
[41] See Wallace, 309.

ARTICULAR ADJECTIVAL CONSTRUCTIONS			
	1ST POSITION	2ND POSITION	3RD POSITION
PREDICATE	Adjective-Article-Noun (ἀγαθὸς ὁ ἄνθρωπος = "the man is **good**")	Article-Noun-Adjective (ὁ ἄνθρωπος ἀγαθός = "the man is **good**")	None
ATTRIBUTIVE	Article-Adjective-Noun (ὁ ἀγαθὸς ἄνθρωπος = "the **good** man")	Article-Noun-Article-Adjective (ὁ ἄνθρωπος ὁ ἀγαθός = "the **good** man")	Noun-Article-Adjective (ἄνθρωπος ὁ ἀγαθός = "the **good** man")

ANARTHROUS ADJECTIVAL CONSTRUCTIONS			
	1ST POSITION	2ND POSITION	4TH POSITION[a]
PREDICATE	Adjective-Noun (ἀγαθὸς ἄνθρωπος = "a man is **good**")	Noun-Adjective (ἄνθρωπος ἀγαθός = "a man is **good**")	None
ATTRIBUTIVE	Adjective-Noun (ἀγαθὸς ἄνθρωπος = "a **good** man")	None	Noun-Adjective (ἄνθρωπος ἀγαθός = "a **good** man")

[a]The reason "fourth position" is used is that there is no article at all in the construction, whereas the first through third attributive positions all have the article.

When it comes to distinguishing the attributive from the predicate use, the following rule applies: *when the adjective is immediately preceded by the article, it is always attributive.*[42] However, the converse does not necessarily follow: if an adjective is *not* preceded by the article, this does *not* necessarily mean it is used predicatively (see anarthrous attributive 1st position). Nevertheless—our second axiom—*when the noun is preceded by the article and the adjective is not, the adjective is always used predicatively* (see articular predicate 1st and 2nd position).

As the above chart makes clear, in Greek there is more than one way to say "the (or a) good man." There are three types of articular attributive constructions—(1) article-adjective-noun (equivalent to English usage); (2) article-noun-article-adjective (literally, "the man, the good [one]"); and (3) noun-article-adjective (literally, "man, the good [one]")—as well as two types of anarthrous (article-less) attributive constructions: (1) adjective-noun, and (2) noun-adjective.

While articular constructions (2) and (3) look awkward for the native English speaker, they clearly illustrate the function of the adjective as further describing the noun and as distinguishing it from other nouns.[43] To use a biblical example, when Jesus identifies himself as "the good shepherd" (ὁ ποιμὴν ὁ καλός; John

---

[42] Of course an articular adjective could be substantival as well. This rule only applies to determining the relationship of adjectives to nouns.

[43] Conventional wisdom has it that the article-adjective-noun construction puts an emphasis on the adjective while the second construction, article-noun-article-adjective, stresses the noun (see, e.g., Wallace, 306, citing Robertson, 776; Young, 81). However, this kind of emphasis is best corroborated from the context rather than inferred from the type of construction alone.

10:11; 2nd position), he both describes himself not merely as a shepherd, but as one who is good, and distinguishes himself from the "hired hands" (i.e., the Jewish leaders) who care nothing for the "sheep" (i.e., God's people: cf. vv. 1–18).

Finally, as you can see in the second chart above (labeled "Anarthrous Adjectival Constructions"), the patterns adjective-noun or noun-adjective, by themselves, are inconclusive; they can be either attributive or predicate (in which the "being verb" would be merely implied). In such instances, context must decide. If you find this array of options bewildering, take heart: not all of these options are equally common—in fact, some of them are rather rare—and context will almost always enable you to render a confident verdict as to the likely translation.

Predicate Use

In the predicate use of the adjective, a quality is predicated about the subject, frequently by way of a linking verb (e.g., Matt 5:3: "**blessed** [are] the poor in spirit"; **μακάριοι** οἱ πτωχοὶ τῷ πνεύματι). As noted above, predicate adjectives are never immediately preceded by the article. A verb, usually a copulative (linking) verb, is used to join a noun or substantive to an adjective which predicates or ascribes a quality to that term. In some instances, the verb is made explicit, as in John 4:11: "the well is **deep**" (τὸ φρέαρ ἐστὶν **βαθύ**). In other cases, the verb is merely implied, as in Mark 9:50: "Salt is **good**" (**καλὸν** τὸ ἅλας). To keep things a bit simpler, in the examples below we will treat uses with or without verbs jointly and focus primarily on whether or not a given instance includes or does not include the article (and in which order the article, the adjective, and the noun are found).

With the Article

ARTICULAR ADJECTIVAL CONSTRUCTIONS			
	1ST POSITION	2ND POSITION	3RD POSITION
PREDICATE	Adjective-Article-Noun (ἀγαθὸς ὁ ἄνθρωπος = "the man is **good**")	Article-Noun-Adjective (ὁ ἄνθρωπος **ἀγαθός** = "the man is **good**")	None

Note that in articular predicate constructions of the adjective, there is an article preceding the noun, though not the adjective (cf. articular attributive constructions of the adjective above).

First Position (Adjective-Article-Noun):

- τί στενὴ <u>ἡ πύλη</u> (Matt 7:14)

  How **narrow** is <u>the gate</u>

- πιστὸς <u>ὁ θεός</u> (1 Cor 1:9)

  <u>God</u> is **faithful**

    See 1 Cor 10:13; 2 Cor 1:18.

Second Position (Article-Noun-Adjective):

- <u>ὁ</u> μὲν <u>θερισμὸς</u> **πολύς**, <u>οἱ</u> δὲ <u>ἐργάται</u> **ὀλίγοι** (Matt 9:37)

  <u>The harvest</u> is **abundant**, but <u>the workers</u> are **few**

    This passage features two juxtaposed second predicate position constructions.

- <u>ὁ</u> μὲν <u>νόμος</u> **ἅγιος** καὶ <u>ἡ ἐντολὴ</u> **ἁγία** καὶ **δικαία** καὶ **ἀγαθή** (Rom 7:12)

  So then, <u>the law</u> is **holy**, and <u>the commandment</u> is **holy** and **just** and **good**

    This passage also has two sets of predicate position constructions, and the second features three adjectives.

Without the Article

ANARTHROUS ADJECTIVAL CONSTRUCTIONS			
	1ST POSITION	**2ND POSITION**	**3RD POSITION**
PREDICATE	Adjective-Noun (**ἀγαθὸς** ἄνθρωπος = "a man is **good**")	Noun-Adjective (ἄνθρωπος **ἀγαθός** = "a man is **good**")	None

As mentioned above, anarthrous predicate constructions of the adjective (whether adjective-noun or noun-adjective) can be distinguished from anarthrous attributive constructions (featured above) only by means of context.

First Position (Adjective-Noun):

- **μακάριος** <u>ἀνὴρ</u> οὗ οὐ μὴ λογίσηται κύριος ἁμαρτίαν (Rom 4:8)

  blessed is the <u>man</u> against whom the Lord will not count his sin (ESV)

    Or, "Blessed is (a) man" (an idiom frequently found in Wisdom literature, such as in Ps 1:1).

- εἰ **ὅλον** <u>ἀκοή</u>, ποῦ ἡ ὄσφρησις; (1 Cor 12:17)

  If the **whole** body were <u>an ear</u>, where would the sense of smell be?

Second Position (Noun-Adjective):

- καὶ ἤδη <u>ὥρα</u> **πολλή** (Mark 6:35)

  and the <u>hour</u> is now **late** (ESV)

- ὅτι <u>οὗτος ὁ υἱός</u> μου **νεκρὸς** ἦν (Luke 15:24)

  because <u>this son</u> of mine was **dead**

  The predicate construction is made explicit by the use of εἰμί.

Attributive Use

In the attributive use, an adjective ascribes a particular quality to a noun or substantive. As we have seen in our discussion above, there are three articular and two non-articular (anarthrous) adjectival constructions. In each instance, the adjective modifies the noun or substantive in such a way that it further describes or distinguishes the substantive by "attributing" a given quality to it. We will give a few examples for each construction.

With the Article

The three articular constructions are: (1) article-adjective-noun, (2) article-noun-article-adjective, and (3) noun-article-adjective. While the first two constructions are frequent in the NT, the third one is rare.

ARTICULAR ADJECTIVAL CONSTRUCTIONS		
1ST POSITION	2ND POSITION	3RD POSITION
Article-Adjective-Noun (ὁ **ἀγαθὸς** ἄνθρωπος = "the **good** man")	Article-Noun-Article-Adjective (ὁ ἄνθρωπος ὁ **ἀγαθός** = "the **good** man")	Noun-Article-Adjective (ἄνθρωπος ὁ **ἀγαθός** = "the **good** man")

First Position (Article-Adjective-Noun):

- οἶδα ὅτι ἀναστήσεται ἐν τῇ ἀναστάσει ἐν <u>τῇ</u> **ἐσχάτῃ** <u>ἡμέρᾳ</u> (John 11:24)

  I know that he will rise again in the resurrection at <u>the</u> **last** <u>day</u>

- οὗτός ἐστιν <u>ὁ</u> **ἀληθινὸς** <u>θεὸς</u> καὶ ζωὴ αἰώνιος (1 John 5:20)

  He is <u>the</u> **true** <u>God</u> and eternal life

Second Position (Article-Noun-Article-Adjective):

- ἄλλα δὲ ἔπεσεν ἐπὶ <u>τὴν γῆν</u> τὴν **καλήν** (Matt 13:8)

  Still other seed fell on **good** <u>ground</u>

- <u>τὸ φῶς</u> τὸ **ἀληθινὸν** ὃ φωτίζει πάντα ἄνθρωπον (John 1:9)

  The **true** <u>light</u>, which enlightens everyone (ESV)

Third Position (Noun-Article-Adjective):

- καὶ καταλιπὼν τὴν Ναζαρὰ ἐλθὼν κατῴκησεν εἰς <u>Καφαρναοὺμ τὴν</u> **παραθαλασσίαν** (Matt 4:13)

  He left Nazareth and went to live in <u>Capernaum</u> **by the sea**

- ἐξενέγκατε <u>στολὴν τὴν</u> **πρώτην** καὶ ἐνδύσατε αὐτόν (Luke 15:22)

  Bring out <u>the</u> **best** <u>robe</u> and put it on him

  Literally, "the robe—the best one."

Without the Article

The anarthrous constructions are: (1) adjective-noun, or (2) noun-adjective. There are close to 2,400 occurrences of this kind of construction in the NT.[44] You will need to determine the type of adjectival use from the context.[45]

ANARTHROUS ADJECTIVAL CONSTRUCTIONS		
1ST POSITION	2ND POSITION	4TH POSITION
Adjective-Noun (**ἀγαθὸς** ἄνθρωπος = "a **good** man")	None	Noun-Adjective (ἄνθρωπος **ἀγαθός** = "a **good** man")

First Position (Adjective-Noun):

- **πολλῶν** <u>στρουθίων</u> διαφέρετε ὑμεῖς (Matt 10:31)

  you are worth more than **many** <u>sparrows</u>

- ἀλλὰ **τιμίῳ** <u>αἵματι</u> [Χριστοῦ] (1 Pet 1:19)

  but with the **precious** <u>blood</u> of Christ

Fourth Position (Noun-Adjective):

- ἐχάρησαν <u>χαρὰν</u> **μεγάλην** σφόδρα (Matt 2:10)

  they rejoiced exceedingly with **great** <u>joy</u> (NASB)

- ἵνα πᾶς ὁ πιστεύων ἐν αὐτῷ ἔχῃ <u>ζωὴν</u> **αἰώνιον** (John 3:15)

  so that everyone who believes in him will have **eternal** <u>life</u>

---

[44] Wallace, 309.
[45] For guidelines, see Wallace, 311–12.

Substantival Use

At times the adjective is used substantivally, that is, it stands on its own and does not modify a noun adjectivally. In terms of form, the adjective takes on the characteristics of a noun and will usually have the article. It will match the noun it is replacing in gender and number. In terms of function, the adjective takes the place of a noun or substantive in a given phrase. Its case is determined by its function in the clause. The substantival use of the adjective is extremely frequent in the NT.

- ὅτι τὸν ἥλιον αὐτοῦ ἀνατέλλει ἐπὶ **πονηροὺς** καὶ **ἀγαθοὺς** καὶ βρέχει ἐπὶ **δικαίους** καὶ **ἀδίκους** (Matt 5:45)

  For he causes his sun to rise on **the evil** and **the good**, and sends rain on **the righteous** and **the unrighteous**

  Anarthrous examples.

- καὶ ἡμεῖς πεπιστεύκαμεν καὶ ἐγνώκαμεν ὅτι σὺ εἶ **ὁ ἅγιος** τοῦ θεοῦ (John 6:69)

  We have believed and have come to know that You are **the Holy One** of God! (NASB)[46]

Adverbial Use

Frequently, an adjective will function adverbially rather than modifying a substantive. In such cases, the adjective is often (though not always) in the accusative case and in the neuter gender. This type of usage pertains to a limited number of Greek words (such as πρῶτον or μόνον) and has a certain affinity with the "accusative of respect" or "accusative of time."[47]

- καὶ προελθὼν **μικρὸν** ἔπεσεν ἐπὶ πρόσωπον αὐτοῦ (Matt 26:39)

  Going a **little farther**, he fell facedown

- ἐκέλευσεν ἔξω **βραχὺ** τοὺς ἀνθρώπους (Acts 5:34)

  [he] ordered the men to be taken outside **for a little while**[48]

---

[46] For other examples of the substantival use of the adjective, see Matt 5:3; 6:13; 7:11; 11:5; Mark 3:14; Luke 6:45; John 6:71; Acts 17:21; Rom 1:14, 17; 5:7, 15; 8:33; 9:22; 1 Cor 1:25; 6:2, 15; 13:10; Col 3:12; 1 Tim 1:15; 6:17; Heb 10:9; 1 John 2:20; 5:20; 3 John 11.

[47] Porter, *Idioms*, 121–22. There are some parallels in colloquial English, such as "I'm good," or "Come quick!" (Wallace, 29; Robertson, 659).

[48] For more examples of the adverbial use of the adjective, see Matt 5:24; 6:33; 9:14; 15:16; Mark 1:19; 6:31; 12:27; Luke 9:36; 17:25; John 1:41; 4:18; 10:40; 13:9, 33; 16:19; Acts 7:12; 27:20; 2 Cor 13:11; Gal 1:23; 6:17; Eph 3:3; 1 Pet 1:6.

THE USE OF THE ADJECTIVE TO SHOW KIND/DEGREE

Comparison is "the method by which an adjective expresses a greater or lesser degree of the same quality."[49] In terms of form, adjectives ending in -τερος or -ιων are comparative, and those ending in -τατος or -ιστος are superlative. Some of the most common comparative and superlative adjectives use alternate forms (similar to: good → better → best): μικρός ("small") → ἐλάχιστος ("smallest"); κακός ("bad") → χείρων ("worse"); καλός ("good") → κάλλιων ("better") → κράτιστος ("best"). As a rule, comparative adjectives compare two items (e.g., he is taller than she) while superlative adjectives compare more than two (he is the tallest of all).[50]

POSITIVE	COMPARATIVE	SUPERLATIVE
wise	wiser	wisest
σοφός	σοφώτερος	σοφώτατος

For example, consider Acts 17:21: "Now all the Athenians and the foreigners residing there spent their time on nothing else but telling or hearing something **new**" (Ἀθηναῖοι δὲ πάντες καὶ οἱ ἐπιδημοῦντες ξένοι εἰς οὐδὲν ἕτερον ηὐκαίρουν ἢ λέγειν τι ἢ ἀκούειν τι **καινότερον**). Is the comparative adjective καινότερον here to be translated as a positive adjective ("new") as in the CSB? Or is the reference to listening to something "newer"? Or to listening to the "newest thing"?[51] In such instances, the interpreter must weigh contextual factors carefully in determining the force of the adjective.

Positive

The positive adjective "focuses on the properties of a noun in terms of *kind*, not degree."[52] For example, "the beautiful girl" identifies the girl as beautiful in and of herself without any indication as to whether she is more beautiful than others. There are over 7,000 positive adjectives in the NT. Per the discussion above, the use of positive adjectives may be attributive, predicate, substantival, or adverbial.

- καὶ ἐν τῷ γενέσθαι τὴν φωνὴν εὑρέθη Ἰησοῦς **μόνος** (Luke 9:36)

  And when the voice had spoken, Jesus was found **alone** (NASB)

  This is an example of the adverbial use of the positive adjective.

---

[49] Black, 61.
[50] Young, 83.
[51] The example is provided by Porter, *Idioms*, 123.
[52] Wallace, 296.

- οἴδαμεν γὰρ ὅτι ὁ νόμος **πνευματικός** ἐστιν (Rom 7:14)

  we know that the law is **spiritual**

  > This is an example of the predicate adjective used with the copulative verb (ἐστιν).

- ἡ **τελεία** ἀγάπη ἔξω βάλλει (1 John 4:18)

  perfect love drives out fear

  > This is an example of a positive adjective used in the attributive position.

Comparative

The comparative adjective compares two persons or objects with regard to their possession of a given attribute, focusing "on the properties of a noun in terms of *degree*, not kind."[53] For example, in the parable of the laborers in the vineyard (Matt 20:1–16), when the time comes for the vineyard owner to pay the group of laborers who were called first, "they assumed they would get **more**" (ἐνόμισαν ὅτι **πλεῖον** λήμψονται; Matt 20:10). Πλεῖον is the comparative of πολύς, "many, much." The workers based their expectation of payment in relation to what that the other laborers had been paid; it was a comparison of degree. Most commonly, the comparison is explicit, in which case the adjective is followed by (1) a genitive of comparison (e.g., John 14:28: "the Father is greater **than I**", ὁ πατὴρ μείζων **μού** ἐστιν) or (2) the particle ἤ with the new things compared expressed in the same case forms ("than"; e.g., 1 John 4:4: "greater is the one in you **than** the one who is in the world", μείζων ἐστὶν ὁ ἐν ὑμῖν **ἤ** ὁ ἐν τῷ κόσμῳ). At other times, the comparative adjective is used substantivally, merely implying the comparison.[54] There are close to 200 comparative adjectives in the NT.

There are two ways to form a comparative in Greek: (1) a third declension ending on a comparative noun: μείζων ("greater"), πλέον ("more"), χείρων ("worse"), κρεῖσσον ("better"), κρείττων ("better"); (2) adding -τερος to a positive degree adjective: ἀσθενής ("weak") → ἀσθενέστερος ("weaker"), ἰσχυρός ("strong") → ἰσχυρότερος ("stronger"), μικρός ("small") → μικρότερος ("smaller"), πρέσβυς ("old") → πρεσβύτερος ("older").

- ἔρχεται ὁ **ἰσχυρότερός** μου ὀπίσω μου (Mark 1:7)

  One who is **more powerful** than I am is coming after me

  > This is an example of the adjective used substantivally; the word "one" is implied. μου is a genitive of comparison.

---

[53] Wallace, 296.
[54] Or, less frequently, παρά or ὑπέρ; Wallace, 299.

- τί γάρ ἐστιν **εὐκοπώτερον**, εἰπεῖν· ἀφίενταί σου αἱ ἁμαρτίαι, ἢ εἰπεῖν· Ἔγειρε καὶ περιπάτει; (Matt 9:5)

  For which is **easier**: to say, 'Your sins are forgiven,' or to say, 'Get up and walk'?

  > Here two entire scenarios are compared. The comparative εὐκοπώτερον is used with the particle ἤ.

- ὅτι τὸ μωρὸν τοῦ θεοῦ **σοφώτερον** τῶν ἀνθρώπων ἐστίν (1 Cor 1:25)

  because God's foolishness is **wiser** than human wisdom

  > The comparative σοφώτερον exhibits a predicate use ("is wiser"); τῶν ἀνθρώπων is a genitive of comparison.

Superlative

The difference between the comparative and the superlative adjective is one of number rather than kind or degree. While comparative adjectives compare two entities, superlative adjectives compare three or more.[55] It is important to note that in Koine Greek, the use of the superlative was gradually diminishing (with the exception of πρῶτος and ἔσχατος).[56] So while there are close to 200 superlatives in the NT, only about half of the superlative *forms* in the NT actually *function* as superlatives.[57] Thus, in the case of superlatives, students must be careful to distinguish between form and function, keeping in mind that many adjectives that are superlative in form will not truly convey a superlative force.

There are two ways of forming a superlative: (1) adding -ιστος to a positive degree adjective: μέγας ("great") → μέγιστος ("greatest"), πολύς ("much") → πλεῖστος ("most"), μικρός ("small") → ἐλάχιστος ("smallest"), ὕψιστος ("highest" or "most high;" this form has no positive form in the NT); (2) adding -τατος to a positive degree adjective: ἅγιος ("holy") → ἁγιώτατος ("holiest"), τίμιος ("valuable") → τιμιώτατος ("most valuable"), ἀκριβής ("strict") → ἀκριβέστατος ("strictest").

- τί ἐμοὶ καὶ σοί, Ἰησοῦ υἱὲ τοῦ θεοῦ τοῦ **ὑψίστου**; (Luke 8:28)

  What do you have to do with me, Jesus, Son of the **Most High** God?[58]

- ὑμεῖς δέ, ἀγαπητοί, ἐποικοδομοῦντες ἑαυτοὺς τῇ **ἁγιωτάτῃ** ὑμῶν πίστει (Jude 20)

  But you, beloved, building yourselves up on your **most holy** faith (NASB)

---

[55] Wallace, 296, 301.
[56] Robertson, 669.
[57] Wallace, 302.
[58] Note that ὕψιστος seems to have a superlative force in the NT whenever referring to God: Matt 21:9; Mark 11:10; Luke 1:32, 35, 76; 2:14; 6:35; 8:28; 19:38; Acts 7:48; 16:17; Heb 7:1 (see Porter, *Idioms*, 123).

- ὁ φωστὴρ αὐτῆς ὅμοιος λίθῳ **τιμιωτάτῳ** (Rev 21:11)

  its radiance like a **most rare** jewel (ESV)

Elative

The elative is "a term used of either the comparative or superlative adjective to describe an *intensification* of the positive notion," often translated with "very."[59] For example, in 2 Peter 1:4, Peter speaks of promises that are μέγιστα (from μέγιστος, the superlativee of μέγας), meaning the "very great" promises, not the "greatest" promises.[60] As a result, the student, when identifying a comparative or superlative adjective in the NT, must always consider the possibility that a given comparative or superlative *form* may not convey a genuine comparative or superlative *force* but rather be elative in nature.

Comparative for Elative

In cases where the comparative is used for the elative, the adjective simply intensifies the quality and no comparison is indicated.[61] For instance, ὁ σοφώτερος ἀνήρ might mean "the *very* wise man" rather than "the wiser man." That is, the focus is on a quality the man possesses in and of himself (kind) rather than on a comparison between him and another person (degree). Although in classical Greek the elative was solely a function of the superlative, in Koine Greek there are a limited number of examples in the comparative.[62]

- κατὰ πάντα ὡς **δεισιδαιμονεστέρους** ὑμᾶς θεωρῶ (Acts 17:22)

  I see that you are **extremely religious** in every respect

  > In context, the idea is not that the Athenians were more religious than other people (degree), but that they were *very religious* (kind).

- **σπουδαιότερος** . . . ἐξῆλθεν (2 Cor 8:17)

  [he] **being very diligent,** went out

Superlative for Elative

As Wallace observes, "Apart from πρῶτος and ἔσχατος, the superlative is used about as frequently for the elative as it is for the superlative."[63]

- καὶ συνάγεται πρὸς αὐτὸν ὄχλος **πλεῖστος** (Mark 4:1)

  a **very large crowd** gathered around him

  > In context, the reference is most likely not to "the greatest crowd" in comparison to others but simply to a very large crowd.

---

[59] Wallace, 296.
[60] The example is from Dana & Mantey, 121.
[61] Wallace, 300.
[62] Moulton & Turner, 30.
[63] Wallace, 303.

- μετάγεται ὑπὸ **ἐλαχίστου** πηδαλίου (Jas 3:4)

they are guided by a **very small** rudder

> The reference is to a "very small" rudder rather than to "the smallest rudder" in comparison to other, larger, rudders.[64]

Special Cases

In addition to the above-mentioned types of usage, the astute Greek student detects in the NT occasional irregularities bound up with Semitic influence in particular or popular speech in general.[65] Similar to English, where we at times violate the strict distinction between comparative and superlative (for example, you may say to your playing partner, "You played the best," even though there were only two players), those kinds of distinctions were increasingly neglected in NT Greek, resulting in various irregularities. In part, this resulted from the fact that the language was increasingly adopted by non-native speakers, leading to Semitic or other non-native Greek influence.

Positive for Comparative

Since the Hebrew and Aramaic lack the comparative form, the comparative (as well as the superlative; see below) is sometimes (rarely) in the NT expressed by the positive. This is often indicated by the presence of the particle ἤ ("than").[66]

- **καλόν** σοί ἐστιν εἰσελθεῖν εἰς τὴν ζωὴν κυλλὸν ἢ χωλόν, ἢ δύο χεῖρας ἢ δύο πόδας ἔχοντα βληθῆναι εἰς τὸ πῦρ τὸ αἰώνιον (Matt 18:8)

It is **better** for you to enter life maimed or lame, <u>than</u> to have two hands or two feet and be thrown into the eternal fire

> Literally, "It is good for you to enter into life maimed or lame." Actually, however, it is *not* "good" in and of itself to enter into life maimed or lame, but *only by comparison* to the alternative (cf. Matt 18:9).[67]

- σὺ τετήρηκας τὸν **καλὸν** οἶνον ἕως ἄρτι (John 2:10)

you have kept the **fine** wine until now

> The idea, in context, is that the *better* wine was served after the inferior one.

---

[64] For other possible examples of the superlative for elative, see Matt 21:8; Luke 1:3; 12:26; 16:10; 19:17; Acts 13:8; 2 Cor 12:9, 15; 2 Pet 1:4; Rev 18:12; 21:11. Note that in some cases the English translation is superlative, but the sense is elative. For example, in Luke 1:3: **"most honorable** Theophilus" (**κράτιστε Θεόφιλε**) does not necessarily mean Theophilus was the *most* honorable from among a number of Roman government officials but merely that he was *very* honorable.

[65] Zerwick, 48.

[66] Zerwick, 48; Robertson, 660.

[67] Wallace, 297.

Positive for Superlative

Since Hebrew and Aramaic also lack the superlative form,[68] at times the superlative is expressed by the positive.

- αὕτη ἐστὶν ἡ **μεγάλη** καὶ πρώτη ἐντολή (Matt 22:38)

  This is the **greatest** and most important command

  > Literally, "this is the **great** . . . command" (ESV), but the idea is superlative (cf. Matt 22:36).

- **εὐλογημένη** σὺ ἐν γυναιξίν (Luke 1:42)

  Blessed are you among women

  > The positive is used Semitically *in the superlative* in speaking of a group or class; thus Elizabeth's greeting to Mary indicates that she is *most blessed*, rather than simply *blessed*.[69]

Comparative for Superlative

In some (rare) cases, the comparative adjective is used in place of the superlative. As Zerwick points out, in popular speech the distinction between comparative (the better of the two) and superlative (the best of three or more) tends not to be strictly observed. While in English the superlative may be used in both cases, in Greek the general tendency was toward the comparative form. What is more, the comparative tended to supplant the superlative even in its elative sense ("very big").[70]

- τίς ἄρα **μείζων** ἐστὶν ἐν τῇ βασιλείᾳ τῶν οὐρανῶν; (Matt 18:1)

  Who then is **greatest** in the kingdom of heaven? (NASB)

  > The idea cannot be who is "greater"; otherwise there would be only two people in the kingdom.

- νυνὶ δὲ μένει πίστις, ἐλπίς, ἀγάπη· τὰ τρία ταῦτα, **μείζων** δὲ τούτων ἡ ἀγάπη (1 Cor 13:13)

  Now these three remain: faith, hope, and love. But the **greatest** of these is love

  > Literally, "the greater." Among the *three* attributes—faith, hope, and love—the greatest is love.[71]

---

[68] See Bruce K. Waltke and M. O'Connor, *An Introduction to Biblical Hebrew Syntax* (Winona Lake, IN: Eisenbrauns, 1990), 267–71 (§14.5).

[69] Zerwick, 48. Other possible instances of the positive for superlatives are Luke 9:48 and 10:42.

[70] Zerwick, 49.

[71] See the discussions in Wallace, 299–301; Porter, *Idioms*, 124. For other possible examples of the comparative for the superlative, see Matt 13:32; 18:1; Mark 9:34; Luke 7:28; 1 Cor 12:23; 1 Tim 4:1. In addition, some discuss the possible use of the superlative for the comparative involving πρῶτος and ἔσχατος (e.g., Matt 21:28; John 20:4; 2 Pet 2:20). However, these terms are not superlative in form. See Baugh, *A First John Reader*, 113 (see preface, n. 4).

SUMMARY

USES OF THE ARTICLE		
WITH SUBSTANTIVES	The article particularizes a substantive or uses it generically.	*Identification:* ποῦ ἐστιν ὁ τεχθεὶς βασιλεὺς τῶν Ἰουδαίων ("Where is **he** who has been born King of the Jews?"; Matt 2:2).
		Par Excellence: ὁ προφήτης εἶ σύ; ("Are you **the** Prophet?"; John 1:21).
		Monadic (One-of-a-Kind): οὕτως γὰρ ἠγάπησεν ὁ θεὸς τὸν κόσμον, ὥστε **τὸν** υἱὸν τὸν μονογενῆ ἔδωκεν ("For God so loved the world, that he gave **his** only Son"; John 3:16 ESV).
		With Abstract Nouns: ἡ σωτηρία ἐκ τῶν Ἰουδαίων ἐστίν ("salvation is from the Jews"; John 4:22).
		Previous Reference (Anaphoric): πόθεν οὖν ἔχεις **τὸ** ὕδωρ τὸ ζῶν ("So where do You get **that** 'living water'?"; John 4:11 ESV).
		Generic: Προσέχετε ἀπὸ **τῶν** ψευδοπροφητῶν ("Be on your guard against false prophets"; Matt 7:15).
AS A PRONOUN	The article functions as a personal, relative, possessive, demonstrative, or alternate pronoun.	*As Personal Pronoun:* οἱ δὲ εἶπαν αὐτῷ ("**They** told him"; Matt 2:5).
		As Relative Pronoun: δοξάσωσιν τὸν πατέρα ὑμῶν **τὸν** ἐν τοῖς οὐρανοῖς ("give glory to your Father **who** is in heaven"; Matt 5:16 ESV).
		As Possessive Pronoun: ὁ δὲ διεῖλεν αὐτοῖς **τὸν** βίον ("And he divided **his** property between them"; Luke 15:12 ESV).
		As Demonstrative Pronoun: οἱ ἐν τῷ πλοίῳ προσεκύνησαν αὐτῷ ("**those** in the boat worshiped him"; Matt 14:33).
		As Alternate Pronoun: αὐτὸς ἔδωκεν **τοὺς** μὲν ἀποστόλους ("He gave **some** as apostles"; Eph 4:11 NASB).

USES OF THE ARTICLE		
ABSENCE OF ARTICLE	The absence of the article may convey that a given substantive is **non-particular** (indefinite or qualitative) or definite. If definite, this may be in conjunction with a proper name, a prepositional object, ordinal numbers, in predicate nominatives, as the complement in an object, complement construction, with monadic (one-of-a-kind) nouns, with abstract or generic nouns, with a pronominal adjective, or with technical expressions.	**Indefinite:** καὶ εἶπεν τοῖς μαθηταῖς αὐτοῦ ἵνα **πλοιάριον** προσκαρτερῇ αὐτῷ ("Then he told his disciples to have **a small boat** ready for him"; Mark 3:9). **Qualitative:** πλήρης **χάριτος** καὶ **ἀληθείας** ("full of **grace** and **truth**"; John 1:14). **Definite:** **Proper Name:** **Παῦλος** καὶ **Σιλᾶς** προσευχόμενοι ("**Paul** and **Silas** were praying"; Acts 16:25). **Prepositional Object:** Χαίρετε ἐν **κυρίῳ** ("Rejoice in **the Lord**"; Phil 4:4). **Predicate Nominative:** θεοῦ εἰμι **υἱός** ("I am **the Son** of God!"; Matt 27:43 ESV).
SPECIAL RULES	**Granville Sharp Rule:** When a single article governs two singular, personal, non-proper substantives of the same case that are joined by καί, they frequently refer to the same person.	τοῦ μεγάλου θεοῦ καὶ σωτῆρος ἡμῶν Ἰησοῦ Χριστοῦ ("our great God and Savior, Jesus Christ"; Titus 2:13).
	Colwell's Rule: A definite predicate nominative does not usually take the article when preceding the copula (linking verb).	θεὸς ἦν ὁ λόγος ("the Word was **God**"; John 1:1).
	Apollonius's Canon: When two nouns are in a genitive construction, both the head noun and the noun in the genitive case either have or lack the article.	ὁ λόγος τοῦ θεοῦ = "**the** Word **of** God" (John 10:35) or λόγος θεοῦ (1 Pet 1:23).

GENERAL USE OF THE ADJECTIVE		
PREDICATE	An adjective that predicates a certain quality to the subject, frequently by way of a copulative (linking) verb.	*With Article:* πιστὸς ὁ θεός ("God is **faithful**"; 1 Cor 1:9). *Without Article:* μακάριος ἀνὴρ οὗ οὐ μὴ λογίσηται κύριος ἁμαρτίαν ("**blessed** is the man against whom the Lord will not count his sin"; Rom 4:8 ESV)

GENERAL USE OF THE ADJECTIVE		
ATTRIBUTIVE	An adjective that ascribes a particular quality to a noun or substantive.	*With Article:* ὁ ἀληθινὸς θεός ("the **true** God"; 1 John 5:20).
		Without Article: πολλῶν <u>στρουθίων</u> διαφέρετε ὑμεῖς ("you are worth more than **many** <u>sparrows</u>"; Matt 10:31).
SUBSTANTIVAL	The adjective normally takes on the characteristics of a noun (e.g., the article) and functions as a noun or substantive in a given phrase.	σὺ εἶ ὁ ἅγιος ("You are **the Holy One**"; John 6:69 NASB).
ADVERBIAL	Use of an adjective (usually in the neuter accusative singular) to modify a verb rather than noun.	καὶ προελθὼν **μικρὸν** ἔπεσεν ἐπὶ πρόσωπον αὐτοῦ ("Going **a little farther**, he fell face-down"; Matt 26:39).

USE OF THE ADJECTIVE TO SHOW KIND/DEGREE		
POSITIVE	Focuses on the properties of a noun in terms of kind rather than degree.	ὁ νόμος **πνευματικός** ἐστιν ("the law is **spiritual**"; Rom 7:14).
COMPARATIVE	Focuses on the properties of a noun in terms of degree rather than kind.	ἔρχεται ὁ **ἰσχυρότερός** μου ὀπίσω μου ("One who is **more powerful** than I am is coming after me"; Mark 1:7).
SUPERLATIVE	Compares the qualities of three or more entities.	τί ἐμοὶ καὶ σοί, Ἰησοῦ υἱὲ τοῦ θεοῦ τοῦ **ὑψίστου**; ("What do you have to do with me, Jesus, Son of the **Most High** God?"; Luke 8:28).
ELATIVE	Use of the comparative or superlative adjective to describe an intensification of the positive notion.	*Comparative for Elative:* σπουδαιότερος . . . ἐξῆλθεν ("**[he] being very diligent**, went out"; 2 Cor 8:17).
		Superlative for Elative: ὄχλος πλεῖστος ("a **very large** crowd"; Mark 4:1).
SPECIAL CASES	Instances where popular speech and/or Semitic influence affected the use of the positive, comparative and superlative for one another.	*Positive for Comparative:* καλόν σοί ἐστιν ("It is **better** for you"; Matt 18:8).
		Positive for Superlative: ἡ μεγάλη καὶ πρώτη ἐντολή ("the **greatest** and most important command"; Matt 22:38).
		Comparative for Superlative: μείζων δὲ τούτων ἡ ἀγάπη ("but the **greatest** of these is love"; 1 Cor 13:13).

PRACTICE EXERCISES

In each of the following examples, (1) identify the form of each underlined article or adjective and (2) determine its specific use.

1. ἐν αὐτῇ δὲ τῇ οἰκίᾳ μένετε ἐσθίοντες καὶ πίνοντες <u>τὰ</u> παρ' αὐτῶν· ἄξιος γὰρ ὁ ἐργάτης τοῦ μισθοῦ αὐτοῦ (Luke 10:7).

2. ἐν αὐτῷ ζωὴ ἦν, καὶ <u>ἡ</u> ζωὴ ἦν <u>τὸ</u> φῶς τῶν ἀνθρώπων (John 1:4).

3. λέγει αὐτῷ Σίμων Πέτρος, Κύριε, μὴ τοὺς πόδας μου μόνον ἀλλὰ καὶ <u>τὰς</u> χεῖρας καὶ <u>τὴν</u> κεφαλήν (John 13:9).

4. ἡ ἀγάπη μακροθυμεῖ, χρηστεύεται <u>ἡ</u> ἀγάπη, οὐ ζηλοῖ, [<u>ἡ</u> ἀγάπη] οὐ περπερεύεται, οὐ φυσιοῦται (1 Cor 13:4).

5. ἀγαπήσεις <u>τὸν</u> πλησίον σου ὡς σεαυτόν (Gal 5:14).

6. κατανοήσατε <u>τὸν</u> ἀπόστολον καὶ ἀρχιερέα τῆς ὁμολογίας ἡμῶν Ἰησοῦν (Heb 3:1).

7. πᾶσα γραφὴ <u>θεόπνευστος</u> καὶ <u>ὠφέλιμος</u> πρὸς διδασκαλίαν (2 Tim 3:16).

8. <u>τυφλοὶ</u> ἀναβλέπουσιν καὶ <u>χωλοὶ</u> περιπατοῦσιν, <u>λεπροὶ</u> καθαρίζονται καὶ <u>κωφοὶ</u> ἀκούουσιν, καὶ <u>νεκροὶ</u> ἐγείρονται καὶ <u>πτωχοὶ</u> εὐαγγελίζονται (Matt 11:5).

9. ὁ δὲ <u>μικρότερος</u> ἐν τῇ βασιλείᾳ τῶν οὐρανῶν <u>μείζων</u> αὐτοῦ ἐστιν (Matt 11:11).

10. <u>καλόν</u> ἐστίν σε κυλλὸν εἰσελθεῖν εἰς τὴν ζωὴν ἢ τὰς δύο χεῖρας ἔχοντα ἀπελθεῖν εἰς τὴν γέενναν (Mark 9:43).

VOCABULARY

Vocabulary to Memorize

ἀδικία, ἡ	unrighteousness, injustice (25)
ἀληθής	true, honest, genuine (26)
ἀναβλέπω	I look up, see again, receive sight (25)
ἄρτι	now (36)
ἀσθενής	weak, powerless, sick (26)
βαστάζω	I bear, endure (27)
γάμος, ὁ	wedding, marriage (16)
γέ	indeed, even (25)
γεύομαι	I taste, experience (15)
γνωρίζω	I make known, reveal, know (25)
δέκα	ten (25)
δένδρον, τό	tree (25)
διάκονος, ὁ	servant, deacon (29)
δουλεύω	I am a slave, serve, obey (25)
ἐκχέω	I pour out, shed (27)
Ἕλλην, -ηνος, ὁ	a Greek, gentile, pagan (25)
ἕνεκα	because of, on account of, for the sake of (26)
ἥκω	I have come (26)
Ἰακώβ, ὁ	Jacob (27)
καθαρός	clean, pure (27)
κεῖμαι	I lie, recline (24)
λυπέω	I grieve, offend (26)
Μαρία, ἡ	Mary (27)
Μαριάμ, ἡ	Mary (27)
μυστήριον, τό	mystery, secret (28)
νικάω	I conquer, overcome (28)
νυμφίος, ὁ	bridegroom (16)
οἶνος, ὁ	wine (34)
πνευματικός	spiritual (26)
πόθεν	from where? (29)
πόσος	how great/much/many (?) (27)
προφητεύω	I prophesy (28)
σός	your (27)
σταυρός, ὁ	cross (27)
στρατιώτης, -ου, ὁ	soldier (26)
συνίημι	I understand, comprehend (26)

τελέω	I finish, complete (28)
φρονέω	I think, ponder (26)
φωνέω	I call (43)
χήρα, ἡ	widow (26)

Vocabulary to Recognize

ἀνά	each (13)
ἀντλέω	I draw (water) (4)
ἄνω	above (9)
ἀρχιτρίκλινος, ὁ	headwaiter (3)
γεμίζω	I fill (8)
ἐλάσσων	inferior, of lesser quality (4)
ἕξ	six (13)
καθαρισμός, ὁ	purification (7)
Κανά, ἡ	Cana (4)
λίθινος	(made of) stone (3)
μεθύσκω	I get drunk (5)
μετρητής, -οῦ, ὁ	measure (1)
ὑδρία, ἡ	water jar (3)
χωρέω	I contain (10)

READING THE NEW TESTAMENT

John 2:1–11

¹ Καὶ τῇ ἡμέρᾳ τῇ τρίτῃ γάμος ἐγένετο ἐν Κανὰ τῆς Γαλιλαίας, καὶ ἦν ἡ μήτηρ τοῦ Ἰησοῦ ἐκεῖ· ² ἐκλήθη δὲ καὶ ὁ Ἰησοῦς καὶ οἱ μαθηταὶ αὐτοῦ εἰς τὸν γάμον. ³ καὶ ὑστερήσαντος οἴνου λέγει ἡ μήτηρ τοῦ Ἰησοῦ πρὸς αὐτόν, Οἶνον οὐκ ἔχουσιν. ⁴ [καὶ] λέγει αὐτῇ ὁ Ἰησοῦς, Τί ἐμοὶ καὶ σοί, γύναι; οὔπω ἥκει ἡ ὥρα μου. ⁵ λέγει ἡ μήτηρ αὐτοῦ τοῖς διακόνοις, Ὅ τι ἂν λέγῃ ὑμῖν ποιήσατε. ⁶ ἦσαν δὲ ἐκεῖ λίθιναι ὑδρίαι ἓξ κατὰ τὸν καθαρισμὸν τῶν Ἰουδαίων κείμεναι, χωροῦσαι ἀνὰ μετρητὰς δύο ἢ τρεῖς. ⁷ λέγει αὐτοῖς ὁ Ἰησοῦς, Γεμίσατε τὰς ὑδρίας ὕδατος. καὶ ἐγέμισαν αὐτὰς ἕως ἄνω. ⁸ καὶ λέγει αὐτοῖς, Ἀντλήσατε νῦν καὶ φέρετε τῷ ἀρχιτρικλίνῳ· οἱ δὲ ἤνεγκαν. ⁹ ὡς δὲ ἐγεύσατο ὁ ἀρχιτρίκλινος τὸ ὕδωρ οἶνον γεγενημένον καὶ οὐκ ᾔδει πόθεν ἐστίν, οἱ δὲ διάκονοι ᾔδεισαν οἱ ἠντληκότες τὸ ὕδωρ, φωνεῖ τὸν νυμφίον ὁ ἀρχιτρίκλινος ¹⁰ καὶ λέγει αὐτῷ, Πᾶς ἄνθρωπος πρῶτον τὸν καλὸν οἶνον τίθησιν καὶ ὅταν μεθυσθῶσιν τὸν ἐλάσσω· σὺ τετήρηκας τὸν καλὸν οἶνον ἕως ἄρτι. ¹¹ Ταύτην ἐποίησεν ἀρχὴν τῶν σημείων ὁ Ἰησοῦς ἐν Κανὰ τῆς Γαλιλαίας καὶ ἐφανέρωσεν τὴν δόξαν αὐτοῦ, καὶ ἐπίστευσαν εἰς αὐτὸν οἱ μαθηταὶ αὐτοῦ.

Reading Notes[72]

Verse 1

- **τῇ ἡμέρᾳ τῇ τρίτῃ** ("On the third day") – This is a dative of time. The expression is one in a series of time markers following several references to "the next day" (1:2, 35, 43). Jesus's sign at the wedding at Cana thus completes an entire week of activity.[73] The articles, together with the numeral, indicate a definite point in time. The adjective τῇ τρίτῃ is attributive modifying τῇ ἡμέρᾳ and uses a common article-noun-article-adjective construction.

- **ἐν Κανὰ τῆς Γαλιλαίας** ("in Cana of Galilee") – τῆς Γαλιλαίας is a partitive genitive, denoting the territory in which the town of Cana is located. Cana is mentioned only in John's Gospel. Jesus's signs in 2:1–11 and 4:43–54 frame the "Cana cycle."

- **ἡ μήτηρ τοῦ Ἰησοῦ** ("Jesus's mother") – τοῦ Ἰησοῦ is a genitive of relationship. Jesus's mother is never named in this Gospel, perhaps to avoid confusion with other Marys (such as Mary Magdalene).[74] In keeping with

---

[72] The English version used in the Reading Notes for this chapter is the CSB.

[73] Andreas J. Köstenberger, *A Theology of John's Gospel*, BTNT (Grand Rapids: Zondervan, 2009), 189–90.

[74] D. A. Carson, *John*, PNTC (Grand Rapids: Eerdmans, 1991), 168.

Apollonius's Canon, the article is found both before μήτηρ and Ἰησοῦ (also in v. 3).

Verse 2

- **ἐκλήθη** ("were invited") – ἐκλήθη (aor pass ind 3rd sg καλέω) agrees with ὁ Ἰησοῦς rather than with the joint subject ὁ Ἰησοῦς καὶ οἱ μαθηταὶ αὐτοῦ (cf. 2:12; 3:22; 18:15). The sense is that Jesus was invited, together with his disciples.[75]

- **καὶ ὁ Ἰησοῦς καὶ οἱ μαθηταὶ αὐτοῦ** ("his disciples") – αὐτοῦ is a genitive of relationship. The articles before both Ἰησοῦς and μαθηταί separate Jesus and the disciples as two separate entities.

- **εἰς τὸν γάμον** ("to the wedding") – Note the article here but not in the previous verse, indicating the demonstrative force of the article in the present instance. In the context of the discourse, the evangelist makes reference to "that wedding," that is, the wedding previously mentioned in v. 1.

Verse 3

- **ὑστερήσαντος οἴνου** ("When the wine ran out") – ὑστερήσαντος (aor act ptc masc gen sg ὑστερέω) is a genitive absolute, conveying a temporal sense ("when") and possibly also a causal idea, with both the noun οἴνου and the participle ὑστερήσαντος in the genitive.

- **λέγει** ("told") – λέγει is a historical present. This is the first of a series of references to people's comments by way of λέγει. There are five additional instances of the verb in verses 4–10.

Verse 4

- **Τί ἐμοὶ καὶ σοί** ("What has this concern of yours to do with me") – ἐμοί and σοί are datives of possession, indicating concern. Biblical parallels in both Testaments typically convey a reproachful connotation.[76]

- **γύναι** ("woman") – Jesus's address of his mother (cf. 19:26, a vocative), together with the phrase τί ἐμοὶ καὶ σοί (see previous note), may serve the purpose of establishing polite distance but need not be viewed as harsh.

---

[75] Wallace says the emphasis is on Jesus, and his disciples "tagged along," though this may be over-interpreting the grammar here (401).

[76] OT: Judg 11:12; 2 Sam 16:10; 1 Kgs 17:18; 2 Kgs 3:13; 2 Chron 35:21; NT: Matt 8:29; Mark 1:24; 5:7; Luke 4:34; 8:28 (Carson, *John*, 170).

Verse 5

- τοῖς διακόνοις ("the servants") – Apparently disregarding Jesus's refusal to act, Mary addresses herself to the servants (first mentioned here). τοῖς διακόνοις is an indirect object in the dative case. The article specifies the identity of the servants (cf. v. 9).

- Ὅ τι ἂν λέγῃ ὑμῖν ("whatever he tells you") – ὅ τι is the neuter accusative singular of the compound indefinite relative pronoun ὅστις. The particle ἂν underscores the indefiniteness of Mary's request, in conjunction with the present subjunctive λέγῃ ("*whatever* he tells you"). Mary, in faith, instructs the servants, not knowing *how* Jesus will meet the need for more wine but believing that he will do whatever he deems appropriate to help.

- ποιήσατε ("Do") – Aor act impv 2nd pl ποιέω.

Verse 6

- ἦσαν . . . κείμεναι ("had been set") – Most likely, this is a periphrastic perfect construction with the imperfect of εἰμι and the participle κείμεναι (pres pass ptc fem nom pl κεῖμαι; "Now there were standing there six stone water jars").[77]

- κατὰ τὸν καθαρισμὸν τῶν Ἰουδαίων ("for Jewish purification") – τῶν Ἰουδαίων is most likely an attributive genitive ("Jewish," as rendered in the CSB). Alternatively, the genitive may be possessive ("of the Jews") or subjective ("practiced by the Jews").[78] In keeping with Apollonius's Canon, articles precede both nouns.

- χωροῦσαι ἀνά ("each contained") – χωροῦσαι (pres act ptc fem nom pl χωρέω) is most likely an attributive participle, modifying λίθιναι ὑδρίαι. ἀνά, in conjunction with numbers, is a distributive particle ("each").

Verse 7

- Γεμίσατε τὰς ὑδρίας ("Fill the jars") – γεμίσατε (aor act impv 2nd pl γεμίζω; cf. ποιήσατε in v. 5) takes τὰς ὑδρίας as its direct accusative object. Mary's faith is rewarded: Jesus now issues orders to the servants as she had hoped. The use of the article before ὑδρίας is functioning to show previous reference, pointing back to the particular jars of water mentioned in verse 6.

---

[77] Alternatively, the two verb forms are independent ("Now there were six stone water jars, standing").

[78] Murray J. Harris, *John,* EGGNT (Nashville: B&H Academic, 2015), 58.

- ὕδατος ("with water") – masc gen sg ὕδωρ. Describes the content with which the servants are to fill the jars. The need is for more *wine*, but Jesus has the servants fill the jars with *water*, setting up the ensuing miracle (v. 9: τὸ ὕδωρ οἶνον γεγενημένον). The reference to water here is generic (no article); compare and contrast the two articular uses of ὕδωρ in v. 9 below.

Verse 8

- Ἀντλήσατε νῦν καὶ φέρετε τῷ ἀρχιτρικλίνῳ ("Now draw some out and take it to the headwaiter") – ἀντλήσατε (aor act impv 2nd pl ἀντλέω, "draw water"; cf. 4:7, 15) is yet another aor impv (cf. vv. 5, 7), while φέρετε breaks the string, shifting to the present imperative (verbs of motion prefer the present tense form).[79] νῦν may imply that the miracle had just taken place. The direct object is to be supplied with φέρετε. The indirect dative object τῷ ἀρχιτρικλίνῳ introduces a new character into the narrative, the headwaiter or master of ceremonies, who was to certify the occurrence of the miracle. The article specifies the identity of the headwaiter here and twice in the following verse.

- οἱ δὲ ἤνεγκαν ("And they did") – The nominative masculine plural article οἱ serves as a personal pronoun, referring to the servants ("they"). ἤνεγκαν (aor act ind 3rd pl φέρω) reiterates φέρετε and is rendered by the CSB simply as "they did."

Verse 9

- τὸ ὕδωρ οἶνον γεγενημένον ("the water [after it had become wine]") – This is a rather oblique reference to the miracle that had just taken place. The entire phrase serves as a direct object to ἐγεύσατο ("tasted"), whereby οἶνον γεγενημένον (per mid ptc neut acc sg γίνομαι) is an attributive participial phrase indicating that the water had been turned into wine ("the having-become-wine water"). The article indicates definiteness (cf. the anarthrous ὕδατος in v. 7 above and the articular τὸ ὕδωρ later in the same verse below).

- καὶ οὐκ ᾔδει πόθεν ἐστίν, οἱ δὲ διάκονοι ᾔδεισαν ("he did not know where it came from—though the servants . . . knew") – The conjunction καί may here, as is not uncommon in the NT, carry an adversative connotation ("but"). The ignorance of the headwaiter is contrasted with the knowledge of the servants who had drawn the water (see the adversative

---

[79] Though there is little discernible interpretive significance to this shift (see Harris, *John*, 59, with reference to Zerwick). As an imperative, φέρω occurs 10 times in the present tense and only once in the aorist tense.

δέ). Both ᾔδει (pluper act ind 3rd sg οἶδα) and ᾔδεισαν (pluper act ind 3rd pl οἶδα) are pluperfect verbs that function as aorists (see chapter 9). The phrase καὶ οὐκ ᾔδει πόθεν ἐστίν, or at least οἱ δὲ διάκονοι ᾔδεισαν, is parenthetical. The servants' and headwaiter's unwitting participation in the miracle jointly serves to underscore its authenticity.

- οἱ ἠντληκότες τὸ ὕδωρ ("who had drawn the water") – οἱ ἠντληκότες (per act ptc masc nom pl ἀντλέω) is an attributive participle that modifies οἱ διάκονοι (cf. vv. 7–8) and is equivalent in function to a relative clause.[80] The perfect participles γεγενημένον and ἠντληκότες in the present verse may serve to highlight the dramatic effect of the performance and revelation of Jesus's miracle.

- ὁ ἀρχιτρίκλινος . . . οἱ διάκονοι . . . τὸν νυμφίον ("the headwaiter . . . the servants . . . the groom") – The evangelist parades a series of characters authenticating the miracle performed by Jesus. The articles specify the identity of these characters.

Verse 10

- Πᾶς ἄνθρωπος πρῶτον τὸν καλὸν οἶνον τίθησιν . . . σὺ τετήρηκας ("Everybody sets out the fine wine first . . . But you have kept") – The adjective πρῶτον functions as an adverbial accusative, modifying the verb τίθησιν (pres act ind 3rd sg τίθημι [gnomic use of the present]). The headwaiter's remarks to the groom establish a dramatic contrast between common practice (πᾶς ἄνθρωπος) and the supposed action of the groom (highlighted by the Johannine misunderstanding motif, conveying irony). The personal pronoun σύ is emphatic (because already implied in τετήρηκας).

- τὸν καλὸν οἶνον . . . τὸν ἐλάσσω . . . τὸν καλὸν οἶνον ("the fine wine . . . the inferior . . . the fine wine") – The articles point to the types of wine by comparing and contrasting them. καλός is a positive adjective functioning as a comparative, though the CSB renders it as a positive ("fine").

- ὅταν μεθυσθῶσιν τὸν ἐλάσσω ("then, after people are drunk, the inferior") – ὅταν (ὅτε + ἄν, "whenever") plus the aorist subjunctive "specifies a fut. action whose accomplishment precedes the action of the principal v[er]b."[81] In the present case, the verb is μεθυσθῶσιν (aor pass sub 3rd pl μεθύσκω; the only passive instance in the NT), meaning "to drink freely" or "to get drunk." ἐλάσσω is masc acc sg (for ἐλάσσονα).

---

[80] Harris, *John,* 59.
[81] Harris, *John,* 60.

Verse 11

- **Ταύτην ἐποίησεν ἀρχὴν τῶν σημείων ὁ Ἰησοῦς** ("Jesus did this, the first of his signs") – The syntax is a bit unusual in that ταύτην . . . ἀρχήν is separated by ἐποίησεν. Also, one might have expected τοῦτο ἐποίησεν, "Jesus did *this*" (cf., e.g., 8:40). However, even though ταύτην is technically a pronoun, not an adjective (which would require ταύτην τὴν ἀρχήν), it agrees by grammatical attraction with the following noun ἀρχήν, which is predicative.[82] Thus, the phrase more literally means "Jesus did this as the beginning (or the first) of his signs" (ταύτην and ἀρχήν serve as a double accusative).

- **ἐν Κανὰ τῆς Γαλιλαίας** ("in Cana of Galilee") – The phrase constitutes an *inclusio* with v. 1, delimiting vv. 1–11 as a literary unit. It also represents an *inclusio* with 4:46, 54, designating 2:1–4:54 as the "Cana cycle."

---

[82] "As a/the beginning" (Harris, *John*, citing Robertson, 701–2, 781; et al.).

//////////////

CHAPTER 6

VERBS: OVERVIEW, SUBJUNCTIVES & IMPERATIVES

GOING DEEPER

Asking a question in Greek can be done in several different ways to elicit various types of responses. In Rom 10:14–15, Paul asks his readers a series of questions: "How, then, can they call (ἐπικαλέσωνται) on him they have not believed in? And how can they believe (πιστεύσωσιν) without hearing about him? And how can they hear (ἀκούσωσιν) without a preacher? And how can they preach (κηρύξωσιν) unless they are sent?" Because Paul uses the subjunctive mood to ask these questions, his goal is not to gain a factual response. The clear implication, for example, is that without a preacher, there is no way the nations will hear the good news of Jesus Christ. But by framing these questions with the subjunctive mood, Paul is not so much eliciting facts, but urging the congregation to reflect on their own personal role in taking the gospel to those who have never heard. Knowing that Paul is using the subjunctive mood (instead of the indicative mood) to ask these rhetorical questions helps us to see that he is not really asking questions of fact, but questions of obligation.

CHAPTER OBJECTIVES

The purpose of this chapter is to provide an overview of the Greek verb system. Some of the material will necessarily be review because our aim is to firm up what has already been studied and, at the same time, offer more in-depth information that will aid the student in the interpretive process. Thus, we will consider all the major components that make up the Greek verb including (1) person and number, (2) voice, (3) mood, (4) tense, and (5) aspect. In the discussion of mood, there will be a more extensive treatment of the Subjunctive and Imperative moods.

INTRODUCTION

The Greek verbal system is perhaps the most complicated and debated portion of Greek grammar. This difficulty is partly due to the fact that Greek verbs are highly inflected. That is, they are able to change or be altered in many different ways. For instance, Greek verbs can add various morphemes (the smallest unit of meaning) such as prefixes (augments, reduplication), suffixes (which communicate person and number), and even infixes (changes that occur directly before the suffix). In addition, the stem (the root form of the verb) can also be slightly altered or even completely transformed. All of these inflections contribute to the complexity of Greek verbs.

Verbs can be categorized as finite or infinite. A finite verb is a word which "both expresses action or state of being *and* which makes an assertion about the subject of a sentence or clause."[1] That is, a finite verb is a verb that can be conjugated because it has person and number and thus is limited to a particular subject (e.g., λύω = pres act ind 1st sg, "I am loosing"). On the other hand, infinite verb forms "express action or state of being, but they make no assertion about the subject of the sentence or clause."[2] Thus, unlike a finite verb, an infinite verb cannot be conjugated (which means it has no person or number), is not limited in form to a particular subject, and therefore cannot form a complete sentence (e.g., λύειν = pres act inf, "to loose").[3]

Another distinction between types of verbs relates to whether a verb is transitive or intransitive. Transitive verbs are verbs that can take a direct object. If someone states, "I see," the listener will naturally want to know what it is that the person saw (e.g., "I see people," βλέπω τοὺς ἀνθρώπους, Mark 8:24). On the other hand, intransitive verbs do not take direct objects to complete their meaning (e.g., "I am going," ESV; ἐγὼ ὑπάγω, John 8:21). It should be noted, however, that some verbs can function as either transitive or intransitive based on the particular context. For example, John 9:25 states, "I was blind, and now I can see!" (τυφλὸς ὢν ἄρτι βλέπω). In this case the verb is intransitive, not taking a direct object.[4]

---

[1] Brooks & Winbery, 131.
[2] Brooks & Winbery, 131.
[3] Functionally, participles and infinitives can (and often do) violate this pattern.
[4] For a more in-depth discussion, see Wallace, 409; Dana & Mantey, 154–55; Robertson, 330, 797.

PERSON & NUMBER

Greek verb endings communicate information regarding the subject of the verb. That is, they communicate the person and number of the one performing the action or the one who is receiving the action. By *person* we are referring to the first person ("I" or "we"), second person ("you" sg or pl), or third person ("he/she/it" or "they").[5] By *number* we are referring to whether there is only one person related to the action of the verb ("I," "you" [sg], or "he/she/it") or more than one person ("we," "you" [pl], or "they").

	SINGULAR	PLURAL
FIRST	I	we
SECOND	you (sg)	you (pl)
THIRD	he, she, it	they

Greek verbs contain more information than English verbs, although there is still some overlap. This overlap can be seen in the fact that English verbs occasionally communicate number. For example, you say, "He *writes*" but not "He *write*." In English the third person singular requires a different form of the verb. And yet, in English you can say, "I write, "You (sg) write," "We write," "You (pl) write," and "They write." With Greek, however, each person and number requires a different verb ending (with some exceptions, of course).

Occasionally, the use of *person* will function more literarily than grammatically. For example, the first person singular ("I") can be employed as a third person generic reference ("someone"). Thus, Paul states, "If **I** rebuild (οἰκοδομῶ) those things that **I** tore down (κατέλυσα), **I** show myself (ἐμαυτὸν συνιστάνω) to be a lawbreaker" (Gal 2:18). In this text Paul is not necessarily referring to himself but is speaking generically. That is, he is in effect saying, "If anyone rebuilds those things that he tore down, that person shows himself to be a lawbreaker." Or even more to the point, "If you Galatians rebuild those things that you tore down, you show yourselves to be lawbreakers" (see also Rom 7:7–25; 1 Cor 10:30; 13:1–3).

A more common literary use of *person* relates to the first person plural "we." Indeed, there are at least three different functions of "we" in the NT: (1) the editorial "we," (2) the exclusive "we," and (3) the inclusive "we."[6] The editorial "we" has the function of "I" and is similar to many books written in English that use "we" when there is only one author (this book, of course, does have more than one author, so the "we" really does mean "we"). This use of the first person plural

---

[5] "If the subject is represented as speaking, the verb is in the first person. If the subject is being spoken to, the verb is in the second person. If the subject is being spoken about, the verb is in the third person" (Brooks & Winbery, 130).

[6] A clear distinction between these categories is not always clear; the context for some first person plurals may arguably allow for more than one understanding.

(sometimes called the "epistolary plural") is often employed in letters or epistles when it seems clear that the author is really only referring to himself. For example, in Rom 1:5 Paul writes, "Through him **we** have received (ἐλάβομεν) grace and apostleship to bring about the obedience of faith for the sake of his name among all the Gentiles."[7] Although Paul uses the first person plural ending (–μεν, "we"), there are several reasons for interpreting this verse as an editorial "we." First, only Paul is mentioned in the opening greeting as the author, even though Timothy was with him (Rom 1:1). Second, the first person singular ("I") is employed consistently throughout the epistle, especially in 1:8–16. Finally, the verse indicates that "we" received an apostleship specifically to bring about the obedience of faith to the nations—a calling that was unique to the apostle Paul.[8]

The exclusive "we" includes both the author and one or more co-authors, co-workers, or cohorts but *excludes* the audience or recipients of the letter. For example, in 1 Cor 3:9 Paul states, "For **we** are (ἐσμεν) God's coworkers. You are God's field, God's building." As the second half of the verse makes clear, Paul was not including his readers with his use of the first person plural verb ending.[9] In contrast, the inclusive "we" refers to both the author(s) and the audience as when the author of Hebrews asks, "How shall **we escape** (ἐκφευξόμεθα) if we neglect such a great salvation?" (Heb 2:3).[10]

For the most part, the Greek verb will agree with the subject of the sentence in both person and number (this is known as *concord*). There are occasions, however, when the subject and the verb do not agree (this is known as *discord*). Perhaps the most common example of discord is when a neuter plural subject takes a singular verb (Greek grammarians referred to this rule as "the animals run" [τὰ ζῷα τρέχει], which was itself an example of the rule).[11] Because a neuter plural noun often referred to something impersonal, the noun was considered as a collective whole. For instance, Acts 1:18 states concerning Judas that "his intestines spilled out" (ἐξεχύθη [sg] πάντα **τὰ σπλάγχνα** [neut pl] αὐτοῦ).[12]

Another example of discord is found when compound subjects (at least one is singular, and together they make a plural) are found with singular verbs. This

---

[7] For more examples of the editorial "we," see Rom 3:28 (λογιζόμεθα); 1 Cor 2:6-7 (λαλοῦμεν), 12–13 (ἐλάβομεν, εἰδῶμεν, λαλοῦμεν), 16 (ἔχομεν); 2 Cor 3:1 (ἀρχόμεθα, χρῄζομεν); 10:3 (στρατευόμεθα), 13 (καυχησόμεθα); 1 Thess 2:18 (ἠθελήσαμεν); 1 John 1:4 (γράφομεν).

[8] So Moo, *The Letter to the Romans*, 2nd ed., 49 (see chap. 3, n. 66); Schreiner, *Romans*, 2nd ed., 38–39 (see chap. 3, n. 40); Wallace, 395.

[9] For more examples of the exclusive "we," see Gal 1:8 (ἡμεῖς… εὐαγγελίζηται, εὐηγγελισάμεθα); Col 1:3 (εὐχαριστοῦμεν); 1 Thess 1:2 (εὐχαριστοῦμεν); Heb 13:18 (πειθόμεθα, ἔχομεν); 2 Pet 1:16 (ἐγνωρίσαμεν).

[10] For more examples of the inclusive "we," see Gal 2:4 (ἔχομεν); 6:10 (ἔχομεν); Eph 1:7 (ἔχομεν); Col 1:14 (ἔχομεν); Heb 2:1 (παραρυῶμεν); 1 John 2:1 (ἔχομεν). Though outside of the epistle genre, Mark (4:30) presents Jesus as using the first person plural to include his hearers (ὁμοιώσωμεν).

[11] See BDF, 73–74 (§133).

[12] For more examples of a neuter plural subject with a singular verb, see Matt 11:27 (πάντα μοι παρεδόθη); Mark 4:4 (ἦλθεν τὰ πετεινὰ καὶ κατέφαγεν); Luke 8:35 (δαιμόνια ἐξῆλθεν); 10:17 (τὰ δαιμόνια ὑποτάσσεται); John 10:25 (ταῦτα μαρτυρεῖ); 17:10 (τὰ ἐμὰ πάντα σά ἐστιν); Jas 3:4 (τὰ πλοῖα … μετάγεται); 2 Pet 2:20 (γέγονεν … τὰ ἔσχατα); Rev 19:14 (τὰ στρατεύματα [τὰ] ἐν τῷ οὐρανῷ ἠκολούθει).

construction was sometimes used to emphasize one of the subjects, with the second subject receiving less focus. For example, John 8:15 states, "Simon Peter and another disciple **were following** (ἠκολούθει, sg) Jesus" (NIV).[13]

Voice

The voice of a verb indicates the way in which the subject relates to the action or state expressed by the verb. In the active voice, the subject performs the action ("I see someone"). In the middle voice, the subject performs the action to or for himself ("I see myself," "I see for myself" or "I myself see"). In the passive voice, the subject receives the action ("I was seen [by someone else]"). The use of the voices in the NT is as follows: the active voice occurs 20,735 times; the middle voice occurs 3,730 times; the passive voice occurs 3,659 times; and 33 forms are debatable as to whether they are middle or passive.

	Simple
ACTIVE VOICE	Causative
	Reflexive
	Reflexive
MIDDLE VOICE	Special Interest
	Permissive
PASSIVE VOICE	Simple
	Permissive

Active Voice

As noted in the statistics above, the active voice is by far the most commonly used voice. With the active voice, the subject performs (or produces or experiences) the action of the verb. Below are the most common uses of the active voice.

Simple Active

The simple active is the most basic and common use of the active voice and indicates that the subject directly performs the action of the verb. In John 3:16 we read, "God **loved** the world" (**ἠγάπησεν** ὁ θεὸς τὸν κόσμον). In this example, the subject (God) performs an action (love), which is focused toward a direct object (the world).

---

[13] For more examples of a compound subject with a singular verb, see Matt 5:18 (παρέλθῃ ὁ οὐρανὸς καὶ ἡ γῆ); 6:19 (ὅπου σὴς καὶ βρῶσις ἀφανίζει); 13:55 (ἡ μήτηρ αὐτοῦ λέγεται Μαριὰμ καὶ οἱ ἀδελφοὶ αὐτοῦ); Mark 4:41 (ὁ ἄνεμος καὶ ἡ θάλασσα ὑπακούει); John 3:22 (ἦλθεν ὁ Ἰησοῦς καὶ οἱ μαθηταὶ αὐτοῦ); 8:52 (Ἀβραὰμ . . . καὶ οἱ προφῆται); 18:15 (ἠκολούθει . . . Σίμων Πέτρος καὶ ἄλλος μαθητής); 20:3 (ἐξῆλθεν οὖν ὁ Πέτρος καὶ ὁ ἄλλος μαθητής).

Causative Active

With the causative active, the subject is not necessarily performing the action but is the source or cause behind it. In Matt 5:45, Jesus states that God "**causes** his sun **to rise** (ἀνατέλλει) on the evil and the good, and **sends rain** (βρέχει) on the righteous and the unrighteous." Notice that God is not the one rising or raining over His creation but is the one who causes the sun to rise or causes the rain to fall on His creation.[14]

Reflexive Active

The reflexive active signifies that the subject performs the action to himself. This construction functions similar to the middle voice but uses the active voice with a reflexive pronoun. In 1 Tim 4:7 Paul encourages his young protégé Timothy, "**Train** yourself in godliness" (**γύμναζε** σεαυτὸν πρὸς εὐσέβειαν).[15]

Middle Voice

The middle voice is sometimes difficult for students of Greek to grasp because there is not an English equivalent.[16] Oftentimes, it is thought that the middle voice communicates mainly a reflexive idea (someone doing something to himself).[17] Although the reflexive idea is occasionally found in the NT, most often the middle is used to convey the idea that the subject directly participates or is involved in the results of the action.[18] In addition, it must be remembered that only aorist and future verbs have separate middle and passive forms. That is, with present, imperfect, and perfect verbs the middle and passive voices share the same forms. Although context usually makes it clear which voice is intended by the author, there are some instances where there is some uncertainty. The following categories (like many of the categories in this grammar) should not be seen as rigid ones. As Dana

---

[14] For more examples of the causative use of the active voice, see John 3:22 (ἐβάπτιζεν); John 19:1 (ἔλαβεν, ἐμαστίγωσεν); Acts 16:3 (περιέτεμεν); 21:11 (δήσουσιν, παραδώσουσιν); 1 Cor 3:6 (ηὔξανεν); 8:13 (σκανδαλίζει); Gal 2:4 (καταδουλώσουσιν); Eph 4:16 (αὔξησιν); 1 Pet 1:22 (ἡγνικότες); Jude 13 (ἐπαφρίζοντα); Rev 7:15 (σκηνώσει); 8:6 (σαλπίσωσιν).

[15] Technically, this usage is not a function of the verb's voice but of the reflexive pronoun. For more examples of the reflexive use of the active voice, see Matt 23:12 (ὑψώσει, ταπεινώσει); Mark 15:30 (σῶσον); John 13:4 (διέζωσεν); 1 Cor 11:28 (δοκιμαζέτω); Gal 6:3 (φρεναπατᾷ); 1 Pet 3:5 (ἐκόσμουν); Rev 19:7 (ἡτοίμασεν).

[16] "Here we approach one of the most distinctive and peculiar phenomena of the Greek language. It is impossible to describe it, adequately and accurately, in terms of English idiom, for English knows no approximate parallel" (Dana & Mantey, 156).

[17] "Grammars sometimes describe the Middle as primarily reflexive. Whether or not this is true for certain periods, it is manifestly not true of N.T. usage" (Moule, 24).

[18] "[T]he middle calls special attention to the subject. . . . [I]n the middle the subject is acting in relation to himself somehow" (Robertson, 804). The middle voice "in some way, relates the action more intimately to the subject" (Dana & Mantey, 157). "The middle voice represents the subject as participating in the results of the action, as acting in relation to itself, as having personal interest in the action, as being intimately involved in the action" (Brooks & Winbery, 111). "*[T]he Greek middle voice expresses more direct participation, specific involvement, or even some form of benefit of the subject doing the action*" (Porter, *Idioms*, 67, emphasis original). "The middle voice represents the subject as acting on, for or towards itself" (McKay, 21).

& Mantey advise, "The student should seek to master the fundamental significance of the middle voice, then interpret each use in the light of its own context and the meaning of the verb."[19]

Reflexive Middle

The reflexive middle is also known as the direct middle because the subject of the verb performs something (directly) *to* himself (or acts *on* himself). Although this form was common in classical Greek, it was gradually replaced with the more explicit (especially for non-native speakers) reflexive active. Perhaps the most commonly noted example is found in Matt 27:5 where the text states that Judas "went out and **hanged himself**" (ἀπελθὼν **ἀπήγξατο**).[20]

Special Interest Middle

The special interest middle is the most common use of the middle voice and is also known as the indirect (or intensive or dynamic) middle. It indicates that the subject performs something *for* himself (i.e., for his own interest). In Luke 10:42 we read, "Mary **has chosen** the good portion" (ESV; Μαριὰμ τὴν ἀγαθὴν μερίδα **ἐξελέξατο**). The middle voice indicates *not* that Mary chose herself (a reflexive meaning) because the text indicates that she chose "the good portion." The middle voice is used here to communicate that Mary chose something that affects her personally. She chose something for herself or for her own interest (this clearly does not mean the person is being selfish, but that they have some stake in the matter). Also see Acts 5:2 (Ananias "**kept back** [for himself] part of the proceeds," **ἐνοσφίσατο** ἀπὸ τῆς τιμῆς) and Eph 1:4 (God "**chose** us [for himself] in him," **ἐξελέξατο** ἡμᾶς ἐν αὐτῷ).

Permissive (Causative) Middle

The permissive middle refers to the subject allowing or permitting something to be done to or for himself. It is also closely associated with what some call the *causative* middle which entails the subject not simply permitting something to be done, but actually causing it to occur.[21] In Acts 22:16 Ananias tells Paul, "Get up and **be baptized** (βάπτισαι) and **wash away** (ἀπόλουσαι) your sins, calling on his name." It is evident that these two verbs are best viewed as permissive (or causative) middles because it is unbiblical for someone to baptize himself (notice how the passive was used in the translation), nor is it sound theology to suggest that a new believer is able to wash away his own sins. Instead, the idea is that Ananias instructs Paul to permit himself to be baptized and allow God to wash away his sins. Also see Luke 2:5 (Joseph went up from Galilee "to be registered," ἀπογράψασθαι); 1 Cor

---

[19] Dana & Mantey, 158.

[20] For more examples of the reflexive middle, see Mark 7:4 (βαπτίσωνται); 14:54 (θερμαινόμενος); Luke 12:15 (φυλάσσεσθε), 37 (περιζώσεται); Acts 12:21 (ἐνδυσάμενος); 1 Cor 14:8 (παρασκευάσεται); 16:16 (ὑποτάσσησθε); Rev 3:18 (περιβάλῃ).

[21] "The *permissive* middle is very close to the *causative* middle. The latter implies ultimate source and often volition; the former suggests that the prompting lay elsewhere and only that consent or permission or toleration was wrung from the subject" (Wallace, 425).

6:11 (Although formerly they were unrighteous, Paul informs the Corinthians, "You were washed," ἀπελούσασθε); 1 Cor 10:2 ("All **were baptized** into Moses," πάντες εἰς τὸν Μωϋσῆν **ἐβαπτίσαντο**[22]); and Gal 5:2 ("If you **get yourself circumcised**, Christ will not benefit you at all," ἐὰν **περιτέμνησθε**, Χριστὸς ὑμᾶς οὐδὲν ὠφελήσει).

Deponent Middle

A typical definition of a deponent verb is one that is middle (or passive) in form, but active in meaning (function). The term *deponent* (from the Latin verb *deponere*) means "to lay aside." Thus, according to the traditional explanation, the original middle or passive meaning of the verb is "laid aside" and is replaced with an active meaning.[23] More recent studies, however, have rightly called into question the concept of deponency.[24] For example, Jonathan Pennington states that the grammatical category of deponent verbs is unhelpful and even erroneous. Instead, he suggests that most verbs that have been traditionally considered "deponent" are truly middle in meaning. He maintains that the category of deponent verbs has been accepted by many grammarians because of two main reasons: (1) the influence of Latin grammar which has no true middle voice but rather only has the categories of active and passive, (2) the unfamiliarity with the middle voice since English also does not have this grammatical category. He offers the example of δέχομαι which is typically listed among deponent verbs because all the extant forms are middle or passive but the meaning is active ("I receive"). And yet, simply because a verb does not occur in the active voice (when its apparent meaning is active) does not necessarily make it deponent.[25] Assuming the category of deponency still has some limited legitimacy, δέχομαι could only be considered deponent if the middle sense was lacking, which is not the case because "I receive" clearly involves the idea of reciprocity (one of the uses of the middle voice).

So, although some grammars assume that the "deponent middle" category is the most common use of the middle, this assessment is based on the faulty assumption

---

[22] Some manuscripts have the passive ἐβαπτίσθησαν (which is more likely original). This example could also be categorized as a causative middle.

[23] So Wallace, 428. Others suggest that what is set aside is not the original middle or passive *meaning*, but the active *form*. For example, Robertson writes that the deponent "is used to mean the laying aside of the active form in the case of verbs that have no active voice" (811–12).

[24] See, e.g., Jonathan T. Pennington, "Deponency in Koine Greek: The Grammatical Question and the Lexicographical Dilemma," *TrinJ* 24 (2003): 55–76; idem, "Setting Aside 'Deponency' and Rediscovering the Greek Middle Voice in New Testament Studies" in *The Linguist as Pedagogue: Trends in the Teaching and Linguistic Analysis of the Greek New Testament*, ed. Stanley E. Porter and Matthew Book O'Donnell, New Testament Monograph 11 (Sheffield: Sheffield Phoenix, 2009), 181–203. For an overview of this topic, see Constantine R. Campbell, *Advances in the Study of Greek: New Insights for Reading the New Testament* (Grand Rapids: Zondervan, 2015), chap. 4.

[25] "There are some verbs that never had an active form, but the true middle force is clearly seen. For example, δέχομαι means *I receive, welcome*—an idea that is inherently reflexive. It is not enough, therefore, to note merely that a verb lacks an active form throughout its history; it must also be demonstrated that the middle *force* is absent" (Wallace, 429; also see similar remarks on p. 421).

that many middle verbs are really odd-looking active verbs.[26] Instead, "The Greek verbal system has a rich and nuanced middle voice capable of communicating any number of actions, attitudes and conditions involving a subject-focused lexical idea."[27] There is also some potential exegetical payoff for appreciating the significance of the middle voice. Consequently, Pennington suggests that we need to rethink the necessity of having a category called *deponent* and instead treat most so-called deponent verbs as true middles.[28]

Recognizing the overlap of middle and passive forms in various paradigms, some grammarians argue it is best to speak of two categories of endings—active and "medio-passive" (or middle/passive). In this textbook, we have tried to present a balanced summary, recognizing the wide use of the category of "deponency" by other Greek scholars, while seeking to bring students to a better understanding of most (and perhaps all) supposed deponent verbs as actually Greek middles.

Passive Voice

As noted earlier, with the passive voice the subject does not perform the action; rather, the subject receives the action (or is acted upon). Thus, the subject of the verb is "passive," and the one performing the action (i.e., the agent) is either implied or referenced using another grammatical construction (usually a prepositional phrase). For example, if someone states, "I am blessed by God," the subject "I" is not performing an action but is receiving something (a blessing). The one performing the act is God, but grammatically he is not the subject of the sentence. Similarly, if someone merely stated, "I am blessed," then God would be the understood or implied agent who gives the blessing.

The most common construction used with the passive voice to communicate the agent of the action is the preposition ὑπό + genitive (sometimes with ἀπό + gen and rarely παρά + gen). With this construction, the agent indicates the person who is ultimately responsible for the action (this is sometimes called the *ultimate agent*).[29]

---

[26] For example, Mounce calculates the deponency rate of middle-passive verbs at approximately 75 percent (Mounce, *Basics of Biblical Greek*, 149 [see chap. 2, n. 4]). Similarly, Wenham maintains that "verbs in the middle are usually deponent." See J. W. Wenham, *The Elements of New Testament Greek* (Cambridge: Cambridge University Press, 1965), 93.

[27] Pennington, "Setting Aside 'Deponency,'" 190. Robertson suggests that the following verbs may be deponent: αἰσθάνομαι ("I understand"), ἀρνέομαι ("I deny"), ἀσπάζομαι ("I greet"), διαβεβαιόομαι ("I speak confidently"), ἐντέλλομαι ("I command"), ἐπιλανθάνομαι ("I forget"), εὔχομαι ("I pray"), ἡγέομαι ("I think"), λογίζομαι ("I reckon"), μαίνομαι ("I am mad"), and μέμφομαι ("I blame") (812). In addition to these verbs, Wallace lists the following verbs that look deponent but most likely are not: ἀποκρίνομαι ("I answer"), βουλεύομαι ("I decide"), δέχομαι ("I receive"), ἐκλέγομαι ("I choose"), καυχάομαι ("I boast"), μιμνήσκομαι ("I remember"), παύσομαι ("I stop"), and προσκαλέομαι ("I summon") (430). Often the verbs in question denote mental activity.

[28] Pennington is building on the work Suzanne Kemmer, *The Middle Voice* (Amsterdam and Philadelphia: John Benjamins, 1993); idem, "Middle Voice, Transitivity, and the Elaboration of Events," in *Voice: Form and Function*, ed. Barbara A. Fox and Paul J. Hopper (Amsterdam and Philadelphia: John Benjamins, 1994); and Rutger J. Allan, *The Middle Voice in Ancient Greece: A Study in Polysemy* (Brill: Leiden, 2003).

[29] See Wallace, 433–39 for a more detailed discussion of agency.

For example, in Acts 10:42 Luke writes, "He is the one appointed **by God** to be the judge" (οὗτός ἐστιν ὁ ὡρισμένος **ὑπὸ τοῦ θεοῦ** κριτής). To communicate that the agent was involved but not ultimately responsible, διά + genitive is used (this is sometimes called the *intermediate agent*). For example, Matt 1:22 states, "What was spoken by the Lord **through the prophet**" (τὸ ῥηθὲν ὑπὸ κυρίου **διὰ τοῦ προφήτου**). This verse offers a good comparison of the two different types of agency. The ultimate agent is "by the Lord" (ὑπὸ κυρίου) because prophecy ultimately comes from God. The intermediate agent is "through the prophet" (διὰ τοῦ προφήτου) because prophets are those who communicate God's Word to the people. Consequently, the evangelists consistently use ὑπό + genitive in relation to God the Father, whereas they use διά + genitive in relation those who deliver God's words and accomplish his will (see also Gal 3:18). Passive verb constructions also sometimes indicate an impersonal means which is communicated by ἐν + dative (or less often ἐκ + gen) or with a simple dative with no preposition. In Eph 2:18, Paul states, "We both have access to the Father through Christ **by one Spirit**" (CEB; ὅτι δι᾽ αὐτοῦ ἔχομεν τὴν προσαγωγὴν οἱ ἀμφότεροι **ἐν ἑνὶ πνεύματι** πρὸς τὸν πατέρα). This construction does not relate to us who the agent is, but rather the means by which the verb was accomplished.

Finally, passive verbs sometimes express no agent or means. This is done for a number of reasons, but when the subject clearly relates to God, the passive is referred to as a "divine passive."[30] The assumption is that God is not mentioned in the context because of the Jewish aversion to using the divine name (lest they use it in vain). For instance, some of the blessings that Jesus offers in the Beatitudes are given in the passive voice with no agent mentioned: "they will be comforted" (παρακληθήσονται; Matt 5:4); "they will be filled" (χορτασθήσονται; Matt 5:6); "they will be shown mercy" (ἐλεηθήσονται; Matt 5:7); "they will be called sons of God" (κληθήσονται; Matt 5:9). In the first example, the understood meaning is that those who mourn will be comforted *by God*. If the sentence were in the active voice, it would state, "God will comfort them." Wallace rightly warns, however, that this construction may have been used not so much to avoid the divine name, but for stylistic reasons. He writes, "Such expressions are obviously not due to any reticence on the part of the author to utter the name of God. It might be better to say that this phenomenon is due to certain collocations that would render the repetition of the divine name superfluous, even obtrusive. . . . That God is behind the scenes is self-evidently part of the worldview of the NT writers. The nature of [the Bible] demands that we see him even when he is not mentioned."[31]

Simple Passive

The simple passive is the most common use of the passive voice and indicates that the subject receives the action. Young indicates that one of the reasons for this

---

[30] Conversely, there are instances in the NT where the implied agent is not God, but Satan (e.g., 1 Tim 2:14 [ἠπατήθη and ἐξαπατηθεῖσα]). This may be called a "diabolical passive."
[31] Wallace, 438.

use is to keep a particular theme at the forefront of the discussion (he calls it "the-matizing the subject"). For example, in order for Paul to keep the "righteousness of God" as the main topic, he is forced to use the passive: "For in it the righteousness of God **is revealed**" (δικαιοσύνη γὰρ θεοῦ ἐν αὐτῷ **ἀποκαλύπτεται**; Rom 1:17).

Permissive Passive
The permissive passive is similar to the permissive middle and implies consent, permission, or even cause of the action and is often used in connection with im-peratives. For example, in Eph 5:18 Paul writes, "Do not get drunk with wine . . . but **be filled** with the Spirit" (ESV; μὴ μεθύσκεσθε οἴνῳ . . . ἀλλὰ **πληροῦσθε** ἐν πνεύματι). Here, Paul gives the Ephesian Christians a passive command (which seems like an oxymoron). In other words, why command someone to do some-thing in which they are passive? The idea is that Christians are commanded to be filled with the Spirit, but the filling itself is not something that the Christian does but something that is done to him when he submits himself to God's will.

Deponent Passive
See the previous discussion concerning deponent verbs under the subheading "Deponent Middle."[32]

MOOD

The mood of a verb is a morphological feature of the verb that indicates the author's or speaker's attitude (i.e., its actuality or potentiality) toward an event.[33] There are four moods in Greek. (1) The *indicative* represents something as certain or asserted ("He went fishing"). (2) The *subjunctive* represents something as prob-able or undefined ("Whenever he goes fishing"). (3) The *optative* represents some-thing as possible or hoped for ("I wish he would go fishing"). (4) The *imperative* represents something as intended or commanded ("Go fishing!").[34] The indicative mood is by far the most common in the NT, occurring 15,674 times.[35] In contrast, the subjunctive mood occurs 1,863 times, the imperative mood occurs 1,648 times,

---

[32] See esp. Allan, *Middle Voice in Ancient Greek*, who notes that the passive category is essen-tially a function of the middle system in Greek. Along this spectrum, reflexive middle would be on one extreme of the middle functions and passive on the other. Among other things, this would help explain θη forms that are not passive in function. See also the perceptive discussions in Robertson, 347, 356–57.

[33] "*Mood is the morphological feature of a verb that a speaker uses to **portray** his or her affirma-tion as to the certainty of the verbal action or state (whether an actuality or potentiality)*" (Wallace, 445; emphasis original).

[34] Technically speaking, participles and infinitives are not moods since they are dependent on main verbs to communicate a particular "mood." For purposes of convenience, however, participles and infinitives are usually labeled as such when parsed.

[35] The number here represents the total of individual tense-forms searched and then added togeth-er. When the search is done for all indicatives regardless of tense-form, the total number is slightly less (15,628). Unless otherwise noted, statistics in this volume are based on searches in a morpholog-ical database created by Michael Bushell, Jean-Noel Aletti, and Andrzej Gieniusz.

and the optative mood occurs only 68 times. It should also be emphasized that, outside of the indicative mood, the element of time is completely absent.[36]

INDICATIVE MOOD	Declarative	
	Interrogative	
	Conditional	
	Cohortative	
	Potential	
SUBJECTIVE MOOD	Dependent Subjunctives	Purpose
		Result
		Conditional
		Indefinite Relative
		Indefinite Temporal
	Independent Subjunctives	Hortatory
		Deliberate
		Emphatic Negation
		Prohibitory
OPTATIVE MOOD	Voluntative	
	Deliberative	
	Potential	
IMPERATIVE MOOD	Command	
	Prohibition	
	Request	
	Permission	
	Conditional	
	Greeting	

Indicative Mood

The indicative mood is used to make an assertion. Statements in the indicative mood do not necessarily indicate a fact. Rather, the indicative has to do with the manner in which a statement is made and not the objective nature or truth of the statement. Thus, it is possible for someone to lie (see Acts 6:13) or be mistaken (see Luke 7:39) while using the indicative mood.

---

[36] "There is but one mood which has essential temporal relations; viz., the indicative. . . . Hence the time element is entirely absent from the potential [i.e., the subjunctive, optative, and impera-tive] moods" (Dana & Mantey, 167). Porter even argues that indicative verbs lack any time element (Porter, *Idioms*, 25, 29–45). See chapter 7 for more information on this topic.

Declarative Indicative

The declarative indicative is the most common use of the indicative and is employed to present an unqualified assertion or statement. For example, John states, "In the beginning **was** the Word" (ἐν ἀρχῇ ἦν ὁ λόγος; John 1:1). In Matt 16:16 Peter confessed, "You **are** the Messiah, the Son of the living God" (σὺ **εἶ** ὁ χριστὸς ὁ υἱὸς τοῦ θεοῦ τοῦ ζῶντος).

Interrogative Indicative

The indicative is often used to ask a question that will also be answered in the indicative mood. Such questions are typically asking for information as opposed to indicating whether something is possible or involves a moral obligation.[37] In John 1:19, the Jews send priests and Levites to John the Baptist in order to ask him, "Who **are** you?" (Σὺ τίς **εἶ**;). It should also be noted that Greek has the ability to indicate whether the anticipated answer to a question is "yes" or "no." If the particle οὐ is used, then the intended answer is usually "yes." For example, in 1 Cor 9:1 Paul asks a series of questions that all demand a positive answer: "Am I **not** free? Am I **not** an apostle? Have I **not** seen Jesus our Lord? Are you **not** my work in the Lord?" (**οὐκ** εἰμὶ ἐλεύθερος; **οὐκ** εἰμὶ ἀπόστολος; **οὐχὶ** Ἰησοῦν τὸν κύριον ἡμῶν ἑόρακα; **οὐ** τὸ ἔργον μου ὑμεῖς ἐστε ἐν κυρίῳ;). By using οὐ, οὐκ, or οὐχί, Paul is clearly indicating a "yes" answer to each question. On the other hand, if the particle μή is used, then the intended answer is usually "no." Paul states in 1 Cor 12:30, "All do **not** speak with tongues, do they?" (NASB; **μὴ** πάντες γλώσσαις λαλοῦσιν;). The English translation of the NASB correctly anticipates a negative answer, "No, all do not speak in tongues." In other cases, a question can be asked, not to gain information, but to draw one's attention to a particular topic. This is known as a rhetorical question (see, e.g., Rom 6:1).

Conditional Indicative

The conditional indicative is found in the protasis (or "if clause") of a conditional sentence (see discussion of the subjunctive mood below). There are roughly 350 uses of this type of indicative in both first class condition clauses (which indicate the assumption of truth for the sake of the argument; more than 300 examples) and second class conditional clauses (which indicate the assumption of an untruth for the sake of argument; fewer than 50 examples). An example of a first class conditional indicative is Col 3:1: "So if **you have been raised** with Christ [and you have], seek the things above" (εἰ οὖν **συνηγέρθητε** τῷ Χριστῷ, τὰ ἄνω ζητεῖτε). An example of a second class conditional indicative is John 5:46, "For if **you believed** Moses [and you don't], you would believe me, because he wrote about me" (εἰ γὰρ **ἐπιστεύετε** Μωϋσεῖ, ἐπιστεύετε ἂν ἐμοί· περὶ γὰρ ἐμοῦ ἐκεῖνος ἔγραψεν).

---

[37] "The interrogative indicative assumes that there is an actual fact which may be stated in answer to the question" (Dana & Mantey, 168).

Cohortative Indicative

The cohortative indicative (sometimes called the indicative of command or a volitive indicative), involves a future indicative that is used as a command. For example, in Jas 2:8 we read, "**You shall love** your neighbor as yourself" (ESV; ἀγαπήσεις τὸν πλησίον σου ὡς σεαυτόν). This obviously is not a future prediction but is a use of the future tense that functions as an imperative.

Potential Indicative

The indicative is often used with verbs of obligation (ὀφείλω, δεῖ), wish (βούλομαι), or desire (θέλω), followed by an infinitive. In 1 Tim 5:14, Paul instructs the church at Ephesus, "**I want** younger women to marry" (**βούλομαι** οὖν νεωτέρας γαμεῖν).

Subjunctive Mood

The subjunctive mood represents the verbal action as indefinite but probable (the mood of probability). Some grammars describe the subjunctive as the mood of uncertainty but this is not altogether accurate. For example, John uses the subjunctive to describe the return of Christ ("when he appears," ἐὰν φανερωθῇ; 1 John 2:28; 3:2). John uses the subjunctive not because the return of Christ is uncertain, but because the time of His return is unknown to us and therefore is indefinite. We should also note that non-indicative verb forms (like the subjunctive) do not involve time of action but are restricted to the kind of action or the author's perspective of the action. Despite the particular tense-form used, the subjunctive often deals with something that *might* take place in the future, whereas the future indicative usually indicates something that *will* take place (at least as portrayed by the one who is making the statement).

Dependent Clause Subjunctives

Purpose or Result Clause. The most common use of the subjunctive is following the particle ἵνα, and the most frequent use of the ἵνα clause is to express purpose.[38] The purpose clause answers the question "Why?" and is usually translated "that," "in order that," or "to" (the last option is translated similar to an infinitive).

- τοῦτο δὲ ὅλον γέγονεν <u>ἵνα</u> **πληρωθῇ** τὸ ῥηθὲν ὑπὸ κυρίου (Matt 1:22)

  Now all this took place [in order] <u>to</u> **fulfill** what was spoken by the Lord

- οὗτος ἦλθεν εἰς μαρτυρίαν <u>ἵνα</u> **μαρτυρήσῃ** περὶ τοῦ φωτός (John 1:7)

  He came as a witness [in order] <u>to</u> **testify** about the light

Closely related to a purpose clause is a result clause (the main difference is that a purpose clause is an intended result and a result clause is something that already

---

[38] Wallace lists seven basic uses of ἵνα: purpose, result, purpose-result, substantival, epexegetical, complementary, and command (471).

actually occurred, whether intended or not). The result clause is usually translated "that," "so that," or "with the result that." In addition to ἵνα, ὅπως is also sometimes used with a result clause.

- τίς ἥμαρτεν, οὗτος ἢ οἱ γονεῖς αὐτοῦ, <u>ἵνα</u> τυφλὸς **γεννηθῇ** (John 9:2)

  Who sinned, this man or his parents, <u>that</u> [<u>as a result</u>] **he was born** blind?

- πιστός ἐστιν καὶ δίκαιος, <u>ἵνα</u> **ἀφῇ** ἡμῖν τὰς ἁμαρτίας (1 John 1:9)

  He is faithful and righteous <u>to</u> **forgive** us our sins

  > Clearly in this context, there is no doubt as to whether God will forgive our sins. The idea here is, "If we confess our sins, He is faithful and just so that [as a result] he forgives our sins."

Conditional Clause. The subjunctive with the particle ἐάν ("if") or ἐὰν μή ("unless") is used in the protasis ("if" clause) of a third class conditional sentence and expresses a probable, though at times hypothetical, future condition.[39] This use of the subjunctive is common, occurring nearly 300 times in the NT.

- <u>ἐὰν μή</u> τις **γεννηθῇ** ἄνωθεν, οὐ δύναται ἰδεῖν τὴν βασιλείαν τοῦ θεοῦ (John 3:3)

  <u>Unless</u> someone **is born** again, he cannot see the kingdom of God

- <u>ἐάν</u> τις τὸν ἐμὸν λόγον **τηρήσῃ**, θάνατον οὐ μὴ θεωρήσῃ εἰς τὸν αἰῶνα (John 8:51)

  <u>If</u> anyone **keeps** my word, he will never see death

- <u>ἐὰν</u> **ὁμολογήσῃς** ἐν τῷ στόματί σου . . . καὶ **πιστεύσῃς** ἐν τῇ καρδίᾳ σου . . . σωθήσῃ (Rom 10:9)

  <u>if</u> you **confess** with your mouth . . . and [<u>if</u> you] **believe** in your heart . . . you will be saved[40]

Indefinite Relative or Temporal Clause. The subjunctive is used after the indefinite relative pronouns ὅστις (ἄν/ἐάν) or ὅς (δ᾽) ἄν. These constructions generally indicate a generic or indefinite subject. That is, they make a relative pronoun (e.g., "who") indefinite or uncertain ("who*ever*").

- <u>ὅστις</u> δ᾽ ἂν **ἀρνήσηταί** με ἔμπροσθεν τῶν ἀνθρώπων, ἀρνήσομαι κἀγὼ αὐτὸν ἔμπροσθεν τοῦ πατρός μου (Matt 10:33)

  <u>But whoever</u> **denies** me before others, I will also deny him before my Father

---

[39] ἐάν is a combination of εἰ + contingent particle ἄν.
[40] For an example of ὅπως + subjunctive expressing purpose, see Heb 2:9.

- ὃς ἂν **ἐπικαλέσηται** τὸ ὄνομα κυρίου σωθήσεται (Acts 2:21)

  <u>everyone who</u> [lit. "whoever"] **calls** on the name of the Lord will be saved (cf. Rom 10:13)

The subjunctive is also used after the temporal conjunction ὅταν or after a temporal adverb or preposition (e.g., ἕως, ἄχρι, μέχρι) and is typically translated "whenever."

- <u>ὅταν</u> γὰρ **λέγῃ** τις, Ἐγὼ μέν εἰμι Παύλου, ἕτερος δέ, Ἐγὼ Ἀπολλῶ, οὐκ ἄνθρωποί ἐστε; (1 Cor 3:4)

  For <u>whenever</u> someone **says**, 'I belong to Paul,' and another, 'I belong to Apollos,' are you not acting like mere humans?

- τὸν θάνατον τοῦ κυρίου καταγγέλλετε <u>ἄχρις</u> οὗ **ἔλθῃ** (1 Cor 11:26)

  you proclaim the Lord's death <u>until</u> he **comes**

Independent Clause Subjunctives

Hortatory Subjunctive. Also known as the volitive subjunctive, the hortatory subjunctive is used when the author wants to command his audience but also include himself in the command. Or better, the author is urging his audience to join with him in a particular course of action. Normally, the imperative is used for commands. The imperative, however, is found in only the second and third persons ("you [sg or pl] loose," or "let him/them loose"). The hortatory subjunctive is an exhortation in the *first person plural* ("let us").[41]

- **ἐργαζώμεθα** τὸ ἀγαθὸν πρὸς πάντας (Gal 6:10)

  Let us do good to everyone (ESV)

- **προσερχώμεθα** οὖν . . . τῷ θρόνῳ τῆς χάριτος (Heb 4:16)

  Therefore **let us approach** the throne of grace

- **ἀγαπῶμεν** ἀλλήλους (1 John 4:7)

  let us love one another

Deliberative Subjunctive. Also known as the dubitative subjunctive, the deliberative subjunctive asks a real or rhetorical question. In the first instance with real questions, the speaker is typically asking for some sort of guidance and therefore expects an answer. The use of the subjunctive signifies some uncertainty or indefiniteness about the answer.

---

[41] There are also five NT instances where the hortatory subjunctive is used with the first person *singular* ("let me"). See Matt 7:4 (ἐκβάλω); Luke 6:42 (ἐκβάλω); Acts 7:34 (ἀποστείλω); Rev 17:1 (δείξω); 21:9 (δείξω; it is likely that Rev 17:1 and 21:9 are future indicatives).

- ποῦ θέλεις **ἐτοιμάσωμέν** σοι φαγεῖν τὸ πάσχα (Matt 26:17)

  Where do you want us **to make preparations** for you to eat the Passover?

  This is a genuine question to which the disciples did not know the answer (uncertainty).

- ἀπελθόντες **ἀγοράσωμεν** δηναρίων διακοσίων ἄρτους καὶ δώσομεν αὐτοῖς φαγεῖν (Mark 6:37)

  Should we go and **buy** two hundred denarii worth of bread and give them something to eat?

  The disciples are seeking an answer but their question is not so much should they go and buy bread (factual or informational) but how they are expected to feed 5,000 people (possible).

The other type of deliberative subjunctive asks a rhetorical question that does not expect an answer. Thus, this type of question is not one in search of facts but is a veiled challenge to the readers to change their behavior or thinking.

- **ἐπιμένωμεν** τῇ ἁμαρτίᾳ, ἵνα ἡ χάρις πλεονάσῃ (Rom 6:1)

  Should we continue in sin so that grace may multiply?

  It is evident that Paul is not seeking information because his immediate response is "Absolutely not!" (μὴ γένοιτο). He is not really asking if we should continue in sin in order that grace may multiply. Instead, he is urging his readers to see that it is not morally acceptable for them to willfully continue to sin against God.

- τί **εἴπω** ὑμῖν; **ἐπαινέσω** ὑμᾶς (1 Cor 11:22)

  What **should I say** to you? **Should I praise** you?

  Again, Paul is not asking for information from his readers but is rebuking them for misusing and abusing the Lord's Supper. He answers the second question by stating, "I do not praise you for this!"[42]

Emphatic Negation Subjunctive. Emphatic negation is expressed by the double negative οὐ μή (the indicative and non-indicative negative particles)[43] plus the aorist subjunctive (or less commonly, the future indicative). As its name suggests, this type of negation is emphatic and strongly denies that something will happen. In fact, it is the strongest way to negate a statement in Greek. About 90 percent of the occurrences are found in the sayings of Jesus and in citations from the Septuagint. It is often translated as "never," "certainly not," or "absolutely not."

---

[42] Also see the "Going Deeper" section at the beginning of this chapter that provides more examples of this category from Rom 10:14–15.

[43] That is, οὐ is used to negate indicative verbs, whereas μή is used to negate non-indicative verbs. When μή is used to negate an indicative verb in a question, it assumes a negative answer to the posed question.

- οὐ μὴ **εἰσέλθητε** εἰς τὴν βασιλείαν τῶν οὐρανῶν (Matt 5:20)

  you will <u>never</u> enter the kingdom of heaven (ESV)

  > To translate this phrase, "you will *not* enter the kingdom of heaven," simply does not do justice to the emphatic form.

- μὴ κρίνετε, καὶ οὐ μὴ **κριθῆτε** (Luke 6:37)

  Do not judge, and **you will <u>not</u> be judged**

  > The Greek is stronger than the English "not." Perhaps a better translation is "Do not judge, and you will *by no means* be judged."

- οὐ μὴ σε **ἀνῶ** οὐδ᾽ *οὐ μή σε* **ἐγκαταλίπω** (Heb 13:5)

  I will <u>never</u> leave you nor [*never*] **forsake** you (ESV)

  > This verse is perhaps the most powerful verse in the Bible due the fact that it contains 5 negatives (2 emphatic negations plus the conjunction οὐδέ ["nor"]). This idea is well captured in the old hymn "How Firm a Foundation" where the last verse reads, "The soul that on Jesus has leaned for repose, I will not, I will not desert to its foes; That soul, though all hell should endeavor to shake, I'll *never, no never, no never* forsake."[44]

Prohibitory Subjunctive. The subjunctive is used as an imperative when two conditions are met: (1) the command is negated (a prohibition), and (2) the subjunctive uses the aorist tense-form. The following chart illustrates the use of the subjunctive:

	COMMAND	PROHIBITION
PRESENT	λυέ (loose)	μὴ λυέ (do not loose)
AORIST	λῦσον (loose)	**μὴ λύσῃς** (do not loose)

Notice that the second person aorist prohibition is not μὴ λῦσον (as one might expect) but is μὴ λύσῃς. It is translated "do not . . ." (i.e., as an imperative) and not "you should not . . ." (i.e., as a typical subjunctive).

By way of illustration, in Luke 18:16 Jesus is recorded as stating, "Let the children come to me, and **do not hinder** (μὴ κωλύετε) them" (ESV). Because the imperative is in the present tense-form (imperfective aspect; κωλύετε), the normal (imperatival) form is used. In contrast, when the aorist is used, the mood switches to the subjunctive. Again, Jesus teaches, "If anyone takes away your coat, **don't hold back** (μὴ κωλύσῃς) your shirt either" (Luke 6:29). Thus, because the command is negated *and* uses the aorist tense-form, the subjunctive (not the imperative) is used.

---

[44] The author of this hymn is unknown. It is found in John Rippon's hymnal (*A Selection of Hymns from the Best Authors*), but where the author's name is normally listed, only the initial "K" is referenced. Some think that this is a reference to the music director, Robert Keene, at Carter's Lane Baptist Church in London, where Rippon was a pastor for more than 50 years.

- μὴ **νομίσητε** ὅτι ἦλθον καταλῦσαι τὸν νόμον ἢ τοὺς προφήτας (Matt 5:17)

  Do not **think** that I have come to abolish the Law or the Prophets (ESV)

  Notice that the text is translated as a prohibition ("Do not think") and not as a normal subjunctive ("You should not think").

- μὴ **θαυμάσῃς** ὅτι εἶπόν σοι, Δεῖ ὑμᾶς γεννηθῆναι ἄνωθεν (John 3:7)

  Do not **be amazed** that I told you that you must be born again

- μὴ **ἅψῃ** μηδὲ γεύσῃ μηδὲ **θίγῃς** (Col 2:21)

  Do not **handle**, Do not **taste**, Do not **touch** (ESV)

Optative Mood

Whereas the subjunctive mood is sometimes described as the mood of *probability*, the optative mood is the mood of *possibility*. Or, "The subjunctive expresses action which is objectively possible, the optative that which is subjectively possible."[45] Thus, the optative is viewed as a "sort of weaker subjunctive" or "less assured in tone."[46] The optative was dying out in the Koine period, becoming absorbed by the subjunctive. Consequently, there are only 68 uses of the optative in the NT, which can be used to express a wish, prayer, or something that is potential.[47]

Voluntative Optative

The voluntative optative is used to express a prayer/benediction, blessing, or wish. Negatively, it can be used to express abhorrence (e.g., μὴ γένοιτο). The voluntative is the most common category of the optative, including 35 of the 68 occurrences (15 of which include μὴ γένοιτο).[48]

1. *Benediction:* χάρις ὑμῖν καὶ εἰρήνη **πληθυνθείη** ("**May** grace and peace **be multiplied** to you"; 1 Pet 1:2).

2. *(Imprecatory) Prayer:* τὸ ἀργύριόν σου σὺν σοὶ **εἴη** εἰς ἀπώλειαν ("May your silver **be** destroyed with you"; Acts 8:20).

3. *Blessing:* **δῴη** ἔλεος ὁ κύριος τῷ Ὀνησιφόρου οἴκῳ ("**May** the Lord **grant** mercy to the household of Onesiphorus"; 2 Tim 1:16).

---

[45] Brooks & Winbery, 124.

[46] The quotes are from Robertson, 936 and Moule, 23, respectively.

[47] Of the 68 occurrences of the optative, 45 are aorists and 23 are presents. In addition, most of the uses are found in Luke and Paul.

[48] 14 of the 15 occurrences are found in Paul's writings (Rom 3:6, 31; 6:2, 15; 7:7, 13; 9:14; 11:1, 11; 1 Cor 6:15; Gal 2:17; 3:21; 6:14). Luke's usage is found in Luke 20:16.

4. ***Abhorrence (μὴ γένοιτο)***: Paul asks the rhetorical question, "What then? Should we sin because we are not under law but under grace?" His response is emphatic: μὴ γένοιτο ("Absolutely not!"; Rom 6:15).[49]

Deliberative Optative

The second most common use of the optative (about 12 occurrences) is with indirect (rhetorical) questions. This usage is found exclusively in Luke's writings.[50]

- αὐτοὶ δὲ ἐπλήσθησαν ἀνοίας καὶ διελάλουν πρὸς ἀλλήλους τί ἂν **ποιήσαιεν** τῷ Ἰησοῦ (Luke 6:11)

    They, however, were filled with rage and started discussing with one another what **they might do** to Jesus

    > Note that this a not a direct question but is an indirect question. A direct question would be: "What will we do?"

- ἐπηρώτων δὲ αὐτὸν οἱ μαθηταὶ αὐτοῦ τίς αὕτη **εἴη** ἡ παραβολή (Luke 8:9)

    And His disciples began questioning Him as to what this parable **might be** (NASB)

    > A direct question would be: "What does this parable mean?"

Potential Optative

The potential optative involves a fourth class conditional clause (possible fulfillment).

- εἰ καὶ **πάσχοιτε** διὰ δικαιοσύνην, μακάριοι (1 Pet 3:14)

    even if **you should suffer** for righteousness, you are blessed

- κρεῖττον γὰρ ἀγαθοποιοῦντας, εἰ **θέλοι** τὸ θέλημα τοῦ θεοῦ, πάσχειν ἢ κακοποιοῦντας (1 Pet 3:17)

    For it is better to suffer for doing good, if that **should be** God's will, than for doing evil[51]

---

[49] Wallace paraphrases this statement: *"You should never conclude such a thing! God forbid that you should think so! No way!"* (482, emphasis original).

[50] For more uses of the deliberative optative, see Luke 1:29 (εἴη); 3:15 (εἴη); 9:46 (εἴη); 18:36 (εἴη); 22:23 (εἴη); Acts 5:24 (γένοιτο); 8:31 (δυναίμην); 17:11 (ἔχοι); 21:33 (εἴη); 25:20 (βούλοιτο).

[51] For more uses of the potential optative, see Luke 1:62 (θέλοι); Acts 5:24 (γένοιτο); 8:31 (δυναίμην); 17:18 (θέλοι), 27 (εὕροιεν); 20:16 (εἴη); 24:19 (ἔχοιεν); 27:12 (δύναιντο), 39 (δύναιντο); 1 Cor 14:10 (τύχοι); 15:37 (τύχοι).

Imperative Mood

The basic concept of the imperative mood is that it expresses a command. It is, however, best described as the mood of *intention* (or volition) and not mood of *command* because the imperative is used in contexts other than a command. "It expresses neither probability nor possibility, but only intention, and is, therefore, the furthest removed from reality."[52]

Command

To state the obvious, the use of the imperative as a command expresses an exhortation or charge and is the most common category of the imperative, occurring five times more than the prohibitory imperative. Like subjunctives, imperatives are found mainly in the present and aorist, though a few perfect imperatives occur in the NT as well.[53] Third person imperatives are normally translated as "let him/her/them" and likewise express a command (and not merely permission as English translations sometimes suggest).

- πάντοτε **χαίρετε**, ἀδιαλείπτως **προσεύχεσθε**, ἐν παντὶ **εὐχαριστεῖτε** (1 Thess 5:16–18)

  Rejoice always, **pray** constantly, **give thanks** in everything

- **πείθεσθε** τοῖς ἡγουμένοις ὑμῶν καὶ **ὑπείκετε** (Heb 13:17)

  Obey your leaders and **submit** to them

- εἰ δέ τις ὑμῶν λείπεται σοφίας, **αἰτείτω** παρὰ . . . θεοῦ (Jas 1:5)

  If any of you lacks wisdom, **let him ask** God (ESV)

  In this context, the force of the command is not merely permission ("let him") but functions closer to a second person imperative. The translation of the CSB is appropriate, "he should ask God."[54] The book of James has the highest frequency of imperatives in the New Testament.[55]

Prohibition

A prohibition is simply a *negative* command and is thus used to forbid an action. Like all non-indicative verbs, the imperative is negated with the particle μή (and

---

[52] Dana & Mantey, 174.

[53] For perfect imperatives, see Mark 4:39 (πεφίμωσο); Acts 15:29 (ἔρρωσθε); 23:30 (ἔρρωσθε, some manuscripts); Eph 5:5 (ἴστε); Heb 12:17 (ἴστε); Jas 1:19 (ἴστε). In the last three texts, it is possible that ἴστε is a perfect indicative.

[54] "The force of the imperative is probably not a mere urging or permission, but a command, in spite of the typical English rendering. An expanded gloss is, 'If anyone of you lacks wisdom, *he must ask* of God.' In other words, lacking wisdom (in the midst of trials [vv 2–4]) does not give one the option of seeking God, but the obligation" (Wallace, 486).

[55] See D. A. Carson and Douglas Moo, *An Introduction to the New Testament*, 2nd ed. (Grand Rapids: Zondervan, 2005), 629. The letter of James contains 54 imperatives and a few prohibitory aorist subjunctives that function as imperatives. Thus, about half of the 108 verses in James contain an imperative.

not οὐ). Because prohibitions in the aorist use the subjunctive mood (see above), nearly all imperative prohibitions are found in the present tense-form (imperfective aspect).[56] Contrary to the claim of many grammars, however, the use of the present tense-form does not usually indicate that the action is already ongoing and is therefore to be stopped.[57]

- μὴ οὖν **βασιλευέτω** ἡ ἁμαρτία ἐν τῷ θνητῷ ὑμῶν σώματι (Rom 6:12)

  Therefore **do not let** sin **reign** in your mortal body

  > There is no grammatical, syntactical, or contextual reason to translate this phrase, "Therefore do not let sin *continue* to reign in your mortal body."

- μὴ **ἀγαπᾶτε** τὸν κόσμον (1 John 2:15)

  Do not love the world

- μὴ παντὶ πνεύματι **πιστεύετε** (1 John 4:1)

  do not believe every spirit

Request (Entreaty)

When a command is given to a superior, it is usually weakened to the level of a mere request. In other words, someone with a lower social status does not usually command a higher-ranking individual to do something but must politely make a request. It is also possible (though not as common) that requests are made by people of higher rank to those below them. This category is therefore fitting for prayers where the petitioner is addressing God. In such prayers the aorist form of the imperative is normally used.[58] It is often appropriate to add the word "please" in the translation to communicate this force of the imperative.

- **ἐλθέτω** ἡ βασιλεία σου· **γενηθήτω** τὸ θέλημά σου. . . . τὸν ἄρτον ἡμῶν τὸν ἐπιούσιον **δὸς** ἡμῖν σήμερον (Matt 6:10–11)

  [May] Your kingdom **come**. [May] Your will **be done**. . . . [Please] **Give** us today our daily bread

  > These imperatives in the Lord's Prayer are not commands but requests to God. Also note that each of the imperatives in the Lord's Prayer is in the aorist tense-form.

---

[56] There are only 8 aorist prohibitions in the NT: Matt 6:3 (μὴ γνώτω); 24:17 (μὴ καταβάτω), 18 (μὴ ἐπιστρεψάτω); Mark 13:15 (μὴ καταβάτω μηδὲ εἰσελθάτω), 16 (μὴ ἐπιστρεψάτω); Luke 17:31 (μὴ καταβάτω, μὴ ἐπιστρεψάτω). Notice that two of these verbs (μὴ καταβάτω) and (μὴ ἐπιστρεψάτω) each occur in the triple tradition.

[57] For example, Brooks & Winbery assert, "The present imperative with μή is used to stop an action already in progress" (116). Young rightly points out that if every present imperative were interpreted in such a manner, "the vast majority of cases would result in forced exegesis" (Young, 144). See chapter 7 for a fuller analysis of the meaning of the present and aorist with non-indicative verbs, especially with imperatives.

[58] Though exceptions are found in Luke 11:3 (δίδου) and 22:42 (γινέσθω) where the present tense-form is used in prayers to God.

- εἴ τι δύνῃ, **βοήθησον** ἡμῖν σπλαγχνισθεὶς ἐφ᾽ ἡμᾶς (Mark 9:22)

  If you can do anything, [please] have compassion on us and **help** us

  > It is obvious from the context that the force of the imperative "help" (βοήθησον) is not that of a command but rather that of an entreaty. The desperate father is asking (even begging) Jesus to heal his demon-possessed son, and thus it would be appropriate to translate the imperative "please help."

- Πάτερ ἅγιε, **τήρησον** αὐτοὺς ἐν τῷ ὀνόματί σου (John 17:11)

  Holy Father, [please] **protect** them by your name

Permissive Imperative

This type of imperative is less common than those previously mentioned and is used to convey permission, allowance, or toleration. The person granting consent may or may not be in favor of the act but, for whatever reason, allows the person to attempt it. In contrast to the imperative of request (see above), this category usually involves a superior granting permission to an inferior. It is often appropriate to add "let" or "may" in the translation.[59]

- **ὑπάγετε** (Matt 8:32)

  [You may] **go**.

  > The Gadarene demoniacs beg Jesus to send them into the herd of pigs. Jesus then grants permission to their request by saying, "Go."

- εἰ ὁ ἄπιστος χωρίζεται, **χωριζέσθω** (1 Cor 7:15)

  If the unbeliever leaves, **let him leave**

- εἰ δέ τις ὑμῶν λείπεται σοφίας, **αἰτείτω** . . . θεοῦ (Jas 1:5)

  Now if any of you lacks wisdom, **he should ask** God

Conditional Imperative

Like the subjunctive, an imperative can be used to state a condition. The construction consists of an imperative followed by a future indicative (or a subjunctive or another imperative—both functioning like a future indicative) connected by καί. Though this use is not common, there are at least 20 such imperatives in the NT.

- ἀλλὰ μόνον **εἰπὲ** λόγῳ, καὶ ἰαθήσεται ὁ παῖς μου (Matt 8:8)

  But just **say** the word, and my servant will be cured

  > The meaning here is "If you say the word, then my servant will be cured."

---

[59] It should be remembered that not all third person imperatives convey permission even though the typical translation is "let him/them" (see note above regarding the imperative of command).

- **ἔρχου** καὶ ἴδε (John 1:46)

  Come and see

  > After Philip tells his brother Nathanael that he has found the Messiah, Nathanael
  > responds, "Can anything good come out of Nazareth?" To this Philip answers, "Come
  > and see." Because the first imperative communicates a condition, it is appropriate to
  > translate the phrase, "If you come, you will see."

- **ἐγγίσατε** τῷ θεῷ καὶ ἐγγιεῖ ὑμῖν (Jas 4:8)

  Draw near to God, and he will draw near to you

  > The idea here is, "If you draw near to God, then he will draw near to you."[60]

Wallace rightly argues that Eph 4:26, "**Be angry** and do not sin" (ὀργίζεσθε
καὶ μὴ ἁμαρτάνετε), does not belong in this category.[61] Grammatically, in all the
other examples, the trailing verb, in this case ἁμαρτάνετε, functions as a future
indicative. The meaning would then be, "If you are angry, you will not sin," which
hardly can be the meaning. In addition, the conditional imperatives still retain their
imperatival force. In other words, the author or speaker is still issuing a command.
In the previous example it would mean, "If you come—and I want you to come—
you will see." With Eph 4:26 it would thus communicate, "If you are angry—and
I want you to be angry—you will not sin." Wallace maintains that the imperatives
should be interpreted as a command and prohibition: "Be angry and do not sin." He
then explains the meaning of this verse: "one should not give a place to the devil *by
doing nothing about the sin in the midst of the believing community.* Entirely opposite of the 'introspective conscience' view, this text seems to be a shorthand expression for church discipline, suggesting that there is biblical warrant for δικαία
ὀργή (as the Greeks put it)—righteous indignation."[62]

Greeting

Greetings are often expressed with a stereotyped imperative. Under this category, the imperatival force has disappeared, being reduced to an exclamation. Such
examples are often found at the end of letters.

- **Χαῖρε**, ῥαββί (Matt 26:49)

  Greetings, Rabbi!

- ἐξ ὧν διατηροῦντες ἑαυτοὺς εὖ πράξετε. **ἔρρωσθε** (Acts 15:29)

  You will do well if you keep yourselves from these things. **Farewell**

---

[60] For more uses of the conditional imperative, see Matt 7:7 (αἰτεῖτε, ζητεῖτε, κρούετε); 8:8
(εἰπέ); John 1:39 (ἔρχεσθε); 2:19 (λύσατε); 7:52 (ἐραύνησον); Luke 6:37–38 (μὴ κρίνετε, μὴ
καταδικάζετε, ἀπολύετε, δίδοτε); Eph 5:14 (ἔγειρε, ἀνάστα); Jas 4:7–8 (ὑποτάγητε, ἀντίστητε,
ἐγγίσατε), 10 (ταπεινώθητε).
[61] Wallace, 491–92.
[62] Wallace, 492 (emphasis original).

TENSE & ASPECT

As mentioned above, the Greek verb system is quite complex. In this section we will only give a very brief summary of the various tenses, going into more detail in the next chapter. There are six tenses in NT Greek: present, future, imperfect, aorist, perfect, and pluperfect.[63] Generally speaking, the *indicative* mood tense consists of two qualities: time (the word "tense" comes from the Latin *tempus*, meaning time) and aspect. Time has to do with when the action occurs (the imperfect, aorist, perfect, and pluperfect usually occur in the past). Aspect has to do with how the author/speaker views or portrays the action. Because time is relevant only in the indicative mood, aspect seems to be the more dominant or primary force of the verb's tense.

SUMMARY

PERSON AND NUMBER (NOMINATIVE)		
	SINGULAR	PLURAL
FIRST	ἐγώ ("I")	ἡμεῖς ("we")
SECOND	σύ ("you" *sg*)	ὑμεῖς ("you" *pl*)
THIRD	αὐτός, –ή, –ό ("he," "she," "it")	αὐτοί, –αί, –ά (they)

ACTIVE VOICE		
SIMPLE	The subject directly performs the action of the verb.	ἠγάπησεν ὁ θεὸς τὸν κόσμον ("God **loved** the world"; John 3:16).
CAUSATIVE	The subject is the cause behind the action of the verb.	τὸν ἥλιον αὐτοῦ **ἀνατέλλει** (God "**causes** His sun **to rise**"; Matt 5:45).
REFLEXIVE	The subject performs the action to himself.	γύμναζε σεαυτὸν πρὸς εὐσέβειαν ("**Train** yourself in godliness"; 1 Tim 4:7).
MIDDLE VOICE		
REFLEXIVE	The subject performs the action to himself.	ἀπελθὼν **ἀπήγξατο** (Judas "went out and **hanged**" himself"; Matt 27:5).

---

[63] The future perfect does occur in the NT, but only in periphrasis (see Matt 16:19 [ἔσται δεδεμένον, ἔσται λελυμένον]; 18:18 [ἔσται δεδεμένα, ἔσται λελυμένα]).

MIDDLE VOICE		
SPECIAL INTEREST	The subject performs the action *for* himself.	Μαριὰμ τὴν ἀγαθὴν μερίδα **ἐξελέξατο** ("Mary has **chosen** the good portion"; Luke 10:42 ESV).
PERMISSIVE	The subject allows something to be done to or for himself.	ἀναστὰς **βάπτισαι** καὶ **ἀπόλουσαι** τὰς ἁμαρτίας σου ("Get up and **be baptized**, and **wash away** your sins"; Acts 22:16).
PASSIVE VOICE		
SIMPLE	The subject receives the action of the verb.	δικαιοσύνη θεοῦ . . . **ἀποκαλύπτεται** ("The righteousness of God **is revealed**"; Rom 1:17).
PERMISSIVE	The subject gives consent or permission regarding the action of the verb.	**πληροῦσθε** ἐν πνεύματι ("**Be filled** with the Spirit"; Eph 5:18 ESV).

INDICATIVE MOOD		
DECLARATIVE	An unqualified assertion or statement.	ἐν ἀρχῇ **ἦν** ὁ λόγος ("In the beginning **was** the Word"; John 1:1).
INTERROGATIVE	A question that will also be answered in the indicative mood.	Σὺ τίς **εἶ**; ("Who **are** you?"; John 1:19).
CONDITIONAL	*First Class:* The protasis ("if" clause) of a first class conditional sentence.	εἰ οὖν **συνηγέρθητε** τῷ Χριστῷ, τὰ ἄνω ζητεῖτε ("So if you have **been raised** with Christ, seek the things above"; Col 3:1).
	Second Class: The protasis of a second class conditional sentence.	εἰ γὰρ **ἐπιστεύετε** Μωϋσεῖ, ἐπιστεύετε ἂν ἐμοί· περὶ γὰρ ἐμοῦ ἐκεῖνος ἔγραψεν ("For if you **believed** Moses, you would believe me, because he wrote about me"; John 5:46).
COHORTATIVE	A future indicative that is used as a command.	**ἀγαπήσεις** τὸν πλησίον σου ("You **shall love** your neighbor"; Jas 2:8 ESV).
POTENTIAL	Used with verbs of obligation, wish, or desire, followed by a complementary infinitive.	**βούλομαι** οὖν νεωτέρας γαμεῖν ("I **want** younger women to marry"; 1 Tim 5:14).

SUBJUNCTIVE MOOD		
PURPOSE	Follows the particle ἵνα (or ὅπως) and expresses purpose (intended result).	<u>ἵνα</u> **μαρτυρήσῃ** περὶ τοῦ φωτός ("[John the Baptist came] <u>to</u> **testify** about the the light"; John 1:7).

SUBJUNCTIVE MOOD		
RESULT	Follows the particle ἵνα (or ὅπως) and expresses result (actual result).	τίς ἥμαρτεν, οὗτος ἢ οἱ γονεῖς αὐτοῦ, ἵνα τυφλὸς γεννηθῇ; ("Who sinned, this man or his parents, <u>that</u> [as a result] he was born blind?"; John 9:2).
CONDITIONAL	Follows the particle ἐάν or ἐὰν μή and is used in the protasis of a third class conditional sentence.	ἐάν τις τὸν ἐμὸν λόγον τηρήσῃ ("<u>If</u> anyone keeps my word"; John 8:51).
INDEFINITE RELATIVE	Used after the indefinite relative pronouns ὅστις (ἄν/ ἐάν) or ὃς (δ') ἄν.	ὃς ἂν ἐπικαλέσηται τὸ ὄνομα κυρίου σωθήσεται ("everyone [lit. "<u>whoever</u>"] calls on the name of the Lord will be saved"; Acts 2:21).
INDEFINITE TEMPORAL	Used after the temporal conjunction ὅταν or after a temporal adverb or preposition (e.g., ἕως, ἄχρι, μέχρι).	ὅταν γὰρ λέγῃ τις ("For <u>whenever</u> someone says"; 1 Cor 3:4).
HORTATORY	The author commands his audience but also includes himself in the command.	ἐργαζώμεθα τὸ ἀγαθὸν πρὸς πάντας ("Let us do good to everyone"; Gal 6:10 ESV).
DELIBERATIVE	Asks a real or rhetorical question.	ἐπιμένωμεν τῇ ἁμαρτίᾳ, ἵνα ἡ χάρις πλεονάσῃ ("Should we continue in sin so that grace may multiply?"; Rom 6:1).
EMPHATIC NEGATION	Expressed by the double negative οὐ μή, it strongly denies that something will happen.	οὐ μὴ εἰσέλθητε εἰς τὴν βασιλείαν τῶν οὐρανῶν ("you will <u>never</u> enter the kingdom of heaven"; Matt 5:20 ESV).
PROHIBITORY	Used when two conditions are met: (1) the command is negated, and (2) the subjunctive uses the aorist tense-form.	μὴ νομίσητε ὅτι ἦλθον καταλῦσαι τὸν νόμον ἢ τοὺς προφήτας ("Do <u>not</u> think that I have come to abolish the Law or the Prophets"; Matt 5:17 ESV).

OPTATIVE MOOD		
VOLUNTATIVE	Expresses a prayer, benediction, blessing, or wish.	χάρις ὑμῖν καὶ εἰρήνη πληθυνθείη ("May grace and peace be multiplied to you"; 1 Pet 1:2).
DELIBERATIVE	Used with indirect (rhetorical) questions.	ἐπηρώτων δὲ αὐτὸν οἱ μαθηταὶ αὐτοῦ τίς αὕτη εἴη ἡ παραβολή ("And His disciples began questioning Him as to what this parable might be"; Luke 8:9 NASB).
POTENTIAL	Involves a fourth class conditional clause.	εἰ καὶ πάσχοιτε διὰ δικαιοσύνην, μακάριοι ("Even if you should suffer for righteousness, you are blessed"; 1 Pet 3:14).

IMPERATIVE MOOD		
COMMAND	An exhortation or charge.	πάντοτε **χαίρετε** ("**Rejoice** always!"; 1 Thess 5:16).
PROHIBITION	A negative command that forbids an action.	μὴ **ἀγαπᾶτε** τὸν κόσμον ("**Do not love** the world"; 1 John 2:15).
REQUEST	A command that is given to a superior and is thus weakened to a request.	εἴ τι δύνῃ, **βοήθησον** ἡμῖν ("If You can do anything . . . **help** us"; Mark 9:22).
PERMISSION	Used to convey permission, allowance, or toleration.	εἰ ὁ ἄπιστος χωρίζεται, **χωριζέσθω** ("If the unbeliever leaves, **let him leave**"; 1 Cor 7:15).
CONDITIONAL	Like the subjunctive, an imperative can be used to state a condition.	**ἔρχου** καὶ ἴδε ("**Come** and see" = "**If you come**, you will see"; John 1:46).
GREETING	Greetings are often expressed with a stereotyped imperative.	**Χαῖρε**, ῥαββί ("**Greetings**, Rabbi!"; Matt 26:49).

TENSE (ONLY IN THE INDICATIVE MOOD)[a]		
PRESENT	λύω	"I am loosing"
FUTURE	λύσω	"I will loose"
IMPERFECT	ἔλυον	"I was loosing"
AORIST	ἔλυσα	"I loosed"
PERFECT	λέλυκα	"I have loosed"
PLUPERFECT	ἐλελύκειν	"I had loosed"

[a]It should be noted that this chart is an oversimplification of the wide diversity of tense-form uses and that students will not always translate verbs in such a manner.

PRACTICE EXERCISES

In each of the following examples, (1) parse the underlined verb, paying special attention to the mood of the verb, and (2) determine the specific use of the various moods based on the information provided in this chapter.

1. ἀμὴν γὰρ λέγω ὑμῖν· ἕως ἂν <u>παρέλθῃ</u> ὁ οὐρανὸς καὶ ἡ γῆ, ἰῶτα ἓν ἢ μία κεραία οὐ μὴ <u>παρέλθῃ</u> ἀπὸ τοῦ νόμου, ἕως ἂν πάντα γένηται (Matt 5:18).

2. λέγει αὐτῇ Ἰησοῦς, μή μου <u>ἅπτου</u>, οὔπω γὰρ ἀναβέβηκα πρὸς τὸν πατέρα (John 20:17).

3. μὴ <u>δῶτε</u> τὸ ἅγιον τοῖς κυσὶν μηδὲ <u>βάλητε</u> τοὺς μαργαρίτας ὑμῶν ἔμπροσθεν τῶν χοίρων (Matt 7:6).

4. λέγει τοῖς μαθηταῖς· <u>ἄγωμεν</u> εἰς τὴν Ἰουδαίαν πάλιν (John 11:7).

5. καὶ ἰδοὺ Ἰησοῦς ὑπήντησεν αὐταῖς λέγων, <u>χαίρετε</u> (Matt 28:9).

6. ἐάν τις <u>ἴδῃ</u> τὸν ἀδελφὸν αὐτοῦ ἁμαρτάνοντα ἁμαρτίαν μὴ πρὸς θάνατον, αἰτήσει καὶ δώσει αὐτῷ ζωήν (1 John 5:16).

7. εἶπέν τις τῶν μαθητῶν αὐτοῦ πρὸς αὐτόν· κύριε, <u>δίδαξον</u> ἡμᾶς προσεύχεσθαι (Luke 11:1).

8. αὐτὸς δὲ ὁ θεὸς τῆς εἰρήνης . . . ὑμῶν τὸ πνεῦμα καὶ ἡ ψυχὴ καὶ τὸ σῶμα ἀμέμπτως ἐν τῇ παρουσίᾳ τοῦ κυρίου ἡμῶν Ἰησοῦ Χριστοῦ <u>τηρηθείη</u> (1 Thess 5:23).

9. <u>ἔστω</u> δὲ ὁ λόγος ὑμῶν ναὶ ναί, οὒ οὔ (Matt 5:37).

10. <u>αἰτεῖτε</u> καὶ δοθήσεται ὑμῖν, <u>ζητεῖτε</u> καὶ εὑρήσετε, κρούετε καὶ ἀνοιγήσεται ὑμῖν (Matt 7:7).

VOCABULARY

Vocabulary to Memorize

ἁμαρτωλός, ὁ	sinner (47)
ἀμπελών, -ῶνος, ὁ	vineyard (23)
ἀνάγω	I lead up, restore (23)
ἀναιρέω	I take away, destroy, kill (24)
ἄπιστος	faithless, unbelieving (23)
ἀσθένεια, ἡ	weakness, sickness, disease (24)
ἀσθενέω	I am weak, sick, in need (33)
ἀστήρ, -έρος, ὁ	star (24)
αὐξάνω	I grow, increase (23)
δέησις, -εως, ἡ	prayer, entreaty, petition (18)
εἰκών, -όνος, ἡ	image, likeness, form (23)
ἐλεύθερος	free (23)
ἐνεργέω	I work, produce (21)
ἑορτή, ἡ	festival (25)
ἐπιστολή, ἡ	letter, epistle (24)
ἐπιστρέφω	I turn (around/back), return (36)
Ἠλίας, ὁ	Elijah (29)
ἰάομαι	I heal, cure, restore (26)
ἰσχύω	I am strong, powerful, able (28)
καταλείπω	I leave (behind), abandon, neglect (24)
κελεύω	I command, order, urge (25)
κρίσις, -εως, ἡ	judgment, condemnation (47)
λευκός	white, bright, shining (25)
μανθάνω	I learn (25)
μήν, -ος, ὁ	month, new moon (18)
μήποτε	never, lest (25)
μήτε	and not, nor (34)
νεφέλη, ἡ	cloud (25)
νοῦς, νοός, ὁ	mind, understanding (24)
ὀμνύω	I swear, take an oath (26)
παῖς, παιδός, ὁ/ἡ	boy, child, son, servant (24)
πάρειμι	I am present, have come (24)
παρουσία, ἡ	coming, arrival (24)
πίμπλημι	I fill, fulfill (24)
πλῆθος, -ους, τό	multitude, large amount, crowd (31)
πορνεία, ἡ	(sexual) immorality (25)

προσευχή, ἡ	prayer (36)
προσέχω	I pay attention to, devote myself to (24)
προσκαλέω	I summon, call, invite (29)
Τιμόθεος, ὁ	Timothy (24)

Vocabulary to Recognize

ἀλείφω	I anoint (9)
βλαστάνω	I produce, sprout (4)
βρέχω	it rains (impers); I send rain (7)
ἔλαιον, τό	(olive) oil (11)
ἐνιαυτός, ὁ	year, era (14)
εὐθυμέω	I am cheerful (3)
εὐχή, ἡ	prayer, oath, vow (3)
εὔχομαι	I pray, wish (7)
ἕξ	six (13)
ἐξομολογέω	I confess, praise; promise, consent (10)
κακοπαθέω	I suffer hardship (3)
καλύπτω	I cover, hide, conceal (8)
κάμνω	I am weary, ill (2)
ὁμοιοπαθής, –ες,	with the same nature, like in every way (2)
ὅρκος, ὁ	oath (10)
πλάνη, ἡ	wandering, error, deception (10)
ὑετός, ὁ	rain (5)
ψάλλω	I sing (praise), make melody (5)

READING THE NEW TESTAMENT

James 5:12–20

¹² Πρὸ πάντων δέ, ἀδελφοί μου, μὴ ὀμνύετε μήτε τὸν οὐρανὸν μήτε τὴν γῆν μήτε ἄλλον τινὰ ὅρκον· ἤτω δὲ ὑμῶν τὸ Ναὶ ναὶ καὶ τὸ Οὒ οὔ, ἵνα μὴ ὑπὸ κρίσιν πέσητε. ¹³ Κακοπαθεῖ τις ἐν ὑμῖν, προσευχέσθω· εὐθυμεῖ τις, ψαλλέτω· ¹⁴ ἀσθενεῖ τις ἐν ὑμῖν, προσκαλεσάσθω τοὺς πρεσβυτέρους τῆς ἐκκλησίας καὶ προσευξάσθωσαν ἐπ' αὐτὸν ἀλείψαντες [αὐτὸν] ἐλαίῳ ἐν τῷ ὀνόματι τοῦ κυρίου. ¹⁵ καὶ ἡ εὐχὴ τῆς πίστεως σώσει τὸν κάμνοντα καὶ ἐγερεῖ αὐτὸν ὁ κύριος· κἂν ἁμαρτίας ᾖ πεποιηκώς, ἀφεθήσεται αὐτῷ. ¹⁶ ἐξομολογεῖσθε οὖν ἀλλήλοις τὰς ἁμαρτίας καὶ εὔχεσθε ὑπὲρ ἀλλήλων ὅπως ἰαθῆτε. πολὺ ἰσχύει δέησις δικαίου ἐνεργουμένη. ¹⁷ Ἠλίας ἄνθρωπος ἦν ὁμοιοπαθὴς ἡμῖν, καὶ προσευχῇ προσηύξατο τοῦ μὴ βρέξαι, καὶ οὐκ ἔβρεξεν ἐπὶ τῆς γῆς ἐνιαυτοὺς τρεῖς καὶ μῆνας ἕξ· ¹⁸ καὶ πάλιν προσηύξατο, καὶ ὁ οὐρανὸς ὑετὸν ἔδωκεν καὶ ἡ γῆ ἐβλάστησεν τὸν καρπὸν αὐτῆς. ¹⁹ Ἀδελφοί μου, ἐάν τις ἐν ὑμῖν πλανηθῇ ἀπὸ τῆς ἀληθείας καὶ ἐπιστρέψῃ τις αὐτόν, ²⁰ γινωσκέτω ὅτι ὁ ἐπιστρέψας ἁμαρτωλὸν ἐκ πλάνης ὁδοῦ αὐτοῦ σώσει ψυχὴν αὐτοῦ ἐκ θανάτου καὶ καλύψει πλῆθος ἁμαρτιῶν.

Reading Notes[64]

Verse 12

- **Πρὸ πάντων** ("above all") – Although some have taken this phrase to mean that this verse is the most important of the letter, it is more likely that it should be viewed as "an emphatic epistolary introduction,"[65] drawing attention to what is said as something of great importance (cf. 1 Pet 4:8). This phrase could also be an indicator that James is drawing his letter to a close.

- **μὴ ὀμνύετε** ("do not swear") – Pres act impv 2nd pl ὀμνύω (prohibitory imperative). The form of the verb ὀμνύετε can be either indicative or imperative. In this context, however, we know that it is imperative because it is negated by μή (which is used to negate non-indicative verbs) and not οὐ (which is used to negate indicative verbs). The present tense-form (imperfective aspect) does not necessarily mean that this action was currently and habitually being performed by James' readers. See commentaries for the discussion of whether James is prohibiting all swearing of oaths or merely voluntary oaths.

---

[64] The English version used in the Reading Notes for this chapter is the CSB.
[65] Peter H. Davids, *The Epistle of James*, NIGTC (Grand Rapids: Eerdmans, 1982), 189.

- **μήτε τὸν οὐρανὸν μήτε τὴν γῆν μήτε ἄλλον τινὰ ὅρκον** ("either by heaven or by earth or with any other oath") – Accusative of oath.

- **ἤτω** ("let … mean") – Pres act impv 3rd sg εἰμί. The CSB is smoothing out the more literal sense of "let … be." Remember that the third person imperative is not merely a suggestion (note NASB "is to be"). This is also true for the following third person imperatives in v. 13 (προσευχέσθω, "he should pray"; ψαλλέτω, "he should sing praises"), v. 14 (προσκαλεσάσθω, "he should call"; προσευξάσθωσαν, "they are to pray"), and v. 20 (γινωσκέτω, "let that person know," conveying the meaning "he should know").

- **τὸ Ναὶ ναὶ καὶ τὸ Οὒ οὔ** ("'yes' … 'yes,' and … 'no' … 'no'") – Notice the function of the article here. It is quite common for the article to make a virtual noun out of almost any part of speech (adverbs, adjectives, prepositional phrases, infinitives, participles, and even finite verbs). In this case the article is "substantizing" (i.e., making something into a substantive or noun) the particles ναί and οὔ.

- **ἵνα μὴ ὑπὸ κρίσιν πέσητε** ("so that you won't fall under judgment") – ἵνα introduces a purpose clause with the following verb πέσητε in the subjunctive mood (aor act sub 2nd pl πίπτω). Also notice that the prepositional phrase ὑπὸ κρίσιν is sandwiched between the negative particle (μή) and the verb it negates (πέσητε).

Verse 13

- **κακοπαθεῖ τις ἐν ὑμῖν** ("Is anyone among you suffering?") – Pres act ind 3rd sg κακοπαθέω. Although it is possible to take this phrase as a declarative statement ("Someone among you suffers"), it is best to take it as an interrogative (cf. 1 Cor 7:18). The same is true for the subsequent phrases εὐθυμεῖ τις ("Is anyone cheerful?") and ἀσθενεῖ τις ἐν ὑμῖν ("Is anyone among you sick?"). Thus, these questions followed by imperatives demonstrate that the questions are equivalent to conditional statements ("*If* any among you is suffering, he should pray").

- **προσευχέσθω** ("he should pray") – Pres mid impv 3rd sg προσεύχομαι. Note the emphasis on prayer: προσευχέσθω ("he should pray," v. 13), προσευξάσθωσαν ("they are to pray," v. 14), ἡ εὐχή ("the prayer," v. 15), εὔχεσθε ("pray," v. 16), δέησις ("prayer," v. 16), προσευχῇ προσηύξατο ("he prayed earnestly," v. 17), προσηύξατο ("he prayed," v. 18).

- **εὐθυμεῖ τις** ("Is anyone cheerful?") – Pres act ind 3rd sg εὐθυμέω.

- **ψαλλέτω** ("He should sing praises") – Pres act impv 3rd sg ψάλλω.

Verse 14

- **ἀσθενεῖ τις ἐν ὑμῖν** ("Is anyone among you sick?") – Pres act ind 3rd sg ἀσθενέω.

- **προσκαλεσάσθω** ("he should call") – Aor mid impv 3rd sg προσκαλέω. The observant student will notice that while the previous imperatives (προσευχέσθω, ψαλλέτω) were in the present tense-form (imperfective aspect), this and the subsequent imperative (προσευξάσθωσαν) are in the aorist tense-form (perfective aspect). Many commentators maintain that such a change in tense-form/aspect (especially when a present imperative is expected) suggests urgency. There is, however, a better explanation that has to do with the nature of the verb and/or the nature of the situation. In the first case with προσκαλεσάσθω, we expect this verb to be found in the aorist because of its usage in the NT. Outside of the indicative mood, προσκαλέω never occurs in the present tense-form. It occurs 22 times as an aorist participle, once as an aorist subjunctive, and once (here in Jas 5:14) as an aorist imperative. Therefore, based on this usage, we would expect προσκαλέω to be found as an aorist and so no special nuance should be read into the verb. In addition, the aorist fits the context best because the action of the verb does not need to be repeated (as the imperfective aspect often implies). In other words, the idea is not that the sick person repeatedly calls upon the elders but rather he should do so on the specific occasion when he is sick.

  In contrast, προσεύχομαι is usually found in the present tense-form (imperfective aspect), probably due to its inherently ongoing nature (the same is true for ψάλλω, "I sing praise"). For example, if someone is suffering, they do not simply pray about it once and then move on but should continue in prayer. Thus, as an imperative, προσεύχομαι occurs 15 times in the present tense-form but only twice in the aorist. One of those occurrences is found here in v. 14. Why then does James switch from the present tense-form in v. 13 to the aorist in v. 14? The reason has to do with the context. When the sick person calls upon the elders to pray for him and anoint him with oil, this is related to a very specific occasion. James is not suggesting that the elders pray only once for this person. Certainly, their prayers will continue. But in the context of visiting the person as a group of elders and praying for healing while anointing the person with oil will occur only on this specific occasion.[66] Thus, an aorist fits this context better. (More on this in the next chapter.)

---

[66] We disagree with Martin, who writes that the aorist form προσευξάσθωσαν "hardly refers to a single invocation; it probably stresses urgency with the invocation." See Ralph P. Martin, *James*, WBC 48 (Waco, TX: Word, 1988), 207.

- **προσευξάσθωσαν** ("they are to pray") – Aor mid impv 3rd pl προσεύχομαι.

- **ἀλείψαντες** ("anointing") – Aor act ptc masc nom pl ἀλείφω. Notice that the main idea related to the visitation of the elders is prayer (προσευξάσθωσαν = main verb), since the anointing with oil is a subordinate participle. The participle could be taken as attendant circumstance (so NIV, "and anoint").

- **ἐλαίῳ** ("with oil") – This is a dative of material and should not be confused with a dative of means. Dative of means indicates the tool by which something is accomplished whereas dative of material indicates the material used to accomplish it. Was the purpose of the oil medicinal (practical) or symbolic? Consult the commentaries for this discussion.

Verse 15

- **ἡ εὐχὴ τῆς πίστεως** ("the prayer of faith") – τῆς πίστεως is an attributive genitive or genitive of description and could be translated as "a prayer characterized by faith." Martin translates this phrase "the request based on faith."[67]

- **σώσει** ("will save") – Fut act ind 3rd sg σῴζω. Notice that the zeta (ζ) was dropped when the sigma (σ) was added to form the future tense.

- **τὸν κάμνοντα** ("the sick person") – This is a substantival participle (pres act ptc masc acc sg κάμνω) which means that the participle (which is a verbal adjective) is not merely functioning as an adjective but as a noun.

- **ἐγερεῖ** ("will raise up") – Fut act ind 3rd sg ἐγείρω. Remember, liquid verbs (i.e., verbs whose stem ends in λ, μ, ν, or ρ) cannot take a sigma that is added to the stem with future (and aorist) tense verbs. To compensate for this, the stem of ἐγείρ was changed to ἐγερ (the iota was dropped). An epsilon replaced the rejected tense formative (σ), and then that epsilon contracted with the 3rd sg ending, as marked by a circumflex.

- **κἄν** ("and if" [CSB omits "and"]) – This word represents the merger of two separate words (known as *crasis*): καί + ἐάν = κἄν. This word also initiates a third class conditional sentence (uncertain of fulfillment, but still likely).

- **ᾖ πεποιηκώς** ("he has committed") – Pres act sub 3rd sg εἰμί and per act ptc masc nom sg ποιέω. This is a periphrastic participial construction (periphrastic means a round-about way of saying something). In other words, instead of using a perfect indicative form of ποιέω (= πεποίηκεν),

---

[67] Martin, *James*, 209.

a longer construction of the present subjunctive form of εἰμί (= ᾖ) with the perfect participle (= πεποιηκώς) is used.

- **ἀφεθήσεται** ("he will be forgiven") – Fut pass ind 3rd sg ἀφίημι. This is an example of the divine passive. "He will be forgiven" is another way of saying "he will be forgiven by God" or "God will forgive him."

Verse 16

- **ἐξομολογεῖσθε . . . καὶ εὔχεσθε** ("confess . . . and pray") – Pres mid impv 2nd pl ἐξομολογέω and pres mid impv 2nd pl εὔχομαι. As mentioned in the notes above (v. 14), the present tense-form (imperfective aspect) is appropriate for (προσ) εὔχομαι as well as ἐξομολογέω due to the nature of these verbs.

- **τὰς ἁμαρτίας** ("your sins") – The article can sometimes function as a possessive pronoun, which is why most English versions translate this phrase as "your sins" and not merely "the sins."

- **ὅπως ἰαθῆτε** ("so that you may be healed") – Aor pass sub 2nd pl ἰάομαι. ὅπως is used in this context to indicate purpose and is followed by the subjunctive mood. Again, the divine passive is used. The idea is, "so that you may be healed by God" or "so that God may heal you."

- **ἐνεργουμένη** ("in its effect" [lit. "working" or "effective"]) – Pres mid/pass ptc fem nom sg ἐνεργέω. There is debate as to whether this participle is adverbial or attributive. If it is adverbial, then there is another issue at stake: is it middle or passive? The middle would mean something like "the prayer is very powerful in its working," whereas the passive would mean that "prayer is very powerful when it is made effective [by God/the Spirit]." Most commentators and English versions take it as middle. The other option (and the one followed by the KJV, NASB, and NKJV) is to take ἐνεργουμένη as an attributive participle modifying δέησις ("prayer"). δέησις seems to be used without any difference in meaning from εὐχή (v. 15) and προσευχή (v. 17). McCartney comments, "It is best to take the participle as modifying 'is powerful [ἰσχύει],'" explaining not under what conditions it is effective [the passive meaning], but in what way prayer has power: it is powerful because it effects change."[68]

Verses 17–18

- **ὁμοιοπαθής** (lit. "a like-nature") – In the NT, this word only occurs here and in Acts 14:15 (but is found in Wisd 7:3; 4 Macc 12:13).

---

[68] Dan G. McCartney, *James*, BECNT (Grand Rapids: Baker, 2009), 258.

- **προσευχῇ προσηύξατο** ("he prayed earnestly") – Aor mid ind 3rd sg προσεύχομαι. In this construction, the noun προσευχή is a cognate dative (which is a subset of dative of manner explaining how something is done). With a cognate dative, both the noun and the verb have the same root. The force of this construction is primarily to emphasize the action of the verb. Thus, "he prayed earnestly" is more accurate than the more literal "in prayer he prayed."

- **τοῦ μὴ βρέξαι** ("that it would not rain") – Aor act inf βρέχω. The infinitive preceded by the article τοῦ usually communicates purpose ("in order that it might not rain"). It is also possible that this is an infinitive of indirect discourse which indicates the content of the prayer.

- **οὐκ ἔβρεξεν** ("it did not rain") – Notice that this verb has an impersonal subject (i.e., "it").

- **ὁ οὐρανὸς ὑετὸν ἔδωκεν** ("the sky gave rain") – Aor act ind 3rd sg δίδωμι. The use of "sky" or "heaven" (οὐρανός) may be a substitution for the divine name (cf. Luke 15:18, 21, "I have sinned against heaven").

- **ἐβλάστησεν** ("produced") – Aor act ind 3rd sg βλαστάνω.

Verse 19

- **ἀδελφοί μου** ("My brothers and sisters") – ἀδελφοί is in the vocative case used for direct address. This use of the vocative probably signals a new section and consequently the end of the letter (cf. 1 John 5:21).

- **ἐάν τις ... πλανηθῇ ... καὶ ἐπιστρέψῃ τις αὐτόν** ("if any ... strays ... and someone turns him back") – ἐάν is followed by two subjunctive verbs πλανηθῇ (aor pass sub 3rd sg πλανάω) and ἐπιστρέψῃ (aor act sub 3rd sg ἐπιστρέφω) and indicates a third class conditional clause.

Verse 20

- **γινωσκέτω** ("let that person know" [conveying "he should know"]) – Pres act impv 3rd sg γινώσκω.

- **ὁ ἐπιστρέψας** ("whoever turns") – Aor act ptc masc nom sg ἐπιστρέφω. This is a substantival participle that is used generically. That is, James is referring to anyone who turns a sinner back from the error of his way and not to a specific individual.

- **ψυχὴν αὐτοῦ ἐκ θανάτου** ("his soul from death") – This phrase is textually disputed. The UBS⁵ favors this reading based on the manuscript evidence (א A P 33 vg) and because it best accounts for the origin of the other readings (ἐκ θανάτου αὐτοῦ ["from death itself"], 𝔓⁷⁴ B 1292 1611

2138 itff; ἐκ θανάτου ["from death"], K L Ψ 81 322 323 *Byz*). Metzger comments, "Perplexed by the ambiguity of ψυχὴν αὐτοῦ (is it the soul of the converter or of the converted?), scribes either (a) transferred αὐτοῦ to follow ἐκ θανάτου . . . or (b) omitted it entirely."[69] See commentaries concerning the debate as to whose soul is saved from death (the one wandering or the one converting?) and whose sins are covered (the one wandering or the one converting?).

- **καλύψει** ("[he will] cover") – Fut act ind 3rd sg καλύπτω.

- **πλῆθος ἁμαρτιῶν** ("a multitude of sins") – Attributed (reversed adjectival) genitive ("many sins").

---

[69] Metzger, *Textual Commentary*, 615.

CHAPTER 7

////////////////

TENSE & VERBAL ASPECT

GOING DEEPER

Because of the extraordinary revelations Paul received, he writes, "A thorn in the flesh was given to me, a messenger of Satan to torment me so that I would not exalt myself" (2 Cor 12:7). The apostle here employs a ἵνα clause to introduce the purpose of the messenger of Satan, ἵνα με κολαφίζῃ ("to torment me"). The verb translated "torment" is the present active subjunctive third person singular of κολαφίζω. One noted commentator remarks on κολαφίζῃ, "The use of the present tense seems to imply that 'the thorn in the flesh' was a permanent affliction under which the apostle continued to suffer."[1] The commentator seems to indicate that, conversely, if Paul had chosen the aorist tense (the only other option for this subjunctive clause), then the "torment" Paul described would have been limited in duration or already past. In fact, while the exegete may be right in his conclusion (i.e., Paul suffered for the remainder of his life), the basis for his argument is invalid. By employing the present tense-form in 2 Cor 12:7, Paul chooses to present his torment in progressive fashion, but does not indicate the time limit (or lack thereof) of that progressive depiction. Unfortunately, it is not uncommon to find such unguarded statements about tense and time in the commentary literature.

Anyone who has tried to learn at least one foreign language (and most of you reading this are in the process of learning one—biblical Greek!) will readily recognize that no two languages will be alike in every respect. At times the word order will vary; proverbs or common sayings may differ (e.g., the functional equivalent

---

[1] Charles Hodge, *An Exposition of the Second Epistle to the Corinthians* (Grand Rapids: Baker, 1980), 285–86. Reprint of 1859 original, published by Robert Carter & Brothers.

of the English expression, "It's still *Greek* to me" is, in German, "Es kommt mir *Spanisch* vor" ["It's still *Spanish* to me"]); the use of the article can create problems; the sentence structure may be more or less complex (e.g., Greek participles), and so on. While we expect foreign languages to play by our rules, more often than not, what is required when learning another language is a willingness to play by the rules of others.

The Greek verb is a case in point. When approaching the translation and interpretation of a given NT verb, most of us will naturally expect that the Greek verb functions according to the rules of English grammar. At a first glance, this seems to be a reasonable assumption. In keeping with the above-registered caution, however, this assumption is unwarranted. Specifically, native English speakers (and speakers of other similar languages) who are accustomed to verb tenses conveying primarily the *time* of a given action will naturally assume that the same equation, "Tense-form = Time," holds true in NT Greek as well. As we'll see below, however, this is not the case. Other factors, especially the way in which a writer views a given action (called "aspect"), play a role in the choice of a particular tense-form in NT Greek as well. This, in turn, renders time proportionally less significant in the use of the Greek verb than the English one (or at least matters are different). In other words, while time plays the most prominent role in English verbs, the most prominent characteristic of Greek tense-forms is aspect.

When in Rome, therefore, do as the Romans do. Or, to adapt this adage, when in Athens, do as the Athenians do. That is, step into learning NT Greek in general, and into interpreting Greek verbs in particular, within the frame of reference of the Greek, rather than your native language, and be open to the evidence as it presents itself, whether morphological, lexical, grammatical, contextual, or otherwise. As we'll see, this is often easier said than done, and even Greek grammarians don't always agree as to the reasons why a given NT writer chose, say, an aorist rather than a present-tense verb form to convey a certain action.[2] What we therefore hope to do in this chapter is to provide a simple framework for understanding how Greek verbs work. On the whole, we recommend that when you analyze NT Greek verbs, leave English mostly aside and put on a new pair of linguistic glasses. This will enable you to get closer to understanding NT verbs the way first-century Greek writers and readers would have done.

CHAPTER OBJECTIVES

In what follows we will address the three major factors that have a bearing on Greek verb forms: (1) verbal aspect, that is, the author's perspective on a given action; (2) the time of the action; and (3) the type of action (including lexical,

---

[2] This, in turn, keeps commentary-writers, not to mention preachers and Christian publishers, in business!

grammatical, and contextual factors). Under the last rubric, we will also provide a brief case study of the use of imperatives in the writings of the NT.

THE GREEK VERB

Author's Perspective on the Action (Aspect)[3]

Definition of Aspect

There is wide consensus in the relevant scholarly literature today that Greek, unlike English, is aspect-prominent.[4] In other words, the Greek speaker or writer chooses to present an action from a certain subjective vantage point. This choice of perspective (verbal aspect) is more prominent in Greek verbs than the *time* at which the action is performed and/or the *way* in which the action is performed (i.e., the action's objective or intrinsic nature).[5]

Let's step back to be clear on the most fundamental question: what is verbal aspect? Most NT grammarians concur on the basic definition.[6] Constantine Campbell writes, "Verbal aspect refers to the manner in which verbs are used to view an action or state."[7] Stanley Porter defines verbal aspect as "a semantic (meaning) category by which a speaker or writer grammaticalizes a perspective on an action by the selection of a particular tense-form in the verbal system."[8] Buist Fanning's definition is similar: "Verbal aspect in NT Greek is that category in the grammar of the verb which reflects the focus or viewpoint of the speaker in regard to the action or condition which the verb describes."[9] Kenneth McKay offers the following

---

[3] Some of the following material is indebted to conversations with Nicholas Ellis and Mark Dubis, under the auspices of the BibleMesh Greek Project (www.biblemesh.com) and related publications. See also the survey of the history of research in Campbell, *Advances in the Study of Greek*, chapter 5 (see chap. 6, n. 24).

[4] See BDF, *Greek Grammar*, 166–67 (§318); Brooks & Winbery, 76; Burton, 6; Dana & Mantey, 177–79; Moule, 5; Moulton, *Grammar*, 108–10; Robertson, 343, 881–82. For a survey of Greek verbal aspect theory, see Constantine R. Campbell, *Basics of Verbal Aspect in Biblical Greek* (Grand Rapids: Zondervan, 2008). Other important contributions include Albert Rijksbaron, *The Syntax and Semantics of the Verb in Classical Greek: An Introduction*, 3rd ed. (Chicago: University of Chicago Press, 2007); D. N. S. Bhat, *The Prominence of Tense, Aspect and Mood*, Studies in Language Companion Series 49 (Philadelphia: John Benjamins, 1999); and the scholarly literature cited below.

[5] The time at which an action occurs is a factor only in the indicative mood.

[6] Note, however, that while the following scholars concur on the basic definition of aspect, they differ considerably on the number of aspects in NT Greek, on the question of whether or not the augment is a time indicator, and other important questions related to the nature and function of NT Greek verbs (see further the discussion below).

[7] Campbell, *Basics of Verbal Aspect*, 6.

[8] Porter, *Idioms*, 21. Elsewhere Porter defines verbal aspect as "a synthetic category (realized in the forms of verbs) used of meaningful oppositions in a network of tense systems to grammaticalize the author's reasoned subjective choice of conception of a process" (*Verbal Aspect*, 88).

[9] Fanning, 84. He continues, "It shows *the perspective from which the occurrence is regarded or the portrayal of the occurrence* apart from the actual or perceived nature of the situation itself" (84–85; emphasis added).

definition: "Aspect in ancient Greek is that category of the verb system by means of which an author (or speaker) shows how he views each event or activity he mentions in relation to its context."[10] From these definitions, it is clear that the central idea with regard to Greek verbal aspect is the *subjective perspective* or *viewpoint* from which an author communicates the action of a given verb.[11]

Aspects in NT Greek

In light of this definition, what are the ways in which ancient Greek writers, and the writers of the GNT in particular, perceive a given action? While grammarians differ on the nomenclature and number of aspects, there is good reason to believe that NT Greek employs two true aspects: the (1) imperfective (present and imperfect tense-forms), and (2) the perfective (aorist tense-form); and these two combine to form (3) the stative (perfect and pluperfect tense-forms), which conjoins these two aspects with respect to a logically preceding event or state of affairs (perfective) and the resulting state (imperfective).[12] In essence, in the *imperfective* aspect (present or imperfect tense-form), the author depicts the action as ongoing; in the *perfective* aspect (aorist tense-form), the author depicts the action as a whole; and in the *stative* aspect (perfect or pluperfect tense-forms), the author depicts some preceding action or state as particularly relevant to the present context.

VERBAL ASPECT		
ASPECT	DEFINITION	TENSE-FORM
Imperfective	Action viewed as in process, ongoing	Present/Imperfect
Perfective	Action viewed as complete, as a whole	Aorist[a]
Stative	State of affairs resulting from a previous action or state	Perfect/Pluperfect

[a]There is widespread agreement that the future tense-form does not neatly fit within an aspectual framework because it grammaticalizes expectation of an event whether or not it in fact will occur (though aspectually and morphologically, the future has affinities with the perfective aorist tense-form). For this reason we will not include the future tense-form in the discussion below. See further the discussion of the future indicative in chapter 8.

---

[10] McKay, 27.

[11] "Verbal aspect is, in general, the portrayal of the action (or state) as to its progress, results, or simple occurrence" (Wallace, 499).

[12] The presentation below is indebted to Nicholas Ellis and Mark Dubis, who call the stative the "combinative aspect" (see further the discussion below). Porter posits three aspects, imperfective, perfective, and stative; Picirilli uses the terminology progressive, wholistic, and stative; Campbell holds to only two aspects, imperfective and perfective (treating the perfect not as a separate aspect but as an imperfective with heightened or remote proximity). Wallace and Fanning both speak of internal and external in the place of imperfective and perfective. See Porter, *Idioms*, 21–22, 29–42; idem, *Verbal Aspect*, 89, 105; Robert E. Picirilli, "The Meaning of Tenses in New Testament Greek: Where Are We?" *JETS* 48, no. 3 (2005): 533–55; Campbell, *Basics of Verbal Aspect*; Campbell, *Verbal Aspect and Non-Indicative Verbs: Further Soundings in the Greek of the New Testament*, SBG 15 (New York: Peter Lang, 2008), 11; Wallace, 501; Fanning, 84–125.

To elaborate, the *imperfective* aspect conveys action in progress or process, whether incomplete ("was or is happening"), inceptive ("started to happen"), durative ("continues to happen"), or some other kind of process. The *perfective* aspect describes a given action simply as occurring or as having occurred without indicating how the action took place ("it happened"). The *stative* aspect combines the perfective and imperfective aspects, correlating a preceding event or state of affairs with its resulting imperfective state ("it has happened, and it is relevant to the present context").

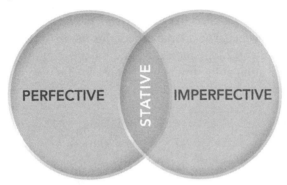

Some of this terminology may appear novel and confusing, but perhaps an analogy with English may help.[13] When I say, "I am jumping" or "I was jumping," I am describing an action as progressing, whether currently or in the past. Neither the beginning nor the end of the action is in view. This is the essence of what we have called the "imperfective aspect" above. When, on the other hand, I say, "I jump" or "I jumped," I simply describe the action as a whole without reference to the beginning, middle, or end, as occurring or as having occurred without regard for *how* it occurred. This is what we have called the "perfective aspect." Finally, when I say, "I have jumped" or "I had jumped," I am correlating a preceding action with the result of having jumped. Perhaps I had jumped but not high or far enough, or just as I had jumped some more important thing happened. Use of stative aspect signals that this resulting state is important to understanding the present context, that something more will be said about it. So while the way in which English expresses aspect (i.e., by the use of helping verbs such as "is" or "was") is different from NT Greek, both languages have ways of conveying both time and aspect, as well as kind of action.

An example of the stative aspect signaling the relevance of the action would be the use of the perfect tense-form ἐλήλυθεν, "he has come," in Luke 7:33–34.[14] John the Baptist and the Son of Man each came in opposite manners, yet the Pharisees rejected both of them. *How* they came is not what is most important; it simply sets the stage for Jesus's comment about the Pharisees' response. The perfect-tense-form signals that these details are key to understanding the "no win"

---

[13] Adapted from conversation with Ellis and Dubis.
[14] We are grateful to Steven Runge for providing the following example.

situation that Jesus faces. The *response* is what is most important in this context, not the *manner* in which Jesus and John came. Had the writer used the aorist instead of the perfect, the ongoing relevance of these details would have been implicit rather than explicit.

Morphologizing Aspect

Now that we have introduced you to the ways of thinking underlying the notion of aspect, let's talk about how grammatical form (morphology) conveys the different Greek aspects. Specifically, the aspectual nature of the verb may be indicated with an aspectual marker, such as the sigma (σ) in the perfective aspect or reduplication in the stative aspect. The stative aspect, for its part, features two aspectual markers in the active voice, one preceding and the other following the verb stem, namely, the reduplication at the front and the Greek letter kappa (κ) affixed to the stem.[15]

ASPECTUAL CATEGORY	IMPERFECTIVE			PERFECTIVE	
	PAST-TIME INDICATOR	ASPECT PREFIX	LEXICAL CORE	ASPECT SUFFIX	PERSONAL ENDING
Imperfective (past)	ε	—	λυ	—	ομεν
Imperfective (non-past)	—	—	λυ	—	ομεν
Perfective (past)	ε	—	λυ	σ	αμεν
Perfective (non-past)	—	—	λυ	σ	ομεν
Stative (past)	ε	λε	λυ	κ	ειμεν
Stative (non-past)	—	λε	λυ	κ	αμεν

The reduplication is found not only in the indicative but in other moods as well, which makes clear that, unlike the augment, the reduplication is not a temporal indicator. In addition, in the indicative mood, as we'll further discuss below, the augment is used to indicate time, that is, whether or not the action occurred in the past.[16]

---

[15] The following chart is based largely on the work of Ellis and Dubis. The terminology "non-past" is used only in this chapter to designate tense-forms where the augment is not present. In terms of background, "Gerhard Mussies offered a proposal in 1971 which is suggestive. Rather than classifying the present as communicating present time, he classified it instead as grammaticalizing *non-past* reference. Porter and Decker acknowledge this usage, but see it as further evidence for the disassociation between Greek tense and time. Comrie also describes the Ancient Greek verbal system as using a past/non-past distinction." See Steven E. Runge, "The Verbal Aspect of the Historical Present Indicative in Narrative," in *Discourse Studies and Biblical Interpretation: A Festschrift in Honor of Stephen H. Levinsohn*, ed. Steven E. Runge (Bellingham, WA: Logos Bible Software, 2011), 217. See also Steven E. Runge, "The Perfect, Markedness, and Grounding" (paper presented at the SBL annual meeting, Baltimore, MD, November 23–26, 2013).

[16] In the following chart, future forms are included in parentheses even though, as mentioned, the future does not neatly fit into the aspectual scheme. It should be noted that there are a number of scholars who claim that time is never an element that is communicated by the verb itself

Given this linguistic framework, some additional comments should be made regarding the stative aspect. We have argued that a combination of the reduplication prefix and a *kappa* suffix effectively combines the perfective aspect of an event and imperfective aspect of an ongoing state. However, an interesting phenomenon takes place in the middle voice where the *kappa* aspect marker is universally absent. Examine the following chart:

PERFECT MIDDLE	IMPERFECTIVE			PERFECTIVE	
	PAST-TIME INDICATOR	ASPECT PREFIX	LEXICAL CORE	ASPECT SUFFIX	PERSONAL ENDING
First Singular	—	λε	λυ	—	μαι
Second Singular	—	λε	λυ	—	σαι
Third Singular	—	λε	λυ	—	ται
First Plural	—	λε	λυ	—	μεθα
Second Plural	—	λε	λυ	—	σθε
Third Plural	—	λε	λυ	—	νται

Note the expected reduplication, given the imperfective emphasis of the verb as well as the fact that the *kappa* is no longer present. Interestingly, in the large majority of middle verbs, the event is no longer consciously in view, only the ongoing state. For example, take the English sentence, "The man is dressed sharply." In this case, the focus is on the man's sharp attire, rather than on the preceding action of putting on clothes. Indeed, with the Greek middle, the event is frequently no longer in view, as indicated by the absence of the *kappa*, while the reduplication remains as an imperfective aspect marker to direct the focus on the resulting state.

MOOD	IMPERFECTIVE	PERFECTIVE	STATIVE
Indicative	λύω / ἔλυον	(λύσω) ἔλυσα	λέλυκα / ἐλελύκειν
Infinitive	λύειν	(λύσειν) λῦσαι	λελυκέναι
Subjunctive	λύω	λύσω	λελύκω
Imperative	λῦε	λῦσον	λέλυκε
Participle	λύων	(λύσων) λύσας	λελυκώς

In moving from thinking in terms of English verbs to internalizing the different way in which Greek verbs function, NT Greek students should get into the habit of

---

and who consequently deny that the augment serves as a time indicator. See Porter, *Verbal Aspect*, 75–109, 208–9; *Idioms*, 20–28; *Studies in the Greek New Testament: Theory and Practice*, Studies in Biblical Greek 6 (New York: Peter Lang, 1996), 21–38; McKay, 30; idem, "Time and Aspect in New Testament Greek," *NovT* 34 (1992): 209–28; Rodney J. Decker, *Temporal Deixis of the Greek Verb in the Gospel of Mark with Reference to Verbal Aspect*, SBG 10 (New York: Peter Lang, 2001).

looking at a given verb form primarily with regard to its three aspects (imperfective, perfective, stative) rather than with regard to tense-forms (present, imperfect, future, aorist, perfect, pluperfect) in light of the fact that aspect, rather than time, serves as the basic framework for the use of NT Greek verbs. The first question, then, that a student should ask is, "What is the aspect of a given verb form?" Correspondingly, students may want to think of

1. the present tense-form as non-past imperfective;

2. the imperfect as past imperfective;

3. the aorist as past perfective;

4. the perfect as non-past stative (a state resulting from past action or event); and

5. the pluperfect as past stative.

IMPERFECTIVE		PERFECTIVE		STATIVE	
λύω	Non-Past Imperfective (Present Tense-Form)	λύσω	Non-Past Perfective (Future Tense-Form)	λέλυκα	Non-Past Stative (Perfect Tense-Form)
ἔλυον	Past Imperfective (Imperfect Tense-Form)	ἔλυσα	Past Perfective (Aorist Tense-Form)	ἐλελύκειν	Past Stative (Pluperfect Tense-Form)

As the above chart indicates, NT Greek in the indicative mood has three tense-forms conveying past action: (1) the past imperfective (imperfect tense-form); (2) the past perfective (aorist tense-form); and (3) the past stative (pluperfect tense-form). In each case, past time is indicated by the augment. Importantly, each of these verb forms conveys action in the past, but the verb forms differ with regard to aspect, that is, the way in which a given NT author chooses to perceive a given action: (1) progressive (past imperfective), (2) wholistic (past perfective), and (3) conveying a state resulting from a preceding completed action (past stative).

Aspect and Discourse

Verbal aspect not only has a *grammatical* function, in all probability it has a *literary* function as well. Most typically in narrative, verbs in the perfective aspect (aorist tense-form) convey the actions that carry forward the mainline of the narrative whereas verbs in the past imperfective (imperfect tense-forms) and the past stative aspect (pluperfect tense-forms) typically provide relevant supporting information. However, more work needs to be done to study the way in which verbs function at the larger discourse level in NT Greek.[17]

A brief example of how aspect may be analyzed on the discourse level comes from the account of the wedding at Cana in John 2:1–11.[18] Throughout the entire pericope, the series of mainline actions carrying forward the narrative is cast in the past perfective aspect (aorist tense-form). A wedding took place in Cana (ἐγένετο, v. 1), and Jesus and his disciples, along with his mother, were invited (ἐκλήθη, v. 2). The aorist is the default tense in narrative proper to simply report the events. The verbs of speaking introducing the dialogue embedded within the narrative is consistently introduced using historical present verbs standing in the place of the aorist (λέγει in vv. 3, 4, 5, 7, 8, 10). This switch from aorist to the historical present adds prominence to the speech it introduces. The presence of Jesus's mother (ἦν, v. 2) and of six stone jars (ἦσαν, v. 6) is indicated by past tense-forms of the verb εἰμί, providing important supporting material but not advancing the mainline of the narrative. The headwaiter's tasting of the wine is once again cast in the past perfective aspect (ἐγεύσατο, aorist tense-form, v. 9), while the transformation of the wine into water is viewed from the stative aspect (γεγενημένον, ἠντληκότες, v. 9) and the headwaiter's summons of the bridegroom is found in the non-past imperfective aspect (φωνεῖ, present tense-form, v. 9). The concluding verse wraps up the pericope with three mainline past perfectives, indicating that Jesus "performed" (ἐποίησεν) his first sign and thus "revealed" himself (ἐφανέρωσεν) to his first disciples who "believed" (ἐπίστευσαν) in him (aorist tense-forms; v. 11).

On the whole, therefore, we see how the setting, the ensuing series of actions, and the conclusion are carrying forward the mainline of the narrative using past perfectives, reporting the action wholistically, that is, without attention to its internal unfolding or processes. We also see how verbs in the past and non-past imperfective and stative aspects may be used to provide various kinds of additional information.

Although aspect provides the basic framework for understanding how Greek verbs work, one important caution must be registered at this point. Asserting that NT Greek is an aspect-prominent language does not necessarily mean that a writer's aspectual choice reigns supreme (i.e., is invariably determinative) or remains unaffected by any other factors or constraints that (in combination with verbal aspect) result in a writer's choice of a given verb form. To the contrary, as we shall see below, not only does time affect tense-form choices in the indicative, but so does type of action of the verb lemma.

---

[17] Scholars continue to differ on matters of terminology and as to whether certain tense-forms convey prominence on the discourse level. For example, some scholars speak of foreground/background, while others speaks of mainline/offline. See p. 57 in Stanley E. Porter, "Prominence: An Overview," in *The Linguist as Pedagogue*, 45–74 (see chap. 6, n. 24).

[18] We will only analyze indicative forms at this point; we will comment on imperatives later on in this chapter. Since this example is designed merely to illustrate the implications of verbal aspect for the analysis of biblical discourse, we will highlight most indicative verb forms without attempting a complete analysis of every single verb form.

Time of Action

Within the above-sketched aspectual framework, time is indicated in NT Greek in the indicative by the presence or absence of the augment. The fact that the augment is found only in the indicative suggests that (absolute) time is of no consequence in the non-indicative moods.[19] In addition, time may be indicated by contextual information such as so-called "deictic indicators" (e.g., adverbs of time).[20]

Type of Action

The third component that may have a bearing on how a given NT Greek verb is used beside aspect and (in the indicative) time is the kind or type of action. Verbal aspect gives us the basic perspective of how an author views the action of the verb (imperfective, perfective, or stative). The presence or absence of the augment in the indicative conveys whether or not an action took place in the past. The kind or type of action may also influence and, at times, even determine the particular verb form that is used.

While NT Greek, as mentioned, is an aspect-prominent language, and time is in the picture in the indicative mood as well, exegetes must therefore also consider the lemma's type or kind of action on a case-by-case basis in order to arrive at a complete understanding of the verb's meaning in a particular context. Put simply, aspect provides one kind of limitation on a verb's meaning on the level of semantics while the type of action provides another limitation based on the contextual or nuanced meaning on the level of contextual usage. Specifically, we must consider lexical, grammatical, and contextual factors.[21]

Lexical Factors

By "lexical factors" we are referring to those elements in the verb's basic form that make it prefer one tense-form over another. This may be in terms of: (1) lexical determination, or (2) lexical influence. When a verb's usage is limited to certain tense-forms, it is said to be *lexically determined*. For example, verbs such as εἰμί, κεῖμαι, κάθημαι, and φημί do not occur in the aorist tense-form because of their inherent meanings or because of idiomatic influence.[22] In addition, a few aorist

---

[19] But see Porter who denies that the augment conveys time (*Verbal Aspect*, 75–109, 208–9; *Idioms*, 20–28).

[20] See Porter, *Verbal Aspect*, 98–102; *Idioms*, 25–26.

[21] Wallace utilizes these three concepts in his grammar and employs them specifically in the discussion concerning type of action. He writes, "In general, we can say that **aspect** *is the unaffected meaning* while **Aktionsart** [type of action] *is aspect in combination with lexical, grammatical, or contextual features.*" Wallace, 499. Campbell helpfully highlights the modern linguistic terminology of *semantics* and *pragmatics*. When referring to verbs, he notes that *semantics* "refers to the values that are encoded in the verbal form" while *pragmatics* "refers to the expression of semantic values in context and in combination with other factors" (*Basics of Verbal Aspect*, 22-23).

[22] In personal correspondence, Constantine Campbell adds a nuance here regarding "verbal suppletion," which, he observes, "is the recognized phenomenon of using a synonymous lexeme to supplete lexemes that do not occur in all tense forms (e.g., the use of ἐγενόμην for εἰμί, since the latter does not have an aorist form)." He points out that "in that case, the use of εἰμί is actually meaningful

imperatives, such as ἴδε and ἰδού ("look"), have lost their verbal nature and have become virtual particles. Thus, in some cases the author's choice of tense-form is determined by the verb itself. Consequently, the fact that in those cases a certain tense-form is used should not be unduly pressed.

In most cases, however, the verb's usage is not lexically restricted to only some tense-forms. And yet, most verbs *prefer* a particular tense-form (or forms) above others. *Lexical influence*, then, refers to the influence of the verb's inherent meaning on its usage in the various tense-forms. For instance, verbs that have a natural terminus may be described as *telic* (moving toward a goal or completion) whereas verbs that have no natural terminus may be characterized as *atelic* (or non-telic, i.e., not moving toward a goal or completion). Some telic verbs refer to an action that is limited in that it conveys a climax, conclusion, or termination and yet still conveys some perceived duration;[23] other telic verbs refer to an action that is performed in a moment without taking any perceived or significant time or duration for the action.[24] Conversely, atelic verbs convey a condition or relationship (personal, temporal, or local), referring not to what someone *does* but what he or she *is* (or a relationship they have).[25] Activities are viewed as having no set limit for their completion (they are "unbounded").[26]

This means that the inherent nature of the verb may affect which verb tense-form is to be expected. All things being equal, telic verbs tend to prefer the perfective aspect (aorist tense-form) whereas atelic verbs prefer the imperfective aspect (present or imperfect). The stative aspect (perfect tense-form) is much less common and often communicates the resulting state of a previous completed action. Thus, aspect and type of action function in tandem in NT Greek verb usage. Occasionally, however, an author will not conform to the expectations directed by the underlying tendency of Greek. It is at this point that we must ask the question why the author is departing from the expected usage (see further the discussion below).

Grammatical Factors

Grammatical factors—such as tense-form, voice, and mood—relate to the form of the verb itself. Perhaps the most significant grammatical factor relates to the verb's *mood*. Each mood should be analyzed independently because different factors influence the verb's tense-form in the various moods. The tense-form of an *indicative* verb is influenced by the time of the action. With the other moods, time

---

because an aorist synonym could have been used if perfective aspect were desired." For development of this, see Campbell's monograph, *Verbal Aspect, the Indicative Mood, and Narrative Soundings in the Greek of the New Testament* (Studies in Biblical Greek 13; New York: Peter Lang, 2008)

[23] E.g., ἀνοίγω ("I open"), δίδωμι ("I give"), ἐνδύσω ("I get dressed"), ἑτοιμάζω ("I prepare"), and καλέω ("I call").

[24] E.g., ἀγοράζω ("I buy"), βάλλω ("I throw"), εὑρίσκω ("I find"), and πίπτω ("I fall").

[25] E.g., ἀγαπάω ("I love"), ἀσθενέω ("I am sick"), εἰμί ("I am"), ἔχω ("I have"), ζάω ("I am alive"), μισέω ("I hate"), οἰκέω ("I dwell"), πιστεύω ("I believe"), πλουτέω ("I am rich"), and φοβέομαι ("I am afraid").

[26] E.g., ἀναγινώσκω ("I am reading"), ἐσθίω ("I am eating"), κηρύσσω ("I am preaching"), λέγω/λαλέω ("I am talking"), περιπατέω ("I am walking"), and ποιέω ("I am doing").

is not a factor. When *infinitives* are studied, attention should be given to verb combinations, especially with complementary infinitives.[27] It is also important to know that infinitives used for indirect discourse should be analyzed as indicative verbs (thus relative time becomes a factor).[28]

The *subjunctive* mood also has some notable features that should be considered. First, the aorist tense-form outnumbers the present tense-form in all the various subjunctive constructions (about 3 to 1).[29] This is especially true for constructions used with οὐ μή, ἕως (ἄν), ἄχρι(ς), and μέχρι(ς).[30] Second, both hortatory subjunctives and prohibitory subjunctives should be analyzed as imperatives.

Imperatives, likewise, must be considered independently of the other moods. First, the aorist imperative is greatly favored in prayers, even when it is used to reference something general in nature (more on this under Contextual Factors). It should also be noted that one author might use a particular form more than other authors (usually based on the literary form).[31]

In addition to mood, other factors should also be considered when relevant. These factors include the voice of the verb, the nature of the subject or object phrase, the use of various adverbs or prepositional modifiers, and relevant features in the broader context.

Contextual Factors

Perhaps the most influential contextual factor that influences a verb's tense-form is the text's literary genre. Certain literary styles are prone to favor certain tense-forms. For example, historical narratives heavily favor the aorist tense-form (perfective aspect). While the aorist serves as the default tense-form for narratives, present, imperfect (imperfective aspect), perfect, or pluperfect forms (stative aspect), as mentioned, are used to provide relevant background information.

Another example relates to the use of imperatives in prayers. In non-prayer texts, present imperatives are normally used to command or forbid a general behavior (general precept) whereas the aorist is used to command or forbid an action on a

---

[27] E.g., the verbs ἄρχομαι and μέλλω are almost always followed by a present infinitive. When the infinitive following one of these verbs is found in the aorist tense, then it is not the default form and can communicate a nuanced meaning.

[28] S. M. Baugh, *Introduction to Greek Tense Form Choice in the Non-Indicative Moods* (pdf edition, 2009), 21. This is a case where the function of the verb is more relevant than the grammatical form.

[29] Perhaps this is due to the verbal idea communicated by purpose statements that tend to look at the situation as a whole or a simple event without any added nuance (e.g., iterative, inceptive, or tendential).

[30] E.g., in the New Testament the use of the subjunctive with οὐ μή occurs 85 times in the aorist and never in the present (though it does occur in the present in the LXX).

[31] For example, Paul uses the present imperative three times more frequently than the aorist imperative. On the other hand, 1 Peter contains twenty-five aorist imperatives but only ten present imperatives. See Robertson, 856; Campbell, *Verbal Aspect and Non-Indicative Verbs*, 87; and Greg W. Forbes, "The Use of the Imperative in 1 Peter" and "Imperatival Participles in 1 Peter," in *1 Peter*, EGGNT (Nashville: B&H Academic, 2014), 4–7.

specific occasion (specific command).[32] In prayers, however, where imperatives are used to make requests to God, the predominant tense-form is the aorist, whether referring to a general precept or a specific occasion. In these cases, the literary genre (prayer) virtually determines the use of the tense-form. Another distinction with imperatives is that present imperatives are the most common form in epistles whereas the aorist is more common in narratives.

Case Study: Imperatives. Before concluding this chapter, it will be helpful to illustrate the importance of considering the type of action in conjunction with aspect by studying the NT use of imperatives.[33] The imperative mood variously expresses a command, prohibition, request, entreaty, or permission.[34] When it comes to tense-form choice, with imperatives the author essentially had only two choices: present and aorist.[35] Also, when speaking of tense-forms for imperatives, because you cannot command someone to do something in the past (or, when you think about it, even the present), all imperatives are essentially future with regard to time. Therefore, the distinction between present and aorist tense-forms is completely unrelated to time and instead communicates the author's *perspective* of the action (aspect) or some specific type of action (kind of action).

The question we should ask ourselves is, "Why does an author use one tense-form over another?" Note, for example, the verse where Jesus commands his disciples, "Untie (λύσατε) [the colt] and bring (φέρετε) it" (Mark 11:2). Why is the first verb (λύσατε) aorist, whereas the second verb (φέρετε) is present? Should the differences between the tense-forms be pressed to highlight a nuanced meaning or should these imperatives be viewed as virtually identical?

In order to answer these questions adequately, we must consider the lexical, grammatical, and contextual factors. First, regarding lexis, we must remember that sometimes a verb's tense-form is lexically determined. For example, a few aorist imperatives, such as ἴδε and ἰδού ("look"), have lost their verbal nature and have become virtual particles. In addition, the imperatives for εἰμί and οἶδα occur only in the present tense-form.[36] We should also note that verbs of motion are almost

---

[32] See, e.g., BDF, 172 (§335); Fanning, 325–88; idem, "Approaches to Verbal Aspect," 55; Zerwick, 79 (§243).

[33] See D. S. Huffman, *Verbal Aspect Theory and the Prohibitions in the Greek New Testament*, SBG 16 (New York: Lang, 2014).

[34] See the previous chapter for an overview of imperatives. Other verbal forms that function as imperatives (such as the hortatory subjunctive, the prohibitory subjunctive, and participles in parallel constructions with imperatival forms) should be considered in this category as well. Future indicatives can also function as imperatives but do not need to be included here because the future tense-form communicates that the event took place simply or categorically and tense-form choice is not an issue.

[35] There are only two perfect imperatives in the NT: πεφίμωσο ("be still," Mark 4:39) and ἔρρωσθε ("farewell," Acts 15:39). The use of the perfect tense-form does not significantly affect the interpretation of these two imperatives.

[36] Although οἶδα is technically a perfect verb, it is a virtual present since "*there is very little distinction between the act and its results*" (Wallace, 580 [emphasis original]). Thus, to parse οἶδα as a perfect verb can be misleading.

always found in the present tense-form when used as imperatives,[37] whereas -μι verbs overwhelmingly prefer the aorist.[38] Therefore, it would be misleading to emphasize that a particular imperative is in the present tense-form if it is a verb of motion since that is the default form.[39]

Another factor to consider is whether a verb's tense-form is lexically influenced, by its inherent semantic nature. As mentioned above, a special nuance should be identified only when the particular form is not the one normally expected. The following charts illustrate how some verbs naturally (lexically) prefer one tense over another based on the particular type of action/state conveyed by the verb.[40]

TELIC EVENTS	PRESENT	AORIST
ἀγοράζω	0	3
ἀφίημι	2	25
βάλλω	0	14
δείκνυμι	0	8
δίδωμι	4	33
ἐνδύω	0	6
ἑτοιμάζω	1	8
λαμβάνω	4	17
πωλέω	0	5
σῴζω	1	9
Total	**12**	**128**

ATELIC EVENTS	PRESENT	AORIST
ἀγαπάω	8	1
ἀκολουθέω	16	2
γρηγορέω	10	1
ἐργάζομαι	4	0
ἔχω	12	1
μνημονεύω	8	0
περιπατέω	14	1
πιστεύω	13	2
προσεύχομαι	15	2
φεύγω	9	0
Total	**109**	**10**

To illustrate, in Matthew 16:24 Jesus calls anyone who would follow him to "deny himself, take up his cross, and follow" him (ἀπαρνησάσθω [aorist] ἑαυτὸν καὶ **ἀράτω** [aorist] τὸν σταυρὸν αὐτοῦ καὶ **ἀκολουθείτω** [present] μοι). In this example, the verbs ἀπαρνέομαι ("deny") and αἴρω ("take up") convey specific actions (note that ἀπαρνέομαι occurs twice as an aorist imperative and never as a present imperative, while αἴρω occurs 22 times as an aorist imperative and only four times as a present imperative). By contrast, ἀκολουθέω is a verb of motion (which are found almost exclusively in the present tense-form in the imperative), occurring 16 times as a present imperative and only twice as an aorist imperative. Or take Mark 2:11 as an example where Jesus tells the paralytic to "get up, take

---

[37] E.g., ἀκολουθέω, ἐγείρω, ἔρχομαι, περιπατέω, πορεύομαι, ὑπάγω, φεύγω, and φέρω.

[38] E.g., ἀφίημι, δίδωμι, ἵστημι, and τίθημι.

[39] Porter unduly emphasizes the present tense as the marked tense with verbs of motion. For example, regarding the use of πορεύεσθε in Matt 25:9 he notes, "The Present Imperative may be used to stress the urgency of the situation or the hardship the maidens face by being compelled to go, or, with a twist of irony, to draw attention to the wise maidens' knowledge that to leave is to risk the bridegroom coming" (*Verbal Aspect*, 352).

[40] These charts include not only imperatives but also hortatory and prohibitory subjunctives.

your mat and go home" (NIV; ἔγειρε [present] ἆρον [aorist] τὸν κράβαττόν σου καὶ ὕπαγε [present] εἰς τὸν οἶκόν σου). Because ἔγειρε and ὕπαγε are verbs of motion, they prefer the present tense-form (imperfective aspect). Ἆρον, on the other hand, is a telic verb and thus prefers the aorist tense-form (perfective aspect).

Second, grammatical factors should be considered. In this case, the most significant factor is that the verb is in the imperative mood. Because of their lexical nature, atelic verbs were often used to command or forbid an action as a general practice (or as a more-than-once occurrence) whereas telic verbs were often used to command or forbid an action or state on a specific occasion (or as unmarked and so could possibly either be performed once or more than once). For example, in John 18:31 Pilate is giving a specific command to the Jewish leaders to be carried out in this one circumstance (telic, aorist tense-form): "**Judge** him according to your law" (κατὰ τὸν νόμον ὑμῶν **κρίνατε** αὐτόν). In Luke 6:37, however, Jesus is not merely stating a one-time command but urging a general or characteristic behavior (atelic; present tense-form), urging his disciples, "Do not **judge**, and you will not be judged" (μὴ **κρίνετε**, καὶ οὐ μὴ κριθῆτε).[41] It is also important to recognize, as mentioned, that certain authors due to personal style may be prone to favor one tense-form over another and that literary genre may be a relevant factor as well. Various other contextual factors may also be relevant.

Conclusion

The above discussion makes clear that the interpretation of Greek verb tenses requires careful consideration of aspect, time, and type of action. Among these, aspect provides the general framework, while time is limited to the indicative, and type of action should be considered in conjunction with aspect. Importantly, aspect does not merely have linguistic significance; it has an important literary function on the discourse level as well.

In analyzing Greek verbs, it should be kept in mind that communication often involves convention rather than conscious choices between a set of linguistic alternatives.[42] Moreover, in interpreting a given verb form, it will be important to determine whether the tense-form of the verb is the expected form or not. This involves consideration of a variety of lexical, grammatical, and contextual factors in interpreting a given verb form or set of forms.

---

[41] In order to bring out the general nature of the command, Baugh helpfully translates this verse: "Do not *go around judging,* then you will not be judged" (*Tense Form Choice,* 41).

[42] See Silva's comments regarding this phenomenon in Moisés Silva, "A Response to Fanning and Porter on Verbal Aspect," in *Biblical Greek Language and Linguistics: Open Questions in Current Research,* ed. Stanley E. Porter and D. A. Carson, JSNTSup 80 (Sheffield: Sheffield Academic Press, 1993), 79.

SUMMARY

VERBAL ASPECT		
ASPECT	DEFINITION	TENSE-FORM
Imperfective	Action viewed as in process, ongoing	Present/Imperfective
Perfective	Action viewed as complete, as a whole	Aorist
Stative	State of affairs resulting from a previous action	Perfect/Pluperfect

ASPECTUAL CATEGORY	PAST-TIME INDICATOR	ASPECT PREFIX	LEXICAL CORE	ASPECT SUFFIX	PERSONAL ENDING
Imperfective (past)	ε	—	λυ	—	ομεν
Imperfective (non-past)	—	—	λυ	—	ομεν
Perfective (past)	ε	—	λυ	σ	αμεν
Perfective (non-past)	—	—	λυ	σ	ομεν
Stative (past)	ε	λε	λυ	κ	ειμεν
Stative (non-past)	—	λε	λυ	κ	αμεν

MOOD	IMPERFECTIVE	PERFECTIVE	STATIVE
Indicative	λύω / ἔλυον	(λύσω) ἔλυσα	λέλυκα / ἐλελύκειν
Infinitive	λύειν	(λύσειν) λῦσαι	λελυκέναι
Subjunctive	λύω	λύσω	λελύκω
Imperative	λῦε	λῦσον	λέλυκε
Participle	λύων	(λύσων) λύσας	λελυκώς

TELIC	Performance	Bounded actions with perceived duration	Prefers **Aorist**
	Punctual	Bounded actions with little perceived duration	
ATELIC	Stative	States and relationships	Prefers **Present/ Imperfect**
	Activity	Actions with no inherent termination	

INTERPRETING IMPERATIVES		
LEXICAL	Determination	When a verb is limited to a particular tense-form (e.g., εἰμί and οἶδα = present; ἴδε and ἰδού = aorist) or is almost always found in a particular tense-form (e.g., verbs of motion occurring in the present tense-form).
	Influence	The impact of a verb's inherent meaning on its usage in various tense-forms. Verbs that convey specific commands prefer the aorist whereas verbs that denote general instructions prefer the present.
GRAMMATICAL	Telic verbs (which naturally prefer the aorist tense) were often used to command or forbid an action on a specific occasion, whereas atelic verbs (which naturally prefer the present tense) were often used to command or forbid a general behavior.	
CONTEXTUAL	Aorist imperatives are preferred in prayers and historical narratives whereas present imperatives are preferred in epistles (except in 1 Peter).	

PRACTICE EXERCISES

Identify the aspect and tense-form of all the verb forms in the following examples and comment on the interpretive significance of these forms (e.g., imperfective aspect views the action in a given example as progressive and ongoing).

1. καὶ <u>ἔρχεται</u> εἰς οἶκον· καὶ <u>συνέρχεται</u> πάλιν [ὁ] ὄχλος (Mark 3:20).

2. καὶ <u>ἤκουσαν</u> οἱ δύο μαθηταὶ αὐτοῦ <u>λαλοῦντος</u> καὶ <u>ἠκολούθησαν</u> τῷ Ἰησοῦ (John 1:37).

3. ὃ <u>ἑώρακεν</u> καὶ <u>ἤκουσεν</u> τοῦτο <u>μαρτυρεῖ</u>, καὶ τὴν μαρτυρίαν αὐτοῦ οὐδεὶς <u>λαμβάνει</u> (John 3:32).

4. καὶ <u>ἥψατο</u> τῆς χειρὸς αὐτῆς, καὶ <u>ἀφῆκεν</u> αὐτὴν ὁ πυρετός, καὶ <u>ἠγέρθη</u> καὶ <u>διηκόνει</u> αὐτῷ (Matt 8:15).

5. <u>ἐξεπορεύετο</u> πρὸς αὐτὸν Ἰεροσόλυμα καὶ πᾶσα ἡ Ἰουδαία . . . καὶ <u>ἐβαπτίζοντο</u> ἐν τῷ Ἰορδάνῃ ποταμῷ ὑπ' αὐτοῦ <u>ἐξομολογούμενοι</u> τὰς ἁμαρτίας αὐτῶν. (Matt 3:5)

In each of the following examples, (1) identify the aspect and tense-form of the underlined verb, (2) identify the verbs as telic or atelic (if possible), and (3) determine whether the tense-form given is the default form or not.

6. <u>παράλαβε</u> (aor act impv) τὸ παιδίον καὶ τὴν μητέρα αὐτοῦ καὶ <u>φεῦγε</u> (pres act impv) εἰς Αἴγυπτον (Matt 2:13).

7. <u>ἴδε</u> (aor mid impv) τὰς χεῖράς μου καὶ <u>φέρε</u> (pres mid impv) τὴν χεῖρά σου καὶ <u>βάλε</u> (aor mid impv) εἰς τὴν πλευράν μου (John 20:27).

8. <u>ἐκραύγασαν</u> οὖν ἐκεῖνοι· <u>ἆρον</u> (aor act impv 2nd sg αἴρω) <u>ἆρον</u>, <u>σταύρωσον</u> (aor act impv 2nd sg σταυρόω) αὐτόν (John 19:15).

9. <u>ἐνδύσασθε</u> (aor mid impv) οὖν . . . σπλάγχνα οἰκτιρμοῦ χρηστότητα ταπεινοφροσύνην . . . <u>ἀνεχόμενοι</u> (pres mid ptc) ἀλλήλων καὶ <u>χαριζόμενοι</u> (pres mid ptc) ἑαυτοῖς (Col 3:12–13).

10. <u>ἑτοίμαζέ</u> (pres act impv) μοι ξενίαν (Phlm 22).

VOCABULARY

Vocabulary to Memorize

ἀγιάζω	I sanctify, make holy, reverence (28)
ἀγνοέω	I do not know, am ignorant (22)
Αἴγυπτος, ἡ	Egypt (25)
ἀναχωρέω	I go away, withdraw (14)
ἀντί	instead of, for, on behalf of (22)
βασιλεύω	I reign, rule (21)
δέομαι	I ask, pray, beg (22)
δοκιμάζω	I examine, test, prove (22)
ἐκλέγομαι	I choose, elect (22)
ἐκλεκτός	chosen, elect (22)
ζῷον, τό	living thing/being, animal (23)
Ἡρῴδης, ὁ	Herod (43)
θεάομαι	I see, look at, behold (22)
θυσιαστήριον, τό	altar (23)
Ἰουδαία, ἡ	Judea (43)
Ἰωσήφ, ὁ	Joseph (35)
καθεύδω	I sleep (22)
κἀκεῖνος	and that one, he also (22)
κατεργάζομαι	I do, achieve, accomplish (22)
κατηγορέω	I accuse (23)
κατοικέω	I live, dwell, reside (44)
κοιλία, ἡ	belly, stomach, womb (22)
κοπιάω	I work hard, labor (23)
κωλύω	I hinder, prevent (23)
Μακεδονία, ἡ	Macedonia (22)
μέρος, -ους, τό	part, share, district (42)
μηκέτι	no longer (22)
νέος	new, fresh, young (23)
πεινάω	I hunger, am hungry (23)
πειρασμός, ὁ	temptation, trial, test (21)
πέραν	on the other side (23)
περιβάλλω	I put on, clothe, dress (23)
πληγή, ἡ	blow, plague, wound (22)
ῥύομαι	I rescue, deliver (17)
σήμερον	today (41)
σκεῦος, τό	vessel, jar, object (23)

τελειόω, τό	I complete, make perfect (23)
φαίνω	I shine, appear (31)
χαρίζομαι	I give freely, grant (23)
χιλιάς, -αδος, ἡ	a thousand (23)

Vocabulary to Recognize

Ἀρχέλαος	Archelaus (1)
εἰσφέρω	I bring in (8)
ἐπιούσιος	daily, for today (2)
θνήσκω	I die (9)
Ναζαρέτ, ἡ	Nazareth (12)
Ναζωραῖος	Nazarene (13)
ὄναρ, τό	dream (6)
ὀφειλέτης, -ου, ὁ	debtor (7)
ὀφείλημα, -ατος, τό	debt (2)
τελευτάω	I die (11)
χρηματίζω	I instruct, warn (9)

READING THE NEW TESTAMENT

Matthew 2:19–23

¹⁹Τελευτήσαντος δὲ τοῦ Ἡρῴδου ἰδοὺ ἄγγελος κυρίου φαίνεται κατ᾽ ὄναρ τῷ Ἰωσὴφ ἐν Αἰγύπτῳ ²⁰λέγων, Ἐγερθεὶς παράλαβε τὸ παιδίον καὶ τὴν μητέρα αὐτοῦ καὶ πορεύου εἰς γῆν Ἰσραήλ· τεθνήκασιν γὰρ οἱ ζητοῦντες τὴν ψυχὴν τοῦ παιδίου. ²¹ὁ δὲ ἐγερθεὶς παρέλαβεν τὸ παιδίον καὶ τὴν μητέρα αὐτοῦ καὶ εἰσῆλθεν εἰς γῆν Ἰσραήλ. ²²ἀκούσας δὲ ὅτι Ἀρχέλαος βασιλεύει τῆς Ἰουδαίας ἀντὶ τοῦ πατρὸς αὐτοῦ Ἡρῴδου ἐφοβήθη ἐκεῖ ἀπελθεῖν· χρηματισθεὶς δὲ κατ᾽ ὄναρ ἀνεχώρησεν εἰς τὰ μέρη τῆς Γαλιλαίας, ²³καὶ ἐλθὼν κατῴκησεν εἰς πόλιν λεγομένην Ναζαρέτ· ὅπως πληρωθῇ τὸ ῥηθὲν διὰ τῶν προφητῶν ὅτι Ναζωραῖος κληθήσεται.

Matthew 6:9–13

⁹Οὕτως οὖν προσεύχεσθε ὑμεῖς·
Πάτερ ἡμῶν ὁ ἐν τοῖς οὐρανοῖς·
ἁγιασθήτω τὸ ὄνομά σου·
¹⁰ἐλθέτω ἡ βασιλεία σου·
γενηθήτω τὸ θέλημά σου,
    ὡς ἐν οὐρανῷ καὶ ἐπὶ γῆς·
¹¹τὸν ἄρτον ἡμῶν τὸν ἐπιούσιον δὸς ἡμῖν σήμερον·
¹²καὶ ἄφες ἡμῖν τὰ ὀφειλήματα ἡμῶν,
    ὡς καὶ ἡμεῖς ἀφήκαμεν τοῖς ὀφειλέταις ἡμῶν·
¹³καὶ μὴ εἰσενέγκῃς ἡμᾶς εἰς πειρασμόν,
ἀλλὰ ῥῦσαι ἡμᾶς ἀπὸ τοῦ πονηροῦ.
[Ὅτι σοῦ ἐστιν ἡ βασιλεία καὶ ἡ δύναμις καὶ ἡ δόξα εἰς τοὺς αἰῶνας.
Ἀμήν.]

Reading Notes[43]

Matthew 2:19

- **Τελευτήσαντος δὲ τοῦ Ἡρῴδου** ("After Herod died") – The temporal genitive absolute consists of the verb τελευτήσαντος (aor act ptc masc gen sg τελευτάω) and the genitive τοῦ Ἡρῴδου, depicting the action wholistically (perfective aspect).[44]

---

[43] The English version used in the Reading Notes for this chapter is the NIV.
[44] Donald A. Hagner, *Matthew 1–13*, WBC 33A (Dallas: Word, 1993), 39 notes the similar language in Exod 2:23 regarding the death of Pharaoh and the near-verbatim agreement with v. 13 (cf. v. 20). Cf. W. D. Davies and Dale C. Allison Jr., *The Gospel according to Saint Matthew*, ICC, 3 vols. (Edinburgh: T&T Clark, 1988), 270.

- ἰδοὺ ἄγγελος κυρίου φαίνεται κατ' ὄναρ ("an angel of the Lord appeared in a dream") – The verb φαίνεται (pres mid ind 3rd sg φαίνω) is a historical present (cf. v. 13).

Matthew 2:20

- Ἐγερθεὶς παράλαβε . . . καὶ πορεύου ("Get up, take . . . and go") – ἐγερθείς (aor pass ptc masc nom sg ἐγείρω) conveys a perfective aspect, depicting the action wholistically and expressing attendant circumstance. παράλαβε (aor act impv 2nd sg παραλαμβάνω) is a perfective imperative, portraying the action wholistically, while πορεύου (pres mid impv 2nd sg πορεύομαι) is imperfective, viewing the action as ongoing (cf. the virtually identical pattern in v. 13). Also note that verbs of motion (such as πορεύομαι) prefer the present-tense form as imperatives.

- τὸ παιδίον καὶ τὴν μητέρα αὐτοῦ ("the child and his mother") – A subtle reference to the fact that while Mary was Jesus's real mother, Joseph was not his biological father (cf. 1:16: "Joseph, the husband of Mary, and Mary . . . the mother of Jesus"; and 1:18–25).

- τεθνήκασιν γὰρ οἱ ζητοῦντες τὴν ψυχὴν τοῦ παιδίου ("for those who were trying to take the child's life are dead") – τεθνήκασιν (perf act ind 3rd pl θνῄσκω) is in the stative aspect, depicting a past event (death) with resulting consequences. Not only are king Herod and his henchmen now dead, their demise also removes the threat on the child Messiah, Jesus. ζητοῦντες (pres act ptc masc nom pl ζητέω), contrary to the conventional understanding of relative time in participles, most likely does not convey contemporaneous action (how could Jesus's enemies seek to kill him when they were dead?) but rather depicts the action (trying to take the child's life) from an imperfective aspect, highlighting the ongoing nature of persecution while Jesus's foes were still alive (i.e., prior to their death, preceding action).[45]

Matthew 2:21

- ὁ δὲ ἐγερθεὶς παρέλαβεν . . . καὶ εἰσῆλθεν ("So he got up, took . . . and went") – The article ὁ functions as a personal pronoun referring to Joseph. The series of verbs (one participle, two indicatives) are all in the perfective aspect, viewing the actions wholistically.[46] The indicatives

---

[45] We are indebted for this insight to Nicholas Ellis. Cf. Davies and Allison, *Gospel according to Saint Matthew*, 272, who observe that "the present participle can connote antecedent time" (with reference to John 12:17; Acts 4:34; Rom 9:30; Gal 1:23; and BDF §339.3). Hagner, *Matthew 1–13*, 39, notes the near-verbatim agreement of this statement with Exod 4:19.

[46] Hagner, *Matthew 1–13*, 39, notes that the "recording of the obedience mirrors the wording of the command in v 20."

παρέλαβεν (aor act ind 3rd sg παραλαμβάνω) and εἰσῆλθεν (aor act ind 3rd sg εἰσέρχομαι) both convey past actions, while the participle ἐγερθείς (see v. 20 above) denotes the perfective aspect as well, with no necessary implication as to time (though from context it is clear that the participle reports an action prior to the indicative).

- τὸ παιδίον καὶ τὴν μητέρα αὐτοῦ ("the child and his mother") – See commentary at v. 20 above.

Matthew 2:22

- **ἀκούσας δὲ ὅτι Ἀρχέλαος βασιλεύει τῆς Ἰουδαίας** ("But when he heard that Archelaus was reigning in Judea") –The temporal participle ἀκούσας (aor act ptc masc nom sg ἀκούω) is in the perfective aspect, viewing the action wholistically. The verb βασιλεύει (pres act ind 3rd sg βασιλεύω) conveys the imperfective aspect, depicting the action as ongoing ("was reigning"; the present tense-form is normal in this statement of indirect discourse).[47] τῆς Ἰουδαίας possibly a genitive of subordination ("he was reigning *over* Judea").

- **ἐφοβήθη ἐκεῖ ἀπελθεῖν** ("he was afraid to go there") – Although Herod had died (v. 19), his son Archelaus, who was now reigning in Judea, remained a threat. Both the indicative ἐφοβήθη (aor pass ind 3rd sg φοβέω) and the infinitive ἀπελθεῖν (aor act inf ἀπέρχομαι) are in the perfective aspect, viewing the actions wholistically.

- **χρηματισθεὶς δέ . . . ἀνεχώρησεν** ("Having been warned . . ., he withdrew") – Again, Matthew uses an aorist participle (χρηματισθείς, aor pass ptc masc nom sg χρηματίζω) followed by an aorist indicative (ἀνεχώρησεν, aor act ind 3rd sg ἀναχωρέω).

Matthew 2:23

- **καὶ ἐλθὼν κατῴκησεν** ("and he went and lived") – This is another instance of juxtaposition of an aorist participle (ἐλθών, aor act ptc masc nom sg ἔρχομαι) followed by an aorist indicative (κατῴκησεν, aor act ind 3rd sg κατοικέω), conveying a series of actions viewed wholistically. See commentary at vv. 20, 21, 22 above. Note that Matthew could have depicted "lived" by way of the imperfective aspect (using, e.g., an imperfect tense-form), but he chose to view the action wholistically rather than as ongoing.

---

[47] See Hagner, *Matthew 1–13*, 39; Davies and Allison, *Gospel according to Saint Matthew*, 273, who note that in "indirect discourse the present tense with verbs of saying takes up the temporal point of view of the speaker. Similarly here the present tense ('rules') with a verb of perception ('hearing') reflects the temporal point of view of Joseph (BDF §324)."

- **πληρωθῇ . . . κληθήσεται** ("was fulfilled . . . he would be called") – This is now the third quotation in Matthew's Gospel demonstrating fulfillment of Old Testament prophecy in Jesus's life, showing him to be the Messiah (cf. 1:22; 2:15). The divine passive πληρωθῇ (aor pass subj 3rd sg πληρόω) suggests that God is the primary agent, sovereignly superintending the fulfillment of his promises issued through the various OT prophets. The shift from the singular διὰ τοῦ προφήτου (1:22; 2:5, 15, 17) to the plural διὰ τῶν προφητῶν may signal that a prophetic theme rather than a single specific text is in view,[48] possibly OT prophecies describing the Messiah as a "branch" (Isa 11:1; cf. Isa 4:2; Jer 23:5; 33:15).[49] κληθήσεται is a fut pass ind 3rd sg of καλέω.

Matthew 6:9

- **Οὕτως** ("this") – The adverb οὕτως means "in this way" or "thus." In the context, it refers to the prayer that follows. Most commentators maintain that this prayer is an example of how to pray rather than an exact prayer that is simply to be repeated verbatim.

- **προσεύχεσθε** ("should pray") – Pres mid impv 2nd pl προσεύχομαι. The present tense is the expected tense-form as praying is an atelic activity and the meaning is that this should be done as a general practice (or done more than once or repeated). Thus, as an imperative, προσεύχομαι occurs in the present tense-form 15 times but only twice as an aorist. Jesus gives an injunction to his disciples here, but remember that the imperative mood does not always convey a command but can convey a request or entreaty (as in the petitions below).

- **ὑμεῖς** ("you") – Emphatic use of the second person personal pronoun which is not needed because the person and number are embedded in the verbal ending. The "you" is probably emphasized in contrast to how hypocrites pray.

- **Πάτερ ἡμῶν** ("Our Father") – Masc voc sg πατήρ. The use of "our" (ἡμῶν) demonstrates the corporate or communal nature of the prayer and also suggests that Jesus was primarily speaking against certain abuses when he stated we should pray in private (Matt 6:6).

- **ὁ ἐν τοῖς οὐρανοῖς** ("in heaven") – The article ὁ makes the prepositional phrase a virtual adjective (substantizing) which then modifies πάτερ. In such constructions, it is usually best to translate the article as a relative pronoun ("Our Father *who* is in heaven").

---

[48] Hagner, *Matthew 1–13*, 40.
[49] See the discussion in Blomberg, *Matthew*, NAC, 70 (see chap. 2, n. 86); Hagner, *Matthew 1–13*, 40–42.

- **ἁγιασθήτω** ("hallowed be") – Aor pass impv 3rd sg ἁγιάζω. Note that the NIV translation, though usually conforming to modern speech patterns, maintains continuity with the KJV here—likely because of the translators' desire to reflect previous English translations in well-known passages. Notice that all of the imperatives in the Lord's Prayer are aorist. Why is this so?

Matthew 6:10

- **ἐλθέτω** ("come") – Aor act impv 3rd sg ἔρχομαι.

- **γενηθήτω** ("be done") – Aor pass impv 3rd sg γίνομαι.

- **ὡς ἐν οὐρανῷ καὶ ἐπὶ γῆς** ("on earth as it is in heaven") – This phrase could simply modify the last petition ("your will be done") or, most likely, it refers to all three. This is especially true if Jesus is using synonymous parallelism so that the three pleas point to the same reality.

Matthew 6:11

- **τὸν ἐπιούσιον** ("daily") – This word is rare in the NT as it occurs only here and in Luke's version of the Lord's Prayer (Luke 11:3). In addition, it does not occur in the LXX and has not been found in literature outside the Bible.

- **δός** ("give") – Aor act impv 2nd sg δίδωμι. The first three petitions were focused on God but now the focus shifts to those praying. This shift is evidenced by the change from the third person imperatives to the second person as well as a switch from the second person personal pronoun "your" (σου) to the first person "our" (ἡμῶν). It is important to remember that the use of the aorist imperative here should not be overinterpreted. For example, Rogers and Rogers state that the aorist looks "at a specific request."[50] Actually, this is a daily (and thus repeated) prayer that would more naturally fit with the present tense-form (imperfective aspect). The aorist is used most likely because the verb form is found in a prayer and is a telic verb.[51] Osborne, following Porter, suggests that the aorist imperative looks "at the action as a single whole."[52] But this usage is probably more related to the literary genre (prayer) and the verb's lexical nature than a conscious effort of the author to offer a particular perspective regarding the action.

---

[50] Cleon L. Rogers Jr. and Cleon L. Rogers, *The New Linguistic and Exegetical Key to the Greek New Testament* (Grand Rapids: Zondervan, 1998), 13.

[51] Interestingly, Luke uses the present tense-form (δίδου) most likely because he uses "each day" or "day by day" (καθ᾽ ἡμέραν) instead of "today" (σήμερον). This is one of the rare exceptions where an aorist form is not used in a prayer. Perhaps this is an example of an adverbial phrase clarifying an imperfective idea.

[52] Osborne, *Matthew*, 228.

Matthew 6:12

- ἄφες ("forgive") – Aor act impv 2nd sg ἀφίημι.

- τὰ ὀφειλήματα ("debts") – Typically, this word refers to a literal debt but here it is used metaphorically. This is confirmed by Luke's version which uses the term "sins" (ἁμαρτίας) instead of "debts" (Luke 11:4).

- ὡς ("as") – Although some suggest translating ὡς "because," it is not likely that our forgiving others is the grounds of our being forgiven. As Osborne comments, "It is not that our forgiveness is the basis of God's forgiveness . . ., but rather that as we experience being pardoned by God, we must exercise in [sic] a greater willingness to pardon others."[53]

- ἡμεῖς ("we") – This is emphatic, stressing the importance of forgiving others (see Matt 18:35).

- ἀφήκαμεν ("have forgiven") – Aor act ind 1st pl ἀφίημι. This is the dramatic use of the aorist that represents an action that recently occurred.

Matthew 6:13

- μὴ εἰσενέγκῃς ("lead us not") – Aor act sub 2nd sg εἰσφέρω. This is a prohibitory subjunctive that is used in the place of an aorist imperative (this is only used when the verb is aorist *and* negated).

- ῥῦσαι ("deliver") – Aor mid impv 2nd sg ῥύομαι.

- τοῦ πονηροῦ ("the evil one") – This term could be either neuter ("evil") or masculine ("evil one"). If the latter is preferred, then the adjective is functioning as a substantive (i.e., as a noun).[54]

- Ὅτι σοῦ ἐστιν ἡ βασιλεία καὶ ἡ δύναμις καὶ ἡ δόξα εἰς τοὺς αἰῶνας. Ἀμήν (KJV: "For thine is the kingdom, and the power, and the glory, forever. Amen.") – The originality of this text is debated. Although it appears in some early manuscripts (K L W Δ Θ Π), it is missing in some of the oldest (and most reliable?) manuscripts (ℵ B D). It is therefore excluded from most modern English versions. Metzger concludes, "The absence of any ascription in early and important representatives of the Alexandrian (ℵ B), the Western (D and most of the Old Latin), and other (f1) types of text, as well as early patristic commentaries on the Lord's Prayer (those of Tertullian, Origen, Cyprian), suggest that an ascription, usually in a threefold form, was composed (perhaps on the basis of 1 Chr 29:11–13) in order to adapt the Prayer for liturgical use in the early church."[55]

---

[53] Osborne, *Matthew*, 230.

[54] Wallace comments, "The devil is in view here, not evil in general. . . . The prayer is not a request for deliverance from evil in general, but from the grasp of the evil one himself" (294).

[55] Metzger, *Textual Commentary*, 14.

////////////////

CHAPTER 8

PRESENT, IMPERFECT & FUTURE INDICATIVES

GOING DEEPER

At times an English translation of the Bible may seem to run contrary to other passages in the Bible. For example, 1 John 3:6 reads, "Everyone who remains in him **does not sin** (οὐχ ἁμαρτάνει); everyone who sins has not seen him or known him." The difficulty with this verse is that it seems to contradict both experience (if we are honest with ourselves) and other passages of Scripture. John himself previously stated, "If we say, 'We have no sin,' we are deceiving ourselves, and the truth is not in us" (1 John 1:8; see also v. 10). There are two main ways to view the present tense-form verb ἁμαρτάνει in 1 John 3:6. It is either to be interpreted as a gnomic present (a general truth) or an iterative present (a repeated or customary action). If it is a gnomic present, then the interpreter has another choice to make. Is John describing something that is an actual possibility (i.e., sinless perfection in this life) or something that is in view of our eschatological hope (i.e., it is not true experientially but in light Christ's death for us, it is true positionally)?

The better option, however, is to view the verb ἁμαρτάνει as an iterative present which involves the idea of a repetitive or customary action. This is the way both the ESV ("No one who abides in him **keeps on sinning**") and the NIV ("No one who lives in him **keeps on sinning**") interpret this verse. But what contextual evidence is there to interpret the verb with such a nuance? First, as we have already seen, John notes that if we claim to be without sin we deceive ourselves. Thus, John already implicitly acknowledges that perfection in this life is impossible.

255

Second, the idea that John is speaking in light of our eschatological hope does not best fit the context of the letter. In this epistle, John offers a series of three repeated tests that serve to give assurance to true believers and expose false believers. The false believers are those who live ungodly lifestyles, do not love others, and consequently continue to live in sin. Thus, John is seeking to contrast the lifestyle of the false teachers with those who are genuine Christians. Third, the iterative nuance is supported by the immediate context where John has been speaking about "everyone who practices sin" (v. 4, NASB; πᾶς ὁ ποιῶν τὴν ἁμαρτίαν), "the one who practices sin" (v. 8, NASB; ὁ ποιῶν τὴν ἁμαρτίαν), and the one who "does not practice sin" (v. 9, author's translation; ἁμαρτίαν οὐ ποιεῖ). In the context, John has not only been referring to those who sin but specifically to those who practice or make a practice of sinning. Thus, John is not making a statement about the possibility of Christian perfectionism in this life or about our eschatological hope based on what Christ has done for us but is giving guidelines for knowing who are the true children of God: they are those who are not characterized by habitual disobedience to God.

CHAPTER OBJECTIVES

The purpose of this and the next chapter is to explain the various nuances sometimes found in indicative mood verbs, with this chapter focusing on the present, imperfect, and future tense-forms.[1] Although these nuances or categories are somewhat artificial (in the sense that the original author or speakers were not necessarily mindful of such categories) it is helpful for us to see how verbs were actually used in certain contexts. The indicative mood is the most common mood in the NT. Of the 15,674 indicative verbs, 5,538 are present, 1,682 are imperfect, 1,609 are future, 5,919 are aorist, 839 are perfect, and 86 are pluperfect.[2]

	Progressive
	Durative
	Iterative
	Gnomic
PRESENT INDICATIVE	Instantaneous
	Historical
	Tendential
	Futuristic
	Perfective

---

[1] We prefer "tense-form" over "tense" because the latter is often associated strictly with the time of the action. In addition, many of the categories discussed in this chapter are applicable to non-indicate verbs, but for the sake of simplicity, we will limit our discussion to the indicative mood.

[2] There is also one future perfect (Heb 8:11, εἰδήσουσίν).

	Progressive
IMPERFECT INDICATIVE	Inceptive
	Iterative
	Tendential
FUTURE INDICATIVE	Predictive
	Imperatival
	Deliberative
	Gnomic
	Progressive

PRESENT INDICATIVE

As mentioned in the previous chapter, the tense-form of the verb includes both the time of action (for indicative verbs) and the author's perspective of the action. For the present indicative, the time of the action normally refers to the present time.[3] There are contexts, however, where the present indicative conveys an action that is in the past (e.g., the historical present), the future, or is omni-temporal (e.g., the gnomic present). The aspect of the present tense-form can be characterized as progressive, internal, or incomplete. That is, it views the action as imperfect (from the Latin *imperfectivum*, "not completed") in the sense that the action is in progress. But this is only the basic or unaffected meaning of the verb's tense-form. There are often other influences (such as lexical, grammatical, and contextual factors) that affect a specific use of a verb. It is only when we consider all of these factors that we can be prepared to address the issue of whether or not a particular verb is being used in a specific manner. The following categories represent those categories that are sometimes found as specific uses of present tense-form verbs. There are 5,538 present indicatives in the NT.

Progressive Present[4]

As its name suggests, this use of the present tense-form conveys an action that is in progress, as opposed to an action performed instantaneously. The action is viewed as continuous but should not be confused with an action that is repeated (iterative), regularly performed (customary), or is a general truth that is timeless (gnomic). The progressive present is consistent with the imperfective aspect in

---

[3] Though it could be argued that the temporal nature of the present tense-form is not "present" but rather "non-past." That is, because the present tense-form lacks the past-time augment, it is unmarked for past time. The historical present is the only exception, but is probably used as a rhetorical device.

[4] The term "Descriptive Present" is used by Robertson, Brooks & Winbery, Young, and Black. Both Robertson and Black have a distinct category called "Progressive Present" but this represents an action that was begun in the past and continues to the present (i.e., present for past action still in progress = durative). Dana & Mantey have a general category called "Progressive Present" and then under this heading are three sub-categories, (a) Present of Description, (b) Present of Existing Result, and (c) Present of Duration.

that it presents an action as in progress or in the process of being accomplished. Consequently, it is usually best translated as a continuous present with the helping verb "is/are." This use is especially common in narratives where the verb occurs in direct (or sometimes indirect) discourse.

- κύριε, σῶσον, **ἀπολλύμεθα** (Matt 8:25)

  Lord, save us! **We are perishing!** (NRSV)

- αἱ λαμπάδες ἡμῶν **σβέννυνται** (Matt 25:8)

  our lamps **are going out**

- Τί **λαλεῖς** μετ᾽ αὐτῆς (John 4:27)

  Why **are you talking** with her?

- θαυμάζω ὅτι οὕτως ταχέως **μετατίθεσθε** (Gal 1:6)

  I am amazed that **you are** so quickly **turning away**

- ἡ σκοτία **παράγεται** καὶ τὸ φῶς τὸ ἀληθινὸν ἤδη **φαίνει** (1 John 2:8)

  the darkness **is passing away** and the true light **is** already **shining**[5]

Durative Present[6]

The basic idea of the durative use of the present tense-form is that it represents an action (or state) that began in the past and continues into the present. This usage should not be confused with the progressive present, which communicates an action that is present but does not have a temporal marker (such as an adverb), indicating that the action began sometime in the past. In addition, the durative use of the present tense-form should not be confused with the perfect tense which often signifies an action that was completed in the past but has ongoing results. In the case of the present tense, the action itself is still ongoing (not simply the consequences of that action). Moulton describes this use of the present tense-form as one that "gathers up past and present time into one phrase."[7] Although the action began in the past and continues into the present, the emphasis is on the present time frame of the verb. These verbs are usually translated as an English present perfect (i.e., have/has + verb).

---

[5] For more examples of the progressive present, see Mark 1:37 (ζητοῦσίν); 2:19 (ἔχουσιν); 3:32 (ζητοῦσιν); John 5:7 (ἔρχομαι, καταβαίνει); Acts 2:8 (ἀκούομεν); 3:12 (θαυμάζετε, ἀτενίζετε); 14:15 (ποιεῖτε); 21:31 (συγχύννεται); Rom 9:1 (λέγω, ψεύδομαι); 1 Cor 14:14 (προσεύχεται); 2 Cor 12:9 (τελεῖται); Gal 4:9 (ἐπιστρέφετε).

[6] As noted above, this category is sometimes labeled as a "Progressive Present" (so Robertson, Fanning, and Black). Burton and Moule label it "Present of Past Action Still in Progress" whereas Wallace calls it an "Extending-from-Past Present."

[7] Moulton, 1:119.

- τρία ἔτη ἀφ᾽ οὗ **ἔρχομαι** (Luke 13:7)

  for three years **I have come**

- τοσαῦτα ἔτη **δουλεύω** σοι (Luke 15:29)

  these many years **I have served** you (ESV)

- ἀπ᾽ ἀρχῆς μετ᾽ ἐμοῦ **ἐστε** (John 15:27)

  you have been with me from the beginning

- Μωϋσῆς . . . κατὰ πόλιν τοὺς κηρύσσοντας αὐτὸν **ἔχει** (Acts 15:21)

  Moses **has had** those who proclaim him in every city

- ἀπ᾽ ἀρχῆς ὁ διάβολος **ἁμαρτάνει** (1 John 3:8)

  the devil **has sinned** from the beginning[8]

Iterative Present[9]

The present tense-form is sometimes used to describe an action that is performed repeatedly, regularly, or customarily or is a state that is ongoing or continuous. This use is quite common and is frequently found with imperative verbs.[10] In order to communicate the iterative use of the present, it is often helpful to supply the words "keep on," "customarily," "normally," or "always" (in many cases, the context itself includes such words).

- πολλάκις **πίπτει** εἰς τὸ πῦρ (Matt 17:15)

  He often **falls** into the fire

  It is clear that the context, not the verb itself, determines its specific usage. Note that the word "often" (πολλάκις) communicates the repeated nature of the action.

---

[8] For more examples of the durative present, see John 5:6 (ἔχει); 14:9 (εἰμι); Acts 27:33 (διατελεῖτε); 2 Cor 12:19 (δοκεῖτε); 2 Tim 3:15 (οἶδας, this is an old perfect form that functioned as a virtual present tense); 2 Pet 3:4 (διαμένει).

[9] Wallace differentiates between the "Iterative" and the "Customary" present (as do Dana & Mantey, though they seem to blur the customary use with the gnomic). He states that the "intervals are shorter with the iterative, and less regular." He goes on, however, to admit that "several passages are difficult to analyze and could conceivably fit in either category" (Wallace, 520).

[10] Matt 7:7: "**Keep on asking**, and you will receive what you ask for. **Keep on seeking**, and you will find. **Keep on knocking**, and the door will be opened to you" (NLT; **αἰτεῖτε** καὶ δοθήσεται ὑμῖν, **ζητεῖτε** καὶ εὑρήσετε, **κρούετε** καὶ ἀνοιγήσεται ὑμῖν); 1 Thess 5:17: "**Pray** constantly" (ἀδιαλείπτως **προσεύχεσθε**). Young explains the significance of the present tense-form in 1 Thess 5:17: "If we understand the verb as an iterative present, then Paul is exhorting us to have a regular prayer life rather than to be continuously in prayer; that is, it refers to an unceasing habit rather than an unceasing activity" (108).

- **νηστεύω** δὶς τοῦ σαββάτου, **ἀποδεκατῶ** πάντα ὅσα **κτῶμαι** (Luke 18:12)

  I fast twice a week; **I give a tenth** of everything **I get**

    It was the customary or habitual pattern of the Pharisees to fast and tithe.

- ὑμεῖς ἀεὶ τῷ πνεύματι τῷ ἁγίῳ **ἀντιπίπτετε** (Acts 7:51)

  You are always **resisting** the Holy Spirit

    Again, the iterative nature is helped by the use of the word "always" (ἀεί).

- ἡμεῖς δὲ **κηρύσσομεν** Χριστὸν ἐσταυρωμένον (1 Cor 1:23)

  but **we preach** Christ crucified

- πᾶς ὁ ἐν αὐτῷ μένων οὐχ **ἁμαρτάνει** (1 John 3:6)

  No one who abides in him **keeps on sinning** (ESV)[11]

Gnomic Present

The present tense-form is sometimes used to make a statement that is timeless (omni-temporal), universal, or generally true. Consequently, "this use of the present occurs in proverbial statements or general maxims about what occurs at *all* times."[12] A similar (but slightly distinct) use is found in "generic or indefinite statements, which relate what occurs generally or at *any* time."[13] In distinction to the iterative (repeated or customary) use of the present which indicates a reoccurring action, the gnomic use of the present refers to a timeless or general fact, not limited to a particular place or time.[14] Because God is eternal and unchanging, truths associated with God's character are often found in this category. In translation, the words "always" and "ever" (or "never") are sometimes supplied.

- πᾶν δένδρον ἀγαθὸν καρποὺς καλοὺς **ποιεῖ** (Matt 7:17)

  every good tree **produces** good fruit

- οὐχ ὁ ὕψιστος ἐν χειροποιήτοις **κατοικεῖ** (Acts 7:48)

  the Most High **does** not **dwell** in sanctuaries made with hands

---

[11] For more examples of the iterative present, see Matt 23:23 (ἀποδεκατοῦτε); Mark 2:18 (νηστεύουσιν); Luke 3:16 (βαπτίζω); John 1:38 (ζητεῖτε); 3:26 (βαπτίζει); 14:17 (μένει); Rom 1:9 (λατρεύω, ποιοῦμαι); 1 Cor 9:25 (ἐγκρατεύεται), 27 (ὑπωπιάζω, δουλαγωγῶ); 10:16 (εὐλογοῦμεν, κλῶμεν); 11:21 (προλαμβάνει), 26 (καταγγέλλετε), 29 (ἐσθίει, πίνει); 15:31 (ἀποθνῄσκω); Phil 1:15 (κηρύσσουσιν); Col 1:3 (εὐχαριστοῦμεν).

[12] Fanning, 208 (emphasis original).

[13] Fanning, 209.

[14] Fanning notes, "[T]he gnomic present is similar to the customary present in that they both express generalized continuing or repeated occurrence . . . , but the gnomic use is *more* general and indefinite, even *less* focused on particular people and restricted circumstances" (Fanning, 210).

- ἱλαρὸν δότην **ἀγαπᾷ** ὁ θεός (2 Cor 9:7)

  God **loves** a cheerful giver

  > This is clearly a general truth and sounds proverbial. The idea is that God always loves a cheerful giver.

- ἕκαστος δὲ **πειράζεται** ὑπὸ τῆς ἰδίας ἐπιθυμίας (Jas 1:14)

  But each person **is tempted** . . . by his own desire (ESV)

- ὁ ὁμολογῶν τὸν υἱὸν καὶ τὸν πατέρα **ἔχει** (1 John 2:23)

  Whoever confesses the Son **has** the Father also (ESV)[15]

Instantaneous Present[16]

This use of the present tense-form involves an action that is done, not progressively as is typical of the present indicative, but instantaneously (similar to some uses of the aorist tense-form). Note that the action is still performed at the present time (not the past) but is perfective (aoristic) with regards to the aspect. Because the Greek verb system does not have a tense to communicate the perfective aspect (i.e., an action completed or viewed as a whole) in the present time, the present tense-form at times functions in that capacity. Consequently, this use of the present tense-form communicates an action that is done in the present time but is completed at the moment of speaking. Thus, the aspect of the verb is suppressed and the time of the action becomes prominent. This category is lexically influenced because certain verbs, such as verbs of saying and thinking, are commonly used in this category. Some grammars refer to this as a "Performative Present" because the verb accomplishes or performs an action by the very fact that it is spoken.[17]

- **ὁρκίζω** σε τὸν θεόν, μή με βασανίσῃς (Mark 5:7)

  I adjure you by God, do not torment me (ESV)

- πάτερ, **εὐχαριστῶ** σοι ὅτι ἤκουσάς μου (John 11:41)

  Father, **I thank** You that you heard me

- **παραγγέλλω** σοι ἐν ὀνόματι Ἰησοῦ Χριστοῦ (Acts 16:18)

  I command you in the name of Jesus Christ

---

[15] For more examples of the gnomic present, see Matt 6:26 (τρέφει, διαφέρετε); Mark 2:21 (ἐπιράπτει), 22 (βάλλει); Luke 3:9 (ἐκκόπτεται, βάλλεται); John 2:10 (τίθησιν); 3:8 (πνεῖ); 7:52 (ἐγείρεται); 1 Cor 9:9 (μέλει); Jas 1:15 (τίκτει, ἀποκύει); Heb 3:4 (κατασκευάζεται); 1 John 3:3 (ἁγνίζει), 8 (ἐστίν), 20 (γινώσκει).

[16] Some grammars label this category the "Aoristic Present" (so BDF, Brooks & Winbery, Black).

[17] So Young, 112.

- Καίσαρα **ἐπικαλοῦμαι** (Acts 25:11)

  I appeal to Caesar![18]

- **συνίστημι** δὲ ὑμῖν Φοίβην τὴν ἀδελφὴν ἡμῶν (Rom 16:1)

  I commend to you our sister Phoebe[19]

Notice several features from these examples. First, most of the instantaneous (or performative) uses of the present tense-form are in the first person.[20] This category should not be confused with the historical present (which often uses λέγω in the present tense); which is different in at least two ways: (1) the historical present typically uses the third person, and (2) is typically used in a narrative that is translated as a past event. Second, the instantaneous present accomplishes the act by the very fact that it is uttered or takes place in the act itself. For example, Paul's appeal to Caesar was accomplished by stating that he appealed to Caesar. Likewise, Phoebe receives a commendation from Paul by the fact that he says he "commends" her.

Historical Present

The present tense-form is sometimes used (especially in historical narratives) to describe a past event which: (1) adds vividness to the event, drawing the reader into the story; or (2) gives literary prominence to some aspect of the story (e.g., change in setting/scene or introduction of new characters). Because the expected tense-form in narratives is the aorist, the use of the present is striking, highlighting something in the story. This could be done intentionally (to highlight some aspect of the narrative) or stereotypically (to add color to the story). Because the verb λέγει is used so often in narratives to introduce direct or indirect discourse, it has become a stereotyped idiom, no longer carrying any interpretive weight. Finally, the historical present will always be found in the third person (singular or plural, typically with verbs of action), is most common in the Gospels of Mark and John, and is translated as a simple past tense.[21]

- καὶ **ἔρχεται** πρὸς τοὺς μαθητὰς καὶ **εὑρίσκει** αὐτοὺς καθεύδοντας, καὶ **λέγει** τῷ Πέτρῳ (Matt 26:40)

  Then **he came** to the disciples and **found** them sleeping. He **asked** Peter

---

[18] The word "hereby" can be added to the translation to test for this category ("I hereby appeal to Caesar").

[19] For more examples of the instantaneous present, see Matt 3:9 (λέγω); 10:42 (λέγω); Luke 17:4 (μετανοῶ); John 3:3 (λέγω); 4:19 (θεωρῶ); Acts 17:22 (θεωρῶ); 19:13 (ὁρκίζω); 24:14 (ὁμολογῶ); 26:17 (ἀποστέλλω); 2 Cor 7:8 (μετεμελόμην); Gal 1:11 (γνωρίζω); Rev 1:8 (λέγει).

[20] There are some exceptions to this pattern: "Jesus told the paralytic, 'Son, your sins **are forgiven**'" (ὁ Ἰησοῦς . . . λέγει τῷ παραλυτικῷ· τέκνον, **ἀφίενταί** σου αἱ ἁμαρτίαι, Mark 2:5); "Aeneas, Jesus Christ **heals** you" (Αἰνέα, **ἰᾶταί** σε Ἰησοῦς Χριστός, Acts 9:34); "**It is permitted** for you to speak for yourself" (**ἐπιτρέπεταί** σοι περὶ σεαυτοῦ λέγειν, Acts 26:1).

[21] One should note the contraexpectational use of the historical present. That is, where one would expect to find an aorist (a form marked for perfective aspect and past time), instead one finds an imperfective aspect form unmarked for past time. The cumulative effect is rhetorical, not semantic or syntactical.

- καὶ **εἰσπορεύονται** εἰς Καφαρναούμ (Mark 1:21)

  Then they **went** into Capernaum

    The use of the present tense-form highlights a new location.

- καὶ **ἔρχονται** φέροντες πρὸς αὐτὸν παραλυτικὸν (Mark 2:3)

  They **came** to him bringing a paralytic

    The use of the present tense-form highlights new participants into the narrative.

- καὶ ἐξῆλθεν ἐκεῖθεν καὶ **ἔρχεται** εἰς τὴν πατρίδα αὐτοῦ, καὶ **ἀκολουθοῦσιν** αὐτῷ οἱ μαθηταὶ αὐτοῦ (Mark 6:1)

  He left there and **came** to his hometown, and his disciples **followed** him

    The use of the present tense-form highlights a change in location.

- τῇ ἐπαύριον **βλέπει** τὸν Ἰησοῦν ἐρχόμενον πρὸς αὐτὸν (John 1:29)

  The next day he **saw** Jesus coming toward him (ESV)[22]

Tendential Present[23]

The tendential use of the present tense-form (non-past imperfective aspect) is found in contexts where an action was begun, attempted, or proposed, but not completed. Thus, the action can be one that is being attempted but will not be completed or one that is being contemplated but may or may not be carried out. The use of the present tense-form is consistent with its imperfective or progressive aspect which views the action as in progress without regard to whether it is completed or not.[24] Indeed, oftentimes the action is attempted, but not completed (although there are some exceptions). The words "trying," "attempting," "going," or "intending" can be supplied in English to express the tendential idea.

- ἐπυνθάνετο παρ᾽ αὐτῶν ποῦ ὁ Χριστὸς **γεννᾶται** (Matt 2:4)

  he . . . asked them where the Christ **would be born**

---

[22] For more examples of the historical present, see Matt 3:1 (παραγίνεται); Mark 1:30 (λέγουσιν), 40 (ἔρχεται); 4:36 (παραλαμβάνουσιν); 11:27 (ἔρχονται); 14:17 (ἔρχεται); Luke 8:49 (ἔρχεται); John 18:28 (ἄγουσιν).

[23] Some grammars name this category "Conative" (so BDF, Burton, Fanning, Moule, Robertson, Wallace), "Voluntative" (Wallace), or "Inchoative" (Robertson). This idiom is more commonly used with the imperfect tense-form.

[24] "The present [= imperfective] aspect views the action from within, without reference to beginning or end-point, and thus it can be used with verbs of a certain lexical type or in particular contexts to denote an action which is continuing, or intended, but which does not reach its termination. The sense of incompletion is a natural concomitant of the 'internal viewpoint'" (Fanning, 219).

- διὰ ποῖον αὐτῶν ἔργον ἐμὲ **λιθάζετε**; (John 10:32)

  for which of them **are you going to stone** me? (ESV)

  > Notice that the Jews were not actually stoning Jesus as he spoke these words but it is something the Jews were contemplating at that time.

- κύριε, σύ μου **νίπτεις** τοὺς πόδας; (John 13:6)

  Lord, are you **going to wash** my feet?

  > As a mere question ("Lord, are you washing my feet?"), this statement makes little sense because it is something that Peter would have known (unless the focus is not on the action of the verb but on the pronouns—"Lord, *you* are washing *my* feet?").

- ἀγνοῶν ὅτι τὸ χρηστὸν τοῦ θεοῦ εἰς μετάνοιάν σε **ἄγει**; (Rom 2:4)

  not recognizing that God's kindness **is intended to lead** you to repentance?

- οἵτινες ἐν νόμῳ **δικαιοῦσθε** (Gal 5:4)

  You who **are trying to be justified** by the law

  > It is clear from the context that the Galatians are not being justified by the law since such a statement would run contrary to Paul's main argument of the epistle. Instead, he is arguing that they are trying or attempting to do that which is, in fact, impossible.[25]

Futuristic Present

The present tense-form is sometimes used to describe a future event. Unlike the tendential use, which indicates that something is attempted, this use usually has the connotation of immediacy or certainty.[26] The future sense can be indicated by "explicit adverbial modifiers" or is "implicit in the larger context."[27] The reason the present tense-form is used in this way may be to add vividness or indicate certainty of the future event (though this is not always the case). It is often used with verbs of action that involve anticipation (e.g., ἔρχομαι) and is sometimes used for prophetic utterances (especially when spoken by Jesus).

- μισθὸν οὐκ **ἔχετε** παρὰ τῷ πατρὶ ὑμῶν τῷ ἐν τοῖς οὐρανοῖς (Matt 6:1)

  you will have no reward from your Father who is in heaven (ESV)

- μετὰ τρεῖς ἡμέρας **ἐγείρομαι** (Matt 27:63)

  After three days **I will rise again**

---

[25] For more examples of the tendential present, see Matt 2:4 (γεννᾶται); Mark 11:23 (γίνεται); John 13:27 (ποιεῖς); Acts 26:28 (πείθεις); 2 Cor 5:11 (πείθομεν); Gal 2:14 (ἀναγκάζεις); 6:12 (ἀναγκάζουσιν).

[26] A similar idiom is found in English. If someone says, "I am going to church on Sunday," this is a futuristic use of the present tense.

[27] Fanning, 221.

- πάλιν **ἔρχομαι** καὶ παραλήμψομαι ὑμᾶς πρὸς ἐμαυτόν (John 14:3)

  I will come again and take you to myself

  > Notice that present tense ἔρχομαι is paralleled with the future tense παραλήμψομαι. This use probably signals the certainty of Jesus's return for His people.

- **ὑπάγω** καὶ **ἔρχομαι** πρὸς ὑμᾶς (John 14:28)

  I am going away and **I am coming** to you

  > As seen from the English translation, this idiom (a present used as a future) is also found in English. When Jesus says this statement, it is clearly a future event ("I will go away and I will come to you").

- ναί, **ἔρχομαι** ταχύ (Rev 22:20)

  Yes, **I am coming** soon

  > Again, Jesus's return is a future event.[28]

Perfective Present[29]

An infrequent use of the present tense-form is to express the present state of a past action (which is normally found with the perfect tense-form). This can be based on lexical reasons (e.g., ἥκω, a present tense-form verb, which means "I have come") or on contextual factors (e.g., λέγει used to introduce an OT quotation).

- **ἀπέχουσιν** τὸν μισθὸν αὐτῶν (Matt 6:2)

  they have received their reward (ESV)

- εἶπεν δὲ Μαριὰμ πρὸς τὸν ἄγγελον, Πῶς ἔσται τοῦτο, ἐπεὶ ἄνδρα οὐ **γινώσκω**; (Luke 1:34)

  Mary asked the angel, "How can this be, since **I have** not **had sexual relations** with a man?"

- Ἠσαΐας γὰρ **λέγει**, Κύριε, τίς ἐπίστευσεν τῇ ἀκοῇ ἡμῶν; (Rom 10:16)

  For Isaiah **says**, "Lord, who has believed our message?"

  > Paul quotes the OT (Isa 53:1) because he believes that it not only was authoritative in the past, but also for the present circumstances for the church at Rome. More often,

---

[28] For more examples of the futuristic present, see Matt 2:4 (γεννᾶται); 17:11 (ἔρχεται); 24:43 (ἔρχεται); 26:2 (παραδίδοται), 18 (ποιῶ), 45 (παραδίδοται); Mark 9:31 (παραδίδοται); 10:33 (ἀναβαίνομεν); Luke 3:9 (ἐκκόπτεται, βάλλεται); 16 (ἔρχεται); 13:32 (ἐκβάλλω, ἀποτελῶ, τελειοῦμαι); John 4:21, 23, 25 (ἔρχεται); 8:14 (ὑπάγω); 11:11 (πορεύομαι); Acts 20:22 (πορεύομαι); Rom 6:9 (ἀποθνῄσκει); 1 Cor 15:32 (ἀποθνῄσκομεν); 16:5 (διέρχομαι); 2 Cor 5:1 (ἔχομεν); 13:1 (ἔρχομαι).

[29] Young labels this category "Present of Existing Results."

OT quotations are introduced with the formulaic perfect tense-form γέγραπται ("it has been written" or "it stands written").[30]

- ὁ υἱὸς τοῦ θεοῦ **ἥκει** καὶ δέδωκεν ἡμῖν διάνοιαν (1 John 5:20)

  the Son of God **has come** and has given us understanding

  Notice that ἥκει (present tense-form) is parallel to δέδωκεν (perfect tense-form).[31]

IMPERFECT INDICATIVE

The imperfect tense-form carries the same aspectual significance as the present tense-form (imperfective aspect).[32] That is, it portrays that action as progressive, internal, or incomplete. In contrast to the aorist tense-form (perfective aspect), it views the action from within as opposed to viewing it as a whole or in summary fashion.[33] Some view the difference between the imperfect and the aorist as similar to the difference between a video and a picture.[34] The imperfect is like a video in the sense that it is ongoing action in progress whereas the aorist is like a picture giving a complete presentation of the event without describing how it actually unfolded. The time of the imperfect is almost always past time due to the fact that it does not occur outside of the indicative mood. Remember, the imperfect is one of three tenses (together with the aorist and pluperfect) that contain an augment in the indicative mood. Because the aspect of the imperfect is the same as the present, the categories here are basically the same as those found with the present tense-form. The majority of the imperfect uses in the NT are found in historical narratives, and especially the Gospel of Mark. There are 1,682 imperfect indicatives in the NT.

---

[30] Wallace suggests the following distinction between λέγει and γέγραπται: "(1) γέγραπται, being a perfect tense, stresses the abiding *authority* of scripture; (2) λέγει, being a present tense, stresses the *applicability* of scripture to the present situation" (533).

[31] For uses of λέγει as an introductory formula, see Rom 9:15; 10:8, 11, 19; 11:9; 12:19; 2 Cor 6:2; Gal 3:16; 4:30; Eph 4:8; 1 Tim 5:18; Jas 4:5, 6. For uses of ἥκω, see Luke 15:27; John 2:4; 4:47; 8:42. For other verbs, see Matt 3:10 (κεῖται); Luke 9:9 (ἀκούω); John 11:28 (πάρεστιν); Acts 17:6 (πάρεισιν); 1 Cor 11:18 (ἀκούω), 21 (πεινᾷ, μεθύει); Gal 1:6 (μετατίθεσθε); 2 Thess 3:11 (ἀκούομεν); 2 Pet 2:20 (ἥττωνται).

[32] Both the present and imperfect tense-forms are built on the first principle part of the verb. Thus, only the present tense-form is typically listed in principle parts—the assumption being that if the present tense-form is known, then the imperfect can be formed by adding an augment and secondary endings to the present tense-form stem.

[33] Just as there are exceptions to virtually every category in Greek grammar, so there are exceptions in the use of the imperfect. For example, Wallace categorizes one use of the imperfect as the "Instantaneous Imperfect" which is also known as the "Aoristic or Punctiliar Imperfect" (542). Because this use is rare and virtually restricted to ἔλεγεν (e.g., Matt 9:24; Mark 4:9; John 5:19) we will not treat it in the categories below.

[34] Robertson describes the imperfect as "a sort of moving panorama, a 'moving-picture show'" (883). He later adds, "The aorist tells the simple story. The imperfect draws the picture. It helps you to see the course of the act. It passes before the eye the flowing stream of history" (Robertson, 883).

Progressive Imperfect[35]

This basic use of the imperfect portrays an action (or state) in the past that is in progress from the perspective of the author. In other words, "it portrays a *specific* situation (action or state) viewed *as it is going on.* . . . [This] produces either vivid narration of a situation in the past or the presentation of an occurrence in close simultaneity with another situation in the past."[36] In a narrative context, "the imperfect highlights the manner of the occurrence while the aorist merely relates the fact of it."[37] Some of the uses may indicate that the action began in the past and continued for some time (= durative use).[38]

- σεισμὸς μέγας ἐγένετο ἐν τῇ θαλάσσῃ . . . αὐτὸς δὲ **ἐκάθευδεν** (Matt 8:24)

  a furious storm came up on the lake . . . but Jesus **was sleeping** (NIV)

- **ἐδίδασκεν** γὰρ τοὺς μαθητὰς αὐτοῦ καὶ **ἔλεγεν** αὐτοῖς (Mark 9:31)

  For **he was teaching** his disciples and **[was] telling** them.

- καὶ πολλοὶ πλούσιοι **ἔβαλλον** πολλα (Mark 12:41)

  Many rich people **were putting** in large sums

- **ἤσθιον, ἔπινον, ἐγάμουν, ἐγαμίζοντο,** ἄχρι ἧς ἡμέρας εἰσῆλθεν Νῶε εἰς τὴν κιβωτὸν (Luke 17:27)

  they were eating, they were drinking, they were marrying, they were being given in marriage, until the day that Noah entered the ark (NASB).

- ὅτι πάντες **ἐδόξαζον** τὸν θεὸν ἐπὶ τῷ γεγονότι (Acts 4:21)

  for all **were praising** God for what had happened (ESV)[39]

---

[35] This category is sometimes labeled "Descriptive Imperfect" (so Brooks & Winbery, Young).

[36] Fanning, 241 (emphasis added).

[37] Fanning, 243.

[38] As opposed to the present tense-form, we will not include a separate category for the durative use. We are thus following Dana & Mantey who list the general category as Progressive and then under this heading have two subcategories (i.e., descriptive and durative). An example of the durative use is 1 John 2:7 which states, "That **you have had** from the beginning" (ἣν **εἴχετε** ἀπ᾽ ἀρχῆς).

[39] For more examples of the progressive imperfect, see Matt 3:4–6 (εἶχεν, ἐξεπορεύετο, ἐβαπτίζοντο); 25:5 (ἐκάθευδον); 26:58 (ἠκολούθει), 63 (ἐσιώπα); Mark 9:28 (ἐπηρώτων); Luke 1:62 (ἐνένευον); 2:49 (ἐζητεῖτε); 6:19 (ἐζήτουν); 7:6 (ἐπορεύετο); 15:16 (ἐπεθύμει); Acts 2:6 (ἤκουον); 3:2 (ἐβαστάζετο); 6:1 (παρεθεωροῦντο); 15:37 (ἐβούλετο); 15:38 (ἠξίου); 16:14 (ἤκουεν).

Inceptive Imperfect[40]

The imperfect tense-form (past imperfective aspect) is often used to emphasize the beginning of an action (or, less common, a state). This inceptive nuance is communicated by the lexical meaning of the verb and the context. Because of the inperfective aspect, the implication is that the action, after it began, continued for some duration. In contrast, the inceptive use of the *aorist*, while also stressing the beginning of the state (or, less common, action), does not imply that the state continued.[41] Like many of the various uses of the imperfect, this use is common in narratives and often indicates a shift in topic or a change in the action.[42] In order to communicate this use, "began" or "started" is usually added to the English translation.

- ἄγγελοι προσῆλθον καὶ **διηκόνουν** αὐτῷ (Matt 4:11)

  angels came and ***began* to minister** to Him (NASB)

- καθίσας δὲ ἐκ τοῦ πλοίου **ἐδίδασκεν** τοὺς ὄχλους (Luke 5:3)

  And He sat down and ***began* teaching** the people from the boat (NASB)

- καὶ ἰδόντες πάντες **διεγόγγυζον** (Luke 19:7)

  All who saw it **began to complain**

- ἐξῆλθον ἐκ τῆς πόλεως καὶ **ἤρχοντο** πρὸς αὐτόν (John 4:20)

  So they left the town and **began coming** to him (NET)

- ἔστη καὶ **περιεπάτει** (Acts 3:8)

  he stood and **began to walk** (ESV)[43]

Iterative Imperfect[44]

The imperfect tense-form is also frequently used for repeated or customary action in the past. A distinction can be made between actions that are repeated over

---

[40] This category is sometimes labeled "Ingressive" (Wallace) or "Inchoative" (Robertson).

[41] Wallace helpfully highlights this significant distinction between the inceptive use of the imperfect and aorist (544).

[42] In addition to noting this use's relation to a change in activity, Wallace also notes that it "is possibly the most common imperfect in narrative because it introduces a topic shift" (Wallace, 544).

[43] For more examples of the inceptive imperfect, see Matt 3:5 (ἐξεπορεύετο), 5:2 (ἐδίδασκεν); Mark 1:21 (ἐδίδασκεν), 35 (προσηύχετο); 5:32 (περιεβλέπετο); 9:20 (ἐκυλίετο); 14:72 (ἔκλαιεν); John 4:30 (ἤρχοντο); 5:10 (ἔλεγον); Acts 7:54 (ἔβρυχον); 26:1 (ἀπελογεῖτο); 27:33 (παρεκάλει).

[44] Wallace differentiates between the "Iterative" and the "Customary" use of the imperfect but acknowledges that "the customary imperfect is a *subset* of the iterative imperfect" (546). An iterative statement conveys repetition of an event at various times whereas a customary (or "habitual") statement conveys that the event is repeated at regular intervals. Wallace adds, "The difference between the customary (proper) and the iterative imperfect is not great" (548).

a short span of time versus actions that are customarily or regularly (habitually) done on a regular basis over a longer period of time. The meaning of the verb along with the context (e.g., adverbs noting a reoccurring action) determines whether or not the verb is used with the iterative force. The tense-form of the verb communicates an action that is portrayed by the author as in progress. Robertson reminds us, "Sometimes it is difficult to tell whether an act is merely descriptive or is a series."[45] This use of the imperfect can also have a literary function, explaining or supplementing the main narrative, thus indicating prominence in the discourse.[46] In English translation, the gloss "kept on," "repeatedly," "used to," "were accustomed to," "customarily," or "continually" is often added to convey this use of the verb.

- καθ᾽ ἡμέραν ἐν τῷ ἱερῷ **ἐκαθεζόμην** διδάσκων (Matt 26:55)

  Every day **I used to sit [customarily]**, teaching in the temple

- **ἐδίδου** τοῖς μαθηταῖς [αὐτοῦ] (Mark 6:41)

  He kept giving [the loaves] to his disciples[47]

- **ἠρώτων** αὐτὸν οἱ μαθηταὶ λέγοντες, Ῥαββί, φάγε (John 4:31)

  the disciples **kept urging** him, "Rabbi, eat something"

- καὶ **ἤρχοντο** πρὸς αὐτὸν καὶ **ἔλεγον**, Χαῖρε ὁ βασιλεὺς τῶν Ἰουδαίων (John 19:3)

  And **they kept coming** up to him and **[repeatedly] saying**, "Hail, King of the Jews!"

- ἑτέροις τε λόγοις πλείοσιν διεμαρτύρατο καὶ **παρεκάλει** αὐτοὺς (Acts 2:40)

  And with many other words he solemnly testified and **kept on exhorting them** (NASB)[48]

---

[45] Robertson, 884.

[46] See Fanning, 247–49.

[47] "[T]he handing out of the bread is described by an imperfect as a continuous process, so that we conclude that having . . . blessed and broken the bread, Our Lord multiplied it by continuing to hand it out without exhausting the scanty stock: the multiplication thus took place in the hands of Our Lord Himself" (Zerwick, 91 [§271]).

[48] For more examples of the iterative imperfect, see Matt 9:21 (ἔλεγεν); 12:23 (ἔλεγον); 15:6 (ἀπέλυεν); 27:30 (ἔτυπτον); Luke 2:41 (ἐπορεύοντο); 6:23 (ἐποίουν); 19:47 (ἐζήτουν); John 3:22 (ἐβάπτιζεν); 4:31 (ἠρώτων); Acts 2:47 (προσετίθει); 3:2 (ἐβαστάζετο, ἐτίθουν); 16:5 (ἐστερεοῦντο); 21:19 (ἐξηγεῖτο); Rom 6:17 (ἦτε); 1 Cor 6:11 (ἦτε); 10:4 (ἔπινον); Gal 1:13 (ἐδίωκον), 14 (προέκοπτον).

Tendential Imperfect[49]

The tendential use of the imperfect tense-form is similar to the present tense-form (both imperfective aspect) use but refers to the past time and is more common. It is found in contexts where an action was begun, attempted, or proposed, but not completed. This category can be divided into two subcategories: (1) actions attempted but not accomplished, or (2) actions desired or wished but not attempted. In the first case (something attempted but not accomplished) "the action is under way and an attempt is being made to succeed in it, but the effort is not consummated—the process is not brought to its conclusion."[50] This use of the imperfect tense-form is consistent with its imperfective aspect which views the action as in progress without regard to whether it is completed. With this use, the words "trying" or "attempting" can be added to the English translation. The second subcategory (something desired but not attempted) "occurs with verbs of *desiring* or *wishing* and has the sense of 'to be on the verge of wanting', 'to contemplate the desire, but fail to bring oneself actually to the point of wishing.'"[51] The words "going," "intending," "could," or "would" can be added to the English translation.

Attempted Action

- **ἐδίδουν** αὐτῷ ἐσμυρνισμένον οἶνον· ὃς δὲ οὐκ ἔλαβεν (Mark 15:23)

  They tried to give him wine mixed with myrrh, but he did not take it

- **ἐκωλύομεν** αὐτόν, ὅτι οὐκ ἀκολουθεῖ μεθ᾽ ἡμῶν (Luke 9:49; cf. Mark 9:38)

  we tried to stop him because he wasn't following us

- καθ᾽ ὑπερβολὴν ἐδίωκον τὴν ἐκκλησίαν τοῦ θεοῦ καὶ **ἐπόρθουν** αὐτήν (Gal 1:13)

  I intensely persecuted God's church and **tried to destroy** it[52]

Desired Action

- **ἐκάλουν** αὐτὸ ἐπὶ τῷ ὀνόματι τοῦ πατρὸς αὐτοῦ Ζαχαρίαν (Luke 1:59)

  they were going to name him Zechariah, after his father

- **ἐβουλόμην** καὶ αὐτὸς τοῦ ἀνθρώπου ἀκοῦσαι (Acts 25:22)

  I would like to hear the man myself

---

[49] This category is sometimes labeled "Conative" (so BDF, Burton, Fanning, Robertson, Wallace).

[50] Fanning, 250.

[51] Fanning, 251.

[52] For more examples of the tendential imperfect (attempted), see Luke 4:42 (κατεῖχον); Acts 7:26 (συνήλλασσεν); 18:4 (ἔπειθεν); 26:11 (ἠνάγκαζον); Gal 1:23 (ἐπόρθει); Heb 11:17 (προσέφερεν).

- ἤθελον δὲ παρεῖναι πρὸς ὑμᾶς ἄρτι (Gal 4:20)

I wish I could be present with you now (ESV)[53]

FUTURE INDICATIVE

The future tense-form is somewhat of an anomaly among Greek verbs because it is regarded (at least by some) as aspectually neutral (though it is recognized by some as being closest to the aorist tense-form).[54] For example, Fanning argues that "the future must be taken as a non-aspectual *tense*-category, indicating occurrence *subsequent* to some reference-point."[55]

Similarly, Porter states that the future is distinct in that it does not constitute "*a verbal aspect in its full sense*."[56] Instead, the future grammaticalizes the author's expectation regarding a possible event (similar to the uses of the various moods in Greek).[57] Because an expectation relates to something that has not yet occurred, the future tense-form primarily refers to a future time frame from the author's perspective (or with participles, in relation to the time of the main verb's action). Although the future tense-form occurs outside the indicative mood, the non-indicative use of the future in the NT is extremely rare. For example, the future participle is found 12 times and the future infinitive is found only 5 times.[58] The future indicative occurs 1,609 times in the NT.

Predictive Future

The predictive use of the future is the most common use of the future tense-form and predicts a future event or at least indicates the expectation that something will take place from the author's perspective. Of course, "The objective certainty of

---

[53] For more examples of the tendential imperfect (desired), see Matt 18:33 (ἔδει); 26:9 (ἐδύνατο); Rom 9:3 (ηὐχόμην); Phlm 13 (ἐβουλόμην).

[54] See, e.g., Dana & Mantey, 191; Wallace, 566–67; Fanning, 120. BDF states that "the future is the only tense which expresses only a level of time and not an *Aktionsart* so that completed and durative action are not distinguished" (178 [§348]). Many have also noted that the future is similar in form to the aorist (addition of the sigma) and that there is evidence that "the future arose from the aorist subjunctive" (Dana & Mantey, 191).

[55] Fanning, 123 (emphasis original).

[56] Porter, *Idioms*, 24 (emphasis original).

[57] "The future indicative is not merely a tense in the true sense of that term, expressing the state of the action. It is almost a mode [i.e., mood] on a par with the subjunctive and imperative" (Robertson, 872). Over time, the future tense-form actually replaced the subjunctive mood.

[58] Future participles: Matt 27:49 (σώσων); Luke 22:49 (ἐσόμενον); John 6:64 (παραδώσων); Acts 8:27 (προσκυνήσων); 20:22 (συναντήσοντα); 22:5 (ἄξων); 24:11 (προσκυνήσων), 17 (ποιήσων); 1 Cor 15:37 (γενησόμενον); Heb 3:5 (λαληθησομένων); 13:17 (ἀποδώσοντες); 1 Pet 3:13 (κακώσων). Future infinitives: Acts 11:28 (ἔσεσθαι); 23:30 (ἔσεσθαι); 24:15 (ἔσεσθαι); 27:10 (ἔσεσθαι); Heb 3:18 (εἰσελεύσεσθαι). The future perfect tense-form is found in Heb 8:11, "because **they will** all **know** me, from the least to the greatest of them" (ὅτι πάντες **εἰδήσουσίν** με ἀπὸ μικροῦ ἕως μεγάλου αὐτῶν). This is the only use of the future perfect in the NT; it was also rare in Koine Greek. Notice that this use of the future perfect has lost its perfect force.

the prediction depends on whether the speaker is deity or a person giving a divine pronouncement."[59]

- **τέξεται** δὲ υἱόν . . . αὐτὸς **σώσει** τὸν λαὸν αὐτοῦ ἀπὸ τῶν ἁμαρτιῶν αὐτῶν (Matt 1:21)

  She will give birth to a son . . . he **will save** his people from their sins

- αὐτὸς **βαπτίσει** ὑμᾶς ἐν πνεύματι ἁγίῳ (Mark 1:8)

  He **will baptize** you with the Holy Spirit

- μετὰ τρεῖς ἡμέρας **ἀναστήσεται** (Mark 9:31)

  after three days **he will rise** (ESV)

- **λήμψεσθε** δύναμιν ἐπελθόντος τοῦ ἁγίου πνεύματος ἐφ᾽ ὑμᾶς καὶ **ἔσεσθέ** μου μάρτυρες (Acts 1:8)

  you will receive power when the Holy Spirit has come on you, and **you will be** my witnesses[60]

- **λυθήσεται** ὁ Σατανᾶς ἐκ τῆς φυλακῆς αὐτοῦ (Rev 20:7)

  Satan **will be released** from his prison[61]

Imperatival Future[62]

The future tense-form is sometimes used to express a command. This is a common use in English. For example, a parent might say to a child, "You *will* clean your room!" This statement does not function as a prediction but as an imperative to the child and is virtually the same as saying, "Clean your room!" In the NT, this usage is most commonly found in the Gospels, especially Matthew. Because this use of the future was common in the OT, NT writers often quote such statements that support their teaching. The force of imperatival future is usually seen as being more emphatic than the imperative mood, containing a universal or timeless quality.[63]

---

[59] Young, 117.

[60] It is possible that the second future (ἔσεσθε) has an imperatival force.

[61] For more examples of a predictive future, see Matt 24:30 (φανήσεται, κόψονται, ὄψονται); Mark 2:20 (ἐλεύσονται, νηστεύσουσιν); 9:31 (ἀποκτενοῦσιν); Luke 2:12 (εὑρήσετε); John 4:14 (δώσω, διψήσει); 14:26 (πέμψει, διδάξει, ὑπομνήσει); Acts 1:11 (ἐλεύσεται); 21:11 (δήσουσιν, παραδώσουσιν); Gal 5:21 (κληρονομήσουσιν); Phil 1:6 (ἐπιτελέσει); 1 Thess 4:16 (ἀναστήσονται); 1 Tim 2:15 (σωθήσεται); Heb 6:14 (εὐλογήσω, πληθυνῶ); 2 Pet 2:2 (ἐξακολουθήσουσιν, βλασφημηθήσεται).

[62] Robertson calls this the "Volitive Future."

[63] Though Smyth maintains, "The tone of the jussive future . . . is generally familiar" (428 [§3]).

- οὐκ **ἐκπειράσεις** κύριον τὸν θεόν σου (Matt 4:7; quoting Deut 6:16; see also Luke 4:12)

  You shall not **tempt** the LORD your God (NKJV)

- κύριον τὸν θεόν σου **προσκυνήσεις** καὶ αὐτῷ μόνῳ **λατρεύσεις** (Matt 4:10; quoting Deut 6:13; see also Luke 4:8)

  You shall worship the Lord your God and him only **shall you serve** (ESV)

- ὃς ἂν θέλῃ ἐν ὑμῖν εἶναι πρῶτος **ἔσται** ὑμῶν δοῦλος (Matt 20:27; see also Matt 20:26; 23:11; Mark 10:44)

  whoever wishes to be first among you **shall be** your slave (NASB)

- οὐ **μοιχεύσεις**, οὐ **φονεύσεις**, οὐ **κλέψεις**, οὐκ **ἐπιθυμήσεις** . . . ἐν τῷ λόγῳ τούτῳ ἀνακεφαλαιοῦται [ἐν τῷ]· **ἀγαπήσεις** τὸν πλησίον σου ὡς σεαυτόν (Rom 13:9; quoting from the ten commandments and Lev 19:18)

  You shall not **commit adultery, you shall** not **murder, you shall** not **steal, you shall** not **covet** . . . all are summed up in this word: **You shall love** your neighbor as yourself (ESV)

- ἅγιοι **ἔσεσθε**, ὅτι ἐγὼ ἅγιός εἰμι (1 Pet 1:16; quoting Lev 11:44)

  You shall be holy, for I am holy (ESV)[64]

Deliberative Future

The deliberative use involves a question with the future tense-form that implies some amount of uncertainty as to the response. The person is not so much asking what will happen but if something can or ought to be done. Because someone is asking a question, the first person (singular or plural) is normally used. The aorist subjunctive occurs more often than the deliberative use of the future. The questions can be divided into real questions and rhetorical questions.

---

[64] For examples of the imperatival future quoting the Ten Commandments, see Matt 5:21 (φονεύσεις), 27 (μοιχεύσεις), 33 (ἐπιορκήσεις); 19:18 (φονεύσεις, μοιχεύσεις, κλέψεις, ψευδομαρτυρήσεις); Rom 7:7 (ἐπιθυμήσεις). For examples quoting Deut 6:5 ("You shall love [ἀγαπήσεις] the Lord your God," ESV), see Matt 22:37; Mark 12:30; Luke 10:27. For examples quoting Lev 19:18 ("You shall love [ἀγαπήσεις] your neighbor as yourself"), see Matt 5:43 (also μισήσεις); 22:39; Gal 5:14; Jas 2:8. For examples quoting other OT texts, see Matt 4:4 (ζήσεται; quoting Deut 8:3); 21:13 (κληθήσεται; quoting Isa 56:7); 1 Tim 5:15 (φιμώσεις; quoting Deut 25:4). For examples not quoting the Old Testament, see Matt 1:21 (καλέσεις); 6:5 (ἔσεσθε); 20:26 (ἔσται); 21:3 (ἐρεῖτε); 27:4 (ὄψῃ), 24 (ὄψεσθε); Mark 9:35 (ἔσται); Luke 1:13, 31 (καλέσεις); 17:4 (ἀφήσεις); Acts 18:15 (ὄψεσθε).

Real Questions

These questions ask for information (factual) or some sort of reply and can often be answered with a "yes" or "no" response.

- ἀπελθόντες ἀγοράσωμεν δηναρίων διακοσίων ἄρτους καὶ **δώσομεν** αὐτοῖς φαγεῖν; (Mark 6:37)

  Should we go and buy two hundred denarii worth of bread and **[should we] give** them something to eat?

  > Note that the first verb (ἀγοράσωμεν) is a subjunctive which is parallel to the future indicative.

- κύριε, εἰ **πατάξομεν** ἐν μαχαίρῃ; (Luke 22:49)

  Lord, **should we strike** with the sword?

Rhetorical Questions

These questions challenge the reader to consider the implications and then to respond appropriately. Such questions are used to take the place of a direct assertion. Occasionally, these questions are used when the author is debating with himself (see the first example below).

- Κύριε, πρὸς τίνα **ἀπελευσόμεθα**; ῥήματα ζωῆς αἰωνίου ἔχεις (John 6:68)

  Lord, who **will we go** to? You have the words of eternal life.

  > The direct assertion would be, "Lord, there is nowhere else for us to go."

- τί οὖν **ἐροῦμεν**; (Rom 6:1; see also 3:5; 9:14).

  What **should we say** then?

- πῶς ἔτι **ζήσομεν** ἐν αὐτῇ; (Rom 6:2)

  How **can we** . . . still **live** in it [= sin]?

  > The direct assertion would be, "We cannot live in sin."[65]

Gnomic Future

The future-tense form is (rarely) used to express a timeless truth or something that will happen if certain circumstances are met. The present and aorist tense-forms are used more often to convey a gnomic idea.

- μόλις γὰρ ὑπὲρ δικαίου τις **ἀποθανεῖται** (Rom 5:7)

  For rarely **will** someone **die** for a just person

---

[65] For more examples of the deliberative future, see Matt 11:16 (ὁμοιώσω); 17:17 (ἀνέξομαι); 18:21 (ἁμαρτήσει, ἀφήσω); 1 Cor 15:29 (ποιήσουσιν); Heb 2:3 (ἐκφευξόμεθα).

- ἕκαστος γὰρ τὸ ἴδιον φορτίον **βαστάσει** (Gal 6:5)

  For each one **will bear** his own load (NASB)[66]

- ἀντὶ τούτου **καταλείψει** ἄνθρωπος [τὸν] πατέρα καὶ [τὴν] μητέρα καὶ **προσκολληθήσεται** πρὸς τὴν γυναῖκα αὐτοῦ, καὶ **ἔσονται** οἱ δύο εἰς σάρκα μίαν (Eph 5:31; quoting Gen 2:24)

  For this reason a man **will leave** his father and mother and **[will]** be joined to his wife, and the two **will become** one flesh[67]

Progressive Future

Occasionally, the future tense-form is used in contexts where an action that was being performed will continue into the future. This usage is especially obvious when the same verb is used first in the present and then in the future tense-form (see Phil 1:18 and 2 Thess 3:4 below).

- ὁ ἐναρξάμενος ἐν ὑμῖν ἔργον ἀγαθὸν **ἐπιτελέσει** ἄχρι ἡμέρας Χριστοῦ Ἰησοῦ (Phil 1:6)

  He who began a good work in you **will [continue to] perfect** it until the day of Christ Jesus (NASB)

- καὶ ἐν τούτῳ χαίρω. ἀλλὰ καὶ **χαρήσομαι** (Phil 1:18)

  And in this I rejoice. Yes, and **I will continue to rejoice**

- ὅτι ἃ παραγγέλλομεν [καὶ] ποιεῖτε καὶ **ποιήσετε** (2 Thess 3:4)

  that you are doing and **will continue to do** what we command[68]

---

[66] It is possible that Gal 6:5 is an imperatival future.

[67] For more examples of the gnomic future, see Matt 6:24 (μισήσει, ἀγαπήσει, ἀνθέξεται, καταφρονήσει); Rom 7:3 (χρηματίσει).

[68] For more examples of the progressive future, see Rom 6:2 (ζήσομεν; this example was also used above as a deliberative future); Rev 9:6 (ζητήσουσιν).

SUMMARY

PRESENT INDICATIVE		
Progressive	An action that is in progress or ongoing.	κύριε, σῶσον, **ἀπολλύμεθα** ("Lord, save us! **We are perishing!**"; Matt 8:25 NRSV).
Durative	An action that began in the past and continues into the present.	ἀπ᾿ ἀρχῆς ὁ διάβολος **ἁμαρτάνει** ("The devil **has sinned** from the beginning"; 1 John 3:8).
Iterative	An action that is performed repeatedly, regularly, or customarily.	πολλάκις **πίπτει** εἰς τὸ πῦρ ("He **often falls** into the fire"; Matt 17:15).
Gnomic	A statement that is timeless (omni-temporal), universal, or generally true.	ἱλαρὸν δότην **ἀγαπᾷ** ὁ θεός ("God **loves** a cheerful giver"; 2 Cor 9:7).
Instantaneous	An action that is done instantaneously, usually by the very fact that it is spoken.	Καίσαρα **ἐπικαλοῦμαι** ("**I appeal** to Caesar!"; Acts 25:11).
Historical	A past event that adds vividness to the event or gives literary prominence to some aspect of the story.	καὶ **ἔρχεται** πρὸς τοὺς μαθητὰς ("Then **he came** to the disciples"; Matt 26:40).
Tendential	An action was begun, attempted, or proposed, but not completed.	οἵτινες ἐν νόμῳ **δικαιοῦσθε** ("**You who are trying to be justified** by the law"; Gal 5:4).
Futuristic	An action that will occur in the future (often adds vividness or certainty).	μετὰ τρεῖς ἡμέρας **ἐγείρομαι** ("After three days **I will rise** again"; Matt 27:63).
Perfective	Emphasizes the present state of a past action.	**ἀπέχουσιν** τὸν μισθὸν αὐτῶν ("**They have received** their reward"; Matt 6:2 ESV).
IMPERFECT INDICATIVE		
Progressive	An action in the past that is in progress from the perspective of the author.	καὶ πολλοὶ πλούσιοι **ἔβαλλον** πολλά ("Many rich people **were putting** in large sums"; Mark 12:41).
Inceptive	Emphasizes the beginning of an action (or state).	ἔστη καὶ **περιεπάτει** ("He stood and **began to walk**"; Acts 3:8 ESV).
Iterative	Repeated or customary action in the past.	**ἐδίδου** τοῖς μαθηταῖς [αὐτοῦ] ("**He kept giving** [the loaves] to his disciples"; Mark 6:41).
Tendential	An action was begun, attempted, or proposed, but not completed.	ἐδίωκον τὴν ἐκκλησίαν τοῦ θεοῦ καὶ **ἐπόρθουν** αὐτήν ("I intensely persecuted God's church . . . and **tried to destroy** it"; Gal 1:13).

FUTURE INDICATIVE		
Predictive	A future event is predicted.	αὐτὸς **βαπτίσει** ὑμᾶς ἐν πνεύματι ἁγίῳ ("He **will baptize** you with the Holy Spirit"; Mark 1:8).
Imperatival	Expresses a command.	ἅγιοι **ἔσεσθε**, ὅτι ἐγὼ ἅγιός εἰμι ("**You shall be** holy, for I am holy"; 1 Pet 1:16 ESV).
Deliberative	A question (real or rhetorical) is asked.	πῶς ἔτι **ζήσομεν** ἐν αὐτῃ; ("How **can we** . . . still **live** in it [= sin]?"; Rom 6:2).
Gnomic	Expresses a timeless truth.	μόλις γὰρ ὑπὲρ δικαίου τις **ἀποθανεῖται** ("For rarely **will** someone **die** for a just person"; Rom 5:7).
Progressive	An action that was being done will continue into the future.	ἀλλὰ καὶ **χαρήσομαι** ("Yes, and **I will continue to rejoice**"; Phil 1:18).

PRACTICE EXERCISES

In each of the following examples, (1) parse each underlined verb and (2) determine the specific use of the verb based on its tense-form and context.

1. ὁ δὲ Ἰησοῦς <u>ἐσιώπα</u> (Matt 26:63).

2. καὶ εὐθὺς τὸ πνεῦμα αὐτὸν <u>ἐκβάλλει</u> εἰς τὴν ἔρημον (Mark 1:12).

3. καὶ προελθὼν μικρὸν ἔπιπτεν ἐπὶ τῆς γῆς καὶ <u>προσηύχετο</u> (Mark 14:35).

4. οὐκ <u>ἀφήσω</u> ὑμᾶς ὀρφανούς, <u>ἔρχομαι</u> πρὸς ὑμᾶς (John 14:18).

5. πῶς <u>κρινεῖ</u> ὁ θεὸς τὸν κόσμον; (Rom 3:6).

6. <u>παραγίνεται</u> ὁ Ἰησοῦς . . . πρὸς τὸν Ἰωάννην τοῦ βαπτισθῆναι ὑπ᾽ αὐτοῦ. ὁ δὲ Ἰωάννης <u>διεκώλυεν</u> αὐτὸν (Matt 3:13–14).

7. ὁ γὰρ θεὸς ἀπείραστός <u>ἐστιν</u> κακῶν, <u>πειράζει</u> δὲ αὐτὸς οὐδένα (Jas 1:13).

8. <u>ἔσεσθε</u> οὖν ὑμεῖς τέλειοι ὡς ὁ πατὴρ ὑμῶν ὁ οὐράνιος τέλειός ἐστιν (Matt 5:48).

9. καὶ τοιαύταις παραβολαῖς πολλαῖς <u>ἐλάλει</u> αὐτοῖς τὸν λόγον (Mark 4:33).

10. <u>σπλαγχνίζομαι</u> ἐπὶ τὸν ὄχλον, ὅτι ἤδη ἡμέραι τρεῖς <u>προσμένουσίν</u> μοι καὶ οὐκ <u>ἔχουσιν</u> τί φάγωσιν (Mark 8:2).

VOCABULARY

Vocabulary to Memorize

αἰτία, ἡ	cause, reason, accusation (20)
ἅπας	all, everybody, everything (34)
ἀπέχω	I have received, am distant (19)
ἀργύριον, τό	silver, money (20)
γενεά, ἡ	generation, family, descent (43)
γένος, -ους, τό	race, descendent, family (20)
γεωργός, ὁ	farmer (19)
γονεύς, -έως, ὁ	parent (20)
διαμαρτύρομαι	I solemnly urge, exhort, warn (15)
διδαχή, ἡ	teaching [as content] (30)
ἑκατοντάρχης, -ου, ὁ	centurion, captain, officer (20)
ἐφίστημι	I stand by, appear (21)
ἡγεμών, -όνος, ὁ	governor, ruler, leader (20)
θερίζω	I reap, harvest (21)
Ἰσαάκ, ὁ	Isaac (20)
ἰχθύς, -ύος, ὁ	fish (20)
καθίστημι	I bring, appoint (21)
κοινωνία, ἡ	fellowship, communion (19)
λατρεύω	I serve, worship (21)
μετανοέω	I repent (34)
μνημονεύω	I remember, think of, mention (21)
νηστεύω	I fast (20)
ξύλον, τό	wood, tree, cross (20)
προάγω	I lead out (20)
προστίθημι	I add (to), increase (18)
πωλέω	I sell (22)
σκηνή, ἡ	tent, booth, tabernacle (20)
σοφός	wise, clever, skillful (20)
στρέφω	I turn, return (21)
συνέδριον, τό	Sanhedrin, council (22)
τέρας, -ατος, τό	wonder (16)
τιμάω	I honor, revere (21)
τοσοῦτος, -αύτη, -οῦτον	so great, so large, so many (20)
τρέχω	I run (20)
τροφή, ἡ	food, nourishment (16)

ὑπακούω	I obey, follow (21)
ὑπηρέτης, -ου, ὁ	servant, helper, assistant (20)
χιλίαρχος, ὁ	military tribune, high ranking officer (21)
χρεία, ἡ	need, lack, necessity (49)
ὡσεί	as, like, about (21)

Vocabulary to Recognize

ἀγαλλίασις, ἡ	gladness, great joy (5)
αἰνέω	I praise (8)
ἀποδέχομαι	I accept (7)
ἀφελότης, -ητος, ἡ	humility, simplicity, sincerity (1)
διαμερίζω	I distribute (11)
δωρεά, ἡ	gift (11)
καθότι	as (6)
κατανύσσομαι	I am pierced, stabbed (1)
κλάσις, -εως, ἡ	breaking (2)
κλάω	I break (14)
κοινός	communal, common (14)
κτῆμα, -ατος, τό	possession (4)
μακράν	far away (10)
μεταλαμβάνω	I share, partake of (7)
ὁμοθυμαζόν	with one mind/purpose (11)
πιπράσκω	I sell (9)
προσκαρτερέω	I am devoted to, continue in, hold fast to (10)
σκολιός	crooked, dishonest (4)
τρισκίλιοι	three thousand (1)
ὕπαρξις, -εως, ἡ	property, possession (2)
χάριν	because of, for the sake of (9)

READING THE NEW TESTAMENT

Acts 2:37–47

³⁷ Ἀκούσαντες δὲ κατενύγησαν τὴν καρδίαν εἶπόν τε πρὸς τὸν Πέτρον καὶ τοὺς λοιποὺς ἀποστόλους, Τί ποιήσωμεν, ἄνδρες ἀδελφοί; ³⁸ Πέτρος δὲ πρὸς αὐτούς, Μετανοήσατε, [φησίν,] καὶ βαπτισθήτω ἕκαστος ὑμῶν ἐπὶ τῷ ὀνόματι Ἰησοῦ Χριστοῦ εἰς ἄφεσιν τῶν ἁμαρτιῶν ὑμῶν καὶ λήμψεσθε τὴν δωρεὰν τοῦ ἁγίου πνεύματος. ³⁹ ὑμῖν γάρ ἐστιν ἡ ἐπαγγελία καὶ τοῖς τέκνοις ὑμῶν καὶ πᾶσιν τοῖς εἰς μακράν, ὅσους ἂν προσκαλέσηται κύριος ὁ θεὸς ἡμῶν. ⁴⁰ ἑτέροις τε λόγοις πλείοσιν διεμαρτύρατο καὶ παρεκάλει αὐτοὺς λέγων, Σώθητε ἀπὸ τῆς γενεᾶς τῆς σκολιᾶς ταύτης. ⁴¹ οἱ μὲν οὖν ἀποδεξάμενοι τὸν λόγον αὐτοῦ ἐβαπτίσθησαν καὶ προσετέθησαν ἐν τῇ ἡμέρᾳ ἐκείνῃ ψυχαὶ ὡσεὶ τρισχίλιαι. ⁴² ἦσαν δὲ προσκαρτεροῦντες τῇ διδαχῇ τῶν ἀποστόλων καὶ τῇ κοινωνίᾳ, τῇ κλάσει τοῦ ἄρτου καὶ ταῖς προσευχαῖς. ⁴³ Ἐγίνετο δὲ πάσῃ ψυχῇ φόβος, πολλά τε τέρατα καὶ σημεῖα διὰ τῶν ἀποστόλων ἐγίνετο. ⁴⁴ πάντες δὲ οἱ πιστεύοντες ἦσαν ἐπὶ τὸ αὐτὸ καὶ εἶχον ἅπαντα κοινὰ ⁴⁵ καὶ τὰ κτήματα καὶ τὰς ὑπάρξεις ἐπίπρασκον καὶ διεμέριζον αὐτὰ πᾶσιν καθότι ἄν τις χρείαν εἶχεν· ⁴⁶ καθ' ἡμέραν τε προσκαρτεροῦντες ὁμοθυμαδὸν ἐν τῷ ἱερῷ, κλῶντές τε κατ' οἶκον ἄρτον, μετελάμβανον τροφῆς ἐν ἀγαλλιάσει καὶ ἀφελότητι καρδίας ⁴⁷ αἰνοῦντες τὸν θεὸν καὶ ἔχοντες χάριν πρὸς ὅλον τὸν λαόν. ὁ δὲ κύριος προσετίθει τοὺς σῳζομένους καθ' ἡμέραν ἐπὶ τὸ αὐτό.

Reading Notes⁶⁹

Verse 37

- **ἀκούσαντες** ("When they heard") – Aor act ptc masc nom pl ἀκούω (temporal). The aorist participle depicts the action from a perfective aspect, viewing the action as simply occurring. Whether the action is antecedent ("after they heard") or contemporaneous ("while/when they heard") depends on the context.

- **κατενύγησαν** ("They were pierced") – Aor pass ind 3rd pl κατανύσσομαι.

- **τὴν καρδίαν** ("to the heart") – This is an accusative of reference or respect which limits or specifies the action of the verb ("they were pierced with respect to the heart"). See LXX Ps 108[9]:16 where the dative is used with the same verb (κατανενυγμένον τῇ καρδίᾳ).

- **τε** ("and") – This term often functions similarly to δέ or καί and occurs mostly in Acts (about 70 percent of all occurrences). Robertson states, "It

---

⁶⁹ The English version used in the Reading Notes for this chapter is the CSB.

seems certain that τε, indicates a somewhat closer unity than does καί. . . .
It is something additional, but in intimate relation with the preceding."[70]

- τὸν Πέτρον ("Peter") – Remember that sometimes proper nouns have a
definite article which need not be reflected in translation.

- ποιήσωμεν ("[what] should we do") – Aor act sub 1st pl ποιέω. This is the
deliberative use of the subjunctive (it could also be described as a hortatory subjunctive used in a question).[71]

- ἄνδρες ἀδελφοί ("Brothers") – ἄνδρες is a vocative noun and "is used
throughout Acts (29 times) as a formal opening to a speech. When it is
followed by another vocative noun identifying the referent [i.e., ἀδελφοί],
it should be left untranslated."[72]

Verse 38

- Πέτρος δὲ πρὸς αὐτούς ("Peter replied to them") – The verb εἶπεν is
omitted but implied from v. 37.

- μετανοήσατε ("Repent") – Aor act impv 2nd pl μετανοέω. The context
calls not for an attitude of repentance, but for a specific act of repentance.
This distinction, however, is based on the context and not the aorist tense.
The only other use of this verb as an aorist imperative in Acts is found in
8:22 where Peter calls for Simon the Sorcerer to repent of his wickedness
(μετανόησον οὖν ἀπὸ τῆς κακίας σου ταύτης). For other aorist imperatives, see Rev 2:5, 16; 3:3, 19.

- φησίν ("said" omitted from CSB) – Pres act ind 3rd sg φημί. This word
is placed in brackets by the editors of the UBS Greek NT because they
were uncertain as to its authenticity. It is included in 𝔓74vid (uncertain)
ℵ A C 81 630 1642* 1704 1729 1891 vg. Because φησίν is located in
various places (e.g., before and after μετανοήσατε) and because ἔφη or
εἶπε is also sometimes added, its originality is questioned. It was included
because of the diversity of early testimony supporting the reading but en-
closed in brackets because of the weight of codex B. Metzger adds, "Only
[the reading with its omission] accounts for the rise of the other readings,
for the absence of an explicit verb of saying prompted copyists to add, at
various places, φησίν or ἔφη or εἶπε; there is no good reason why any of
these verbs, if original, should have been omitted or altered to a different
verb. It ought to be noted also that elsewhere Luke occasionally dispenses
with a verb of saying (25.22a; 26.28)."[73]

---

[70] Robertson, 1178–79; see also BDF, 229–30 (§443).
[71] So Moule, 22.
[72] Mikeal C. Parsons and Martin M. Culy, *Acts: A Handbook on the Greek Text* (Waco, TX: Baylor
University Press, 2003), 11.
[73] Metzger, *Textual Commentary*, 261.

- **βαπτισθήτω** ("be baptized") – Aor pass impv 3rd sg βαπτίζω. Notice the switch between the second person plural imperative (μετανοήσατε) to this third person singular imperative. Barrett writes, "μετανοήσατε, which, in the plural, is presumably addressed to the whole house of Israel (v. 35), and βαπτισθήτω ἕκαστος ὑμῶν, which is specifically directed to the individual members of the crowd."[74] The aorist tense-form fits the telic nature of the verb. This verb could be classified as a permissive passive indicating that the command involves allowing someone else to baptize an individual (see also σώθητε in v. 40).

- **ἐπὶ τῷ ὀνόματι** ("in the name") – This is the only case of ἐπί being used in conjunction with the verb βαπτίζω. Normally the preposition εἰς or ἐν is used. The phrase ἐπὶ τῷ ὀνόματι, however, is used 14 times in the NT, including 9 times in Luke/Acts. It usually designates the authority by which an action is performed.

- **εἰς ἄφεσιν τῶν ἁμαρτιῶν ὑμῶν** ("for the forgiveness of your sins") – The preposition εἰς is often used to communicate purpose ("for") but can also communicate grounds ("on the basis of"). See Wallace for a lengthy discussion of the theological significance of this phrase in its context.[75] The genitive τῶν ἁμαρτιῶν is an objective genitive ("[God] forgives sins").

- **λήμψεσθε** ("you will receive") – Fut mid ind 2nd pl λαμβάνω (predictive future).

- **τὴν δωρεὰν τοῦ ἁγίου πνεύματος** ("the gift of the Holy Spirit") – The genitive phrase τοῦ ἁγίου πνεύματος is in apposition to the noun τὴν δωρεὰν meaning that the gift itself is the Holy Spirit ("the gift, that is, the Holy Spirit").

Verse 39

- **ὑμῖν** ("for you") – Dative of possession ("the promise is yours." This same category also applies to τοῖς τέκνοις ὑμῶν and πᾶσιν τοῖς εἰς μακράν). The placement of this personal pronoun at the beginning of the sentence makes it emphatic.

- **πᾶσιν τοῖς εἰς μακράν** ("for all who are far off") – The article τοῖς turns εἰς μακράν into a virtual noun. This phrase could refer to those Jews who were scattered but most likely is a euphemism for Gentiles.[76]

[74] C. K. Barrett, *The Acts of the Apostles*, vol. 1, ICC (Edinburgh: T&T Clark, 1994), 153–54.
[75] Wallace, 369–71.
[76] So Barrett, *Acts*, 155–56; I. Howard Marshall, *The Acts of the Apostles*, TNTC (Leicester: InterVarsity; Grand Rapids: Eerdmans, 1980), 82; John B. Polhill, *Acts*, NAC 26 (Nashville: Broadman, 1992), 117.

- **προσκαλέσηται** ("will call") – Aor mid sub 3rd sg προσκαλέομαι. The subjunctive is used with the indefinite relative pronoun ὅσους ἄν. Remember that the subjunctive mood does not communicate uncertainty (as if God may or may not call some) but rather indefiniteness (he will call some but we have yet to find out precisely whom).

Verse 40

- **ἑτέροις λόγοις πλείοσιν** ("with many other words") – λόγοις is a dative of means (instrument).

- **διεμαρτύρατο** ("he testified") – Aor mid ind 3rd sg διεμαρτύρομαι.

- **παρεκάλει** ("strongly urged") – Impf act ind 3rd sg παρακαλέω. This is possibly an iterative use of the imperfect tense-form signifying repeated exhortation (he "kept on exhorting them," NASB; he "continued to exhort them," ESV).

- **σώθητε** ("Be saved") – Aor pass impv 2nd pl σῴζω. The passive sense ("be saved") is to be preferred over the middle connotation ("save yourselves," so ESV).

Verse 41

- **μὲν οὖν** ("So") – There is debate as to whether the paragraph division should be placed between vv. 40 and 41 (CSB; NKJV), vv. 41 and 42 (NA[28]; ESV; NIV), or vv. 42 and 43 (UBS[4]; NASB). Barrett argues for the first option based on "Luke's use in v. 41 of μὲν οὖν . . . his usual method of resuming a narrative."[77]

- **οἱ ἀποδεξάμενοι** ("those who accepted") – Aor mid ptc masc nom pl ἀποδέχομαι (substantival).

- **ἐβαπτίσθησαν** ("were baptized") – Aor pass ind 3rd pl βαπτίζω.

- **προσετέθησαν** ("were added") – Aor pass ind 3rd pl προστίθημι.

- **ψυχαὶ ὡσεὶ τρισχίλιαι** ("about three thousand people") – This phrase functions as the subject of the preceding verbs. ψυχαί ("souls") is a synecdoche (part for the whole) for people (see also v. 43).

Verse 42

- **ἦσαν προσκαρτεροῦντες** ("they devoted themselves") – This is a periphrastic construction of the imperfect form of εἰμί in combination with the participle of προσκαρτερέω (pres act ptc masc nom pl). It is possible

---

[77] Barrett, *Acts*, 159.

that this construction in its present context carries an iterative connotation ("they were continually devoting themselves," NASB; "And they continued steadfastly," NKJV).

- τῇ διδαχῇ τῶν ἀποστόλων ("to the apostles' teaching") – This is the first of four items to which the early Christian community devoted themselves. Each of these is in the dative case because the verb προσκαρτερέω takes its direct object in the dative (instead of accusative) case. Witherington suggests that "the breaking of bread" and "prayers" (note the plural; see below) further defines "fellowship."[78] τῶν ἀποστόλων is a subjective genitive ("the apostles taught [others]").

- τῇ κοινωνίᾳ ("to fellowship") – This could refer to the close mutual relationships among believers or the sharing of resources (see. v. 44) or both.

- τῇ κλάσει τοῦ ἄρτου ("to the breaking of bread") – This could refer to eating together generally or, more likely, is a reference to the Lord's Supper.[79] τοῦ ἄρτου is an objective genitive ("[they] broke bread").

- ταῖς προσευχαῖς ("to prayer") – Because the definite article is given it is possible that this specifically refers to the Jewish prayers at the temple (see v. 46; 3:1).

Verse 43

- ἐγίνετο ... φόβος ("[Everyone] was filled wth awe") – Impf mid ind 3rd sg γίνομαι. The CSB smooths out the more literal rendering of "awe came upon" (so ESV). It is possible that this construction in its present context carries an iterative connotation ("Everyone kept feeling a sense of awe," NASB). One should be careful, however, of overinterpreting such verbs (as the NASB is prone to do). More likely it has a inceptive idea (so CSB, ESV, NKJV, NRSV).

- πάσῃ ψυχῇ ("everyone") – This is probably dative of possession.[80]

- πολλά τέρατα καὶ σημεῖα ("many wonders and signs") – These neuter plural nouns are the subject of the second use of ἐγίνετο (which is singular). Remember that a neuter plural subject can take a singular verb. Note that the more common construction is "signs and wonders."

- διὰ τῶν ἀποστόλων ("through the apostles") – Instrumental genitive (intermediate agent).

---

[78] Ben Witherington III, *The Acts of the Apostles: A Socio-Rhetorical Commentary* (Grand Rapids: Eerdmans; Carlisle, UK: Paternoster, 1998), 160.

[79] See Acts 20:7, 11; so Witherington, *Acts*, 161.

[80] Wallace, 149; see also Robertson, 541.

Verses 44–45

- οἱ πιστεύοντες ("the believers") – Pres act ptc masc nom pl πιστεύω (substantival).

- ἐπὶ τὸ αὐτὸ ("together") – This phrase literally means "at the same [place]" (see Acts 1:15; 2:1, 47; 4:26). "The intent of using the phrase is to say something about the unity or togetherness of the early Christians, even if the precise translation may be debated. . . . It refers to a gathered group in harmony with one another."[81]

- εἶχον ("had") – Impf act ind 3rd pl ἔχω. This could be an iterative use of the imperfect tense-form (see also v. 45, εἶχεν).

- τὰ κτήματα ("their possessions") – The article is used as a personal pronoun ("their"). This term probably refers to their property (real estate) whereas ὑπάρξεις refers to possessions.[82]

- ἐπίπρασκον ("they sold") – Impf act ind 3rd pl πιπράσκω. This could be an inceptive use of the imperfect tense-form ("they began selling," NASB; also with διεμέριζον). Another possibility is to take it as an iterative imperfect. Polhill writes, "The imperfect tense is used, indicating that this was a recurrent, continuing practice."[83]

- διεμέριζον ("distributed") – Impf act ind 3rd pl διαμερίζω. This is an iterative use of the imperfect (the church would customarily distribute goods to those who had need).

Verse 46

- καθ' ἡμέραν ("every day") – Distributive use of the preposition κατά to form a common idiom meaning "daily," "day by day," or "every day" (also v. 47).

- προσκαρτεροῦντες ("they devoted themselves") – Pres act ptc masc nom pl προσκαρτερέω (attendant circumstance). It is also possible that ἦσαν is understood (cf. v. 42).

- κλῶντές ("broke") – Pres act ptc masc nom pl κλάω. Because these early Christians broke bread "every day" many note that this phrase does not refer to the Lord's Supper.[84]

- κατ' οἶκον ("from house to house") – Distributive use of the preposition κατά.

---

[81] Witherington, *Acts*, 161.
[82] So Polhill, *Acts*, 121.
[83] Polhill, *Acts*, 121; so also Witherington, *Acts*, 162.
[84] So Barrett, *Acts*, 170; Witherington, *Acts*, 163; contrary to Polhill, *Acts*, 121; Marshall, *Acts*, 85.

- **μετελάμβανον** ("ate") – Impf act ind 3rd pl μεταλαμβάνω (iterative imperfect, "they repeatedly ate"). The verb means "share" or "partake of" and takes a genitive direct object (τροφῆς).

- **ἐν ἀγαλλιάσει καὶ ἀφελότητι καρδίας** ("with joyful and sincere hearts") – The preposition governs both dative phrases (dative of manner). καρδίας is an attributed genitive (sometimes called a reversed adjectival genitive) so that "sincerity of heart" = "a sincere heart."

Verse 47

- **αἰνοῦντες** ("praising") – Pres act ptc masc nom pl αἰνέω (attendant circumstance of μετελάμβανον, v. 46).

- **ἔχοντες** ("enjoying) – Pres act ptc masc nom pl ἔχω (attendant circumstance of μετελάμβανον, v. 46). Lit. "having" (so ESV and NASB).

- **προσετίθει** ("added") – Impf act ind 3rd sg προστίθημι. This is probably the iterative use of the imperfect tense-form. In v. 41 the aorist form was used (προσετέθησαν, "were added") because it referred to those who were saved and added to the church on a particular day (ἐν τῇ ἡμέρᾳ ἐκείνῃ), depicting the action from a perfective aspect as simply having occurred. In this verse, however, the context tells us that people were being saved and added to the church every day (καθ᾽ ἡμέραν). Thus, it could be translated, "The Lord was continually adding to the church those who were being saved."[85]

- **τοὺς σῳζομένους** ("those who were being saved") – Pres pass ptc masc acc pl σῳζω (substantival).

---

[85] So Robertson, 1116; Wallace, 546–47.

//////////////

CHAPTER 9

AORIST, PERFECT & PLUPERFECT INDICATIVES

GOING DEEPER

B ecause no two languages have identical grammatical and syntactical structures, it is often difficult to translate concepts from one language to another. This difficulty is sometimes seen when translating Greek perfect verbs into English. The Greek perfect tense-form is often described as conveying an action completed in the past that has continuing results. That is, the action itself is no longer being performed but the consequences of that action still exist in the present (in relation to the time of the author). As Zerwick notes, the perfect tense-form is used for "indicating not the past action as such but the present 'state of affairs' resulting from the past action."[1] It is difficult, however, to convey such a meaning of the verb in English. Without knowledge of the Greek verbal system, the significance or emphasis of an author's use of the perfect can be lost in translation.

For example, in John 16:33 Jesus states, "I **have conquered** the world" (ἐγὼ **νενίκηκα** τὸν κόσμον). The meaning here is not merely that Jesus conquered the world, but that it is still under his conquest. Mounce comments, "The perfect tense . . . emphasizes the abiding nature of that victory."[2] Based on this emphasis Carson explains, "The decisive battle has been waged and won. The world continues its wretched attacks, but those who are in Christ share the victory he has won. They

---

[1] Zerwick, 96.
[2] Robert H. Mounce, "John," in *Luke–Acts*, EBC 10, rev. ed. (Grand Rapids: Zondervan, 2007), 596.

cannot be harmed by the world's evil, and they know who triumphs in the end."[3] A second example is found in 1 Cor 15:4: **"He was raised** on the third day according to the Scriptures" (ἐγήγερται τῇ ἡμέρᾳ τῇ τρίτῃ κατὰ τὰς γραφὰς). Writing more than twenty years after Jesus's resurrection, Paul indicates that Jesus "has been raised" (ἐγήγερται, perfect tense-form) from the dead. In the immediate previous context, Paul noted that Jesus "died" (ἀπέθανεν) and "was buried" (ἐτάφη). What is significant is that both of these verbs are in the aorist tense-form (perfective aspect). Thus, the use of the perfect is noticeably contrasted with these aorist verbs. Fee asserts, "The verb in this instance is a perfect passive ('he has been raised'), implying that he was both raised from the dead *and still lives.*"[4]

CHAPTER OBJECTIVES

In the previous chapter we looked at the various uses in the indicative mood for the present, imperfect, and future tense-forms. The purpose of this chapter is to explain the various nuances sometimes found in indicative mood verbs of the aorist, perfect, and pluperfect tense-forms.

AORIST INDICATIVE	Constative
	Inceptive
	Culminative
	Gnomic
	Epistolary
	Futuristic
	Dramatic
PERFECT INDICATIVE	Intensive
	Consummative
	Dramatic
	Present State
	Gnomic
	Iterative
PLUPERFECT INDICATIVE	Intensive
	Consummative
	Past State

---

[3] D. A. Carson, *Gospel According to John*, PNTC (Grand Rapids: Eerdmans; Leicester: InterVarsity, 1991), 550.

[4] Gordon D. Fee, *1 Corinthians*, NICNT (Grand Rapids: Eerdmans, 1987), 726.

AORIST INDICATIVE

The aorist tense-form (perfective aspect) is used when the author wants to portray the action in its entirety or as a whole.[5] In contrast, the present and imperfect tense-forms portray an action that is ongoing or is in progress. "The fundamental significance of the aorist is to denote action simply as occurring, without reference to its progress. . . . It states the *fact* of the action or event without regard to its *duration*."[6] In narratives, the aorist is the most commonly used tense-form in the indicative mood and as such can be viewed as the unmarked or default form.[7] The aorist tense-form (perfective aspect) often carries the main story of the narrative whereas the present and imperfect tense-forms (imperfective aspect) are used to introduce significant characters, background information, or to emphasize certain features of a story.[8] The time of the action for the aorist tense-form is usually in the past, which (according to the traditional view) is demonstrated grammatically by an augment (ἔλυσα = "I loosed"). Absolute time, however, is limited to the indicative mood.

The aorist tense-form has suffered from misunderstanding and abuse, especially in preaching. It has often been touted from the pulpit that the aorist tense-form conveys a "once-for-all action." Even a modern grammar asserts, "The aorist tense expresses punctiliar action."[9] However, as Young rightly cautions, "The 'punctiliar' or 'point' terminology should be avoided, since it can lead to the erroneous idea that the aorist refers to action that occurred at one particular moment of time."[10] The idea that the aorist tense-form conveys a once-for-all or punctiliar action is a confusion of a verb's type of action (*Aktionsart*) with aspect. The aorist tense-form only conveys the aspect of the verb which relates to the way in which the author portrays the action. In the case of the aorist, the action is portrayed as a simple action or as a whole. The tense-form, however, does not tell us how the action actually unfolded in history. For example, in Rom 5:14 Paul writes, "death **reigned** from Adam to Moses" (**ἐβασίλευσεν** ὁ θάνατος ἀπὸ Ἀδὰμ μέχρι Μωϋσέως). This text makes it clear that the action of the verb was not punctiliar since it spans many years (even centuries!). Paul's reason for using the aorist was not to communicate a once-for-all action, but to focus on the action *as a whole* (perfective aspect), without detailing how it actually unfolded in history. Another example is found in Rev 20:4 where John states that "**they . . . reigned** with Christ for a thousand

---

[5] Greek, ἀ-όριστος = "without boundaries" or "undefined."

[6] Dana & Mantey, 193.

[7] "The aorist . . . is not the only way of expressing indefinite (undefined) action, but it is the normal method of doing so. . . . [T]he aorist is the tense used as a matter of course, unless there was special reason of using some other tense" (Robertson, 831).

[8] This is not necessarily the case in other types of literature or in non-indicative moods.

[9] Brooks & Winbery, 98. Moule similarly comments that "the chief function of the Aorist tense is to indicate an action viewed as instantaneous" (10).

[10] Young, 121.

years" (ἐβασίλευσαν μετὰ τοῦ Χριστοῦ χίλια ἔτη). In these cases, the aorist is used to present the action as a whole or in its entirety.

When considering how to best interpret or translate a sentence or phrase, it is also important to remember that there are more factors to consider than merely the tense-form of the verb. Although the aspect is often the most significant feature regarding the function and meaning of a verb, as was highlighted in chapter 7, we must also consider lexical, grammatical, and contextual factors. Thus, the tense-form (aspect) of the verb cannot be analyzed in isolation but must take many other factors into consideration.[11] It is only when these other factors are considered that we can determine whether a nuanced meaning of the verb is intended.[12] In the case of the aorist tense-form, the context may indicate that the emphasis of the action of the verb is its inception, completion, or some other nuanced meaning. There are 5,919 aorist indicatives in the NT.

Constative Aorist[13]

The most basic use of the aorist tense-form is to present the action as a whole (the perfective). The constative use focuses on the action in its entirety without regard to its beginning or end, or the length of time it took to accomplish the action.[14] Thus, the aorist does not communicate whether the action was momentary, repetitive, or took place over an extended period of time. Such nuances are only detected by the lexical nature of the verb and other features found in the context (such as adverbs or prepositional phrases, so-called "deictic indicators"), and not the aorist tense-form itself.[15]

- οἱ πατέρες ἡμῶν ἐν τῷ ὄρει τούτῳ **προσεκύνησαν** (John 4:20)

  Our fathers **worshiped** on this mountain

    Notice that the action would have taken place repeatedly over a long period of time, but the function of the aorist is simply to represent the action in a summary fashion.

---

[11] "The use of the aorist in any given situation depends, then, on its combination with other linguistic features" (Wallace, 556).

[12] "[T]he verbal idea as well as the context usually affects very decidedly the significance of the aorist" (Dana & Mantey, 196). "[T]he presence of the aorist does not in itself give any hint as to the nature of the action behind it. Contextual factors are primary for any attempt to go behind the aorist to the nature of the action itself." See Frank Stagg, "The Abused Aorist," *JBL* 91 (1972): 231.

[13] Some grammars label this category the "Historical Aorist" (Burton), "Global Aorist" (Zerwick), "Complexive Aorist" (BDF), or "Indefinite Aorist" (Burton).

[14] "[T]he aorist indicative makes a summary reference to a past action or state as a whole without emphasis on any of the actional features which may be involved in the internal constituency of the occurrence" (Fanning, 256). "The 'constative' aorist just *treats* the act as a single whole entirely irrespective of the parts or time involved" (Robertson, 832).

[15] "Thus, the constative aorist can be used of situations which are either durative or instantaneous, either single or multiple. In each case the sense is dependent on the lexical character of the verb and other features, not on the use or non-use of the aorist" (Fanning, 259).

- ἐνέμεινεν δὲ διετίαν ὅλην (Acts 28:30)

  Then **he stayed** two full years (NASB)

- πολλάκις **προεθέμην** ἐλθεῖν πρὸς ὑμᾶς, καὶ **ἐκωλύθην** ἄχρι τοῦ δεῦρο (Rom 1:13)

  I often **planned** to come to you (but was **prevented** until now)

  > The context clearly indicates (primarily through the use of the word "often" [πολλάκις]) that the actions took place repeatedly.

- πεντάκις τεσσεράκοντα παρὰ μίαν **ἔλαβον** (2 Cor 11:24)

  Five times **I received** . . . forty lashes minus one

  > Again, the action took place repeatedly but the aorist presents the action as a whole.

- ἐπέμεινα πρὸς αὐτὸν ἡμέρας δεκαπέντε (Gal 1:18)

  I stayed with him fifteen days

  > This is obviously not a once-for-all or punctiliar action because it took place over the course of two weeks.[16]

Inceptive Aorist[17]

The aorist tense-form is often found in contexts that emphasize the beginning of a state (or, less common, an action). This inceptive (or ingressive) nuance is communicated by the lexical meaning of the verb and the context. In contrast to the inceptive use of the imperfect, the aorist does not specify whether or not the action continued for some duration. In English, the inceptive idea can be expressed by the terms "began" (with action verbs) or "came/became" (with stative verbs).[18]

- ὁ ἀδελφός σου οὗτος νεκρὸς ἦν καὶ **ἔζησεν** (Luke 15:32)

  for this brother of yours was dead and **_has begun_** to live (NASB)

---

[16] For more examples of the constative aorist, see Matt 8:3 (ἥψατο); Luke 4:43 (ἀπεστάλην); John 1:21 (ἠρώτησαν); 2:20 (οἰκοδομήθη); Acts 9:40 (ἤνοιξεν, ἀνεκάθισεν); 12:23 (ἐπάταξεν); 18:11 (ἐκάθισεν); Rom 5:14 (ἐβασίλευσεν); 2 Cor 11:25 (ἐρραβδίσθην, ἐλιθάσθην, ἐναυάγησα); Eph 2:4 (ἠγάπησεν); Heb 11:13 (ἀπέθανον), 23 (ἐκρύβη); Rev 20:4 (ἐβασίλευσαν).

[17] Some grammars label this category the "Ingressive Aorist" (BDF, Black, Brooks & Winbery, Dana & Mantey, Moule, Moulton, Wallace, Young) or as the "Inchoative Aorist" (Robertson).

[18] It should be noted that these categories (e.g., constative, inceptive, etc.) can apply to aorist verbs in non-indicative moods.

- ἐδάκρυσεν ὁ Ἰησοῦς (John 11:35)

  Jesus **began to weep** (NRSV)

  > Many scholars have noted that this phrase is perhaps best translated, "Jesus burst into tears."[19]

- ἤδη ἐπλουτήσατε, χωρὶς ἡμῶν ἐβασιλεύσατε (1 Cor 4:8)

  Already **you have become rich**! Without us **you have become kings**! (ESV)

- δι᾽ ὑμᾶς ἐπτώχευσεν πλούσιος ὤν, ἵνα ὑμεῖς τῇ ἐκείνου πτωχείᾳ πλουτήσητε (2 Cor 8:9)

  though he was rich, for your sake **he became poor**, so that by his poverty you might **become rich**[20]

  > The second verb (πλουτήσητε) is an aorist subjunctive (thus no augment), but is also an inceptive aorist.

- ὁ πρῶτος καὶ ὁ ἔσχατος, ὃς ἐγένετο νεκρὸς καὶ ἔζησεν (Rev 2:8)

  The First and the Last, the one who was dead and **came to life**[21]

Culminative Aorist[22]

In contrast to the inceptive use of the aorist that emphasizes the beginning of an action or state, the culminative aorist emphasizes the cessation of an action or state. This usage can be detected by the presence of certain verbs whose lexical nature lends itself to this usage (i.e., verbs whose inherent meanings imply effort or a process) or by the context where an action was already in progress but the aorist verb signals its conclusion. It is often the case that the act was stopped more than that it was completed, though the lexical meaning of the verb and the context can signal completion as well. Such verbs are often translated with the English perfect tense.

- οἱ δὲ ἀρχιερεῖς καὶ οἱ πρεσβύτεροι ἔπεισαν τοὺς ὄχλους (Matt 27:20)

  The chief priests and the elders, however, **persuaded** the crowds

---

[19] Robertson translates a similar verb in Luke 19:41 (ἔκλαυσεν) as "burst into tears" and then references John 11:35 (834).

[20] Young aptly comments, "The aorist ἐπτώχευσεν in this context cannot mean 'he was poor,' Christ was exceedingly rich, but for us He became poor, that is, He left one state and entered into another" (123).

[21] For more examples of the inceptive aorist, see Matt 9:27 (ἠκολούθησαν); 22:7 (ὠργίσθη); Luke 19:41 (ἔκλαυσεν); John 1:14 (ἐγένετο); 4:52 (ἔσχεν); 11:31 (ἠκολούθησαν); Acts 7:60 (ἐκοιμήθη); 15:12 (ἐσίγησαν); Rom 14:9 (ἔζησεν); Rev 1:8 (ἐγενόμην); 13:14 (ἔζησεν); 20:4 (ἔζησαν).

[22] Some grammars label this category the "Consummative Aorist" (Wallace), "Effective Aorist" (Black, Moulton, Robertson, Zerwick), or "Resultative Aorist" (Burton).

- κατὰ ἀποκάλυψιν **ἐγνωρίσθη** μοι τὸ μυστήριον (Eph 3:3)

  The mystery **was made known** to me by revelation

- ἐγὼ γὰρ **ἔμαθον** ἐν οἷς εἰμι αὐτάρκης εἶναι (Phil 4:11)

  for **I have learned** to be content in whatever circumstances I find myself

- ἡ σκοτία **ἐτύφλωσεν** τοὺς ὀφθαλμοὺς αὐτοῦ (1 John 2:11)

  the darkness **has blinded** his eyes

- ἰδοὺ **ἐνίκησεν** ὁ λέων ὁ ἐκ τῆς φυλῆς Ἰούδα (Rev 5:5)

  Look, the Lion from the tribe of Judah, the Root of David, **has conquered**[23]

Gnomic Aorist

Occasionally the aorist tense-form is used to communicate a timeless or universal truth. In this case, the verb does not communicate that a particular event or state occurred but that it does occur (all the time). As such, it is often used to express axioms or proverbs. Because of this nuance, the gnomic use of the aorist is typically translated with a present tense verb.[24]

- ἐπὶ τῆς Μωϋσέως καθέδρας **ἐκάθισαν** οἱ γραμματεῖς καὶ οἱ Φαρισαῖοι (Matt 23:2)

  The scribes and the Pharisees **sit** on Moses' seat (ESV)

- **ἐδικαιώθη** ἡ σοφία ἀπὸ πάντων τῶν τέκνων αὐτῆς (Luke 7:35)

  wisdom **is vindicated** by all her children

- οὐδεὶς ποτε τὴν ἑαυτοῦ σάρκα **ἐμίσησεν** (Eph 5:29)

  no one ever **hates** his own flesh

---

[23] For more examples of the culminative aorist, see Matt 2:2 (ἤλθομεν); 7:28 (ἐτέλεσεν); 22:7 (ἐνέπρησεν); 25:20 (ἐκέρδησα); Mark 5:12 (παρεκάλεσαν), 39 (ἀπέθανεν); Luke 1:1 (ἐπεχείρησαν); 19:16 (παρεγένετο), 42 (ἐκρύβη); 24:17 (ἐστάθησαν); John 1:42 (ἤγαγεν); Acts 5:4 (ἔθου), 39 (ἐπείσθησαν); 7:36 (ἐξήγαγεν); 27:43 (ἐκώλυσεν); 28:14 (παρεκλήθημεν); Rom 1:13 (ἐκωλύθην); Eph 3:3 (ἐγνωρίσθη); 1 Pet 3:18 (ἔπαθεν).

[24] Fanning suggests that the difference between the present and aorist gnomic verb is that "the present looks at multiple occurrences of the event and abstracts to a general principle, while the aorist points to a single instance as typical of many" (266–67). He continues, "[T]he aorist tends to occur with verbs of instantaneous meaning and thus state a more vivid, sudden occurrence" (267).

- ἀνέτειλεν γὰρ ὁ ἥλιος σὺν τῷ καύσωνι καὶ **ἐξήρανεν** τὸν χόρτον καὶ τὸ ἄνθος αὐτοῦ **ἐξέπεσεν** καὶ ἡ εὐπρέπεια τοῦ προσώπου αὐτοῦ **ἀπώλετο** (Jas 1:11)

  For the sun **rises** with a scorching wind and **withers** the grass; and its flower **falls off**, and the beauty of its appearance **is destroyed** (NASB)[25]

- **ἐξηράνθη** ὁ χόρτος καὶ τὸ ἄνθος **ἐξέπεσεν** (1 Pet 1:24)

  The grass **withers**, and the flower **falls**[26]

Epistolary Aorist

The aorist tense-form is sometimes used in epistles whereby the author writes from the perspective of the readers.[27] In this case, the present tense-form ("I am writing,") or the future tense-form ("I will send") is not used but rather the aorist tense-form is preferred ("I wrote" or "I sent"). So, although the author is currently writing something (or going to be sending someone in the future), by the time the recipients receive the letter, it will already have been written (or the person will have already been sent). Exegetically, this distinction is important because it makes a difference as to whether the author is referring to something that is currently being written (true epistolary aorist), something that was just written in the same epistle (e.g., Rom 15:15; Eph 3:3; 1 Pet 5:12), or something that was written in a previous epistle (e.g., 1 Cor 5:9; 2 Cor 2:3–4, 9; 7:12; 3 John 9).

- οὐκ **ἔγραψα** δὲ ταῦτα, ἵνα οὕτως γένηται ἐν ἐμοί (1 Cor 9:15)

  Nor **have I written** this to make it happen that way for me

    The ESV, NASB, NIV and NRSV all translate the verb in the present tense ("I am not writing").

- ἴδετε πηλίκοις ὑμῖν γράμμασιν **ἔγραψα** τῇ ἐμῇ χειρί (Gal 6:11)

  Look at what large letters I use as **I write** to you in my own handwriting

    The ESV, NASB, and NRSV all have "I am writing" (the NIV states, "as I write").

---

[25] It should be noted that this and the next example are influenced by the Hebrew perfect which stands behind the LXX.

[26] For more examples of the gnomic aorist, see Matt 7:24–27 (ᾠκοδόμησεν, κατέβη, ἦλθον, ἔπνευσαν, προσέπεσαν, ἔπεσεν, προσέκοψαν); 13:44 (ἔκρυψεν); 18:23 (ὡμοιώθη); Mark 1:11 (εὐδόκησα); John 15:6 (ἐβλήθη, ἐξηράνθη), 8 (ἐδοξάσθη); Gal 5:24 (ἐσταύρωσαν); Jas 1:24 (κατενόησεν). Some grammars place Mark 1:11 and parallels under the category of dramatic aorist (so Black, Brooks & Winbery, Dana & Mantey, and Wallace [tentatively]).

[27] "[T]he writer courteously projects himself in imagination into the position of the readers, for whom actions contemporaneous with the time of writing will be past" (Moule, 12). Porter, who sees no temporal significance to the aorist indicative, maintains that the author is not writing from the perspective of the readers but rather the author is referring to "the entire writing process" (*Idioms*, 37).

- [Τύχικον] **ἔπεμψα** πρὸς ὑμᾶς (Eph 6:22)

  I am sending [Tychicus] to you

  > As the bearer of the letter, Tychicus was still with Paul when the letter was being written. But, by the time the church in Ephesus read the letter, the sending of Tychicus would have been a past event (see also Col 4:8).

- σπουδαιοτέρως οὖν **ἔπεμψα** αὐτόν (Phil 2:28)

  Therefore **I have sent** him all the more eagerly (NASB)

- ἐγὼ Παῦλος **ἔγραψα** τῇ ἐμῇ χειρί (Phlm 19)

  I, Paul, **write** this with my own hand[28]

Futuristic Aorist[29]

In a few cases, the aorist tense-form is used to describe events that have not yet taken place (i.e., future) as if they had already occurred. By using the aorist as a future, an author stresses the certainty of the event by picturing it as if the event was in the past (thus sometimes called the prophetic aorist).

- ἐὰν μή τις μένῃ ἐν ἐμοί, **ἐβλήθη** ἔξω ὡς τὸ κλῆμα καὶ **ἐξηράνθη** (John 15:6)

  If anyone does not remain in me, **he is thrown** aside like a branch and **he withers**

  > Because these aorist verbs occur in the apodosis of a conditional statement, they necessarily will occur in the future.

- ἐν τούτῳ **ἐδοξάσθη** ὁ πατήρ μου (John 15:8)

  My Father **is glorified** by this

  > This verse could be translated, "My Father will be glorified by this" because of the following phrase which states, "that you produce much fruit and prove to be My disciples."

- οὓς δὲ ἐδικαίωσεν, τούτους καὶ **ἐδόξασεν** (Rom 8:30)

  and those he justified, **he** also **glorified**

  > The glorification has not yet occurred but is considered certain.

---

[28] For more examples of the epistolary aorist, see Acts 23:30 (ἔπεμψα); 1 Cor 5:11 (ἔγραψα); 2 Cor 8:17 (ἐξῆλθεν), 18 (συνεπέμψαμεν), 22 (συνεπέμψαμε); 9:3 (ἔπεμψα), 5 (ἡγησάμην); Phil 2:25 (ἡγησάμην); Phlm 12 (ἀνέπεμψα), 19 (ἔγραψα); 1 John 2:21 (ἔγραψα), 26 (ἔγραψα).

[29] Some grammars label this category the "Proleptic Aorist" (Wallace and Zerwick).

- ἦλθεν κύριος ἐν ἁγίαις μυριάσιν αὐτοῦ (Jude 14)

  The Lord **comes** with tens of thousands of his holy ones

    This is clearly future: "The Lord will come with tens of thousands of his holy ones."

- ὅταν μέλλῃ σαλπίζειν, καὶ **ἐτελέσθη** τὸ μυστήριον τοῦ θεοῦ (Rev 10:7)

  when [he] will blow his trumpet, then the mystery of God **will be completed**[30]

Dramatic Aorist[31]

In some contexts, the aorist indicative is used to refer to an event that recently occurred and thus has present consequences. "In this use an aorist of a verb of *emotion* or *understanding* appears in dialogue, expressing a state of feeling or of comprehension reached either in the immediate past or exactly contemporary with the utterance."[32] Often contextual markers will be included, especially the adverbs of time such as ἄρτι and νῦν. Typically, the perfect (and sometimes the present) tense will be used in the English translation.

- ἡ θυγάτηρ μου <u>ἄρτι</u> **ἐτελεύτησεν** (Matt 9:18)

  My daughter **has** <u>just</u> **died** (ESV)

- **ἔγνων** τί ποιήσω (Luke 16:4)

  I have decided what to do (ESV)

    In the context, the unjust (but shrewd) manager makes a strategic decision that will help him in the future. This is a decision that just came to his mind. It is a past action that recently happened but is not limited to the past since his knowing continues into the present.

- ἐνέγκατε ἀπὸ τῶν ὀψαρίων ὧν **ἐπιάσατε** <u>νῦν</u> (John 21:10)

  Bring some of the fish that **you have** <u>just</u> **caught** (ESV)

- καθὼς **προέγραψα** ἐν ὀλίγῳ (Eph 3:3)

  as I have briefly **written** above

    Paul could be referring to an earlier (unknown) letter but most interpreters take this as a reference to an earlier part of Ephesians (2:11–22). The CSB favors this interpretation by supplying the word "above" to make that point clear.

---

[30] For more examples of the futuristic aorist, see Matt 18:15 (ἐκέρδησας); Mark 11:24 (ἐλάβετε); John 13:31 (ἐδοξάσθη, ἐδοξάσθη); 17:18 (ἀπέστειλα); 1 Cor 7:28 (ἥμαρτες, ἥμαρτεν); Gal 5:4 (κατηργήθητε, ἐξεπέσατε); Heb 4:10 (κατέπαυσεν); Jas 2:4 (διεκρίθητε, ἐγένεσθε); 1 Pet 3:6 (ἐγενήθητε).

[31] Wallace also calls this the "Immediate Past Aorist."

[32] Fanning, 275 (emphasis original).

- ἄρτι **ἐγένετο** ἡ σωτηρία καὶ ἡ δύναμις καὶ ἡ βασιλεία τοῦ θεοῦ ἡμῶν καὶ ἡ ἐξουσία τοῦ Χριστοῦ αὐτοῦ (Rev 12:10)

  <u>Now</u> the salvation and the power and the kingdom of our God and the authority of his Christ **have come** (ESV)[33]

PERFECT

The perfect tense-form (stative aspect) is often described as conveying a completed action in the past that has continuing results. That is, the action itself is no longer being performed but the consequences of that action still exist in the present (in relation to the time of the author). Thus, γέγραπται (the perfect of γράφω) does not so much mean "it was written" as "it stands written."[34] The idea conveyed by the perfect is that what was written in the past has abiding consequences or implications for the recipients.

As noted in chapter 7, the aspect of the perfect is described as stative, which is used when the author wants to focus on the state of being that results from a previous action (a combination of the perfective and imperfective aspects). Porter notes, "The perfect and the pluperfect tense forms occur in contexts where the user of Greek wishes to depict the action as reflecting a given (often complex) state of affairs."[35] According to Wallace, with the stative aspect the "*action* is portrayed *externally* (summary), while the *resultant state* proceeding from the action is portrayed *internally* (continuous state)."[36] Others have described the perfect tense-form as a combination of the aorist (completed action, perfective aspect) and the present (progressive nature, imperfective aspect) tense-form.[37] It is often the goal of the interpreter to determine which of these two features is being emphasized in a particular context.[38]

Although the perfect is less common than the present, imperfect, future, and aorist tense-forms, its presence is often more significant.[39] Dana & Mantey comment,

---

[33] For more examples of the dramatic aorist, see Matt 6:12 (ἀφήκαμεν); 26:65 (ἠκούσατε); Mark 1:8 (ἐβάπτισα); 5:35 (ἀπέθανεν); 16:6 (ἠγέρθη); Luke 1:47 (ἠγαλλίασεν); 1 Cor 4:18 (ἐφυσιώθησαν).

[34] Wallace offers what he calls a *very* loose paraphrase: "Although this scripture was written long ago, its authority is still binding on us" (576).

[35] Porter, *Idioms*, 39.

[36] Wallace, 501, 573 (emphasis original).

[37] E.g., BDF maintains that the "perfect combines in itself, so to speak, the present and the aorist in that it denotes the *continuance* of *completed action*" (175 [§340], emphasis original). See also the discussion of the stative aspect as a combination of the perfective and imperfect aspects in chapter 7.

[38] "Emphasis, as indicated by the context or the meaning of the verb root, may be on either the completion of the action or on its finished results" (Dana & Mantey, 201).

[39] Moulton notes that the perfect tense-form is "the most important, exegetically, of all the Greek Tenses" (1:140).

"It is best to assume that there is a reason for the perfect wherever it occurs."[40] Typically, the perfect tense-form is translated into English using the helping verb "have/has." But because there is no English equivalent to the Greek perfect, this method is not always sufficient. For example, because the perfect often focuses on the resulting state, a present tense English translation is often preferred. Attention has to be given to the context and the inherent meaning of the verb to see how it is best translated. There are 839 perfect indicatives in the NT.

Intensive Perfect[41]

The intensive use of the perfect emphasizes the present state of the verb brought about by a past action. The focus is on the resultant state (stative aspect) rather than on the completed action. "When special attention is thus directed to the results of the action, stress upon the existing fact is intensified."[42] As such, it is usually best to translate this type of perfect with the English present tense.[43]

- **ἀφέωνταί** σοι αἱ ἁμαρτίαι σου (Luke 5:20)

  your sins **are forgiven**

- οὕτως **γέγραπται** παθεῖν τὸν χριστὸν (Luke 24:46)

  Thus **it is written**, that the Christ should suffer (ESV)

- ἐγὼ **πεπίστευκα** ὅτι σὺ εἶ ὁ χριστὸς ὁ υἱὸς τοῦ θεοῦ (John 11:27)

  I believe you are the Messiah, the Son of God

- εἰ δὲ ἀνάστασις νεκρῶν οὐκ ἔστιν, οὐδὲ Χριστὸς **ἐγήγερται** (1 Cor 15:13)

  But if there is no resurrection of the dead, then Christ **is not risen** (NKJV)[44]

- ὅτι λέγεις ὅτι Πλούσιός εἰμι καὶ **πεπλούτηκα** (Rev 3:17)

  For you say, "I'm rich; **I have become wealthy**"

---

[40] Dana & Mantey, 200. They continue, "We should certainly in fairness take it for granted that the New Testament writer intended the differentiation of meaning which is represented in this distinction [between the perfect and the aorist], whether we are able to understand fully his reason or not" (201).

[41] Some grammars label this category the "Perfect of Existing State" (Burton) or the "Perfect of Resulting State" (Fanning).

[42] Dana & Mantey, 202.

[43] Wallace warns, "One ought to be careful when translating the perfect into English to resist the temptation to translate it as an English perfect at all times" (575).

[44] For more examples of the intensive perfect, see Mark 5:33 (γέγονεν); 6:14 (ἐγήγερται); John 5:45 (ἠλπίκατε); 17:7 (ἔγνωκαν); Acts 8:14 (δέδεκται); 3:10 (γέγραπται); 5:2 (ἐσχήκαμεν); 14:23 (κατακέκριται); 15:4 (ἐγήγερται); 2 Cor 1:10 (ἠλπίκαμεν); 6:11 (πεπλάτυνται); Heb 3:14 (γεγόναμεν).

Consummative Perfect[45]

Whereas the intensive use of the perfect emphasizes the resulting state of a past action, the consummative use emphasizes the completed action that brought about the resulting state. In other words, "the accomplishment of the action is so emphasized that the resulting state is merely the vague condition of 'the occurrence having actually taken place on a particular occasion or, more generally, at least once in the past.'"[46] Verbs that fit into this category are often transitive in nature (i.e., they can take a direct object). It is usually best to translate this type of perfect with the English present perfect ("have/has" + past tense).

- ἡ πίστις σου **σέσωκέν** σε (Mark 10:52)

  Your faith **has saved** you

- **ἑώρακα** καὶ **μεμαρτύρηκα** ὅτι οὗτός ἐστιν ὁ υἱὸς τοῦ θεου (John 1:34)

  I have seen and **testified** that this is the Son of God!

- **τετέλεσται** (John 19:30)

  It is finished!

  > The lexical meaning ("finish") and the perfect tense-form combine to emphasize the completion of Jesus's mission.[47]

- ὡς **προειρήκαμεν** καὶ ἄρτι πάλιν λέγω (Gal 1:9)

  As **we have said before,** I now say again

- τὸν καλὸν ἀγῶνα **ἠγώνισμαι**, τὸν δρόμον **τετέλεκα**, τὴν πίστιν **τετήρηκα** (2 Tim 4:7)

  I have fought the good fight, **I have finished** the race, **I have kept** the faith[48]

---

[45] Some grammars label this category the "Extensive Perfect" (Robertson and Wallace).

[46] Fanning, 297. With this use of the perfect, "it is not merely the process which is denoted, but a consummated process, and consummation implies result" (Dana & Mantey, 203).

[47] Young notes that if this is a consummative perfect, the meaning is that "Jesus was looking backward to the state of affairs that had just been drawn to a close: the Old Testament sacrifices, rituals, typology, as well as His own life and sufferings" (127–28).

[48] For more examples of the consummative perfect, see Mark 5:33 (γέγονεν); John 2:10 (τετήρηκας); 5:33 (ἀπεστάλκατε, μεμαρτύρηκεν); 10:29 (δέδωκεν); 17:6 (τετήρηκαν); 19:22 (γέγραφα); Acts 5:28 (πεπληρώκατε); Rom 5:5 (ἐκκέχυται); 16:7 (γέγοναν); 2 Cor 7:3 (προείρηκα); 1 John 1:10 (ἡμαρτήκαμεν); Jude 6 (τετήρηκεν).

Dramatic Perfect[49]

The perfect tense-form is sometimes used to vividly portray a past event or state of affairs. As Robertson explains, "Here an action completed in the past is conceived in terms of the present time for the sake of vividness."[50] This usage is similar to the historical present which describes a past event with the present tense-form by adding vividness to the event and draws the reader into the story or gives literary prominence to some aspect of the story. It is also similar to the dramatic use of the aorist which refers to an event that occurred recently, and thus has present consequences.[51] Due to the nature of the dramatic use of the perfect, it occurs exclusively in narrative contexts (sometimes the narrative is found in an epistle) and is usually translated into English as a simple past tense.

- ἀπελθὼν **πέπρακεν** πάντα ὅσα εἶχεν (Matt 13:46)

  he went and **sold** everything he had

- Ἰωάννης μαρτυρεῖ περὶ αὐτοῦ καὶ **κέκραγεν** (John 1:15)

  John testified concerning him and **exclaimed**

    The fact that the perfect κέκραγεν is paralleled with the historical present μαρτυρεῖ demonstrates its affinity with its use and meaning.

- οὐκ **ἔσχηκα** ἄνεσιν τῷ πνεύματί μου (2 Cor 2:13)

  I had no rest in my spirit

- τρὶς ἐραβδίσθην, ἅπαξ ἐλιθάσθην, τρὶς ἐναυάγησα, νυχθήμερον ἐν τῷ βυθῷ **πεποίηκα** (2 Cor 11:25)

  Three times I was beaten with rods. Once I received a stoning. Three times I was shipwrecked. **I have spent** a night and a day in the open sea

    The previous three verbs are in the aorist tense-form. Paul seems to shift to the perfect to highlight his experience of being adrift at sea.

---

[49] Some grammars label this category the "Aoristic Perfect" (Wallace) or the "Historical Perfect" (Burton). In addition, some grammars treat the dramatic/historical perfect and the aoristic perfect as separate categories (e.g., Brooks & Winbery, Burton, and Robertson), but there is some doubt as to whether the separate category of aoristic perfect is legitimate. Robertson himself states, "I conclude by saying that the N. T. writers may be guilty of this idiom, but they have not as yet been proved to be" (902).

[50] Robertson, 896. Brooks & Winbery add, "The narrator describes the past event in such a way that his hearers or readers are led to think for a moment that they are present and witnessing it" (96).

[51] "The historical present and the dramatic aorist are also used in a sense similar to this, but for this purpose the perfect is the most forcible of the three" (Dana & Mantey, 204).

- καὶ ἦλθεν καὶ **εἴληφεν** [τὸ βιβλίον] (Rev 5:7)

  He went and **took** [the scroll][52]

Present State Perfect[53]

This category applies to certain verbs that are stative in nature with no implication of a previous act that produced the state. Verbs found in this category include οἶδα, ἕστηκα, πέποιθα, and μέμνημαι.[54] "The reason why such perfects have the same semantics as presents is frequently that *there is very little distinction between the act and its results*."[55] Or to put it differently, "the results have become the act."[56] Thus, this category is lexically influenced and verbs found in this category should be treated as virtual present tense-form verbs.

- ἡ μήτηρ σου καὶ οἱ ἀδελφοί σου **ἑστήκασιν** ἔξω (Luke 8:20)

  Your mother and your brothers **are standing** outside

- τὰς ἐντολὰς **οἶδας** (Luke 18:20)

  You know the commandments

- νῦν **ἐγνώκαμεν** ὅτι δαιμόνιον ἔχεις (John 8:52)

  Now **we know** you have a demon

- **οἶδα** καὶ **πέπεισμαι** ἐν κυρίῳ Ἰησοῦ (Rom 14:14)

  I know and **am persuaded** in the Lord Jesus

- ἐπαινῶ δὲ ὑμᾶς ὅτι πάντα μου **μέμνησθε** (1 Cor 11:2)

  Now I praise you because **you remember** me in everything[57]

---

[52] For more examples of the dramatic perfect, see Matt 25:6 (γέγονεν); Luke 9:36 (ἑώρακαν); John 1:32 (τεθέαμαι), 41 (εὑρήκαμεν); 12:29 (λελάληκεν); Acts 7:35 (ἀπέσταλκεν); 21:28 (κεκοίνωκεν); 2 Cor 1:9 (ἐσχήκαμεν); 7:5 (ἔσχηκεν); 12:17 (ἀπέσταλκα); Jas 1:24 (ἀπελήλυθεν); Rev 7:14 (εἴρηκα); 8:5 (εἴληφεν); 19:3 (εἴρηκαν).

[53] Some grammars label this category the "Perfect with (a) Present Force" (Moulton and Wallace) but most grammars do not include this category.

[54] οἶδα is the most common of these perfects, accounting for more than 25 percent of all perfect tense-forms in the NT.

[55] Wallace, 579–80.

[56] Wallace, 580.

[57] For more examples of the present state perfect, see Matt 27:43 (πέποιθεν); Luke 4:34 (οἶδα); John 1:26 (ἕστηκεν, οἴδατε); 3:2 (οἴδαμεν); 16:30 (οἴδαμεν, οἶδας); Acts 1:11 (ἑστήκατε); 26:27 (οἶδα); Rom 2:19 (πέποιθας); 8:38 (πέπεισμαι); 1 Cor 11:2 (μέμνησθε); 16:9 (ἀνέῳγεν); 2 Cor 1:24 (ἑστήκατε); 6:11 (ἀνέῳγεν); Gal 5:10 (πέποιθα); Phil 2:24 (πέποιθα); Heb 6:9 (πεπείσμεθα); 10:11 (ἕστηκεν); Jas 1:6 (ἔοικεν), 23 (ἔοικεν); Rev 3:20 (ἕστηκα); 19:12 (οἶδεν). The following represents the use of this category with participles: Matt 16:28 (ἑστώτων); Luke 9:27 (ἑστηκότων); 2 Cor 2:3 (πεποιθώς); Phlm 21 (πεποιθώς); Jas 3:1 (εἰδότες); 2 Pet 1:12 (εἰδότας).

Gnomic Perfect

As with the gnomic use of the other tense forms, the perfect gnomic is used to communicate a customary or general truth. "The basic sense of the perfect is preserved in this use, but the 'existing result of an antecedent occurrence' is not limited to a particular time or occasion; instead, it refers to a generic situation which could be true on numerous occasions."[58] As such, it is often used to express axioms or proverbs. Some of the following examples may also fit into other categories (especially the intensive use of the perfect). Those examples which are found in the apodosis of a conditional clause could also be categorized as the futuristic use of the perfect.[59]

- ὁ δὲ μὴ πιστεύων ἤδη **κέκριται** (John 3:18)

  but anyone who does not believe **is** already **condemned**

- ὁ δὲ διακρινόμενος ἐὰν φάγῃ **κατακέκριται** (Rom 14:23)

  But whoever has doubts **is condemned** if he eats (ESV)

- γυνὴ **δέδεται** ἐφ' ὅσον χρόνον ζῇ ὁ ἀνὴρ αὐτῆς (1 Cor 7:39)

  A wife **is bound** as long as her husband is living

- κατενόησεν γὰρ ἑαυτὸν καὶ **ἀπελήλυθεν** καὶ εὐθέως ἐπελάθετο ὁποῖος ἦν (Jas 1:24)

  for he looks at himself, **goes away**, and immediately forgets what kind of person he was

- ᾧ γάρ τις **ἥττηται**, τούτῳ **δεδούλωται** (2 Pet 2:19)

  For whatever **overcomes** a person, to that he **is enslaved** (ESV)[60]

Iterative Perfect

When the context suggests that the action of the verb occurred at intervals, the verb is said to be an iterative perfect. This use could also be seen as a subdivision of the consummative use of the perfect which emphasizes the past action (rather than the resulting present state). As seen from the examples below, this usage occurs mostly in the Johannine corpus.

---

[58] Fanning, 304.

[59] E.g., John 20:23; Rom 14:23; Jas 2:10; 1 John 2:5. This use is also sometimes called the proleptic perfect (Fanning and Wallace).

[60] For more examples of the gnomic perfect, see John 5:24 (μεταβέβηκεν); 20:23 (ἀφέωνται, κεκράτηνται); Rom 7:2 (δέδεται, κατήργηται); 13:8 (πεπλήρωκεν); Jas 2:10 (γέγονεν); 1 John 2:5 (τετελείωται).

- θεὸν οὐδεὶς **ἑώρακεν** πώποτε (John 1:18)

  No one **has** ever **seen** God

- ὁ πέμψας με πατὴρ ἐκεῖνος **μεμαρτύρηκεν** περὶ ἐμοῦ (John 5:37)

  The Father who sent me **has** himself **testified** about me

- οὐδενὶ **δεδουλεύκαμεν** πώποτε (John 8:33)

  we have never **been enslaved** to anyone

- εἰ μὲν οὖν ἀδικῶ καὶ ἄξιον θανάτου **πέπραχά** τι, οὐ παραιτοῦμαι τὸ ἀποθανεῖν (Acts 25:11)

  If then I am a wrongdoer, and **have committed** anything worthy of death, I do not refuse to die (NASB)

- ὃ ἦν ἀπ' ἀρχῆς, ὃ **ἀκηκόαμεν**, ὃ **ἑωράκαμεν** τοῖς ὀφθαλμοῖς ἡμῶν (1 John 1:1)

  What was from the beginning, what **we have heard**, what **we have seen** with our eyes

  "The state of affairs in which the disciples were in the very presence of the Lord occurred at repeated intervals for a period of three and a half years."[61]

PLUPERFECT

The pluperfect (past stative aspect) can be described as "a *past* state of affairs constituted by an action still further in the past."[62] That is, when a narrator is telling a story, that story is already a past event. But when the narrator needs to describe something that took place prior to this narrative, then the pluperfect is often used. For example, in Luke 8:2 we read that among the women who had been cured of evil spirits and diseases was "Mary (called Magdalene) from whom seven demons had come out" (ἐξεληλύθει). As the author narrates the story, he explains that Jesus traveled from town to town preaching the gospel using past-referring verb forms. But in order to describe an event that occurred before these past events he uses the pluperfect.

The aspectual significance of the pluperfect is similar to that of the perfect. Both tense-forms emphasize the resulting state of a previous action or event. The main difference relates to time. Whereas the perfect typically indicates the *present* state of a past event (from the perspective of the author), the pluperfect indicates the

---

[61] Young, 127. For another example, see 2 Cor 12:17 (ἀπέσταλκα).

[62] Zerwick, 98 (§290). BDF notes, "The pluperfect equals the aorist plus the imperfect" (177 [§347]).

past state of a past event.[63] It is possible, however, that the results of the past action continue into the present (from the perspective of the author) but such conclusions are reached based on other features in the context and not from the tense-form of the verb.

The pluperfect occurs only in the indicative mood and is used only 86 times in the NT (not including pluperfect periphrastic constructions which consist of the imperfect form of εἰμί + perfect participle). While the pluperfect is not a common tense form, where it does occur it is fairly easy to recognize due to the fact that the form includes: (1) an augment;[64] (2) reduplication; and (3) a distinct variable vowel diphthong (e.g., ἐλελύκειμεν).

Intensive Pluperfect[65]

Like the intensive perfect, the emphasis of the intensive pluperfect is on the results brought about by a past action. With the pluperfect, however, both action *and* the results are in the past. "The focus here is upon a *state* which existed in the past, with implications of a prior occurrence which produced it."[66] This use is different from the aorist because the aorist does not give information about the resulting state of a past action. It is usually best to translate this use as a simple past tense.[67] These verbs are usually found in historical narratives.

- εἰ δὲ **ἐγνώκειτε** τί ἐστιν (Matt 12:7)

  If **you had known** what this means

- ἤγαγον αὐτὸν ἕως ὀφρύος τοῦ ὄρους ἐφ᾽ οὗ ἡ πόλις **ᾠκοδόμητο** αὐτῶν (Luke 4:29)

  They . . . brought him to the edge of the hill that their town **was built** on

- ἤρχοντο πέραν τῆς θαλάσσης εἰς Καφαρναούμ. καὶ σκοτία ἤδη **ἐγεγόνει** καὶ οὔπω ἐληλύθει πρὸς αὐτοὺς ὁ Ἰησοῦς (John 6:17)

  [They] started across the sea to Capernaum. **It was** now dark, and Jesus had not yet come to them (ESV).

  > The first pluperfect is intensive because it focuses on the resulting state but the second (ἐληλύθει) is consummative because it focuses on the action.

---

[63] "The perfect looks back on the past from a standpoint of the present; the pluperfect looks back on the past from the standpoint of the past" (Brooks & Winbery, 108).

[64] The augment is found on most, but not all, forms.

[65] Fanning labels this category as the "Pluperfect of resulting state."

[66] Fanning, 306.

[67] "Here stress is laid upon the reality of the fact, which enables it to be presented with more force than could be done with the aorist, but the only device for construing it in English is the simple past" (Dana & Mantey, 205–6).

Aorist, Perfect & Pluperfect Indicatives //////////////// 307

- ἐξῆλθεν ὁ τεθνηκὼς . . . ἡ ὄψις αὐτοῦ σουδαρίῳ **περιεδέδετο** (John 11:44)

  The dead man came out . . . with his face **wrapped** in a cloth

- παρέθεντο αὐτοὺς τῷ κυρίῳ εἰς ὃν **πεπιστεύκεισαν** (Acts 14:23)

  they committed them to the Lord in whom **they had believed**[68]

Consummative Pluperfect[69]

This use of the pluperfect emphasizes the completion of a past action rather than the results brought about by that action (= intensive pluperfect). It is usually best to translate the consummative pluperfect with an English past perfect ("have/had" + verb). The Fourth Gospel often employs this use of the pluperfect, and it usually occurs with active transitive verbs.

- **δεδώκει** δὲ ὁ παραδιδοὺς αὐτὸν σύσσημον αὐτοῖς (Mark 14:44)

  His betrayer **had given** them a signal

- οἱ μαθηταὶ αὐτοῦ **ἀπεληλύθεισαν** εἰς τὴν πόλιν (John 4:8)

  His disciples **had gone** into town

- ἤδη γὰρ **συνετέθειντο** οἱ Ἰουδαῖοι (John 9:22)

  since the Jews **had** already **agreed**

- ἰδοὺ ἀνὴρ Αἰθίοψ εὐνοῦχος . . . ὃς **ἐληλύθει** προσκυνήσων εἰς Ἰερουσαλήμ (Acts 8:27)

  There was an Ethiopian man, a eunuch . . . [who] **had come** to worship in Jerusalem[70]

- ὀδυνώμενοι μάλιστα ἐπὶ τῷ λόγῳ ᾧ **εἰρήκει** (Acts 20:38)

  being sorrowful most of all because of the word **he had spoken** (ESV)

---

[68] For more examples of the intensive pluperfect, see Matt 12:7 (ἐγνώκειτε); Mark 10:1 (εἰώθει); Luke 4:41 (ᾔδεισαν); Acts 14:23 (πεπιστεύκεισαν). For periphrastic pluperfects, see Matt 9:36 (ἦσαν ἐσκυλμένοι); Luke 4:17 (ἦν γεγραμμένον), 15:24 (ἦν ἀπολωλώς); Acts 14:26 (ἦσαν παραδεδομένοι); Gal 4:3 (ἤμεθα δεδουλωμένοι).

[69] Some grammars label this category the "Extensive Pluperfect" (Robertson and Wallace) or the "Pluperfect of completed action" (Fanning).

[70] For more examples of the consummative perfect, see Luke 8:2 (ἐξεληλύθει); 22:13 (εἰρήκει); John 6:17 (ἐγεγόνει, ἐληλύθει); 11:13 (εἰρήκει); Acts 4:22 (γεγόνει); 9:21 (ἐληλύθει); 19:32 (συνεληλύθεισαν). For periphrastic pluperfects, see Mark 15:46 (ἦν λελατομημένον); Luke 8:2 (ἦσαν τεθεραπευμέναι); John 1:24 (ἀπεσταλμένοι ἦσαν).

Past State Pluperfect

This category applies to certain verbs that convey a past state with no antecedent action. This type of usage is found with verbs that are stative in nature with no implication of a previous act that produced the state. Verbs in this category are οἶδα, ἵστημι, εἴωθα, πείθω, and παρίστημι. Because of the frequent use of the pluperfect form of οἶδα (occurring 33 times), this is the most common pluperfect category.[71]

- οἱ ἀδελφοὶ αὐτοῦ **εἰστήκεισαν** ἔξω (Matt 12:46)

  His mother and brothers **were standing** outside

- κατὰ δὲ ἑορτὴν **εἰώθει** ὁ ἡγεμὼν ἀπολύειν ἕνα τῷ ὄχλῳ δέσμιον (Matt 27:15)

  Now at the feast the governor **was accustomed** to release for the crowd any one prisoner (ESV)

- οὐκ ἤφιεν λαλεῖν τὰ δαιμόνια, ὅτι **ᾔδεισαν** αὐτόν (Mark 1:34)

  He would not permit the demons to speak, because **they knew** him

- τὴν πανοπλίαν αὐτοῦ αἴρει ἐφ᾽ ᾗ **ἐπεποίθει** (Luke 11:22)

  he takes from him all his weapons **he trusted in**

- ἄνδρες δύο **παρειστήκεισαν** αὐτοῖς (Acts 1:10)

  two men . . . **stood** by them[72]

SUMMARY

AORIST INDICATIVE		
Constative	An action is portrayed in its entirety without regard to its beginning or end, or the length of time it took to accomplish the action.	ἐβασίλευσεν ὁ θάνατος ἀπὸ Ἀδὰμ μέχρι Μωϋσέως ("Death **reigned** from Adam to Moses"; Rom 5:4 ESV).
Inceptive	Emphasizes the beginning of an action or a state.	ἐπτώχευσεν πλούσιος ὤν ("Though He was rich . . . **he became poor**"; 2 Cor 8:9).

---

[71] The occurrence of the other verbs are as follows: ἵστημι occurs 14 times; εἴωθα occurs 2 times; πείθω occurs 1 time; and παρίστημι occurs 1 time.

[72] For more examples of the past state perfect of (1) ἵστημι, see Matt 13:2; Luke 23:10, 35, 49; John 1:35; 7:37; 18:5, 16, 18; 19:25; 20:11; Acts 9:7; Rev 7:11; (2) εἴωθα, see Mark 10:1. For periphrastic pluperfects, see Luke 5:1 (ἦν ἑστώς); Acts 16:9 (ἦν ἑστώς).

AORIST INDICATIVE		
Culminative	Emphasizes the cessation of an action or state.	ἐγὼ γὰρ **ἔμαθον** . . . αὐτάρκης εἶναι ("For I **have learned** to be content"; Phil 4:11).
Gnomic	A statement that is timeless, universal, or generally true.	ἐδικαιώθη ἡ σοφία ἀπὸ πάντων τῶν τέκνων αὐτῆς ("Wisdom **is vindicated** by all her children"; Luke 7:35).
Epistolary	The author writes from the perspective of the readers and thus uses the aorist instead of the expected present.	ἐγὼ Παῦλος **ἔγραψα** τῇ ἐμῇ χειρί ("I, Paul, **write** this with my own hand"; Phlm 19).
Futuristic	Describes an event that has not yet taken place as if it had already occurred.	**ἦλθεν** κύριος ἐν ἁγίαις μυριάσιν αὐτοῦ ("The Lord **comes** with tens of thousands of his holy ones"; Jude 14).
Dramatic	Refers to an event that recently occurred, having present consequences.	ἡ θυγάτηρ μου **ἄρτι ἐτελεύτησεν** ("My daughter has just **died**"; Matt 9:18 ESV).
PERFECT INDICATIVE		
Intensive	Emphasizes the present state of the verb brought about by a past action.	**ἀφέωνταί** σοι αἱ ἁμαρτίαι σου ("your sins **are forgiven** you"; Luke 5:20).
Consummative	Emphasizes the completed action that brought about the resulting state.	τὸν καλὸν ἀγῶνα **ἠγώνισμαι** ("I **have fought** the good fight"; 2 Tim 4:7).
Dramatic	Vividly portrays a past event or state of affairs.	ἀπελθὼν **πέπρακεν** πάντα ὅσα εἶχεν ("he went and **sold** everything he had"; Matt 13:46).
Present State	Used with certain verbs that lost their perfect significance and conveys a present tense-form meaning.	τὰς ἐντολὰς **οἶδας** ("**You know** the commandments"; Luke 18:20).
Gnomic	Communicates a customary or general truth.	ὁ δὲ μὴ πιστεύων ἤδη **κέκριται** ("but anyone who does not believe **is** already **condemned**"; John 3:18).
Iterative	The action of the verb occurred at intervals.	ὃ **ἑωράκαμεν** τοῖς ὀφθαλμοῖς ἡμῶν ("What **we have seen** with our eyes"; 1 John 1:1).
PLUPERFECT INDICATIVE		
Intensive	Emphasizes the (past) results brought about by a past action.	εἰς ὃν **πεπιστεύκεισαν** ("in whom **they had believed**"; Acts 14:23).
Consummative	Emphasizes the completion of a past action.	οἱ μαθηταὶ αὐτοῦ **ἀπεληλύθεισαν** εἰς τὴν πόλιν ("His disciples **had gone** into town"; John 4:8).
Past State	Used with certain verbs that convey a past state with no antecedent action.	ὅτι **ᾔδεισαν** αὐτόν ("because **they knew** him"; Mark 1:34).

PRACTICE EXERCISES

In each of the following examples, (1) parse each underlined verb and (2) determine the specific use of the verb based on its tense-form and context.

1. ἐὰν μή τις μένῃ ἐν ἐμοί, <u>ἐβλήθη</u> ἔξω . . . ἐν τούτῳ <u>ἐδοξάσθη</u> ὁ πατήρ μου (John 15:6, 8).

2. Ἰησοῦ Χριστοῦ . . . ὃν ὁ θεὸς ἤγειρεν ἐκ νεκρῶν, ἐν τούτῳ οὗτος <u>παρέστηκεν</u> ἐνώπιον ὑμῶν ὑγιής (Acts 4:10).

3. Τύχικος . . . ὃν <u>ἔπεμψα</u> πρὸς ὑμᾶς (Col 4:7–8).

4. θεὸν οὐδεὶς πώποτε <u>τεθέαται</u> (1 John 4:12).

5. καὶ <u>ἔζησαν</u> καὶ <u>ἐβασίλευσαν</u> μετὰ τοῦ Χριστοῦ χίλια ἔτη (Rev 20:4).

6. πολλοὶ ψευδοπροφῆται <u>ἐξεληλύθασιν</u> εἰς τὸν κόσμον (1 John 4:1).

7. Ἔτι αὐτοῦ λαλοῦντος τοῖς ὄχλοις ἰδοὺ ἡ μήτηρ καὶ οἱ ἀδελφοὶ αὐτοῦ <u>εἱστήκεισαν</u> ἔξω (Matt 12:46).

8. γυνὴ <u>δέδεται</u> ἐφ᾽ ὅσον χρόνον ζῇ ὁ ἀνὴρ αὐτῆς (1 Cor 7:39).

9. Μαρία ἡ καλουμένη Μαγδαληνή, ἀφ᾽ ἧς δαιμόνια ἑπτὰ <u>ἐξεληλύθει</u> (Luke 8:2).

10. ὁ λόγος σὰρξ <u>ἐγένετο</u> καὶ <u>ἐσκήνωσεν</u> ἐν ἡμῖν (John 1:14).

VOCABULARY

Vocabulary to Memorize

ἀδελφή, ἡ	sister (26)
ἀληθῶς	truly, really (18)
Ἀντιόχεια, ἡ	Antioch (18)
ἀποκάλυψις, -εως, ἡ	revelation (18)
ἀπώλεια, ἡ	destruction, ruin (18)
ἀριθμός, ὁ	number, total (18)
Ἀσία, ἡ	Asia (18)
βλασφημία, ἡ	blasphemy, slander (18)
δεσμός, ὁ	bond, chain, prison (18)
δῶρον, τό	gift, present, offering (19)
εἰσπορεύομαι	I go in, enter (18)
ἐπαίρω	I lift up (19)
ἐπάνω	above, over (19)
ἐπιβάλλω	I throw over, lay on, put on (18)
εὐχαριστέω	I give thanks, am thankful (38)
θυμός, ὁ	passion, anger, rage (18)
καταγγέλλω	I proclaim, make known (18)
κατακρίνω	I condemn, pass judgment on (18)
κενός	empty, vain (18)
κλαίω	I weep, cry (40)
κληρονομέω	I inherit, obtain (18)
κοιμάω	I (fall) asleep, die (18)
κρείττων	better (19)
κριτής, -οῦ, ὁ	judge (19)
κτίσις, -εως, ἡ	creation, creature (19)
κώμη, ἡ	village, small town (27)
Λάζαρος, ὁ	Lazarus (15)
μαρτύριον, τό	testimony, witness, proof (19)
μεριμνάω	I am anxious, worry (19)
μνημεῖον, τό	grave, tomb (40)
οὔπω	not yet (26)
παλαιός	old, former (19)
πάντοτε	always (41)
παράπτωμα, -ατος, τό	transgression, trespass, sin (19)
παρατίθημι	I place before (19)
πότε	when? (19)

προφητεία, ἡ	prophecy (19)
συνέρχομαι	I come/travel together, go with (30)
ταράσσω	I stir up, disturb, trouble (17)
φιλέω	I love, like, kiss (25)

Vocabulary to Recognize

ἄνω	up(wards) (9)
δακρύω	I weep (1)
δεῦρο	come out (9)
ἐμβριμάομαι	I am deeply moved (with anger), sternly warn (5)
ἐπίκειμαι	I lie on (7)
θνήσκω	I die (9)
κειρία, ἡ	binding material, wrappings (1)
κραυγάζω	I cry out (9)
Μάρθα, ἡ	Martha (13)
ὄζω	I smell, give off an odor (1)
ὄψις, -εως, ἡ	face, countenance (3)
περιδέω	I bind, wrap around (1)
περιΐστημι	I stand around (4)
σουδάριον, τό	face cloth (4)
σπήλαιον, τό	cave, den (6)
τελευτάω	I die (11)
τεταρταῖος	happening on the fourth day (1)
ὑπαντάω	I meet (10)

READING THE NEW TESTAMENT

John 11:30–44

³⁰ οὔπω δὲ ἐληλύθει ὁ Ἰησοῦς εἰς τὴν κώμην, ἀλλ᾽ ἦν ἔτι ἐν τῷ τόπῳ ὅπου ὑπήντησεν αὐτῷ ἡ Μάρθα. . . . ³² ἡ οὖν Μαριὰμ ὡς ἦλθεν ὅπου ἦν Ἰησοῦς ἰδοῦσα αὐτὸν ἔπεσεν αὐτοῦ πρὸς τοὺς πόδας λέγουσα αὐτῷ, Κύριε, εἰ ἧς ὧδε οὐκ ἄν μου ἀπέθανεν ὁ ἀδελφός. ³³ Ἰησοῦς οὖν ὡς εἶδεν αὐτὴν κλαίουσαν καὶ τοὺς συνελθόντας αὐτῇ Ἰουδαίους κλαίοντας, ἐνεβριμήσατο τῷ πνεύματι καὶ ἐτάραξεν ἑαυτὸν ³⁴ καὶ εἶπεν, Ποῦ τεθείκατε αὐτόν; λέγουσιν αὐτῷ, Κύριε, ἔρχου καὶ ἴδε. ³⁵ ἐδάκρυσεν ὁ Ἰησοῦς. ³⁶ ἔλεγον οὖν οἱ Ἰουδαῖοι, Ἴδε πῶς ἐφίλει αὐτόν. ³⁷ τινὲς δὲ ἐξ αὐτῶν εἶπαν, Οὐκ ἐδύνατο οὗτος ὁ ἀνοίξας τοὺς ὀφθαλμοὺς τοῦ τυφλοῦ ποιῆσαι ἵνα καὶ οὗτος μὴ ἀποθάνῃ; ³⁸ Ἰησοῦς οὖν πάλιν ἐμβριμώμενος ἐν ἑαυτῷ ἔρχεται εἰς τὸ μνημεῖον· ἦν δὲ σπήλαιον καὶ λίθος ἐπέκειτο ἐπ᾽ αὐτῷ. ³⁹ λέγει ὁ Ἰησοῦς, Ἄρατε τὸν λίθον. λέγει αὐτῷ ἡ ἀδελφὴ τοῦ τετελευτηκότος Μάρθα, Κύριε, ἤδη ὄζει, τεταρταῖος γάρ ἐστιν. ⁴⁰ λέγει αὐτῇ ὁ Ἰησοῦς, Οὐκ εἶπόν σοι ὅτι ἐὰν πιστεύσῃς ὄψῃ τὴν δόξαν τοῦ θεοῦ; ⁴¹ ἦραν οὖν τὸν λίθον. ὁ δὲ Ἰησοῦς ἦρεν τοὺς ὀφθαλμοὺς ἄνω καὶ εἶπεν, Πάτερ, εὐχαριστῶ σοι ὅτι ἤκουσάς μου. ⁴² ἐγὼ δὲ ᾔδειν ὅτι πάντοτέ μου ἀκούεις, ἀλλὰ διὰ τὸν ὄχλον τὸν περιεστῶτα εἶπον, ἵνα πιστεύσωσιν ὅτι σύ με ἀπέστειλας. ⁴³ καὶ ταῦτα εἰπὼν φωνῇ μεγάλῃ ἐκραύγασεν, Λάζαρε, δεῦρο ἔξω. ⁴⁴ ἐξῆλθεν ὁ τεθνηκὼς δεδεμένος τοὺς πόδας καὶ τὰς χεῖρας κειρίαις καὶ ἡ ὄψις αὐτοῦ σουδαρίῳ περιεδέδετο. λέγει αὐτοῖς ὁ Ἰησοῦς, Λύσατε αὐτὸν καὶ ἄφετε αὐτὸν ὑπάγειν.

Reading Notes[73]

Verse 30

- **οὔπω δὲ ἐληλύθει ὁ Ἰησοῦς εἰς τὴν κώμην** ("Jesus had stayed outside the village") – Literally, "But Jesus had not yet come into the village." ἐληλύθει (pluper act ind 3rd sg of ἔρχομαι) is an example of the consummative use of the pluperfect which emphasizes the completion of a past action. In this case, however, the action was not yet performed.

- **ὑπήντησεν** ("met") – Aor act ind 3rd sg ὑπαντάω. Although this verb is aorist, many translations, including the ESV, CSB, and the NIV render it as a pluperfect ("had met") because the action of the verb took place before the time of the storyline. Robertson explains, "The aorist sometimes occurs where the context 'implies completion before the main action,' where in English we prefer the past perfect."[74]

---

[73] The English version used in the Reading Notes for this chapter is the NLT.
[74] Robertson, 840.

- **αὐτῷ** ("him") – This dative singular third person personal pronoun functions as the direct object of the verb ὑπήντάω. Normally, the direct object of a verb is found in the accusative case, but some verbs prefer their direct objects in the dative case (e.g., ἀκολουθέω, ἀποκρίνομαι, πιστεύω, προσκυνέω, and ὑποτάσσω).

- **ἡ Μάρθα** ("Martha") – Often the article is included with proper nouns in Greek. In this case, it is not necessary to translate the article because personal names are already definite. See also v. 32 (ἡ Μαριάμ) and v. 39 (ὁ Ἰησοῦς).

Verse 32

- **ἰδοῦσα** ("saw") – Aor act ptc fem nom sg βλέπω/ὁράω. This is most likely a temporal adverbial participle ("when she saw him").

- **ἔπεσεν** ("fell") – Aor act ind 3rd sg πίπτω.

- **λέγουσα** ("said") – Pres act ptc fem nom sg λέγω.

- **Κύριε** ("Lord") – Masc voc sg κύριος. Remember that the vocative is used for direct address. See also the same term in vv. 34, 39 and Λάζαρε ("Lazarus") in v. 43.

- **εἰ ἦς ὧδε** ("if only you had been here") – εἰ here introduces a second class conditional statement (an assumption contrary to fact for the sake of argument).

- **οὐκ ἄν μου ἀπέθανεν ὁ ἀδελφός** ("my brother would not have died") – This phrase forms the apodosis (i.e., the "then" statement) which for a second class (contrary to fact) conditional sentence usually includes ἄν plus a past tense (aorist or imperfect) in the indicative mood. ἀπέθανεν (aor act ind 3rd sg of ἀποθνήσκω) is a second aorist verb, which means that it follows the imperfect endings but there has been a spelling change of the stem.

Verse 33

- **εἶδεν** ("saw") – Aor act ind 3rd sg βλέπω/ὁράω.

- **κλαίουσαν** ("weeping") – Pres act ptc fem acc sg κλαίω. This is a temporal adverbial participle that conveys the action in the imperfective aspect as ongoing. The same use is found with the following participle κλαίοντας (pres act ptc masc acc pl κλαίω).

- **τοὺς συνελθόντας αὐτῇ Ἰουδαίους κλαίοντας** ("the other people wailing with her") – Literally, "the Jews who had come together with her also weeping." συνελθόντας (aor act ptc masc acc pl συνέρχόμαι) is an attributive participle that modifies τοὺς . . . Ἰουδαίους ("the Jews"). αὐτῇ is a dative of association.

- ἐνεβριμήσατο τῷ πνεύματι ("a deep anger welled up within him") – ἐνεβριμήσατο (aor mid ind 3rd sg ἐμβριμάομαι) is translated in various ways: "he was deeply moved" (CSB, ESV, NASB, NIV), and "he was greatly disturbed" (NRSV). τῷ πνεύματι is a dative of sphere ("in his spirit").

- ἐτάραξεν ἑαυτὸν ("he was deeply troubled") – Aor act ind 3rd sg ταράσσω. The reflexive pronoun ἑαυτόν functions to intensify the meaning of the verb.

Verses 34–35

- εἶπεν ("he asked") – Aor act ind 3rd sg λέγω.

- τεθείκατε ("have you put") – Per act ind 2nd pl τίθημι. This is an example of the consummative use of the perfect (stative aspect) which emphasizes the completed action that brought about the resulting state.

- λέγουσιν ("told") – Pres act ind 3rd pl λέγω. The present tense-form is sometimes used (especially in historical narratives) to describe a past event which adds vividness to the event, drawing the reader into the story, or highlights something in the story (= historical use of the present). See also λέγει in vv. 39 (2x), 40, and 44 and ἔρχεται in v. 38.

- ἔρχου καὶ ἴδε ("come and see") – Pres mid impv 2nd sg ἔρχομαι and aor act impv 2nd sg βλέπω/ὁράω (see also v. 36). It should be noted that these two imperatives are in different tense-forms. Based on the context, one would expect the aorist form since the command given is for a specific occasion and not a general practice. Verbs of motion (such as ἔρχομαι), however, prefer the present tense-form regardless of the type of command given. Fanning concludes, "Thus, ἔρχομαι in NT usage departs from the general/specific rule in a way similar to other verbs of motion."[75] Also note that this is a conditional imperative (meaning, "If you come, you will see") and based on the context, these imperatives are not commands but polite requests.

- ἐδάκρυσεν ("wept") – Aor act ind 3rd sg δακρύω. This is probably an example of an inceptive aorist, "Jesus began to weep" (so NRSV).[76] Verse 35 (ἐδάκρυσεν ὁ Ἰησοῦς) is the shortest verse in the NT.

---

[75] Fanning, 345.
[76] Cf. Andreas J. Köstenberger, who translates: "Jesus burst into tears." *John*, BECT (Grand Rapids: Baker, 2004), 341.

Verse 36

- ἔλεγον ("said") – Impf act ind 3rd pl λέγω. This is possibly an inceptive use of the imperfect, "they began saying."

- οἱ Ἰουδαῖοι ("The people who were standing nearby") – Literally, "the Jews."

- ἐφίλει ("loved") – Impf act ind 3rd sg φιλέω. This is an iterative use of the imperfect that here refers to a customary or habitual action.

Verse 37

- τινὲς ἐξ αὐτῶν ("some") – Literally, "some of them." αὐτῶν is a partitive genitive in combination with the preposition ἐκ.

- εἶπαν ("said") – Aor act ind 3rd pl λέγω. The regular 2nd aorist form is εἶπον. The alpha (εἶπαν) has replaced the omicron (εἶπον), assimilating to the first aorist form (i.e., ἔλυσαν).

- ἐδύνατο . . . ποιῆσαι (Literally, "able . . . to make") – The verb ἐδύνατο (impf mid ind 3rd sg δύναμαι) is a verb that usually takes a complementary infinitive such as ποιῆσαι (aor act inf ποιέω).

- ὁ ἀνοίξας τοὺς ὀφθαλμοὺς τοῦ τυφλοῦ ("healed a blind man") – Literally, "the one who opened the eyes of the blind." ὁ ἀνοίξας (aor act ptc masc nom sg ἀνοίγω) is an attributive participle modifying οὗτος ("this man") in the perfective aspect, viewing the action wholistically.

- οὗτος ("Lazarus") – The first use of the near demonstrative pronoun οὗτος in this verse is translated as "this man," referring to Jesus. This second use, however, refers to Lazarus as the editors of the NLT indicate in their translation.

- ἀποθάνῃ ("dying") – Aor act sub 3rd sg ἀποθνήσκω. The subjunctive mood was triggered by the use of ἵνα which is used to introduce a result clause.

Verse 38

- ἐμβριμώμενος ("angry") – Pres mid ptc masc nom sg ἐμβριμάομαι. This is probably a causal adverbial participle and could be translated "because he was angry."

- ἔρχεται ("he arrived") – Pres mid ind 3rd sg ἔρχομαι (historical present).

- ἐπέκειτο ("rolled across") – Impf mid ind 3rd sg ἐπίκειμαι. Literally, "was lying."

Verse 39

- Ἄρατε τὸν λίθον ("Roll the stone aside") – Literally, "Take away the stone." Because ἄρατε (aor act impv 2nd pl αἴρω) is a liquid verb (i.e., a verb whose stem ends with λ, μ, ν, or ρ), the sigma is dropped (not αἴρσατε) and to compensate for the missing sigma, the iota is also dropped. The aorist form is expected, since it is a telic verb and the command given is for a specific occasion and not for a general practice.

- τοῦ τετελευτηκότος ("dead man's") – Per act ptc masc gen sg τελευτάω. This is a substantival participle, meaning that the participle functions like a noun.

- ἤδη ὄζει ("The smell will be terrible") – Literally, "he already stinks." ὄζει (pres act ind 3rd sg ὄζω) is a NT *hapax legomenon*.

Verse 40

- Οὐκ ("Didn't") – The indicative negative particle indicates the expectation of a positive response to the question. Thus, the question could be translated, "I told you that if you believed you would see the glory of God, didn't I?"

- ἐὰν πιστεύσῃς ("if you believe") – Aor act sub 2nd sg πιστεύω. The subjunctive mood is triggered by the use of the indefinite conjunction ἐάν which introduces a third class conditional statement (uncertain of fulfillment but still likely).

- ὄψῃ ("you would see") – Fut mid ind 2nd sg ὁράω. This is the apodosis of the earlier protasis ("if you believed"). The NLT reverses the order found in the Greek text.

Verse 41

- ἦραν ("they rolled . . . aside") – Aor act ind 3rd pl αἴρω ("take up, remove"). A different form (ἦρεν, aor act ind 3rd sg αἴρω) of the same verb is used later in this verse in conjunction with the adverb ἄνω and is translated "looked up."

- ὁ δὲ Ἰησοῦς ἦρεν τοὺς ὀφθαλμοὺς ἄνω ("Then Jesus looked up to heaven") – Literally, "Then Jesus lifted up his eyes" The definite article (τούς) is used as a personal pronoun ("his") in some translations.

- Πάτερ ("Father") – Masc voc sg πατήρ.

- εὐχαριστῶ σοι ("[I] thank you") – Pres act ind 1st sg εὐχαριστέω. This is an example of the instantaneous (or performative) use of the present tense-form which involves an action that is done, not progressively, but instantaneously. In this case, the verb accomplishes or performs an action by the very fact that it is spoken. This verb also takes its direct object in the dative case (i.e., σοι) instead of the normal accusative case.

- ὅτι ἤκουσάς μου ("for hearing me") – Literally, "because you heard me." ἤκουσάς (aor act ind 2nd sg ἀκούω) is a dramatic use of the aorist tense-form (perfective aspect) which is used to refer to an event that recently occurred and thus has present consequences. ἀκούω frequently takes its direct object in the genitive case (i.e., μου) (see also v. 42).[77]

Verse 42

- ἐγὼ δὲ ᾔδειν ὅτι πάντοτέ μου ἀκούεις ("You always hear me") – Literally, "I know that you always hear me." Although many resources parse ᾔδειν as a pluperfect, it is probably better to parse it as an aorist (aor act ind 1st sg οἶδα). The reason for this confusion is one related to form versus function. That is, the form was originally pluperfect but it later took on an aorist meaning (= past state use of the pluperfect). Because ἐγὼ ("I") is not needed, its inclusion most likely signifies emphasis. This phrase ("I know") is left untranslated in the NLT.

- τὸν περιεστῶτα ("standing here") – Per act ptc masc acc sg περιΐστημι. This is an attributive participle that modifies τὸν ὄχλον ("these people," literally, "the crowd").

- πιστεύσωσιν ("will believe") – Aor act sub 3rd pl πιστεύω.

- σύ . . . ἀπέστειλας ("You sent") – Aor act ind 2nd sg ἀποστέλλω. Remember that when a verb begins with a prepositional prefix, such as ἀπό (ἀποστέλλω), the augment occurs after the prepositional prefix (ἀπέστειλας). In addition, because this verb is a liquid verb, the sigma is dropped (not ἀπέστειλσας) and to compensate for the missing sigma, the first lambda is changed to an iota (ἀπέστειλας). Because σύ ("You") is not needed, its inclusion most likely signifies emphasis.

Verse 43

- καὶ ταῦτα εἰπών ("[and after saying these things]") – εἰπών (aor act ptc masc nom sg λέγω) is a temporal adverbial participle that conveys the action in the perfective aspect as complete, and in this context as taking place prior to the action of the main verb ("after He said this, [then] He shouted . . ."). Interestingly, the NLT drops this phrase.

---

[77] About half of the time ἀκούω takes its direct object in the accusative case.

- **φωνῇ μεγάλῃ** ("[with a loud voice]") – This is a dative of means indicating the means by which Jesus shouted. This phrase is left untranslated in the NLT.

- **ἐκραύγασεν** ("shouted") – Aor act ind 3rd sg κραυγάζω.

- **δεῦρο** ("come out") – Technically, δεῦρο is an adverb, but it functions here like an imperative.

Verse 44

- **ὁ τεθνηκώς** ("the dead man") – Per act ptc masc nom sg τελευτάω. This perfect participle conveys a stative aspect, denoting the result of a preceding action (i.e., dying). This is also a substantival participle meaning that the participle functions like a noun.

- **δεδεμένος** ("bound") – Per pass ptc masc nom sg δέομαι. This is an adverbial participle that indicates Lazarus's condition (stative aspect) while he walked.

- **τοὺς πόδας καὶ τὰς χεῖρας** ("his hands and feet") – This is an accusative of respect (or reference) which indicates how Lazarus was bound. Notice that nearly all English translations reverse the order (Literally, "feet and hands").

- **κειρίαις** ("with graveclothes") – Literally, "with linen strips." This is a dative of means indicating the means by which Lazarus was bound.

- **σουδαρίῳ** ("in a headcloth") – This is a dative of means indicating the means by which Lazarus's face was wrapped.

- **περιεδέδετο** ("wrapped") – Pluper pass ind 3rd sg περιδέω. This is the intensive use of the pluperfect which emphasizes the results brought about by a past action (past stative aspect) and is usually translated as a simple past tense.

- **Λύσατε . . . ἄφετε** ("Upwrap . . . let") – Aor act impv 2nd pl λύω and ἀφίημι, respectively. The aorist form is expected because of the lexical nature of the verbs (= telic) and that the command given is for a specific occasion and not for a general practice.

- **ὑπάγειν** ("go") – Pres act inf ὑπάγω. This most likely functions as an infinitive of purpose.

//////////////

CHAPTER 10

PARTICIPLES

GOING DEEPER

Virtually every student in beginning Greek is warned about the difficulty of participles. This difficulty arises from at least three factors. (1) Participles are verbal adjectives. This means that they are part verb and also part adjective. Consequently, they not only have a tense, voice, and can take an object, but also have gender, case, and number. (2) Participles can have a variety of functions in a sentence. They can serve as nouns, adjectives, adverbs, or verbs. (3) Participles usually take more than one word to translate. With a noun, for example, often a one-to-one correspondence between Greek and English can be made (ἄγγελος = angel). With a participle, however, up to six words might be needed (ὁ τεχθείς = "the one who has been born"). But the payoff for properly understanding participles is well worth the effort, especially since there are 6,658 participles in the NT.[1]

As will be discussed below, participles function in a variety of ways, modifying both nouns and verbs. When a participle functions adverbially (i.e., modifying a verb), it is grammatically subordinate or dependent on the main verb of the sentence or clause. Typically, the main verb will be in the indicative, imperative, or subjunctive mood. Adverbial participles often indicate the means, manner, or results of the action of the main verb. This usage can be seen in Eph 5:18–21. In this passage Paul exhorts the Ephesian Christians,

---

[1] There are 4,614 in the nominative case (69%), 738 in the genitive case (11%), 354 in the dative case (5%), 946 in the accusative case (14%), and 6 in the vocative case (<1%). Regarding the tense-forms used, there are 3,688 in the present tense (55%), 12 in the future tense (<1%), 2,285 in the aorist tense (34%), and 673 in the perfect tense (10%).

And <u>don't get drunk</u> with wine, which *leads to* reckless living, but <u>be filled</u> by the Spirit: **speaking** to one another in psalms, hymns, and spiritual songs, **singing** and **making music** with your heart to the Lord, **giving thanks** always for everything to God the Father in the name of our Lord Jesus Christ, **submitting** to one another in the fear of Christ.

καὶ <u>μὴ μεθύσκεσθε</u> οἴνῳ, ἐν ᾧ ἐστιν ἀσωτία, ἀλλὰ <u>πληροῦσθε</u> ἐν πνεύματι, **λαλοῦντες** ἑαυτοῖς [ἐν] ψαλμοῖς καὶ ὕμνοις καὶ ᾠδαῖς πνευματικαῖς, **ᾄδοντες** καὶ **ψάλλοντες** τῇ καρδίᾳ ὑμῶν τῷ κυρίῳ, **εὐχαριστοῦντες** πάντοτε ὑπὲρ πάντων ἐν ὀνόματι τοῦ κυρίου ἡμῶν Ἰησοῦ Χριστοῦ τῷ θεῷ καὶ πατρί.[2] **ὑποτασσόμενοι** ἀλλήλοις ἐν φόβῳ Χριστοῦ.

The underlined words "don't get drunk" (μὴ μεθύσκεσθε) and "be filled" (πληροῦσθε) are imperatives and are the main verbs of the passage. The bold-type words "speaking" (λαλοῦντες), "singing" (ᾄδοντες), "making music" (ψάλλοντες), "giving thanks" (εὐχαριστοῦντες), and "submitting" (ὑποτασσόμενοι) are all participles and indicate the results of someone who is filled with the Spirit. The CSB rightly and helpfully translates each of the participles as dependent on the main verb, which is indicated by using one sentence.

Unfortunately, the NIV translates some of the participles as main verbs:

<u>Do not get drunk</u> on wine, which leads to debauchery. Instead, <u>be filled</u> with the Spirit, **speaking** to one another with psalms, hymns, and songs from the Spirit. <u>Sing</u> and **make music** from your heart to the Lord, always **giving thanks** to God the Father for everything, in the name of our Lord Jesus Christ. **Submit** to one another out of reverence for Christ.

Note that two of the verbs are translated as dependent verbs (i.e., "speaking" and "giving thanks") whereas three are translated as independent verbs or imperatives (i.e., "sing," "make music," and "submit"). Even more surprising is the decision of the editors of the NIV to make a paragraph break before verse 21. O'Brien rightly notes,

Although the point is often missed in the English translations, verses 18–21 form one long sentence, with five participles modifying the imperative "be filled with the Spirit". . . . Although these participles have been understood as imperatival (particularly the last one, "submit [yourselves to one another]," v. 21), it is better to regard them as dependent participles of result which describe the overflow or outworking of the Spirit's filling believers. Spirit-filled Christians are people whose lives are characterized by singing, thanksgiving, and mutual submission.[3]

---

[2] Unfortunately, the UBS[5] and NA[28] add a period here.

[3] Peter T. O'Brien, *The Letter to the Ephesians*, PNTC (Grand Rapids: Eerdmans; Leicester: Apollos, 1999), 386–88. Though this commentary is no longer in print, we acknowledge the helpful insight here.

Similarly, Wallace comments,

> Result participles are invariably present participles that follow the main verb; as well, the idea of result here would suggest that the way in which one measures his/her success in fulfilling the command of 5:18 is by the participles that follow (notice the progressive difficulty: from speaking God's word to being thankful for all, to being submissive to one another; such progression would, of course, immediately suggest that this filling is not instantaneous and absolute but progressive and relative).[4]

CHAPTER OBJECTIVES

The purpose of this chapter is to provide a basic overview of participles. Participles can be broken down into two main categories: (1) adjectival, and (2) adverbial. Adjectival participles can further be divided into attributive participles (which modify an expressed noun) and substantival participles (which function in the place of an unexpressed noun). Adverbial participles, as the name implies (ad-verbial), relate to the main verb or main action of the sentence.

VERBAL QUALITIES OF PARTICIPLES

Aspect

In chapter 7, we have learned that Greek is aspect-prominent and that Greek has three aspects: imperfective, perfective, and stative. In the indicative, time is indicated by the tense-form as well by the presence or absence of the augment. However, the augment is absent in the non-indicative moods, including participles. At the same time, aspect continues to be conveyed by the various tense-forms essentially in the same way as in the indicative. That is, aorist participles portray an action wholistically (perfective aspect); present participles depict an action progressively (imperfective aspect); and stative participles present a state resulting from a preceding action (stative aspect).

What this means is that students, when encountering a given participial form in the text, should first of all ask the question, which aspect is used: perfective (aorist tense-form), imperfective (present tense-form), or stative (perfect tense-form)? Once the aspect is determined, the next question should be, how is the action portrayed? The answer will be, depending on the tense-form, wholistically, that is, as simply occurring (aorist participle), as ongoing or occurring continuously (present participle), or as the result of a preceding action (perfect participle).

---

[4] Wallace, 639.

Paul's lengthy introduction to the book of Ephesians may serve to illustrate the aspectual nature of participles. The majority of participles in Eph 1:3–14 are in the perfect aspect (aorist tense-form): ὁ εὐλογήσας, προορίσας, γνωρίσας, προορισθέντες, ἀκούσαντες, and πιστεύσαντες. All of these actions are portrayed as simply having occurred. The context indicates that these actions took place in the past, but past time is indicated not by the aorist tense-form (note that there is no augment affixed to participles) but by the discourse context. God's work is depicted as ongoing in the imperfect aspect (present participle, τοῦ ἐνεργοῦντος), while the stative aspect is used with two participles, τῷ ἠγαπημένῳ and τοὺς προηλπικότας, presenting the state resulting from preceding actions.

Time

There are three major theories as to how time works in participles. The traditional view is that participles convey relative time, that is, the time of action in relation to the time conveyed by the main verb.[5] Specifically, aorist participles communicate antecedent action, present participles communicate contemporaneous action, and perfect participles communicate a state resulting from preceding action. In keeping with this theory, students see an aorist participle and think "antecedent action"; see a present participle and think "contemporaneous action"; and see a perfect participle and think "state resulting from preceding action." However, the problem with this theory is: (1) that it does not sufficiently recognize the role of aspect in participles (see the discussion above); (2) while accounting for 80–90 percent of participial forms, it does not account for the remaining 10–20 percent; and (3) it insufficiently takes account of the fact that the augment, which indicates time in the indicative, is missing in the non-indicative moods (including participles).

The second theory holds that word order is often determinative in explaining the function of Greek participles. Porter has put forth the theory that the tense of the participle does not communicate (relative) time, but that time is indicated by the order of the participle. That is, antecedent time is communicated by placing the participle (whether aorist or present) before the main verb and contemporaneous time is communicated by placing the participle (whether present or aorist) after the main verb. He explains: "If a participle occurs before the finite verb on which it depends (or another verb which forms the governing or head term of the construction), the participle tends to refer to antecedent (preceding) action. If a participle occurs after the finite (or other) verb on which it depends, it tends to refer to concurrent (simultaneous) or subsequent (following) action."[6] Although Porter does acknowledge that this is merely a trend ("tends to") and later states that it is "only a generalization," he nevertheless concludes that this theory "holds in a surprisingly large proportion of instances where temporal reference is at issue."[7]

---

[5] "In general, *time is absolute in the indicative, relative in the participle, and nonexistent in the other moods*" (Wallace, 498; emphasis original).

[6] Porter, *Idioms*, 188.

[7] Porter, *Idioms*, 188.

Robert Picirilli, however, applied this theory to the adverbial (circumstantial) participles found in the Gospel of Mark and Luke and concluded that "the positioning of circumstantial participles before or after their primary verbs does not point to a temporal relationship."[8]

Espousing the third theory as to how time works in participles, Picirilli maintains that participles never communicate time (even relative time) but that the time of the participle can only be determined by context. Nevertheless, his analysis of the adverbial participles in the Gospels of Mark and Luke demonstrates a fairly consistent pattern: about 80 percent of aorist adverbial participles precede the action of the main verb and about 90 percent of present adverbial participles are contemporaneous with the action of the main verb.

How do we adjudicate between these three views? What we do know is that aspect continues to be a factor in the non-indicative mood. Specifically, as mentioned in our discussion of aspect, the perfective aspect (aorist participle) conveys an action wholistically, the imperfective aspect (present participle) conveys an action progressively, and the stative aspect (perfect participle) conveys a state resulting from preceding action. Context comes into play in a number of ways as well. For example, if a series of actions is portrayed in which the first is a participle and subsequent verb forms are in the indicative, the action conveyed by an aorist participle is preceding not because it is in the aorist but because it is mentioned first in a series of actions. Type of action or lexical considerations may enter into the picture as well.

Conversely, the traditional understanding of participles, while accounting for the majority of NT uses of participles, insufficiently considers the role of aspect and does not adequately explain instances where aorist participles are not conveying antecedent action and where present participles are not conveying contemporaneous action. The notion that the aorist, present, or perfect tense-forms convey "relative time" with regard to the main verb must therefore be regarded as doubtful, especially since alternate explanations exist that adequately account for the presence of aorist or present tense-forms in given discourse contexts (see the example of Eph 1:3–14) above. For this reason the third, aspectual view is to be preferred.

---

[8] Robert E. Picirilli, "Time and Order in the Circumstantial Participles of Mark and Luke," *BBR* 17 (2007): 256. See also idem, "Order and Relative Time in the Participles of the Greek New Testament," *JETS* 57 (2014): 99–110.

ADJECTIVAL PARTICIPLES	Attributive	
	Substantival	
VERBAL PARTICIPLES	Adverbial	Temporal
		Means
		Manner
		Cause
		Condition
		Concession
		Purpose
		Result
	Other Verbal	Attendant Circumstance
		Genitive Absolute
		Imperatival
		Pleonastic
		Complementary
		Indirect Discourse
	Periphrastic	Present
		Imperfect
		Future
		Perfect
		Pluperfect
		Future Perfect

ADJECTIVAL PARTICIPLES

When functioning as an adjective, a participle can function attributively or substantively. An attributive participle modifies a noun (or other substantive) whereas a substantival participle functions as a noun itself. The key for identifying an adjectival participle (both adjectival and substantive) is the presence of an article in front of the participle—though there are exceptions as we will see below. The article is typically directly in front of the participle but may be separated from the participle if it is negated (ὁ μὴ ἀγαπῶν, "the one who does not love"), is found at the beginning of a sentence or phrase with a postpositive conjunction (ὁ δὲ ἀγαπῶν, "and the one who loves"), or is modified by other material (ὁ ἐμὲ ἀγαπῶν, "the one who loves me").

Attributive Participles

In this category, the participle functions as a typical adjective since it modifies an expressed noun (or other substantive). If there is no article, then most likely it is adverbial but it may be attributive. And just like an adjective, an attributive participle will agree with the noun it is modifying in gender, case, and number. An attributive participle should normally be translated with a relative clause (e.g., "the Father **who** sent Him," τὸν πατέρα τὸν **πέμψαντα** αὐτόν).[9]

- ὁ δὲ ἐχθρὸς ὁ **σπείρας** αὐτά (Matt 13:39)

  and the enemy **who sowed** them

- οἱ δὲ ὄχλοι οἱ **προάγοντες** αὐτόν (Matt 21:9)

  And the crowds **that went ahead of** him

- ὅμοιός ἐστιν ἀνθρώπῳ **οἰκοδομοῦντι** οἰκίαν (Luke 6:48)

  he is like a man **building** a house

  > Though the participle lacks the article, context identifies it as attributive.

- ὁ ἄρτος ὁ ἐκ τοῦ οὐρανοῦ **καταβαίνων** (John 6:50)

  the bread that **comes down** from heaven[10]

- τὸν **κοπιῶντα** γεωργόν (2 Tim 2:6)

  The **hardworking** farmer

  > Typically, when the participle precedes the noun, the article is not repeated (article-participle-noun).

Substantival Participles

In this category an adjectival participle does not function as an adjective (thus modifying a noun) but independently as a noun (or substantive) itself. These participles can function as subjects, direct objects, indirect objects, objects of prepositions, etc. The key for identifying a substantival participle is the presence of an article directly in front of the participle with no accompanying noun that the participle modifies—though like adjectival participles, subtantival participles may appear without an article (anarthorous). Substantival participles can be translated

---

[9] It is also possible for an adjectival participle to function as a predicate participle, although this usage is rare (occurring about 20 times) and sometimes difficult to distinguish with the anarthrous use of the attributive participle. Whereas the attributive participle usually has an article, the predicate participle never has it. One clear example is Heb 4:12, "the word of God is **living**" (ζῶν γὰρ ὁ λόγος τοῦ θεοῦ). Oftentimes this use is also confused with (or difficult to distinguish from) a periphrastic participle. For more examples, see Acts 7:56 (διηνοιγμένους); Rom 12:1 (ζῶσαν); Jas 2:15 (λειπόμενοι); Rev 1:18 (ζῶν).

[10] For more examples of attributive participles, see Matt 2:2 (ὁ **τεχθεὶς** βασιλεύς); 27:52 (τῶν **κεκοιμημένων** ἁγίων); 28:5 (Ἰησοῦν τὸν **ἐσταυρωμένον**); Luke 10:11 (τὸν κονιορτὸν τὸν **κολληθέντα**); John 6:22 (ὁ ὄχλος ὁ **ἑστηκώς**); 11:42 (διὰ τὸν ὄχλον τὸν **περιεστῶτα**); Rom 1:3 (τοῦ υἱοῦ αὐτοῦ τοῦ **γενομένου**); 3:25 (τῶν **προγεγονότων** ἁμαρτημάτων); 8:24 (ἐλπὶς δὲ **βλεπομένη**); Phil 4:7 (ἡ εἰρήνη τοῦ θεοῦ ἡ **ὑπερέχουσα**); Rev 15:1 (ἀγγέλους ἑπτὰ **ἔχοντας** πληγὰς ἑπτά).

"the one who," "he who," or "that which" plus the meaning of the participle translated as a finite verb (e.g., ὁ λέγων = "the one who says"). Sometimes it is best to translate such participles as mere nouns (e.g., ὁ σπείρων = "the sower" [instead of "the one who sows"]). In addition to aspect, one must also be sensitive to the context. This usage is very common.[11]

- προσεύχεσθε ὑπὲρ τῶν **διωκόντων** ὑμᾶς (Matt 5:44)

  pray for those **who persecute** you

  The participle functions as the object of a prepositional phrase.

- ὃν ἐπηγγείλατο τοῖς **ἀγαπῶσιν** αὐτόν (Jas 1:12)

  that God has promised to those **who love** him

  The participle functions as the indirect object of the verb ἐπηγγείλατο.

- πᾶς ὁ **μισῶν** τὸν ἀδελφὸν αὐτοῦ ἀνθρωποκτόνος ἐστίν (1 John 3:15)[12]

  Everyone who hates his brother or sister is a murderer[13]

- Καὶ εἶδον ἐπὶ τὴν δεξιὰν τοῦ **καθημένου** ἐπὶ τοῦ θρόνου (Rev 5:1)

  then I saw in the right hand of the **one seated** on the throne

  The participle functions in a genitive construction.

- ὁ **νικῶν** κληρονομήσει ταῦτα (Rev 21:7)

  The one **who conquers** will inherit these things

  The participle functions as the subject.

VERBAL PARTICIPLES[14]

Sometimes participles function more as verbs than as adjectives. The largest category is the adverbial participle but there are also several other uses of the participle that emphasize the verbal over the adjectival nature.

---

[11] Boyer maintains there are 1,467 substantival participles in the NT (James L. Boyer, "The Classification of Participles: A Statistical Study," *GTJ* 5 [1984]: 165n3).

[12] 1 John has 49 substantival participles out of a total of 58 participles.

[13] For more examples of substantival participles, see Matt 2:6 (τοῖς ἡγεμόσιν, ἡγούμενος); 5:22 (ὁ ὀργιζόμενος); 10:37 (ὁ φιλῶν); 23:37 (ἡ ἀποκτείνουσα); 26:46 (ὁ παραδιδούς); Luke 8:45 (ὁ ἁψάμενός); 11:10 (ὁ αἰτῶν, ὁ ζητῶν, τῷ κρούοντι); 12:33 (τὰ ὑπάρχοντα); John 5:23 (ὁ μὴ τιμῶν); 8:18 (ὁ μαρτυρῶν, ὁ πέμψας); Acts 2:41 (οἱ . . . ἀποδεξάμενοι); Rom 1:32 (οἱ . . . πράσσοντες); 2:1 (ὁ κρίνων); Eph 3:20 (τῷ . . . δυναμένῳ, τὴν ἐνεργουμένην); 6:24 (τῶν ἀγαπώντων); Jas 5:20 (ὁ ἐπιστρέψας); 1 John 2:26 (περὶ τῶν πλανώντων); Rev 1:3 (ὁ ἀναγινώσκων, οἱ ἀκούοντες, τηροῦντες).

[14] The order of adverbial participles followed by Dan Wallace (1996) and Richard Young (1994) seems the most logically and pedagogically useful and is closely paralleled by many Greek grammars over recent decades. We will be following that order.

Adverbial Participles

The adverbial participle is grammatically subordinate to or dependent on the main verb of the sentence or clause. Similar to an adverb, the participle modifies the main verb by answering questions such as "When?" (temporal), "Why?" (purpose or cause), or "How?" (manner or means). The key to recognizing adverbial participles is that they are never preceded by an article (predicate position) and often occur at the beginning of a sentence or clause. Perhaps the greatest difficulty with this type of participle is identifying its particular nuance. Below we will discuss eight different types of adverbial participles, and the only factors used to distinguish a particular use are the context and the lexical nature of the verb. In other words, there is nothing in the grammatical form that identifies the adverbial force, and so we must analyze the relationship between the participle, main verb, and the context.[15] When a particular nuance is identified, the participle is then usually translated as a finite verb. For example, the clause ἐγὼ ἐλθὼν θεραπεύσω αὐτόν (Matt 8:7) cannot be translated "I, coming, will heal him." Instead, the temporal participle ἐλθών is translated as a finite verb, "When I come, I will heal him" (author's translation). Also notice that the subject of the verb (ἐγώ) is also the subject of the participle. Thus, the ESV translates the phrase, "I will come and heal him."

Temporal

A temporal adverbial participle answers the question "When?" in relation to the main or controlling verb.[16] Based on its aspect, the participle can communicate the perfective (aorist participle), imperfective (present participle), or stative aspect (perfect participle).[17] Perfective participles depict a given action wholistically, that is, as simply having occurred; imperfect participles portray an action progressively, that is, as ongoing or customary; and stative participles depict a state resulting from a preceding action or event.

At times, participles appear first, followed by a series of imperatives or indicatives. In this case, they may convey antecedent action, not because they are in the

---

[15] "In itself, it must be distinctly noted, the participle does not express time, manner, cause, purpose, condition or concession. These ideas are not in the participle, but are merely suggested by the context, if at all, or occasionally by a particle" (Robertson, 1124). "The logical relation of the circumstantial participle to the rest of the sentence is not expressed by the participle itself . . . but is to be deduced from the context" (BDF, 215 [§417]). "The various ideas which may be expressed by the adverbial participle are not inherent in the participle itself but arise from its relationship to the main verb and even to the larger context" (Brooks & Winbery, 146). The context of a participle may clearly reflect the idea of time, manner, cause, purpose, condition or concession. Yet, at times the biblical interpreter is challenged by degrees of ambiguity when the context arguably supports more than one category for the participle.

[16] Wallace helpfully includes these various questions addressed by the different uses of the adverbial participle (When?, How?, Why?, etc.) which serves to further clarify how each use is functioning in a particular context (622-40).

[17] Fanning reminds us of the aspectual significance of the aorist participle: "The aorist participle does not in itself denote a time-value, but such a 'summary aspect,' since it takes in the whole occurrence including the end-point, most naturally yields a secondary sense of sequenced occurrence or occurrence antecedent to the verb to which it is related" (413).

aorist tense-form but because they are first in the series. Take Matthew's narrative of Jesus's flight from Egypt as an example: ἐγερθεὶς <u>παράλαβε</u> τὸ παιδίον καὶ τὴν μητέρα αὐτοῦ καὶ <u>πορεύου</u> (Matt 2:20; "**Get up**, <u>take</u> the child and his mother and <u>go</u>" [NIV]). In this instance, the aorist participle ἐγερθεὶς (translated as an imperative, "Get up," in the NIV) denotes a preceding action followed by two additional verb forms, the imperatives παράλαβε ("take") and πορεύου ("go"). The aorist participle, while conveying antecedent action, does so not because of relative time, or even context, but primarily because it portrays the action wholistically, that is, from a perfective aspect as simply having occurred. In this case, the participle has imperatival force. In the very next verse, recording Joseph's obedience to the angel's command, the participle is followed by two indicatives: ὁ δὲ **ἐγερθεὶς** <u>παρέλαβεν</u> τὸ παιδίον καὶ τὴν μητέρα αὐτοῦ καὶ <u>εἰσῆλθεν</u> (Matt 2:21; "So he **got up**, <u>took</u> the child and his mother and <u>went</u>" [NIV]).[18]

Perfective Aspect

- **νηστεύσας** . . . ὕστερον ἐπείνασεν (Matt 4:2)

  After he had fasted . . . he was hungry

- **ἰδὼν** ὁ Ἰησοῦς τὴν πίστιν αὐτῶν εἶπεν τῷ παραλυτικῷ (Matt 9:2)

  when Jesus **saw** their faith, he said to the paralytic (ESV)

- καθαρισμὸν τῶν ἁμαρτιῶν **ποιησάμενος** ἐκάθισεν (Heb 1:3)

  After making purification for sins, he sat down[19]

Imperfective Aspect

- **παράγων** εἶδεν ἄνθρωπον (John 9:1)

  As he **was passing by**, he saw a man

- καὶ **διερχόμενος** εὐηγγελίζετο τὰς πόλεις πάσας (Acts 8:40)

  as he passed through he preached the gospel to all the towns (ESV)

- ἐχθροὶ **ὄντες** κατηλλάγημεν τῷ θεῷ (Rom 5:10)

  while we **were** enemies, we were reconciled to God[20]

---

[18]   See further the discussion of attendant circumstance adverbial participles below.

[19]   For more examples of perfective aspect participles, see Matt 2:10 (ἰδόντες), 11 (ἐλθόντες); Mark 5:22 (ἰδών); Luke 10:33 (ἰδών); 11:33 (ἅψας); John 9:11(ἀπελθὼν . . . νιψάμενος); John 4:47 (ἀκούσας); Acts 11:26 (εὑρών); Eph 1:15 (ἀκούσας); 4:8 (ἀναβάς); Heb 11:23 (γεννηθείς); Rev 1:12 (ἐπιστρέψας).

[20]   For more examples of imperfective aspect participles, see Matt 6:17 (νηστεύων); Mark 1:19 (καταρτίζοντας); 2:14 (παράγων); Luke 8:8 (λέγων); 24:36 (λαλούντων); Acts 1:4 (συναλιζόμενος); 8:40 (διερχόμενος); 1 Cor 8:12 (ἁμαρτάνοντες); 2 Cor 10:1 (ἀπών).

Means[21]

The adverbial participle of means answers the question "How?" the main verb was accomplished. The participle is usually translated with the phrase "by" or "by means of." Unlike the participle of manner, this usage is not merely conveying the mental or emotional state someone experienced while performing an action, but the actual way in which it was completed. The participle usually follows the main verb. This usage is common.

- ἀπόλουσαι τὰς ἁμαρτίας σου **ἐπικαλεσάμενος** τὸ ὄνομα αὐτοῦ (Acts 22:16)

  Have your sins washed away **by calling** on the name of the Lord (NLT)

- ἀλλὰ ἑαυτὸν ἐκένωσεν μορφὴν δούλου **λαβών**, ἐν ὁμοιώματι ἀνθρώπων **γενόμενος** (Phil 2:7)

  but made himself nothing, **[by] taking** the form of a servant, **[by] being born** in the likeness of men (ESV)[22]

- τοῦτο γὰρ **ποιῶν** καὶ σεαυτὸν σώσεις καὶ τοὺς ἀκούοντάς σου (1 Tim 4:16)

  for **in doing** this you will save both yourself and your hearers

- οἵτινες ὅλους οἴκους ἀνατρέπουσιν **διδάσκοντες** ἃ μὴ δεῖ (Titus 1:11)

  they are ruining entire households **by teaching** what they shouldn't

- ταπεινώθητε οὖν ὑπὸ τὴν κραταιὰν χεῖρα τοῦ θεοῦ . . . πᾶσαν τὴν μέριμναν ὑμῶν **ἐπιρίψαντες** ἐπ᾽ αὐτόν (1 Pet 5:6–7)

  Humble yourselves therefore under the mighty hand of God . . . **[by] casting** all your care upon him[23]

---

[21] Some grammars label this category the "Instrumental Participle" (Brooks & Winbery, Dana & Mantey).

[22] Hawthorne comments, "Paradoxically, then, Christ's self-giving was accomplished by his taking, his self-emptying was achieved by becoming what he was not before . . . not by subtracting from but by adding to." Gerald F. Hawthorne, *Philippians*, WBC (Waco, TX: Word, 1983), 86.

[23] For more examples of the participle of means, see Matt 6:27 (μεριμνῶν); 27:4 (παραδούς); Luke 15:13 (ζῶν); John 20:31 (πιστεύοντες); Acts 5:30 (κρεμάσαντες); 9:8 (χειραγωγοῦντες), 22 (συμβιβάζων); 16:16 (μαντευομένη); 27:38 (ἐκβαλλόμενοι); Rom 12:20 (ποιῶν); 1 Cor 4:12 (ἐργαζόμενοι); Eph 1:20 (ἐγείρας); 2:14–15 (καταργήσας); 4:28 (ἐργαζόμενος); 6:14 (περιζωσάμενοι); Phil 1:30 (ἔχοντες); 2:2 (ἔχοντες, φρονοῦντες), 8 (γενόμενος); 1 Tim 1:6 (ἀστοχήσαντες), 12 (θέμενος); Heb 2:18 (πειρασθείς); 2 Pet 2:15 (καταλίποντες); 3:6 (κατακλυσθείς).

Manner[24]

An adverbial participle of manner answers the question "How?" the main verb was performed. Because the participle of means answers this same question, there is often confusion between these two uses. The participle of manner refers to the way in which an action is carried out, often translated as an adverb. It often conveys an emotion or attitude. In contrast, the participle of means relates to the method by which something was completed. The participle of manner may employ the particle ὡς ("as"). This category is much less common than the participle of means.

- ἀπῆλθεν **λυπούμενος** (Matt 19:22)

  he went away **grieving**

  > Notice that the participle does not convey the means by which he went away (e.g., walking) but the manner in which he went away (grieving).

- ἦν διδάσκων αὐτοὺς ὡς ἐξουσίαν **ἔχων** (Mark 1:22)

  He was teaching them as one **having** authority (NASB)

- Μαρία δὲ εἱστήκει πρὸς τῷ μνημείῳ ἔξω **κλαίουσα** (John 20:11)

  But Mary stood **weeping** outside the tomb (ESV)

- ἐπορεύοντο **χαίροντες** (Acts 5:41)

  they went out . . . **rejoicing**

- οὕτως πυκτεύω ὡς οὐκ ἀέρα **δέρων** (1 Cor 9:26)

  I do not fight like a man **beating** the air (NIV)[25]

Cause[26]

The causal adverbial participle conveys why the action of the main verb occurred. Specifically, it tells the reader the cause, reason, or grounds by which the action is accomplished.[27] If the context supports understanding a participle as causal, this idea can be reflected in translation by adding the words "because," "since,"

---

[24] Some grammars label this category the "Modal Participle" (Black, Brooks & Winbery, and Dana & Mantey). Robertson combines this category with attendant circumstance.

[25] For more examples of the participle of manner, see Luke 1:64 (εὐλογῶν); 2:48 (ὀδυνώμενοι); 7:38 (κλαίουσα); 8:47 (τρέμουσα); 19:5 (σπεύσας); Acts 2:13 (διαχλευάζοντες); Phil 3:18 (κλαίων).

[26] Some grammars label this category the "Reason Participle" (Young).

[27] Young includes grounds as a separate category, distinct from reason/causal participles. This distinction has some validity because something can be the grounds for a conclusion or exhortation without necessarily being the reason or cause behind it. For example, in Rom 5:1 Paul states, "Therefore, **since we have been declared righteous** by faith, we have peace with God" (**δικαιωθέντες** οὖν ἐκ πίστεως εἰρήνην ἔχομεν πρὸς τὸν θεόν). The point here is not so much that believers have peace with God *because* they have been declared righteous, but that peace with God is grounded on the fact that they have been declared righteous. See also Gal 4:9 (γνόντες) and Phlm 9 (ὤν).

or "for." Note that this participle will usually precede the main verb and that adverbial participles in the perfect tense are almost always a causal participle.[28]

- πλανᾶσθε μὴ **εἰδότες** τὰς γραφὰς μηδὲ τὴν δύναμιν τοῦ θεοῦ (Matt 22:29)

  You are mistaken, **because you do** not **know** the Scriptures or the power of God

- πολλοὶ ἐπίστευσαν εἰς τὸ ὄνομα αὐτοῦ **θεθροῦντες** αὐτοῦ τὰ σημεῖα ἃ ἐποίει (John 2:23)

  many believed in his name **because they saw** the signs that he was doing (NRSV)

- ἡμεῖς δὲ ἡμέρας **ὄντες** νήφωμεν (1 Thess 5:8)

  But **since we are** of the day, we must be sober (NASB)

- ἡ εὐσέβεια πρὸς πάντα ὠφέλιμός ἐστιν ἐπαγγελίαν **ἔχουσα** ζωῆς τῆς νῦν καὶ τῆς μελλούση (1 Tim 4:8)

  Godliness is beneficial in every way, **since it holds** promise for the present life and also for the life to come

- σὺ δὲ μένε ἐν οἷς ἔμαθες καὶ ἐπιστώθης, **εἰδὼς** παρὰ τίνων ἔμαθες (2 Tim 3:14)

  But as for you, continue in what you have learned and have become convinced of, **because you know** those from whom you learned it (NIV)[29]

Condition

This participle introduces a condition which, if fulfilled, will result in certain consequences indicated by the controlling verb. This construction is normally equivalent to a third class conditional clause typically expressing a sense of uncertainty.[30] Thus, the participial phrase functions as the protasis ("if" clause) of a conditional statement. In translation the term "if" is added to convey the conditional idea. This usage is relatively common.

---

[28] Wallace, 631. He also highlights that, even though translated as a present, this is a common usage with the perfect verb οἶδα (εἰδώς).

[29] For more examples of causal participles, see Matt 2:22 (ἀκούσας); 25:25 (φοβηθείς); Luke 10:29 (θέλων); 23:20 (θέλων); John 20:20 (ἰδόντες); Rom 5:1 (δικαιωθέντες); 9:22 (θέλων); 2 Cor 4:14 (εἰδότες); 5:4 (βαρούμενοι); Gal 2:12 (φοβούμενος); Eph 1:11 (προορισθέντες); 2:4 (ὤν), 10 (κτισθέντες); 4:25 (ἀποθέμενοι); 6:8 (εἰδότες); Phi 1:14 (πεποιθότας); Col 1:4 (ἀκούσαντες); 3:24 (εἰδότες); Jas 3:1 (εἰδότες); Rev 12:12 (εἰδώς).

[30] Wallace, 632

- τί γὰρ ὠφελεῖται ἄνθρωπος **κερδήσας** τὸν κόσμον ὅλον (Luke 9:25)

  For what does it benefit someone **if he gains** the whole world[31]

- ὁ γὰρ ἐσθίων καὶ πίνων κρίμα ἑαυτῷ ἐσθίει καὶ πίνει μὴ **διακρίνων** τὸ σῶμα (1 Cor 11:29)

  For he who eats and drinks, eats and drinks judgment to himself **if he does not judge** the body rightly (NASB)

- οὐδὲν ἀπόβλητον μετὰ εὐχαριστίας **λαμβανόμενον** (1 Tim 4:4)

  nothing is to be rejected **if it is received** with thanksgiving

- **ἔχοντες** δὲ διατροφὰς καὶ σκεπάσματα, τούτοις ἀρκεσθησόμεθα (1 Tim 6:8)

  If we have food and clothing, we will be content with these

- ταῦτα γὰρ **ποιοῦντες** οὐ μὴ πταίσητέ ποτε (2 Pet 1:10)

  because **if you do** these things you will never stumble[32]

Bible interpreters have vigorously debated as to whether Heb 6:6 belongs in this category. After a series of four substantival participles all grammatically linked by one article and the term καί (or τε), a fifth participle is then added (τοὺς . . . φωτισθέντας, γευσαμένους τε . . . καὶ . . . γενηθέντας . . . καὶ . . . γευσαμένους . . . καὶ **παραπεσόντας**). The question is whether this fifth participle is adverbial or substantival. If adverbial, it could be taken as conditional ("and if they fall away")[33] or temporal ("and then they fall away").[34] This construction (the parallelism of καί + aorist participles), however, favors reading this participle as substantival.[35] In this case, the author is listing a series of five characteristics of apostates (**"those who were once enlightened, who tasted** the heavenly gift, **who shared** in the Holy Spirit, **tasted** God's good word and the powers of the coming age, and **who have fallen away"**).[36]

---

[31] Cf. Matt 16:26 where the parallel passage uses the subjunctive instead of the conditional participle (τί γὰρ ὠφεληθήσεται ἄνθρωπος ἐὰν τὸν κόσμον ὅλον **κερδήσῃ**).

[32] For more examples of conditional participles, see Matt 21:22 (πιστεύοντες); Luke 15:4 (ἀπολέσας); Acts 15:29 (διατηροῦντες); Rom 2:27 (τελοῦσα); 7:3 (τελοῦσα); 1 Cor 6:1 (ἔχων); 8:10 (ὄντος); Gal 6:9 (ἐκλυόμενοι); Phil 1:27 (ἐλθών, ἰδών, ἀπών); Col 2:20 (ζῶντες); 1 Tim 3:10 (ὄντες); 4:6 (ὑποτιθέμενος); Heb 2:3 (ἀμελήσαντες); 7:12 (μετατιθεμένης); 10:26 (ἁμαρτανόντων); 11:32 (διηγούμενον); 1 Pet 3:6 (ἀγαθοποιοῦσαι).

[33] So NIV84, RSV, KJV, NKJV.

[34] So ESV, NASB, NRSV.

[35] So CSB, NIV.

[36] So Wallace, 633; Young, 156.

Concession

With a concessive participle, the state or action of the main verb takes place in spite of the circumstances related to the participle. In other words, because of the situation described by the participle, one would not normally expect the action of the main verb to be realized. In translation the terms "although," "even though," or "though" are added to the beginning of the phrase to convey the concessive idea. Occasionally the particles καίπερ, καίτοι, or καί γε are used to clarify the concessive force of the participle. Sometimes it is difficult to decide whether a particular particle is concessive or causal, though the meanings are very different.[37]

- τυφλὸς **ὢν** ἄρτι βλέπω (John 9:25)

  though I was blind, now I see (ESV)

- **γνόντες** τὸν θεὸν οὐχ ὡς θεὸν ἐδόξασαν (Rom 1:21)

  though they knew God, they did not glorify him as God

- ἐν σαρκὶ γὰρ **περιπατοῦντες** οὐ κατὰ σάρκα στρατευόμεθα (2 Cor 10:3)

  For **though we walk** in the flesh, we are not waging war according to the flesh (ESV)

- ὃς ἐν μορφῇ θεοῦ **ὑπάρχων** (Phil 2:6)

  who, **though he was** in the form of God (ESV)

- καὶ γὰρ **ὀφείλοντες** εἶναι διδάσκαλοι διὰ τὸν χρόνον, πάλιν χρείαν ἔχετε τοῦ διδάσκειν ὑμᾶς τινὰ (Heb 5:12)

  For **though** by this time **you ought** to be teachers, you need someone to teach you again (ESV)[38]

Purpose[39]

This use of the participle indicates the purpose (or end goal) of the main verb's action and is similar to ἵνα + subjunctive or a purpose infinitive.[40] Consequently, in translation the terms, "in order to," "so that," or "that" will be added. There is a

---

[37] For such ambiguity see, Gal 2:3 (ὤν); Phlm 9 (ὤν).

[38] For more examples of concessive participles, see Matt 14:9 (λυπηθείς); Mark 8:18 (ἔχοντες); John 10:33 (ὤν); Acts 5:7 (εἰδυῖα); 13:28 (εὑρόντες); 14:18 (λέγοντες); Rom 1:32 (ἐπιγνόντες); 5:10 (ὄντες); 1 Cor 9:19 (ὤν); Eph 2:1 (ὄντας); 1 Tim 1:7 (νοοῦντες); 3:14 (ἐλπίζων); Phlm 8 (ἔχων); Jas 3:4 (ὄντα); 1 Pet 1:8 (ἰδόντες); Jude 5 (εἰδότας). For examples with καίπερ, see Phil 3:4 (ἔχων); Heb 5:8 (ὤν); 7:5 (ἐξεληλυθότας); 12:17 (ἐκζητήσας); 2 Pet 1:12 (εἰδότας). For examples with καίτοι or καί γε, see Heb 4:3 (γενηθέντων) and Acts 17:27 (ὑπάρχοντα), respectively.

[39] Some grammars label this category the "Telic" (or "Final") Participle (BDF, Black, Brooks & Winbery, Dana & Mantey, and Moulton).

[40] Young, 156.

strong authorial preference for present tense participles to convey purpose, though future tense is also used. In fact, as Wallace notes, all future adverbial participles belong to this category.[41] Because purpose generally points to a future intended result, perhaps this pattern indicates that the aorist and perfect tense participles were generally considered not the best choice for future references. Because perfect participles occur prior to the action of the main verb, they will never be purpose participles (since the action of the participle has not been completed).[42] Similarly, aorist participles almost never communicate purpose.[43] Also, whereas the casual participle will usually precede the main verb, the purpose participle will almost always follow the main verb.[44] Finally, note that some verbs, especially "seek" (ζητέω) and "tempt" (πειράζω), are lexically influenced and inherently convey the idea of purpose.[45]

- καὶ ἐπηρώτησεν εἷς ἐξ αὐτῶν [νομικὸς] **πειράζων** αὐτόν (Matt 22:35)

  And one of them, an expert in the law, asked a question **to test him**

- ἀπέστειλεν πρὸς αὐτὸν πρεσβυτέρους τῶν Ἰουδαίων **ἐρωτῶν** αὐτόν (Luke 7:3)

  he sent some respected Jewish elders **to ask** him (NLT)

- ἦλθον εἰς Καφαρναοὺμ **ζητοῦντες** τὸν Ἰησοῦν (John 6:24)

  they came into Capernaum **to search for** Jesus[46]

- ὃς ἐληλύθει **προσκυνήσων** εἰς Ἰερουσαλήμ (Acts 8:27)

  He had come **to worship** in Jerusalem

- πορεύομαι εἰς Ἰερουσαλὴμ **διακονῶν** τοῖς ἁγίοις (Rom 15:25)

  I am traveling to Jerusalem **to serve** the saints[47]

---

[41] Wallace, 636. He notes that there are only 12 future participles in the NT and only five are adverbial: Matt 27:49 (σώσων); Acts 8:27 (προσκυνήσων); 22:5 (ἄξων); 24:11 (προσκυνήσων), 17 (ποιήσων). The other seven future participles are substantival: Luke 22:49 (τὸ ἐσόμενον); John 6:64 (ὁ παραδώσων); Acts 20:22 (συναντήσοντα); 1 Cor 15:37 (τὸ γενησόμενον); Heb 3:5 (τῶν λαληθησομένων); 13:17 (ἀποδώσοντες); 1 Pet 3:13 (ὁ κακώσων). A possible thirteenth future participle is found in Rom 8:34 (ὁ κατακρινῶν). Because it is a liquid verb, the sigma is dropped making it impossible to distinguish from the present form.

[42] Wallace, 635–36.

[43] See Acts 25:13 (ἀσπασάμενοι) for an exception.

[44] Wallace, 635–36.

[45] Wallace, 635–36.

[46] Author's translation.

[47] For more examples of purpose participles, see Mark 10:2 (πειράζοντες); Luke 2:45 (ἀναζητοῦντες); John 6:6 (πειράζων); 12:33 (σημαίνων). Further examples of participles whose context likely indicate the idea of purpose include Matt 2:13 (λέγων); 3:1 (κηρύσσων); Mark 1:14 (κηρύσσων); 3:31 (καλοῦντες); 10:32 (ἀναβαίνοντες); Luke 7:6 (λέγων); 22:43 (ἐνισχύων); 1 Peter 5:8 (ζητῶν); Jude 3 (παρακαλῶν).

Result

This use of the participle is similar to the purpose participle except that it indicates the *actual* result (and not merely the *intended* result) of the main's verb action. Sometimes it is difficult to distinguish between purpose and result, especially if the actual result was intended. Wallace notes two types of result participle. The result that is accomplished can either be a logical result of the main verb's action (e.g., Eph 2:15) or a temporal result (e.g., Mark 9:7).[48] Result participles are consistently found (1) in the present tense-form and (2) after the main verb.[49] In translation the terms "so that," or "with the result that," or "that" can be added. This use is less common than the purpose participle.[50]

- οὐκέτι ἀφίετε αὐτὸν οὐδὲν ποιῆσαι τῷ πατρὶ ἢ τῇ μητρί, **ἀκυροῦντες** τὸν λόγον τοῦ θεοῦ (Mark 7:12–13)

  you no longer permit him to do anything for his father or mother, **thus [as a result] making** void the word of God (ESV)

- καὶ ἐπλήσθησαν φόβου **λέγοντες** ὅτι εἴδομεν παράδοξα σήμερον (Luke 5:26)

  and they were filled with awe and **[as a result] said**, "We have seen incredible things today."

- ἵνα ἦτε τέλειοι καὶ ὁλόκληροι ἐν μηδενὶ **λειπόμενοι** (Jas 1:4)

  so that you may be mature and complete, **[and as a result] lacking** nothing

- ἁμαρτίαν ἐργάζεσθε **ἐλεγχόμενοι** ὑπὸ τοῦ νόμου ὡς παραβάται (Jas 2:9)

  you commit sin and **[as a result] are convicted** by the law as transgressors

- ξενίζονται μὴ συντρεχόντων ὑμῶν εἰς τὴν αὐτὴν τῆς ἀσωτίας ἀνάχυσιν **βλασφημοῦντες** (1 Pet 4:4)

  they are surprised that you don't join them in the same flood of wild living, and **[as a result] they slander you**.[51]

---

[48] Wallace, 638. He clarifies these two types noting the logical result participle "indicates an *implication* of the action of the controlling verb" and the temporal result participle indicates "the *chronological* outcome of the verb."

[49] Wallace, 638.

[50] Interestingly, many grammars do not even include this category (Black, Brooks & Winbery, Burton, Dana & Mantey, and Robertson). Though the result category is mentioned by both Young (1994) and Porter (1994), Wallace is apparently the first to identify and develop it (637–39).

[51] Wallace notes the participle of result is "somewhat common" (637) and includes the following examples (among others) (638–39): Mark 9:7 (ἐπισκιάζουσα); Eph 5:19–21 (λαλοῦντες, ᾄδοντες,

Other Verbal Participles

Attendant Circumstance[52]

The attendant circumstance participle communicates an action that is coordinate to the main verb, thus taking on the mood of this verb (sometimes labeled "parallel" participles). Instead of being translated as an adverbial participle, it is sometimes translated as a finite verb with "and" inserted between the two verbal ideas (i.e., between the participle and the main verb). For example, in Matt 9:6 Jesus commands the paralytic, "**Get up**, take your stretcher, and go home" (ἐγερθεὶς ἆρόν σου τὴν κλίνην καὶ ὕπαγε εἰς τὸν οἶκόν σου). In this verse, the participle ἐγερθεὶς takes on the qualities of the main verb ἆρον. Because ἆρον is an imperative, ἐγερθεὶς functions as an imperative and is translated accordingly. The next verse states, "So **he got up** and went home" (καὶ ἐγερθεὶς ἀπῆλθεν εἰς τὸν οἶκον αὐτοῦ, Matt 9:7). The participle ἐγερθεὶς is once again used as an attendant circumstance but this time it parallels ἀπῆλθεν. Consequently, because ἀπῆλθεν is an indicative verb, ἐγερθεὶς is also translated as an indicative verb with "and" inserted between the two verbal expressions. Wallace lists five rules that *all* occur in at least 90 percent of the instances of attendant circumstance:[53]

1. The tense of the participle is usually *aorist*.

2. The tense of the main verb is usually *aorist* (one exception is the historical present).

3. The mood of the main verb is usually *imperative* (including hortatory subjunctives) or *indicative*.

4. The participle will *precede the main verb*.

5. The participle occurs frequently in *historical narratives* but infrequently elsewhere.

If all five of these criteria are not met, there must be strong evidence to support one's conclusion. Finally, even though the participle and the main verb are translated as coordinate verbs, the participle is still grammatically subordinate with emphasis falling on the main verb.

ψάλλοντες, εὐχαριστοῦντες, ὑποτασσόμενοι); Heb 12:3 (ἐκλυόμενοι); 2 Pet 2:1 (ἐπάγοντες), 6 (τεθεικώς). Further examples of possible result participles include Matt 6:31 (λέγοντες); 21:10 (λέγουσα); 26:8 (λέγοντες); Mark 6:2 (λέγοντες); 7:37 (λέγοντες); Luke 1:9 (εἰσελθών); 21:12 (παραδιδόντες); Rom 1:27 (κατεργαζόμενοι, ἀπολαμβάνοντες); Col 3:13 (ἀνεχόμενοι, χαριζόμενοι).

[52] Some grammars label this category the "Circumstantial Participle" (Brooks & Winbery, Dana & Mantey).

[53] Wallace, 642. There are at least two main problems with Wallace's so-called "rules." (1) He limits his analysis to biblical Greek. (2) His numbers work only if one accepts the examples he offers as conveying this meaning.

- **ἐγερθεὶς** παράλαβε τὸ παιδίον καὶ τὴν μητέρα αὐτοῦ καὶ φεῦγε εἰς Αἴγυπτον (Matt 2:13)

  Get up! Take the child and his mother, flee to Egypt

- ὁ δὲ **ἐγερθεὶς** παρέλαβεν τὸ παιδίον καὶ τὴν μητέρα αὐτοῦ νυκτὸς καὶ ἀνεχώρησεν εἰς Αἴγυπτον (Matt 2:14)

  So he **got up**, took the child and his mother during the night, and escaped to Egypt

- **πορευθέντες** οὖν μαθητεύσατε πάντα τὰ ἔθνη (Matt 28:19)

  Go, therefore, and make disciples of all nations

- **ἀφέντες** πάντα ἠκολούθησαν αὐτῷ (Luke 5:11)

  they . . . **left** everything, and followed him

- ὄγκον **ἀποθέμενοι** πάντα . . . τρέχωμεν (Heb 12:1)

  let us lay aside every hindrance . . . and run

  > Note that the main verb τρέχωμεν is a hortatory subjunctive which is functionally the same as an imperative.[54]

Genitive Absolute

A genitive absolute is a special use of the adverbial participle that provides background information or describes concurrent action. It is "absolute" because it is not grammatically dependent on the rest of the sentence.[55] Because the subject of the main verb and the subject of the participle are distinct, the genitive case is employed. In the following example (which is *not* a genitive absolute), the subject of the participle is also the subject of the main verb: "**Seeing** their faith, Jesus told the paralytic" (Matt 9:2; **ἰδὼν** ὁ Ἰησοῦς τὴν πίστιν αὐτῶν εἶπεν τῷ παραλυτικῷ). In this example, Jesus is the subject of ἰδών ("seeing") and εἶπεν ("told") and so the participle is naturally put in the nominative case. But if an author wants to communicate background information or a concurrent action involving a different subject, the genitive case is used so that the subject of the main verb is

---

[54] For more examples of the participle of attendant circumstance, see Matt 2:8 (πορευθέντες), 20 (ἐγερθείς); 9:6–7 (ἐγερθείς), 13 (πορευθέντες), 18 (ἐλθών); 11:4 (πορευθέντες); 17:7 (ἁψάμενος), 27 (λαβών); 21:2 (λύσαντες); 22:13 (δήσαντες); 25:25 (φοβηθείς, ἀπελθών); 28:7 (πορευθεῖσαι); Mark 1:7 (κύψας), 18 (ἀφέντες); 16:20 (ἐξελθόντες); Luke 4:40 (ἐπιτιθείς); 5:14 (ἀπελθών); 7:22 (πορευθέντες); 13:32 (πορευθέντες); 14:10 (πορευθείς); 16:6 (καθίσας); 17:7 (παρελθών), 14 (πορευθέντες), 19 (ἀναστάς); 19:5 (σπεύσας), 30 (λύσαντες); 22:8 (πορευθέντες); Acts 2:23 (προσπήξαντες); 5:5 (πεσών), 6 (ἐξενέγκαντες); 9:11 (ἀναστάς); 10:13 (ἀναστάς), 20 (ἀναστάς); 16:9 (διαβάς); 2 Tim 4:11 (ἀναλαβών).

[55] Some grammars also include the "Nominative Absolute" as a category of the participle. Unlike the genitive absolute, the nominative absolute is always a substantival participle (see John 7:38, πιστεύων).

not grammatically confused with the subject of the participle. For example, "**As He was saying** these things, many believed in Him" (John 8:30; ταῦτα αὐτοῦ λαλοῦντος πολλοὶ ἐπίστευσαν εἰς αὐτόν). Because the subject of λαλοῦντος ("He") is different from the subject of the main verb ἐπίστευσαν ("many"), the genitive is used to distinguish the two. The genitive absolute contains the following features:

1. The participle and its subject are in the genitive case.

2. The participle is always adverbial and will therefore be anarthrous.

3. The participle is usually temporal.[56]

4. The construction will typically be at the beginning of a verse or sentence.

5. The construction is found most frequently in narratives.

It should also be noted that not all genitive participles are genitive absolutes.

- **ἐκπορευομένων** αὐτῶν ἀπὸ Ἰεριχὼ ἠκολούθησεν αὐτῷ ὄχλος πολύς (Matt 20:29)

  As they were leaving Jericho, a large crowd followed him

- **συνηγμένων** δὲ τῶν Φαρισαίων ἐπηρώτησεν αὐτοὺς ὁ Ἰησοῦς (Matt 22:41)

  While the Pharisees **were together**, Jesus questioned them

- **καθημένου** δὲ αὐτοῦ . . . προσῆλθον αὐτῷ οἱ μαθηταὶ (Matt 24:3)

  While he **was sitting** . . . the disciples approached him[57]

Imperatival

Sometimes the participle functions independently as an imperative. This is grammatically different from attendant circumstance where a participle is used as

---

[56] The temporal use occurs in about 90 percent of genitive absolutes (so Wallace, 655; cf. Henry Anselm Scomp, "The Case Absolute in the New Testament," *BSac* [January 1902]: 325–40). Robertson adds, "All varieties of the circumstantial [adverbial] participle can appear in the absolute participle" (1130). For examples, see 1 Pet 4:1 (παθόντος = causal), Heb 10:26 (ἁμαρτανόντων = conditional); John 20:26 (κεκλεισμένων = concession); Eph 2:20 (ὄντος = attendant circumstances).

[57] For more examples of genitive absolutes, see Matt 8:1 (καταβάντος), 5 (εἰσελθόντος), 16 (γενομένης), 28 (ἐλθόντος); 9:18 (λαλοῦντος), 32 (ἐξερχομένων), 33 (ἐκβληθέντος); 17:14 (ἐλθόντων), 22 (συστρεφομένων), 24 (ἐλθόντων), 18:24 (ἀρξαμένου), 25 (ἔχοντος); 21:10 (εἰσελθόντος), 23 (ἐλθόντος); Mark 5:2 (ἐξελθόντος), 18 (ἐμβαίνοντος), 21 (διαπεράσαντος), 35 (λαλοῦντος); 15:33 (γενομένης); Luke 11:14 (ἐξελθόντος); 18:36 (διαπορευομένου), 40 (ἐγγίσαντος); Acts 13:2 (λειτουργούντων, νηστευόντων); 1 Pet 3:20 (κατασκευαζομένης).

an imperative if the main verb is also an imperative.[58] In this case, the participle is not dependent on a main verb but functions as the main verb.[59] One view is that the imperatival participle is used in order to communicate a softer, gentler appeal than the imperative mood. This view, however, has recently been challenged by Travis Williams who maintains that *"the function is used to engage the volition of the recipients in order to direct them toward a particular action"* and thus, "the participle use is essentially equivalent to the finite imperative."[60] He concludes, "Most who have dealt with the issue have assumed that an author's employment of a form other than the finite verb brings with it a weakened force, or that in some sense he/she is holding back his/her authority. An examination of the evidence reveals that this is not the case, however."[61] Most of the NT occurrences are found in Romans 12 and 1 Peter.[62]

- τῇ ἐλπίδι **χαίροντες**, τῇ θλίψει **ὑπομένοντες**, τῇ προσευχῇ **προσκαρτεροῦντες** (Rom 12:12)

  Rejoice in hope; **be patient** in affliction; **be persistent** in prayer

  The fact that imperatives are used in v. 14 (εὐλογεῖτε, μὴ καταρᾶσθε) demonstrates the imperatival use of the participles in this passage.

- [αἱ] γυναῖκες, **ὑποτασσόμεναι** τοῖς ἰδίοις ἀνδράσιν (1 Pet 3:1)

  Wives . . . **submit yourselves** to your own husbands

- οἱ ἄνδρες . . . **συνοικοῦντες** κατὰ γνῶσιν ὡς ἀσθενεστέρῳ σκεύει τῷ γυναικείῳ (1 Pet 3:7)

  Husbands . . . **live with** your wives in an understanding way, as with a weaker partner[63]

---

[58] Robertson reminds us, "In general it may be said that no participle should be explained in this way that can properly be connected with a finite verb" (1133–34). Similarly, Brooks & Winbery note, "Certainly no participle should be explained as an independent participle if there is any other way to explain it" (138).

[59] The participle can also function independently as an indicative but we will not treat this category separately. An example of a participle used as indicative in found is Rev 1:16: "**He had** seven stars in his right hand" (ἔχων ἐν τῇ δεξιᾷ χειρὶ αὐτοῦ). For more examples, see Rom 5:11 (καυχώμενοι); 12:6 (ἔχοντες); 2 Cor 4:8 (θλιβόμενοι, στενοχωρούμενοι, ἀπορούμενοι, ἐξαπορούμενοι); 5:6 (θαρροῦντες, εἰδότες); 9:11 (πλουτιζόμενοι); Rev 4:7 (ἔχων); 10:2 (ἔχων); 12:2 (ἔχουσα); 17:5 (γεγραμμένον); 19:12 (ἔχων); 21:12 (ἔχουσα), 14 (ἔχων), 19 (κεκοσμημένοι).

[60] Travis B. Williams, "Reconsidering the Imperatival Participle in 1 Peter," *WTJ* (2011): 74–75 (emphasis original).

[61] Williams, "Reconsidering the Imperatival Participle in 1 Peter," 75.

[62] Some have challenged this category, especially in 1 Peter. See, for example, Paul J. Achtemeier, *1 Peter*, Hermeneia (Minneapolis: Fortress, 1996), 194, 209, 217, 223.

[63] For more examples of imperatival participles, see Mark 5:23 (ἐλθών); Rom 12:9 (ἀποστυγοῦντες, κολλώμενοι), 10 (προηγούμενοι), 11 (ζέοντες, δουλεύοντες), 13 (κοινωνοῦντες, διώκοντες), 16 (φρονοῦντες, φρονοῦντες, συναπαγόμενοι), 17 (ἀποδιδόντες, προνοούμενοι), 18 (εἰρηνεύοντες), 19 (ἐκδικοῦντες); 2 Cor 8:24 (ἐνδεικνύμενοι); 1 Pet 2:18 (ὑποτασσόμενοι); Heb 13:5 (ἀρκούμενοι).

Pleonastic

A pleonastic expression is an expression that involves redundancy. With a participle, this expression typically employs a verb of saying (ἀποκριθείς or λέγων), a Semitic idiom brought into Greek. Because this idiom is not employed in English, it is usually translated into English with a single word, choosing either the participle or the main verb.[64] For example, **ἀποκριθεὶς** δὲ ὁ Ἰησοῦς εἶπεν πρὸς αὐτόν is rendered "Jesus answered him" (Matt 3:15). This use of the participle is mostly found in the Synoptic Gospels.[65]

- καὶ ἰδοὺ ἔκραξαν **λέγοντες** (Matt 8:29)

  Suddenly they shouted

- **ἀποκριθεὶς** δὲ ὁ Πέτρος εἶπεν αὐτῷ (Matt 15:15)

  But Peter said to him (ESV)

- ᾧ καὶ εἶπεν **μαρτυρήσας** (Acts 13:22)

  of whom he testified (ESV)[66]

Complementary

As its name suggests, a complementary participle *completes* the idea of another (main) verb. Certain verbs, especially verbs that lexically communicate completion such as παύομαι ("I cease") or τελέω ("I finish"), require another verb to complete the verbal idea. Typically an infinitive is used but sometimes (rarely) a participle is used.

- καὶ ἐγένετο ὅτε ἐτέλεσεν ὁ Ἰησοῦς **διατάσσων** (Matt 11:1)

  When Jesus had finished **giving instructions**

- ὡς δὲ ἐπαύσατο **λαλῶν** (Luke 5:4)

  When he had finished **speaking**

---

[64] Zerwick comments that the pleonastic participle (particularly ἀποκριθεὶς εἶπεν) "became to such an extent an empty formula that it is even sometimes used where there is nothing preceding to which an 'answer' can be referred" (127).

[65] John tends to use two main verbs (**ἀπεκρίθη** Ἰησοῦς καὶ **εἶπεν** αὐτῷ, "Jesus answered and said to him," John 1:48 NASB).

[66] For more examples of the pleonastic participle, see Matt 11:25 (ἀποκριθείς); 12:28 (λέγοντες); 13:3 (λέγων), 11 (ἀποκριθείς); 15:22 (λέγουσα), 23 (λέγοντες); 26:70 (λέγων); Mark 1:7 (λέγων); 9:5 (ἀποκριθείς); 11:14 (ἀποκριθείς); Luke 5:22 (ἀποκριθείς); 7:22 (ἀποκριθείς); 13:2 (ἀποκριθείς); 19:40 (ἀποκριθείς); John 1:26 (λέγων); Acts 1:24 (προσευξάμενοι).

- οὐ παύομαι **εὐχαριστῶν** (Eph 1:16)

  I never stop **giving thanks**[67]

Indirect Discourse[68]

Indirect discourse is a statement of what someone said. In English, such a report would be communicated using the third person ("He said he was hungry"). In contrast, direct discourse involves directly quoting what someone said in the first person ("He said, 'I am hungry'"). Typically, indirect discourse is formed with ὅτι followed by an indicative verb but can also be formed with a participle (or infinitive). There are several features to look for when considering if a participle is used to communicate indirect discourse: (1) The participle will be in the accusative case and will be anarthrous. (2) The noun or pronoun that functions as the subject of the participle will also be in the accusative case. (3) It will usually follow a verb of perception or communication.

- ἀκούσας δὲ Ἰακὼβ **ὄντα** σιτία εἰς Αἴγυπτον (Acts 7:12)

  When Jacob heard **there was** grain in Egypt

- ἀκούομεν γάρ τινας **περιπατοῦντας** ἐν ὑμῖν ἀτάκτως (2 Thess 3:11)

  For we hear that some among you **walk** in idleness (ESV)

- πᾶν πνεῦμα ὃ ὁμολογεῖ Ἰησοῦν Χριστὸν ἐν σαρκὶ **ἐληλυθότα** ἐκ τοῦ θεοῦ ἐστιν (1 John 4:2)

  Every spirit that confesses that Jesus Christ **has come** in the flesh is from God[69]

Periphrastic Participles

A periphrastic participle involves a finite verb (εἰμί) + a participle. The term *periphrastic* relates to the "round-about" way of expressing the verbal idea (περί ["around"] + φράζω ["I explain"]). In other words, instead of simply using one verb to express the action (ἐδίδασκεν = "he was teaching"), a verb plus a participle is used (ἦν διδάσκων = "he was teaching").

Before we discuss the specific types of periphrastic participles, it will be helpful to discuss some common characteristics of this construction.

---

[67] For more examples of complementary participles, see Matt 6:16 (νηστεύοντες); John 8:7 (ἐρωτῶντες); Acts 5:42 (διδάσκοντες, εὐαγγελιζόμενοι); 6:13 (λαλῶν); 12:16 (κρούων); 13:10 (διαστρέφων); 20:31 (νουθετῶν); 21:32 (τύπτοντες); Col 1:9 (προσευχόμενοι); Heb 10:2 (προσφερόμεναι).

[68] Some grammars include this category as a subcategory of "Complementary Participles" (Brooks & Winbery, Dana & Mantey).

[69] For more examples of indirect discourse participles, see Luke 14:18 (παρῃτημένον); Acts 9:21 (δεδεμένους); Phil 2:3 (ὑπερέχοντας); 2 Cor 8:22 (ὄντα); 2 John 7 (ἐρχόμενον).

1. The finite verb found in a periphrastic construction is usually a form of the verb εἰμί.[70]

2. The finite verb can occur in the present, imperfect, or future tense-forms.

3. The participle will be either present or perfect and will usually occur in the nominative case.[71]

4. The participle usually follows the indicative verb (only rarely will the participle precede the main verb).[72]

5. This construction is often used to highlight verbal aspect.[73]

6. It is most common in Mark's, John's, and especially Luke's writings.[74]

7. The most common form in the NT is the imperfect periphrastic.[75]

PERIPHRASTIC PARTICIPLES				
FINITE VERB (εἰμί)	+	PARTICIPLE	=	FINITE TENSE EQUIVALENT
Present	+	Present	=	Present
Imperfect	+	Present	=	Imperfect
Future	+	Present	=	Future
Present	+	Perfect	=	Perfect
Imperfect	+	Perfect	=	Pluperfect
Future	+	Perfect	=	Future Perfect

Present Periphrastic (present form of εἰμί + present participle)

• οἱ ἄνδρες . . . **εἰσὶν** . . . **διδάσκοντες** τὸν λαόν (Acts 5:25)

  The men . . . **are** . . . **teaching** the people

---

[70] γίνομαι is sometimes used instead of εἰμί. See Mark 9:3 (ἐγένετο στίλβοντα); 2 Cor 6:14 (γίνεσθε ἑτεροζυγοῦντες); Col 1:18 (γένηται πρωτεύων); Heb 5:12 (γεγόνατε ἔχοντες); Rev 3:2 (γίνου γρηγορῶν); 16:10 (ἐγένετο ἐσκοτωμένη).

[71] According to Boyer, the NT contains 153 present participles, 115 perfect participles, and only two (possible) aorist participles (Luke 23:19; 2 Cor 5:19) that are found in periphrastic constructions ("The Classification of Participles," 172).

[72] Boyer lists two examples found in the accusative case (Luke 9:18; Col 1:21) and 28 instances where the participle precedes the verb ("The Classification of Participles," 172).

[73] "Periphrasis occasionally provides a rhetorically more forceful expression" (BDF, 179 [§352]).

[74] "The use of the periphrastic construction has in the NT a distribution which gives more than a half of the total number of occurrences to the writings of Luke alone" (Zerwick, 125–26). See also BDF, 179 (§353).

[75] So Robertson, 879; Fanning, 313. Fanning counts 89 imperfect periphrastics in the NT (with a few containing multiple participles after one occurrence of εἰμί).

- καθὼς καὶ ἐν παντὶ τῷ κόσμῳ **ἐστὶν καρποφορούμενον** (Col 1:6)

  as indeed in the whole world it **is bearing fruit** (ESV)[76]

Imperfect Periphrastic (imperfect form of εἰμί [ἤμην] + present participle)

- **ἦν** γὰρ **διδάσκων** αὐτοὺς (Matt 7:29)

  because **he was teaching** them

- ταῦτα ἐν Βηθανίᾳ ἐγένετο . . . ὅπου **ἦν** ὁ Ἰωάννης **βαπτίζων** (John 1:28)

  All this happened in Bethany . . . where John **was baptizing**[77]

Future Periphrastic (future form of εἰμί [ἔσομαι] + present participle)[78]

- καὶ **ἔσεσθε μισούμενοι** ὑπὸ πάντων διὰ τὸ ὄνομά μου (Matt 10:22)[79]

  You will be hated by everyone because of my name

- καὶ οἱ ἀστέρες **ἔσονται** ἐκ τοῦ οὐρανοῦ **πίπτοντες** (Mark 13:25)

  the stars **will be falling** from the sky[80]

Perfect Periphrastic (present form of εἰμί + perfect participle)

- οὗ γάρ **εἰσιν** δύο ἢ τρεῖς **συνηγμένοι** εἰς τὸ ἐμὸν ὄνομα (Matt 18:20)

  For where two or three **are gathered** together in my name

- τῇ γὰρ χάριτί **ἐστε σεσῳσμένοι** διὰ πίστεως (Eph 2:8)

  For by grace **you are saved** through faith (ESV)[81]

---

[76] For more examples of present periphrastics, see Matt 1:23 (ἐστιν μεθερμηνευόμενον; the same phrase also occurs in Mark 5:41; 15:22; Luke 6:43 (ἐστιν ποιοῦν); John 1:41; Acts 4:36); 27:33 (ἐστιν λεγόμενος); 2 Cor 2:17 (ἐσμεν καπηλεύοντες); 9:12 (ἐστιν προσαναπληροῦσα); Gal 4:24 (ἐστιν ἀλληγορούμενα); Col 2:23 (ἐστιν ἔχοντα); 3:1 (ἐστιν καθήμενος); Rev 1:18 (ζῶν εἰμι).

[77] For more examples of imperfect periphrastics, see Matt 19:22 (ἦν ἔχων); Mark 1:22 (ἦν διδάσκων); 5:5 (ἦν κράζων); 9:4 (ἦσαν συλλαλοῦντες); 10:32 (ἦσαν ἀναβαίνοντες . . . προάγων); Luke 1:10 (ἦν προσευχόμενος), 21 (ἦν προσδοκῶν); 2:51 (ἦν ὑποτασσόμενος); 4:20 (ἦσαν ἀτενίζοντες); 19:47 (ἦν διδάσκων); John 13:23 (ἦν ἀνακείμενος); Acts 1:10 (ἀτενίζοντες ἦσαν); 2:2 (ἦσαν καθήμενοι); 8:1 (ἦν συνευδοκῶν); 22:19 (ἤμην φυλακίζων . . . δέρων); Gal 1:22 (ἤμην ἀγνοούμενος). Fanning lists the following occurrences: Matthew (6), Mark (15), Luke (28), John (10), Acts (25), 2 Corinthians (1), Galatians (2), Philippians (1), and 1 Peter (1) [*Verbal Aspect in New Testament Greek*, 316].

[78] Unlike a simple future tense, the future periphrastic conveys a progressive action.

[79] The same phrase (ἔσεσθε μισούμενοι) also occurs in Matt 24:9; Mark 13:13; Luke 21:17.

[80] For more examples of future periphrastics, see Luke 1:20 (ἔσῃ σιωπῶν); 5:10 (ἔσῃ ζωγρῶν); 21:24 (ἔσται πατουμένη); 22:69 (ἔσται καθήμενος); 1 Cor 14:9 (ἔσεσθε λαλοῦντες).

[81] For more examples of perfect periphrastics, see Matt 10:26 (ἐστιν κεκαλυμμένον); 18:20 (εἰσιν συνηγμένοι); Luke 12:6 (ἐστιν ἐπιλελησμένον); 14:8 (ἢ κεκλημένος); 20:6 (πεπεισμένος ἐστιν); 23:15 (ἐστιν πεπραγμένον); John 3:27 (ἢ δεδομένον); 6:31 (ἐστιν γεγραμμένον; the same phrase also occurs in 2:17; 6:45; 10:34; 12:14; 20:30); 16:14 (ἢ πεπληρωμένη); 17:23 (ὦσιν τετελειωμένοι);

Pluperfect Periphrastic (imperfect form of εἰμί [ἤμην] + perfect participle)

- ἔθηκεν αὐτὸν ἐν μνημείῳ ὃ **ἦν λελατομημένον** ἐκ πέτρας (Mark 15:46)

  [Joseph] laid him in a tomb that **had been cut out** of the rock (ESV)

- ἐπίστευσαν ὅσοι **ἦσαν τεταγμένοι** εἰς ζωὴν αἰώνιον (Acts 13:48)

  and all who **were appointed** to eternal life believed[82]

Future Perfect Periphrastic (future form of εἰμί [ἔσομαι] + perfect participle)

- ὃ ἐὰν δήσῃς ἐπὶ τῆς γῆς **ἔσται δεδεμένον** ἐν τοῖς οὐρανοῖς, καὶ ὃ ἐὰν λύσῃς ἐπὶ τῆς γῆς **ἔσται λελυμένον** ἐν τοῖς οὐρανοῖς (Matt 16:19)

  whatever you bind on earth **shall have been bound** in heaven, and whatever you loose on earth **shall have been loosed** in heaven (NASB)

  See also Matt 18:18 where a similar statement occurs [ἔσται δεδεμένα . . . ἔσται λελυμένα]).[83]

- ἐγὼ **ἔσομαι πεποιθὼς** ἐπ᾽ αὐτῷ (Heb 2:13)

  I **will trust** in him[84]

Acts 2:13 (μεμεστωμένοι εἰσίν), 17 (μεμεστωμένοι εἰσίν); 21:33 (ἐστιν πεποιηκώς); 25:10 (ἐστώς εἰμι); Rom 7:14 (εἰμι πεπραμένος); 2 Cor 4:3 (ἔστιν κεκαλυμμένον); Eph 2:5 (ἐστε σεσωσμένοι); Heb 4:2 (ἐσμεν εὐηγγελισμένοι); Jas 5:15 (ᾖ πεποιηκώς); 1 John 1:4 (ᾖ πεπληρωμένη). There are about 40 instances of this construction in the NT (so Robertson, 903; Burton, 40).

[82] For more examples of pluperfect periphrastics, see Matt 9:36 (ἦσαν ἐσκυλμένοι . . . ἐρριμμένοι); 26:43 (ἦσαν βεβαρημένοι); Mark 1:6 (ἦν ἐνδεδυμένος); Luke 2:26 (ἦν κεχρηματισμένον); 4:16 (ἦν τεθραμμένος); 5:17 (ἦσαν ἐληλυθότες); 8:2 (ἦσαν τεθεραπευμέναι); 9:45 (ἦν παρακεκαλυμμένον); 15:24 (ἦν ἀπολωλώς); 23:53 (ἦν κείμενος); John 1:24 (ἀπεσταλμένοι ἦσαν); 3:24 (ἦν βεβλημένος); 19:11 (ἦν δεδομένον), 19 (ἦν γεγραμμένον), 41 (ἦν τεθειμένος); Acts 8:16 (ἦν ἐπιπεπτωκός); 21:29 (ἦσαν προεωρακότες); Gal 4:3 (ἤμεθα δεδουλωμένοι).

[83] Fanning comments, "The two texts in Matthew have engendered some discussion over the sense of the future perfect in Greek. The grammar does not require that these denote the sense of action 'already determined' in heaven *before* Peter and the apostolic company act. Instead, in bolstering the position of leaders in the Christian community, these verses emphasize the *permanence* of their actions: whatever they decide will be confirmed in heaven" (322–23).

[84] This category is rare and only includes the five examples given above along with Luke 12:52 (ἔσονται διαμεμερισμένοι). There is also some doubt as to the validity of this category.

SUMMARY

ADJECTIVAL PARTICIPLES		
Attributive	Modifies an expressed noun (agreeing with it in gender, case, and number) and usually has a definite article.	ὁ δὲ ἐχθρὸς ὁ **σπείρας** αὐτά ("and the enemy **who sowed** them"; Matt 13:39).
Substantival	Usually has a definite article but becomes a virtual noun (substantive).	ὁ **νικῶν** κληρονομήσει ταῦτα ("The one **who conquers** will inherit these things"; Rev 21:7).
VERBAL PARTICIPLES (ADVERBIAL)		
Temporal	The aorist participle communicates perfective aspect, depicting an action as simply occurring or having occurred.	*Perfective aspect:* καθαρισμὸν τῶν ἁμαρτιῶν **ποιησάμενος** ἐκάθισεν ("**After making** purification for sins, he sat down"; Heb 1:3).
	The present participle communicates imperfective aspect, portraying an action as ongoing.	*Imperfective aspect:* **παράγων** εἶδεν ἄνθρωπον ("As he **was passing by**, he saw a man"; John 9:1).
Means	Answers the question "How?" the main verb was accomplished (add "by" or "by means of").	ἀπόλουσαι τὰς ἁμαρτίας σου **ἐπικαλεσάμενος** τὸ ὄνομα αὐτοῦ ("Have your sins washed away **by calling** on the name of the Lord"; Acts 22:16 NLT).
Manner	Answers the question "How?" the main verb was performed and is often translated as an adverb.	ἐπορεύοντο **χαίροντες** ("they went out . . . **rejoicing**"; Acts 5:41).
Cause	Answers the question "Why?" providing the cause, reason, or grounds by which an action is accomplished (add "because," "since," or "for").	ἡμεῖς δὲ ἡμέρας **ὄντες** νήφωμεν ("But **since we are** of the day, we must be sober"; 1 Thess 5:8 NASB).
Condition	The participial phrase functions as the protasis ("if" clause) of a conditional statement (add "if").	οὐδὲν ἀπόβλητον μετὰ εὐχαριστίας **λαμβανόμενον** ("nothing is to be rejected **if it is received** with thanksgiving"; 1 Tim 4:4).
Concession	The action of the main verb takes place in spite of the circumstances related to the participle (add "although," "even though," or "though").	τυφλὸς **ὢν** ἄρτι βλέπω ("**though I was** blind, now I see"; John 9:25 ESV).
Purpose	Indicates the purpose of the main verb's action (add "in order to," "so that," or "that").	ὃς ἐληλύθει **προσκυνήσων** εἰς Ἰερουσαλήμ ("He had come **to worship** in Jerusalem"; Acts 8:27).
Result	Indicates the *actual* result (and not merely the *intended* result) of the main verb's action (add "so that," "with the result that," or "that").	ἵνα ἦτε τέλειοι καὶ ὁλόκληροι ἐν μηδενὶ **λειπόμενοι** ("so that you may be mature and complete, **[and as a result] lacking** nothing"; Jas 1:4).

VERBAL PARTICIPLES (OTHERS)		
Attendant Circumstance	Coordinate to the main verb, thus taking on the mood of this verb (whether indicative, imperative, or subjunctive).	ἐγερθεὶς παράλαβε τὸ παιδίον ("**Get up!** Take the child"; Matt 2:13).
Genitive Absolute	A special use of the adverbial participle found in the genitive case that provides background information.	καθημένου δὲ αὐτοῦ . . . προσῆλθον αὐτῷ οἱ μαθηταὶ ("**While** he **was sitting** . . . the disciples approached him"; Matt 24:3).
Imperatival	The participle functions independently as an imperative.	[αἱ] γυναῖκες, ὑποτασσόμεναι τοῖς ἰδίοις ἀνδράσιν ("Wives . . . **submit yourselves** to your own husbands"; 1 Pet 3:1).
Pleonastic	A redundant expression usually employing ἀποκριθείς or λέγων, often untranslated, as in example.	ἀποκριθεὶς δὲ ὁ Πέτρος εἶπεν αὐτῷ ("but Peter said to him"; Matt 15:15 ESV).
Complementary	Completes the idea of another (main) verb, usually verbs of completion.	ὡς δὲ ἐπαύσατο λαλῶν ("When he had finished **speaking**"; Luke 5:4).
Indirect Discourse	A statement of what someone said. The participle will be in the accusative case and will be anarthrous.	πᾶν πνεῦμα ὃ ὁμολογεῖ Ἰησοῦν Χριστὸν ἐν σαρκὶ ἐληλυθότα ἐκ τοῦ θεοῦ ἐστιν ("Every spirit that confesses that Jesus Christ **has come** in the flesh is from God"; 1 John 4:2).
PERIPHRASTIC PARTICIPLES		
Present	Present of εἰμί + present ptc	οἱ ἄνδρες . . . εἰσὶν . . . διδάσκοντες τὸν λαόν ("The men . . . **are . . . teaching** the people"; Acts 5:25).
Imperfect	Imperfect of εἰμί [ἤμην] + present ptc	ἦν διδάσκων αὐτοὺς ("**He was teaching** them"; Matt 7:29).
Future	Future of εἰμί [ἔσομαι] + present ptc	καὶ ἔσεσθε μισούμενοι ὑπὸ πάντων διὰ τὸ ὄνομά μου ("**You will be hated** by everyone because of my name"; Matt 10:22).
Perfect	Present of εἰμί + perfect ptc	τῇ γὰρ χάριτί ἐστε σεσῳσμένοι διὰ πίστεως ("For by grace **you are saved** through faith"; Eph 2:8 ESV).
Pluperfect	Imperfect of εἰμί [ἤμην] + perfect ptc	ἐπίστευσαν ὅσοι ἦσαν τεταγμένοι εἰς ζωὴν αἰώνιον ("all who **were appointed** to eternal life believed"; Acts 13:48).
Future Perfect	Future of εἰμί [ἔσομαι] + perfect ptc	ὃ ἐὰν λύσῃς ἐπὶ τῆς γῆς ἔσται λελυμένον ἐν τοῖς οὐρανοῖς ("Whatever you loose on earth **shall have been loosed** in heaven"; Matt 16:19 NASB).

PRACTICE EXERCISES

In each of the following examples, (1) parse each underlined participle and (2) determine its specific use based on the information provided in this chapter.

1. καὶ <u>θέλων</u> αὐτὸν ἀποκτεῖναι ἐφοβήθη τὸν ὄχλον, ὅτι ὡς προφήτην αὐτὸν εἶχον (Matt 14:5).

2. <u>ἀκούσας</u> δὲ ὁ νεανίσκος τὸν λόγον ἀπῆλθεν <u>λυπούμενος</u>· ἦν γὰρ <u>ἔχων</u> κτήματα πολλα (Matt 19:22).

3. καὶ <u>ἐλθόντος</u> αὐτοῦ εἰς τὸ ἱερὸν προσῆλθον αὐτῷ <u>διδάσκοντι</u> οἱ ἀρχιερεῖς καὶ οἱ πρεσβύτεροι τοῦ λαοῦ (Matt 21:23).

4. <u>ἀποκριθεὶς</u> δὲ Σίμων Πέτρος εἶπεν· σὺ εἶ ὁ χριστὸς ὁ υἱὸς τοῦ θεοῦ τοῦ <u>ζῶντος</u> (Matt 16:16).

5. οἱ δὲ λοιποὶ ἔλεγον, Ἄφες ἴδωμεν εἰ ἔρχεται Ἠλίας <u>σώσων</u> αὐτόν (Matt 27:49).

6. <u>πορευθέντες</u> οὖν μαθητεύσατε πάντα τὰ ἔθνη, <u>βαπτίζοντες</u> αὐτοὺς εἰς τὸ ὄνομα τοῦ πατρὸς καὶ τοῦ υἱοῦ καὶ τοῦ ἁγίου πνεύματος, <u>διδάσκοντες</u> αὐτοὺς τηρεῖν πάντα ὅσα ἐνετειλάμην ὑμῖν (Matt 28:19–20).

7. τί γὰρ ὠφελεῖται ἄνθρωπος <u>κερδήσας</u> τὸν κόσμον ὅλον ἑαυτὸν δὲ <u>ἀπολέσας</u> ἢ <u>ζημιωθείς</u>; (Luke 9:25).

8. τοῦτο <u>γινώσκοντες</u> ὅτι ὁ παλαιὸς ἡμῶν ἄνθρωπος συνεσταυρώθη (Rom 6:6).

9. πλατεῖα ἡ πύλη καὶ εὐρύχωρος ἡ ὁδὸς ἡ <u>ἀπάγουσα</u> εἰς τὴν ἀπώλειαν καὶ πολλοί εἰσιν οἱ <u>εἰσερχόμενοι</u> δι᾽ αὐτῆς (Matt 7:13).

10. αὐτὸς ἐδίδασκεν ἐν ταῖς συναγωγαῖς αὐτῶν <u>δοξαζόμενος</u> ὑπὸ πάντων (Luke 4:15).

VOCABULARY

Vocabulary to Memorize

ἀνθίστημι	I resist, oppose (14)
ἀποκαλύπτω	I reveal, uncover (26)
ἀρέσκω	I please (17)
βρῶμα, -ατος, τό	food (17)
γρηγορέω	I am awake alert, watchful (22)
διάβολος, ὁ	devil, accuser, slanderous (adj) (37)
ἐξίστημι	I amaze, confuse (17)
ἐπαύριον	tomorrow (17)
ἕτοιμος	ready, prepared (17)
θησαυρός, ὁ	treasure, storehouse (17)
ἵππος, ὁ	horse (17)
Καισάρεια, ἡ	Caesarea (17)
κἄν	and if, even if, if only (17)
καταλύω	I throw down, destroy, abolish (17)
κατέχω	I hold back, restrain, hold fast, possess (17)
κόπος, ὁ	work, labor (18)
κρυπτός	hidden, secret (17)
κρύπτω	I hide, conceal, cover (18)
μήτι	[interrogative particle expecting a negative answer] (18)
νίπτω	I wash (17)
οἰκοδομή, ἡ	edification, building (18)
ὀλίγος	little, few (40)
ὁμοίως	likewise, similarly (30)
οὔ	no (17)
πάθημα, -ατος, τό	suffering (16)
παραχρῆμα	at once, immediately (18)
πάσχω	I suffer (42)
περιτέμνω	I circumcise (17)
πλήρωμα, -ατος, τό	fullness, fulfillment (17)
ποιμήν, ένος, ὁ	shepherd (18)
πόλεμος, ὁ	war, battle, fight (18)
πολλάκις	often, frequently, many times (18)
πυλών, -ῶνος, ὁ	gate, entrance (18)
στέφανος, ὁ	crown, wreath, reward (18)
τίκτω	I bear, give birth to, bring forth (18)
τύπος, ὁ	type, example, pattern (15)

ὑποτάσσω	I subject (38)
ὑψόω	I exalt, lift up (20)
φανερός	manifest, visible, clear (18)
χρυσοῦς	golden (18)

Vocabulary to Recognize

ἀντίδικος, ὁ	adversary, opponent (5)
ἀντιτάσσω	I oppose, resist (5)
ἀρχιποίμην, -ενος, ὁ	chief shepherd (1)
ἐγκομβόομαι	I put on (1)
ἑκουσίως	willingly (2)
ἐπιρίπτω	I cast upon (2)
ἐπισκοπέω	I oversee, care for (2)
ἐπιτελέω	I complete, finish (10)
θεμελιόω	I make firm, establish (5)
κατακυριεύω	I am master/lord over, rule (4)
καταπίνω	I devour, drink down (7)
καταρτίζω	I restore (13)
κλῆρος, ὁ	portion, share, lot (11)
κοινωνός	partner, sharer (10)
κομίζω	I receive (10)
κραταιός	powerful, mighty (1)
κράτος, τό	power, dominion (12)
λέων, ὁ	lion (9)
μέλει	it is a care/concern (10)
μέριμνα, -ης, ἡ	care, anxiety, worry (6)
νεώτερος	younger (11)
νήφω	I am sober, self-controlled (6)
ποιμαίνω	I shepherd (11)
ποίμνιον, τό	flock (5)
προθύμως	eagerly (1)
σθενέω	I strengthen (1)
στερεός	firm, steadfast (4)
στηρίζω	I establish, confirm (13)
συμπρεσβύτερος	fellow-elder (1)
ταπεινός	humble (8)
ταπεινοφροσύνη, ἡ	humility (7)
ταπεινόω	I humble (14)

ὑπερήφανος	proud, arrogant, haughty (5)
χάριν	because of, for the sake of (9)
ὠρύομαι	I roar (1)

READING THE NEW TESTAMENT

1 Peter 5:1–11

¹ Πρεσβυτέρους τοὺς ἐν ὑμῖν παρακαλῶ ὁ συμπρεσβύτερος καὶ μάρτυς τῶν τοῦ Χριστοῦ παθημάτων, ὁ καὶ τῆς μελλούσης ἀποκαλύπτεσθαι δόξης κοινωνός· ² ποιμάνατε τὸ ἐν ὑμῖν ποίμνιον τοῦ θεοῦ [ἐπισκοποῦντες] μὴ ἀναγκαστῶς ἀλλὰ ἑκουσίως κατὰ θεόν, μηδὲ αἰσχροκερδῶς ἀλλὰ προθύμως, ³ μηδ᾽ ὡς κατακυριεύοντες τῶν κλήρων ἀλλὰ τύποι γινόμενοι τοῦ ποιμνίου· ⁴ καὶ φανερωθέντος τοῦ ἀρχιποίμενος κομιεῖσθε τὸν ἀμαράντινον τῆς δόξης στέφανον. ⁵ Ὁμοίως, νεώτεροι, ὑποτάγητε πρεσβυτέροις· πάντες δὲ ἀλλήλοις τὴν ταπεινοφροσύνην ἐγκομβώσασθε, ὅτι [Ὁ] θεὸς ὑπερηφάνοις ἀντιτάσσεται, ταπεινοῖς δὲ δίδωσιν χάριν. ⁶ Ταπεινώθητε οὖν ὑπὸ τὴν κραταιὰν χεῖρα τοῦ θεοῦ, ἵνα ὑμᾶς ὑψώσῃ ἐν καιρῷ, ⁷ πᾶσαν τὴν μέριμναν ὑμῶν ἐπιρίψαντες ἐπ᾽ αὐτόν, ὅτι αὐτῷ μέλει περὶ ὑμῶν. ⁸ Νήψατε, γρηγορήσατε. ὁ ἀντίδικος ὑμῶν διάβολος ὡς λέων ὠρυόμενος περιπατεῖ ζητῶν [τινα] καταπιεῖν· ⁹ ᾧ ἀντίστητε στερεοὶ τῇ πίστει εἰδότες τὰ αὐτὰ τῶν παθημάτων τῇ κόσμῳ ὑμῶν ἀδελφότητι ἐπιτελεῖσθαι. ¹⁰ Ὁ δὲ θεὸς πάσης χάριτος, ὁ καλέσας ὑμᾶς εἰς τὴν αἰώνιον αὐτοῦ δόξαν ἐν Χριστῷ, ὀλίγον παθόντας αὐτὸς καταρτίσει, στηρίξει, σθενώσει, θεμελιώσει. ¹¹ αὐτῷ τὸ κράτος εἰς τοὺς αἰῶνας, ἀμήν.

Reading Notes[85]

Verse 1

- **Πρεσβυτέρους** ("elders") – This term can refer to older men or to office holders in the church. That office holders are in view is supported by (1) the official use of the term elsewhere;[86] (2) the shepherding duty of the elders (vv. 2–3); and (3) the authority of the elders that requires members of the church, especially the younger men, to "submit" (ὑποτάγητε) to them (v. 5).

- **παρακαλῶ** ("I exhort") – Pres act ind 1st sg παρακαλέω.

- **ὁ συμπρεσβύτερος καὶ μάρτυς** ("a fellow elder and witness") – This represents an example of the Granville Sharp rule which states that two singular nouns modified by one article communicates that both nouns refer to the same person. συμπρεσβύτερος is a biblical *hapax legomenon* and, because there is no evidence of the term before this usage, was possibly coined by Peter.

---

[85] The English version used in the Reading Notes for this chapter is the CSB.
[86] See Acts 11:30; 14:23; 15:2, 4, 6, 22–23; 16:4; 20:17; 21:18; 1 Tim 4:14; 5:17, 19; Titus 1:5; Jas 5:14.

- ὁ ... μάρτυς τῶν τοῦ Χριστοῦ παθημάτων ("witness to the sufferings of Christ") – The genitive τῶν ... παθημάτων is an objective genitive meaning Peter witnessed the sufferings. The other genitive (τοῦ Χριστοῦ) is a subjective genitive meaning the sufferings experienced by Christ (= Christ suffered). The genitive constructions form the first of several "sandwich" structures where an article (τῶν) and noun (παθημάτων) are separated and "stuffed" with material that is syntactically related to the noun (i.e., τοῦ Χριστοῦ).

- ὁ καὶ τῆς μελλούσης ἀποκαλύπτεσθαι δόξης κοινωνός ("as well as one who shares in the glory about to be revealed") – This phrase includes another "sandwich" structure where the article (ὁ) is separated from the noun (κοινωνός). In addition, there is another sandwich with the article τῆς separated from the noun δόξης. This entire phrase is in apposition to the phrase ὁ συμπρεσβύτερος καὶ μάρτυς. The genitive τῆς ... δόξης is an objective genitive. μελλούσης (pres act ptc fem gen sg μέλλω) is an attributive participle modifying δόξης. ἀποκαλύπτεσθαι (pres pass inf ἀποκαλύπτω) is a complementary infinitive.

Verse 2

- ποιμάνατε ("shepherd") – Aor act impv 2nd pl ποιμαίνω. This exhortation is reminiscent of Jesus's command to Peter to "shepherd My sheep" (ποίμαινε τὰ πρόβατά μου, John 21:16). What is interesting here is that the author uses an aorist imperative where a present is expected. Shepherding is an atelic verb that is found in the present tense five times in the non-indicative moods but is never found in the aorist tense (except here). Davids writes, "By using the ingressive aorist, [the author] indicates that this is something that needs to be done with ever new vigor rather than as a routine undertaking."[87] It is also possible that the author is merely viewing the action as a whole, especially since the author has a propensity to use the aorist imperative rather than the present imperative (see, e.g., 1 Pet 5:5 [ὑποτάγητε, ἐγκομβώσασθε]; 6 [ταπεινώθητε]; 8 [νήψατε, γρηγορήσατε]; 9 [ἀντίστητε]).

- τὸ ἐν ὑμῖν ποίμνιον τοῦ θεοῦ ("God's flock among you") – This phrase includes another "sandwich" structure where the article (τό) is separated from the noun (ποίμνιον) with ἐν ὑμῖν put in between. The noun ποίμνιον in a cognate accusative of the verb ποιμάνατε.

- [ἐπισκοποῦντες] ("overseeing") – Pres act ptc masc nom pl ἐπισκοπέω. This is an adverbial participle of means describing how the elders are (or are not) to shepherd the flock. The textual variant ἐπισκοποῦντες is

---

[87] Peter H. Davids, *The First Epistle of Peter*, NICNT (Grand Rapids: Eerdmans, 1990), 178.

omitted in ℵ* B and 33, but is retained in 𝔓72 ℵ² A P Ψ the Old Latin versions, and the Latin Vulgate. Favoring its inclusion, Michaels comments, "It is difficult to see why scribes would have added it if it were not original since the verse reads quite smoothly without it."[88] He argues that the witness of Codex Vaticanus (B) should be used with caution since it "exhibits a remarkably short text throughout vv. 1–4." Michaels also observes that the author often places an imperative before a participle. Davids likewise writes, "Either some copyist added it from 2:25 and passages like Acts 20:28, where it is paired with 'shepherd,' or else it was dropped later when it came to mean 'exercise the office of a bishop' and was thus seen as improper as a command to mere elders. While the textual evidence is balanced, the fact that the author's mind did tend to pair the two words (in 2:25, a passage remote enough that one would not expect a copyist to note the connection) makes the second explanation more likely."[89]

Verse 3

- **μηδ' ὡς κατακυριεύοντες** ("not lording it over") – Pres act ptc masc nom pl κατακυριεύω. This is an adverbial participle of manner explaining the way in which the elders are not to shepherd the flock.

- **κλήρων** ("those entrusted to you") – Literally, "the shares." This noun originally referred to the "lot" which was cast and then to the thing which was gained by the casting of the lot (i.e., the "share" or "portion"). It then took on a meaning of "share" however assigned (i.e., with or without the casting of lots). Here it refers to the local congregation or those who are allotted or entrusted to the elders, thus making the elders responsible for them. This metaphor may be used to express the idea of divine appointment.[90]

- **τύποι γινόμενοι τοῦ ποιμνίου** ("being examples") – γινόμενοι (pres mid ptc masc nom pl γινόμαι) is also an adverbial participle of means explaining the way in which the elders are to shepherd the flock. τοῦ ποιμνίου is an objective genitive.

Verse 4

- **φανερωθέντος τοῦ ἀρχιποίμενος** ("when the chief Shepherd appears") – This is an example of a genitive absolute which is a genitive adverbial (temporal) participial phrase that introduces background information.

---

[88] J. Ramsey Michaels, *1 Peter*, WBC 49 (Waco, TX: Word, 1988), 276.
[89] Davids, *First Epistle of Peter*, 178.
[90] So BDAG, 548.

Thus, both the participle (aor pass ptc masc gen sg φανερόω) and the noun occur in the genitive case but are translated as nominatives.

- **κομιεῖσθε** ("you will receive") – Fut mid ind 2nd pl κομίζω.

- **τὸν ἀμαράντινον τῆς δόξης στέφανον** ("the unfading crown of glory") – The genitive construction τῆς δόξης is probably best categorized as a genitive of apposition.[91] In other words, the unfading crown is the glory of Christ that believers share.[92]

Verse 5

- **νεώτεροι** ("you who are younger") – The referent of νεώτεροι is debated. It could refer to (1) a distinct order of ministers who are subordinate to the elders; (2) recent baptized converts or neophytes in the faith; (3) the rest of the congregation who would be younger than the elders; or (4) men who are literally younger in age. Grudem, who holds to this last view, maintains that the author singles out young people because they "were generally those who would most need a reminder to be submissive to authority within the church."[93]

- **ὑποτάγητε** ("be subject to") – Aor pass impv 2nd pl ὑποτάσσω.

- **ἐγκομβώσασθε** ("clothe yourselves") – Aor mid impv 2nd pl ἐγκομβόομαι (reflexive middle).

- **ἀντιτάσσεται** ("resists") – Pres mid ind 3rd sg ἀντιτάσσω (gnomic present).

- **δίδωσιν** ("gives") – Pres act ind 3rd sg δίδωμι (gnomic present).

Verse 6

- **ταπεινώθητε** ("Humble yourselves") – Aor pass impv 2nd pl ταπεινόω. One would expect the middle voice here but instead the passive is used. Wallace calls this the causative or permissive passive and translates it "allow yourselves to be humbled."[94]

- **ὑψώσῃ** ("He may exalt") – Aor act sub 3rd sg ὑψόω.

---

[91] Cf. Jas 1:12 and Rev 2:10, "crown of life" (τὸν στέφανον τῆς ζωῆς); 2 Tim 4:8, "crown of righteousness" (ὁ τῆς δικαιοσύνης στέφανος); and 1 Thess 2:19, "crown of boasting" (στέφανος καυχήσεως).

[92] So Michaels, *1 Peter*, 287; Davids, *First Epistle of Peter*, 182; Schreiner, *1, 2 Peter, Jude*, NAC, 236 (see chap. 4, n. 4); Robertson, 498.

[93] Wayne Grudem, *The First Epistle of Peter*, TNTC 17 (Leicester: InterVarsity; Grand Rapids: Eerdmans, 1988), 193. This position is also held by Davids, *First Epistle of Peter*, 184; and Schreiner, *1, 2 Peter, Jude*, 237.

[94] Wallace, 441.

Verse 7

- ἐπιρίψαντες ("casting") – Aor act ptc masc nom pl ἐπιρίπτω. Most likely this adverbial participle functions as a participle of means (also called an instrumental participle = "by casting"). Wallace writes, "Although treated as an independent command in several modern translations (e.g., RSV, NRSV, NIV), the participle should be connected with the verb of v. 6, ταπεινώθητε. As such, it is not offering a new command, but is defining *how* believers are to humble themselves. Taking the participle as means enriches our understanding of both verbs: Humbling oneself is not a negative act of self-denial per se, but a positive one of active dependence on God for help."[95] Likewise, Schreiner notes, "The participle should be understood as an instrumental participle, and it explains *how* believers can humble themselves under God's strong hand. Seeing the relationship between the main verb ('humble yourselves,' v. 6) and the participle ('casting all your anxiety upon him,' NASB) is important because it shows that giving in to worry is an example of pride. The logical relationship between the two clauses is as follows: believers humble themselves *by casting* their worries on God. Conversely, if believers continue to worry, then they are caving in to pride."[96]

- ὅτι αὐτῷ μέλει περὶ ὑμῶν ("because he cares about you") – Literally, "because it is a care to him concerning you." The verb μέλει is an impersonal verb and is thus always used in the third person singular form.

Verse 8

- νήψατε, γρηγορήσατε ("Be soberminded, be alert!") – As mentioned above, both of these verbs are aorist imperatives. We would expect νήψατε (aor act impv 2nd pl νήφω) to be a present imperative because it is a stative (atelic) verb and is normally found in the present tense-form in non-indicative moods. For example, it occurs twice as a present imperative (1 Thess 5:8 [= hortatory subjunctive]; 2 Tim 4:5), once as a present subjunctive (1 Thess 5:6), and once as a present participle (1 Pet 1:13). The only other aorist imperative is found in 1 Peter 4:7 (νήψατε) which again suggests that Peter heavily favors the aorist over the present imperative, even for imperatives that are given as a general precept. The same is true for γρηγορήσατε (aor act impv 2nd pl γρηγορέω) which occurs ten times as a present imperative but only once (here in 1 Pet 5:8) as an aorist imperative. Therefore, Davids may be overinterpreting these imperatives when he states that both "are ingressive aorist imperatives, calling on the

---

[95] Wallace, 630.
[96] Schreiner, *1–2 Peter, Jude*, 240.

believers to begin being alert and watchful and to continue doing that until the return of Christ."[97]

- ὠρυόμενος . . . ζητῶν ("roaring . . . looking") – Both ὠρυόμενος (pres mid ptc masc nom sg ὠρύομαι) and ζητῶν (pres act ptc masc nom sg ζητέω) are adverbial participles of manner modifying the main verb περιπατεῖ ("is prowling," pres act ind 3rd sg περιπατέω).

- καταπιεῖν ("he can devour") – Aor act inf καταπίνω. This is probably an infinitive communicating purpose ("in order to devour") or perhaps an epexegetical infinitive explaining the seeking ("that is, to devour").

Verse 9

- ᾧ ("him") – This is a relative pronoun (functioning as a personal pronoun) that refers back to the Devil. It is in the dative case because the verb ἀνθίστημι takes its direct object in the dative instead of the accusative case.

- ἀντίστητε ("Resist") – Aor act impv 2nd pl ἀνθίστημι. Although some have interpreted this verb with the added inceptive nuance, caution should be used so as not to read too much into the verb form. This verb never occurs in the present tense outside of the indicative mood and is thus seen as a telic verb. The aorist form is therefore the expected or default form. Thus, Peter uses the aorist form here, which is often used with commands for a specific occasion, even though the Christian is to continually resist the Devil.

- στερεοὶ τῇ πίστει ("firm in the faith") – The adjective στερεοί is influenced by the imperatival force of ἀντίστητε and has the sense of "be firm."[98] τῇ πίστει is a dative of respect ("[be] firm with respect to the faith").

- εἰδότες ("knowing that") – Per act ptc masc nom pl οἶδα. This is a causal adverbial participle giving the reason ("because you know") the readers should stand firm in their faith.

- τὰ αὐτὰ τῶν παθημάτων ("the same kind of sufferings") – When αὐτός is in the attributive position (i.e., preceded by an article), it functions as an identical adjective and is translated "same." There is probably an understood noun related to the pronoun so that Peter is referring to "the same kind of suffering" (as reflected here in the CSB) or "the same experiences of suffering" (NASB). Another option is that this is an attributed (reversed adjectival) genitive and should be translated as "the same sufferings."

---

[97] Davids, *First Epistle of Peter*, 189; see also Michaels, *1 Peter*, 297.
[98] So Michaels, *1 Peter*, 300.

- **τῇ ἐν κόσμῳ ὑμῶν ἀδελφότητι** ("by your fellow believers throughout the world") – This is another example of a "sandwich" construction. The article τῇ is grammatically connected with the noun ἀδελφότητι ("fellow believers"). This noun is then further modified by the "stuff" in the middle (ἐν κόσμῳ ὑμῶν) explaining what type of fellow believers (i.e., the in-the-world-of-you fellow believers). τῇ ἀδελφότητι could be interpreted as a dative of respect ("with respect to your fellow believers" or "in your fellow believers"), a dative of agent ("by your fellow believers"), or a dative of disadvantage ("on/against your fellow believers").[99] Notice that the noun τῇ ἀδελφότητι ("fellow believers," "brothers," or "brotherhood") is feminine and not masculine, which is common with abstract nouns.

- **ἐπιτελεῖσθαι** ("are being experienced") – Pres pass inf ἐπιτελέω. It is possible that the form here is middle but most commentators take it as passive. Because this infinitive functions as a finite verb, some manuscripts (א A B* and others) have the indicative form ἐπιτελεῖσθε. Although the external evidence is strong for the indicative, the infinitive reading is stronger and is most likely the original.[100]

Verse 10

- **Ὁ δὲ θεὸς πάσης χάριτος** ("The God of all grace") – The genitive χάριτος is a genitive of product ("the God who produces all grace").

- **ὁ καλέσας** ("who called") – Aor act ptc masc nom sg καλέω. This is a substantival participle ("the one who called").

- **παθόντας** ("after you have suffered") – Aor act ptc masc acc pl πάσχω. This is a temporal adverbial participle depicting the action from the perfective aspect, that is, as simply occurring.

- **αὐτὸς** ("himself") – Emphatic use of the third person personal pronoun conveyed with the reflexive pronoun "himself."

- **καταρτίσει, στηρίξει, σθενώσει, θεμελιώσει** ("will . . . restore, establish, strengthen, and support") – All of these verbs are fut act ind 3rd sg (καταρτίζω, στηρίζω, σθενόω, θεμελιόω). Michaels writes, "The verse has the appearance of a benediction except that the verbs are not optatives . . . but future indicatives."[101]

---

[99] Michaels favors the dative of respect (*1 Peter*, 301) whereas Davids prefers the dative of disadvantage (*First Epistle of Peter*, 193).

[100] So Michaels, *1 Peter*, 293; Schreiner, *1, 2 Peter, Jude*, 243.

[101] Michaels, *1 Peter*, 302.

///////////////

CHAPTER 11

INFINITIVES

GOING DEEPER

Not every English translation is created equal. While the English language is certainly blessed to have an abundance of accurate and reliable Bible translations, they all have strengths and weaknesses—and some are better than others in particular areas. Of course, the goal in producing a new translation is to maximize the strengths while minimizing the weaknesses. One area of debate is how to translate an idiom or a figure of speech. Some translations favor a more literal or word-for-word rendering, while others seek to translate the meaning or thought behind the idiom.

For example, let us compare how various translations render 1 Cor 7:1:

- NASB: "It is good for a man not **to touch** a woman."
- CSB: "It is good for a man not **to have sexual relations with** a woman."
- NIV84: "It is good for a man not **to marry**."
- NLT: "It is good to abstain from **sexual relations**."

The Greek reads, καλὸν ἀνθρώπῳ γυναικὸς μὴ **ἅπτεσθαι**. The main verb ("is") is not supplied in the Greek but is understood. The present infinitive ἅπτεσθαι ("to touch") is grammatically functioning as the subject of the sentence. Thus, the sentence could be translated, "Not to touch a woman is good for a man." Nearly all translations, however, supply an impersonal subject ("it") with the implied verb.

We can see that the NASB offers a very wooden rendering, leaving the idiom unexplained. The problem with this approach is that this text could be misunderstood if that particular idiom is not known by the reader. The question, then, is what does Paul mean by this statement? First, we must recognize that Paul is most likely quoting a slogan that comes from the Corinthians in the letter that they had written to Paul. First Corinthians 7:1 begins, "About the things you wrote" (περὶ δὲ ὧν ἐγράψατε). Thus, the Corinthians were downplaying the value of physical relations, probably being influenced by Greek philosophy and perhaps distorting Paul's own teaching on the topic. Second, the infinitive ἅπτεσθαι ("to touch") is a euphemism for sexual intercourse. A euphemism is a more dignified way of communicating a harsher reality or "the substitution of a less offensive word for the more direct but harsh one"[1] and is a common tool used by Paul. For example, later he writes, "Then [Jesus] appeared to over five hundred brothers and sisters at one time, most of them are still alive, but some have **fallen asleep**" (ἐκοιμήθησαν, 1 Cor 15:6). When Paul states that some have fallen asleep, this is a more dignified way of saying that some have died.[2] So when the Corinthians wrote to Paul, apparently they affirmed the slogan, "It is good for man not to touch a woman."

The question that a translator has to wrestle with is whether the idiom "to touch a woman" would be correctly understood by the average English reader. Because this idiom is not used in the English vernacular today, both the CSB and the NLT ("[to have] sexual relations") choose to render the meaning of the idiom instead of the idiom itself. The rendering of the NIV84, however, creates some problems.[3] The question the Corinthians were asking was not, "Is it good not **to marry**?" But even within the bounds of marriage, is it good to cut off all sexual relations with one's spouse? If this is the case, they reasoned, then perhaps believers should not marry at all. Or, if they are already married, then perhaps they should practice abstinence within marriage. And if that is too difficult, then perhaps they should divorce—especially if the spouse is an unbeliever. Gordon Fee states the Corinthian position:

> Since you yourself are unmarried, and are not actively seeking marriage, and since you have denied *porneia* in your letter to us, is it not so that one is better off not to have sexual intercourse at all? After all, in the new age which we have already entered by the Spirit, there is neither marrying nor giving in marriage. Why should we not 'be as the angels' now? Besides, since the body counts for nothing, if some wish to fulfill physical needs there are always the prostitutes.[4]

Paul's response, of course, is that they are only partially correct in their thinking. Yes, it can be good for a man not to have relations with a woman, but only if that is his calling and if he is not yet married. Otherwise, Paul's exhortation is that

---

[1] Young, 240.

[2] Cf. Matt 9:24; 27:52; John 11:11–13; Acts 7:60; 13:36; 1 Cor 7:39; 11:30; 15:18–20; 15:51; 1 Thess 4:13–15; 5:10; 2 Pet 3:4.

[3] It should be noted that the NIV2011 reads, "It is good for a man not to have sexual relations with a woman" (1 Cor 7:1).

[4] Fee, *The First Epistle to the Corinthians*, NICNT, 276 (see chap. 9, n. 4).

they should stay as they are (i.e., married) and fulfill their conjugal duties to their spouse.

CHAPTER OBJECTIVES

The purpose of this chapter is to provide an overview of the specific uses of the infinitive. This will be accomplished by looking at: (1) adverbial infinitives, (2) substantival infinitives, and (3) independent infinitives. Adverbial infinitives account for the greatest number of infinitives and include complementary, purpose, result, temporal (previous time, contemporaneous time, and subsequent time), cause, and means infinitives. Substantival infinitives (i.e., infinitives used as nouns or other substantives) include subject, direct object, indirect discourse, and explanatory (appositional and epexegetic) infinitives. The final division, independent infinitives, are less common, and include imperatival and absolute infinitives.[5]

INTRODUCTION

An infinitive is usually defined as a verbal noun.[6] Thus, some of its features and functions follow more closely the verb while others the noun. Similar to a verb, an infinitive: (1) has aspect (perfective, imperfective, or stative) and voice; (2) can take a direct object or be modified by an adverb; and (3) is negated by μή (like all other non-indicative mood verbs). The subject of the infinitive is in the accusative case rather than the nominative case.[7] The time of the infinitive is not established by its tense-form but must be determined by the context (often by prepositions used in infinitive constructions). Unlike finite verbs, however, an infinitive is indeclinable, meaning that it has no person and number.[8] A finite verb is declinable because each form is limited to a particular subject (first, second, third person singular or plural). In contrast, because an infinitive has no person and number, there is only one form for each of the various tense-forms.[9]

---

[5] This organizational approach of the various uses of the infinitive follows, with modifications, the thorough and logical approach reflected in Wallace (1996). As footnotes will show, we are also indebted to these additional scholars whose writings have contributed clarity and insight concerning the Greek infinitives: Smyth (1984), Dana & Mantey (1946) [1927], Burton (1900), Brooks & Winbery (1979), Blass, Dubrunner, and Funk (1961), Moule (1953), Robertson (1934), Porter (1992), and Young (1994).

[6] Most grammarians agree that the infinitive has its origin in the locative or dative case of a noun. This consensus is affirmed, in part, by the article often associated with the infinitive.

[7] An exception is Rev 12:7 where the subject of the infinitive is in the nominative case (ὁ Μιχαὴλ καὶ οἱ ἄγγελοι αὐτοῦ τοῦ πολεμῆσαι μετὰ τοῦ δράκοντος).

[8] Strictly speaking, an infinitive also does not have a mood (similar to a participle) since it is a verbal *noun*. For the sake of simplicity and parsing, however, it is categorized as a mood.

[9] "The word *infinitive* denotes a verbal form without any limitations (*finis*) of number and person" (Smyth, 437 [§1966]).

TENSE[a]	VOICE	INFINITIVE	TRANSLATION
PRESENT	Active	λύειν	to be loosing
	Middle Passive	λύεσθαι	to loose (for) oneself to be loosed
AORIST	Active	λῦσαι	to loose
	Middle	λύσασθαι	to loose (for) oneself
	Passive	λυθῆναι	to be loosed

[a]The perfect tense-form is not included in the chart above because there are only 49 occurrences in the NT. Although the perfect infinitive of λύω does not occur in the NT, its forms are: λελυκῆναι (active) and λελύσθαι (middle/passive).

Similar to a noun, an infinitive (1) can take an article (which is always neuter and singular = τό, τοῦ, and τῷ);[10] (2) can have a variety of different case functions; and (3) can occur after a preposition.[11] When it occurs after a preposition, the infinitive is always articular and functions adverbially.[12] As such, it is often misleading to characterize an infinitive as a verbal noun, especially when it is translated as a main verb (e.g., οὐκ ἔχετε διὰ τὸ **μὴ αἰτεῖσθαι** ὑμᾶς = "You do not have because you **do not ask**").[13] Although they are virtually nonexistent in modern Greek, infinitives appear quite frequently in the NT. There are 2,291 infinitives in the NT (1,977 anarthrous infinitives and 314 articular infinitives). Of these infinitives 1,241 are aorist, 996 are present, 49 are perfect, and 5 are future.[14] In the following discussion we will consider (1) adverbial, (2) substantival, and (3) independent infinitives.

ADVERBIAL INFINITIVES	Complementary	
	Purpose	
	Result	
	Temporal	Previous Time
		Contemporaneous Time
		Subsequent Time
	Cause	
	Means	

---

[10] The infinitive is never used with the vocative case.

[11] The following prepositions are used with infinitives in the NT: εἰς (72x), ἐν (55x), διά (33x), μετά (15x), πρός (12x), πρό (9x), ἀντί (1x), ἕνεκεν (1x), ἐκ (1x), and ἕως (1x). See Brooks & Winbery, 120. The preposition followed by an articular infinitive is an idiomatic construction and cannot usually be translated word-for-word.

[12] The infinitive is not always articular after a preposition in both the LXX and in extrabiblical literature during the Koine period.

[13] It is also impossible to translate the phrase literally with a word-for-word correspondence. Dana & Mantey write, "The exact translation of such a construction into English is not possible, so the student must learn to sense the force of the Greek idiom" (209).

[14] The 5 future infinitives are found in Acts 11:28; 23:30; 24:15; 27:10; Heb 3:18.

SUBSTANTIVAL INFINITIVES	Subject
	Direct Object
	Indirect Discourse
	Explanatory
INDEPENDENT IMPERATIVES	Imperatival
	Absolute

ADVERBIAL INFINITIVES

Complementary[15]

This is the most common category of infinitives. A complementary infinitive is an infinitive that "completes" the verbal idea of another verb. This usage is paralleled in English. For example, if someone says, "I am able to read the book," the main verb "am able" is completed by the infinitive "to read." This type of infinitive is easy to identify because certain verbs require or often take a complementary infinitive. Such verbs include: ἄρχομαι ("I am beginning"), βούλομαι ("I desire"), δύναμαι ("I am able"), ἐπιτρέπω ("I permit"), ζητέω ("I am seeking"), θέλω ("I am wanting"), μέλλω ("I am about to"), and ὀφείλω ("I ought to"). Note that many are volitional verbs—just as in English. This type of infinitive is always anarthrous and is usually (though not always) found after the main verb (note 1 Tim 2:21 below as an exception).[16]

- Καὶ πάλιν <u>ἤρξατο</u> **διδάσκειν** παρὰ τὴν θάλασσαν (Mark 4:1)

  Again <u>he began</u> **to teach** by the sea

- <u>βούλομαι</u> οὖν **προσεύχεσθαι** τοὺς ἄνδρας ἐν παντὶ τόπῳ (1 Tim 2:8)

  Therefore <u>I want</u> the men in every place **to pray**

- **διδάσκειν** δὲ γυναικὶ οὐκ <u>ἐπιτρέπω</u> οὐδὲ **αὐθεντεῖν** ἀνδρός (1 Tim 2:12)

  <u>I do</u> not <u>allow</u> a woman **to teach** or **to have authority** over a man

---

[15] Some grammars include the complementary infinitive under the broader category of direct object infinitives (so Brooks & Winbery, Dana & Mantey).

[16] It is possible to categorize some complementary infinitives as purpose (or result) infinitives. For the sake of simplicity, however, any infinitive that completes another verb is categorized as a complementary infinitive even if it also conveys purpose (see BDF, 199 [§392]).

- τῷ δὲ <u>δυναμένῳ</u> **φυλάξαι** ὑμᾶς ἀπταίστους (Jude 24)

  Now to him who <u>is able</u> **to protect** you from stumbling

  In this case, the head verb is a substantival participle.[17]

- καὶ ἡμεῖς <u>ὀφείλομεν</u> ἀλλήλους **ἀγαπᾶν** (1 John 4:11)

  <u>we</u> also <u>ought</u> **to love** one another (NASB)

Purpose[18]

A purpose infinitive communicates the goal or intent of an action or state expressed by the controlling verb.[19] Students oftentimes have difficulty distinguishing between a purpose and a result infinitive. The main difference·is that a purpose infinitive indicates an *intended* result, whereas a result infinitive indicates what has actually already resulted (or a conceived result). The function of a purpose infinitive is similar to ἵνα + subjunctive. A purpose infinitive can be tested by adding the words "in order to" or "for the purpose of" directly in front of the infinitive. In addition, purpose infinitives can be identified when they are the objects of prepositions. Although they can occur as simple infinitives (i.e., without an article or preposition), they also occur with the article τοῦ or after the prepositions εἰς τό and πρὸς τό.[20] It is usually sufficient simply to translate the purpose infinitive with "to" + the verbal meaning. At times, it might be better to use "that," "so that," "in order that," or "in order to." "Purpose clauses often occur after verbs of motion (such as ἔρχομαι, -βαίνω, and πορεύομαι), sending (such as ἀποστέλλω), giving (such as δίδωμι), and choosing (such as ἐκλέγομαι)."[21]

---

[17] For more examples of complementary infinitives, see Matt 19:12 (χωρεῖν); 22:46 (ἀποκριθῆναι); Mark 1:45 (κηρύσσειν, διαφημίζειν); 3:23 (ἐκβάλλειν); 12:34 (ἐπερωτῆσαι); Luke 3:8 (λέγειν, ἐγεῖραι); 6:42 (λέγειν); 9:31 (πληροῦν); 10:24 (ἰδεῖν, ἀκοῦσαι); 19:4 (διέρχεσθαι); John 6:15 (ἔρχεσθαι, ἁρπάζειν); 13:14 (νίπτειν); 18:32 (ἀποθνῄσκειν); 21:23 (μένειν); Acts 17:5 (προαγαγεῖν); 18:15 (εἶναι); Rom 1:13 (ἀγνοεῖν); 2 Cor 10:12 (ἐγκρῖναι, συγκρῖναι); Eph 3:4 (νοῆσαι), 20 (ποιῆσαι); Col 1:27 (γνωρίσαι); 1 Thess 4:1 (περιπατεῖν, ἀρέσκειν); Rev 2:2 (βαστάσαι), 10 (πάσχειν); 3:8 (κλεῖσαι).

[18] Moule labels this the "final" infinitive.

[19] It is possible for the infinitive to be related to a verb that is not the "main" verb of a sentence or phrase. For example, in John 1:33 it is related to a substantival participle (ὁ πέμψας με βαπτίζειν). In this example, the controlling verb is a substantival participle.

[20] Purpose infinitives are rarely found after ὥστε or ὡς (see Matt 10:1 [ὥστε ἐκβάλλειν . . . θεραπεύειν]; 15:33 [ὥστε χορτάσαι]; 24:24 [ὥστε πλανῆσαι]; 27:1 [ὥστε θανατῶσαι]; Luke 4:29 [ὥστε κατακρημνίσαι]; 9:52 [ὡς ἑτοιμάσαι]; 20:20 [ὥστε παραδοῦναι]; Acts 20:24 [ὡς τελειῶσαι]). It should also be noted that εἰς τό and πρὸς τό + infinitive do not always communicate purpose but can communicate result (Rom 4:18 [εἰς τὸ γενέσθαι]), indirect discourse (1 Thess 2:12 [εἰς τὸ περιπατεῖν]), manner (Matt 5:28 [πρὸς τὸ ἐπιθυμῆσαι]; Rom 12:3 [εἰς τὸ σωφρονεῖν]), reference (Luke 18:1 [πρὸς τὸ δεῖν πάντοτε προσεύχεσθαι αὐτοὺς καὶ μὴ ἐγκακεῖν]), or can be used epexegetically to explain an adjective (1 Thess 4:9 [εἰς τὸ ἀγαπᾶν]; Jas 1:19 [εἰς τὸ ἀκοῦσαι . . . εἰς τὸ λαλῆσαι]).

[21] Young, 168.

- μὴ νομίσητε ὅτι ἦλθον **καταλῦσαι** τὸν νόμον (Matt 5:17)

  Don't assume that I came **to abolish** the Law

  > This is an example of a simple purpose infinitive. It could be translated, "Don't assume that I came *in order to abolish* the Law."

- προσέχετε [δὲ] τὴν δικαιοσύνην ὑμῶν μὴ ποιεῖν ἔμπροσθεν τῶν ἀνθρώπων <u>πρὸς τὸ</u> **θεαθῆναι** αὐτοῖς (Matt 6:1)

  Be careful not to practice your righteousness in front of others **to be seen** by them

- ἀπήγαγον αὐτὸν <u>εἰς τὸ</u> **σταυρῶσαι** (Matt 27:31)

  [they] led him away **to crucify** him

  > When the infinitive is preceded by εἰς τό, it will often carry the idea of purpose. Notice that the final pronoun "him" is implied in the Greek.

- ὁ υἱὸς τοῦ ἀνθρώπου οὐκ ἦλθεν **διακονηθῆναι** ἀλλὰ **διακονῆσαι** καὶ **δοῦναι** τὴν ψυχὴν αὐτου (Mark 10:45)

  the Son of Man did not come **to be served**, but **to serve**, and **to give** his life

- Σίμων Σίμων, ἰδοὺ ὁ Σατανᾶς ἐξητήσατο ὑμᾶς <u>τοῦ</u> **σινιάσαι** ὡς τὸν σῖτον (Luke 22:31)

  Simon, Simon, look out! Satan has asked **to sift** you like wheat

  > Luke uses τοῦ + infinitive about 40 times, more than any other NT writer.[22]

Result[23]

As mentioned above, the result infinitive is very similar to the purpose infinitive. The main difference is that the result infinitive indicates something that actually resulted (or a conceived result),[24] whereas the purpose infinitive is intended but may

---

[22] For more examples of the purpose infinitive, see Matt 2:2 (προσκυνῆσαι); 6:1 (πρὸς τὸ θεαθῆναι); 13:3 (τοῦ σπείρειν), 30 (πρὸς τὸ κατακαῦσαι); Mark 1:24 (ἀπολέσαι); 14:55 (εἰς τὸ θανατῶσαι); Luke 2:22 (παραστῆσαι); 4:16 (ἀναγνῶναι); 15:15 (βόσκειν); 18:10 (προσεύξασθαι); Acts 3:2 (τοῦ αἰτεῖν), 19 (εἰς τὸ ἐξαλειφθῆναι); 7:42 (λατρεύειν); Rom 1:11 (εἰς τὸ στηριχθῆναι); 3:26 (εἰς τὸ εἶναι); 4:11 (εἰς τὸ εἶναι ... εἰς τὸ λογισθῆναι), 16 (εἰς τὸ εἶναι); 6:6 (τοῦ ... δουλεύειν); 7:4 (εἰς τὸ γενέσθαι); 8:29 (εἰς τὸ εἶναι); 15:8 (εἰς τὸ βεβαιῶσαι), 13 (εἰς τὸ περισσεύειν), 16 (εἰς τὸ εἶναι); 1 Cor 1:17 (βαπτίζειν ... εὐαγγελίζεσθαι); Eph 6:11 (πρὸς τὸ δύνασθαι); Phil 3:10 (τοῦ γνῶναι); 1 Thess 2:12 (εἰς τὸ περιπατεῖν); 3:5 (εἰς τὸ γνῶναι); Jas 3:3 (εἰς τὸ πείθεσθαι); 1 Pet 3:7 (εἰς τὸ μὴ ἐγκόπτεσθαι).

[23] Some grammars label this the "consecutive" infinitive (so Moule).

[24] "Where it is clearly result, it may be actual or hypothetical. The hypothetical is the natural or conceived result" (Robertson, 1089). "In this case the result is thought of as that which the action of the principal verb is adapted or sufficient to produce, and it is the context or the nature of the case only which shows that this result is actually produced" or "is one which the action of the principal

or may not result.[25] The result can be either intentional ("He preached the gospel so that many were saved and baptized") or unintentional ("He preached so long that he became weak"). Another difficulty in differentiating purpose and result infinitives is that they both can use the same constructions. Young adds, "The problem is compounded when it involves divine action, for with the omnipotent and omniscient God who dwells beyond time, His purposes are always realized."[26] They can occur as a simple infinitive (i.e., without an article or preposition), with the article τοῦ, after the prepositions εἰς τό, or after ὥστε or ὡς. In order to communicate the meaning of the infinitive, the words "so that," "so as to," "as a result," or "with the result that" can be used in translation.

- ἦλθον καὶ ἔπλησαν ἀμφότερα τὰ πλοῖα <u>ὥστε</u> **βυθίζεσθαι** αὐτά (Luke 5:7)

  they came and filled both the boats, <u>so that</u> they **began to sink** (ESV)

  > Notice that it was not the intention of the disciples for the boat to sink but the result of too many fish being loaded on board. The use of the infinitive with ὥστε is the most common way to express result with infinitives.[27]

- τί ἐπλήρωσεν ὁ σατανᾶς τὴν καρδίαν σου, **ψεύσασθαί** σε τὸ πνεῦμα τὸ ἅγιον (Acts 5:3)

  why has Satan filled your heart **to lie** to the Holy Spirit

  > This is an example of a simple infinitive and obviously expresses result and not merely purpose since it already happened.

- διὸ παρέδωκεν αὐτοὺς ὁ θεὸς ἐν ταῖς ἐπιθυμίαις τῶν καρδιῶν αὐτῶν . . . <u>τοῦ</u> **ἀτιμάζεσθαι** τὰ σώματα αὐτῶν (Rom 1:24)

  Therefore God delivered them over in the desires of their hearts . . . <u>so that</u> their bodies **were degraded**

  > The CSB interprets this as a result infinitive, though some take this as a purpose or epexegetical infinitive.

- μὴ οὖν βασιλευέτω ἡ ἁμαρτία ἐν τῷ θνητῷ ὑμῶν σώματι <u>εἰς τὸ</u> **ὑπακούειν** ταῖς ἐπιθυμίαις αὐτου (Rom 6:12)

  Therefore do not let sin reign in your mortal body, <u>so that</u> **you obey** its desires

  > Only rarely is εἰς τό + infinitive used to convey result. Because it usually communicates purpose, when in doubt, choose purpose.

---

verb is adapted or sufficient to produce, though the actual production is either left in doubt, or is indicated by the context not to have taken place" (Burton, 148).

[25] "Purpose is only 'intended result,' . . . It is hard to draw a line between conceived result and intended result. . . . The line of distinction is often very faint, if not wholly gone" (Robertson, 1089).

[26] Young, 170.

[27] "[N]early all of the 62 examples of ὥστε and the inf. in the N. T. have the notion of result" (Robertson, 1090).

- ἐὰν ἔχω πᾶσαν τὴν πίστιν <u>ὥστε</u> ὄρη **μεθιστάναι** (1 Cor 13:2)

  if I have all faith, <u>so that</u> I **can move** mountains

  This is a conceived result of having "all faith."[28]

Temporal

The use of the infinitive can convey the relative time of the action of the main verb in relation to the action of the infinitive. In other words, the temporal use can convey when the action occurs, conveying to the reader that the action of the infinitive occurs before (previous or antecedent time) during (contemporaneous time) or after (subsequent time) the action of the infinitive. As Wallace notes, it is important for the interpreter not only to label an infinitive as "temporal" but more specifically which type of temporal relationship exists.[29] In addition, we must note that the time of the action of the infinitive is not based on the tense-form of the infinitive but on contextual factors, such as its relation to the main verb and the use of various prepositions.[30]

Previous Time

Previous time is communicated by μετὰ τό + infinitive. The confusing feature here is that the word μετά is translated "after" and indicates that the action of the infinitive occurs "before" that of the main verb. What is important to remember is that the *time of the infinitive is defined in relation to the main verb* (and not vice versa). Unfortunately, this usage is often mislabeled as "subsequent time" in many grammars which label the action in accordance with the time of the main verb.[31] Thus, in the phrase "After he had suffered (μετὰ τὸ παθεῖν), he also presented Himself alive to them" (Acts 1:3), the suffering occurs *before* (i.e., previous time) Jesus presented himself to his disciples.

---

[28] For more examples of the result infinitive, see Matt 13:32 (ὥστε ἐλθεῖν); 21:32 (πιστεῦσαι); Mark 1:27 (ὥστε συζητεῖν), 45 (ὥστε . . . δύνασθαι); 3:20 (ὥστε . . . δύνασθαι); 4:37 (ὥστε . . . γεμίζεσθαι); 9:26 (ὥστε . . . λέγειν); Luke 12:1 (ὥστε καταπατεῖν); Acts 16:26 (ὥστε σαλευθῆναι); Rom 1:20 (εἰς τὸ εἶναι); 4:18 (εἰς τὸ γενέσθαι); 7:3 (τοῦ . . . εἶναι), 5 (εἰς τὸ καρποφορῆσαι); 1 Cor 8:10 (εἰς τὸ . . . ἐσθίειν); 2 Cor 8:6 (εἰς τὸ παρακαλέσαι); Gal 3:17 (εἰς τὸ καταργῆσαι); Eph 6:19 (γνωρίσαι); Col 4:6 (εἰδέναι); 1 Thess 1:7 (ὥστε γενέσθαι), 8 (ὥστε . . . ἔχειν); Heb 6:10 (ἐπιλαθέσθαι); 11:3 (εἰς τὸ . . . γεγονέναι), 8 (ἐξελθεῖν); 13:6 (ὥστε . . . λέγειν); Rev 2:20 (πορνεῦσαι, φαγεῖν); 5:5 (ἀνοῖξαι).

[29] In addition to distinguishing the three subcategories Wallace rightly emphasizes this need for specificity when addressing a temporal infinitive (594–96).

[30] Dana & Mantey, 215.

[31] So Brooks & Winbery, 123–24; Dana & Mantey, 215–16; Porter, *Idioms*, 201; Robertson, 1091–92; Young, 166–67. Wallace helpfully highlights this confusion concerning the labeling of the temporal infinitive (594, 596). This grammar follows Wallace in labeling the temporal infinitive in accordance with the time of the infinitive.

- μετὰ δὲ τὸ **παραδοθῆναι** τὸν Ἰωάννην ἦλθεν ὁ Ἰησοῦς εἰς τὴν Γαλιλαίαν (Mark 1:14)

  <u>After</u> John **was arrested**, Jesus went to Galilee

  > Notice the order: John is first arrested, then, after that, Jesus went to Galilee. Thus, the action of the infinitive occurs before the action of the main verb.

- μετὰ τὸ **ἐγερθῆναί** με προάξω ὑμᾶς εἰς τὴν Γαλιλαίαν (Mark 14:28)

  <u>after</u> I **have been raised**, I will go ahead of you to Galilee (NASB)

- ἑκουσίως γὰρ ἁμαρτανόντων ἡμῶν <u>μετὰ τὸ</u> **λαβεῖν** τὴν ἐπίγνωσιν τῆς ἀληθείας (Heb 10:26)

  For if we deliberately go on sinning <u>after</u> **receiving** the knowledge of the truth[32]

Contemporaneous Time

With the contemporaneous time use of the infinitive, the action of the infinitive occurs *simultaneously* or *at the same time* as the action of the main or controlling verb and is expressed by ἐν τῷ + infinitive.[33] The prepositional phrase is usually translated with the English word "while," "as," or "when."

- <u>ἐν τῷ</u> **σπείρειν** αὐτὸν ἃ μὲν ἔπεσεν παρὰ τὴν ὁδόν (Matt 13:4)

  <u>As</u> he **sowed**, some seeds fell along the path

- ἐν δὲ <u>τῷ</u> **καθεύδειν** τοὺς ἀνθρώπους ἦλθεν αὐτοῦ ὁ ἐχθρὸς (Matt 13:25)

  But <u>while</u> people **were sleeping**, his enemy came

- ἐν δὲ <u>τῷ</u> **λαλῆσαι** ἐρωτᾷ αὐτὸν Φαρισαῖος ὅπως ἀριστήσῃ παρ' αὐτῷ (Luke 11:37)

  <u>As</u> he **was speaking**, a Pharisee asked him to dine with him[34]

---

[32] For more examples of the previous time infinitive, see Luke 12:5 (μετὰ τὸ ποκτεῖναι); Acts 7:4 (μετὰ τὸ ἀποθανεῖν); 10:41 (μετὰ τὸ ἀναστῆναι); 15:13 (μετὰ . . . τὸ σιγῆσαι); 19:21 (μετὰ τὸ γενέσθαι); 20:1 (μετὰ . . . τὸ παύσασθαι); 22:20 (μετὰ τὸ δειπνῆσαι); 1 Cor 11:25 (μετὰ τὸ δειπνῆσαι). Luke's writings account for over half of the uses (8 of 15).

[33] A few uses of ἐν τῷ + infinitive do not communicate contemporaneous time but means (Acts 3:26 [ἐν τῷ ἀποστρέφειν]) or are epexegetical (Luke 12:15 [ἐν τῷ περισσεύειν]).

[34] For more examples of the contemporaneous time infinitive, see Luke 1:8 (ἐν τῷ ἱερατεύειν), 21 (ἐν τῷ χρονίζει); 3:21 (ἐν τῷ βαπτισθῆναι); 17:11 (ἐν τῷ πορεύεσθαι); 24:51 (ἐν τῷ εὐλογεῖν); Acts 2:1 (ἐν τῷ συμπληροῦσθαι); 8:6 (ἐν τῷ ἀκούειν); 9:3 (ἐν . . . τῷ πορεύεσθαι); Rom 3:4 (ἐν τῷ κρίνεσθαι); 1 Cor 11:21 (ἐν τῷ φαγεῖν); Heb 2:8 (ἐν τῷ . . . ὑποτάξαι); 3:15 (ἐν τῷ λέγεσθαι). Luke–Acts account for 41 of the 54 NT occurrences.

Subsequent Time

With the subsequent time use of the infinitive, the action of the infinitive occurs *after* the action of the main or controlling verb and is expressed by πρὸ τοῦ or πρίν (ἤ) + infinitive.[35] As was mentioned in the discussion for the previous time use of the infinitive, this category is often mislabeled. Because the action of the infinitive takes place after the action of the main verb, the word "before" is used in translation. Thus, before the action of the infinitive occurred, the action of the main verb took place.

- πρὸ τοῦ σε Φίλιππον φωνῆσαι . . . εἶδόν σε (John 1:48)

  <u>Before</u> Philip **called** you . . . I saw you

  > Notice the order: Jesus saw Nathaniel before Philip called him. Thus, the action of the infinitive occurs after the action of the main verb.

- πρὶν Ἀβραὰμ γενέσθαι ἐγὼ εἰμι (John 8:58)

  <u>Before</u> Abraham **was**, I am

- ὁ ἥλιος μεταστραφήσεται εἰς σκότος . . . <u>πρὶν</u> **ἐλθεῖν** ἡμέραν κυρίου (Acts 2:20)

  the sun shall be turned to darkness . . . <u>before</u> the day of the Lord **comes** (ESV)[36]

Cause[37]

The causal infinitive communicates the (usually unintentional) reason or ground for the action of the controlling verb, answering the question "Why?" The most common construction for this type of infinitive is διὰ τό + infinitive (τοῦ + infinitive is rarely used).[38] Such infinitival constructions are best translated using "because," "since," or "for" plus the appropriate finite verb.

- διὰ τὸ μὴ **ἔχειν** ῥίζαν ἐξηράνθη (Matt 13:6)

  <u>since</u> they **had** no root, they withered (ESV)

---

[35] There are 20 uses in the NT: πρὸ τοῦ (9x), πρίν (8x), and πρίν ἤ (3x).

[36] For more examples of the subsequent time infinitive, see Matt 1:18 (πρὶν ἤ συνελθεῖν); 6:8 (πρὸ τοῦ . . . αἰτῆσαι); Mark 14:30 (πρὶν ἤ . . . φωνῆσαι); Luke 22:15 (πρὸ τοῦ . . . παθεῖν); John 4:49 (πρὶν ἀποθανεῖν); 13:19 (πρὸ τοῦ γενέσθαι); 14:29 (πρὶν γενέσθαι); Acts 7:2 (πρὶν ἤ κατοικῆσαι); 23:15 (πρὶν τοῦ ἐγγίσαι); Gal 2:12 (πρὸ τοῦ . . . ἐλθεῖν); 3:23 (πρὸ τοῦ . . . ἐλθεῖν). There is also one example of ἕως τοῦ + infinitive (Acts 8:40), which Robertson calls "the prospective future" (1092).

[37] Some grammars label this category "reason" (so Young).

[38] The dative article (τῷ) + infinitive expresses cause in 2 Cor 2:13 ("I had no rest in my spirit <u>because</u> I **did** not **find** my brother Titus" [οὐκ ἔσχηκα ἄνεσιν τῷ πνεύματί μου τῷ μὴ **εὑρεῖν** με Τίτον τὸν ἀδελφόν μου]). Young maintains ἐν τῷ + infinitive (Acts 2:1; Rom 15:13; Heb 2:8; 8:13) and ἕνεκεν τοῦ + infinitive (2 Cor 7:12) are used as causal infinitives, but these examples are unlikely causal (167). Porter includes 2 Cor 8:11 (ἐκ τοῦ ἔχειν) but this example is likely dubious (*Idioms*, 200).

- διά γε τὸ **παρέχειν** μοι κόπον τὴν χήραν ταύτην ἐκδικήσω αὐτήν (Luke 18:5)

  yet because this widow keeps **pestering** me, I will give her justice

- γὰρ ἐξ ἱκανῶν χρόνων θέλων ἰδεῖν αὐτὸν διὰ τὸ **ἀκούειν** περὶ αὐτοῦ (Luke 23:8)

  for a long time he had wanted to see him because **he had heard** about him

- Καθώς ἐστιν δίκαιον ἐμοὶ τοῦτο φρονεῖν ὑπὲρ πάντων ὑμῶν διὰ τὸ **ἔχειν** με ἐν τῇ καρδίᾳ ὑμᾶς (Phil 1:7)

  it is right for me to think this way about all of you, because I **have** you in my heart

- οὐκ ἔχετε διὰ τὸ μὴ **αἰτεῖσθαι** ὑμᾶς (Jas 4:2)

  You do not have because you **do** not **ask**[39]

Means

On a few occasions, ἐν τῷ + infinitive (normally used to communicate contemporaneous time) or a simple infinitive is used to convey the way in which the action of the controlling verb is performed, answering the question "How?" This meaning will usually be translated with "by" plus the infinitival verb in the form of a gerund (i.e., verbal idea + "ing").

- ὁ θεὸς . . . ἀπέστειλεν αὐτὸν εὐλογοῦντα ὑμᾶς ἐν τῷ **ἀποστρέφειν** ἕκαστον ἀπὸ τῶν πονηριῶν ὑμῶν (Acts 3:26)

  God . . . sent him . . . to you to bless you by **turning** each of you from your evil ways

- δὸς τοῖς δούλοις σου μετὰ παρρησίας πάσης λαλεῖν τὸν λόγον σου, ἐν τῷ τὴν χεῖρά [σου] **ἐκτείνειν** (Acts 4:29–30)

  grant to Your servants that with all boldness they may speak Your word, by **stretching** out Your hand (NKJV)

  Most translations interpret the infinitive as temporal (contemporaneous, "while").

---

[39] For more examples of the causal infinitive, see Matt 13:5 (διὰ τὸ . . . ἔχειν); Mark 5:4 (διὰ τὸ . . . δεδέσθαι); Luke 6:48 (διὰ τὸ . . . οἰκοδομῆσθαι); 9:7 (διὰ τὸ λέγεσθαι); 11:8 (διὰ τὸ εἶναι). Luke's writings account for 18 of the 32 occurrences of this construction (Young, 167).

- τί πειράζετε τὸν θεὸν **ἐπιθεῖναι** ζυγὸν ἐπὶ τὸν τράχηλον τῶν μαθητῶν (Acts 15:10)

  why are you putting God to the test <u>by</u> **placing** a yoke on the neck of the disciples (ESV)

  > This is an example of a simple infinitive expressing means or instrument. Another possible example is Rev 2:14 (φαγεῖν, πορνεῦσαι; so NKJV, NIV).[40]

SUBSTANTIVAL INFINITIVES

Whereas adverbial infinitives are syntactically related to verbs, substantival infinitives function as nouns or other substantives. We will cover four uses of the substantival infinitive: (1) subject; (2) direct object; (3) indirect discourse; and (4) explanatory (appositional and epexegetical).

Subject

It is common for an infinitive (or infinitival phrase) to function as the subject (or predicate nominative) of a finite verb. In such instances, the infinitive may be either articular or anarthrous (but never in a prepositional phrase). When testing as to whether a particular infinitive functions as a subject, try substituting any noun in the place of the infinitive. For example, in the phrase, "to study is important," the subject is the infinitive "to study." The noun "godliness" could replace the infinitive and the resulting sentence would read "godliness is important." The verbs εἰμί, δεῖ, ἔξεστιν, or δοκεῖ are often used in the context.

- ὑμῖν δέδοται **γνῶναι** τὰ μυστήρια τῆς βασιλείας τῶν οὐρανῶν (Matt 13:11)

  To you it has been given **to know** the secrets of the kingdom of heaven (ESV)

  > "To know" is the subject of the passive verb δέδοται ("it has been given").

- ἔξεστιν τοῖς σάββασιν ἀγαθὸν **ποιῆσαι** ἢ **κακοποιῆσαι**, ψυχὴν **σῶσαι** ἢ **ἀποκτεῖναι**; (Mark 3:4)

  Is it lawful to do good on the Sabbath or **to do evil, to save** life or **to kill**?

---

[40] For other possible examples of the infinitive of means, see Heb 2:8 (ἐν τῷ . . . ὑποτάξαι); 8:13 (ἐν τῷ λέγειν). It is possible that ἐκ τοῦ + infinitive conveys means in 2 Cor 8:11 (so NASB).

- οὐ γάρ ἐστιν καλὸν **λαβεῖν** τὸν ἄρτον τῶν τέκνων καὶ τοῖς κυναρίοις **βαλεῖν** (Mark 7:27)

  because it isn't right **to take** the children's bread and **throw** it to the dogs

  > The two infinitives "to take" and "to throw" are the subjects of the predication "isn't right."

- **εὐαγγελίσασθαί** με δεῖ τὴν βασιλείαν τοῦ θεοῦ (Luke 4:43)

  I must **preach** the good news of the kingdom of God (ESV)

  > Literally, "To preach the kingdom of God is necessary for me."

- τὸ ζῆν Χριστὸς καὶ **τὸ ἀποθανεῖν** κέρδος (Phil 1:21)

  to live is Christ, and **to die** is gain (ESV)

  > Notice that the verbs are implied in the Greek and added to the English translation for clarity. The RSV translates the verse as "living is Christ and dying is gain."[41]

Direct Object

In various grammars, this category is described as both rare or quite common. The variances of this category are determined by what sub-categories are included. For example, Wallace maintains that this category is "rare" because he treats both complementary infinitives and infinitives used for indirect discourse under separate categories, though he recognizes that technically the category of indirect discourse is a sub-category of direct object.[42] Others, such as Brooks & Winbery, include both of those sub-categories under the general heading, "The Infinitive as the Direct Object of a Verb."[43] Because the use of the infinitive as indirect discourse is common and is more difficult to translate, we will treat it as a separate category.

On a few occasions the infinitive (or infinitival phrase) functions as the direct object of a finite verb. Although this category is rare, the examples that do exist are exegetically significant. This usage of the infinitive may be either articular or anarthrous (but never in a prepositional phrase).

- οὕτως καὶ τῷ υἱῷ ἔδωκεν ζωὴν **ἔχειν** ἐν ἑαυτῷ (John 5:26)

  so also he has granted to the Son **to have** life in himself

  > The anarthrous infinitive ἔχειν is the direct object of the verb ἔδωκεν.

---

[41] For more examples of the infinitive used in indirect discourse, see Matt 19:7 (δοῦναι, ἀπολῦσαι); Mark 6:27 (ἐνέγκαι); 8:6 (ἀναπεσεῖν), 7 (παρατιθέναι); Luke 5:3 (ἐπαναγαγεῖν), 14 (εἰπεῖν); 9:21 (λέγειν); 12:13 (μερίσασθαι); 19:15 (φωνηθῆναι); 20:27 (εἶναι); 22:31 (σινιάσαι); 24:23 (ἑωρακέναι); Acts 25:4 (τηρεῖσθαι, μέλλειν), 24 (δεῖν); Rom 2:19 (εἶναι); 1 Cor 9:14 (ζῆν); 11:18 (ὑπάρχειν); Eph 4:22–24 (ἀποθέσθαι, ἀνανεοῦσθαι, ἐνδύσασθαι); 1 Tim 2:1 (ποιεῖσθαι); 2 Tim 2:18 (γεγονέναι); Heb 11:24 (λέγεσθαι); Jas 4:17 (ποιεῖν); Rev 3:9 (εἶναι); 13:14 (ποιῆσαι).

[42] Wallace, 601.

[43] Brooks & Winbery, 127.

- οὐ παραιτοῦμαι **τὸ ἀποθανεῖν** (Acts 25:11)

  I do not refuse **to die** (NASB)

- θεὸς γάρ ἐστιν ὁ ἐνεργῶν ἐν ὑμῖν καὶ **τὸ θέλειν** καὶ **τὸ ἐνεργεῖν** ὑπὲρ τῆς εὐδοκίας (Phil 2:13)

  For it is God who is working in you, [enabling you] both **to will** and **to work** for his good purpose

  > Wallace translates this phrase, "For the one producing in you both the willing and the working (for [his] good pleasure) is God."[44] This verse indicates, then, that although the believer is supposed to "work out [his] own salvation with fear and trembling" (Phil 2:12), the basis of this ability comes from God and thus leaves no room for boasting.[45]

Indirect Discourse

The infinitive is used with verbs of speaking or perception to communicate indirect discourse (i.e., not a direct quotation in the first person ["He said, 'I am hungry'"] but in the third person ["He said that he was hungry"]). In Greek this meaning can be communicated by using a few different grammatical expressions such as ὅτι + indicative, ἵνα + subjunctive, or an anarthrous infinitive. When the infinitive is used in indirect discourse, the sentence often cannot be translated literally or "word-for-word." For example, 1 John 2:6 reads, ὁ λέγων ἐν αὐτῷ μένειν. This phrase could literally be translated, "The one who says in him to remain," but such a translation makes little sense. Instead we should render it, "the one who says he remains in him" (see also 1 John 2:9). Notice that the infinitive is translated as a third person indicative verb ("he remains"). Some of the most common verbs used in this type of construction include: δοκέω, ἐρωτάω, κελεύω, κρίνω, λέγω, νομίζω, παραγγέλλω, and παρακαλέω.

- τότε ὁ Πιλᾶτος <u>ἐκέλευσεν</u> **ἀποδοθῆναι** (Matt 27:58)

  Then Pilate <u>ordered</u> it **to be given** (to him) (ESV)

- <u>ἐπηγγείλαντο</u> αὐτῷ ἀργύριον **δοῦναι** (Mark 14:11)

  <u>they promised</u> **to give** him money

  > A direct quotation would be, "We will give you money." But as an indirect discourse, Mark is reporting a third person account of what they promise.

---

[44] Wallace, 602.

[45] For other possible examples of the infinitive as the direct object, see Matt 19:14 (ἐλθεῖν); Luke 1:9 (τοῦ θυμιᾶσαι); 2 Cor 8:11 (τὸ ποιῆσαι); Phil 2:6 (τὸ εἶναι); 4:10 (τὸ φρονεῖν).

- καὶ <u>ἀπεκρίθησαν</u> μὴ **εἰδέναι** πόθεν (Luke 20:7)

  So <u>they answered</u> that **they did** not **know** where it came from (ESV)

  > The direct discourse would have used the first person, "We do not know where it came from."

- <u>ἠρώτων</u> **ἀπελθεῖν** ἀπὸ τῆς πόλεως (Acts 16:39)

  <u>they urged</u> them **to leave** town

- καὶ ἀπῆλθα πρὸς τὸν ἄγγελον <u>λέγων</u> αὐτῷ **δοῦναί** μοι τὸ βιβλαρίδιον (Rev 10:9)

  So I went to the angel and <u>told</u> him **to give** me the little scroll (ESV)

Explanatory (Appositional or Epexegetical)[46]

Under this category we will treat both appositional and epexegetical infinitives. An appositional infinitive further *defines* a noun, pronoun, or substantival adjective by giving more specific information. One way to translate this category is to supply "namely" or "that is" in front of the infinitive. Another method is simply to use a colon. An epexegetical infinitive further *clarifies* or *qualifies* a noun or adjective. The appositional and epexegetical uses are very similar (and sometimes indistinguishable). Robertson states that "there is no essential difference between the appositional and the epexegetical use of the infinitive."[47] Wallace readily admits, "The use of the [epexegetical] infinitive is easy to confuse with the appositional infinitive."[48] Porter, noting that some grammars such as Moule distinguish between these two uses of the infinitives, treats them under one category.[49] Likewise, we have decided to deal with these categories under the general heading of "explanatory" infinitives.

Appositional

- ὁ δὲ θεός, ἃ προκατήγγειλεν διὰ στόματος πάντων τῶν προφητῶν **παθεῖν** τὸν Χριστὸν αὐτοῦ, ἐπλήρωσεν οὕτως (Acts 3:18)

  In this way God fulfilled what he had predicted through all the prophets— that his Messiah **would suffer**[50]

---

[46] Brooks & Winbery label this category under the heading, "The Infinitive as a Modifier" (128–29). Young has a separate category for "apposition" but includes his discussion of epexegetical infinitives under the heading "Infinitives Functioning as Adjectives" (175).

[47] Robertson, 1086. Earlier he writes, "The inf. in apposition is that with nouns; the epexegetical inf. is used with verbs. But at bottom the two uses are one" (Robertson, 1078).

[48] Wallace, 607.

[49] Porter, *Idioms*, 198.

[50] For more examples of appositional infinitives, see Acts 3:18 (παθεῖν); 15:20 (τοῦ ἀπέχεσθαι), 29 (ἀπέχεσθαι); 26:16 (προχειρίσασθαι); Rom 4:13 (εἶναι); 14:13 (τὸ . . . τιθέναι); 15:23 (τοῦ ἐλθεῖν); 1 Cor 7:37 (τηρεῖν); 2 Cor 2:1 (ἐλθεῖν); Heb 9:8 (πεφανερῶσθαι); Jas 1:27 (ἐπισκέπτεσθαι,

- ὑμῖν ἐχαρίσθη τὸ ὑπὲρ Χριστοῦ, οὐ μόνον **τὸ** εἰς αὐτὸν **πιστεύειν** ἀλλὰ καὶ **τὸ** ὑπὲρ αὐτοῦ **πάσχειν** (Phil 1:29)

  it has been granted to you on Christ's behalf not only **to believe** in him, but also **to suffer** for him

  > "[T]he articular infinitives are in apposition to a substantival prepositional phrase functioning as the subject."[51]

- τοῦτο γάρ ἐστιν θέλημα τοῦ θεοῦ, ὁ ἁγιασμὸς ὑμῶν, **ἀπέχεσθαι** ὑμᾶς ἀπὸ τῆς πορνείας (1 Thess 4:3)

  For this is God's will, your sanctification: **that** you **keep away** from sexual immorality

Epexegetical

- ἐζήτει εὐκαιρίαν **τοῦ παραδοῦναι** αὐτὸν (Luke 22:6)

  he . . . started looking for a good opportunity **to betray** him

  > In this example, the opportunity is the betrayal. As noted above, there is a fine line between this usage and purpose (or result). For example, another way to understand this verse is that Judas was looking for an opportunity *in order to* betray Jesus.[52]

- ἔδωκεν αὐτοῖς ἐξουσίαν τέκνα θεοῦ **γενέσθαι** (John 1:12)

  He gave them the right **to be** children of God

- ἔχω **φαγεῖν** ἣν ὑμεῖς οὐκ οἴδατε (John 4:32)

  I have food **to eat** that you don't know about[53]

τηρεῖν); Rev 2:14 (βαλεῖν, φαγεῖν). It should be noted that some of these examples could also be considered as purpose infinitives.

[51] Wallace, 607.

[52] Regarding the examples they offer concerning epexegetical infinitives, Brooks & Winbery comment, "It is possible to explain all of the following examples in some other way, namely as adverbial infinitives of purpose or result" (142). Likewise, Moule notes, "It will be observed how thin the boundary wears here and there between epexegetic (that is, explanatory and extensive) Infinitives and consecutive [that is, result] Infinitives" (*Idiom Book*, 127). He then adds, "*Note* also that a ἵνα-clause can be used as an alternative for such epexegetic Infinitives."

[53] For more examples of epexegetical infinitives, see Matt 3:14 (βαπτισθῆναι); Mark 2:10 (ἀφιέναι); Luke 10:19 (τοῦ πατεῖν); 24:25 (τοῦ πιστεύειν); John 19:10 (ἀπολῦσαι); Acts 14:9 (τοῦ σωθῆναι); 1 Cor 7:39 (γαμηθῆναι); 10:9 (τοῦ μετέχειν); Jas 1:19 (ἀκοῦσαι, λαλῆσαι).

INDEPENDENT INFINITIVES

Imperatival

On a few occasions the infinitive functions as an imperative (or hortatory subjunctive). In such cases the infinitive is not dependent on any other verb but is independent.

- χαίρειν μετὰ χαιρόντων, **κλαίειν** μετὰ κλαιόντων (Rom 12:15)

  Rejoice with those who rejoice; **weep** with those who weep

- πλὴν εἰς ὃ ἐφθάσαμεν, τῷ αὐτῷ **στοιχεῖν** (Phil 3:16)

  Only **let us hold true** to what we have attained (ESV)[54]

Absolute

Similar to other absolute constructions, the infinitive absolute functions independently of the rest of the sentence, having no syntactical relation to other words or phrases. The most common infinitive used in this manner is χαίρειν and it is usually found in the introductory section of a letter. Because it functions similarly to an interjection, it is not translated "to rejoice" but has the stereotyped meaning of "Greetings!"

- οἱ ἀπόστολοι καὶ οἱ πρεσβύτεροι ἀδελφοὶ τοῖς κατὰ τὴν Ἀντιόχειαν καὶ Συρίαν καὶ Κιλικίαν ἀδελφοῖς τοῖς ἐξ ἐθνῶν **χαίρειν** (Acts 15:23)

  From the apostles and the elders, your brothers, To the brothers and sisters from among the Gentiles in Antioch, Syria, and Cilicia: **Greetings**

- Κλαύδιος Λυσίας τῷ κρατίστῳ ἡγεμόνι Φήλικι **χαίρειν** (Acts 23:26)

  Claudius Lysias, To the most excellent governor Felix: **Greetings**

- Ἰάκωβος θεοῦ καὶ κυρίου Ἰησοῦ Χριστοῦ δοῦλος ταῖς δώδεκα φυλαῖς ταῖς ἐν τῇ διασπορᾷ **χαίρειν** (Jas 1:1)

  James, a servant of God and of the Lord Jesus Christ: To the twelve tribes in the dispersed abroad. **Greetings**[55]

---

[54] Some debated examples include Matt 5:34 (ὁμόσαι); Luke 9:3 (ἔχειν); 2 Thess 3:14 (συναναμίγνυσθαι); 2 Tim 2:14 (λογομαχεῖν); Titus 2:2 (εἶναι).

[55] See also Heb 7:9 (εἰπεῖν).

SUMMARY

ADVERBIAL INFINITIVES		
Complementary	"Completes" the verbal idea of another verb.	καὶ ἡμεῖς <u>ὀφείλομεν</u> ἀλλήλους **ἀγαπᾶν** ("<u>we</u> also <u>ought</u> **to love** one another"; 1 John 4:11 NASB).
Purpose	Communicates the goal or intent of an action or state expressed by the controlling verb.	μὴ νομίσητε ὅτι ἦλθον **καταλῦσαι** τὸν νόμον ("Don't think that I came **to abolish** the Law"; Matt 5:17).
Result	Communicates the actual or conceived result of an action or state expressed by the controlling verb.	ἔπλησαν ἀμφότερα τὰ πλοῖα <u>ὥστε</u> **βυθίζεσθαι** αὐτά ("they . . . filled both the boats, <u>so that</u> they **began to sink**"; Luke 5:7 ESV)
Temporal		
Previous Time	The action of the infinitive occurs *before* the action of the controlling verb (μετὰ τό + infinitive).	<u>μετὰ</u> δὲ <u>τὸ</u> **παραδοθῆναι** τὸν Ἰωάννην ἦλθεν ὁ Ἰησοῦς εἰς τὴν Γαλιλαίαν ("<u>After</u> John **was arrested**, Jesus went to Galilee"; Mark 1:14).
Contemporaneous Time	The action of the infinitive occurs *simultaneously* with the action of the controlling verb (ἐν τῷ + infinitive).	<u>ἐν τῷ</u> **σπείρειν** αὐτὸν ἃ μὲν ἔπεσεν παρὰ τὴν ὁδόν ("As he **sowed**, some seed fell along the path"; Matt 13:4).
Subsequent Time	The action of the infinitive occurs *after* the action of the controlling verb (πρὸ τοῦ or πρίν [ἤ] + infinitive).	<u>πρὸ τοῦ</u> σε Φίλιππον **φωνῆσαι** . . . εἶδόν σε ("<u>Before</u> Philip **called** you . . . I saw you"; John 1:48).
Cause	Communicates the reason or ground for the action of the controlling verb, answering "Why?" (διὰ τό + infinitive).	οὐκ ἔχετε <u>διὰ τὸ</u> μὴ **αἰτεῖσθαι** ὑμᾶς ("You do not have <u>because</u> you **do** not **ask**"; Jas 4:2).
Means	Conveys the way in which the action of the controlling verb is performed, answering "How?" (ἐν τῷ + infinitive).	ὁ θεὸς . . . ἀπέστειλεν αὐτὸν εὐλογοῦντα ὑμᾶς <u>ἐν τῷ</u> **ἀποστρέφειν** ἕκαστον ἀπὸ τῶν πονηριῶν ὑμῶν ("God . . . sent him . . . to you to bless you <u>by</u> **turning** each of you from your evil ways"; Acts 3:26).

SUBSTANTIVAL INFINITIVES		
Subject	Functions as the subject (or predicate nominative) of a finite verb.	τὸ ζῆν Χριστὸς καὶ τὸ ἀποθανεῖν κέρδος ("**to live** is Christ, and **to die** is gain"; Phil 1:21 ESV).
Direct Object	Functions as the direct object of a finite verb.	ὁ πατὴρ . . . τῷ υἱῷ ἔδωκεν ζωὴν ἔχειν ἐν ἑαυτῷ ("The Father . . . has granted to the Son to **have** life in himself"; John 5:26).
Indirect Discourse	Used with verbs of speaking or perception to communicate indirect discourse.	καὶ <u>ἀπεκρίθησαν</u> μὴ **εἰδέναι** πόθεν ("So <u>they answered</u> that **they did** not **know** where it came from"; Luke 20:7 ESV).
Explanatory	Further defines, clarifies, or qualifies a noun or adjective.	ἔδωκεν αὐτοῖς ἐξουσίαν τέκνα θεοῦ **γενέσθαι** ("He gave them the right **to be** children of God"; John 1:12).

INDEPENDENT INFINITIVES		
Imperatival	Functions as an imperative (or hortatory subjunctive).	**χαίρειν** μετὰ χαιρόντων ("**Rejoice** with those who rejoice"; Rom 12:15).
Absolute	Functions independently of the rest of the sentence, having no syntactical relation to other words or phrases.	Ἰάκωβος . . . ταῖς δώδεκα φυλαῖς ταῖς ἐν τῇ διασπορᾷ **χαίρειν** ("James . . . To the twelve tribes dispersed abroad. **Greetings**"; Jas 1:1).

PRACTICE EXERCISES

In each of the following examples, (1) parse each underlined infinitive and (2) determine its specific use based on the information provided in this chapter.

1. ὁ δὲ ἐξελθὼν ἤρξατο <u>κηρύσσειν</u> πολλὰ καὶ <u>διαφημίζειν</u> τὸν λόγον, ὥστε μηκέτι αὐτὸν <u>δύνασθαι</u> φανερῶς εἰς πόλιν <u>εἰσελθεῖν</u> (Mark 1:45).

2. καὶ ἐποίησεν δώδεκα . . . ἵνα ὦσιν μετ᾽ αὐτοῦ καὶ ἵνα ἀποστέλλῃ αὐτοὺς <u>κηρύσσειν</u> καὶ <u>ἔχειν</u> ἐξουσίαν <u>ἐκβάλλειν</u> τὰ δαιμόνια (Mark 3:14–15).

3. καὶ ἤρξατο <u>διδάσκειν</u> αὐτοὺς ὅτι δεῖ τὸν υἱὸν τοῦ ἀνθρώπου πολλὰ <u>παθεῖν</u> καὶ <u>ἀποδοκιμασθῆναι</u> ὑπὸ τῶν πρεσβυτέρων καὶ τῶν ἀρχιερέων καὶ τῶν γραμματέων καὶ <u>ἀποκτανθῆναι</u> καὶ μετὰ τρεῖς ἡμέρας <u>ἀναστῆναι</u> (Mark 8:31).

4. εἰ δὲ καὶ ὁ Σατανᾶς ἐφ᾽ ἑαυτὸν διεμερίσθη, πῶς σταθήσεται ἡ βασιλεία αὐτοῦ; ὅτι λέγετε ἐν Βεελζεβοὺλ <u>ἐκβάλλειν</u> με τὰ δαιμόνια (Luke 11:18).

5. προσθεὶς εἶπεν παραβολὴν διὰ τὸ ἐγγὺς <u>εἶναι</u> Ἰερουσαλὴμ αὐτὸν καὶ <u>δοκεῖν</u> αὐτοὺς ὅτι παραχρῆμα μέλλει ἡ βασιλεία τοῦ θεοῦ <u>ἀναφαίνεσθαι</u> (Luke 19:11).

6. ἀπ᾽ ἄρτι λέγω ὑμῖν πρὸ τοῦ <u>γενέσθαι</u>, ἵνα πιστεύσητε ὅταν γένηται ὅτι ἐγώ εἰμι (John 13:19).

7. παρέστησεν ἑαυτὸν ζῶντα μετὰ τὸ <u>παθεῖν</u> αὐτὸν (Acts 1:3).

8. ἐν δὲ τῷ <u>ἄρξασθαί</u> με <u>λαλεῖν</u> ἐπέπεσεν τὸ πνεῦμα τὸ ἅγιον ἐπ᾽ αὐτοὺς (Acts 11:15).

9. μηκέτι οὖν ἀλλήλους κρίνωμεν· ἀλλὰ τοῦτο κρίνατε μᾶλλον, <u>τὸ μὴ</u> <u>τιθέναι</u> πρόσκομμα τῷ ἀδελφῷ ἢ σκάνδαλον (Rom 14:13).

10. ἐγερθήσονται γὰρ ψευδόχριστοι καὶ ψευδοπροφῆται καὶ δώσουσιν σημεῖα μεγάλα καὶ τέρατα ὥστε <u>πλανῆσαι</u>, εἰ δυνατόν, καὶ τοὺς ἐκλεκτούς (Matt 24:24).

VOCABULARY

Vocabulary to Memorize

ἀθετέω	I nullify, reject, set aside (16)
ἀνακρίνω	I judge, examine, call to account (16)
δείκνυμι	I show (33)
δεῖπνον, τό	dinner, supper, banquet (16)
δέσμιος, ὁ	prisoner (16)
δηνάριον, τό	denarius (16)
διαλογίζομαι	I consider, ponder, reason (16)
διατάσσω	I order, direct, command (16)
διψάω	I am thirsty, long for (16)
διώκω	I pursue (45)
ἐκτείνω	I stretch out (16)
ἐλπίζω	I hope (31)
ἐμβαίνω	I go in, step in, embark (16)
ἔπειτα	then, next (16)
ἐπιθυμέω	I desire, long for, lust for (16)
ἐπιλαμβάνομαι	I take hold of, catch, arrest (19)
ἐπιμένω	I stay, remain, persevere (16)
ἐργάτης, -ου, ὁ	laborer, worker (16)
εὐλογία, ἡ	blessing, praise (16)
εὐσέβεια, ἡ	godliness, piety (15)
Ἔφεσος, ἡ	Ephesus (16)
ζῆλος, ὁ/τό	jealousy, envy (16)
θεμέλιος, ὁ	foundation (15)
κακῶς	badly, wrongly, wickedly (16)
κατέρχομαι	I come down, arrive, put in (16)
μέχρι	until (17)
ὁμολογέω	I confess, profess (26)
παραγγέλλω	I command, charge (32)
παρέχω	I offer, grant (16)
πλησίον	neighbor (17)
πλούσιος	rich, wealthy (28)
πλοῦτος, ὁ/τό	wealth, riches (22)
ῥίζα, ἡ	root, source, shoot, descendent (17)
τιμή, ἡ	honor, value, price (41)
ὑποκριτής, -οῦ, ὁ	hypocrite, pretender (17)
ὑπομένω	I remain, endure (17)

ὑπομονή, ἡ	endurance, perseverance, patience (32)
φεύγω	I flee, avoid (29)
χάρισμα, -ατος, τό	gift, favor (17)
ὦ	O (direct address) (17)

Vocabulary to Recognize

ἀγαθοεργέω	I do good (2)
ἀγών, -ῶνος, ὁ	fight, struggle (6)
ἀγωνίζομαι	I fight, struggle (8)
ἀδηλότης, -ητος, ἡ	uncertainty (1)
ἀθανασία, ἡ	immortality (3)
ἀνεπίλημπτος	above reproach, blameless (3)
ἀποθησαυρίζω	I store, lay up (1)
ἀπόλαυσις, -εως, ἡ	enjoyment (2)
ἀπρόσιτος	unapproachable (1)
ἄσπιλος	spotless, pure (4)
δυνάστης, -ου, ὁ	ruler, sovereign (3)
ἐπιφάνεια, ἡ	appearance (6)
εὐμετάδοτος	generous (1)
ζῳογονέω	I give life to, preserve life (3)
κοινωνικός	generous (1)
κράτος, τό	power, dominion (12)
κυριεύω	I rule (7)
οἰκέω	I inhabit, dwell (9)
ὁμολογία, ἡ	confession (6)
ὄντως	really (10)
πλουσίως	richly (4)
πλουτέω	I am rich (12)
Πόντιος, ὁ	Pontius (3)
πραϋπαθία, ἡ	gentleness (1)
ὑψηλοφρονέω	I am proud, conceited, haughty (1)

READING THE NEW TESTAMENT

1 Timothy 6:11–19

¹¹ Σὺ δέ, ὦ ἄνθρωπε θεοῦ, ταῦτα φεῦγε· δίωκε δὲ δικαιοσύνην εὐσέβειαν πίστιν, ἀγάπην ὑπομονὴν πραϋπαθίαν. ¹² ἀγωνίζου τὸν καλὸν ἀγῶνα τῆς πίστεως, ἐπιλαβοῦ τῆς αἰωνίου ζωῆς, εἰς ἣν ἐκλήθης καὶ ὡμολόγησας τὴν καλὴν ὁμολογίαν ἐνώπιον πολλῶν μαρτύρων. ¹³ παραγγέλλω [σοι] ἐνώπιον τοῦ θεοῦ τοῦ ζῳογονοῦντος τὰ πάντα καὶ Χριστοῦ Ἰησοῦ τοῦ μαρτυρήσαντος ἐπὶ Ποντίου Πιλάτου τὴν καλὴν ὁμολογίαν, ¹⁴ τηρῆσαί σε τὴν ἐντολὴν ἄσπιλον ἀνεπίλημπτον μέχρι τῆς ἐπιφανείας τοῦ κυρίου ἡμῶν Ἰησοῦ Χριστοῦ, ¹⁵ ἣν καιροῖς ἰδίοις δείξει ὁ μακάριος καὶ μόνος δυνάστης, ὁ βασιλεὺς τῶν βασιλευόντων καὶ κύριος τῶν κυριευόντων, ¹⁶ ὁ μόνος ἔχων ἀθανασίαν, φῶς οἰκῶν ἀπρόσιτον, ὃν εἶδεν οὐδεὶς ἀνθρώπων οὐδὲ ἰδεῖν δύναται· ᾧ τιμὴ καὶ κράτος αἰώνιον, ἀμήν. ¹⁷ Τοῖς πλουσίοις ἐν τῷ νῦν αἰῶνι παράγγελλε μὴ ὑψηλοφρονεῖν μηδὲ ἠλπικέναι ἐπὶ πλούτου ἀδηλότητι ἀλλ᾽ ἐπὶ θεῷ τῷ παρέχοντι ἡμῖν πάντα πλουσίως εἰς ἀπόλαυσιν, ¹⁸ ἀγαθοεργεῖν, πλουτεῖν ἐν ἔργοις καλοῖς, εὐμεταδότους εἶναι, κοινωνικούς, ¹⁹ ἀποθησαυρίζοντας ἑαυτοῖς θεμέλιον καλὸν εἰς τὸ μέλλον, ἵνα ἐπιλάβωνται τῆς ὄντως ζωῆς.

Reading Notes[56]

Verse 11

- Σὺ ("you") – Second person personal pronoun and (emphatic) subject of φεῦγε.

- δέ ("But") – This postpositive conjunction is adversative and contrasts the rich (especially the false teachers) with Timothy. This is the first time Paul uses this device (σὺ δέ) in his letters to Timothy and Titus to contrast his associates with the opponents (see 2 Tim 3:10, 14; 4:5; Titus 2:1). Towner notes, "[T]his polemical-rhetorical device is designed to emphasize a break with, and to create distance from, the opponents."[57]

- ὦ ("O") – This interjection indicates deep emotion but is untranslated in most English translations. Zerwick comments, "This is but a little particle, but it casts such a light on the state of Our Lord and of His apostles, that no one surely, in reading the Scriptures, would wish to neglect its indications."[58] Some versions, such as the CSB, NIV, and NRSV, omit this interjection.

---

[56] The English version used in the Reading Notes for this chapter is the ESV.
[57] Philip H. Towner, *The Letters to Timothy and Titus*, NICNT (Grand Rapids: Eerdmans, 2006), 407.
[58] Zerwick, 12 (§35).

- **ἄνθρωπε** ("man") – The use of the vocative signals a change in subject (from a warning to the rich to Timothy) and thus begins a new section or paragraph.

- **θεοῦ** ("of God") – Genitive of relationship. The phrase ἄνθρωπε θεοῦ is used only here and in 1 Tim 3:17 in the NT but is more commonly found in the LXX.

- **ταῦτα** ("these things") – Direct object of φεῦγε. Refers to the vices, especially the desire for wealth and the accompanying temptations, found in 6:3–10.

- **φεῦγε** ("flee") – Pres act impv 2nd sg φεῦγω (see discussion in v. 12 on ἐπιλαβοῦ). This section has four imperatives: φεῦγε ("flee," v. 11); δίωκε ("pursue," v. 11); ἀγωνίζου ("fight," v. 12); and ἐπιλαβοῦ ("take hold," v. 12).

- **δίωκε** ("pursue") – Pres act impv 2nd sg δίωκω (see discussion in v. 12 on ἐπιλαβοῦ). For a similar pattern of φεῦγε . . . δίωκε, see 2 Tim 2:22 (cf. Titus 2:12). These verbs "were stock items in Greek ethical teaching, and were sometimes juxtaposed as here."[59]

- **δικαιοσύνην εὐσέβειαν πίστιν, ἀγάπην ὑπομονὴν πραϋπαθίαν** ("righteousness, godliness, faith, love, steadfastness, and gentleness") – These six virtues (accusative direct objects of δίωκε) either form three sets of two or two sets of three. πραϋπαθίαν ("gentleness") is a NT *hapax* (though a cognate appears in 2 Tim 2:25; Titus 3:2). These are qualities that the false teachers are lacking.

Verse 12

- **ἀγωνίζου** ("fight") – Pres mid impv 2nd sg ἀγωνίζομαι (see discussion on ἐπιλαβοῦ below). Some resources parse this as a deponent verb, but Neva Miller points out that Greek prefers the middle voice for verbs of reciprocity (i.e., actions that inherently require two or more parties such as "fighting").[60]

- **τὸν καλὸν ἀγῶνα** ("the good fight") – Direct object of ἀγωνίζου (see also 2 Tim 4:7 where this phrase occurs). ἀγωνίζου . . . ἀγῶνα . . . ὡμολόγησας . . . ὁμολογίαν: both of these accusatives (ἀγῶνα and ὁμολογίαν) are cognate accusatives.

- **τῆς πίστεως** ("of the faith") – This genitive phrase is difficult to interpret. Marshall interprets this is an appositional genitive so that it refers "to faith

---

[59] Towner, *Letters to Timothy and Titus*, 408.

[60] Neva F. Miller, "Appendix 2: A Theory of Deponent Verbs," in *Analytical Lexicon of the Greek New Testament*, ed. Timothy Friberg, Barbara Friberg, and Neva F. Miller (Grand Rapids: Baker, 2000), 427.

as the characteristic quality of the Christian life that must be maintained to the end, rather than to 'the faith' as an object to be defended."[61] Knight maintains that Paul is speaking "of the struggle in which the Christian engages *because of* his or her faith and *through* his or her faith."[62] Johnson translates the phrase, "Engage the noble athletic contest for the faith."[63]

- ἐπιλαβοῦ ("take hold of") – Aor mid impv 2nd sg ἐπιλαμβάνομαι. Nearly all commentators interpret this imperative as a punctiliar aorist. For example, Knight paraphrases the verse: "Continually struggle the struggle of the faith, i.e. persevere, (and at the end) then once-and-for-all lay hold of eternal life." Guthrie writes, "*Take hold of* (*epilabou*) denotes a single complete event." Kelly adds, "Timothy can lay hold on eternal life . . . immediately, in a single act." Finally, Quinn and Wacker maintain, "The aorist *epilabou* designates the decisive act of laying hold on eternal life in this life."[64] But the view that Paul switches to the aorist tense to describe a punctiliar (or once-and-for-all) command is overly simplistic because it fails to consider the inherent lexical meaning of the verb.

The three preceding verbs (φεῦγω, διώκω, and ἀγωνίζομαι) are all in the present tense. This makes sense since the verbal action of each is viewed as atelic (thus favoring the present tense-form). This distinction is reflected in the actual usage of these three verbs. φεῦγω occurs 29 times in the NT and 9 times as an imperative. Interestingly, all 9 of these imperatives are in the present tense-form. διώκω occurs 45 times in the NT, and in the non-indicative mood the present tense-form occurs 17 times and the aorist tense-form occurs only 3 times (including 6 present imperatives [one of which is a hortatory subjunctive] and only one aorist imperative [which is a quote from Ps 34:14]). ἀγωνίζομαι occurs 8 times in the NT, including 6 times in the present tense-form and never in the aorist tense-form in any mood. On the other hand, ἐπιλαμβάνομαι occurs 19 times in the NT, and in non-indicative moods is found 15 times in the aorist tense-form but never in the present tense-form (λαμβάνω and its compounds occur 17 times as an aorist imperative and only 4 times as a present imperative).

Therefore, Paul's use of the aorist ἐπιλαβοῦ in v. 12 is at least partly determined by the lexical meaning of the verb. In other words, the verb,

---

[61] I. Howard Marshall (in collaboration with Philip H. Towner), *A Critical and Exegetical Commentary on the Pastoral Epistles*, ICC (Edinburgh: T&T Clark, 1999), 659; so also Towner, *Letters to Timothy and Titus*, 411.

[62] George Knight, *The Pastoral Epistles*, NIGTC (Grand Rapids: Eerdmans, 1992), 263.

[63] L. T. Johnson, *Letters to Paul's Delegates: 1 Timothy, 2 Timothy, Titus* (Valley Forge, PA: Trinity Press International, 1996), 305.

[64] Knight, *Pastoral Epistles*, 263; Donald Guthrie, *The Pastoral Epistles*, rev. ed., TNTC 14 (Leicester, UK: InterVarsity; Grand Rapids: Eerdmans, 1990), 127; J. N. D. Kelly, *A Commentary on the Pastoral Epistles*, BNTC (London: Adam & Charles Black, 1963), 141; Jerome D. Quinn and William C. Wacker, *The First and Second Letters to Timothy*, ECC (Grand Rapids: Eerdmans, 2000), 529.

because of the nature of its meaning, fits with the aorist because "taking hold" is viewed (metaphorically) as a telic action. Paul changes tenses not so much because he is thinking of a once-and-for-all or punctiliar action, but because of the inherent meaning of the verb strongly favors the aorist tense (because the action is completed, at least conceptually, in a short period of time).

- τῆς αἰωνίου ζωῆς ("the eternal life") – Genitive direct object of ἐπιλαβοῦ (see also ζωῆς in v. 19).

- εἰς ἣν ("to which") – ἣν is a fem acc sg relative pronoun whose antecedent is τῆς αἰωνίου ζωῆς and is the object of the preposition εἰς.

- ἐκλήθης ("you were called") – Aor pass ind 2nd sg καλέω. The understood agent is God (divine passive).

- ὡμολόγησας ("you made") – Aor act ind 2nd sg ὁμολογέω ("I confess").

- τὴν καλὴν ὁμολογίαν ("the good confession") – Direct object of ὡμολόγησας. This "good confession" could refer to (1) Timothy's baptism or (2) Timothy's ordination or appointment (cf. 1 Tim 1:18; 4:14).

Verse 13

- παραγγέλλω [σοι] – ("I charge you") – Pres act ind 1st sg παραγγέλλω. It is questionable as to whether σοι is original. It is included in ℵ2 A D H *Byz* but omitted by ℵ* F G Ψ 6 33 1739. "It appears to be a later insertion because of the difficulty of having the verbal idea begin with παραγγέλλω, 'I urge,' and not be completed until τηρῆσαί σε, 'you to keep,' in the next verse."[65]

- τοῦ ζῳογονοῦντος ("who gives life") – Pres act ptc masc gen sg ζῳογονέω (attributive participle modifying τοῦ θεοῦ). This participle could also be translated as "who preserves life" (cf. Luke 17:33). The imperfective aspect depicts the action as ongoing: God continually gives life.

- τοῦ μαρτυρήσαντος ("who in his testimony . . . made") – Aor act ptc masc gen sg μαρτυρέω (attributive participle modifying Χριστοῦ Ἰησοῦ).

- ἐπὶ ("before") – This could refer to (1) a spatial meaning "before" or (2) "in the time of."[66]

---

[65] William D. Mounce, *Pastoral Epistles*, WBC 46 (Thomas Nelson: Nashville, 2000), 351.

[66] Knight (*Pastoral Epistles*, 265) and Towner (*Letters to Timothy and Titus*, 413) argue for the former while Mounce (*Pastoral Epistles*, 358) argues for the latter.

Verse 14

- **τηρῆσαί** ("to keep") – Aor act inf τηρέω. This is an indirect discourse infinitive that completes the idea of παραγγέλλω [σοι] in v. 13 ("I charge you . . . to keep"). Remember that indirect discourse infinitives usually follow verbs of speech or command such as παραγγέλλω.

- **σε** ("you" [untranslated in the ESV]) – This second person personal pronoun is the subject of the infinitive τηρῆσαί. Remember that the subject of an infinitive occurs in the accusative case instead of the nominative case. The NASB renders this phrase: "I charge you . . . that <u>you</u> keep."

- **τὴν ἐντολὴν** ("the commandment") – Knight lists eight options for the meaning of this phrase but opts for "the gospel viewed as a rule of life" (i.e., the Christian faith).[67] Similarly, Mounce argues that it refers to a general (not specific) command and therefore refers to "Timothy's commitment to Christ and his ministry, a commitment to preach the gospel. . . ."[68]

- **τῆς ἐπιφανείας τοῦ κυρίου ἡμῶν Ἰησοῦ Χριστοῦ** ("the appearing of our Lord Jesus Christ") – ἐπιφανείας occurs 6 times in the NT and is used only by Paul. In every instance it refers to Christ's appearance, both of his incarnation (2 Tim 1:10) and mostly of his future return (2 Thess 2:8; 1 Tim 4:16; 2 Tim 4:1, 8; Titus 2:13). τοῦ κυρίου is a subjective genitive. Ἰησοῦ Χριστοῦ is in apposition to τοῦ κυρίου.

Verse 15

- **ἥν** ("which") – Fem acc sg relative pronoun whose antecedent is τῆς ἐπιφανείας and is the object of δείξει.

- **δείξει** ("he will display") – Fut act ind 3rd sg δείκνυμι.

- **ὁ . . . δυνάστης** ("the . . . Sovereign") – This term can also be translated "ruler" and occurs only three times in the NT (Luke 1:52; Acts 8:27; in both of these occurrences it is used of humans). The two adjectives μακάριος and μόνος modify δυνάστης as is evidenced by the use of only one article.

- **ὁ βασιλεὺς . . . καὶ κύριος** ("the King . . . and Lord") – This is an example of the Granville Sharp rule, which states that one article governing two (personal, singular, and non-proper) nouns connected by καί, refers to the same person. That is, in the context, the king and the lord both refer to God. This phrase is in apposition to ὁ μακάριος καὶ μόνος δυνάστης (the same is true for ὁ μόνος ἔχων ἀθανασίαν . . . in the v. 16).

---

[67] Knight, *Pastoral Epistles*, 267.
[68] Mounce, *Pastoral Epistles*, 359.

- **τῶν βασιλευόντων . . . τῶν κυριευόντων** ("of kings . . . of lords") – Pres act ptc masc gen pl βασιλεύω and κυριεύω (substantival participles). This could be translated literally as "the King of those who reign as kings and Lord of those who rule as lords." The genitives are best taken as genitives of subordination ("King <u>over</u> Kings"). It is possible that some of the language in this verse is directed against emperor worship. Mounce comments that this phrase "places Timothy's God in direct opposition to the imperial cult."[69]

Verse 16

- **ὁ . . . ἔχων** ("who . . . has") – Pres act ptc masc nom sg ἔχω (subsantival participle).

- **φῶς οἰκῶν ἀπρόσιτον** ("who dwells in unapproachable light") – This clause is governed by the article ὁ at the beginning of the verse. Thus, οἰκῶν (pres act ptc masc nom sg οἰκέω), like ἔχων, is a substantival participle.

- **ὅν** ("whom") – Masc acc sg relative pronoun whose antecedent is the two preceding substantival participles (ὁ . . . ἔχων . . . οἰκῶν).

- **ἰδεῖν δύναται** ("can see") – ἰδεῖν (aor act inf βλέπω/ὁράω) is a complementary infinitive because it *completes* the idea of another verb (δύναται, pres mid ind 3rd sg δύναμαι). Typically, the complementary infinitive will occur after the verb it completes, though in this case it occurs before it. This is also the same root verb that occurred earlier (εἶδεν, aor act ind 3rd sg βλέπω/ὁράω).

- **ᾧ** ("to him") – This masc dat sg relative pronoun is the subject of vv. 15–16 (i.e., God the Father).

Verse 17

- **παράγγελλε** ("charge") – Pres act impv 2nd sg παράγγελλω. This is the main verb followed by five infinitives (two in v. 17 and three in v. 18).

- **ὑψηλοφρονεῖν** ("to be haughty") – Pres act inf ὑψηλοφρονέω (NT *hapax legomenon*). This is an indirect discourse infinitive that completes the idea of παράγγελλε and is a compound word from ὑψηλός ("haughty, lofty") and φρονέω ("to think").

---

[69] Mounce, *Pastoral Epistles*, 361.

- **ἠλπικέναι** ("to set . . . hopes") – Per act inf ἐλπίζω (indirect discourse). This is the present state use of the perfect (stative aspect) which stresses "the continuing character of the hope formed."[70]

- **τῷ παρέχοντι** ("who . . . provides") – Pres act ptc masc dat sg παρέχω (substantival participle, gnomic use of the present tense).

- **ἡμῖν** ("us") – Dative of advantage.

- **εἰς ἀπόλαυσιν** ("to enjoy") – This word occurs only two times in the NT. In Heb 11:25 it is used negatively of the fleeting pleasures of sin.

Verse 18

- **ἀγαθοεργεῖν** ("to do good") – Pres act inf ἀγαθοεργέω (indirect discourse). Because the three infinitives in this verse are dependent on the verb παράγγελλε ("instruct") in v. 17, the CSB and NASB repeat the verb. The NASB uses italics to note that it is not in the original (*"Instruct them* to do good").

- **πλουτεῖν ἐν ἔργοις καλοῖς** ("to be rich in good works") – Pres act inf πλουτέω (indirect discourse). Notice the play on words: "Instruct those who are rich (τοῖς πλουσίοις) in the present age not to be arrogant or to set their hope on the uncertainty of wealth, but on God, who richly (πλούτου) provides us with all things to enjoy. [Instruct them] to do good, to be rich (πλουτεῖν) in good works, to be generous, willing to share." ἐν ἔργοις καλοῖς is a dative of respect ("be rich with respect to good works").

- **εὐμεταδότους εἶναι** ("to be generous") – Pres act inf εἰμί (indirect discourse). εὐμεταδότους ("generous") a biblical *hapax legomenon*.

- **κοινωνικούς** ("ready to share") – This term, also a biblical *hapax*, means "generous, liberal." The verb εἶναι is probably understood ("*to be* willing to share") and this is most likely an amplification of the previous command "to be generous."

Verse 19

- **ἀποθησαυρίζοντας** ("thus storing up") – Pres act ptc masc acc pl ἀποθησαυρίζω. This is an adverbial participle most likely expressing result. That is, a result or consequence of those who do good, are rich in good works, and are generous is that they store up for themselves a good foundation (so ESV, NIV, NRSV).

- **ἑαυτοῖς** ("for themselves") – Masc dat pl third person reflexive pronoun (dative of advantage).

---

[70] BDF, 176 (§341).

- **εἰς τὸ μέλλον** ("for the future") – Literally, "for the about to come [age]." αἰών ("age") is understood from v. 17. μέλλον is a pres act ptc neut acc sg μέλλω (substantival participle).

- **ἐπιλάβωνται** ("they may take hold of") – Aor mid sub 3rd pl ἐπιλαμβάνομαι. This verb is in the subjunctive mood because of the term ἵνα which precedes it.

//////////////

CHAPTER 12

PRONOUNS, PREPOSITIONS, CONJUNCTIONS, ADVERBS & PARTICLES

GOING DEEPER

At prayer meetings, funerals, and weddings, a pastor sometimes leads people in a recitation of "the Lord's Prayer" (Matt 6:9–13). Words memorized in childhood pour forth reflexively, "Our Father which art in heaven . . ." (Matt 6:9 KJV). In the final petition, congregants pray, "And lead us not into temptation, but deliver us from evil" (Matt 6:13 KJV). Interestingly, several modern English versions render the underlying Greek of verse 13 slightly differently. The NIV, for example, translates the verse: "And lead us not into temptation, but deliver us from *the evil one*" (emphasis added). This variation in translation raises a question: in the Lord's Prayer, are we asking God to deliver us from "evil" (perhaps in an abstract or impersonal sense) or from "the evil one" (i.e., from Satan)?

The divergent English translations cannot be traced back to a textual variant in the ancient Greek manuscripts. The Greek text of Matthew 6:13 unequivocally reads: καὶ μὴ εἰσενέγκῃς ἡμᾶς εἰς πειρασμόν, ἀλλὰ ῥῦσαι ἡμᾶς ἀπὸ τοῦ πονηροῦ. The point of dispute is the meaning of the final prepositional phrase— ἀπὸ τοῦ πονηροῦ. Should these words be translated "from evil" or "from the evil one"? Either rendering is grammatically possible; τοῦ πονηροῦ could be neuter or masculine. Greek grammarian Maximilian Zerwick, however, notes that the verb ῥύομαι followed by the preposition ἀπό more commonly has a personal refer-ence.[1] Thus, translating the contested phrase as "from the evil one" is more like-ly. Furthermore, literary context favors this translation. Matthew has prepared his reader to understand τοῦ πονηροῦ as a reference to Satan by structuring his Gospel so that the "first mention of temptation (4:1–11) is unambiguously connected with the devil."[2] This interpretive issue raises a practical question—do you pray regu-larly for the Lord to deliver you from your malevolent demonic foe?

CHAPTER OBJECTIVES

The purpose of this chapter is to introduce students to other parts of speech not covered previously in the text. We will survey pronouns, prepositions, conjunc-tions, adverbs, and particles.[3]

PRONOUNS

A pronoun is a word that stands in for a noun.[4] Pronouns allow for an economy in speech, so that writers do not have to repeat previously introduced nouns or explicitly state nouns understood from context. For example, someone could say, "John is taking Greek, and John is very excited, because John is going to see John's parents at the beach after final exams." Much more pleasant to the ear, however, is this: "John is taking Greek, and *he* is very excited, because *he* is going to see *his* parents at the beach after final exams."

There are many different subcategories of pronouns. In decreasing order of fre-quency, the seven main categories of pronouns are discussed below.[5] Paradigms for pronouns will not be included below, and the student is encouraged to review all pronoun paradigms in his or her introductory Greek textbook. Indeed, some scholars have questioned the benefit of studying pronouns as a separate category in intermediate Greek, since they function in the same ways that nouns do.[6]

---

[1] Zerwick, 29 (§89).

[2] Carson, "Matthew," EBC, 208 (see chap. 2, n. 76).

[3] For a new short lexicon which focuses on these small but significant units of speech, see G. K. Beale, Daniel J. Brendsel, and William A. Ross, *An Interpretive Lexicon of New Testament Greek: Analysis of Prepositions, Adverbs, Particles, Relative Pronouns, and Conjunctions* (Grand Rapids: Zondervan, 2014). This mini-lexicon (96 pages) mainly summarizes previous reference works, but it also adopts a system of labeling words' logical relationships employed in the method of bracketing or arcing popularized by John Piper. See www.biblearc.com.

[4] "The word pronoun is derived from two Latin words, the preposition *pro* which means for and the noun *nomen* which means name. A pronoun therefore is a word which stands for or in the place of or instead of a noun" (Brooks & Winbery, 80).

[5] Wallace lists pronouns by frequency (320).

[6] Brooks & Winbery remark, "Inasmuch as pronouns take the place of nouns, they are used in much the same way as nouns are used. It is unnecessary therefore to provide separate syntactical categories for them" (80).

We will begin looking at each class of pronouns by identifying samples of that pronoun in English and Greek. Then, a few more explanatory comments and illustrative biblical passages will be given.

Personal Pronouns

Personal pronouns (e.g., ἐγώ, σύ, αὐτοῦ, ἡμεῖς) are pronouns that refer to people (usually), but may also refer to things (e.g., αὐτό, "it"): A personal pronoun may be used to express emphasis, intensity, or an identical ("same") relationship. Each of these functions is illustrated below.

Emphatic Use

Because a Greek verb ending usually conveys clearly the person and number of the subject, the presence of an explicit personal pronoun *as subject* often communicates emphasis. Two exceptions should be noted to the emphatic use. (1) In non-subject positions, personal pronouns are frequently used for stylistic brevity (i.e., so that previously introduced nouns do not have to be repeated). (2) With the verb εἰμί, a personal pronoun *as subject* should be expected without emphasis.[7] In other words, to include the explicit personal pronoun with the verb εἰμί is usually an unconscious stylistic pattern in Greek, not a conscious choice to communicate emphasis.

- ὁ δὲ ἐγερθεὶς παρέλαβεν τὸ παιδίον καὶ τὴν μητέρα **αὐτοῦ** (Matt 2:14)

  So he got up, took the child and **his** mother

  > Matthew employs the third person singular personal (possessive) pronoun αὐτοῦ ("his") as opposed to repeating the proper name Ἰησοῦς ("Jesus") in the genitive case. This is an example of using the personal pronoun for brevity.

- **ἐγὼ** χρείαν ἔχω ὑπὸ σοῦ βαπτισθῆναι, καὶ **σὺ** ἔρχῃ πρός με; (Matt 3:14)

  I need to be baptized by you, and yet **you** come to me?

  > Here the Greek verb endings convey clearly the person and number of the subjects. Yet, the explicit addition of the nominative personal pronouns further emphasizes the contrast between John the Baptist and Jesus.

- **ἡμεῖς** δὲ οὐκ ἐσμὲν ὑποστολῆς εἰς ἀπώλειαν (Heb 10:39)

  But **we** are not like those who turn away from God to their own destruction (NLT)

  > Here, following a normal Greek stylistic pattern with no intended emphasis, the personal pronoun is employed with a form of εἰμί.

---

[7] S. M. Baugh writes, "With copulative verbs (usually εἰμί) a nominative personal pronoun was often supplied *without emphasis*, whereas the inclusion of the nominative personal pronoun with most other verbs signified some sort of emphasis." See *A First John Reader*, 93 (see preface, n. 4) (emphasis original). Baugh is the only grammarian I have found who has noted this important pattern. Perhaps his observation should be named "Baugh's rule."

Intensive Use

In the predicate position,[8] the third person personal pronoun (αὐτός, αὐτή, αὐτό) intensifies the noun to which it is linked. In English translation, such intensification is usually communicated with the addition of an intensive pronoun (e.g., "himself," "herself," "itself," "yourself," "themselves," etc.).

- ὅτι **αὐτὸς** ὁ κύριος . . . καταβήσεται ἀπ᾽ οὐρανοῦ (1 Thess 4:16)

  For the Lord **himself** will descend from heaven

  > The third person personal pronoun (αὐτός) in the predicate position intensifies another noun (ὁ κύριος).[9]

- πίστει καὶ **αὐτὴ** Σάρρα στεῖρα δύναμιν εἰς καταβολὴν σπέρματος ἔλαβεν (Heb 11:11)

  By faith even Sarah **herself** received ability to conceive (NASB)

- καὶ **αὐτοὶ** ἅγιοι ἐν πάσῃ ἀναστροφῇ γενήθητε (1 Pet 1:15)

  be holy **yourselves** also in all *your* behavior (NASB)

  > The implied subject of γενήθητε ("be") is ὑμεῖς. In context, ὑμεῖς is understood as masculine plural (i.e., the mixed congregation of men and women whom Peter addresses). So, the implied pronoun ὑμεῖς is intensified with the masculine plural αὐτοί.

Identical ("Same") Use

The third person personal pronoun (αὐτός, αὐτή, αὐτό) is used in the attributive position[10] to communicate an identical relationship. It is usually translated as "same" in English.

- ἐκ τοῦ **αὐτοῦ** στόματος ἐξέρχεται εὐλογία καὶ κατάρα (Jas 3:10)

  Out of the **same** mouth come praise and cursing (NIV)

- ὑμεῖς τὴν **αὐτὴν** ἔννοιαν ὁπλίσασθε (1 Pet 4:1)

  arm yourselves also with the **same** understanding

  > αὐτήν ("same") modifies ἔννοιαν ("understanding"). The personal pronoun ὑμεῖς ("you") is used emphatically.

---

[8] Usually, the "predicate position" means the form of αὐτός does not have an article and the noun it is intensifying does have the article. In some situations, neither the form of αὐτός nor the noun it is intensifying is preceded by an article. Or, a form of αὐτός may intensify an implied subject of a verb (e.g., 1 Pet 1:15).

[9] Wallace lists "intensive pronouns" as a separate category of pronouns (348–50). I have chosen to categorize the intensive pronoun as a function of the personal pronoun.

[10] Usually, the "attributive position" means the form of αὐτός has an article and the noun it is modifying may, or may not, have the article. In some situations, neither the form of αὐτός nor the noun it is modifying is preceded by an article.

- εἰδότες τὰ **αὐτὰ** τῶν παθημάτων . . . ἐπιτελεῖσθαι (1 Pet 5:9)

  knowing that the **same** kind of sufferings are being experienced

Demonstrative Pronouns

Demonstrative pronouns (this [masc, οὗτος], these [fem, αὗται], that [neut, ἐκεῖνο], those [masc, ἐκεῖνοι]) are the "pointing out" pronouns (Latin: *demonstro*, "I point out"). They can be further subdivided into near demonstrative pronouns ("this, these") and far demonstrative pronouns ("that, those"). Near demonstrative pronouns refer to things or people that are near spatially or conceptually to the speaker. Far demonstrative pronouns refer to things or people that are spatially or conceptually distant from the speaker. When employing a demonstrative pronoun, the author is often drawing some emphasis or contrast. Sometimes the demonstrative pronoun has an anaphoric (previous reference) function. Other times, the author may simply use the demonstrative pronoun in a personal stylistic pattern, as the apostle John does in his Gospel and epistles.

Near Demonstrative Pronouns

- **ταῦτα** δὲ αὐτοῦ ἐνθυμηθέντος (Matt 1:20)

  But after he had considered **these things**

  > Here the demonstrative pronoun is used absolutely—as a substantive.

- παρεισέδυσαν γάρ τινες ἄνθρωποι, οἱ πάλαι προγεγραμμένοι εἰς **τοῦτο** τὸ κρίμα (Jude 4)

  For some people, who were designated for **this** judgment long ago, have come in by stealth

  > The demonstrative pronoun, functioning adjectivally, modifies the noun τὸ κρίμα. When used adjectivally, the demonstrative pronoun usually appears in the predicate position (lacking the article and modifying a noun preceded by the article).

Far Demonstrative Pronouns

- ἐν δὲ ταῖς ἡμέραις **ἐκείναις** παραγίνεται Ἰωάννης ὁ βαπτιστὴς (Matt 3:1)

  In **those** days John the Baptist came

- καθὼς **ἐκεῖνος** δίκαιός ἐστιν (1 John 3:7)

  just as **he** is righteous (NRSV)

  > Here the NRSV translation renders the demonstrative pronoun as a personal pronoun ("he") in English. A more literal translation would read, "just as *that one* is righteous."

Relative Pronouns

A relative pronoun (e.g., οἵ, ἧς, ὅ) is a pronoun that (usually) "relates back" to an antecedent noun and allows the writer to make an additional explanatory comment about that noun. The entire clause introduced by the relative pronoun is called a relative clause. The relative pronoun is normally translated in English as "who," "which," or "that." Sometimes the antecedent of the relative pronoun is not stated or the relative pronoun points forward to a postcedent.

One should note that a relative pronoun (like all pronouns) matches the gender and number of its antecedent. Thus, for example, when the antecedent to a relative pronoun is masculine singular, the relative pronoun will be masculine singular. When translating from Greek into English, however, if a masculine or feminine relative pronoun is not referring to a personal entity, the translator should use "which" or "that." For example, Mark 4:31 (ESV) reads, "It is like a grain of mustard seed, **which**, when sown on the ground . . ." The highlighted English word ("which") is a translation of a *masculine* relative pronoun (ὅς). Consider how odd this verse would sound if the relative pronoun had been translated as "who"!

Examples of relative pronouns from the GNT are provided below.

- ἀνδρὶ μωρῷ, **ὅστις** ᾠκοδόμησεν αὐτοῦ τὴν οἰκίαν ἐπὶ τὴν ἄμμον (Matt 7:26)

  a foolish man **who** built his house on the sand

  > ὅστις is an alternate form of the masculine singular relative pronoun (ὅς) with little, if any, difference in meaning.[11]

- ὑμεῖς ἐστε οἱ υἱοὶ τῶν προφητῶν καὶ τῆς διαθήκης **ἧς** διέθετο ὁ θεὸς πρὸς τοὺς πατέρας ὑμῶν (Acts 3:25)

  You are the sons of the prophets and of the covenant **that** God made with your ancestors

  > If following standard "rules of grammar,"[12] the relative pronoun in this sentence should be feminine accusative singular. It would be feminine and singular because it refers back to the feminine singular noun, διαθήκη ("covenant"). It would be accusative (ἥν) because it is functioning as the direct object of the verb διέθετο ("[he] made"). Relative pronouns are, however, sometimes "attracted" to the case of the antecedent, especially when the antecedent is genitive, as here.[13]

---

[11] BDAG notes that though the form ὅστις is frequently used interchangeably with ὅς, in some contexts, it appears to have a more generalizing sense or refer to a class with shared characteristics (729–30). Similar alternate relative pronoun forms exist for the feminine (ἥτις) and neuter (ὅ τι). Such alternate forms usually occur in the nominative (sg or pl) in the Koine period (BDAG, 729).

[12] This phrase is put in quotes because true grammatical study is fundamentally a descriptive (not prescriptive) exercise.

[13] Brooks & Winbery also use Acts 3:25 as an example of a relative pronoun's attraction to its antecedent (80).

- ὃ ἦν ἀπ᾽ ἀρχῆς, ὃ ἀκηκόαμεν, ὃ ἑωράκαμεν τοῖς ὀφθαλμοῖς ἡμῶν (1 John 1:1)

  That which was from the beginning, **which** we have heard, **which** we have seen with our eyes (NIV)

  Notice in this example that there is no antecedent for the relative pronouns.

Interrogative Pronouns

Interrogative pronouns are questioning pronouns: who? (masc/fem sg τίς), of whom? (masc/fem sg τίνος), what/why? (τί).

- τίς γὰρ ἐξ ὑμῶν θέλων πύργον οἰκοδομῆσαι οὐχὶ πρῶτον καθίσας ψηφίζει τὴν δαπάνην (Luke 14:28)

  For **which** of you, wanting to build a tower, doesn't first sit down and calculate the cost

- ἰδοὺ ὕδωρ, τί κωλύει με βαπτισθῆναι; (Acts 8:36)

  Look, here is water! **What** is to prevent me from being baptized? (NRSV)

Indefinite Pronouns

Unlike personal pronouns, which identify a particular person ("he") or persons ("they"), indefinite pronouns are "indefinite" in their identification: someone/anyone (masc sg, τις), certain ones (masc pl, τινες).[14] Interestingly, the paradigms for indefinite and interrogative pronouns are exactly the same except for accents. Interrogative pronouns always have an acute accent over their initial iota. Any other accentuation (or lack of accentuation) identifies the form as an indefinite pronoun.

- καὶ ἰδού **τινες** τῶν γραμματέων εἶπαν ἐν ἑαυτοῖς, Οὗτος βλασφημεῖ (Matt 9:3)

  At this, **some** of the scribes said to themselves, "He's blaspheming!"

- ἐάν **τις** εἴπῃ ὅτι Ἀγαπῶ τὸν θεὸν καὶ τὸν ἀδελφὸν αὐτοῦ μισῇ, ψεύστης ἐστίν (1 John 4:20)

  If **anyone** says, "I love God," and hates his brother, he is a liar (ESV)

---

[14] In his *English Grammar for Language Students*, Braun defines an indefinite pronoun as "a pronoun that does not denote any particular person or thing, such as: any, both, few, many, much, other, several, some, etc." Frank X. Braun, *English Grammar for Language Students: Basic Grammatical Terminology Defined and Alphabetically Arranged* (Ann Arbor, MI: n.p., 1947; repr. Eugene, OR: Wipf & Stock, 2013), 9.

Reflexive Pronouns

Reflexive pronouns "reflect back" to the subject of the verb, usually as a direct object of a verb: "myself" (ἐμαυτόν), "yourselves" (masc, ἑαυτούς), "to themselves" (masc, ἑαυτοῖς). Though the English translations of reflexive and intensive pronouns sound the same *without any literary context* (e.g., "myself"), intensive pronouns do not involve a reflexive action. Rather, intensive pronouns intensify another noun as an identity marker.[15] For example, an author could say, "I, **myself**, will write this chapter!" In this English example, with the intensive pronoun, the author is seeking to mark himself off as having a distinct identity as one who will write this chapter—in contrast to others who are apparently *not* writing this chapter. A reflexive use would be: "I congratulated myself upon finishing the chapter."

In reviewing the paradigms for reflexive pronouns, the student should note that there is only *one* set of plural forms (gen, dat, acc). Literary context must make clear whether the author intends his readers to understand the plural reflexive pronoun as a first person ("ourselves"), second person ("yourselves"), or third person ("themselves").

- κἀγὼ ἐὰν ὑψωθῶ ἐκ τῆς γῆς, πάντας ἑλκύσω πρὸς **ἐμαυτόν** (John 12:32)

  As for me, if I am lifted up from the earth I will draw all people to **myself**

- **ἑαυτοὺς** πειράζετε εἰ ἐστὲ ἐν τῇ πίστει (2 Cor 13:5)

  Examine **yourselves** to see whether you are in the faith (NIV)

  As noted above, the accusative plural reflexive pronoun ἑαυτούς ("yourselves") could, in other contexts, be translated "ourselves" or "themselves."

Reciprocal Pronouns

A reciprocal pronoun indicates interchange or reciprocity between two or more people: one another (ἀλλήλων). A reciprocal pronoun is always plural and never in the nominative case, thus the lexical form of the reciprocal pronoun is the genitive plural, ἀλλήλων.

- φοβηθέντες δὲ ἐθαύμασαν λέγοντες πρὸς **ἀλλήλους**, Τίς ἄρα οὗτός ἐστιν (Luke 8:25)

  They were fearful and amazed, asking **one another**, "Who can this be?"

- ἀνεχόμενοι **ἀλλήλων** (Col 3:13)

  accepting **one another**

---

[15] Matthew S. DeMoss, *Pocket Dictionary for the Study of New Testament Greek* (Downers Grove: InterVarsity, 2001), 73.

Pronominal Adjectives

Pronominal adjectives ("my" [ἐμός], "your" [sg, σός], "our" [ἡμέτερος], "your" [pl, ὑμέτερος]) are sometimes listed as an additional category of "possessive pronouns,"[16] but they are rightly classified as pronominal adjectives.[17] As adjectives, they match the nouns they modify in gender, case, and number (e.g., Mark 8:38, τοὺς ἐμοὺς λόγους ["My words"]). Pronominal adjectives, however, do overlap *in function* with the possessive personal pronoun, perhaps with added emphasis (e.g., 1 John 1:3, "*our* fellowship," καὶ ἡ κοινωνία . . . ἡ **ἡμετέρα**).[18]

PREPOSITIONS

Brooks & Winbery remark, "Prepositions are function words which assist substantives in expressing their case relationship."[19] That is, a preposition helps clarify the relationship that a substantive has with the rest of the sentence. Together, the preposition and its substantive object constitute a prepositional phrase. A bit more precisely, it is probably best to consider how an *entire prepositional phrase* functions in relation to the rest of the sentence.[20] Prepositional phrases usually function adverbially[21] but can also be adjectival. In Elementary Greek, students are introduced to the idea that Greek prepositions have case-specific meanings. For example, διά followed by the genitive is translated as "through," while διά followed by the accusative is translated "because." Also, in an introductory Greek class, students usually learn only one or two glosses (brief definitions) for each case-specific meaning of a preposition. What semantic riches of the preposition await the student's discovery! In intermediate Greek, it is important for students to begin broadening their understanding of a preposition's semantic range (field of meaning).

Below, we will briefly review the two main functions of prepositional phrases. Next, we will discuss the semantic range of Greek prepositions in more detail.

---

[16] So DeMoss (*Pocket Dictionary*, 103) and Wallace (348), though Wallace rightly recognizes them as adjectives.

[17] Moule, 120.

[18] Emphasis added.

[19] Brooks & Winbery, 2.

[20] Young writes, "In koine Greek the preposition gained more independent force, while the case lost some of its significance. It is best to consider the prepositional phrase as a syntactical unit that must be analyzed as a whole in light of various factors" (85).

[21] Robertson approvingly quotes P. Giles, *A Short Manual of Comparative Philology for Classical Students* (London/New York: Macmillan, 1901): "The preposition therefore is only an adverb specialized to define a case-usage" (301).

Functions of Prepositional Phrases

Adverbial

The most common function of prepositional phrases is adverbial, answering questions about the action in the sentence such as "When?" "Where?" "Why?" or "How?"

- εἰσελθόντες **εἰς τὸν οἶκον** Φιλίππου (Acts 21:8)

  we entered **[into] the house** of Philip

  > The prepositional phrase answers the question: Where did we enter?

- **μετὰ ἔτη τρία** ἀνῆλθον **εἰς Ἱεροσόλυμα** (Gal 1:18)

  after three years I went up **to Jerusalem** (ESV)

  > The prepositional phrases answer the questions: When did Paul go up? and Where did Paul go up?

- **τούτου χάριν** κάμπτω τὰ γόνατά μου πρὸς τὸν πατέρα (Eph 3:14)

  For this reason I bow my knees before the Father (NASB)

  > The prepositional phrase answers the question: Why did Paul bow his knees [in prayer]? Note the preposition χάριν is preceded by its object.

- αἰτείτω δὲ **ἐν πίστει** μηδὲν διακρινόμενος (Jas 1:6)

  But let him ask **in faith** without doubting

  > The prepositional phrase answers the question: How should a person ask [pray]? The answer: "in faith," i.e., in a believing posture.

Adjectival

A prepositional phrase can also modify an explicit noun (or other substantive), answering the question "Which?" or "What kind of"?

- ἵνα ἡ **κατ᾽ ἐκλογὴν** πρόθεσις τοῦ θεοῦ μένῃ (Rom 9:11)

  so that God's purpose **according to election** might stand

  > The prepositional phrase κατ᾽ ἐκλογὴν ("according to election") modifies πρόθεσις ("purpose").

- τῇ **κατ᾽ εὐσέβειαν** διδασκαλίᾳ (1 Tim 6:3)

  the teaching **that promotes godliness**

  > The prepositional phrase κατ᾽ εὐσέβειαν (lit., "according to godliness") is placed in the attributive adjective position, modifying the noun διδασκαλίᾳ. Paul is not discussing the "good" teaching or the "bad" teaching, but the "according to godliness" teaching.

Substantival

Greek authors turned almost any grammatical unit into a substantive by placing an article in front of it. The prepositional phrase was no exception. Prepositional phrases are sometimes substantized (nominalized) and function as nouns.

- μὴ ἀγαπᾶτε τὸν κόσμον μηδὲ **τὰ ἐν τῷ κόσμῳ** (1 John 2:15)

  Do not love the world or **the things in the world** (ESV)

  > Because the prepositional phrase is substantized by a *neuter* accusative plural article, the translators have added "the things . . ." in English. This use of the prepositional phrase is akin to the substantive use of the adjective.

- ὃς ἔκτισεν τὸν οὐρανὸν καὶ **τὰ ἐν αὐτῷ** καὶ τὴν γῆν καὶ **τὰ ἐν αὐτῇ** καὶ τὴν θάλασσαν καὶ **τὰ ἐν αὐτῇ** (Rev 10:6)

  who created heaven and **what is in it**, the earth and **what is in it**, and the sea and **what is in it**

  > Here, neuter accusative plural articles substantize several phrases. To capture the comprehensiveness of the reference (i.e., "what is in the earth" = all created matter and entities on earth), the translators have employed the English word "what." An English rendering of "τά . . ." as "the things . . ." might wrongly leave the modern reader with the impression that only non-personal creation was referenced by the biblical author.

The Semantic Domain of Proper Prepositions

Grammarians divide prepositions into two categories—proper and improper prepositions. Proper prepositions are those that occur both in prepositional phrases (e.g., ἐκ τοῦ οὐρανοῦ, "from heaven," Matt 16:11) and as prefixes to compound verbs (e.g., ἐκβάλλω, "I throw out"). The term "improper preposition" refers to a preposition that is never prefixed to a verbal stem to create a compound verb (e.g., ἐνώπιον, "before").

When a preposition is prefixed to a verb stem to make a compound verb, there are four possible effects that the preposition may have on the original verb: (1) additional meaning, (2) intensive meaning, (3) no added meaning, or (4) unrelated meaning. First, sometimes the addition of a preposition provides an added meaning (i.e., the meaning of the verb + the meaning of the preposition = the compound verb's meaning). For example, one would expect ἀναβαίνω to mean "I go up," because ἀνά means "up" and βαίνω means "go." And, in fact, that is what the word does mean. Second, there are other situations where the prepositional prefix was added to the verb stem to communicate a more intensive action, and the verb maintains that intensive sense in the Koine period. For example, ἐσθίω means "I eat," while κατεσθίω (κατά + ἐσθίω) has a more intensive sense of "I devour." Third, sometimes the addition of a prepositional prefix offers no noticeable meaning to the verb *in the Koine period*. The prepositional prefix, however, may have communicated additional nuances of meaning at an earlier period in the Greek language.

In fact, as the Greek language evolved, originally intensive compounds sometimes lost some, or all, of their intensive sense. This semantic shift of the intensive compound towards a non-intensive meaning is sometimes contemporaneous with the disappearance of the original uncompounded verb. So, for example, in the Koine period, ἀνοίγω means simply "I open" (not "I rip open") while the uncompounded form (οἴγω) has fallen out of usage. Finally, on some occasions, the addition of a prepositional prefix creates an unrelated meaning that "defies exact explanation."[22] For example, since ἀνά means "up" and γινώσκω means "I know," one might guess that ἀναγινώσκω means . . . "I know up"? In fact, it actually means, "I read."

COMPOUND VERBS IN KOINE GREEK		
Function	**Examples**	**Definition**
Additional Meaning	ἀναβαίνω	I go up
Intensive Meaning	κατεσθίω	I devour
No Added Meaning	ἀνοίγω	I open
Unrelated Meaning	ἀναγινώσκω	I read

Proper prepositions are extremely common. For instance, ἐν is the most common with nearly three thousand occurrences in the GNT. At the intermediate level of studying Greek, students should begin broadening their understanding of the semantic domains (fields of meaning) of common prepositions. At the same time, there are practical limits as to how comprehensive such a study can be. In BDAG (the best lexicon for the GNT), there are eighteen definitions listed for ἐπί, not to mention many levels of sub-definitions.[23] Louw and Nida (another influential lexicon for the GNT) lists twenty-one distinct semantic categories for ἐπί, along with seventeen idiomatic uses of the preposition in combination with other Greek words.[24] A comprehensive look at uses of the preposition ἐπί in the GNT might be longer than this textbook! So, what follows is a pedagogical compromise—offering a deeper understanding while not overwhelming the student with a multiplicity of categories.

The seventeen proper prepositions found in the GNT are enumerated below. Listed immediately to their right is their frequency in the GNT and the case(s) in which they take their object(s). To broaden students' understanding of the semantic range of prepositions, we have included three to five diverse examples of each preposition's common functions from the GNT. Verses are listed in canonical order. After each verse, the precise function of the preposition is listed along with additional English gloss(es) used to convey this function. In creating this heuristic list, we are drawing upon BDAG, Louw & Nida, Murray Harris's *Prepositions*

---

[22] Moule, 89.
[23] BDAG, 362–67.
[24] Louw and Nida, 2:96–97.

and Theology in the Greek New Testament,[25] and our own personal research. It is important to remember that prepositions are extremely flexible in meaning, and careful consideration of the literary context is essential in determining the nuance of a preposition.

ἀνά (13x, object: acc)

- ἦλθεν αὐτοῦ ὁ ἐχθρὸς καὶ ἐπέσπειρεν ζιζάνια **ἀνὰ μέσον τοῦ σίτου** ("his enemy came, sowed weeds **among the wheat**" [lit.: "among the midst of the wheat"]; Matt 13:25). Location: in the middle of, between.

- *ἀνα*βαίνω πρὸς τὸν πατέρα μου καὶ πατέρα ὑμῶν καὶ θεόν μου καὶ θεὸν ὑμῶν ("I am ascending to My Father and your Father—to My God and your God"; John 20:17). ἀνά used as a prepositional prefix to a compound verb expressing upward movement.

- καὶ οἱ δώδεκα πυλῶνες δώδεκα μαργαρῖται, **ἀνὰ** εἷς ἕκαστος τῶν πυλώνων ἦν ἐξ ἑνὸς μαργαρίτου ("The twelve gates are twelve pearls; **each** individual gate was made of a single pearl"; Rev 21:21). Distribution (in lists): in turn, apiece.

ἀντί (22x, object: gen)

- ἀκούσας δὲ ὅτι Ἀρχέλαος βασιλεύει τῆς Ἰουδαίας **ἀντὶ τοῦ πατρὸς** αὐτοῦ Ἡρῴδου ("But when he heard that Archelaus was ruling over Judea **in place of his father** Herod"; Matt 2:22). Contrasting Alternative: instead of, for.

- **ἀνθ' ὧν** ὅσα ἐν τῇ σκοτίᾳ εἴπατε ἐν τῷ φωτὶ ἀκουσθήσεται ("**Therefore**, whatever you have said in the dark will be heard in the light"; Luke 12:3). Inferential: thus, so. The preposition ἀντί is followed by the neuter genitive plural relative pronoun ὧν.

- **ἀντὶ τούτου** καταλείψει ἄνθρωπος [τὸν] πατέρα καὶ [τὴν] μητέρα καὶ προσκολληθήσεται πρὸς τὴν γυναῖκα αὐτοῦ ("**For this reaso**n a man will leave his father and mother and be united to his wife"; Eph 5:31 NIV). Cause: because of, for the purpose of.

ἀπό (646x, object: gen)

- **ἀπὸ τότε** ἤρξατο ὁ Ἰησοῦς κηρύσσειν ("**From then on** Jesus began to preach"; Matt 4:17). Time: since.

- ὅταν δὲ τὸ ἀκάθαρτον πνεῦμα ἐξέλθῃ **ἀπὸ τοῦ ἀνθρώπου** ("When an unclean spirit comes **out of a person**"; Matt 12:43). Source: from.

---

[25] Harris, *Prepositions and Theology* (see chap. 2, n. 69).

- ἐζήτει ἰδεῖν τὸν Ἰησοῦν τίς ἐστιν καὶ οὐκ ἠδύνατο **ἀπὸ τοῦ ὄχλου** ("He was trying to see who Jesus was, but he was not able **because of the crowd**"; Luke 19:3). Cause: on account of.

- Ἰωσὴφ δὲ ὁ ἐπικληθεὶς Βαρναβᾶς **ἀπὸ τῶν ἀποστόλων** ("Thus Joseph, who was also called **by the apostles** Barnabas"; Acts 4:36 ESV). Agency: through.

- ηὐχόμην γὰρ ἀνάθεμα εἶναι αὐτὸς ἐγὼ **ἀπὸ τοῦ Χριστου** ("For I could wish that I myself were cursed and cut off **from Christ**"; Rom 9:3). Dissociation: separated from.

διά (667x, object: gen or acc)

- ἐν ἐκείνῳ τῷ καιρῷ ἐπορεύθη ὁ Ἰησοῦς τοῖς σάββασιν **διὰ τῶν σπορίμων** ("At that time Jesus passed **through the grainfields** on the Sabbath"; Matt 12:1). Extension: along.

- ἄγγελος δὲ κυρίου **διὰ νυκτὸς** ἀνοίξας τὰς θύρας τῆς φυλακῆς ("But an angel of the Lord opened the doors of the jail **during the night**"; Acts 5:19). Time: throughout.

- μὴ δυναμένου δὲ αὐτοῦ γνῶναι τὸ ἀσφαλὲς **διὰ τὸν θόρυβον** ("Since he was not able to get reliable information **because of the uproar**"; Acts 21:34). Cause: on account of, for this reason.

- πολλὰ ἔχων ὑμῖν γράφειν οὐκ ἐβουλήθην **διὰ χάρτου καὶ μέλανος** ("Though I have many things to write to you, I do not want to do so **with paper and ink**"; 2 John 12 NASB). Means: by, through.

εἰς (1768x, object: acc)

- καὶ ἔτυπτον **εἰς τὴν κεφαλὴν** αὐτοῦ ("and kept hitting him **on the head**"; Matt 27:30). Location: inside, among, at.

- ἐξῆλθεν οὖν ὁ Πέτρος καὶ ὁ ἄλλος μαθητὴς καὶ ἤρχοντο **εἰς τὸ μνημεῖον** ("So Peter went out with the other disciple, and they were going **toward the tomb**"; John 20:3 ESV). Extension: to, into, in the direction of.

- Δαυὶδ γὰρ λέγει **εἰς αὐτόν** ("For David says **concerning him**"; Acts 2:25 ESV). Reference: about, with respect to, with reference to.

- παρεκάλουν **εἰς τὸ μεταξὺ σάββατον** λαληθῆναι αὐτοῖς τὰ ῥήματα ταῦτα ("the people invited them to speak further about these things on the **next Sabbath**"; Acts 13:42 NIV). Time: until, for, throughout.

- ἔνδειγμα τῆς δικαίας κρίσεως τοῦ θεοῦ **εἰς τὸ καταξιωθῆναι ὑμᾶς** τῆς βασιλείας τοῦ θεοῦ ("*This is* a plain indication of God's righteous

judgment **so that you will be considered worthy** of the kingdom of God";
2 Thess 1:5 NASB). Result: so, with the result that.

ἐκ (914x, object: gen)

- ἀλλὰ τὸ ἐκπορευόμενον **ἐκ τοῦ στόματος** τοῦτο κοινοῖ τὸν ἄνθρωπον ("but what comes **out of the mouth**—this defiles a person"; Matt 15:11). Extension: from, out from.

- ἑαυτοῖς ποιήσατε φίλους **ἐκ τοῦ μαμωνᾶ τῆς ἀδικίας** ("make friends for yourselves **by means of the wealth of unrighteousness**"; Luke 16:9 NASB). Means: by, with.

- ἀλλ' ἵνα τηρήσῃς αὐτοὺς **ἐκ τοῦ πονηρου** ("but that you protect them **from the evil one**"; John 17:15). Dissociation: apart from, free from.

- ἐξαπέστειλεν ὁ θεὸς τὸν υἱὸν αὐτοῦ, γενόμενον **ἐκ γυναικός** ("God sent his Son, born **of a woman**"; Gal 4:4). Source: from.

- ἕκαστος καθὼς προῄρηται τῇ καρδίᾳ, μὴ **ἐκ λύπης** ἢ **ἐξ ἀνάγκης** ("Each person should do as he has decided in his heart—not **reluctantly** or **out of compulsion**"; 2 Cor 9:7). Manner: with.

ἐν (2752x, object: dat)[26]

- καὶ ἐξῆλθεν ὁ λόγος οὗτος **ἐν ὅλῃ τῇ Ἰουδαίᾳ** περὶ αὐτου ("And this report about him spread **through the whole of Judea**"; Luke 7:17 ESV). Extension: into.

- εἰ περιτομὴν λαμβάνει ἄνθρωπος **ἐν σαββάτῳ** ("If a man receives circumcision **on the Sabbath**"; John 7:23). Time: at, while, during, when.

- ὅτι **ἐν πυρὶ** ἀποκαλύπτεται ("because it will be revealed **by fire**"; 1 Cor 3:13). Means: with, by means of.

- καθίσας **ἐν δεξιᾷ αὐτοῦ** ἐν τοῖς ἐπουρανίοις ("seating him **at his right hand** in the heavens"; Eph 1:20). Location: in, on, among.

- μὴ . . . τις ὑμᾶς κρινέτω **ἐν βρώσει καὶ ἐν πόσει** ("don't let anyone judge you **in regard to food and drink**"; Col 2:16). Respect: concerning, with respect to.

---

[26] A. T. Robertson remarks, "*En* and *eis* are really the same root only slightly altered by the addition of *s*. *En* is older and originally was alone employed either with the locative case or the accusative, as *in* in Latin. *Eis* was a later development for the accusative idiom alone, but the two uses were not sharply distinguished. . . . In the New Testament there is no absolute line of cleavage." *The Minister and His Greek New Testament* (repr., Grand Rapids: Baker, 1977), 50–51.

ἐπί (890x, object: gen, dat or acc)

- καὶ αὐτὸς ἦν ἐν τῇ πρύμνῃ **ἐπὶ τὸ προσκεφάλαιον** καθεύδων ("He was in the stern, sleeping **on the cushion**"; Mark 4:38). Location: upon, at, near.

- **ἐπ᾽ ἐσχάτου χρόνου** ἔσονται ἐμπαῖκται ("**In the end time** there will be scoffers"; Jude 18). Time: at the time of, at, on.

- ἡ πόλις ἡ μεγάλη ἡ ἔχουσα βασιλείαν **ἐπὶ τῶν βασιλέων** τῆς γῆς ("the great city that has an empire **over the kings** of the earth"; Rev 17:18). Superintendence: in authority over.

- χαρὰν γὰρ πολλὴν ἔσχον καὶ παράκλησιν **ἐπὶ τῇ ἀγάπῃ σου** ("I have great joy and encouragement **because of your love**"; Phlm 7 CEB). Cause: on account of.

- ὁ σπείρων **ἐπ᾽ εὐλογίαις ἐπ᾽ εὐλογίαις** καὶ θερίσει ("the person who sows **generously** will also reap **generously**"; 2 Cor 9:6). Manner: with.

κατά (473x, object: gen or acc)

- ὥρμησεν πᾶσα ἡ ἀγέλη **κατὰ τοῦ κρημνοῦ** εἰς τὴν θάλασσαν ("the whole herd rushed **down the steep bank** into the sea"; Matt 8:32). Extension (downward): down from, along, toward.

- καὶ ὅτε ἐπλήσθησαν αἱ ἡμέραι τοῦ καθαρισμοῦ αὐτῶν **κατὰ τὸν νόμον Μωϋσέως** ("And when the days of their purification **according to the law of Moses** were finished"; Luke 2:22). Correspondence/Conformity: in accordance with, in conformity to.

- αὐτοὺς ἐξηγεῖτο **καθ᾽ ἓν ἕκαστον**, ὧν ἐποίησεν ὁ θεὸς ἐν τοῖς ἔθνεσιν ("he related **one by one** the things that God had done among the Gentiles" [lit.: according to each one]; Acts 21:19 ESV). Distribution: in detail, each, at a time.

- περὶ τοῦ υἱοῦ αὐτοῦ τοῦ γενομένου ἐκ σπέρματος Δαυὶδ **κατὰ σάρκα** ("concerning his Son, who was descended from David **according to the flesh**"; Rom 1:3 ESV). Respect: with regard to, with respect to, concerning.

- ἐξαλείψας τὸ **καθ᾽ ἡμῶν** χειρόγραφον τοῖς δόγμασιν ("He erased the certificate of debt, with its obligations, that was **against us**"; Col 2:14). Opposition: opposite, down upon.

μετά (469x, object: gen or acc)

- τότε προσῆλθεν αὐτῷ ἡ μήτηρ τῶν υἱῶν Ζεβεδαίου **μετὰ τῶν υἱῶν αὐτῆς** ("Then the mother of Zebedee's sons approached him **with her sons**"; Matt 20:20). Association: among, in the company of.

- **μετὰ ἡμέρας ἓξ** παραλαμβάνει ὁ Ἰησοῦς τὸν Πέτρον καὶ τὸν Ἰάκωβον καὶ τὸν Ἰωάννην ("**After six days** Jesus took Peter, James, and John"; Mark 9:2). Time (after): following, subsequent to.

- ὡσαύτως [καὶ] γυναῖκας ἐν καταστολῇ κοσμίῳ **μετὰ αἰδοῦς καὶ σωφροσύνης** κοσμεῖν ἑαυτάς ("Also, the women are to dress themselves in modest clothing, **with decency and good sense**"; 1 Tim 2:9). Attendant Circumstance or Manner: accompanied by.

παρά (194x, object: gen, dat, or acc)

- ἵνα **παρὰ τῶν γεωργῶν** λάβῃ ἀπὸ τῶν καρπῶν τοῦ ἀμπελῶνος ("in order to receive *some* of the produce of the vineyard **from the vine-growers**"; Mark 12:2 NASB). Source: of.

- ἐπιλαβόμενος παιδίον ἔστησεν αὐτὸ **παρ' ἑαυτῷ** ("took a little child and had him stand **next to him**"; Luke 9:47). Location: at, by, beside, near, with.

- τὸ πνεῦμα τῆς ἀληθείας ὃ **παρὰ τοῦ πατρὸς** ἐκπορεύεται ("the Spirit of truth who proceeds **from the Father**"; John 15:26). Extension: from the side of.

- λέγοντες ὅτι **παρὰ τὸν νόμον** ἀναπείθει οὗτος τοὺς ἀνθρώπους σέβεσθαι τὸν θεόν ("saying, 'This man is persuading people to worship God **contrary to the law**'"; Acts 18:13 ESV). Opposition: against.

- θρησκεία καθαρὰ καὶ ἀμίαντος **παρὰ τῷ θεῷ** καὶ πατρὶ αὕτη ἐστίν ("Pure and undefiled religion **in the sight of *our* God** and Father is this"; Jas 1:27 NASB). Estimation: in the sight of, in the judgment of, in the opinion of.

περί (333x, object: gen or acc)

- καὶ ἐξελθὼν **περὶ τρίτην ὥραν** ("And going out **about the third hour**"; Matt 20:3 ESV). Time (approximating): around.

- καλόν ἐστιν αὐτῷ μᾶλλον εἰ περίκειται μύλος ὀνικὸς **περὶ τὸν τράχηλον** ("it would be better for him if a heavy millstone were hung **around his neck**"; Mark 9:42). Location: about, near.

- πίστει καὶ **περὶ μελλόντων** εὐλόγησεν Ἰσαὰκ τὸν Ἰακὼβ καὶ τὸν Ἡσαῦ ("By faith Isaac blessed Jacob and Esau **concerning things to come**"; Heb 11:20). Reference: about, with reference to, with regard to.

πρό (47x, object: gen)

- τε **πρὸ τῆς θύρας** ἐτήρουν τὴν φυλακήν ("while the sentries **in front of the door** guarded the prison"; Acts 12:6). Location: before, at.

- ἐξελέξατο ἡμᾶς ἐν αὐτῷ **πρὸ καταβολῆς κόσμου** ("He chose us in him, **before the foundation of the world**"; Eph 1:4). Time (prior): earlier than, prior to.

- **πρὸ πάντων** δέ, ἀδελφοί μου, μὴ ὀμνύετε ("But **above all**, my brothers, do not swear"; Jas 5:12 ESV). Position (above): especially, over.

πρός (700x, object: gen, dat, or acc)

- **πρὸς τὸ ἀποπλανᾶν**, εἰ δυνατόν, τοὺς ἐκλεκτούς ("**in order to lead astray**, if possible, the elect"; Mark 13:22 NASB). Purpose: so that, for the purpose of.

- ἀνέπεμψεν αὐτὸν **πρὸς Ἡρῴδην** ("he sent him **to Herod**"; Luke 23:7). Extension: towards.

- ὑμεῖς δὲ ἠθελήσατε ἀγαλλιαθῆναι **πρὸς ὥραν** ἐν τῷ φωτὶ αὐτου ("and you were willing to rejoice **for a while** in his light" [lit.: for an hour]; John 5:35). Temporal (duration): for the length of, during.

- ἐν τούτῳ καὶ αὐτὸς ἀσκῶ ἀπρόσκοπον συνείδησιν ἔχειν **πρὸς τὸν θεὸν καὶ τοὺς ἀνθρώπους** διὰ παντός ("So I strive always to keep my conscience clear **before God and man**"; Acts 24:16 NIV). Estimation: in the sight of, in the judgment of.

- ὅτε **πρὸς ὑμᾶς** ἦμεν ("when we were **with you**"; 1 Thess 3:4). Location/ Association: near, at, close at hand, around.

σύν (128x, object: dat)

- ἡ δὲ Μαριὰμ πάντα **συνετήρει** τὰ ῥήματα ταῦτα ("But Mary was **treasuring up** all these things"; Luke 2:19). σύν here communicates intensity as a prepositional prefix to a compound verb. As a prepositional prefix, σύν frequently expresses association (συγχαίρω, "rejoice with") and assistance (συνεργέω, "work together with").[27]

---

[27] Harris, *Prepositions and Theology*, 204.

- ἀλλά γε καὶ **σὺν πᾶσιν τούτοις** τρίτην ταύτην ἡμέραν ἄγει ἀφ᾽ οὗ ταῦτα ἐγένετο ("**Besides all this**, it's the third day since these things happened"; Luke 24:21). Accompaniment/Addition: besides, in addition to.

- ἐὰν ἔλθωσιν **σὺν ἐμοὶ** Μακεδόνες ("if any Macedonians come **with me**"; 2 Cor 9:4). Association: accompanying.

ὑπέρ (150x, object: gen or acc)

- Ἡσαΐας δὲ κράζει **ὑπὲρ τοῦ Ἰσραήλ** ("But Isaiah cries out **concerning Israel**"; Rom 9:27). Reference/Content: about, with reference to, with regard to.

- τί βλασφημοῦμαι **ὑπὲρ οὗ** ἐγὼ εὐχαριστω ("why should I be denounced **because of that for which** I give thanks?"; 1 Cor 10:30 NRSV). Cause: on account of.

- καὶ αὐτὸν ἔδωκεν κεφαλὴν **ὑπὲρ πάντα** ("and appointed him as head **over everything**"; Eph 1:22). Position: above, beyond, more than.

- ὅς ἐστιν πιστὸς **ὑπὲρ ὑμῶν** διάκονος τοῦ Χριστοῦ ("He is a faithful minister of Christ **on your behalf**"; Col 1:7). Benefaction: for the sake of, for.

ὑπό (220x, object: gen or acc)

- οὐδὲ καίουσιν λύχνον καὶ τιθέασιν αὐτὸν **ὑπὸ τὸν μόδιον** ("No one lights a lamp and puts it **under a basket**"; Matt 5:15). Location (under): beneath.

- τότε **ὑπέβαλον** ἄνδρας ("Then they **secretly** persuaded some men"; Acts 6:11 NIV). Here, the prepositional prefix ὑπό communicates secrecy. As a prepositional prefix, ὑπό frequently conveys position ("under") or motion ("up").[28]

- τὸ εὐαγγέλιον τὸ εὐαγγελισθὲν **ὑπ᾽ ἐμοῦ** ὅτι οὐκ ἔστιν κατὰ ἄνθρωπον ("the gospel preached **by me** is not of human origin"; Gal 1:11). Agency: through.

The Semantic Domain of Improper Prepositions

Improper prepositions are those prepositions never found in combination with a verb stem to form a compound verb. So, for example, ἔμπροσθεν ("in front of," "before," "in the presence of") is an improper preposition, so we will never find a verb such as ἐμπροσθένβαλλω ("I throw in front of"). There are forty-two improper prepositions in the GNT.

---

[28] Harris, *Prepositions and Theology*, 223.

Improper prepositions sometimes *function* as adverbs or conjunctions. Moule, for example, remarks that ἅμα is used only once in the GNT as a preposition (Matt 13:29); in its nine other occurrences it functions as an adverb.[29] This observation reminds us of the close functional overlap among prepositions, conjunctions, and adverbs. In the chart below, the left column lists the forty-two improper prepositions in alphabetical order. The frequency of the word's occurrence in the NT is given (e.g., ἐγγύς, 31x), and if the word's frequency *as a preposition* differs from its total occurrences, this smaller number is given in parentheses with the comment, "as a prep" (e.g., ἐγγύς, 12x as a prep.). The middle column lists the case(s) of the preposition's object—overwhelming the genitive case. The right column gives some meanings of the preposition and limited Scripture references.[30]

IMPROPER PREPOSITIONS		
Preposition	**Case of Object**	**Meaning**
ἅμα 10x (1x as prep.)	Dative	together with Matt 13:29
ἄνευ 3x	Genitive	without, without the consent of Matt 10:29; 1 Pet 4:9
ἄντικρυς 1x	Genitive	opposite, offshore from Acts 20:15
ἀντιπέρα 1x	Genitive	opposite, across from Luke 8:26
ἀπέναντι 5x	Genitive	opposite, in front of, across from Matt 27:24; Acts 3:16; Rom 3:18
ἄτερ 2x	Genitive	apart from, without Luke 22:6, 35
ἄχρι(ς) 49x (44x as prep.)	Genitive	until, as far as Luke 2:15; Phil 1:5; Heb 6:11
ἐγγύς 31x (12x as prep.)	Genitive or Dative	near, close to John 3:23, 11:54; Acts 9:38
ἐκτός 8x (4x as prep.)	Genitive	outside, except Acts 26:22; 1 Cor 15:27
ἔμπροσθεν 48x (44x as prep.)	Genitive	in front of, before, in the presence of Gal 2:14; 1 Thess 3:9; Rev 22:8

---

[29] Statistics on occurrence are from Harris's *Prepositions and Theology* (241–42) and Warren C. Trenchard, *The Student's Complete Vocabulary Guide to the Greek New Testament: Complete Frequency Lists, Cognate Groupings and Principal Parts* (Grand Rapids: Zondervan, 1992), 291–92. Statistics were checked with searches on Friberg's morphologically tagged text of the Greek New Testament.

[30] Due to the space limitations of this chapter, we cannot provide a more comprehensive semantic discussion of this comparatively rarer class of prepositions. Definitions below are drawn from BDAG, Louw & Nida, Murray Harris's *Prepositions and Theology*, and our own evaluation of prepositional usage in the GNT. For a fuller treatment of these words, students are encouraged to consult for themselves the relevant reference works.

IMPROPER PREPOSITIONS		
Preposition	Case of Object	Meaning
ἔναντι 2x	Genitive	in front of, before, in the judgment of Luke 1:8; Acts 8:21
ἐναντίον 8x (5x as prep.)	Genitive	before, in the judgment of Luke 1:6; 20:26; Acts 7:10
ἕνεκα, ἕνεκεν, εἵνεκεν 26x	Genitive	because of, for the sake of Acts 26:21; Rom 8:36; 2 Cor 7:12
ἐντός 2x (1x as prep.)[a]	Genitive	within, among Luke 17:21
ἐνώπιον 94x	Genitive	before, in the sight of, in the judgment of Acts 10:30; 1 Pet 3:4; 3 John 1:6
ἔξω 63x (19x as prep.)	Genitive	outside, out of Matt 10:14; Luke 4:29; Acts 4:15
ἔξωθεν 13x (3x as prep.)	Genitive	outside, from outside Mark 7:15; Rev 11:2; 14:20
ἐπάνω 19x (16x as prep.)	Genitive	above, over, on, superior to Matt 2:9; Luke 19:17; John 3:31
ἐπέκεινα 1x	Genitive	at a more advanced point, beyond, farther on Acts 7:43
ἔσω[b] 9x (1x as prep.)	Genitive	inside Mark 15:16
ἕως 146x (90x as prep.)	Genitive	until, to, up to, as far as Matt 11:13; Acts 1:22; 2 Cor 12:2
κατέναντι 8x (7x as prep.)	Genitive	opposite, in the judgment of, before Mark 13:3; Rom 4:17; 2 Cor 2:17
κατενώπιον 3x	Genitive	in the presence of, in the judgment of, before Eph 1:4; Col 1:22; Jude 24
κυκλόθεν 3x (1x as prep.)	Genitive	in a circle, around Rev 4:3, 4
κύκλῳ 8x (3x as prep.)	Genitive	around Rev 4:5; 5:11; 7:11
μέσον[c] 58x (1x as prep.)	Genitive	in the middle of Phil 2:15[d]
μεταξύ 9x (7x as prep.)	Genitive	between, among Matt 18:15; Acts 12:6; Rom 2:15
μέχρι(ς) 17x (16x as prep.)	Genitive	as far as, to the point of, up to, until Luke 16:16; Phil 2:8; Heb 3:14
ὄπισθεν 7x (2x as prep.)	Genitive	after, behind Matt 15:23; Luke 23:26

IMPROPER PREPOSITIONS		
Preposition	Case of Object	Meaning
ὀπίσω 35x (26x as prep.)	Genitive	behind, after, following John 1:15; Jude 7; Rev 12:15
ὀψέ 3x (1x as prep.)	Genitive	after Matt 28:1[e]
παραπλήσιον[f] 1x	Dative	alongside, near, close to Phil 2:27
παρεκτός 3x (2x as prep.)	Genitive	apart from, except for Matt 5:32; Acts 26:29
πέραν 23x (15x as prep.)	Genitive	beyond, across from, on the other side Matt 4:15; Mark 5:1; John 6:1
πλήν 31x (4x as prep.)	Genitive	except, only, apart from Mark 12:32; Acts 8:1; 27:22
πλησίον 17x (1x as prep.)	Genitive	near, close by John 4:5
ὑπεράνω 3x	Genitive	far above Eph 1:21; 4:10; Heb 9:5
ὑπερέκεινα 1x	Genitive	beyond 2 Cor 10:16
ὑπερεκπερισσοῦ 3x (1x as prep.)	Genitive	far beyond Eph 3:20
ὑποκάτω 11x	Genitive	beneath, under, below Mark 7:28; Heb 2:8; Rev 12:1
χάριν 9x	Genitive	because of, for the sake of, on behalf of Gal 3:19; 1 Tim 5:14; Titus 1:5
χωρίς 41x (40x as prep.)	Genitive	without, apart from 1 Cor 4:8; Phlm 14; Jas 2:18

[a] Murray Harris labels both occurrences of ἐντός as prepositional, but in Matt 23:26, ἐντός appears to be an adverbial substantive. So Moule, 83 .

[b] A comparative form of ἔσω appears in Acts 16:24 (ἐσωτέραν, "inner") and Heb 6:19 (ἐσώτερον, "inner"), though neither word functions as a preposition. Nevertheless, Trenchard lists ἐσώτερος as a distinct improper preposition (*Vocabulary Guide*, 291). BDAG lists a prepositional usage of ἐσώτερος in 1 Sam 24:4 [LXX] (398).

[c] The neuter accusative singular of the adjective μέσος ("middle").

[d] Moule notes that μέσον also occurs as a preposition in variant readings of Matt 14:24, Luke 8:7, and Luke 10:3 (*Idiom Book*, 85).

[e] Matt 28:1 begins, "After the Sabbath" (ὀψὲ δὲ σαββάτων). Moule notes that ὀψέ could also be understood here as adverbial ("late on the Sabbath"; see Moule, 86).

[f] Moule (*Idiom Book*, 86), Trenchard (*Vocabulary Guide*, 292), and Harris (*Prepositions*, 242) list παραπλήσιον ("near") as an improper preposition with one occurrence in the NT (Phil 2:27). Nevertheless, it seems more likely that παραπλήσιον is an adverb followed by a dative of reference (θανάτῳ, "to death").

Conjunctions

Conjunctions are indeclinable words used to link words, phrases, clauses, and larger discourse (communication) units.[31] Thus, they are "the joints of speech."[32] A conjunction cues the reader to the relationship between discourse units—whether they are being placed side-by-side as equal assertions, or whether one unit is somehow dependent on the other.[33] (Note that in chapter 13 we will give more attention to separating the text into discourse units and seeing how conjunctions help the reader trace the flow of the author's argument.) In introductory Greek classes, students usually memorize a "gloss" (unnuanced definition) for the most common conjunctions. At the intermediate level, students should grow in their awareness of the semantic range of conjunctions (e.g., καί does not mean simply "and") and give more careful thought to the way an author's various assertions are related to each other. A few points of guidance will help. (1) In determining the meaning of conjunctions, give primacy to the literary context over lexical definitions. (2) Be aware of recent studies in discourse analysis that seek to define words inductively with greater attention to function rather than simply choosing the most fitting gloss offered in the standard lexicons.[34] (3) Slow down in your Greek reading and occasionally look up conjunctions in the best Greek lexicons (BDAG, LSJ, or Louw and Nida).[35] Read through all the definitions. Take notes on the range of meaning, especially possible nuances of which you were unaware.

We will continue by looking at the two main categories of conjunctions—coordinating and subordinating conjunctions.

Coordinating Conjunctions

A coordinating conjunction communicates a parallel ("equal rank") relationship between the words, phrases, or clauses that it links. Common coordinating conjunctions in English are *and*, *but*, and *or*.[36] The most common coordinating conjunctions in Greek are (in decreasing frequency): καί ("and," "also"), δέ ("and,"

---

[31] To someone raised on School House Rock cartoons, the lyrics of a song come to mind: "Conjunction Junction, what's your function? Hooking up words and phrases and clauses."

[32] Robertson, 1177. Robertson writes, "[Conjunctions] have a very good name, since they bind together (*con-jungo*) the various parts of speech not otherwise connected, if they need connection, for asyndeton was always possible to the speaker or writer. The point here is to interpret each conjunction as far as possible so that its precise function is made clear."

[33] Young observes that most "sentences in the Greek New Testament begin with a conjunction. The New Testament writers follow the classical practice of using conjunctions to indicate semantic relations between sentences and paragraphs" (179).

[34] The most readable work in this area is Runge's *Discourse Grammar* (see chap. 2, n. 46). Note, for example, Runge's discussion of δέ and τότε: "Since both δέ and τότε mark new developments, the question arises of how they differ from one another. Based on the idea of default verses marked, δέ should be viewed as a default development marker, the one used when there is no desire to specify the exact nature of the development. Due to the semantic nature of τότε, it makes explicit that the development that follows is temporal in nature. At times this may end up being a generic transition in time, but it is still temporal in nature" (38).

[35] See chapter 14 on word studies, which explains these tools in more detail.

[36] Braun, *English Grammar for Language Students*, 6.

"but"), γάρ ("for"), ἀλλά ("but"), οὖν ("therefore"), ἤ ("or"), τέ ("and so"), οὐδέ ("and not"), οὔτε ("and not"), and εἴτε ("if," "whether").[37] Listed below are syntactical functions performed by coordinating conjunctions. Under each function is a list of common conjunctions that communicate that function. For pedagogical purposes, an English gloss is given with each Greek conjunction, but students should be forewarned: such glosses are simplistically misleading! Conjunctions have a wide range of meaning and function. The same Greek conjunction can mean nearly opposite things in different contexts. Also, one illustrative text from the GNT is listed under each functional category.[38] Note: some of the conjunctions listed are rarely found in isolation; they usually function as a unit together with other particles (e.g., μέν).

Copulative (joining together)[39]

- καί ("and," "also"), δέ ("and"), οὐδέ ("and not"), μηδέ ("and not"), τέ ("and so"), οὔτε ("and not"), μήτε ("and not")

- ὃ γὰρ ἐὰν σπείρῃ ἄνθρωπος, τοῦτο **καὶ** θερίσει ("For whatever a person sows he will **also** reap"; Gal 6:7).

Disjunctive (giving alternatives)

- ἤ ("or"), εἴτε ("if," "whether")

- μή τις ἐκ τῶν ἀρχόντων ἐπίστευσεν εἰς αὐτὸν **ἢ** ἐκ τῶν Φαρισαίων; ("Have any of the rulers **or** Pharisees believed in him?"; John 7:48).

Adversative (contrasting)

- ἀλλά ("but"), δέ ("but"), μέν ("but"), μέντοι ("nevertheless"), πλήν ("but," "except"), εἰ μή ("except"), ὅμως ("yet"), καίτοι ("yet")

- οὐκ ἦλθον καταλῦσαι **ἀλλὰ** πληρῶσαι ("I did not come to abolish **but** to fulfill"; Matt 5:17).

Inferential (drawing a logical conclusion based on previous discussion)

- οὖν ("therefore," "so"), ἄρα ("then"), διό ("for this reason"), δή ("therefore")

---

[37] Wallace, 669.

[38] The categories for coordinating and subordinating conjunctions, as well as the lists of conjunctions under each category, are (with minor changes) from John D. Grassmick, *Principles and Practice of Greek Exegesis: A Classroom Manual* (n.p.: Dallas Theological Seminary, 1976), 86. The illustrative texts are from our own reading of the GNT.

[39] Sometimes called "continuative" conjunctions.

- ἐγὼ ὅσους ἐὰν φιλῶ ἐλέγχω καὶ παιδεύω· ζήλευε **οὖν** καὶ μετανόησον ("As many as I love, I rebuke and discipline. **So** be zealous and repent"; Rev 3:19).

Explanatory (marker of clarification)

- γάρ ("for")[40]

- ἦσαν **γὰρ** ὡσεὶ ἄνδρες πεντακισχίλιοι ("**For** about five thousand men were there"; Luke 9:14).

Subordinating Conjunctions

A subordinating conjunction is a word that links a word, phrase, or clause in an unequal or dependent relationship with another word, phrase, or clause. Common subordinating conjunctions in English are *although, because, if,* and *since.*[41] The most common Greek subordinating conjunctions employed with indicative verbs (in decreasing frequency) are: ὅτι ("that," "because"), εἰ ("if"), καθώς ("just as"), ὡς ("as," "like"), γάρ ("because," "since"), and ὅτε ("when"). Common subordinating conjunctions used with subjunctive verbs (again, in decreasing frequency) are: ἵνα ("in order that," "so that"), ὅταν ("whenever"), ἐάν ("if"), ὅπως ("that"), ἕως ("until"), μή ("that," "lest"),[42] and μήποτε ("that . . . not," "lest").[43] As noted above, providing a gloss (unnuanced definition) for a conjunction is a pedagogical accommodation and can be misleading. Common functions of subordinating conjunctions are listed below, accompanied by a list of conjunctions that introduce such functions and illustrations from the GNT.

Purpose (giving the purpose of)

- ἵνα ("in order that," "so that"), ὅπως ("that")

- διὰ τοῦτο ἐκ πίστεως, **ἵνα** κατὰ χάριν ("This is why the promise is by faith, **so that** it may be according to grace"; Rom 4:16).

Result (giving the result of)

- ὥστε ("so that"), ὅπως ("that")

- καὶ ἰδοὺ σεισμὸς μέγας ἐγένετο ἐν τῇ θαλάσσῃ, **ὥστε** τὸ πλοῖον καλύπτεσθαι ὑπὸ τῶν κυμάτων ("Suddenly a furious storm came up on the lake, **so that** the waves swept over the boat"; Matt 8:24 NIV).

---

[40] In certain literary contexts γάρ can be classified both as a coordinating conjunction and as a causal or inferential particle.

[41] Braun, *English Grammar for Language Students,* 6.

[42] For μή used as a conjunction after verbs of fearing, see BDAG, 646.

[43] Wallace lists conjunctions in this way by frequency (669).

Causal (giving the cause of)

- ὅτι ("that," "because"), διότι ("because"), ἐπεί ("because," "since"), ἐπειδή ("because")

- ὅτι τὸ μωρὸν τοῦ θεοῦ σοφώτερον τῶν ἀνθρώπων ἐστὶν ("**because** God's foolishness is wiser than human wisdom"; 1 Cor 1:25).

Comparative (drawing a comparison between)

- ὡς ("as," "like"), ὥσπερ ("just as"), καθώς ("as," "just as"), καθάπερ ("just as")

- **καθὼς** εὐοδοῦταί σου ἡ ψυχή ("**just as** your soul prospers"; 3 John 2 NASB).

Conditional (giving a condition)

- εἰ ("if"), ἐάν ("if"), εἴπερ ("if indeed")

- ὅτι νῦν ζῶμεν **ἐὰν** ὑμεῖς στήκετε ἐν κυρίῳ ("For now we live, **if** you stand firm in the Lord"; 1 Thess 3:8).

Concessive (making a concession)

- εἰ καί ("even if"), καὶ εἰ ("even if"), κἄν ("even though"), καίπερ ("although")

- **καίπερ** ὢν υἱός, ἔμαθεν ἀφ᾽ ὧν ἔπαθεν τὴν ὑπακοήν ("**Although** he was a son, he learned obedience through what he suffered"; Heb 5:8 ESV).

Declarative (giving the content of a declaration)

- ὅτι ("that"), ἵνα ("that," also sometimes untranslated or communicated with a dash or colon)

- αὕτη γάρ ἐστιν ἡ ἀγάπη τοῦ θεοῦ, **ἵνα** τὰς ἐντολὰς αὐτοῦ τηρῶμεν ("For this is the love of God, **that** we keep his commandments"; 1 John 5:3 ESV).

Temporal (telling the time of)

- ὅτε ("when"), ἕως ("until"), ὅταν ("whenever"), πρίν ("before")

- **πρὶν** ἀλέκτορα φωνῆσαι σήμερον ἀπαρνήσῃ με τρίς ("**Before** the rooster crows today, you will deny me three times"; Luke 22:61).

Local (giving the location of)

- οὗ ("where"), ὅπου ("where"), ὅθεν ("from where," "whence")

- τότε λέγει, Εἰς τὸν οἶκόν μου ἐπιστρέψω **ὅθεν** ἐξῆλθον ("Then it says, 'I will return to my house **from which** I came'"; Matt 12:44 ESV).

ADVERBS

An adverb is a word that modifies a verb, adjective, or adverb (e.g., he was studying *diligently*). Adverbs are usually not inflected; they are "fixed-case forms."[44] The most common adverb ending is -ως (genitive plural adjective ending with ν replaced by ς), followed by -ον (neuter accusative employed as adverb).[45] Adverbs answer questions such as: "Where?"; "When?"; "How often?"; "How intensely?"; and "In what way?" Indeed, many different constructions in Greek can function adverbially.[46] For example, prepositional phrases usually function adverbially (e.g., Acts 21:8, "[we] entered **[into] the house**," εἰσελθόντες **εἰς τὸν οἶκον**). Participles and infinitives also frequently function adverbially (e.g., Luke 8:47, "she came **trembling**," **τρέμουσα** ἦλθεν). In this subsection on adverbs, however, we will focus on individual words lexically classified as adverbs.

Adverbs can be subdivided in a number of different ways. We will consider adverbs under two questions: (1) What is the adverb modifying?, and (2) How is the adverb functioning?

What Is the Adverb Modifying?

An adverb can modify: (1) a verb, or (2) an adjective or adverb. It will be helpful to consider a few examples under these two categories.

Adverbs Modifying Verbs

Adverbs usually modify verbs. In simplifying matters for beginning Greek students, Samuel Lamerson defines an adverb as, "A word that describes a verb or tells how the action was accomplished (e.g., the man was running *fast*)."[47] As we consider this common use of adverbs, we should note that adverbs modify not only indicative verbs, but also imperative verbs, subjunctive verbs, verbal nouns (infinitives) and verbal adjectives (participles).

---

[44] Robertson, 294. For further information on the historical origins of adverbs in the Greek language and their orthographic patterns, see Robertson, 294–96. Though adverbs do not inflect (as, e.g., the noun λόγος does with its various case endings), some adverbs are found with minor variations in their endings—e.g., οὕτως ("thus, so, in this manner") and οὕτω.

[45] For more discussion on the orthographic patterns and formation of adverbs, see Dana & Mantey, 235–39.

[46] Dana & Mantey remark, "The term adverb is so general in its scope that it includes a wide range in grammatical usage. In a broad, nontechnical sense, all prepositions, conjunctions, particles, and interjections are adverbs" (Dana & Mantey, 234–35).

[47] Samuel Lamerson, *English Grammar to Ace New Testament Greek* (Grand Rapids: Zondervan, 2004), 100.

Adverbs Modifying Indicative Verbs

- πάλιν γέγραπται, Οὐκ ἐκπειράσεις κύριον τὸν θεόν σου (Matt 4:7)

  It is **also** written: Do not test the Lord your God

- οὕτως γὰρ ἠγάπησεν ὁ θεὸς τὸν κόσμον (John 3:16)

  For God loved the world **in this way**

- οὐρανοὶ ἦσαν **ἔκπαλαι** καὶ γῆ ἐξ ὕδατος καὶ δι᾽ ὕδατος συνεστῶσα τῷ τοῦ θεοῦ λόγῳ (2 Pet 3:5)

  By the word of God the heavens came into being **long ago** and the earth was brought about from water and through water

- ὁ θάνατος οὐκ ἔσται **ἔτι** (Rev 21:4)

  Death will be no **more** (NRSV)

- ναί, ἔρχομαι **ταχύ** (Rev 22:20)

  Yes, I am coming **quickly** (NASB)

Adverbs Modifying Non-indicative Verbs

- Ἰωσὴφ . . . ἐβουλήθη **λάθρᾳ** ἀπολῦσαι αὐτήν (Matt 1:19)

  Joseph . . . decided to divorce her **secretly**

  The adverb λάθρᾳ (secretly) modifies the infinitive ἀπολῦσαι ("to divorce").

- ὁ σπείρων **φειδομένως** φειδομένως καὶ θερίσει (2 Cor 9:6)

  the person who sows **sparingly** will also reap sparingly

  The adverb in bold modifies the participle ὁ σπείρων ("the person who sows"). The same adverb is repeated in this short sentence to modify an indicative verb, θερίσει ("reap").

- ἐπίστηθι **εὐκαίρως ἀκαίρως** (2 Tim 4:2)

  be ready in season and out of season (ESV)

  Two adverbs here modify the imperative ἐπίστηθι ("be ready").

- ἵνα . . . **σωφρόνως** καὶ **δικαίως** καὶ **εὐσεβῶς** ζήσωμεν ἐν τῷ νῦν αἰῶνι (Titus 2:12)

  to live in a **sensible**, **righteous**, and **godly way** in the present age

  Paul here employs three adverbs to modify the subjunctive verb ζήσωμεν ("live").

- αἰτείτω παρὰ τοῦ διδόντος θεοῦ πᾶσιν **ἁπλῶς** (Jas 1:5)

  he should ask God—who gives to all **generously**

  > The adverb modifies the participle διδόντος, describing the way in which God gives to his people.[48]

Adverbs Modifying Adverbs and Adjectives

Adverbs can modify adverbs or adjectives, though this construction is comparatively less common in the NT.

- [ἦσαν] χαλεποὶ **λίαν**, ὥστε μὴ ἰσχύειν τινὰ παρελθεῖν διὰ τῆς ὁδοῦ ἐκείνης (Matt 8:28)

  They were **so** violent that no one could pass that way

  > The adverb λίαν ("so, very") modifies the adjective χαλεποί ("violent").

- οὕτως **καὶ** ὁ υἱὸς τοῦ ἀνθρώπου μέλλει πάσχειν ὑπ᾽ αὐτῶν (Matt 17:12)

  So **also** the Son of Man will certainly suffer at their hands (ESV)

  > Here καί functions adverbially ("also") modifying the adverb οὕτως ("so, thus").

- καὶ πρωῒ ἔννυχα **λίαν** ἀναστὰς ἐξῆλθεν καὶ ἀπῆλθεν εἰς ἔρημον τόπον (Mark 1:35)

  Very early in the morning, while it was still dark, he got up, went out, and made his way to a deserted place

  > Jesus arose to pray not just early (πρωῒ), but very early (πρωῒ λίαν).

- ἦν γὰρ πλούσιος **σφόδρα** (Luke 18:23)

  for he was **very** rich (NLT)

  > The adverb σφόδρα ("very") modifies the predicate adjective πλούσιος ("rich").

- **πολλῷ** μᾶλλον καταλλαγέντες σωθησόμεθα ἐν τῇ ζωῇ αὐτοῦ (Rom 5:10)

  then how **much** more, having been reconciled, will we be saved by his life!"

  > Here πολλῷ ("much") functions adverbially further intensifying μᾶλλον ("more").

---

[48] Though ἁπλῶς is translated "generously" in numerous modern English translations (CSB, ESV, NASB, NIV), the word more likely means "unwaveringly" or "without hesitation." James is here contrasting God with the fickle human petitioner (Jas 1:6).

How Is the Adverb Functioning?

Another way to classify adverbs is according to their function. That is, what question is the adverb answering in the sentence? (1) When? (2) To what degree? (3) In what way? (4) Where?[49]

Adverbs of Time (When?)

- **ἔπειτα** ἦλθον εἰς τὰ κλίματα τῆς Συρίας καὶ τῆς Κιλικίας (Gal 1:21)

  Afterward, I went to the regions of Syria and Cilicia

- **σήμερον** ἐὰν τῆς φωνῆς αὐτοῦ ἀκούσητε, μὴ σκληρύνητε τὰς καρδίας ὑμῶν (Heb 4:7)

  Today, if you hear his voice, do not harden your hearts

Adverbs of Intensity or Degree (To What Degree? How Much?)

- ἐγὼ ἦλθον ἵνα ζωὴν ἔχωσιν καὶ **περισσὸν** ἔχωσιν (John 10:10)

  I came that they may have life, and have *it* **abundantly** (NASB)

- ἐχάρην γὰρ **λίαν** ἐρχομένων ἀδελφῶν καὶ μαρτυρούντων σου τῇ ἀληθείᾳ (3 John 3)

  For I was **very** glad when fellow believers came and testified to your fidelity to the truth

  > John was not just glad (ἐχάρην); he was very glad (ἐχάρην **λίαν**). The adverb **λίαν** intensifies the verb.

Adverbs of Manner (How? In What Way?)

- **ὁμοίως** ὁ ἐλεύθερος κληθεὶς δοῦλός ἐστιν Χριστου (1 Cor 7:22)

  Likewise he who is called as a free man is Christ's slave.

- ὁ θέλων λαβέτω ὕδωρ ζωῆς **δωρεάν** (Rev 22:17)

  Let the one who desires take the water of life **freely**

---

[49] Linguists commonly divide adverbs into four classes according to function. For example, see Braun, *English Grammar for Language Students*, 1. Gary Long, in discussing adverbs in English, proposes six categories: (1) adverbs of time [when?], (2) adverbs of place [where?], (3) adverbs of quantity [how much? how well?], (4) adverbs of manner [how?], (5) adverbs of intensity [to what degree?], and (6) adverbs of cause or purpose [why? what for?]. See Gary A. Long, *Grammatical Concepts 101 for Biblical Greek: Learning Biblical Greek Grammatical Concepts through English Grammar* (Peabody, MA: Hendrickson, 2006), 177–78.

Adverbs of Place (Where?)

- καὶ ἦν **ἐκεῖ** ἄνθρωπος ἐξηραμμένην ἔχων τὴν χεῖρα (Mark 3:1)

  and a man was **there** who had a shriveled hand

- σὺ κάθου **ὧδε** καλῶς (Jas 2:3)

  Sit **here** in a good place

Adverbs Functioning as Nouns or Adjectives

Occasionally, an adverb functions as a noun or adjective. Adverbs used as nouns seem especially common in prepositional phrases expressing time.

- εἰ **οὕτως** ἐστὶν ἡ αἰτία τοῦ ἀνθρώπου μετὰ τῆς γυναικός (Matt 19:10)

  If the relationship of a man with his wife is **like this**

  οὕτως functions as a predicate adjective.[50]

- ἵνα γένηται καὶ **τὸ ἐκτὸς** αὐτοῦ καθαρόν (Matt 23:26)

  so **the outside** of it may also become clean

  The adverb ἐκτός acts as a noun.

- ἀπὸ **τοῦ νῦν** μακαριοῦσίν με πᾶσαι αἱ γενεαί (Luke 1:48)

  from **now on** all generations will call me blessed

  The adverb νῦν functions as the object of a preposition (i.e., as a noun).

- πρὸς τὴν ἔνδειξιν τῆς δικαιοσύνης αὐτοῦ ἐν **τῷ νῦν** καιρῷ (Rom 3:25)

  to demonstrate his righteousness at the **present** time (NIV)

  The adverb νῦν functions as an attributive adjective.

- οἵτινες οὐ μόνον τὸ ποιῆσαι ἀλλὰ καὶ τὸ θέλειν προενήρξασθε ἀπὸ **πέρυσι** (2 Cor 8:10)

  Last year you were the first not only to give but also to have the desire to do so (NIV)

  The adverb πέρυσι acts as a noun, functioning as the object of the preposition ἀπό. The entire prepositional phrase ἀπὸ πέρυσι (lit., "from last year") functions adverbially to communicate time.

Adverbs can sometimes express nuances beyond the main categories explored above, so the exegete should always be attentive to the immediate literary context.

---

[50] So BDF, 224 (§434 [1]).

PARTICLES

Vaughan and Gideon note that the Greek category of "particle" has never been clearly defined.[51] Robertson wisely counsels, "Certainly it is not easy nor practicable always to distinguish sharply between the adverb and preposition, conjunction, interjections and other particles."[52] Nevertheless, we shall mark out the distinct category of "particle" as a class of usually short words, sometimes untranslated, which could often also be categorized as adverbs, conjunctions, or interjections. Because of this overlap of categories, no attempt will be made below to provide a comprehensive list of particles. Finally, we should note that some particles are postpositive (e.g., δέ ["and," "but'], γάρ ["for"])—meaning they never occur as the first word in a clause, even splitting a noun and its article (e.g., Matt 3:14, ὁ **δὲ** Ἰωάννης διεκώλυεν αὐτὸν ["**But** John tried to stop him"]).

Particles of Negation

These particles, which could also be classified as adverbs, function to negate a verb or some other discourse unit. There are particles of negation for the indicative mood (e.g., οὐ, οὐκ, οὐχ, οὐχί) and for the non-indicative moods (e.g., μή, μήποτε ["never"]), though Koine Greek writers occasionally felt free to deviate from this grammatical "rule."

- **μὴ** κρίνετε, ἵνα **μὴ** κριθῆτε (Matt 7:1)

  Do **not** judge, so that you **won't** be judged

- **οὐκ** ἐτόλμησεν κρίσιν ἐπενεγκεῖν βλασφημίας (Jude 9)

  he did **not** presume to pronounce a blasphemous judgment (ESV)

Particles of Mood

The particles ἄν and ἐάν function alongside orthographic (spelling) changes in the verb and specific subordinate conjunctions to cue the reader that the statement is made in the subjunctive mood. Such particles often are untranslated in English (as below).

- πάντα οὖν ὅσα **ἐὰν** θέλητε ἵνα ποιῶσιν ὑμῖν οἱ ἄνθρωποι (Matt 7:12)

  Therefore, whatever you want others to do for you

- ἐν ᾧ δ' **ἄν** τις τολμᾷ (2 Cor 11:21)

  But in whatever anyone dares to boast

---

[51] Curtis Vaughan and Virtus E. Gideon, *A Greek Grammar of the New Testament: A Workbook Approach to Intermediate Greek* (Nashville: Broadman, 1979), 18.

[52] Robertson, 293.

Particles of Connection

Some particles help stitch together words, phrases, and clauses. Such particles can also be classified as conjunctions. See earlier in this chapter for an extensive classification of coordinating and subordinating conjunctions.

- οὓς **μὲν** δέροντες, οὓς **δὲ** ἀποκτέννοντες (Mark 12:5)

  some they beat, and others they killed

  > The μέν . . . δέ construction often communicates contrast or development between clauses. Translators sometimes render it (somewhat laboriously), "on the one hand . . . on the other hand."

- ὅτι σκεῦος ἐκλογῆς ἐστίν μοι οὗτος τοῦ βαστάσαι τὸ ὄνομά μου ἐνώπιον ἐθνῶν **τε** καὶ βασιλέων υἱῶν **τε** Ἰσραήλ (Acts 9:15)

  For this man is my chosen instrument to take my name to Gentiles, kings, and the Israelites

  > The particle τε (overwhelmingly used in Acts) functions as a coordinate conjunction, stitching together parallel discourse units. The τε . . . τε construction is sometimes translated "not only . . . but also."

Particles of Intensification

Some Greek particles serve to express an intensification of the statement. This class of particles includes ἀμήν ["amen"], γέ ["even"], and ναί ["yes!"].

- **ναὶ** ἐρωτῶ καὶ σέ, γνήσιε σύζυγε, συλλαμβάνου αὐταῖς (Phil 4:2)

  Yes, I also ask you, true partner, to help these women

- **ἀμήν**, ἔρχου κύριε Ἰησοῦ (Rev 22:20)

  Amen! Come, Lord Jesus!

Particles of Attention (Interjections)

Some Greek particles draw the reader's attention and could also be classified as interjections, such as ἰδού ("look!"), οὐαί ("woe!"), and ὦ ("O!").

- **ὦ** γύναι, μεγάλη σου ἡ πίστις (Matt 15:28)

  O woman, great is your faith! (ESV)

- **ἰδοὺ** ὁ κριτὴς πρὸ τῶν θυρῶν ἕστηκεν (Jas 5:9)

  Look, the judge stands at the door!

SUMMARY

PRONOUNS		
TYPE	SAMPLE FORMS	NT EXAMPLE
Personal	ἐγώ ("I"); μου ("my"); σύ (sg, "you"); ὑμῶν (pl, "your"); αὐτοῦ ("his").	**ἡμεῖς** δὲ οὐκ ἐσμὲν ὑποστολῆς εἰς ἀπώλειαν ("But **we** are not like those who turn away from God to their own destruction"; Heb 10:39 NLT).
Demonstrative	**Near:** οὗτος (masc, "this"); αὗται (fem, "these").	**ταῦτα** δὲ αὐτοῦ ἐνθυμηθέντος ("But after he had considered **these things**"; Matt 1:20).
	Far: ἐκεῖνο (neut, "that"); ἐκεῖνοι (masc, "those").	ἐν δὲ ταῖς ἡμέραις **ἐκείναις** παραγίνεται Ἰωάννης ὁ βαπτιστὴς ("In **those** days John the Baptist came"; Matt 3:1).
Relative	οἵ (masc pl, "who"); ἧς (fem sg, "of whom"); ὅ (neut sg, "which").	ἀνδρὶ μωρῷ, **ὅστις** ᾠκοδόμησεν αὐτοῦ τὴν οἰκίαν ἐπὶ τὴν ἄμμον ("a foolish man **who** built his house on the sand"; Matt 7:26).
Interrogative	τίς (masc/fem sg, "who?"); τίνος (masc/fem sg, "of whom?"); τί ("what/why?").	**τί** κωλύει με βαπτισθῆναι; ("**What** is to prevent me from being baptized?"; Acts 8:36 NRSV).
Indefinite	τις (masc sg, "anyone, someone"); τινες (masc pl, "certain ones").	ἐάν **τις** εἴπῃ . . . ("If **anyone** says . . ."; 1 John 4:20).
Reflexive	ἐμαυτόν ("myself"); ἑαυτούς (masc, "yourselves"); ἑαυτοῖς (masc, "to themselves").	**ἑαυτοὺς** πειράζετε εἰ ἐστὲ ἐν τῇ πίστει ("Examine **yourselves** to see whether you are in the faith"; 2 Cor 13:5 NIV).
Reciprocal	ἀλλήλων ("one another").	ἀνεχόμενοι **ἀλλήλων** ("bearing with **one another**"; Col 3:13).

FUNCTIONS OF PREPOSITIONAL PHRASES	
Adverbial (modifying a verb)	αἰτείτω δὲ **ἐν πίστει** ("But let him ask **in faith**"; Jas 1:6).
Adjectival (modifying a noun)	τῇ **κατ᾽ εὐσέβειαν** διδασκαλίᾳ ("the teaching **that promotes godliness**"; 1 Tim 6:3).
Substantival (acting as a noun)	Μὴ ἀγαπᾶτε τὸν κόσμον μηδὲ **τὰ ἐν τῷ κόσμῳ** ("Do not love the world or **the things in the world**"; 1 John 2:15 ESV).

THE 17 PROPER PREPOSITIONS			
PREPOSITION	FREQUENCY IN GNT	CASE OF OBJECT	GLOSSES
ἀνά	13	acc	each, in turn, up
ἀντί	22	gen	in place of, instead of
ἀπό	646	gen	from, of
διά	667	gen acc	through because of
εἰς	1768	acc	into, in, at
ἐκ	914	gen	from, out of
ἐν	2752	dat	in, into, by
ἐπί	890	gen dat acc	on, upon upon against
κατά	473	gen acc	against according to
μετά	469	gen acc	with after
παρά	194	gen dat acc	from with beside
περί	333	gen acc	concerning around
πρό	47	gen	before, at
πρός	700	gen dat acc	for at to
σύν	128	dat	with
ὑπέρ	150	gen acc	for, above
ὑπό	220	gen acc	by, under

CONJUNCTION TYPE	COMMON CONJUNCTIONS AND GLOSSES
Copulative	καί ("and," "also"); δέ ("and"); οὐδέ ("and not"); μηδέ ("and not"); τέ ("and so"); οὔτε ("and not"); μήτε ("and not").
Disjunctive	ἤ ("or"); εἴτε ("if," "whether").
Adversative	ἀλλά ("but"); δέ ("but"); μέν ("but"); μέντοι ("nevertheless"); πλήν ("but," "except"); εἰ μή ("except"); ὅμως ("yet"); καίτοι ("yet").
Inferential	οὖν ("therefore," "so"); ἄρα ("then"); διό ("for this reason"); δή ("therefore").
Explanatory	γάρ ("for").

CONJUNCTION TYPE	COMMON CONJUNCTIONS AND GLOSSES
Purpose	ἵνα ("in order that," "so that"); ὅπως ("that").
Result	ὥστε ("so that"); ὅπως ("that").
Causal	ὅτι ("that," "because"); διότι ("because"); ἐπεί ("because," "since"); ἐπειδή ("because").
Comparative	ὡς ("as," "like"); ὥσπερ ("just as"); καθώς ("as," "just as"); καθάπερ ("just as").
Conditional	εἰ ("if"); ἐάν ("if"); εἴπερ ("if indeed").
Concessive	εἰ καί ("even if"); καὶ εἰ ("even if"); κἄν ("even though"); καίπερ ("although").
Declarative	ὅτι ("that"); ἵνα ("that"). Conjunctions sometimes untranslated or communicated with a dash, colon, or quotation marks.
Temporal	ὅτε ("when"); ἕως ("until"); ὅταν ("whenever"); πρίν ("before").
Local	οὗ ("where"); ὅπου ("where"); ὅθεν ("from where," "whence").

ADVERBS MODIFYING A VERB	
Indicative	ὁ θάνατος οὐκ ἔσται **ἔτι** ("Death will be no **more**"; Rev 21:4 NRSV).
Infinitive	Ἰωσὴφ . . . ἐβουλήθη **λάθρᾳ** ἀπολῦσαι αὐτήν ("Joseph . . . decided to divorce her **secretly**"; Matt 1:19).
Participle	ὁ σπείρων **φειδομένως** φειδομένως καὶ θερίσει ("The person who sows **sparingly** will also reap sparingly"; 2 Cor 9:6).
Imperative	ἐπίστηθι **εὐκαίρως ἀκαίρως** ("be ready **in season** and **out of season**"; 2 Tim 4:2 ESV).
Subjunctive	ἵνα . . . **σωφρόνως** καὶ **δικαίως** καὶ **εὐσεβῶς** ζήσωμεν ἐν τῷ νῦν αἰῶνι ("to live in a **sensible**, **righteous**, and **godly** way in the present age"; Titus 2:12).

ADVERBS MODIFYING AN ADJECTIVE OR ADVERB	
Adjective	[ἦσαν] χαλεποὶ **λίαν**, ὥστε μὴ ἰσχύειν τινὰ παρελθεῖν διὰ τῆς ὁδοῦ ἐκείνης ("They were **so** violent that no one could pass that way"; Matt 8:28).
Adverb	καὶ πρωῒ ἔννυχα **λίαν** ἀναστὰς ἐξῆλθεν καὶ ἀπῆλθεν εἰς ἔρημον τόπον ("**Very** early in the morning, while it was still dark, he got up, went out, and made his way to a deserted place"; Mark 1:35).

USES OF THE ADVERB	
Time (When?)	**ἔπειτα** ἦλθον εἰς τὰ κλίματα τῆς Συρίας καὶ τῆς Κιλικίας ("**Afterward**, I went to the regions of Syria and Cilicia"; Gal 1:21).
Degree (How much?)	ἐγὼ ἦλθον ἵνα ζωὴν ἔχωσιν καὶ **περισσὸν** ἔχωσιν ("I came that they may have life, and have it **abundantly**"; John 10:10 NASB).

USES OF THE ADVERB	
Manner **(In what way?)**	ὁμοίως ὁ ἐλεύθερος κληθεὶς δοῦλός ἐστιν Χριστου ("**Likewise** he who is called as a free man is Christ's slave"; 1 Cor 7:22).
Place (Where?)	σὺ κάθου **ὧδε** καλῶς ("Sit **here** in a good place"; Jas 2:3).

ADVERBS USED AS NOUNS OR ADJECTIVES	
Noun	ἵνα γένηται καὶ **τὸ ἐκτὸς** αὐτοῦ καθαρόν ("so **the outside** of it may also become clean"; Matt 23:26).
Adjective	πρὸς τὴν ἔνδειξιν τῆς δικαιοσύνης αὐτοῦ ἐν τῷ **νῦν** καιρῷ ("to demonstrate his righteousness at the **present** time"; Rom 3:25 NIV).

PRACTICE EXERCISES

In each of the following examples, (1) identify the part of speech of the under-lined word(s) and (2) determine the specific function of the word(s).

1. ἐν ᾧ θελήματι ἡγιασμένοι ἐσμὲν <u>διὰ</u> τῆς προσφορᾶς τοῦ σώματος Ἰησοῦ Χριστοῦ <u>ἐφάπαξ</u> (Heb 10:10).

2. σπεῦσον καὶ ἔξελθε ἐν τάχει <u>ἐξ</u> Ἰερουσαλήμ, <u>διότι</u> οὐ παραδέξονταί <u>σου</u> μαρτυρίαν περὶ ἐμου (Acts 22:18).

3. <u>ἡμεῖς</u> <u>δὲ</u> ὀφείλομεν εὐχαριστεῖν τῷ θεῷ πάντοτε περὶ <u>ὑμῶν</u> (2 Thess 2:13).

4. ἰδὼν ὅτι <u>καλῶς</u> ἀπεκρίθη αὐτοῖς ἐπηρώτησεν <u>αὐτόν</u>, Ποία ἐστὶν ἐντολὴ πρώτη πάντων; (Mark 12:28).

5. καὶ διελογίζοντο <u>πρὸς</u> <u>ἀλλήλους</u> ὅτι Ἄρτους <u>οὐκ</u> ἔχουσιν (Mark 8:16).

6. θεὸς γάρ ἐστιν ὁ ἐνεργῶν ἐν <u>ὑμῖν</u> καὶ τὸ θέλειν καὶ τὸ ἐνεργεῖν <u>ὑπὲρ</u> τῆς εὐδοκίας (Phil 2:13).

7. <u>ὃς</u> <u>δ᾽</u> <u>ἂν</u> τηρῇ αὐτοῦ τὸν λόγον, ἀληθῶς <u>ἐν</u> τούτῳ ἡ ἀγάπη τοῦ θεοῦ τετελείωται (1 John 2:5).

8. μὴ φοβοῦ, ἀλλὰ λάλει καὶ μὴ σιωπήσῃς (Acts 18:9).

9. καὶ ἐγένετο ὅτε ἐτέλεσεν ὁ Ἰησοῦς τοὺς λόγους τούτους (Matt 7:28).

10. ἰδοὺ ἡ παρθένος ἐν γαστρὶ ἕξει καὶ τέξεται υἱόν, καὶ καλέσουσιν τὸ ὄνομα αὐτοῦ Ἐμμανουήλ, ὅ ἐστιν μεθερμηνευόμενον Μεθ' ἡμῶν ὁ θεός (Matt 1:23).

VOCABULARY

Vocabulary to Memorize

ἀνέχω	I endure, bear with (15)
ἀνομία, ἡ	lawlessness (15)
ἀπάγω	I lead away, bring before (15)
βλασφημέω	I blaspheme, defame, slander (34)
γνωστός	known, notable (15)
γυμνός	naked, poorly dressed (15)
Δαμασκός, ἡ	Damascus (15)
δέρω	I skin, beat (15)
διδασκαλία, ἡ	teaching, instruction (21)
εἶτα	then, furthermore (15)
ἐντέλλομαι	I command (15)
ἐπαγγέλλομαι	I announce, proclaim, promise (15)
εὐχαριστία, ἡ	thankfulness, thanksgiving (15)
καταλαμβάνω	I seize, attain, overtake (15)
Καφαρναούμ, ἡ	Capernaum (16)
κλείω	I shut, close, lock (16)
κλέπτης, -ου, ὁ	thief (16)
κληρονόμος, ὁ	heir (15)
κτίζω	I create, make (15)
λῃστής, -οῦ, ὁ	robber, bandit, revolutionary (15)
λύπη, ἡ	grief, sorrow, pain (16)
μοιχεύω	I commit adultery (15)
νομίζω	I think, suppose (15)
ξηραίνω	I dry (up), wither (15)
ὅθεν	from where (15)
οἰκουμένη, ἡ	world, inhabited earth, humankind (15)
ὁμοιόω	I compare, make like (15)
οὐδέποτε	never (16)
περισσότερος	greater, more (16)
πλήρης	filled, full, complete (16)
προσδοκάω	I wait for, look for, expect (16)
σεαυτοῦ	yourself (43)
σκοτία, ἡ	darkness (16)
συκῆ, ἡ	fig tree (16)
συλλαμβάνω	I arrest, catch, become pregnant (16)
συνίστημι	I recommend, commend (16)

σφραγίς, -ῖδος, ἡ	seal, mark, inscription (16)
τολμάω	I dare, am courageous (16)
χορτάζω	I feed, satisfy (16)
ὡσαύτως	likewise, similarly (17)

Vocabulary to Recognize

ἁγνός	pure, holy (8)
ἀκατάγνωστος	beyond reproach (1)
ἀντιλέγω	I speak against (11)
ἀφθορία, ἡ	soundness (1)
δεσπότης, -ου, ὁ	master (10)
δουλόω	I enslave (8)
ἐναντίας	opposed, contrary (8)
ἐνδείκνυμι	I show (11)
ἐντρέπω	I shame (9)
ἐπιταγή	authority (7)
εὐάρεστος	pleasing (9)
ἱεροπρεπής	reverent (1)
καλοδιδάσκαλος	teaching what is good (1)
κατάστημα, -ατος, τό	behavior (1)
κοσμέω	I adorn (10)
νέος	young woman (1)
νεώτερος	young man (11)
νηφάλιος	self-controlled (3)
νοσφίζω	I keep back (3)
οἰκουργός	worker at home (1)
πρέπει	it is fitting (7)
πρεσβύτης, -ου, ὁ	old man (3)
πρεσβῦτις, -ιδος, ἡ	older woman (1)
σεμνός	worthy of respect (4)
σεμνότης, -τητος, ἡ	dignity (3)
σώφρων	prudent (4)
σωφρονέω	I am sensible (6)
σωφρονίζω	I encourage (1)
ὑγιαίνω	I am correct (12)
ὑγιής	healthy, sound (11)
φαῦλος	base (6)
φίλανδρος	loving one's husband (1)
φιλότεκνος	loving one's children (1)

READING THE NEW TESTAMENT

Titus 2:1–10

¹ Σὺ δὲ λάλει ἃ πρέπει τῇ ὑγιαινούσῃ διδασκαλίᾳ. ² πρεσβύτας νηφαλίους εἶναι, σεμνούς, σώφρονας, ὑγιαίνοντας τῇ πίστει, τῇ ἀγάπῃ, τῇ ὑπομονῇ· ³ πρεσβύτιδας ὡσαύτως ἐν καταστήματι ἱεροπρεπεῖς, μὴ διαβόλους μὴ οἴνῳ πολλῷ δεδουλωμένας, καλοδιδασκάλους, ⁴ ἵνα σωφρονίζωσιν τὰς νέας φιλάνδρους εἶναι, φιλοτέκνους ⁵ σώφρονας ἁγνὰς οἰκουργοὺς ἀγαθάς, ὑποτασσομένας τοῖς ἰδίοις ἀνδράσιν, ἵνα μὴ ὁ λόγος τοῦ θεοῦ βλασφημῆται. ⁶ τοὺς νεωτέρους ὡσαύτως παρακάλει σωφρονεῖν ⁷ περὶ πάντα, σεαυτὸν παρεχόμενος τύπον καλῶν ἔργων, ἐν τῇ διδασκαλίᾳ ἀφθορίαν, σεμνότητα, ⁸ λόγον ὑγιῆ ἀκατάγνωστον, ἵνα ὁ ἐξ ἐναντίας ἐντραπῇ μηδὲν ἔχων λέγειν περὶ ἡμῶν φαῦλον. ⁹ δούλους ἰδίοις δεσπόταις ὑποτάσσεσθαι ἐν πᾶσιν, εὐαρέστους εἶναι, μὴ ἀντιλέγοντας, ¹⁰ μὴ νοσφιζομένους, ἀλλὰ πᾶσαν πίστιν ἐνδεικνυμένους ἀγαθήν, ἵνα τὴν διδασκαλίαν τὴν τοῦ σωτῆρος ἡμῶν θεοῦ κοσμῶσιν ἐν πᾶσιν.

Reading Notes[53]

Verse 1

- **Σὺ δέ** ("But as for you") – The Greek personal pronoun σύ ("you") is emphatic and together with the conjunction δέ ("but") draws a sharp contrast between Titus and the false teachers mentioned in 1:10–16.[54]

- **ἃ πρέπει τῇ ὑγιαινούσῃ διδασκαλίᾳ** ("the things which are fitting for sound doctrine") – πρέπει ("what are fitting"; cf. 1 Tim 2:10) governs the dative τῇ ὑγιαινούσῃ διδασκαλίᾳ, a dative of respect[55] that expresses the implied subject.[56] The content is spelled out in vv. 2–10.

Verse 2

- **πρεσβύτας . . . πρεσβύτιδας** ("older men" . . . "older women"; vv. 2, 3) – Older, more mature Christian men and women are to set the example and mentor τὰς νέας ("young women"; v. 4) and τοὺς νεωτέρους ("young

---

[53] The English version used in the Reading Notes for this chapter is the NASB.

[54] Mounce says that "δέ, 'but,' has its full adversative force," citing 1 Tim 6:1; 2 Tim 3:10, 14; 4:5 as parallels (Mounce, *Pastoral Epistles*, 408). For succinct commentary on Titus 2:1–10, see Andreas J. Köstenberger, "1–2 Timothy, Titus," in *Ephesians–Philemon*, EBC, rev. ed., vol. 12 (Grand Rapids: Zondervan, 2006), 613–18.

[55] Marshall notes that this phrase "indicates that in respect of which Titus's teaching is to be 'appropriate.'" I. H. Marshall, *The Pastoral Epistles*, ICC (Edinburgh: T&T Clark, 1999), 238.

[56] Marshall, *Pastoral Epistles*, 238n9, who also cites 1 Tim 2:10; Heb 7:26.

men"; v. 6) in cultivating Christian virtues and in developing Christ-honoring relationships in the church, God's family or household.

- **πρεσβύτας νηφαλίους εἶναι** ("Older men are to be temperate") – εἶναι is an infinitive of indirect discourse.

- **ὑγιαίνοντας τῇ πίστει, τῇ ἀγάπῃ, τῇ ὑπομονῇ** ("sound in faith, in love, in perseverance") – Paul is fond of using this kind of triadic structure (cf. 1 Tim 6:11; 2 Tim 3:10; 1 Thess 1:3; see also "faith, hope, and love" in 1 Cor 13:13).[57] In the present instance, the three nouns are all in the dative case (cf. πρέπει τῇ ὑγιαινούσῃ διδασκαλίᾳ in v. 1), datives of respect (i.e., sound *with reference to* faith, love, and endurance).[58]

Verse 3

- **ὡσαύτως** ("likewise") – The word links together Paul's instructions for older men and women on the one hand (v. 3) and his directives for young women and men on the other (v. 6). Paul's instructions to Timothy regarding men and women in the church follow a similar pattern (cf. 1 Tim 2:9; 3:8, 11).

- **ἐν καταστήματι** ("in their behavior") – In this instance, Paul uses the preposition ἐν plus the dative (cf. 1:13: ἐν τῇ πίστει), connoting reference or sphere,[59] rather than the simple dative as in v. 2 (τῇ πίστει, etc.). καταστήματι is a *hapax legomenon* (occurring only here in the NT; cf. καταστολή in 1 Tim 2:9).

- **μὴ οἴνῳ πολλῷ δεδουλωμένας** ("not enslaved to much wine") – δεδουλωμένας is a per pass ptc acc fem pl of δουλόω ("to enslave"; cf. 2 Pet 2:19; see the use of δουλεύω at 3:3). The dative οἴνῳ πολλῷ modifies δεδουλωμένας and indicates respect ("enslaved *with respect to* much wine").

- **καλοδιδασκάλους . . . φιλάνδρους . . . φιλοτέκνους** ("teaching what is good," "to love their husbands, to love their children"; vv. 3, 4) – Paul produces a whole series of compound adjectives not found elsewhere in the NT (*hapax legomena*).[60]

---

[57] Mounce, *Pastoral Epistles*, 409.
[58] Marshall, *Pastoral Epistles*, 240n12.
[59] Marshall, *Pastoral Epistles*, 243n22: "ἐν gives the sense 'as far as X is concerned,' 'in the sphere of'" (citing Eph 2:4; Heb 13:21; Jas 1:4, 8).
[60] "This word (καλοδιδάσκαλος) occurs only here in Greek literature and may have been coined by Paul." Mounce, *Pastoral Epistles*, 410; cf. φιλάγαθος in Titus 1:8. Marshall cites similar coinages in the Apostolic Fathers: κακοδιδασκαλέω in 1 Clement 10.5 and κακοδιδασκαλία in Ignatius, *To the Philadelphians* 2.1 (Marshall, *Pastoral Epistles*, 246).

Verse 4

- **ἵνα σωφρονίζωσιν τὰς νέας** ("so that they may encourage the young women") – Older women are to cultivate Christian virtues not merely as ends in themselves but so that they may encourage the young women in the church to be self-controlled and circumspect. See also the comment on παρακάλει σωφρονεῖν at v. 6 below.

- **φιλάνδρους εἶναι, φιλοτέκνους** ("to love their husbands, to love their children") – A young woman's primary responsibilities are to her husband and children, with the husband having pride of place. "Love" (φιλ-) is the all-encompassing virtue. These qualities were also highly prized in ancient Greco-Roman and Jewish cultures as the mark of a good wife.[61] Εἶναι is an infinitive of indirect discourse. The word order is interesting, with εἶναι completing the ἵνα clause and φιλοτέκνους continuing the list of virtues.

Verse 5

- **οἰκουργούς** ("workers at home") – The textual variant οἰκουρούς ("keepers at home") is adopted by most Church Fathers and the Textus Receptus and adopted in the KJV, but οἰκουργούς is more widely attested in the earliest MSS and most likely original.[62] "Working at home" contrasts with those "younger Ephesian widows who were lazy and ran from house to house" (1 Tim 5:13); the passage "does not require a woman to work only at home . . . but does state that she does have duties at home."[63] In fact, it may be argued that a woman's domestic and familial duties are to be her center of gravity (e.g., 1 Tim 2:15; cf. Gen 3:16; Prov 31:10–31).

- **ὑποτασσομένας τοῖς ἰδίοις ἀνδράσιν** ("being subject to their own husbands") – ὑποτασσομένας (pres pass ptc acc fem pl ὑποτάσσω) governs the dative τοῖς ἰδίοις ἀνδράσιν.[64] Wifely submission to one's husband is standard NT teaching (cf. Eph 5:22; Col 3:18; 1 Pet 3:1, 5–6).

- **ἵνα μὴ ὁ λόγος τοῦ θεοῦ βλασφημῆται** ("so that the word of God will not be dishonored") – This is the first of three times in this letter where Paul urges the church to guard its reputation in the unbelieving world (see vv. 8, 10). ἵνα may indicate purpose ("in order that"), not merely result and is followed by the subjunctive verb βλασφημῆται (pres pass sub 3rd sg βλασφημέω).

---

[61] For parallels, see Marshall, *Pastoral Epistles*, 248n42.

[62] Bruce M. Metzger, *A Textual Commentary on the Greek New Testament*, 2nd ed. (Stuttgart: German Bible Society, 1994), 585.

[63] Mounce, *Pastoral Epistles*, 411.

[64] Marshall notes that "the middle voice implies willing subjection" (*Pastoral Epistles*, 247).

Verse 6

- ὡσαύτως ("likewise") – See comment at v. 3 above.

- παρακάλει σωφρονεῖν ("urge . . . to be sensible") – Paul's instruction regarding young men is similar to that regarding women, with παρακάλει σωφρονεῖν serving as a synonym to σωφρονίζω ("encourage") in v. 4 (σωφρονεῖν is an infinitive of indirect discourse). Marshall plausibly contends that "the idea is that of self-control rather than prudence."[65]

Verse 7

- περὶ πάντα ("in all things") – It is not easy to decide whether this phrase is to be construed with the preceding (CSB) or the following clause (NASB), with the former option being perhaps more likely (cf. ἐν πᾶσιν in v. 9a and at the end of v. 10; note also that σωφρονεῖν is an all-encompassing term). If so, σεαυτόν would be emphatic.[66]

- σεαυτὸν παρεχόμενος τύπον καλῶν ἔργων ("show yourself to be an example of good deeds") – παρεχόμενος (pres mid ptc masc nom sg παρέχω) urges Titus, Paul's apostolic delegate, to undergird his teaching with his personal example (cf. 1 Tim 4:12; Phil 3:17; 1 Thess 1:7; 2 Thess 3:9; 1 Pet 5:3). Notice that the participle παρεχόμενος is translated as an imperative. In the original Greek, the participle appears to adverbially modify the command παρακάλει from v. 6 (see above). The genitive καλῶν ἔργων is descriptive of the kind of example Paul wants Titus to be. Good works are commended by the apostle throughout the letter as a proper expression of believers' faith (cf. 1:16; 2:14; 3:1, 8, 14).

- ἐν τῇ διδασκαλίᾳ ("in doctrine") – NIV: "in your teaching." The phrase seems to denote the sphere of the following qualities, with the verb παρεχόμενος being implied from the previous verse.[67] Teaching, both by explicit verbal instruction and by personal example, is Paul's main burden in this passage. See the references to teaching in vv. 1, 4, here, and in v. 10 below.

Verse 8

- λόγον ὑγιῆ ἀκατάγνωστον ("sound in speech which is beyond reproach") – Mounce calls this "a grammatically awkward construction" by which Paul continues the force of παρεχόμενος from the previous verse.[68]

---

[65] See Excursus 3 in Marshall, *Pastoral Epistles*, 182–91.
[66] See the discussion in Mounce, *Pastoral Epistles*, 412.
[67] See Marshall for an excellent discussion of possible ways of understanding the syntax in this verse (*Pastoral Epistles*, 254).
[68] Mounce, *Pastoral Epistles*, 413.

ἀκατάγνωστον occurs only here in the NT (cf. ἀνέγκλητος in 1 Tim 3:10; Titus 1:6, 7 and ἀνεπίλημπτον in 1 Tim 3:2; 5:7; 6:14).

- **ἵνα ὁ ἐξ ἐναντίας ἐντραπῇ μηδὲν ἔχων λέγειν περὶ ἡμῶν φαῦλον** ("so that the opponent will be put to shame, having nothing bad to say about us") – On the ἵνα-clause, most likely conveying purpose, see the comment at v. 5 above. ἐξ ἐναντίας means literally "opposite someone," an idiom denoting an opponent. λέγειν is an infinitive of direct object.

- **ἐντραπῇ** ("will be put to shame") – Aor pass sub 3rd sg ἐντρέπω. Paul's challenge to Titus is to put his opponents to shame by being above reproach (cf. 2 Thess 3:14).

- **ἔχων** ("having") – Pres act ptc masc nom sg ἔχω. As an adverbial participle, it may be causal ("because they have nothing bad to say about us"), result ("with the result that they have nothing bad to say about us"), or express an attendant circumstance ("and have nothing bad to say about us").

Verses 9–10

- **δούλους ἰδίοις δεσπόταις ὑποτάσσεσθαι ἐν πᾶσιν** ("*Urge* bond-slaves to be subject to their own masters in everything") – Paul's instructions to slaves echo his directives to wives (ὑποτασσομένας τοῖς ἰδίοις ἀνδράσιν; v. 5). In both cases, he calls for submission to authority. The dative ἰδίοις δεσπόταις is required by the verb ὑποτάσσω. The infinitive ὑποτάσσεσθαι (indirect discourse; also εἶναι in the next phrase) is probably governed by παρακάλει from v. 6.[69] ἐν πᾶσιν most likely modifies ὑποτάσσεσθαι.

- **εὐαρέστους εἶναι, μὴ ἀντιλέγοντας, μὴ νοσφιζομένους, ἀλλὰ πᾶσαν πίστιν ἐνδεικνυμένους ἀγαθήν** ("to be well-pleasing, not argumentative, not pilfering, but showing all good faith") – εὐαρέστου ("well-pleasing") is spelled out in two negative terms and one positive term, all three in the form of present adjectival participles functioning predicatively: ἀντιλέγοντας, νοσφιζομένους, and ἐνδεικνυμένους.[70]

- **ἵνα τὴν διδασκαλίαν τὴν τοῦ σωτῆρος ἡμῶν θεοῦ κοσμῶσιν ἐν πᾶσιν** ("so that they will adorn the doctrine of God our Savior in every respect") – Again, the ἵνα-clause conveys purpose (cf. vv. 5, 8). τοῦ σωτῆρος ἡμῶν θεοῦ (cf. 1 Tim 1:1) is an objective genitive ("doctrine

---

[69] Cf. the similar phrase in Col 3:22: ὑπακούετε κατὰ πάντα; see also comment on περὶ πάντα at v. 7 above and ἐν πᾶσιν at the end of v. 10 below.

[70] ἀντιλέγοντας (pres act ptc masc acc pl ἀντιλέγω) is an active participle; νοσφιζομένους (pres mid ptc masc acc pl νοσφίζομαι, found elsewhere in the NT only at Acts 5:2, 3 with reference to Ananias and Sapphira) is in the middle voice (perhaps denoting self-interest, "keeping for themselves"); ἐνδεικνυμένους (pres mid ptc masc acc pl ἐνδείκνυμι) is in the middle as well ("showing themselves").

about God our Savior"; τοῦ σωτῆρος = genitive of apposition). κοσμέω is used in a literal sense for women's adornment in 1 Tim 2:9. Slaves (who were part of the ancient household) were to commend the gospel in their community by proper submission to their masters.[71]

---

[71] For other NT instructions to slaves and masters, see Eph 6:5–9; Col 3:22; 1 Tim 6:1–2; 1 Pet 2:18–25.

///////////////

CHAPTER 13

SENTENCES, DIAGRAMMING & DISCOURSE ANALYSIS

GOING DEEPER

Matthew 28:18–20 (the "Great Commission") is frequently used to challenge people to follow Jesus overseas as full-time career missionaries. Such teaching often places the emphasis on "going." And, from reading the Great Commission in English Bible translation (e.g., CSB, ESV, NASB, NIV), one does get the sense that the imperative "Go" is emphasized by the biblical author.[1] A look at the Greek text, however, reveals a slightly different emphasis. Matthew 28:19–20a reads:

πορευθέντες οὖν **μαθητεύσατε** πάντα τὰ ἔθνη, **βαπτίζοντες** αὐτοὺς εἰς τὸ ὄνομα τοῦ πατρὸς καὶ τοῦ υἱοῦ καὶ τοῦ ἁγίου πνεύματος, **διδάσκοντες** αὐτοὺς τηρεῖν πάντα ὅσα ἐνετειλάμην ὑμῖν.

Go, therefore, and **make disciples** of all nations, **baptizing** them in the name of the Father and of the Son and of the Holy Spirit, **teaching** them to observe everything I have commanded you.

The student will note that there is only one explicit imperative in the Greek text, μαθητεύσατε ("make disciples"). There are three participles, πορευθέντες ("go"), βαπτίζοντες ("baptizing"), and διδάσκοντες ("teaching"). Matthew frequently

---

[1] The apostle Matthew wrote this passage and is intending to teach his readers through it. Yet, we assume Matthew was a faithful conveyor of Jesus's intent.

uses participles that communicate attendant circumstances alongside main verbs.[2] Bible translators are correct to see here contextual markers pointing to πορευθέντες ("go") being employed to communicate attendant circumstance—functioning imperatively alongside the main imperative verb, μαθητεύσατε ("make disciples").[3] Nevertheless, in translating πορευθέντες ("go") as an imperative, a structural nuance from the original Greek is lost. Had Matthew wanted to line up imperatives side by side, he easily could have (e.g., 2 Tim 4:2). Yet, by using one imperative and three grammatically dependent participles, Matthew emphasizes the centrality of "making disciples" in Jesus's final instructions. Certainly, disciples cannot be made without "locomotive initiative" (going); neither are disciples made without initiation/formal declaration of allegiance (baptizing) or instruction (teaching). However, the "neon flashing sign" in the Greek text is the word μαθητεύσατε ("make disciples").[4] When we teach or preach a text such as Matthew 28:19–20, we need to ask not only if we are faithfully conveying the meaning/content of the original text, but also if we are emphasizing what the inspired author emphasized. In this chapter, we will learn methods of studying the Greek text that help reveal the author's emphasis.

CHAPTER OBJECTIVES

The purpose of this chapter is to equip students to think more carefully about the structure of the Greek language as recorded in the NT. We will begin by examining parts of the Greek sentence and word order within sentences.[5] Next, we will introduce several methods for analyzing the structure of the Greek text more systematically. Finally, we will provide a brief discussion of a growing field in Greek studies—discourse analysis.

GREEK SENTENCES

As students begin to study Greek, many feel the poverty of their grammatical background in English. Indeed, a student once remarked, "I didn't really learn English grammar until I took Greek!" Thankfully, a number of accessible resources

---

[2] See chapter 10 for a fuller explanation of the participle of attendant circumstance.

[3] The other two participles, βαπτίζοντες ("baptizing"), and διδάσκοντες ("teaching"), may also communicate attendant circumstances (functioning imperatively), or they may communicate means. That is, one makes disciples by baptizing and teaching.

[4] Note also other instances in Matthew's Gospel where a (passive) participial form of πορεύομαι precedes an imperative, such as Matt 2:8 (a possible *inclusio* with Matt 28:19); 9:13; 10:7; 11:4; 17:27; 18:12; and 28:7. In each case, the primary emphasis lies, not on the participle of πορεύομαι, but on the following imperative.

[5] Although some scholars encourage looking at the "colon" or "period" as the standard informational unit of ancient Greek, I will be looking at sentences—possibly sacrificing precision for the sake of intelligibility to intermediate Greek students.

have recently been published to aid students with weak backgrounds in English grammar.[6] One area where students regularly face challenges is in understanding the parts of a sentence—subject, predicate, dependent clause, etc. The purpose of this section of the chapter is to overview the main components and types of Greek sentences. Students are not expected to develop an exhaustive knowledge of Greek sentence structure but to develop familiarity with common patterns.

The Components of Sentences

While linguistic scholars may debate what exactly a sentence is,[7] the following definition is helpful: a sentence is a complete grammatical unit that includes or implies a subject and a predicate. A subject is a person, place, or thing about which something is said. The predicate is the part of the sentence that says something about the subject (i.e., conveys information about the subject). For example, John 11:35 reads: ἐδάκρυσεν ὁ Ἰησοῦς ("Jesus wept").[8] In this short verse, ὁ Ἰησοῦς is the subject and ἐδάκρυσεν is the predicate. We also note that Greek verbs include subject information in their endings, so ἐδάκρυσεν ("he wept") alone could function as a complete sentence. In this case, the subject is conveyed by the third person singular ending of the verb (-εν).

Beyond simply labeling one part of the sentence as "subject" and another part as "predicate," we can think of sentences as being made up of smaller pieces—words, phrases, and clauses. We will now briefly define and comment on these components.

Word

We all know what a word is when we see it or say it, but it is a bit more challenging to provide a technical definition.[9] A word is a foundational sound unit (lex)[10]

---

[6] E.g., Lamerson, *English Grammar to Ace New Testament Greek* (see chap. 12, n. 47); Douglas S. Huffman, *The Handy Guide to New Testament Greek: Grammar, Syntax, Diagramming* (Grand Rapids: Kregel, 2012); Long, *Grammatical Concepts 101 for Biblical Greek* (see chap. 12, n. 49); Peter James Silzer and Thomas John Finley, *How Biblical Languages Work: A Student's Guide to Learning Hebrew and Greek* (Grand Rapids: Kregel, 2004). For short definitions of many grammatical terms, see DeMoss, *Pocket Dictionary for the Study of New Testament Greek* (see chap. 12, n. 15). Also note the classic and affordable pamphlet by Braun, *English Grammar for Language Students* (see chap. 12, n. 14).

[7] Young observes, "A sentence can be defined as a grammatically complete unit consisting of one or more words. The traditional definition that a sentence expresses a complete thought is now being discarded by linguists as a misleading and erroneous idea. Complete thoughts are expressed by larger discourse units within situational contexts" (205).

[8] When choosing a text from the GNT to illustrate a sentence, I immediately thought of the "shortest verse in the Bible"—"Jesus wept" (John 11:35). Later, I noticed that Richard Young uses the same verse to illustrate sentence structure, though I was not conscious of being influenced by him.

[9] Some grammarians offer us unhelpful definitions for "word" such as "a grammatical unit which can stand alone" (Silzer and Finley, *How Biblical Languages Work*, 251).

[10] About the lex(eme), Long writes, "[It] is the typically foundational element of a word or lexical item. The idea of a lex(eme) is not the easiest to comprehend. In English it is typically represented as the dictionary form of any word. For example, a person learning English may encounter the word *kicked* in a text; the dictionary will have the word entered simply as *kick*. *Kick*, represented on the page as k-i-c-k, is the *lex*, while the (emic) concept behind the word, 'kick,' is the *lexeme*. The notion

with other functional sound units (morphemes)[11] sometimes combined with it, so that a native speaker recognizes it as a grammatical entity referring to a person, place, thing, or action, or functioning in some other way in his language. For our purposes, a precise linguistic definition of a word is unnecessary. Simply pointing to a printed word on the page and noting that it is a singular letter (e.g., ὁ, "the") or group of letters (λόγος, "word") that has space on either side is sufficient. What is important for us to note is that a word alone, apart from any context, conveys no information about the author's intent in using it. If we were to provide a student with a word from the GNT and ask what it meant, he could provide us with a semantic range for the word in the Koine Greek period, but that is all. In addition, sometimes literary context can push a word to the edge (or over the edge) of its normal semantic range. Additional context is essential in determining meaning. Examples of Greek words are below:

- Matt 1:21 – καί ("and"). A conjunction.
- Mark 4:2 – ἐδίδασκεν ("He taught"). An indicative verb.
- Rom 16:1 – Φοίβην ("Phoebe"). A proper noun.
- 2 Thess 1:5 – καταξιωθῆναι ("be counted worthy"). An infinitive.
- Heb 2:14 – τό ("the"). An article.

Again, apart from context, we can only give a brief "gloss" of a word—essentially a guess based on the Greek word's semantic domain. For instructions on how to do a Greek word study, see the next chapter.

Phrase

A phrase is two or more words functioning together as a discrete grammatical unit, though lacking the sufficient components to be called a clause or sentence (i.e., phrases usually lack a subject, a predicate, or both). In non-technical usage, the labels "phrase" and "clause" sometimes overlap, and perhaps it is best not to be overly dogmatic in delimiting the term.[12] Common phrase types and accompanying examples are listed below.

---

of lex(eme) is similar to Biblical Greek. The lexeme 'reverence' is represented by the lex ἀγ, which underlies ἅγιος *holy* and ἁγιασμός *sanctification*. Commonly, Biblical Greek grammarians give the label *root* to what I am here calling a lex(eme). Unlike English, however, Biblical Greek has some roots that are *not* a simple dictionary form" (Long, *Grammatical Concepts*, 4–5).

[11] About the morpheme, Long explains, "[It] is the *smallest* or *minimal* block of language that is *meaningful* and recurrent for word-building in a language" (*Grammatical Concepts*, 4).

[12] Even some respected grammarians define a phrase in significantly different ways—e.g., some allowing for the inclusion of a verbal element, others not so. Porter says a phrase may consist of only one word (*Idioms*, 312). Elsewhere, Porter defines a clause as "a complete grammatical construction consisting of one or more phrases" (Porter, *Idioms*, 309).

Prepositional Phrase

- τοῦ λοιποῦ, ἐνδυναμοῦσθε **ἐν κυρίῳ** καὶ **ἐν τῷ κράτει τῆς ἰσχύος αὐτοῦ** (Eph 6:10)

  Finally, be strong **in the Lord** and **in the strength of His might** (NASB)

Noun Phrase

- **ἡ χάρις τοῦ κυρίου Ἰησοῦ Χριστοῦ** . . . μετὰ πάντων ὑμῶν (2 Cor 13:13)

  The grace of the Lord Jesus Christ . . . be with all of you

Adverbial Phrase

- ἀνθρώπῳ οἰκοδεσπότῃ, ὅστις ἐξῆλθεν **ἅμα πρωῒ** μισθώσασθαι ἐργάτας εἰς τὸν ἀμπελῶνα αὐτοῦ (Matt 20:1)

  a landowner who went out **early in the morning** to hire workers for his vineyard

Adjectival Phrase

- ἔσται σκεῦος εἰς τιμήν, ἡγιασμένον, **εὔχρηστον τῷ δεσπότῃ**, εἰς πᾶν ἔργον ἀγαθὸν ἡτοιμασμένον (2 Tim 2:21)

  he will be a special instrument, set apart, **useful to the Master**, prepared for every good work

  > Here the adjective εὔχρηστος is further limited by a dative of reference, δεσπότῃ ("to the Master").

Verbal Phrase[13]

- **καὶ χρηματισθέντες κατ᾽ ὄναρ μὴ ἀνακάμψαι πρὸς Ἡρῴδην**, δι᾽ ἄλλης ὁδοῦ ἀνεχώρησαν εἰς τὴν χώραν αὐτῶν (Matt 2:12)

  And being warned in a dream not to go back to Herod, they returned to their own country by another route

  > Though the participle χρηματισθέντες ("being warned") lacks an explicit subject, the subject is clearly implied. One could also describe this participial phrase as a dependent adverbial temporal clause (see below).

---

[13] Huffman says that a phrase is a "syntactically functioning group of words without a verb" (*Handy Guide to New Testament Greek*, 88), but he is at odds with other grammarians in this definition. DeMoss lists a "verb phrase" as one type of phrase (98).

Clause

A clause is a portion of a sentence that contains (or implies) a subject and predicate. In other words, a clause is a recognizable grammatical unit in a sentence that has both a subject and verb (or implies one or the other, if it is lacking). By using the label "clause," we imply that the grammatical unit we are labeling makes up only a portion of the sentence. Otherwise, we would call it a sentence. Clauses can be divided into two different kinds: (1) independent clauses and (2) dependent clauses. In illustrations of independent and dependent clauses below, sentences have been extracted from larger grammatical relationships in the GNT. If any words are missing from the middle of a quoted verse, they are marked with the sign of an ellipsis (. . .).

Independent Clause

An independent clause is a portion of a sentence that contains (or implies) a subject or predicate and is not subordinated to another portion of the sentence. In other words, an independent clause can stand on its own. In fact, if you put a period at the end of an independent clause, it will become a sentence. The independent clauses below are in bold.

- **μακάριοί ἐστε** ὅταν ὀνειδίσωσιν ὑμᾶς καὶ διώξωσιν καὶ εἴπωσιν πᾶν πονηρὸν καθ᾽ ὑμῶν [ψευδόμενοι] ἕνεκεν ἐμου (Matt 5:11)

  You are blessed when they insult and persecute you and falsely say every kind of evil against you because of me

  > The second person plural subject ὑμεῖς ("you") is implied by the second person plural form ἐστε ("[you] are").

- **γρηγορεῖτε** καὶ **προσεύχεσθε**, ἵνα μὴ εἰσέλθητε εἰς πειρασμόν (Matt 26:41)

  Stay awake and **pray**, so that you won't enter into temptation

  > Both γρηγορεῖτε ("[you] stay awake") and προσεύχεσθε ("[you] pray") are independent (imperative) clauses linked with a coordinating conjunction, καί ("and"). This compound sentence has an additional dependent (purpose) clause. Together, the compound sentence with a dependent clause forms a compound-complex sentence (see below).

- ἡνίκα δὲ ἐὰν ἐπιστρέψῃ πρὸς κύριον, **περιαιρεῖται τὸ κάλυμμα** (2 Cor 3:16)

  But whenever anyone turns to the Lord, **the veil is taken away** (NIV)

Dependent Clause

A dependent clause is a portion of a sentence that contains (or implies) a subject or predicate and is subordinated to another portion of the sentence. It cannot stand alone as a complete thought. If you were to put a period at the end of a dependent clause, it would not be a sentence; it would be an incomplete thought. Many Greek dependent clauses are introduced with explicit subordinating words such as ὅτε ("when"), ἵνα ("in order that"), ὥστε ("so that"), or ὅτι ("that," "because").[14] Adverbial participles often introduce dependent clauses, and translators frequently render them in English with dependent introductory words (e.g., "when," "because," "if"), though such an explicit function word is lacking in Greek. In the sentences below, the dependent clauses are in bold.

- **κατακειμένου αὐτοῦ** ἦλθεν γυνὴ ἔχουσα ἀλάβαστρον μύρου νάρδου πιστικῆς πολυτελοῦς (Mark 14:3)

  as he was reclining at the table, a woman came with an alabaster jar of very expensive perfume of pure nard

  > A temporal clause (genitive absolute) expressing contemporaneous activity ("as," "when," "while").

- πιστὸς δέ ἐστιν ὁ κύριος, **ὃς στηρίξει ὑμᾶς καὶ φυλάξει ἀπὸ τοῦ πονηροῦ** (2 Thess 3:3)

  The Lord, **who will establish you and will guard you from the evil one**, is faithful (author's translation)

  > A relative clause ("who," "which," "that").

- **εἰ δέ τις ὑμῶν λείπεται σοφίας**, αἰτείτω παρὰ τοῦ διδόντος θεοῦ πᾶσιν ἁπλῶς καὶ μὴ ὀνειδίζοντος (Jas 1:5)

  If any of you lacks wisdom, let him ask God, who gives generously to all without reproach (ESV)

  > A conditional clause ("if," "unless").

As can be seen from the examples above, many dependent clauses are introduced by small connecting words which clarify the explicit relationship between the dependent and independent clauses.[15] Except in the case of the relative pronoun ("who," "which," "that"), these little function words are called subordinating conjunctions. For a list of common Greek subordinating conjunctions, brief definitions of them, and grammatical labels of their functions, see the section on conjunctions in chapter 12.

Conditional Clauses ("If" Clauses)

Conditional clauses are a special subset of dependent clauses that set up conditions which, if met, result in an articulated set of circumstances or demand a certain response. Depending on contextual markers, an adverbial participle can be

---

[14] See the list of common subordinating conjunctions in chapter 12.

[15] Of course, in the case of adverbial participial clauses, such function words are lacking in Greek. See chapter 10 on the adverbial uses of the participle.

translated as a conditional clause.[16] Conditional clauses are also frequently introduced with an explicit conditional particle (translated "if"). Traditionally, grammarians have classified Koine Greek as having four kinds or "classes" of conditional sentences.[17] In spite of limitations of this traditional classification system,[18] it is still useful and (from our experience) largely correct. In the chart below, the protasis is the "if" part of the sentence (the dependent conditional clause). The apodosis is the "then" part of the sentence (the resulting set of circumstances if the condition in the protasis has been met).

CLASS	CONDITIONAL PARTICLE	PROTASIS ("IF . . .")	APODOSIS ("THEN . . .")	MEANING
1st	εἰ	**Tense:** any **Mood:** ind "If your hand or your foot causes you to fall away" (εἰ δὲ ἡ χείρ σου ἢ ὁ πούς σου σκανδαλίζει σε).	**Tense:** any **Mood:** any "cut it off and throw it away" (ἔκκοψον αὐτὸν καὶ βάλε ἀπὸ σου, Matt 18:8).	The speaker or writer presents the protasis as true for the sake of argument. "If (and let us assume that this is true) . . ."
2nd	εἰ	**Tense:** impf, aor, or pluper **Mood:** ind "For if the miracles that were done in you had been done in Sodom" (ὅτι εἰ ἐν Σοδόμοις ἐγενήθησαν αἱ δυνάμεις αἱ γενόμεναι ἐν σοί).	**Tense:** impf, aor, or pluper **Mood:** ἄν + ind "it would have remained until today" (ἔμεινεν ἂν μέχρι τῆς σήμερον, Matt 11:23).	The condition is "contrary-to-fact." "If (and I, the speaker, do not think this is true) . . ." The particle ἄν is not always present in a contrary-to-fact condition. Always pay attention to context.
3rd	ἐάν	**Tense:** any **Mood:** sub "And if anyone takes away from the words of the book of this prophecy" (καὶ ἐάν τις ἀφέλῃ ἀπὸ τῶν λόγων τοῦ βιβλίου τῆς προφητείας ταύτης).	**Tense:** any **Mood:** any "God will take away his share of the tree of life" (ἀφελεῖ ὁ θεὸς τὸ μέρος αὐτοῦ ἀπὸ τοῦ ξύλου τῆς ζωῆς, Rev 22:19).	The event in the protasis is presented somewhat more hypothetically by the speaker. It is more tentative than the 1st class conditional.

---

[16] For example, Luke 9:25: "What does it benefit someone **if he gains** the whole world" (τί γὰρ ὠφελεῖται ἄνθρωπος **κερδήσας** τὸν κόσμον).

[17] This four-part classification system for NT Greek dates back at least to A. T. Robertson, who drew upon the classical Greek grammarian, Gildersleeve (Young, 226).

[18] See Young's criticisms (227–30). We might summarize Young's criticisms thus: Do not slavishly follow a grammatical template. Pay attention to context and discourse function. The conditional sentence chart in this chapter is similar to one I created for an online Greek program.

CLASS	CONDITIONAL PARTICLE	PROTASIS ("IF ...")	APODOSIS ("THEN ...")	MEANING
4th	εἰ	**Tense:** any **Mood:** opt "But even if you should suffer for righteous- ness" (ἀλλ᾽ εἰ καὶ πάσχοιτε διὰ δικαιοσύνην).	**Tense:** any **Mood:** opt "you are bless- ed" ([εἴης ἂν] μακάριοι, 1 Pet 3:14).	The event in the protasis is depicted as an extremely remote possibility. **Note:** There is no complete example of a 4th class conditional sentence in the GNT.

Types of Sentences According to Components

Words, phrases, and clauses can be combined in many different ways to produce a wide variety of Greek sentences. As students grow in their understanding
of Greek structure, it will be helpful to keep in mind the major types of sentences
below.[19]

Simple Sentence

A simple sentence has one word or group of words functioning as *the* subject and
one word or group of words functioning as *the* predicate. That is, there is only one
clause—an independent clause with a period (or other final punctuation) at the end,
marking it as a complete grammatical unit.

- ὁ οὐρανὸς καὶ ἡ γῆ παρελεύσονται (Mark 13:31)

  Heaven and earth will pass away

  Here the simple sentence has a compound subject, "heaven and earth." A simple
  sentence may have a compound subject and/or compound predicate. For example, in
  English, "Bill and Mary will sing and dance," is still a simple sentence with both a
  compound subject and compound predicate. "Bill will sing, and Mary will dance,"
  however, is a compound sentence, having two independent clauses (see below).

- ἔπειτα ἦλθον εἰς τὰ κλίματα τῆς Συρίας καὶ τῆς Κιλικίας (Gal 1:21)

  Afterward, I went to the regions of Syria and Cilicia

  Here the subject ("I") is communicated by the first person singular verb ending of
  ἦλθον. The verb ἦλθον ("I went") alone would constitute a simple sentence, but in
  the example above, the sentence contains additional information. We find an adverbial
  temporal modifier (ἔπειτα, "afterward") and a prepositional phrase communicating
  location or extension (εἰς τὰ κλίματα τῆς Συρίας καὶ τῆς Κιλικίας, "to the regions of

---

[19] As above, sometimes verses are presented in edited form to highlight sentence types. In other
words, a simple sentence below may have been extracted from what was originally a compound or
complex sentence. Any words missing from the middle of the verses will be marked with the sign of
an ellipsis (. . .).

Syria and Cilicia"). Simple sentences (as well as other sentence types) can be expanded by adding various modifiers or dependent elements.[20]

- ἐπεφάνη γὰρ ἡ χάρις τοῦ θεοῦ σωτήριος πᾶσιν ἀνθρώποις (Titus 2:11)

  For the grace of God has appeared bringing salvation for all people

Compound Sentence

A compound sentence is composed of two or more independent clauses (clauses that could "stand alone" if followed by a period) connected by one or more coordinating conjunctions. A coordinating conjunction is a word like "and" or "but" that puts independent clauses on equal footing.[21]

- καὶ εὐθὺς ἀπῆλθεν ἀπ' αὐτοῦ ἡ λέπρα, καὶ ἐκαθαρίσθη (Mark 1:42)

  Immediately the leprosy left him, and he was made clean

  > Here we have two independent clauses: (1) καὶ εὐθὺς ἀπῆλθεν ἀπ' αὐτοῦ ἡ λέπρα ("immediately the leprosy left him"), and (2) ἐκαθαρίσθη ("he was made clean"). If followed by a period, either clause could function as a stand-alone sentence. The coordinating conjunction καί ("and") links the two independent clauses. The first independent clause includes two additional modifiers—the adverb εὐθύς ("immediately") and a prepositional phrase communicating source, ἀπ' αὐτοῦ (lit., "from him").

- λέγω ὑμῖν ὅτι καὶ Ἡλίας ἐλήλυθεν, καὶ ἐποίησαν αὐτῷ ὅσα ἤθελον (Mark 9:13)

  I tell you that Elijah has come, and they did whatever they pleased to him

- συνέκλεισαν πλῆθος ἰχθύων πολύ, διερρήσσετο δὲ τὰ δίκτυα αὐτῶν (Luke 5:6)

  they caught a great number of fish, and their nets began to tear

  > Here δέ ("and") functions as a coordinating copulative conjunction.

Complex Sentence

A complex sentence includes both an independent clause and a subordinate (dependent) clause. In other words, one portion of the sentence (the independent clause), if followed by a period, would be a complete sentence. The other portion (the dependent clause) could not stand alone as a sentence, even if followed by a period.

---

[20] See Young, 206–11. We should recognize, of course, that adding certain dependent elements may result in sentences being categorized as a different type. For example, adding a dependent clause to a simple sentence will change it to a complex sentence (see below).

[21] See chapter 12 for a list of common coordinating conjunctions, brief definitions of them, and grammatical labels of their functions.

- μετανοεῖτε· ἤγγικεν γὰρ ἡ βασιλεία τῶν οὐρανῶν (Matt 3:2)

  Repent, because the kingdom of heaven has come near!

  The conjunction γάρ here introduces a dependent causal clause.

- καὶ ἐγερθεὶς ἀπῆλθεν εἰς τὸν οἶκον αὐτοῦ (Matt 9:7)

  And, after he arose, he departed to his house (author's translation)

  In this complex sentence, there is an independent clause (ἀπῆλθεν εἰς τὸν οἶκον αὐτοῦ, "he departed to his house") and a dependent participial clause expressing subsequent time (καὶ ἐγερθεὶς, "And, after he arose"). The words "he departed to his house" could stand alone as a sentence if followed by a period. The words "And, after he arose" could not stand alone as a sentence, even if followed by a period.

- εἷς ὁ θεὸς ὃς δικαιώσει περιτομὴν ἐκ πίστεως καὶ ἀκροβυστίαν διὰ τῆς πίστεως (Rom 3:30)

  there is one God who will justify the circumcised by faith and the uncircumcised through faith

  The independent clause here (εἷς ὁ θεὸς) has an implied copulative verb ἐστιν ("is"). The relative clause (ὃς δικαιώσει . . .) is dependent and cannot stand alone.

Copulative Sentence[22]

A copulative sentence is a sentence that links two substantives with a copulative verb (i.e., εἰμί, γίνομαι, ὑπάρχω). One of the substantives, or the copulative verb itself, may be implied. When two substantives are present, one substantive serves as the subject and the other as the predicate nominative or predicate adjective. The copulative verb can also serve to assert the existence of the subject (i.e., the "existential" use), in which case there is no predicate nominative or predicate adjective.

- ὑμεῖς ἐστε τὸ φῶς τοῦ κόσμου (Matt 5:14)

  You are the light of the world

  ("You") is the subject, ἐστε ("are") is the copulative verb, and τὸ φῶς is the predicate nominative—here, further qualified by a genitival modifier, τοῦ κόσμου ("of the world").

- ἐγώ εἰμι ὁ ἄρτος τῆς ζωῆς (John 6:35)

  I am the bread of life

  Here, ἐγώ serves as the subject, εἰμι ("am") is the copulative verb, and ὁ ἄρτος (the bread) is the predicate nominative.

---

[22] Copulative sentences are also called nonactive, stative, assertive, or equative sentences (with slight differences in meaning). See Young, 207–8.

- μακάριόν ἐστιν μᾶλλον διδόναι ἢ λαμβάνειν (Acts 20:35)

  It is more blessed to give than to receive

    Here the infinitive διδόναι (to give) functions as the subject of ἐστιν (is). μακάριον ("blessed") is a predicate adjective, modified by the adverb μᾶλλον ("more"). A literal rendering of the sentence to highlight the Greek grammatical structure is: "To give is more blessed than to receive."

Additional combinations of the sentence types above occur throughout the GNT. For example, a compound sentence (two independent clauses joined with a coordinating conjunction) often occurs with one or more dependent clauses. Such a sentence is called a compound-complex sentence. Complex sentences frequently occur with multiple dependent clauses.

Types of Sentences According to Function

Sentences can be classified as above—according to the presence, absence, or number of independent and dependent clauses, or the kinds of verbs in those clauses (i.e., the presence or absence of a copulative verb). Sentences can also be classified according to their function. Below we will survey the four main functional categories of sentences: declarative, interrogative, imperative, and exclamatory. We should note these functional categories are based on the explicit grammatical forms in the sentence. Sometimes strict grammatical function and discourse function (the way the sentence is employed by the author to convey meaning) will differ.

Declarative

A declarative sentence makes a statement of fact (or is at least portrayed as factual). Nevertheless, we should not think of declarations as cold, objective assertions apart from the author's purposes. Speech act theorists remind us that all language is inherently action-oriented in some way—commanding, reassuring, rebuking, etc.[23]

- πάντες γὰρ οἱ προφῆται καὶ ὁ νόμος ἕως Ἰωάννου ἐπροφήτευσαν (Matt 11:13)

  For all the prophets and the law prophesied until John came

    Jesus's summary of redemptive history serves to highlight the importance of John, and thus Jesus implicitly commands his hearers to heed John's testimony.

---

[23] See the discussion of speech act theory in Question 38 of Plummer, *40 Questions about Interpreting the Bible* (see chap. 1, n. 38).

- ὁ μὴ τιμῶν τὸν υἱὸν οὐ τιμᾷ τὸν πατέρα τὸν πέμψαντα αὐτόν (John 5:23)

  Anyone who does not honor the Son does not honor the Father who sent him

  > Although this statement is declarative in grammatical form, it has an undeniable imperatival function. Jesus implicitly instructs his hearers to honor the Son.

Interrogative

An interrogative sentence asks a question. Sometimes questions in the GNT are genuine queries (Acts 16:30); other times they function as rebukes, commands, exclamations, etc.

- ἄρας οὖν τὰ μέλη τοῦ Χριστοῦ ποιήσω πόρνης μέλη; (1 Cor 6:15)

  Shall I then take the members of Christ and unite them with a prostitute? (NIV)

  > Though *grammatically* a question, Paul's words here certainly *function* (at a discourse level) as a rebuke of the Corinthians' sexual behavior.

- ποῦ σου, θάνατε, τὸ νῖκος; ποῦ σου, θάνατε, τὸ κέντρον; (1 Cor 15:55)

  Where, death, is your victory? Where, death, is your sting?

  > Although questions in a strict grammatical sense, these queries that personify "Death" are not genuinely seeking information. Paul uses the interrogative rhetorically, essentially exclaiming, "Death, you have no victory! Death, you have no sting!"

Imperative

An imperative sentence makes a command or request.

- αἴτησόν με ὃ ἐὰν θέλῃς (Mark 6:22)

  Ask me whatever you want

- σὺ κάθου ὧδε καλῶς (Jas 2:3)

  Sit here in a good place

Exclamatory

Exclamatory sentences communicate an expression of strong feeling.

- ὄφελον καὶ ἀποκόψονται οἱ ἀναστατοῦντες ὑμᾶς (Gal 5:12)

  I wish those who are disturbing you might also let themselves be mutilated!

- μὴ γένοιτο (Rom 9:14)

  May it never be! (NASB)

Word Order within Sentences

Greek grammars regularly note two things about the order of the Greek language: (1) Because Greek is an inflected language (i.e., nouns have case endings to tell the reader how they are functioning), word order matters much less in conveying meaning than in a language like English. (2) There are some regular patterns of Greek word order, though these patterns can be set aside for stylistic variation, emphasis, or some other literary purposes.[24]

The English language undoubtedly follows a SVO (subject-verb-object) word order.[25] Grammarians frequently assert that Greek basically follows a VSO (verb-subject-object) word order.[26] Stanley Porter, however, is right to call this claim into question. Porter accuses grammarians of skewing the evidence by considering only Greek sentences where verb, subject, and object are *all* explicitly present. Thus, scholars are not adequately taking into account the many sentences lacking one or more of those grammatical units. Porter also contends that scholars have sometimes distorted the data by assuming the placement of a lacking item (i.e., a lacking verb, subject, or object). Porter argues we should start with the explicit constructions in the Greek text rather than linguistic templates such as SVO (subject-verb-object) and VSO (verb-subject-object).[27]

Drawing heavily upon the work of K. J. Dover,[28] Porter asserts that discussions of Greek word order have not adequately taken into account the monolectic nature of Greek verbs (i.e., Greek verbs convey person and number by their endings, so an explicit subject is not grammatically necessary). In his discussion of Greek word order, Porter uses the term "complement," which he defines as "the element which completes (or complements) a predicate."[29] Practically speaking, the complement in the sentence is frequently a direct object or predicate nominative. Porter is not being overly pedantic; he is seeking to describe the structure of the Greek language in light of its own constituent elements.

---

[24] David Alan Black writes, "Word, phrase, and clause order in New Testament Greek are fairly well-defined, and variations from the norm are often used for purposes of conveying emphasis." *Learn to Read New Testament Greek*, 3rd ed. (Nashville: B&H, 2009), 201.

[25] E.g., Jim (subject) threw (verb) the ball (direct object).

[26] Black, *Learn to Read New Testament Greek*, 201. So also BDF, 248 (§472); Young, 218; Silzer and Finley, *How Biblical Languages Work*, 138. Silzer and Finley note their dependence on Timothy Friberg, *New Testament Greek Word Order in Light of Discourse Consideration* (Ph.D. diss., University of Minnesota, 1982).

[27] Porter, *Idioms*, 293.

[28] K. J. Dover, *Greek Word Order* (Cambridge: Cambridge University Press, 1960), esp. chap. 2.

[29] Porter, *Idioms*, 310. His definition continues: "The complement is often equated with the object of a verb (either direct or indirect). In clause structure, the complement is one of the three major components (the others being subject and predicate) and consists of at least one phrase" *Idioms*.

Porter maintains that the two most common base sentence constructions in the GNT are:[30]

Predicate (with no explicit subject or complement)	

Predicate	Complement

Porter says the next two most common sentence patterns are:

Complement	Predicate

Subject	Predicate

Porter also helpfully reminds us that NT authors had their own distinctive styles. He observes,

> In the Greek of the New Testament, the adjectival modifier follows its noun approximately 75% of the time in Luke and Mark, whether it is in attributive or predicate structure. It precedes its noun approximately 65% of the time in Paul. Thus the normal Lukan structure occurs in Lk. 15.13: χώραν μακράν (a distant land), the normal Markan structure in Mk 4.41 φόβον μέγαν (great fear), and the normal Pauline structure in Rom. 1.13 ἐν τοῖς λοιποῖς ἔθνεσιν (among the remaining nations).[31]

Such caveats about individual stylistic differences must be kept in mind even as we tentatively make some observations about regular word order in the GNT. Below is a chart which lists possible *emphatic* orders (i.e., word orders that deviate from the norm). Context must clarify the purpose of the deviation. Possibly a new topic is being introduced, or a contrast is being drawn. Only the literary context can clarify the author's purpose in deviating from typical Greek word order. The exegete should also consider the possibility that an ancient author is unconsciously varying his style.

---

[30] The vertical order within these two charts is not intended to convey the prominence of one construction over the other. Porter lists them as equally prominent (*Idioms*, 293–94). For his statistical analysis, Porter relies upon M. E. Davison, "NT Greek Word Order," *Literary and Linguistic Computing* 4 (1989): 19–28. Davison looks primarily at the writings of Luke and Paul.

[31] Porter, *Idioms*, 290–91.

POSSIBLY EMPHATIC WORD ORDERS[a]		NT EXAMPLES
Direct Object	Verb	αὐτὸν ἐσταύρωσαν ("they crucified him," John 19:18)
Subject	Verb[b]	θεὸν οὐδεὶς ἑώρακεν ("No one has ever seen God," John 1:18)
Predicate nominative or Predicate adjective	Subject or Verb	ὁ θεὸς φῶς ἐστιν ("God is light," 1 John 1:5)
Genitive modifier[c]	Noun	θεοῦ δύναμιν ("power of God," 1 Cor 1:24)
Noun	Attributive adjective[d]	ὁ ποιμὴν ὁ καλός ("the good shepherd," John 10:11)
Noun	Attributive demonstrative[e]	τὴν γενεὰν ταύτην ("this generation," Matt 11:16)
Subject or Object	Imperative verb	τὸν ἄρτον ἡμῶν τὸν ἐπιούσιον δὸς ἡμῖν σήμερον ("Give us today our daily bread," Matt 6:11)
Prepositional phrase	Verb	ἐπὶ ταύτῃ τῇ πέτρᾳ οἰκοδομήσω μου τὴν ἐκκλησίαν ("on this rock I will build My church," Matt 16:18)
Indirect object	Verb	κἀγὼ ὑμῖν παραδώσω αὐτόν ("if I hand him over to you," Matt 26:15)
Clauses introduced by: ἄχρι ("until"), γάρ (causal use: "because"), ἐάν μή ("except"), ἐπεί ("since"), ἕως ("until"), ἵνα ("so that"), καθώς ("just as"), ὅπου ("where"), ὅπως ("so that"), ὅτι ("that"), ὡς ("as")	Verb	ἐγὼ δὲ ὅτι τὴν ἀλήθειαν λέγω, οὐ πιστεύετέ μοι ("Yet because I tell the truth, you do not believe me," John 8:45)
Verb	Clauses introduced by: ἐάν ("if"), εἰ ("if"), ὅταν ("whenever"), ὅτε ("when")	καὶ εἶδον ὅτε ἤνοιξεν τὸ ἀρνίον μίαν ἐκ τῶν ἑπτὰ σφραγίδων ("Then I saw when the Lamb broke one of the seven seals," Rev 6:1 NASB)

a. The material in this chart (with some changes and additions) is drawn from Black, *Learn to Read New Testament Greek*, 202–4. Editorial changes were influenced by Young, 214–18; Silzer and Finley, *How Biblical Languages Work*, 139–41; Porter, *Idioms*, 286–97; and John D. Grassmick, *Principles and Practice of Greek Exegesis: A Classroom Manual* (n.p.: Dallas Theological Seminary, 1976), 88.

b. This subject-verb order is sometimes used to introduce a new topic with no intended emphasis.

c. Porter observes that the genitival modifier follows its noun 96% of the time in Paul and 99% of the time in Luke–Acts (*Idioms*, 291).

d. As noted above, the attributive adjective normally follows its noun in Luke–Acts and Mark (75% of the time), so one must take into account a NT author's stylistic tendencies in applying this pattern (*Idioms*, 290).

e. Porter notes that an attributive demonstrative follows its noun 85% of the time in Paul and 78% of the time in Luke–Acts (*Idioms*, 291).

Analyzing Grammatical and Literary Structure

Students study Greek not so that they can take vocabulary tests, but so they can read the GNT, savor its message, and deliver that message faithfully to others. One essential part of discerning the meaning of any particular biblical text is understanding how the assertions and arguments within that text fit together. What is the author's main point? What appeals does he use to support his point? (e.g., logical? scriptural? emotional?) Also, it is important to consider how any discrete section of text relates to the sections around it and to the author's overarching purposes for his writing.

Biblical authors wrote their works to be read aloud to communities (Col 4:16). The original audiences, who mostly would have spoken Greek as a native language, unconsciously responded to the author's literary clues—discerning the author's purposes, arguments, and emphases. As modern persons who approach the culture and language of the GNT from a marked distance, we need to think more consciously and deliberately about the text's structure.

Greek scholars and teachers have developed several methods to discern and analyze the structure of the Greek text. At best, such methods simply help the reader to see clearly and think carefully about the literary clues that the biblical authors give us. Below, we will briefly survey line diagramming, arcing, and phrase diagramming. Finally, we will introduce discourse analysis.

Line Diagramming

Students who were forced to do line diagramming in elementary school sometimes feel a rush of anxiety in encountering it again. Others who have never been instructed in the mysterious art admire line diagrams from a distance, as if looking at cuneiform tablets in a museum, believing they will never be able to understand or produce such works. In fact, a line diagram is nothing other than a visual representation of the various syntactical relationships in a text. By placing words and phrases on lines and connecting those lines, we are able to show visually how the various parts of a sentence work together—and also how sentences fit together.

Let anxious students calm their hearts. Line diagramming is not an entrance requirement into heaven. Neither did the apostle Paul ever diagram a text. There is no inerrant method of line diagramming; scholars vary their methods. Below, we will give a rudimentary lesson in line diagramming. Then, students will be referred to other resources which teach and model line diagramming in more detail.

When a student starts to diagram a verse, he should look first for the main verb and then check to see if there is an explicit subject. These components will usually be found in an independent clause, and the verb will be indicative, or less frequently imperative or subjunctive. Subject and verb are then placed on a base line with a line intersecting the base line to separate subject from predicate. If there is a direct object, a line is drawn above the base line to the right of the verb, and the direct object is placed to the right of this line.

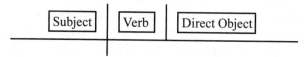

Various dependent elements in the sentence (e.g., adverbs, prepositional phrases, genitival modifiers, dependent clauses) are then placed on lower lines connected to the items they are modifying:

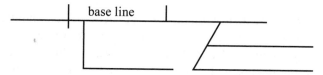

The base line can also be split to allow for compound elements:

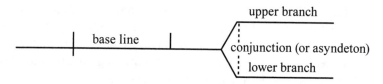

At the risk of overwhelming the reader, we will include a template below showing virtually all possible syntactical relationships that can be represented in a line diagram.

Line Diagramming Master Template[32]

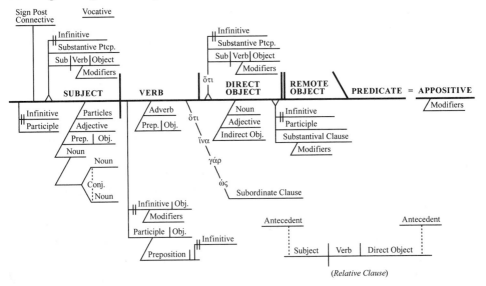

One of the benefits of diagramming is that students cannot "fake" their understanding of the text by parroting English translations. Diagramming forces the student to demonstrate that he knows how each word, phrase, and clause functions in the sentence. Indeed, when producing a line diagram, it is advisable to jot down syntactical functions alongside the visual schema. In other words, don't simply attach a line with an adverbial dependent participle below the base line—also jot down a functional label beside it, such as "temporal" or "causal." Whatever helps you discern and analyze the structure of the text is encouraged.

When first learning to diagram, use a large piece of paper and write in pencil, because much erasing will be needed. As skills grow, students might prefer to use the "cut and paste" features in the diagramming modules of a Bible software program. The complete diagramming of the GNT by Dr. Randy Leedy can now be purchased directly from the author's website: ntgreekguy.com.[33] Although students should not slavishly rely on another's work, viewing an expert's diagrams can sharpen one's own skills. Also, if the student reaches different syntactical conclusions from the pre-packaged diagrams, he has the option of altering the diagrams and saving his altered work.

Diagramming is like swimming—you can't learn unless you jump in, nearly drown, and try it for yourself! Nevertheless, most students are also aided by a gentle step-by-step approach which exceeds the space limitations of this chapter. Thankfully, there are several resources that can help carry the student forward. For print resources, we recommend chapter 5 of Tom Schreiner's *Interpreting the*

---

[32] Denny Burk's summary of John D. Grassmick's diagramming method. Used by permission.

[33] Accordance Bible software offers an add-on module that includes a growing number of diagrams for books in the Greek New Testament. Logos Bible Software also includes sentence diagramming tools with drag and drop capabilities.

Pauline Epistles.[34] There are several free online resources which similarly walk the student step-by-step through diagramming a multiplicity of syntactical relationships.[35] Students should note that while line diagrams are very helpful in technical analysis at the sentence level, they are less effective at visually representing the relationships between sentences and larger discourse units.[36]

Tracing an Argument (Arcing and Bracketing)

Tracing is a method of following a biblical author's argument and representing it through arcing or bracketing. The aim is to show the logical relationship between propositions in the Greek text. This approach breaks a text into propositions, connects those propositions with a series of arcs or brackets, labels the propositions according to function, and finally produces a preaching and/or teaching outline based on one's study. This method of analyzing the text has been popularized by influential pastor John Piper, who credits his seminary professor, Dan Fuller, with first developing the arcing method. Students who employ arcing/bracketing will want to make use of the handy new lexicon which labels connecting words according to Piper's method.[37] Below is a sample arc and bracket of the same passage, Matthew 5:13–16. The arcing and bracketing below were done by Brian Tabb.

---

[34] Thomas R. Schreiner, *Interpreting the Pauline Epistles*, 2nd ed. (Grand Rapids: Baker, 2011).

[35] http://www.chioulaoshi.org/BG/Diagrams/diagramming.html; www.dailydoseofgreek.com/wp-content/uploads/sites/2/2018/07/Diagramming-Handbook.pdf. These links are current as of January 2020. In the event that these links fail, updated links will be made available at www.deepergreek.com.

[36] About line diagramming, Young writes, "This method excels at what it was designed to accomplish, to analyze the grammatical relation of each word in a sentence. Beyond that, its value is dubious. It is a tool designed for sentence-based grammar and is not capable of handling large segments of text without becoming *overly* cumbersome. Since it adheres rigidly to the surface structure, it ignores possible skewing between form and meaning. Hence, line diagramming fails to provide semantic perspective to the text and is therefore inadequate for exegetical purposes" (267).

[37] Beale, Brendsel, and Ross, *An Interpretive Lexicon of New Testament Greek* (see chap. 12, n. 3).

Salt and Light

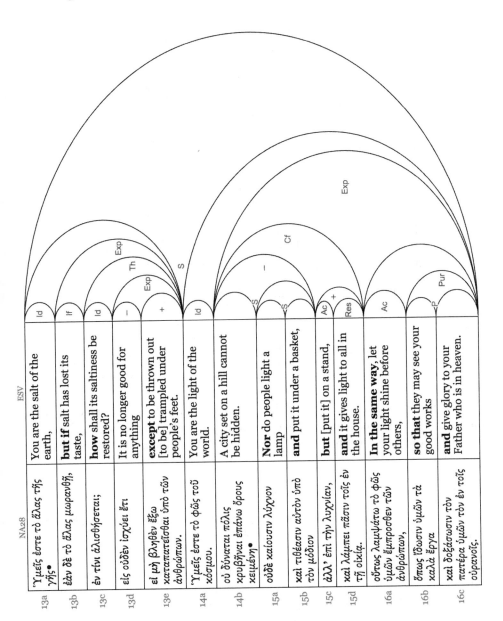

Disciples of Jesus are salt and light in the world.

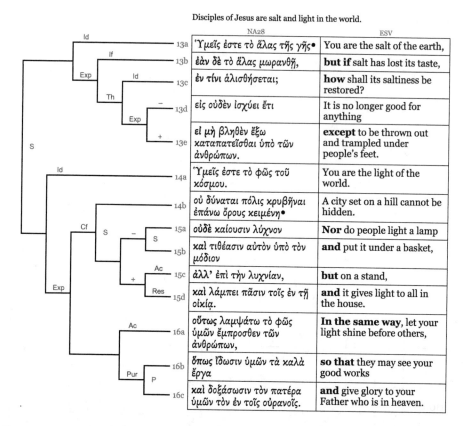

	NA28	ESV
13a	Ὑμεῖς ἐστε τὸ ἅλας τῆς γῆς·	You are the salt of the earth,
13b	ἐὰν δὲ τὸ ἅλας μωρανθῇ,	**but if** salt has lost its taste,
13c	ἐν τίνι ἁλισθήσεται;	**how** shall its saltiness be restored?
13d	εἰς οὐδὲν ἰσχύει ἔτι	It is no longer good for anything
13e	εἰ μὴ βληθὲν ἔξω καταπατεῖσθαι ὑπὸ τῶν ἀνθρώπων.	**except** to be thrown out and trampled under people's feet.
14a	Ὑμεῖς ἐστε τὸ φῶς τοῦ κόσμου.	You are the light of the world.
14b	οὐ δύναται πόλις κρυβῆναι ἐπάνω ὄρους κειμένη·	A city set on a hill cannot be hidden.
15a	οὐδὲ καίουσιν λύχνον	**Nor** do people light a lamp
15b	καὶ τιθέασιν αὐτὸν ὑπὸ τὸν μόδιον	**and** put it under a basket,
15c	ἀλλ' ἐπὶ τὴν λυχνίαν,	**but** on a stand,
15d	καὶ λάμπει πᾶσιν τοῖς ἐν τῇ οἰκίᾳ.	**and** it gives light to all in the house.
16a	οὕτως λαμψάτω τὸ φῶς ὑμῶν ἔμπροσθεν τῶν ἀνθρώπων,	**In the same way**, let your light shine before others,
16b	ὅπως ἴδωσιν ὑμῶν τὰ καλὰ ἔργα	**so that** they may see your good works
16c	καὶ δοξάσωσιν τὸν πατέρα ὑμῶν τὸν ἐν τοῖς οὐρανοῖς.	**and** give glory to your Father who is in heaven.

For an explanation of the various labels above, students are referred to www.biblearc.com. The website includes free training modules on tracing. For the "Arcing 101" course, a student will take an estimated 5–8 hours to complete the 44 short lessons.

Phrase Diagrams

For detailed instruction in sentence diagramming and arcing, students have been pointed to additional print and online resources. It is our hope, however, to provide here sufficient instruction in phrase diagramming that the student can apply the method immediately without additional training. Phrase diagrams are also called "sentence-flow," "thought-flow," or "argument" diagrams. Like the methods above, phrase diagramming visually represents the structure of the Greek text. Yet, phrase diagrams are not as elaborate or detailed as line diagrams or arcs, so they are more likely to be employed by the average student or pastor. Andy Naselli, associate professor of systematic theology and New Testament at Bethlehem College and Seminary, has called phrase diagramming "the single most important aspect about knowing New Testament Greek."[38]

---

[38] Naselli made this written comment while reviewing a pre-publication copy of this manuscript. See also: http://andynaselli.com/languages. Naselli prefers the term "argument diagrams."

In phrase diagramming, the exegete breaks the text down into "phrases"—recognizable related units. Here we are using "phrase" in a non-technical sense, essentially referring to a portion of a sentence. The phrases are then indented and aligned to elucidate the structure. Some phrase diagrammers draw arrows between related grammatical elements to help make those relationships more visually explicit. Others syntactically label the phrase diagram to record the functional relationship among the parts.

Below are some basic principles for phrase diagramming.[39]

1. Main or governing propositions should be further to the left on the page.

2. Dependent elements are indented under the word(s) they modify.

3. Parallel grammatical elements are indented the same distance on the page.

In English, we might represent a simple phrase diagram like this:

I sent the letter
    to my mother
    about my new job
    with a gift card enclosed

The student should note that no attempt is made to account for every syntactical relationship. Phrases need not be broken up more than is helpful in observing the author's flow of thought.[40]

A new technical series analyzing the GNT, The Exegetical Guide to the Greek New Testament (EGGNT), includes phrase diagrams of the biblical text. Suggested homiletical outlines based on the Greek structure are also provided. Below is a Greek diagram of 1 Peter 1:1–2 by Greg Forbes from the EGGNT series, followed by an English phrase diagram that mimics the Greek structure.[41] Forbes's suggest-

---

[39] These steps (worded slightly differently) are listed by William D. Mounce, *A Graded Reader of Biblical Greek* (Grand Rapids: Zondervan, 1996), xv. For additional instruction in phrase diagramming, students are referred to Mounce, *Graded Reader*, xv–xxiii; Huffman, *Handy Guide to New Testament Greek*, 84–106; Young, 268–73; Gordon D. Fee, *New Testament Exegesis: A Handbook for Students and Pastors*, rev. ed. (Louisville, KY: Westminster/John Knox, 1993), 65–80; George H. Guthrie and J. Scott Duvall, *Biblical Greek Exegesis: A Graded Approach to Learning Intermediate and Advanced Greek* (Grand Rapids: Zondervan, 1998), 27–37. See also the diagrams in the EGGNT volumes (on which see further below) and chap. 12 in Andreas J. Köstenberger and Richard D. Patterson, *Invitation to Biblical Interpretation: Exploring the Hermeneutical Triad of History, Literature, and Theology* (Grand Rapids: Kregel, 2011).

[40] Huffman says that students attempting a phrase diagram should remember this "freeing question": *"How can I diagram the phrases of this paragraph so its structure is more visible to me?"* (*Handy Guide to New Testament Greek*, 86; emphasis original).

[41] Forbes, *1 Peter*, EGGNT, 11 (see chap. 7, n. 31). The English phrase diagram and translation are the authors's. The diagramming format for the EGGNT series was developed by Andreas J. Köstenberger.

ed homiletical outline from the EGGNT volume appears below the English phrase diagram.[42]

1   Πέτρος
    ἀπόστολος Ἰησοῦ Χριστοῦ   ἐκλεκτοῖς παρεπιδήμοις διασπορᾶς . . .
2   κατὰ πρόγνωσιν θεοῦ πατρὸς
                                     ἐν ἁγιασμῷ πνεύματος
                                   εἰς ὑπακοὴν καὶ ῥαντισμὸν
                                            αἵματος Ἰησοῦ
                                                  Χριστοῦ,

  χάρις ὑμῖν καὶ εἰρήνη πληθυνθείη.

1   Peter
    an apostle of Jesus Christ   to the elect sojourners of the dispersion . . .
2   according to the foreknowledge
                                   of God the Father
                                 by the sanctification of the Spirit
                                 unto obedience and sprinkling
                                       of the blood of Jesus
                                                Christ,

  May grace and peace be multiplied to you.

Salutation (1–2)

    1. The author: Peter (v. 1a)

    2. The recipients: Christians in northern Asia Minor (v. 1b)

    3. Statement of election (v. 2a)

        (a) Its basis/origin (κατά): the foreknowledge of God

        (b) Its effecting (ἐν): the sanctifying work of the Spirit

        (c) Its purpose (εἰς): obedience

    4. The greeting: grace and peace (v. 2b)

Discourse Analysis

Beginning in the early 1970s, an academic discipline known as discourse analysis or text linguistics began to influence studies of the GNT.[43] The word "discourse" simply means an organized act of communication (usually larger than a sentence). Thus, "discourse analysis" is analyzing a communicative act—in our case, a

---

[42] Forbes, *1 Peter*, 16.

[43] See, for example, Johannes P. Louw, "Discourse Analysis and the Greek New Testament," *The Bible Translator* 24 (1973): 101–18.

portion of the NT. Of course, the term "discourse analysis" also carries with it the connotation that one is employing the insights and vocabulary of modern linguistics. Though some studies in discourse analysis are difficult for the non-specialist to understand, the purpose of the discipline is simply to elucidate the author's intended message in the NT. Moisés Silva observes, "Discourse analysis seeks to understand the ways in which clauses, sentences, and paragraphs are formally related to one another in order to convey meaning."[44] Below are some of the main issues in discourse analysis.[45] We gratefully acknowledge our dependence on Richard Young's excellent discussion of discourse analysis in our presentation below.[46]

Discourse Boundaries

What objective basis do we have for saying that Paul begins a new argument or that his letter breaks into three main sections? Discourse analysis looks at some of the following features:[47]

- ***Uniformity of Content.*** An author's repeated use of the same feature could indicate a unit of material. Subcategories of uniformity include: (1) grammatical (same person/number, tense, voice); (2) lexical (same or similar words); (3) informational (same participants, concepts, events, setting, etc.); (4) teleological (same purpose or goal).

- ***Initial Markers.*** There are certain stylistic features that an author uses to start a new section. These include: (1) orienters ("Now I do not want you to be unaware," 1 Cor 10:1; "Truly, truly I say to you," John 1:51 [ESV]); (2) vocatives (Col 3:18–4:1); (3) topic statements ("now concerning," 1 Cor 7:1, 25; 8:1; 12:1; 16:1, 25 [ESV]); (4) conjunctions (οὖν, διό, δέ); and (5) new settings.

- ***Final Markers.*** There are also certain stylistic features that an author uses to conclude a section. These include: (1) doxologies (Rom 11:33–36); (2) summaries (Heb 11:39–40); (3) tail-head links ("angels" in Heb 1:4–5 or "endure" in Heb 12:2–3).

Practically speaking, properly noting discourse boundaries should influence what portion of text a preacher selects for a sermon—i.e., he should choose a length of text that respects the biblical author's communicative structure.

Beginning with the fourth edition of the United Bible Society's GNT, a "discourse segmentation apparatus" appears at the bottom of the page. This apparatus allows the reader to quickly compare the text segmentation of 16 editions of the

---

[44] Moisés Silva, *Explorations in Exegetical Method: Galatians as a Test Case* (Grand Rapids: Baker, 1996), 82.

[45] Porter lists three of the main focuses of discourse analysis as (1) discourse boundaries; (2) prominence; and (3) cohesion. Our summary of the literature is influenced by his helpful observations (*Idioms*, 301–6).

[46] Young, 247–66.

[47] Most of the following examples come from Young, 251–54.

Bible (Greek New Testaments or modern translations). Below is a list of the main abbreviations used in the apparatus. For more detail on how to use the apparatus, see the introductory section of the most recent edition of the United Bible Society's GNT.

UBS DISCOURSE SEGMENTATION APPARATUS ABBREVIATIONS	
SP	Subparagraph
P	Paragraph
S	Section
MS	Major Section

Prominence

What is the author's main point, and what are his supporting points? Through careful attention to explicit markers in the text, discourse analysis seeks to ground arguments for prominence in textual data. Below are features to consider:[48]

- *Word Order.* See earlier in this chapter for more information.

- *Certain Words.* Such as emphatic particles (οὐχί, "not!"), emphatic pronouns (ἐμοῦ), or superlatives (λίαν ["very"], σφόδρα ["extremely"]).

- *Grammatical Features.* Such as finite verbs, passive voice, relative clauses, and historical present tense.

- *Figures of Speech.* Such as hyperbole ("all Jerusalem"), hendiadys ("rejoice and be glad" = "be very glad"), epizeuxis ("holy, holy, holy" = very holy), litotes ("no insignificant city" = "a very important city").

- *Rhetorical Questions.* "Should we continue in sin in order that grace may multiply?" (Rom 6:1).

- *Discourse Proportion.* Larger or longer sections are often more prominent.

From a homiletical perspective, the preacher should be interested in prominence because he should stress the main point that the biblical author emphasizes.

Cohesion (Interconnectedness)

How do the various pieces fit together within a text? What is the author's flow of thought, and how does this section of text relate to the sections around it? While questions such as these have been asked by careful exegetes since antiquity, discourse analysis seeks to make sure that a modern reader's perspective on a passage's flow of thought is based on clearly labeled objective data in the text.[49]

---

[48] Most of the following examples come from Young, 262–64.

[49] See George H. Guthrie, "Discourse Analysis," in *Interpreting the New Testament: Essays on Methods and Issues*, ed. David Alan Black and David S. Dockery (Nashville: B&H, 2001), 253–71; idem, *The Structure of Hebrews: A Text-Linguistic Analysis* (Grand Rapids: Baker, 1998).

From our observations, discourse analysis has mainly appealed to linguistically inclined scholars who write technical articles for their peers. Thankfully, helpful insights from discourse analysis are beginning to trickle down to the average NT scholar, with promise for future students and pastors. One of the main scholars effectively bridging insights from discourse analysis to non-specialists is Steven Runge, who produced an accessible grammar teaching some principles of discourse analysis.[50] Runge also served as the editor of the *Lexham Discourse Greek New Testament* and the *Lexham High Definition New Testament* (ESV translation).[51] These resources mark discourse features in every verse in the NT. While we have little confidence that pastors will ever use terms like "sequential head," "conjoining head," and "alternating head," we do look forward to helpful insights from discourse analysis finding their way into the preaching of the church.

SUMMARY

COMPONENTS OF A GREEK SENTENCE		
COMPONENT	DEFINITION	EXAMPLE
Word	A foundational sound unit (lex) with other functional sound units (morphemes) sometimes combined with it, so that a native speaker recognizes it as a grammatical entity referring to a person, place, thing, or action, or functioning in some other way in his language.	Φοίβην ("Phoebe"; Rom 16:1).
Phrase	Two or more words functioning together as a discrete grammatical unit, though lacking the sufficient components to be called a clause or sentence. Various kinds of phrases: Prepositional, Noun, Adverbial, Adjectival, Verbal.	τοῦ λοιποῦ, ἐνδυναμοῦσθε **ἐν κυρίῳ** καὶ **ἐν τῷ κράτει τῆς ἰσχύος αὐτοῦ** ("Finally, be strong **in the Lord** and **in the strength of His might**"; Eph 6:10 NASB).
Independent Clause	A portion of a sentence that contains (or implies) a subject or predicate and is not subordinated to another portion of the sentence.	ἡνίκα δὲ ἐὰν ἐπιστρέψῃ πρὸς κύριον, **περιαιρεῖται τὸ κάλυμμα** ("But whenever anyone turns to the Lord, **the veil is taken away**"; 2 Cor 3:16 NIV).

---

[50] Runge, *Discourse Grammar* (see chap. 2, n. 46). See Runge's blog at www.ntdiscourse.org. See also chapters 7 and 8 (discussing discourse anyalysis) of Campbell's *Advances in the Study of Greek* (see chap. 6, n. 24).
[51] These digital resources are available at www.logos.com.

COMPONENTS OF A GREEK SENTENCE		
COMPONENT	DEFINITION	EXAMPLE
Dependent Clause	A portion of a sentence that contains (or implies) a subject or predicate and is subordinated to another portion of the sentence.	σὺ ὃ σπείρεις, οὐ ζῳοποιεῖται **ἐὰν μὴ ἀποθάνῃ** ("What you sow does not come to life **unless it dies**"; 1 Cor 15:36)

Note: The conditional sentences chart presented in the chapter (pp. 448–49) is not repeated here.

TYPES OF GREEK SENTENCES (BY COMPONENTS)		
TYPE	DEFINITION	EXAMPLE
Simple	A sentence that has one word or group of words functioning as the subject and one word or group of words functioning as the predicate.	ὁ πλοῦτος ὑμῶν σέσηπεν ("Your riches have rotted"; Jas 5:2 ESV).
Compound	A sentence composed of two or more independent clauses connected by one or more coordinating conjunctions.	καὶ εὐθὺς ἀπῆλθεν ἀπ᾽ αὐτοῦ ἡ λέπρα, καὶ ἐκαθαρίσθη ("Immediately the leprosy left him, and he was made clean"; Mark 1:42).
Complex	A sentence that includes both an independent clause and a subordinate (dependent) clause.	καὶ ἐγερθεὶς ἀπῆλθεν εἰς τὸν οἶκον αὐτοῦ ("And, after he arose, he departed to his house"; Matt 9:7 author's translation).
Copulative	A sentence that links two substantives with a copulative verb (i.e., εἰμί, γίνομαι, ὑπάρχω).	ὑμεῖς ἐστε τὸ φῶς τοῦ κόσμου ("You are the light of the world"; Matt 5:14).

TYPES OF GREEK SENTENCES (BY FUNCTION)		
TYPE	DEFINITION	EXAMPLE
Declarative	Makes a statement of fact.	πάντες γὰρ οἱ προφῆται καὶ ὁ νόμος ἕως Ἰωάννου ἐπροφήτευσαν ("For all the prophets and the law prophesied until John came"; Matt 11:13).
Interrogative	Asks a question.	ποῦ σου, θάνατε, τὸ νῖκος ("Where, death, is your victory?"; 1 Cor 15:55).
Imperative	Gives a command or makes a request.	αἴτησόν με ὃ ἐὰν θέλῃς ("Ask me whatever you want"; Mark 6:22).
Exclamatory	Communicates an expression of strong feeling.	μὴ γένοιτο ("May it never be!"; Rom 9:14 NASB).

Note: Charts from the chapter related to Greek word order (p. 456) are not duplicated here.

METHODS FOR ANALYZING A TEXT'S STRUCTURE		
METHOD	STRENGTH(S)	WEAKNESS(ES)
Line Diagramming	Good for dealing exhaustively with syntactical connections at the sentence level and below.	Poor at showing relationship between sentences and larger discourse units.
Arcing/Bracketing	Extremely detailed method for labeling the function of phrases and clauses in an author's flow of thought.	Method takes several hours to learn. Categories of modern discourse analysis not fully employed.
Phrase Diagramming	Simple "indentation" method which allows the student to plot quickly a biblical author's flow of thought.	Not good for detailed syntactical study at sentence level and below.
Discourse Analysis	Employing insights from modern linguistics, discourse analysis provides an objective basis for arguing for boundaries, prominence, and cohesion in a text.	Much literature on discourse analysis is overly technical.

PRACTICE EXERCISES

In each of the following examples, (1) Identify the underlined portions of the sentences as a word, phrase, dependent clause, or independent clause; and, (2) based only on the words provided below (not the broader context in the GNT), identify each sentence as simple, compound, complex, or copulative. (Note: sometimes more than one label will apply. A sentence can be compound and complex, for example.) In addition to the exercises below, attempt a phrase diagram of a previous "Reading the New Testament" passage covered earlier this semester.

1. οὗτοί <u>εἰσιν</u> γογγυσταὶ μεμψίμοιροι (Jude 16).

2. ἀγαπητέ, περὶ πάντων εὔχομαί σε εὐοδοῦσθαι καὶ ὑγιαίνειν, <u>καθὼς εὐοδοῦταί σου ἡ ψυχή</u> (3 John 2).

3. τὰ τέκνα, <u>ὑπακούετε τοῖς γονεῦσιν ὑμῶν [ἐν κυρίῳ]</u>· τοῦτο γάρ ἐστιν δίκαιον (Eph 6:1).

4. οὗτός ἐστιν ὁ γενόμενος ἐν τῇ ἐκκλησίᾳ <u>ἐν τῇ ἐρήμῳ</u> μετὰ τοῦ ἀγγέλου τοῦ λαλοῦντος αὐτῷ ἐν τῷ ὄρει Σινα (Acts 7:38).

5. καὶ εἶδον <u>ὅτε ἤνοιξεν τὸ ἀρνίον μίαν ἐκ τῶν ἑπτὰ σφραγίδων</u> (Rev 6:1).

6. καί τινες κατελθόντες <u>ἀπὸ τῆς Ἰουδαίας ἐδίδασκον τοὺς ἀδελφοὺς</u> (Acts 15:1).

7. <u>ὡς δὲ ἐκρίθη τοῦ ἀποπλεῖν ἡμᾶς εἰς τὴν Ἰταλίαν</u>, παρεδίδουν τόν τε Παῦλον καί τινας ἑτέρους δεσμώτας ἑκατοντάρχῃ ὀνόματι Ἰουλίῳ σπείρης <u>Σεβαστῆς</u> (Acts 27:1).

8. <u>καὶ</u> τῇ τρίτῃ ἡμέρᾳ ἐγερθήσεται (Matt 20:19).

9. ἐπειδὴ ἐπλήρωσεν πάντα τὰ ῥήματα αὐτοῦ εἰς τὰς ἀκοὰς τοῦ λαοῦ, <u>εἰσῆλθεν εἰς Καφαρναούμ</u> (Luke 7:1).

10. ἤγγιζεν δὲ ἡ ἑορτὴ τῶν ἀζύμων <u>ἡ λεγομένη πάσχα</u> (Luke 22:1).

VOCABULARY

Vocabulary to Memorize

ἄκανθα, ἡ	thorn (14)
ἀκοή, ἡ	hearing, report, ear (24)
ἀλλότριος	strange, foreign (14)
ἀμφότεροι	both, all (14)
ἀναγγέλλω	I report, announce, proclaim (14)
ἀνάκειμαι	I lie, recline (14)
ἀνάστασις, -εως, ἡ	resurrection (42)
ἀπειθέω	I disobey (14)
ἀτενίζω	I look intently (14)
αὔριον	tomorrow, soon (14)
ἀφίστημι	I mislead, go away, fall away (14)
γράμμα, -ατος, τό	letter (of alphabet), document (14)
διαλογισμός, ὁ	thought, opinion, dispute (14)
ἕκτος	sixth (14)
ἐλάχιστος	smallest, least, insignificant (14)
ἐπεί	because, since, for (25)
ἐπιτρέπω	I allow, permit (18)
ἐπουράνιος	heavenly, in heaven (19)
κρίμα, -ατος, τό	judging, judgment (27)
νήπιος, ὁ	infant, child (15)
ὀφείλω	I owe, ought (35)
ὀψία	late, evening (15)
παρθένος, ἡ/ὁ	virgin (15)
παύω	I stop, cease (15)
πέτρα, ἡ	rock, stone (15)
ποτίζω	I water, give to drink (15)
προλέγω	I tell beforehand (15)
πώς	somehow, perhaps (15)
ῥαββί	rabbi, master, teacher (15)
σαλεύω	I shake (15)
Σαῦλος, ὁ	Saul (15)
σκάνδαλον, τό	stumbling block, trap, temptation (15)
συμφέρω	I bring together (15)
σφραγίζω	I seal, mark, certify (15)
ταχέως	quickly, soon, hastily (15)
τέλειος	perfect, complete, mature, adult (19)

τράπεζα, ἡ	table, meal, food (15)
ὑπακοή, ἡ	obedience (15)
χόρτος, ὁ	grass, hay (15)
ὠφελέω	I help, aid, benefit (15)

Vocabulary to Recognize

ἀδύνατος	impossible (10)
αἰσθητήριον, τό	faculty (1)
ἀνακαινίζω	I renew, restore (1)
ἀνασταυρόω	I crucify (1)
ἄπειρος	unacquainted with, unaccustomed to (1)
βαπτισμός, ὁ	washing (4)
γάλα, γάλακτος, τό	milk (5)
γυμνάζω	I train, undergo discipline (4)
διάκρισις, -εως, ἡ	distinguishing, differentiation (3)
δυσερμήνευτος	hard to explain (1)
δωρεά, ἡ	gift, bounty (11)
ἐάνπερ	if (3)
ἕξις, -εως, ἡ	maturity, training (1)
ἐπίθεσις, -εως, ἡ	laying on (4)
καταβάλλω	I lay (a foundation), throw down (2)
λόγιον, τό	a saying, oracle (4)
μετέχω	I share in, eat, drink, enjoy (8)
μέτοχος	sharing, participating (6)
νωθρός	lazy, sluggish (2)
παραδειγματίζω	I expose, make an example of (1)
παραπίπτω	I fall away, commit apostasy (1)
στερεός	firm, hard, solid, strong (4)
στοιχεῖον, τό	fundamental principles (7)
τελειότης, -ητος, ἡ	perfection, completeness, maturity (2)
φωτίζω	I enlighten, give light to, shed light upon (11)

READING THE NEW TESTAMENT

Hebrews 5:11–6:6

¹¹ Περὶ οὗ πολὺς ἡμῖν ὁ λόγος καὶ δυσερμήνευτος λέγειν, ἐπεὶ νωθροὶ γεγόνατε ταῖς ἀκοαῖς. ¹² καὶ γὰρ ὀφείλοντες εἶναι διδάσκαλοι διὰ τὸν χρόνον, πάλιν χρείαν ἔχετε τοῦ διδάσκειν ὑμᾶς τινὰ τὰ στοιχεῖα τῆς ἀρχῆς τῶν λογίων τοῦ θεοῦ καὶ γεγόνατε χρείαν ἔχοντες γάλακτος [καὶ] οὐ στερεᾶς τροφῆς. ¹³ πᾶς γὰρ ὁ μετέχων γάλακτος ἄπειρος λόγου δικαιοσύνης, νήπιος γάρ ἐστιν· ¹⁴ τελείων δέ ἐστιν ἡ στερεὰ τροφή, τῶν διὰ τὴν ἕξιν τὰ αἰσθητήρια γεγυμνασμένα ἐχόντων πρὸς διάκρισιν καλοῦ τε καὶ κακοῦ. 6:¹ Διὸ ἀφέντες τὸν τῆς ἀρχῆς τοῦ Χριστοῦ λόγον ἐπὶ τὴν τελειότητα φερώμεθα, μὴ πάλιν θεμέλιον καταβαλλόμενοι μετανοίας ἀπὸ νεκρῶν ἔργων καὶ πίστεως ἐπὶ θεόν, ² βαπτισμῶν διδαχῆς ἐπιθέσεώς τε χειρῶν, ἀναστάσεώς τε νεκρῶν καὶ κρίματος αἰωνίου. ³ καὶ τοῦτο ποιήσομεν, ἐάνπερ ἐπιτρέπῃ ὁ θεός. ⁴ Ἀδύνατον γὰρ τοὺς ἅπαξ φωτισθέντας, γευσαμένους τε τῆς δωρεᾶς τῆς ἐπουρανίου καὶ μετόχους γενηθέντας πνεύματος ἁγίου ⁵ καὶ καλὸν γευσαμένους θεοῦ ῥῆμα δυνάμεις τε μέλλοντος αἰῶνος ⁶ καὶ παραπεσόντας, πάλιν ἀνακαινίζειν εἰς μετάνοιαν, ἀνασταυροῦντας ἑαυτοῖς τὸν υἱὸν τοῦ θεοῦ καὶ παραδειγματίζοντας.

Reading Notes[52]

Verse 11

- The discourse segmentation apparatus in the United Bible Society GNT notes that several critical editions of the GNT and modern translations begin a new paragraph (P) at the beginning of Hebrews 5:11. What textual data led translation committees to see textual boundaries between vv. 10 and 11?

- **Περὶ οὗ πολὺς ἡμῖν ὁ λόγος** ("We have a great deal to say about this") – Literally, "Concerning whom our message [is] much." The prepositional phrase περὶ οὗ communicates reference or respect (i.e., the author of Hebrews says that there is much to convey *with reference to* Jesus in his high priestly "Melchizedekian" role).[53] ἡμῖν is a dative of possession, so ἡμῖν ὁ λόγος means "the message which belongs to us," that is, "our message."

---

⁵² The English version used in the Reading Notes for this chapter is the CSB.

⁵³ Concerning Heb 5:11, O'Brien writes, "The relative pronoun οὗ could be understood as masculine ('him' or 'whom'), referring to Melchizedek (so Calvin, Bruce, and Ellingworth), though on balance it is preferable to take it as neuter ('this' or 'which'), referring to Christ's priesthood, 5:5–10, and chaps. 7–10 (Attridge, Lane, Koester; note TNIV, NRSV). The expression indicates that the author was aware of the breadth of the subject." Peter T. O'Brien, *The Letter to the Hebrews*, PNTC 16 (Grand Rapids: Eerdmans; Nottingham: Apollos, 2010), 205n98.

If you own Randy Leedy's diagrams (see ntgreekguy.com), open the pre-made line diagram of Heb 5:11. Does viewing the diagram help you understand the syntax of v. 11?

• **καὶ δυσερμήνευτος λέγειν** ("and it's difficult to explain") – The copulative conjunction καί introduces a second predicate adjective δυσερμήνευτος ("difficult," a biblical hapax). The passage literally reads: "The message is lengthy *and* (καί) difficult." λέγειν is an epexegetical infinitive (pres act) explaining in what way the message is δυσερμήνευτος ("difficult").[54]

• **ἐπεὶ νωθροὶ γεγόνατε ταῖς ἀκοαῖς** ("since you have become too lazy to understand") – ἐπεί ("since"), a subordinating conjunction, introduced a dependent causal clause. γεγόνατε is per act ind 2nd pl of γίνομαι. ταῖς ἀκοαῖς is a dative of reference, limiting the scope of the adjective νωθροί (lit., "lazy, with reference to hearing").[55]

Verse 12

• **καὶ γὰρ ὀφείλοντες εἶναι διδάσκαλοι διὰ τὸν χρόνον** ("Although by this time you ought to be teachers") – γάρ introduces an explanatory clause—referring to all of v. 12 and giving reasons that the author of Hebrews has much to say and the material is difficult to explain (v. 11). The CSB leaves the γάρ untranslated. ὀφείλοντες (pres act ptc masc nom pl ὀφείλω) introduces a dependent adverbial clause, rendered in English concessively ("although . . ."). εἶναι (pres act inf εἰμί) is a complementary infinitive, completing the idea of the participle ὀφείλοντες ("ought").

• **πάλιν χρείαν ἔχετε τοῦ διδάσκειν ὑμᾶς τινὰ τὰ στοιχεῖα τῆς ἀρχῆς τῶν λογίων τοῦ θεοῦ** ("you need someone to teach you the basic principles of God's revelation again") – πάλιν is an adverb modifying τοῦ διδάσκειν (pres act inf διδάσκω), which functions as an explanatory or epexegetical infinitive,[56] clarifying the extent of the χρείαν ("need") that the recipients of the letter have. τινά ("someone") is the subject accusative of the infinitive. Verbs like "teach" often take a double accusative—an accusative of person (ὑμᾶς, "you") and an accusative of thing (τὰ στοιχεῖα, "principles").[57] τῆς ἀρχῆς is an attributive genitive ("basic [beginning]

---

[54] William L. Lane notes that λέγειν functions as an epexegetical infinitive. *Hebrews 1–8*, WBC 47A (Dallas: Word, 1991), 130. So, too, BDF, 202 (§393 [6]); Robertson, 1076.

[55] Lane comments, "The pl form ἀκοαῖς ('ears' as organs of hearing) . . . denotes receptivity and understanding" (*Hebrews 1–8*, 131).

[56] So Moulton & Turner, 3:141. Another option is a purpose infinitive.

[57] Paul Ellingworth writes, "It is likely that the στοιχεῖα τῆς ἀρχῆς τῶν λογίων τοῦ θεοῦ are broadly the same as the 'milk' of v. 12b, the ἀρχή τοῦ Χριστοῦ λόγον in 6:1, and perhaps the λόγος δικαιοσύνης in v. 13. Repetition for emphasis on a smaller scale is provided by the redundant τῆς ἀρχῆς." See *The Epistle to the Hebrews: A Commentary on the Greek Text*, NIGTC (Grand Rapids: Eerdmans; Carlisle, UK: Paternoster, 1993), 303.

principles"). The genitival phrase τῶν λογίων τοῦ θεοῦ communicates source or origin, i.e., basic principles that *come from* or *are found in* God's revelation.

- **γεγόνατε χρείαν ἔχοντες** ("You need") – Literally, "you have become those having need." γεγόνατε is a per act ind 2nd pl of γίνομαι. The particle ἔχοντες (pres act ptc masc nom pl ἔχω) functions substantively as a predicate nominative ("those having . . .").

- **γάλακτος [καὶ] οὐ στερεᾶς τροφῆς** ("milk, not solid food") – Both γάλακτος ("milk") and τροφῆς ("food") are in the genitive case, following χρεία ("need *of* "), as required by Greek idiom. στερεᾶς ("solid") is an attributive adjective.

Verse 13

- **πᾶς γὰρ ὁ μετέχων γάλακτος** ("Now everyone who lives on milk") – NASB: "For everyone who partakes *only* of milk." ὁ μετέχων (pres act ptc masc nom sg μετέχω, "share," "partake") is a substantival participle. The Greek verb μετέχω takes a genitive of direct object, here, γάλακτος ("milk").

- **ἄπειρος λόγου δικαιοσύνης** ("is inexperienced with the message about righteousness") – ἄπειρος ("inexperienced") is a predicate adjective with an implied copulative verb. The adjective ἄπειρος is regularly followed by the genitive, limiting the frame of reference. The author of Hebrews indicts the recipients for being inexperienced with regard to the λόγου δικαιοσύνης, ("the message about righteousness").[58] In this translation, the CSB interprets δικαιοσύνης as a genitive of content. This phrase has been interpreted a wide variety of ways, but perhaps the best understanding is that it refers to God's revelation of himself, rightly understood and obeyed.[59]

- **νήπιος γάρ ἐστιν** ("because he is an infant") – Drawing from the categories introduced in this chapter, here we find (1) an explanatory clause introduced with the conjunction γάρ ("because") and (2) a copulative sentence.

Verse 14

- **τελείων δέ ἐστιν ἡ στερεὰ τροφή** ("But solid food is for the mature") – A copulative sentence, introduced with the copulative conjunction δέ ("but"), functioning adversatively. τελείων ("the mature") is the masc

---

[58] O'Brien also understands λόγου δικαιοσύνης as communicating reference/respect and cites Wallace (128) in support (*Letter to the Hebrews*, 208n117).
[59] See O'Brien, *Letter to the Hebrews*, 208–9.

gen pl of the adjective τέλειος ("mature," "perfect," "complete"). Here, τελείων functions substantively, in the slot of the predicate nominative. Yet, as a genitive, τελείων communicates possession. Solid food belongs to mature Christians.

- τῶν διὰ τὴν ἕξιν τὰ αἰσθητήρια γεγυμνασμένα ἐχόντων ("for those whose senses have been trained to distinguish between good and evil")– τῶν . . . ἐχόντων (pres act ptc masc gen pl ἔχω, "who . . . have") functions as a substantive, appositional to τελείων ("the mature"). The prepositional phrase διὰ τὴν ἕξιν ("because of practice")[60] functions adverbially, modifying the participle ἐχόντων ("have"). γεγυμνασμένα (per pass ptc acc neut pl γυμνάζω, "train") is an attributive participle modifying τὰ αἰσθητήρια ("their senses"). (Note the ESV rendering—"for the mature, for those who have their powers of discernment trained by constant practice.") The possessive pronoun ("their"), as noted in the ESV, is implied from context, as is often the case with constituent elements of the human person. In such situations when the possessive pronoun is implied, the article is usually present, as here. Some grammarians prefer to speak of the Greek article functioning as a possessive pronoun.

- πρὸς διάκρισιν καλοῦ τε καὶ κακοῦ ("to distinguish between good and evil") – The prepositional phrase πρὸς διάκρισιν expresses purpose. The purpose of the mature Christian's training of their senses is *so that* they can discern good from evil. The noun διάκρισιν (fem acc sg, "distinguishing," "differentiation") is regularly followed by the genitive(s) of the thing(s) differentiated, as here. BDAG notes that τὲ . . . καί is used for "connecting concepts, usually of the same kind or corresponding as opposites."[61]

Chapter 6, Verse 1

- Διὸ ἀφέντες τὸν τῆς ἀρχῆς τοῦ Χριστοῦ λόγον ("Therefore, let us leave the elementary message about Christ") – διό ("therefore") is an inferential conjunction. ἀφέντες (aor act ptc masc nom pl ἀφίημι) is best understood as a participle of attendant circumstances. The CSB and ESV translators understood it this way, translating it imperatively along with the main verb ("Therefore let us leave").[62] Some structural emphasis is potentially lost if ἀφέντες is not recognized as an adverbial participle dependent on the main imperative φερώμεθα ("let us . . . go on"). τῆς ἀρχῆς is an attributive genitive (lit., "*beginning* word/doctrine"). Because genitive modifiers (e.g., τῆς ἀρχῆς) normally follow the nouns to which they are

---

[60] Lane comments, "The presence of the ptcp γεγυμνασμένα, 'trained,' seems to require that ἕξις be interpreted in the active sense as 'exercise, practice, long use'" (*Hebrews 1–8*, 131).

[61] BDAG, 993.

[62] Lane also agrees that ἀφέντες has an imperatival sense (*Hebrews 1–8*, 131).

attached, perhaps the genitive is drawn forward to emphasize the unexpected and blameworthy nature of the recipients' *very basic* knowledge. Alternately, it is possible that the wide separation between the noun λόγον and its genitival modifier τῆς ἀρχῆς is an example of hyperbaton—"a wider than necessary separation of two or more syntactically closely connected words or groups of words, for signaling or reinforcing the end of syntactical or semantic units in Greek."[63] τοῦ Χριστοῦ is a genitive of content, that is, "teaching *about Christ*" (so NASB) or an objective genitive.

- **ἐπὶ τὴν τελειότητα φερώμεθα** ("[let us] go on to maturity") – φερώμεθα (pres mid/pass sub 1st pl φέρω, "carry," "lead," "be moved") is a hortatory subjunctive ("[let us] go on to maturity") and is either mid (CSB: "let us ... go on") or pass (NIV: "let us . . . be taken"). In Greek usage, words for movement often occur in the middle (e.g., ἔρχομαι, πορεύομαι). The prepositional phrase ἐπὶ τὴν τελειότητα expresses extension ("toward," "in the direction of").

- **μὴ πάλιν θεμέλιον καταβαλλόμενοι μετανοίας** ("not laying again a foundation of repentance") – μή negates a non-indicative mood verb, here καταβαλλόμενοι (pres mid ptc masc nom pl καταβάλλω; mid: "lay [a foundation]"). μετανοίας functions as a genitive of apposition, i.e., "a foundation of repentance" means "a foundation which is none other than repentance." The participle probably expresses attendant circumstances.[64] It derives an imperatival sense from the hortatory subjunctive, φερώμεθα ("[let us] go on").

- **ἀπὸ νεκρῶν ἔργων** ("from dead works") – The prepositional phrase functions to communicate dissociation, that is, turning in repentance *away from* dead works.

- **καὶ πίστεως ἐπὶ θεόν** ("faith in God") – πίστεως is a genitive of apposition, the second of three genitives in a compound expression begun with μετανοίας above. The foundation that the author speaks of is none other than repentance and faith (and also teaching, see below in v. 2).

Verse 2

- **διδαχῆς** ("teaching") – This genitive is the final of three compound genitives in apposition to θεμέλιον ("foundation"). That is, the foundation is repentance, faith, and teaching. Line or phrase diagramming can help a student decipher the challenging syntax here.

---

[63] Daniel Markovic, "Hyperbaton in the Greek Literary Sentence," *Greek, Roman, and Byzantine Studies* 46 (2006): 127.

[64] As reflected in the CEB translation: "Let's not lay a foundation of turning away from dead works."

- **βαπτισμῶν . . . ἐπιθέσεώς τε χειρῶν, ἀναστάσεώς τε νεκρῶν καὶ κρίματος αἰωνίου** ("about ritual washings, laying on of hands, the resurrection of the dead, and eternal judgment") – This string of genitives (βαπτισμῶν, ἐπιθέσεώς, ἀναστάσεώς, κρίματος) gives the content of the teaching ("teaching about"). Some grammarians label them as objective genitives. Both χειρῶν ("of hands") and νεκρῶν ("of the dead") are subjective genitives. Note the author's generous use of coordinating conjunctions (τὲ . . . τὲ . . . καί). About the "washings" here, Attridge writes, "It may be that the formula refers to the distinction between Christian baptism and pagan lustral rites or, more likely, Jewish rituals of purification, including John's baptism."[65]

Verse 3

- **καὶ τοῦτο ποιήσομεν** ("And we will do this") – ποιήσομεν is a fut act ind 1st pl of ποιέω. In Greek, direct objects frequently occur after verbs, so placing τοῦτο ("this") before the verb heightens this already emphatic statement.

- **ἐάνπερ ἐπιτρέπῃ ὁ θεός** ("if God permits") – The subordinating conjunction ἐάνπερ ("if") occurs only three times in the GNT, all in Hebrews.[66] Louw and Nida observe that ἐάνπερ is "an emphatic marker of condition, with the implication of reduced probability."[67] Perhaps the word should be translated as "if indeed," to communicate this nuance. ἐπιτρέπῃ ("permits") is a pres act sub 3rd sg of ἐπιτρέπω. Although from a strict grammatical perspective ἐάνπερ introduces a dependent conditional clause, the clause functions as an implicit rebuke of the letter's recipients, recognizing their dullness of hearing and the need for divine empowering to move forward in Christian maturity.

Verse 4

- **Ἀδύνατον γὰρ** ("For it is impossible") – ἀδύνατόν functions as the predicate adjective of an implied copulative verb, ἐστιν ("is"). The subject of the copulative verb is an infinitival construction not found in the Greek until v. 6, but appearing earlier in most English translations: πάλιν ἀνακαινίζειν εἰς μετάνοιαν ("to renew to repentance"). Thus, the foundational grammatical structure of vv. 4–6 is: "to renew to repentance [is] impossible."

---

[65] Harold W. Attridge, *The Epistle to the Hebrews*, Hermeneia (Philadelphia: Fortress, 1989), 164.
[66] Heb 3:6 (textually debated), 14; 6:3.
[67] Louw and Nida, 1:786 (§89.68).

- τοὺς ἅπαξ φωτισθέντας, γευσαμένους τε τῆς δωρεᾶς τῆς ἐπουρανίου καὶ μετόχους γενηθέντας πνεύματος ἁγίου ("those who were once enlightened, who tasted the heavenly gift, who shared in the Holy Spirit") – The masc acc pl article τούς governs five aorist substantival participles connected with a series of coordinating conjunctions (τὲ . . . καὶ . . . καὶ . . . τὲ . . . καί). The lengthy accusative construction serves as the "subject accusative" of the pres act inf ἀνακαινίζειν ("to renew") in v. 6. The participle of γεύομαι ("taste") takes a genitive direct object, τῆς δωρεᾶς, "gift." τῆς ἐπουρανίου is an attributive genitive, "heavenly gift." γενηθέντας (aor pass ptc masc acc pl γίνομαι) has μετόχους ("companions") as a complement (lit. "became companions"). The noun μέτοχος ("companion") is regularly followed by the genitive of the person with whom one is a companion, as here (πνεύματος ἁγίου, "Holy Spirit"). Similar to the CSB ("shared in"), the ESV and NIV translate μετόχους γενηθέντας πνεύματος ἁγίου as "have shared in the Holy Spirit." Scholars debate whether this verse *necessarily* describes a genuine Christian (and thus this passage warns against actual loss of salvation) or whether the passage warns nominal (false) Christians or whether it addresses a hypothetical possibility. Regardless of the view one takes on this issue, we can agree that the author of Hebrews warns strongly against an immature faith and emphasizes that the only locus of salvation is Jesus Christ.[68] No words of hope or encouragement are offered to those who depart from the visible church or faith in Jesus as Savior and Messiah.

Verse 5

- καὶ καλὸν γευσαμένους θεοῦ ῥῆμα ("tasted God's good word") – the sequence of accusative substantival participles governed by τούς (v. 4) continues here with γευσαμένους (aor mid ptc masc acc pl γεύομαι). Neva Miller notes that Greek verbs sometimes favor the middle voice when the subject of the verb is "the receiver of sensory perception."[69] The word order here is a bit unusual, with the attributive adjective καλόν ("good") pulled forward, apparently for emphasis. Also, a genitive modifier usually follows the noun it is attached to, unlike here, θεοῦ ῥῆμα ("God's . . . word").[70]

---

[68] A careful discussion of these issues exceeds the space limitations of these reading notes. Students are referred to O'Brien, *Letter to the Hebrews*, 219–27. Also, see Attridge's excursus ("The Impossibility of Repentance for Apostates") in *Epistle to the Hebrews*, 168–69.

[69] Miller, "Appendix 2: A Theory of Deponent Verbs," 429 (see chap. 11, n. 60). Miller gives ἐπακροάομαι ("listen to") and θεάομαι ("see") as two further examples of this class of middle verbs ("Class 5: Receptivity").

[70] Attridge comments, "For the synonymous use of λόγος and ῥῆμα, cf. Philo *Fug.* 137 and *Leg. all.* 3.169, 174–75" (*Epistle to the Hebrews*, 170n56).

- **δυνάμεις τε μέλλοντος αἰῶνος** ("and the powers of the coming age") – δυνάμεις (fem acc pl) is the second half of a compound direct object following the participle γευσαμένους. μέλλοντος (pres act ptc masc gen sg μέλλω) is an attributive participle and modifies αἰῶνος (masc gen sg noun, "age").

Verse 6

- **καὶ παραπεσόντας** ("and who have fallen away") – παραπεσόντας (aor act ptc masc acc pl παραπίπτω) can be taken as an adverbial or as a substantival participle. Furthermore, as an adverbial ptc, it has been understood as conditional ("if they fall away"; so NIV84, RSV, KJV, NRSV) or temporal ("then they fall away"; so ESV, NASB, NRSV). More likely, however, this ptc is substantival ("who have fallen away"; so CSB, NIV).[71] The chain of conjunctions in vv. 5–6 (see note on v. 4) indicates that παραπεσόντας is the final of five substantival participles (all governed by the article τούς in v. 4) which together describe the person for whom renewal to repentance is impossible.

- **πάλιν ἀνακαινίζειν** ("to renew") – Pres act inf ἀνακαινίζω (complementary infinitive; see comments on the function of this infinitive in v. 4). The adverb πάλιν ("again") is pleonastic (or emphatic) as the verb ἀνακαινίζω already contains the idea of "again."

- **εἰς μετάνοιαν** ("to repentance") – This prepositional phrase expresses purpose or result, i.e., to renew the persons *for the purpose of* or *resulting in* repentance. This phrase is translated in v. 4 in the CSB.

- **ἀνασταυροῦντας ἑαυτοῖς τὸν υἱὸν τοῦ θεοῦ καὶ παραδειγματίζοντας** ("This is because, to their own harm, they are recrucifying the Son of God and holding him up to contempt") – The two adverbial participles in this dependent clause are causal, thus "because" or "since" is added in most English translations. The participles modify the base copulative sentence that is stretched through vv. 4–6, "to renew to repentance is impossible." ἀνασταυροῦντας ("again crucify") is pres act ptc masc acc pl of ἀνασταυρόω. ἑαυτοῖς ("to themselves") is a dative of disadvantage,[72] thus the CSB reads "to their own harm," and the NIV has "to their loss." παραδειγματίζοντας "holding him up to contempt" (NASB rendering: "put . . . to open shame") is a pres act ptc masc acc pl of παραδειγματίζω. Perhaps the author of Hebrews employs present participles to depict the despicable thought of re-crucifying Jesus in dramatic unfolding fashion (cf. Mark's use of the present σταυροῦσιν ["crucified"] in Mark 15:24).

---

[71] See also Wallace, 633 and Young, 156.

[72] Also called the *dativus incommodi*. See Robertson, *Greek Grammar*, 539, who so labels ἑαυτοῖς in this verse.

CHAPTER 14

//////////////

WORD STUDIES

GOING DEEPER

In 1 John 2:15, John commands, μὴ **ἀγαπᾶτε** τὸν **κόσμον** ("Do not **love** the **world**"). In John 3:16, the apostle famously writes, οὕτως γὰρ **ἠγάπησεν** ὁ θεὸς τὸν **κόσμον** ("For God **loved** the **world** in this way"). Students of Greek will note that, in both passages, the verbs translated "love" (ἀγαπάω) and the nouns translated "world" (κόσμος) are derived from the same respective lexical forms. Are Christians, then, commanded *not* to do something ("love the world") that God does?

First John 2:15 and John 3:16 illustrate that every word has a range of meaning (a "semantic range") and also a specific meaning that can only be determined when considering the context in which the word is used. In 1 John 2:15–16, the apostle's explanatory comments clarify how we should understand his command not to love the world. John writes,

> ἐάν τις ἀγαπᾷ τὸν κόσμον, οὐκ ἔστιν ἡ ἀγάπη τοῦ πατρὸς ἐν αὐτῷ· ὅτι πᾶν τὸ ἐν τῷ κόσμῳ, ἡ ἐπιθυμία τῆς σαρκὸς καὶ ἡ ἐπιθυμία τῶν ὀφθαλμῶν καὶ ἡ ἀλαζονεία τοῦ βίου, οὐκ ἔστιν ἐκ τοῦ πατρὸς ἀλλ᾽ ἐκ τοῦ κόσμου ἐστίν.

> If anyone loves the world, love for the Father is not in him. For everything in the world—the lust of the flesh, the lust of the eyes, and the pride in one's possessions—is not from the Father, but is from the world.

Thus, the "love" that John speaks of in 1 John 2:15 ("Do not love the world") stands in contrast with devotion to God and is characterized by the lust and boastful pride of humanity's fallen nature. Similarly, "the world" here must mean the things in this world that entice and gratify the longings of humanity's sinful nature. "Do not love the world" (1 John 2:15) means "Do not sinfully long to satisfy yourself with the blandishments of this wicked, fallen order."

With significantly different contextual clues in John 3:16b–17, the apostle clarifies both who "the world" is and the way in which (οὕτως) God loved this world. John writes:

ὥστε τὸν υἱὸν τὸν μονογενῆ ἔδωκεν, ἵνα πᾶς ὁ πιστεύων εἰς αὐτὸν μὴ ἀπόληται ἀλλ' ἔχῃ ζωὴν αἰώνιον. οὐ γὰρ ἀπέστειλεν ὁ θεὸς τὸν υἱὸν εἰς τὸν κόσμον ἵνα κρίνῃ τὸν κόσμον, ἀλλ' ἵνα σωθῇ ὁ κόσμος δι' αὐτοῦ.

He gave his one and only Son, so that everyone who believes in him will not perish but have eternal life. For God did not send his Son into the world to condemn the world, but to save the world through him.

So, in John 3:16–17, "the world" is not the sinful allurements of this fallen age, but humans in their desperate lost state. God's "loving" these sinful humans speaks of his activity and desire to rescue them. All words have a range of meaning, and the broader literary context is absolutely essential in determining a word's or phrase's meaning in any given passage.

CHAPTER OBJECTIVES

The purpose of this chapter is to introduce students to the basic concepts, tools, methods, and potential dangers of word study. Depending on their class schedules, professors may choose to cover this material at different points in the semester, perhaps in conjunction with an exegesis paper assignment.

GREEK WORD STUDIES

Introduction of Concepts

Never in the history of the world has there been less need for Greek word studies than in twenty-first-century English-speaking North America. Many excellent Bible translations exist in the English language, ranging from the more functionally equivalent (NLT) to the more formally equivalent (NASB, ESV), with plenty of translations in between (CSB, NIV).[1] Wise Christians will employ this wealth of resources by comparing biblical passages in various translations. Much

---

[1] For a helpful discussion of modern English Bible translations and translation theory, see Dave Brunn, *One Bible, Many Versions: Are All Translations Created Equal?* (Downers Grove: InterVarsity, 2013). For a comparison of various translations, see Andreas J. Köstenberger and David A. Croteau, eds., *Which Bible Translation Should I Use? A Comparison of 4 Major Recent Versions* (Nashville: B&H, 2012).

misunderstanding could be corrected through simply reading the same passage in parallel Bible translations. For example, a youth minister once asked me (Rob) if 1 Timothy 4:12 taught that the church should not look down upon the "youth group." He was apparently using the New King James Version, which translates 1 Timothy 4:12 as: "Let no one despise your youth, but be an example to the believers in word, in conduct, in love, in spirit, in faith, in purity." Nevertheless, it is not a group of "youth" or young people to which Paul is referring, but to Timothy's young age (or "youthfulness"). My youth minister friend could have avoided confusion by reading a few other translations, such as the NASB, which renders the text helpfully: "Let no one look down on your youthfulness, but *rather* in speech, conduct, love, faith *and* purity, show yourself an example of those who believe."[2]

With all that said, one caveat is in order: though reading more than one translation is beneficial, there is still the matter of judging which translation is best. When reading multiple translations we must be careful not to choose the one that simply sounds best or perhaps makes the point we want it to make.

Nevertheless, as you develop greater facility in Greek and in particular word studies, you should be cautious in presenting your insights. A pastor should never undermine the congregation's trust in English Bible translations through comments such as, "The ESV gets this really wrong here" or "I can't believe the NIV says . . ." It is arrogant and detrimental for the pastor to present himself as the infallible pope of Bible translation. If the pastor is convinced that the Bible version that the church normally uses does not best capture the meaning of the underlying Greek text, he should identify another major translation that renders the text well. Then, the pastor can introduce the alternate translation with words like this: "The meaning of 1 Timothy 4:12 is made very clear by the New American Standard Bible translation. Listen to these words. . . ." By this respectful approach, the pastor is also teaching his congregation to acquire and reference other Bible translations. As a general rule, the pastor's study of the Greek text should be like undergarments—providing support but not publicly visible.

Principles for Word Studies

"Reading the Bible in translation is like kissing your new bride through a veil."[3] So says a Jewish proverb. As students grow in their ability in Greek, they become rightly dissatisfied with a brief definition ("gloss") of a Greek word. They want to plumb the depths of the biblical text's meaning—which includes attention to the nuances of particular words. Below are some key principles students should keep in mind as they engage in Greek word studies.

---

[2] Emphasis original. In its approach to translation, the NASB employs italics to mark words that do not have a one-to-one correspondence with underlying Greek words. As italics are usually used in English to mark stressed words, this method is potentially confusing.

[3] The saying is widely attributed to Jewish poet Hayim Nahman Balik (1873–1934).

1. Don't Make Any Word Mean More Than the Author Intends

Linguist Martin Joobs has summarized this linguistic principle with the influential phrase: "The least meaning is the best meaning."[4] This principle sounds odd at first, but after further thought, it makes sense.[5] Words all carry a variety of potential meanings, but the best reader-discerned meaning for any word is the one that least disturbs the broader literary context. The surrounding words and phrases prepare the reader to understand any particular word. No word can be defined in isolation.

The opposite of the linguistic principle "The least meaning is the best meaning" is the linguistic fallacy called illegitimate totality transfer.[6] When a reader engages in this fallacy, he illegitimately (wrongly) ascribes to a word the totality of what the word could mean in each individual instance of that word's usage. We have all heard preachers do this before—when, for example, the pastor says, "The Greek word here is κόσμος. This word means 'adornment,' 'order,' 'the world,' 'the universe,' 'the sum total of all beings above the level of animals,' 'planet earth,' 'humanity,' 'the system of human existence in its many aspects,' and 'totality.'"[7] Of course, words do not mean the totality of what they could mean in any context; each word only means what the author cues his readers to understand in that particular literary setting. We see the foolishness of illegitimate totality transfer when we apply it to English. Imagine a preacher saying, "The man answered his cell phone. What does 'cell' mean? It means (a) a small chamber of incarceration, (b) a blob of protoplasm, (c) a mobile communications network, and (d) a square in a spreadsheet. How rich in meaning was this man's phone!"

2. Prioritize Synchrony Over Diachrony[8]

When we study a word synchronically, we compare usages from the same time period (σύν [with] + χρόνος [time]). When we study a word diachronically, we consider usages from various time periods (διά [through] + χρόνος [time]). Valuing synchrony over diachrony means that we have a much greater chance of rightly understanding a word's meaning if we rely on parallel uses from the same time period. All languages evolve over time, and part of that evolution is the change in meaning of individual words.

---

[4] This linguistic principle is also called "the rule of maximal redundancy." Cited in Moisés Silva, *Biblical Words and Their Meaning: An Introduction to Lexical Semantics*, rev. ed. (Grand Rapids: Zondervan, 1994), 153–54.

[5] Though I did not consciously recall Silva's words when writing this paragraph, he makes nearly the same point (see Silva, *Biblical Words and Their Meaning*, 154).

[6] See D. A. Carson's discussion of this linguistic fallacy in *Exegetical Fallacies*, 2nd ed. (Grand Rapids: Baker, 1984), 53; Grant R. Osborne, *The Hermeneutical Spiral: A Comprehensive Introduction to Biblical Interpretation*, rev. and exp. (Downers Grove: InterVarsity, 2006), 84, 105; Köstenberger and Patterson, *Invitation to Biblical Interpretation*, 645–47 (see chap. 13, n. 39).

[7] Various definitions taken from BDAG, 561–63.

[8] See Silva's helpful discussion in *Biblical Words and Their Meaning*, 35–38.

The translators of the King James Version rendered Jas 2:3 as: "Ye have respect to him that weareth the gay clothing, and say unto him, Sit thou here in a good place; and say to the poor, Stand thou there, or sit here under my footstool." In the early seventeenth century, the word "gay" meant "fine" or "luxurious." The word "gay" has experienced a dramatic "semantic shift" (change in meaning) over the last 400 years; its primary meaning now is "homosexual." In the same way, one must always remember that the words in the NT are a photograph of a moving target, that is, a snapshot of language in the process of change. For this reason, we should not cite Homer (ca. 8th century, BC) as the most authoritative source for the meaning of a NT Greek word, but should rather seek more contemporaneous sources to inform us. The best Greek lexicographers understand this principle, and it informs their work.

The priority of synchrony in defining NT Greek words also has an obverse fallacy—the etymological fallacy.[9] The etymological fallacy is the false claim that knowing the etymology (historical origins) of a word gives us deeper insights into its meaning. Many congregations are accustomed to being fed the etymological fallacy as part of their regular homiletical diet. Such supposed insights are introduced by the pastor with phrases such as, "The Greek word here *really* means . . ." Congregations tolerate absurdities that would be laughable in their own language. For example, the English word "lasagna" apparently derives from a Greek word λάσανον, a small pot used as a portable bedroom toilet. How many of us have considered this etymology while enjoying a dish of baked pasta? The word "dandelion" comes from the French "dent de lion" (tooth of a lion). When you spray weed killer on the dandelions in your yard, do you imagine yourself as a lion tamer? Similarly, when the apostle Paul wrote a word, he was almost certainly not thinking about the origin of that word. He was unconsciously assuming the contemporary semantic range and then narrowing that range further through cues in the surrounding literary context.

In recent years, some biblical scholars have argued that the emphasis on synchrony in word study has failed to account for biblical authors's reflections on the etymology of some words. This criticism is valid insofar as it points us to an ancient author's *consciously intended* allusion to a word's prior history. One must always ask: How has the author led the reader to consider the origins or historical echoes in this word? For example, in Matthew 1:21, the Gospel author reports that an angel tells Joseph, "[Mary] will give birth to a son, and you are to name him Jesus, because he will save his people from their sins." Matthew clearly intends his audience to understand the etymological origin of Jesus's Hebrew name ("YHWH saves") as significant. In the Scriptures, the etymological meaning of proper names is often viewed as important by biblical authors. We know that fact because of the

---

[9] For a discussion of the etymological fallacy, see Carson, *Exegetical Fallacies*, 28–33; Osborne, *Hermeneutical Spiral*, 84–89; Köstenberger and Patterson, *Invitation to Biblical Interpretation*, 631–35.

inspired authors's *explicit indications* in the text (e.g., Gen 25:26; 27:36; John 9:7–11; Heb 7:2).[10]

3. Do Not Confuse Words and Concepts

Students sometimes search for every instance of a particular word in an effort to understand a theological concept. For example, a student will write a paper on prayer that examines every instance of προσεύχομαι in the NT. Such a student fails to consider, however, that the idea of prayer is mentioned in many places where the actual word προσεύχομαι is not used. In fact, the biblical authors employ many Greek words for prayer (e.g., δέησις, εὐχή, εὔχομαι), and the concept of prayer is sometimes present even when no explicit "prayer words" are used (John 11:41–42).

4. Do Not View Word Study Tools as Inerrant

The number of excellent Greek word study tools available is nearly intoxicating. At the same time, we must remember that these resources are created by fallible human beings who sometimes show their mental frailty or theological biases. Louw and Nida's *Greek-English Lexicon of the New Testament Based on Semantic Domains* is an excellent resource, but like all such resources, it is not perfect. For example, under the word λόγος, Louw and Nida rightly list "gospel" as one of the potential meanings of the word.[11] Under the word ῥῆμα, however, "gospel" is not listed as a possible meaning,[12] even though ῥῆμα carries those connotations in multiple contexts (e.g., Rom 10:8, 17, 18; Eph 5:26; 6:17).

Theological bias can also show up in lexicons. In the entry for ἱλασμός, Louw and Nida argue against the English rendering "propitiation" (wrath-appeasing) because "in the NT God is never the object of propitiation since he is already on the side of people."[13] While the idea that God is not wrathful towards sinners may be popular in certain theological circles, it directly contradicts NT teaching and is not based on linguistic evidence.[14]

To remind myself of the fallible nature of Greek lexicons, I (Rob) keep a hand-written list of my suggested corrections on the blank pages in the back of my lexicons. If you use digital lexicons, perhaps you could keep a digital file of your critiques.

---

[10] Etymological studies are usually a last resort, often most helpful with rare words and proper names.

[11] Louw and Nida, 2:153.

[12] Louw and Nida, 2:217.

[13] Louw and Nida, 2:504.

[14] E.g., John 3:36, "The one who believes in the Son has eternal life, but the one who refuses to believe in the Son will not see life; instead, the wrath of God remains on him" (see also Rom 1:18).

Resources for Word Studies

Most students who continue using Greek in ministry will likely read the GNT via a computer, tablet, or smart phone—giving them easy access to parsing assistance and resources. While the digital versions of older lexicons (e.g., Thayer) are often available at no charge, the best and most up-to-date Greek resources are rarely free. A student should grow his Greek library through careful purchases over time, as budgetary constraints allow. Whether in print or in digital form, the best tools cost money. Listed below are brief descriptions of key resources for Greek word study. The items are listed in a recommended order of acquisition. At the bottom of the list is a subset of more technical and expensive items that perhaps only a NT scholar would acquire.

Items Recommended for Students and Pastors

- **Danker, Frederick William, rev. and ed.** *A Greek-English Lexicon of the New Testament and Other Early Christian Literature*, **3rd ed. Chicago: University of Chicago Press, 2000.** This Greek lexicon (dictionary), known as "BDAG" is the best NT Greek lexicon available. Danker's changes in the third edition have made this text much more user-friendly. The second edition of this text (1979) was known as BAGD because of key scholars who had contributed to it (Walter Bauer, William F. Arndt, F. Wilbur Gingrich, and Frederick W. Danker). In the shorthand title for the third edition of this text (BDAG), Danker's name is now listed second to Bauer, who compiled the German lexicon upon which later editions were based. After purchasing a critical edition of the GNT, BDAG should be next on a student's wishlist.[15]

- **Silva, Moisés, ed.** *New International Dictionary of New Testament Theology and Exegesis.* **5 vols. Grand Rapids: Zondervan, 2014.** Silva's extensive revision of *The New International Dictionary of New Testament Theology* (ed. Colin Brown, 1975–78), has made a valuable linguistic resource even better. For a pastor looking for a scholarly, reliable Greek resource with an eye to theological application in the church, *NIDNTTE* is unsurpassed.[16]

- **Balz, H., and G. Schneider.** *Exegetical Dictionary of the New Testament*, **3 vols. Grand Rapids: Eerdmans, 1990–93.** *EDNT*, a translation and revision of a German lexicon, is an excellent dictionary set that covers the entire vocabulary of the GNT but focuses attention on significant theological terms.

---

[15] See Rod Decker's extensive review of BDAG, as well as online resources to help students learn to use the lexicon, accessed October 20, 2019, http://ntresources.com/blog/?page_id=2526.

[16] For a free 45-page primer on *NIDNTTE*, see https://zondervanacademic.com/blog/free-resources-collection, accessed October 21, 2019.

- **Louw, Johannes P., and Eugene A. Nida.** *Greek-English Lexicon of the New Testament Based on Semantic Domains,* **2 vols. New York: United Bible Societies, 1988.** In "Louw and Nida," words with similar meaning are grouped in meaning categories (semantic domains), and then individual nuances of meaning are delineated. Knowing that this resource was created to assist Bible translators helps to clarify the thinking behind some otherwise oddly-worded definitions. Louw and Nida is part of the base package in many Bible software programs, and a free partial digital version of it can be accessed at www.laparola.net/greco/louwnida.php.

Additional Items Recommended for Scholars

- **Kittel, G., and G. Friedrich, ed.** *Theological Dictionary of the New Testament,* **10 vols. Translated and edited by G. W. Bromiley. Grand Rapids: Eerdmans, 1964–76.** *TDNT* or "Kittel" is not an exhaustive dictionary but concentrates on terms with theological significance. This work gives extensive treatment of the usage of the term in Hellenism, the OT (LXX), and early Judaism. *TDNT* groups cognate terms together but does not include synonyms. Many articles in *TDNT* were written by Germans with liberal theological predilections and therefore must be read with caution.

- **Spicq, Ceslas.** *Theological Lexicon of the New Testament.* **Translated and Edited by James D. Ernest. Peabody, MA: Hendrickson, 1994.** Translated from French, this 3-volume lexicon was prepared by the famous linguist Ceslas Spicq. The work provides a series of short studies on theologically significant words.

- **Liddell, Henry George, and Robert Scott.** *A Greek-English Lexicon with a Revised Supplement,* **rev. Henry Stuart Jones. Oxford: Clarendon, 1996.** Indispensable lexicon for working in Greek literature outside the NT, especially from the classical period. This lexicon is referred to with a variety of abbreviations and identifiers—LSJ, Liddell-Scott-Jones, or simply Liddell-Scott. There is a shortened version of LSJ sometimes called "Middle Liddell" and an even further abbreviated version called "Little Liddell." The full-length LSJ was intended as a comprehensive lexicon of ancient Greek and does give LXX and NT word meanings in many of its entries.

- **Montari, Franco, et., *The Brill Dictionary of Ancient Greek.* Translated from Italian. English Edition edited by Madeleine Goh and Chad Schroeder. Leiden: Brill, 2015.** Heralded by some scholars as "the new LSJ" (see above) and criticized by others as LSJ recycled (through Italian and back into English), *The Brill Dictionary of Ancient Greek* is still being assessed by scholars. I (Rob) have personally found the formatting appealing and information useful in the few times I have used it. The work is intended to cover both the classical and koine periods. Perhaps the dominant way to refer to this new lexicon is "BrillDAG"

- **Moulton, J. H., and G. Milligan. *The Vocabulary of the Greek New Testament.* Peabody, MA: Hendrickson, 1997.** This dictionary, originally published as one volume in 1930 by Hodder & Stoughton, gives information on NT words based on ancient papyri and inscriptions. A Scripture index can be found in the back. This work is referred to as "Moulton & Milligan."

- *New Documents Illustrating Early Christianity.* **Sydney, Australia: Macquarie University, 1981–present.** As of 2019, the Ancient History Documentary Research Centre of Macquarie University, Sydney, Australia, has published 10 volumes of *NewDocs*. This series continues the Moulton and Milligan tradition of illustrating the meaning of NT Greek words through ancient papyri and inscriptions. The first volume of *NewDocs* (published in 1981 by Liverpool University Press) discusses inscriptions and papyri published in 1976. The most recent volume of *NewDocs* was published in 2012 by Eerdmans and discusses papyri and inscriptions published between 1988–1992.

- *Thesaurus Linguae Graecae.* (www.tlg.uci.edu) Known as *TLG* and overseen by the University of California, Irvine, this database currently boasts a comprehensive, searchable collection of Greek writings from the time of Homer to the fall of Byzantium in AD 1453.

- **Lust, J., E. Eynikel, and K. Hauspie, eds. *A Greek-English Lexicon of the Septuagint,* rev. ed. Stuttgart: Deutsche Bibelgesellschaft, 2003.** One of two lexicons for the Septuagint, sometimes called Lust-Eynikel-Hauspie or LEH. In LEH definitions, the editors are asking: "Based upon translation technique, what is the meaning intended by the *translators* of the LXX?"

- **Muraoka, T. *A Greek-English Lexicon of the Septuagint.* Leuven: Peeters, 2009.** The other major lexicon for the Septuagint. Muraoka looks to secular Greek sources as the background for the meaning of words in the LXX. In his definitions, Muraoka is asking: "How did an *early reader* (who had no access to the parent text of the LXX) understand these words?"

A Strategy for Word Studies

Greek grammars can sometimes present unrealistic guidelines for word studies. What pastor would actually have the time and tools to engage in the studies prescribed? Below is an attempt to provide a realistic method for Greek word studies that could be employed regularly by a pastor or layperson in their weekly preparation to preach or teach. Students are recommended to follow the ordered steps below.

1. Consider the Immediate and Broader Literary Context in Determining the Meaning of a Word

For example, imagine that you are preparing a lesson or sermon on Luke chapter 21. As you study verse 34, you come upon a puzzling word, κραιπάλη. As this word only occurs once in the NT, you have likely never seen it. The CSB translates verses 34–36 as:

> Be on your guard, so that your minds are not dulled from *carousing*, drunkenness, and worries of life, or that day will come on you unexpectedly like a trap. For it will come on all who live on the face of the whole earth. But be alert at all times, praying that you may have strength to escape all these things that are going to take place and to stand before the Son of Man. (emphasis added)

"Carousing?" you think. "What is carousing?" In context, Jesus is warning against sinful behaviors that should not mark his followers as they await his return. Clearly, "carousing" is a negative term. It is something that Jesus condemns. Also, we note specifically that Jesus warns against their minds (Greek: ὑμῶν αἱ καρδίαι) being weighed down (βαρηθῶσιν) or dulled by carousing, drunkenness, and worries.

2. Compare English Bible Translations of the Passage in Question

How do other English translations render κραιπάλη?

ENGLISH BIBLE VERSION	RENDERING OF κραιπάλη
Common English Bible	"drinking parties"
English Standard Version	"dissipation"
King James Version	"surfeiting"
New International Reader's Version	"wasteful living"
New Jerusalem Bible	"debauchery"
New Living Translation	"carousing"

Interestingly, most Bible translations (except for the CEB and NIRV) render κραιπάλη with an obscure English word. Arguably, most modern readers would not understand the meaning of "surfeiting," "debauchery," "carousing," or "dissipation." When looked up in a modern dictionary, all of these words have, as part of their semantic range, the nuance of excessive alcohol consumption. Though this alcohol-specific meaning is apparently intended by the translators of the various English translations noted above, in dictionaries of modern English, "excessive drinking" is sometimes listed as a tertiary or archaic definition of the word in question.[17]

The NIRV's translation ("wasteful living") is understandable but ambiguous. Does "wasteful living" refer to wasting money? Wasting natural resources? Wasting one's potential? The CEB's "drinking parties" is by far the most understandable translation, but is it accurate? Does κραιπάλη refer not just to excessive drinking, but immoderate drinking and wild behavior in a group setting?

In the final version cited in the chart above (the NLT), the punctuation and translation imply that the translators understand "drunkenness" (μέθη, Luke 21:34) as connected tightly with "carousing" (κραιπάλη). The NLT reads, "By carousing and drunkenness, and by the worries of this life." In other words, "carousing and drunkenness" are likely being presented by the NLT translators as a hendiadys, that is, two terms used to express one underlying reality. For example, if someone says, "That man has plunged into wickedness and sin," you do not understand them as referring to two realities—that is, that the man plunged into (1) wickedness and then (possibly at a later time), also plunged into (2) sin. Rather, the phrase "wickedness and sin" refers to one reality, and the speaker likely employs two near synonyms to intensify or possibly slightly broaden the reference.

In addition to comparing modern English translations in stage two of a word study, a student may also choose to look at technical commentaries, which should discuss any significant or debated words. The Luke volume of Baylor University Press's Handbook on the Greek Text series provides this comment on Luke 21:34, "The term κραιπάλη, which occurs only here in the NT, refers to 'drunken behavior which is completely without moral restraint' (LN 88.286)."[18] In his commentary on Luke, Darrell Bock comments, "The NT *hapax legomenon*[19] κραιπάλη refers to dizziness or carousing associated with drunkenness."[20]

3. Consider the Same Biblical Author's Other Uses of the Word

Neither Luke nor any other NT author employs κραιπάλη. In studying other words, however, this step can be very important in determining meaning. A search for other uses of a word can be performed in any major Bible software program within a matter of seconds.

4. List the Possible Definitions of the Word According to Standard Lexicons and Word Study Tools

For the sake of this brief study, we will only look at the tools recommended for students above.

---

[17] Accessed December 16, 2019, www.merriam-webster.com.

[18] Martin M. Culy, Mikeal C. Parsons, and Joshua J. Stigall, *Luke*, BHGNT (Waco, TX: Baylor University Press, 2010), 659. The abbreviation "LN" stands for Louw and Nida, so in this case, by referencing a commentary, we are overlapping with step 4 (lexicons and word study tools).

[19] *Hapax legomenon* (Greek: "said once") refers to the unique occurrence of a word in a specified body of literature—here, in the NT.

[20] Darrell L. Bock, *Luke 9:51–24:53*, BECNT 3B (Grand Rapids: Baker, 1996), 1693n48.

- BDAG: "both 'carousing, intoxication' and its result 'drunken headache, hangover' are associated with the term, since it means 'dizziness, staggering' when the head refuses to function . . . **unbridled indulgence in a drinking party, *drinking bout* . . .**" (bold and italics original).[21]

- *NIDNTTE* (ed., Moisés Silva): has an insightful discussion of various Greek words for drunkenness and the broader New Testament teaching on inebriation in volume 3, pages 258–60. It is in the earlier edition of *NIDNTT* (ed., Colin Brown), that we find this additional helpful paragraph: "*kraipalē* (intoxication) occurs in a few Hellenistic sources (e.g., Aristophanes), and can also be used of the effects of intoxication—dizziness and staggering. In the NT *kraipalē* occurs only once, and in conjunction with *methē* (Lk. 21:34). The effect of drunkenness is probably intended (thus 'dissipation' RSV). The context, as in Matt. 24:49; Luke 12:45, is readiness for the day of the Lord's coming."[22]

- *EDNT*: "intoxication, dizziness, staggering"[23]

- Louw & Nida:[24] As noted by a resource referenced above, Louw & Nida define κραιπάλη as "drunken behavior which is completely without moral restraint." It is helpful to have actually looked up the word in Louw and Nida, though, because we find this additional comment: "In a number of languages it may be possible to translate κραιπάλη as 'bad things people do when they are very drunk.'"[25]

5. Identify Other Words in the Same Semantic Domain

Sometimes this exercise will bring the particular nuances of a word into clearer focus. In the semantic field of "drunkenness" (§§88.283–88.288), Louw and Nida list the following Greek words related to inebriation:

- μεθύω, μέθη ("to become drunk on alcoholic beverages," "drunkenness")

- οἰνοφλυγία ("drunkenness, implying the consumption of large quantities of wine")

- μεθύσκομαι ("to become intoxicated")

- κῶμος, πότος ("drinking parties involving unrestrained indulgence in alcoholic beverages and accompanying immoral behavior")

- μέθυσος, οἰνοπότης, πάροινος ("a person who habitually drinks too much and thus becomes a drunkard").

---

[21] BDAG, 564.

[22] *NIDNTT*, 514.

[23] *EDNT*, 2:314.

[24] Reminder: the student should start with the alphabetical index of Greek words in vol. 2, which will direct him to the proper semantic domain [meaning field] in volume 1. In this case, the entry for κραιπάλη on p. 146 of vol. 2, directs us to section 88.286 in vol. 1.

[25] Louw and Nida, 1:773 (§88.286).

It seems that a significant nuance of κραιπάλη is immoral behavior viewed by others that accompanies drunkenness.

In considering the Greek terms for drunkenness, *NIDNTTE* discusses briefly the historical and cultural context, as well as considering metaphorical uses of the words. Silva provides some theological synthesis on the NT's teaching on drunkenness, as well as noting linguistic patterns (e.g., "the noun μέθη ("drunkenness") occurs 3x alongside synonyms").[26]

6. Consider Uses of the Word Throughout the NT and LXX

A quick search in Accordance or Logos turns up no other occurrences of κραιπάλη in the NT or LXX. It should be noted that when a word does appear in the LXX, occurrences there can provide very helpful background for the NT authors's uses. Nevertheless, even if a word does not occur in the LXX, if a student has a Bible software program, additional searches in synchronous Greek literature is relatively easy. For example, one can search morphologically tagged Greek texts of the Apostolic Fathers, Josephus, Philo, and the OT Pseudepigrapha. A search of the Apostolic Fathers turns up one occurrence in Hermas Mandate 6.2.5.[27] There an angelic messenger instructs an early Christian named Hermas:

> ὅταν ὀξυχολία σοί τις προσπέσῃ ἢ πικρία γίνωσκε ὅτι αὐτός ἐστιν ἐν σοί εἶτα ἐπιθυμία πράξεων πολλῶν καὶ πολυτέλειαι ἐδεσμάτων πολλῶν καὶ μεθυσμάτων καὶ **κραιπαλῶν** πολλῶν καὶ ποικίλων τρυφῶν καὶ οὐ δεόντων καὶ ἐπιθυμίαι γυναικῶν καὶ πλεονεξία καὶ ὑπερηφανία πολλή τις καὶ ἀλαζονεία καὶ ὅσα τούτοις παραπλήσιά ἐστι καὶ ὅμοια ταῦτα οὖν ὅταν ἐπὶ τὴν καρδίαν σου ἀναβῇ γίνωσκε ὅτι ὁ ἄγγελος τῆς πονηρίας ἐστὶν ἐν σοί (bold added)

Michael Holmes translates the above passage as follows:

> When some angry temperamental outburst or bitterness comes over you, recognize that [the angel of wickedness] is in you. Then comes the desire for much business, and extravagant kinds of food and drink, and much **drunkenness**, and various kinds of unnecessary luxuries, and the desire for women, and greed and arrogance and pretentiousness, and whatever else resembles or is similar to these things. So whenever these things enter your heart, you know that the angel of wickedness is with you.[28]

From this passage, it is clear the κραιπάλη is a word that belongs in Christian "vice lists," along with greed and arrogance. We are right to see it as a behavior evaluated negatively by early Christians. It is interesting that, unlike the occurrence in Luke 21:34, here κραιπάλη occurs in the plural with the modifier πολύς ("much"). Because the context provides little detail, it is difficult to say much more about the word.

---

[26] *NIDNTTE* 3:259.

[27] Also cited in BDAG's entry for κραιπάλη (564).

[28] Michael W. Holmes, ed., *The Apostolic Fathers: Greek Texts and English Translations* (Grand Rapids: Baker, 2007), 523–24 (bold added).

No occurrence of κραιπάλη turns up in Josephus or the OT Pseudepigrapha, but the word is found once in Philo's "The Posterity and Exile of Cain."[29] In this text, Philo discusses the drunken behavior of Lot whereby he impregnated his two daughters (Gen 19:30–38). The word κραιπάλη is connected with immoral behavior accompanying the stupor of extreme drunkenness.

7. State Clearly and Succinctly What You Have Discovered About the Word in Question

Give thought to practical exhortation that conveys what you have learned. Beware of reductionistic theologizing. What other biblical words, concepts, and passages touch on the topic you are considering? As one person has said, "A mist in the pulpit is a fog in the pew." If we as teachers of God's Word are not clear on what we are saying, how can we hope for others to understand? Part of the discipline of doing a word study is pausing to prayerfully and carefully summarize your insights. You should not enlist the congregation to glean with you in the field of linguistic study, but rather you should deliver to them the finished product—grain threshed, ground, and baked into bread.

Looking at κραιπάλη, we can conclude that the word refers not just to drunkenness in the abstract, but visible immoral behavior that often accompanies the clouded faculties of an inebriated person. The ancient texts above present such immoral behavior in relation to other persons, that is, the way a drunk person sins against others through foolish talk, violence, and sexual exploitation.

In Luke 21:34–36, Jesus warns about the things that can dull the hearts and minds of his followers as they await his return. One of these is anxiety or worry. And indeed, forgetting there is a sovereign Lord who will return to right all wrongs could lead one to frightful anxiety. Another false spiritual path is escapism—drinking and partying, "living it up." Neither despair nor escapism is the Christian response to the current broken world, but faithful and prayerful discipleship. In preparing a sermon on Luke 21:34–36, one will want to consider other forms of escapism that are treated in the Bible, especially those that capture the hearts of people to whom you are ministering. For example, many people find meaning through parading their wealth and success (1 John 2:16). Not only drunkenness, but the idolatry of prestige and luxury can intoxicate us and render us ineffective and unfaithful.

CONCLUSION

Faithful Christians revere the words of the Bible as the very words of God. Every single word in the Hebrew and Greek autographs was exactly the word that God wanted written. These are the words that "cannot be broken" (John 10:35) and that point us to Jesus Christ (John 5:39), where we find life, truth, forgiveness, and joy

---

[29] *De posteritate Caini* 1.176. For an affordable English translation of this text, see *The Works of Philo: New Updated Edition*, trans. C. D. Yonge (Peabody, MA: Hendrickson, 1993), 150.

(John 14:6). It is only fitting, then, that we should be zealous to understand the nuances of every word in the Bible—especially theologically or contextually significant words or phrases. Next time you encounter a puzzling or significant word in your reading of the Bible, don't just rely on the reflections of others; follow the word study procedures presented above. Discover with the psalmist that the words of the Lord are more precious than thousands of pieces of gold and silver (Ps 119:72).

SUMMARY

PRINCIPLES FOR WORD STUDY
1. Don't make any word mean more than you have to. ("The least meaning is the best meaning.")
2. Prioritize synchrony over diachrony. Study word usage contemporaneous with your text.
3. Do not confuse word and concept.
4. Do not view word study tools as inerrant.

RESOURCES FOR WORD STUDY	
RESOURCE	**DESCRIPTION**
BDAG	Best NT Greek lexicon.
NIDNTTE	5-volume word study tool, excellent linguistically and theologically.
EDNT	3-volume lexicon with focus on theologically-significant terms.
Louw and Nida	2-volume work, groups words by "semantic domain" (field of meaning).
TDNT or "Kittel"	10-volume work, extremely detailed diachronic study, some entries have a liberal German bias.
Spicq (Theological Lexicon of the NT)	3-volume work by French linguist.
Liddell-Scott-Jones (LSJ)	Detailed lexicon indispensable for ancient Greek outside the GNT.
The Brill Dictionary of Ancient Greek (BrillDAG)	Translated from Italian. Heralded by some as "the new LSJ." Criticized by others.
Moulton & Milligan	Lexicon illustrating NT vocabulary through ancient papyri and inscriptions.
NewDocs	10 volumes (as of 2015), continuing the tradition of Moulton & Milligan by illustrating NT vocabulary through Greek papyri and inscriptions.

RESOURCES FOR WORD STUDY	
RESOURCE	DESCRIPTION
Thesaurus Linguae Graecae (*TLG*)	Searchable database of Greek writings from the time of Homer to the fall of Byzantium.
Lust-Eynikel-Hauspie (LEH)	LXX lexicon, concerned with the meaning intended by the *translators* of the LXX.
Muraoka	LXX lexicon, concerned with how an early *reader* would have understood the LXX translation.

A STRATEGY FOR WORD STUDY	
1.	Consider the immediate and broader literary context.
2.	Compare English Bible translations.
3.	Consider the same biblical author's other uses of the word.
4.	List the possible definitions of the word according to standard lexicons and word study tools.
5.	Identify other words in the same semantic domain.
6.	Consider uses of the word throughout the NT and LXX.
7.	State clearly and succinctly your discoveries. Beware of theologizing in a reductionistic way.

PRACTICE EXERCISES

Following the seven steps outlined above, complete word studies for the following words:

1. τὰ σπλάγχνα (Phlm v. 20).

2. τῆς ἀνομίας (2 Thess 2:7). Hint: think not only about this specific word, but also about the phrases in which it appears (e.g., "man of lawlessness" [2 Thess 3:3] and "mystery of lawlessness" [2 Thess 3:7]).

3. σπουδάζω (2 Tim 2:15).

/////////////

CHAPTER 15

CONTINUING WITH GREEK

INTRODUCTION

In the conclusion to the best-selling leadership book *What Got You Here Won't Get You There*, Marshall Goldsmith challenges his readers to picture themselves at ninety-five years of age facing imminent death.[1] He says to imagine you can go back in time and talk to yourself at your current age. What advice, warnings, and encouragements would you give to yourself? That's a healthy reflective exercise for any person, but let's focus that advice on Greek. What would you (at age ninety-five) say to yourself (now) about Greek? Maybe this:

> Stick with reading and studying God's Word in Greek because you will spend your life feasting on exegetical treasures and sharing those delicacies with others. Take as many Greek courses as you can now; and after you graduate from school, develop a disciplined life of incorporating the GNT into your devotional and ministry life.

CHAPTER OBJECTIVES

The purpose of this chapter is to help students think deliberately about how to become people who spend their entire lives reading, studying, and teaching from the GNT. Two of the authors of *Going Deeper with New Testament Greek* (Merkle and Plummer) have written a "paperback personal trainer" to assist you

---

[1] Marshall Goldsmith, with Mark Reiter, *What Got You Here Won't Get You There: How Successful People Become Even More Successful* (New York: Hyperion, 2007), 221–24.

in learning, retaining, or reviving Greek skills. We've poured our passion and decades of teaching experience into that book and recommend it as a supplement to your ongoing Greek study. It is entitled *Greek for Life: Strategies for Learning, Retaining, and Reviving New Testament Greek* (Baker, 2017).

START WHERE YOU ARE

Studying Greek in college or seminary takes place in an artificial environment. Tests and quizzes hold you accountable, you are paying for the instruction, and your regular life is somewhat "on hold" as you focus on acquiring more knowledge and skills. You have a peer group around you, helping move you forward. You (presumably) have a brilliant and inspiring professor. And, if you don't keep up with your Greek, you'll get a poor grade or fail. These outside strictures are a blessing—working together to bring students to an acceptable skill level in NT Greek.

From our experience, it is good for students to take a Greek class every semester—and not just because that keeps Greek professors employed! When beginning the study of Greek, students need to be mentored. A student left to himself after one or two semesters is rarely able to continue faithfully with the language; his proficiency level is so low that he will get frustrated when he strikes out on his own. Also, if a student fails to include a Greek course in his schedule every semester, the rigorous demands of other classes will likely end Pollyanna plans to continue self-study in Greek. Four to six semesters of Greek study usually provides sufficient skill and practice for a student to launch out on a lifetime of reading the GNT.

Students in the midst of an academic program should step back and ask these questions: (1) Do I want to lose the Greek skills I have worked so hard to obtain? (2) How can I arrange my remaining academic schedule to maximize my exposure to the GNT?

Beginning Greek classes are often the most challenging, as students spend numerous hours memorizing paradigms and syntactical categories. Upper-level classes focus more on applying those morphological and syntactical skills to studying biblical texts. Greek knowledge is thus able to percolate into the student's long-term memory at the same time that exegetical insights from the text encourage the student to continue study. Many upper-level Greek students have feasted upon spiritual manna from the GNT.

If you are reading this chapter just prior to graduation, don't despair. You simply need to face with stark honesty the danger of your apostasy from the language you have come to love. Then, apply diligently the methods and plans suggested below.

If you knew a tornado was coming, what would you do to ensure the safety of your family and possessions? We've got news for you: A tornado of distractions *is* coming! Your Greek skills are in danger. Don't let what you have worked so hard for be blown away!

GEAR FOR THE JOURNEY

When we go on road trips with our families, the quality of our journey is greatly influenced by what we bring with us. Have we brought sufficient snacks for the children? Did our wives bring the magazines or books they planned to read? Did we remember to bring the ipads with downloaded videos for the kids? Similarly, your lifetime journey with the GNT can be helped or hindered by the quality of the "gear" you bring along. Depending on your personal budget, some of the items below may need to be acquired over time.

Texts

One cannot read the GNT without a copy of the Greek text! This goes without saying, perhaps, but there are many options that can aid in reading for the long haul.

A Reader's Greek New Testament

Recognizing that inexperienced readers of the GNT are often frustrated by unfamiliar vocabulary words, several publishers are now offering a "reader's edition" of the GNT, with uncommon vocabulary words listed verse-by-verse at the bottom of each page. Two of the most popular readers' editions are:

1. *The Greek New Testament: A Reader's Edition* (UBS[5] text).[2] The Greek text is the United Bible Societies' critical text of the GNT.[3] The volume includes glosses (brief definitions) at the bottom of each page for words that occur thirty times or less. Parsing information with difficult grammatical forms is also sometimes provided. Very abbreviated information about the most significant textual variants is given.

2. *Crossway's The Greek New Testament, Produced at Tyndale House, Cambridge, Reader's Edition* (2018). See chapter 1 for discussion of the differences between the UBS and Tyndale House edition of the GNT (or, see this video: https://vimeo.com/313496503). The THGNT reader's edition is very nicely formatted and provides parsings of difficult verbs and definitions of vocabulary words occurring 25 times or less. An appendix provides a brief glossary of more common words in the GNT. The ordering of the NT books, as well as formatting and spelling within the THGNT reflects some features of early Greek manuscripts.

---

[2] *The Greek New Testament: A Reader's Edition* (Stuttgart: Deutsche Bibelgesellschaft, 2015). The running Greek-English dictionary was compiled by Barclay M. Newman. The textual notes were compiled by Florian Voss. Various printings of the UBS GNT are available, from a top grain leather edition to an inexpensive paperback.

[3] See chapter 1 for a discussion of the UBS Greek text, Nestle-Aland, etc.

If students don't mind having a second print volume open alongside their GNT, a "reader's lexicon" can provide the same assistance as the vocabulary helps of a reader's GNT—sometimes with additional usage statistics and more extensive definitions. The best GNT reader's lexicon available is *A New Reader's Lexicon of the Greek New Testament* by Michael H. Burer and Jeffrey E. Miller.[4] Definitions (drawn from BDAG and other sources) are provided for all words that occur fewer than fifty times.

Students may also opt for a diglot version of the GNT, which offers the Greek text on one page and an English Bible translation on the facing page. Zondervan's *Greek-English New Testament: UBS 5th Revised Edition and NIV* (2015) offers the UBS text (with full text-critical apparatus) side-by-side with a standard English translation. Another widely-used diglot is the *New Testament: New English Translation, Novum Testamentum Graece* (Deutsche Bibelgesellschaft and NET Bible Press, 2004). Similar to a diglot are interlinear versions, which usually offer English definitions right above the Greek words or vice versa. A top-selling, user-friendly interlinear is Crossway's *English-Greek Reverse Interlinear New Testament* (ESV translation).

If a reader's version of the GNT is a helpful crutch, then a diglot is a manual wheelchair, and an interlinear version is a motorized wheelchair.[5] Just as a person with limited mobility will find their physical abilities deteriorating through disuse, it is possible to receive too much assistance in reading the GNT so that one's skills actually begin to erode. Please note: If your current skill level demands an interlinear or diglot text, employ one without shame! At the same time, consider how you can exercise your Greek muscles so that you can be less reliant on assistance.

Digital Texts

Not long ago, no one knew what these things were: an app, an iPad, a Kindle. If you are reading these words a decade or more after we write them, perhaps you don't know what they are either! Technology changes quickly. Nevertheless, one thing that will remain constant is the ability to read the GNT and access Greek resources digitally. The majority of students who continue faithfully reading their GNTs do so in digital format because of (1) ease of access and (2) linking of resources. First, while it is inconvenient to carry a printed edition of the GNT, one can easily access a digital text on one's smartphone, tablet, or computer. In our current culture, the smartphone is becoming the ubiquitous digital assistant—replacing cameras, books, wallets, and even printed GNTs! Second, many digital texts have search features that mirror concordance capabilities and are linked with lexicons, parsing information, and even grammatical diagrams so that students can quickly gain assistance with the text.[6] We realize that any digital recommenda-

---

[4] Michael H. Burer and Jeffrey E. Miller, *A New Reader's Lexicon of the Greek New Testament* (Grand Rapids: Kregel, 2008).

[5] Analogy suggested by Andy Naselli, private correspondence, March 18, 2014.

[6] See the section on Greek word study in chapter 14 to learn about concordance-type searches of the text. For a printed concordance of the GNT, we recommend John R. Kohlenberger, Edward

tions will quickly become outdated, but we tentatively offer below our "best of the best" recommendations.

RECOMMENDED DIGITAL TOOLS	
DEVICE/FORMAT	RECOMMENDATION
Computer software	Logos or Accordance
Smartphone app	Olive Tree "Bible Study" app or Logos app
Kindle	SBL Greek NT (free download)

Students are encouraged to visit the following websites to keep up on the latest in digital Greek resources and tools:

- Free ancillary resources keyed to this textbook: www.deepergreek.com
- Daily Dose of Greek, by Rob Plummer: www.dailydoseofgreek.com
- NT Gateway, by Mark Goodacre: www.ntgateway.com
- NT Resources, established by Rodney Decker, maintained by Wayne Slusser: www.ntresources.com
- NT Discourse, by Steve Runge: www.ntdiscourse.org
- NT Greek Portal, by Dave Black: www.newtestamentgreekportal.blog-spot.com

Commentaries

At the end of a second-semester Greek Syntax class, a student confided in me (Rob), "I will never be a Greek scholar, but this class will enable me to sniff out fallacious linguistic arguments when I'm reading commentaries." In fact, being able to employ the most technical NT commentaries (which engage the Greek text) is a huge benefit to any pastor or church leader. As a pastor begins teaching through a book in the NT, he should acquire at least three of the best technical commentaries to serve as dialogue partners alongside his own reflections on the text. Personal study of the text should always come first, but good commentaries can point out insights a pastor missed as well as save him from missteps. Two new commentary series that extensively discuss Greek grammatical and syntactical issues in relationship to a text's meaning are as follows (in order of recommendation):

- The Exegetical Guide to the Greek New Testament (EGGNT) series, by B&H Academic
- A Handbook on the Greek New Testament series, by Baylor University Press

W. Goodrick and James A. Swanson, *The Exhaustive Concordance to the Greek New Testament* (Grand Rapids: Zondervan, 1995). Another helpful tool is Köstenberger and Bouchoc, *The Book Study Concordance* (see preface, n. 3).

A one-volume grammatical aid to the GNT that has been used by students for decades is Max Zerwick and Mary Grosvenor's *Grammatical Analysis of the Greek New Testament*.[7] Similar to Zerwick and Grosvenor's fine text is *The New Linguistic and Exegetical Key to the Greek New Testament*, by Cleon L. Rogers Jr. and Cleon L. Rogers III.[8] Both single-volume grammatical guides, however, are quickly being supplanted by the more extensive and up-to-date grammatical commentaries in the two new series listed above.

Alongside the helpful recommendations at www.bestcommentaries.com, two print resources to help the pastor select more traditional technical commentaries are:

- *New Testament Commentary Survey*, by D. A. Carson. The 7th edition of this Baker Academic text came out in 2013. Revisions of this text have come out every few years, and pastors have come to find Carson an indispensable and trustworthy guide.

- *Best Bible Books: New Testament Resources*, by John Glynn (Kregel, 2018)

Lexicons

Students too easily rely on the glosses (brief definitions) they memorized during their early academic study. Every serious reader of the GNT should aspire to own the best NT Greek lexicon (dictionary): *A Greek-English Lexicon of the New Testament and Other Early Christian Literature*, rev. and ed. by Frederick William Danker. This resource is commonly referred to as BDAG, after the initials of four key scholars who worked on the lexicon (or its precursors). BDAG is available for purchase in either print or digital format, but it is expensive. See the previous chapter for guidelines on doing Greek word studies.

Grammars

The footnotes of this book provide students with the titles of many Greek grammars, from the very basic to the most advanced. A beleaguered student may think he never wants to look at a Greek textbook again, but Greek grammars can, in fact, be quite helpful for ongoing study and reading of the GNT. Listed below are the most common ways that lifetime readers of the GNT will employ grammars:

1. Every few years, a pastor may choose to read through a beginning or intermediate Greek grammar to refresh his understanding and point out blind spots in his knowledge. Not everyone will find reading a Greek grammar relaxing, but some will!

---

[7] Max Zerwick and Mary Grosvenor, *A Grammatical Analysis of the Greek New Testament*, rev. ed. (Rome: Biblical Institute Press, 1981).

[8] Rogers Jr. and Rogers III, *New Linguistic and Exegetical Key to the Greek New Testament* (see chap. 7, n. 50)

2. More likely, a pastor may have questions about a particular Greek form or syntactical issue. Using a grammar's table of contents or indices, he can look up and read about a particular issue when it arises.

3. Many Greek grammars have a Scripture index. Whenever a pastor works through a particular text, he can make it his habit to see if that text is cited in the Scripture index of a chosen grammar or grammars. Once this "Greek index check" becomes a study habit, the pastor will hardly notice the extra time it takes. Learning and reviewing Greek grammar in "bite size chunks" in the midst of ministry preparation is both manageable and relevant. Moreover, learning Greek grammar *in situ* (in the context of a particular textual study) helps the ideas take hold more securely in one's mind.

Vocabulary Resources

Eager Greek students sometimes proclaim grandiose plans to review vocabulary during their summer or winter breaks. Such plans usually fail because it is difficult to maintain joy and a sense of purpose when reviewing vocabulary apart from reading the GNT as God's inspired Word. Nevertheless, to the motivated students reading this chapter, a few comments are in order. Thankfully, it has never been easier to study vocabulary "on the go" with the various Greek vocabulary apps now available for smartphones. Perhaps the best Greek vocabulary apps are "Flash Greek Pro" by Danny Zacharias and "Bible Vocab" by Robert Turnbull.

While there is no substitute for rote memorization, many find it easier to learn Greek vocabulary by seeing the relationship between Greek words built off the same root. In *Building Your New Testament Greek Vocabulary*, Robert E. Van Voorst has done a great service for students by grouping together Greek words in common families to aid in vocabulary acquisition.[9]

Another vocabulary resource worth mentioning is Mark's Wilson's *Mastering New Testament Greek Vocabulary through Semantic Domains*.[10] This book groups vocabulary according to shared fields of meaning. For example, all common Greek words that communicate joy, happiness, or gladness are listed together with conceptual nuances noted. There is one thing to keep in mind, however, about acquiring vocabulary—as helpful as vocabulary resources can be, the very best way to acquire and maintain Greek vocabulary is through regular time reading the Greek text.

---

[9] Robert E. Van Voorst, *Building Your New Testament Greek Vocabulary*, 3rd ed., Resources for Biblical Study 43, ed. Beverly R. Gaventa (Atlanta: Society of Biblical Literature, 2001).

[10] Mark Wilson, with Jason Oden, *Mastering New Testament Greek Vocabulary through Semantic Domains* (Grand Rapids: Kregel, 2003).

A LIFETIME JOURNEY

The authors of this textbook are on a lifetime journey to read, study, and teach the GNT. We hope you will join us. Below are a few suggestions to help make this journey a success:

1. Read the GNT as part of your daily devotions.[11] Don't be afraid to use the digital tools or reading helps mentioned above. Some Christians will be able to read a chapter of Greek every day; others could aim for five to ten verses. Some daily readers of the GNT like to overlap with the previous day's reading to help solidify unfamiliar vocabulary.

2. Include Greek study in your weekly ministerial preparations. Whether preparing for a Sunday School lesson, exposition of a text in a denominational newspaper, or a sermon, the pastor should make study of the GNT a regular part of his teaching preparations. When study of the GNT is incorporated into both your private devotions and formal ministry preparations, you have a good chance of faithfully journeying in the GNT for the rest of your life.

3. Take a "Greek retreat" once or twice a year in which you read longer sections of the GNT, a technical Greek resource, or a Greek grammar. The Greek retreat need not last more than a day. If you want to get up to speed on recent debates and developments in New Testament Greek scholarship, take a weekend to read Con Campbell's *Advances in the Study of Greek: New Insights for Reading the New Testament*.[12]

4. Consider what elements of accountability and self-discipline may be applied to incorporate study of the GNT into your life. For example, consider the following suggestions:

   - Do not eat breakfast until you have done your daily devotional reading in the GNT.

   - On a sermon preparation day, do not check your phone or email until you have completed a pre-set amount of time in the text of the GNT.

   - Formalize a Greek accountability relationship with a fellow pastor who wishes to journey for a lifetime in the GNT. Clarify

---

[11] See J. Scott Duvall and Verlyn D. Verbrugge, eds., *Devotions on the Greek New Testament: 52 Reflections to Inspire & Instruct* (Grand Rapids: Zondervan, 2012); Paul N. Jackson, ed. *Devotions on the Greek New Testament: 52 Reflections to Inspire & Instruct,* vol 2 (Grand Rapids: Zondervan, 2017). See also Heinrich Bitzer, ed., *Light on the Path: Daily Scripture Readings in Hebrew and Greek* (Grand Rapids: Baker, 1982); and David W. Baker and Elaine A. Heath, with Morven Baker, *More Light on the Path: Daily Scripture Readings in Hebrew and Greek* (Grand Rapids: Baker, 1998).

[12] Campbell, *Advances in the Study of Greek* (see chap. 6, n. 24).

expectations, goals, and how those matters will be reported to your accountability partner. Have repercussions for failing to meet your goals—buying an expensive Greek resource for your accountability partner, for example!

- Take (or audit) an online or intensive Greek exegesis course at a seminary or college. If you live near a college or seminary campus, choose an upper-level elective book study and preach through that book as you sit in the class.

- Sign up for the free daily two-minute Greek screencast at www. DailyDoseOfGreek.com. In each daily video, Rob Plummer reads, translates, and comments on one verse from the GNT.

5. Teach Greek. One of the best ways to learn something is to teach it. Teach Greek to your children, at a local Christian school, or at a Christian college or seminary. You can also volunteer to tutor Greek students in different settings. Create YouTube videos of yourself teaching Greek. Perhaps no one will watch them, but you will know the material better!

STRAYING FROM THE ROAD

In John Bunyan's classic book *Pilgrim's Progress*, the characters Christian and Hopeful stray from the road at one point, thinking they have found a shortcut. Upon discovering they are lost, Hopeful groans and cries out, "Oh, that I had kept on my way!"[13] Similarly, some currently eager Greek students will someday find themselves looking with shame upon their dust-covered GNTs, lamenting wasted months or years. The good news in such situations is that most students have retained more Greek than they realize, and the GNT is always there waiting to embrace returning apostates! Even if a student has to dig out his Elementary Greek grammar and begin by reviewing the alphabet, there is no shame! The most zealous students of the GNT are prodigals who have returned from the far country. If this is your story and you are reading this paragraph now, welcome back! Read some of the inspiring quotes below to strengthen and inspire you for the joyful journey ahead.[14]

---

[13] John Bunyan, *The Pilgrim's Progress: Complete and Unabridged* (n.p.: Barbour, 1993), 127.

[14] See also Jason S. DeRouchie, "The Profit of Employing the Biblical Languages: Scriptural and Historical Reflections," *Themelios* 37 (2012): 32–50. Available at https://thegospelcoalition. org/article/themelios-37-1/ (PDF: http://tgc-documents.s3.amazonaws.com/themelios/37-1/ Themelios37.1.pdf).

INSPIRING QUOTES: STUDYING THE GREEK NEW TESTAMENT

In his book on fasting and prayer, John Piper includes an extensive appendix of inspiring quotes. He writes, "Sometimes just a passing comment can have as much impact on us as a whole chapter of a book. It may be that God would use one of these brief statements to awaken in someone *A Hunger for God*."[15] Similarly, we, the authors of this textbook, hope the quotes below might awaken in you, the reader, a hunger for reading the GNT. For now, our task of helping you "go deeper" with NT Greek is done. We commend you to the Lord's grace as you strive to become workers who do not need to be ashamed because you are making every effort to handle God's word of truth accurately.

> *Be diligent to present yourself approved to God, a worker who doesn't need to be ashamed, correctly teaching the word of truth.*[16]
>
> the apostle Paul (died ca. AD 66/67)

> *It was not for empty fame or childish pleasure that in my youth I grasped at the polite literature of the ancients, and by late hours gained some slight mastery of Greek and Latin. It has been my cherished wish to cleanse the Lord's temple of barbarous ignorance, and to adorn it with treasures brought from afar, such as may kindle in hearts a warm love for the Scriptures.*[17]
>
> Erasmus (1466–1536)

> *In so far as we love the Gospel, to that extent let us study the ancient tongues. And let us notice that without the knowledge of the languages we can scarcely preserve the Gospel. Languages are the sheath which hides the sword of the Spirit, they are the chest in which this jewel is enclosed, the goblet holding this draught.*
>
> *So although the Faith and the Gospel may be proclaimed by preachers without the knowledge of languages, the preaching will be feeble and ineffective. But where the languages are studied, the proclamation will be fresh and powerful, the Scriptures will be searched, and the Faith will be constantly rediscovered through ever new words and deeds.*[18]
>
> Martin Luther (1483–1546)

---

[15] John Piper, *A Hunger for God: Desiring God Through Fasting and Prayer* (Wheaton: Crossway, 1997), 183.

[16] 2 Tim 2:15.

[17] Yamauchi, "Erasmus' Contributions to New Testament Scholarship," 8 (see chap. 1, n. 23), citing P. S. Allen, *Erasmus: Lectures and Wayfaring Sketches* (Oxford: Clarendon, 1934), 42–43.

[18] Quoted by John Héring, *The First Epistle of Saint Paul to the Corinthians*, trans. A. W. Heathcote and P. J. Allock (London: Epworth Press, 1962), vi. The quotes are drawn from Luther's essay, "To the Councilmen of All Cities in Germany That They Establish and Maintain Christian Schools" (1524), available in *Luther's Works*, vol. 45, 340–78.

In theology, too, it is important how education is performed. If any field of studies, then theology requires especially talent, training, and conscientiousness. The aroma of God's salve supersedes all the aromas of human knowledge. Led by the Holy Spirit, but accompanied by humanistic studies, one should proceed to theology. But since the Bible is written in part in Hebrew and in part in Greek . . . we drink from the stream of both—we must learn these languages, unless we want to be "silent" persons as theologians. Once we understand the significance and the weight of the words, the true meaning of Scripture will light up for us as the midday sun. Only if we have clearly understood the language will we clearly understand the content if we put our minds to the [Greek and Hebrew] sources, we will begin to understand Christ rightly.[19]

Melanchthon (1497–1560)

Do I understand Greek and Hebrew? Otherwise, how can I undertake, as every Minister does, not only to explain books which are written therein but to defend them against all opponents? Am I not at the mercy of everyone who does understand, or even pretends to understand, the original? For which way can I confute his pretense? Do I understand the language of the Old Testament? critically? at all? Can I read into English one of David's Psalms, or even the first chapter of Genesis? Do I understand the language of the New Testament? Am I a critical master of it? Have I enough of it even to read into English the first chapter of St. Luke? If not, how many years did I spend at school? How many at the University? And what was I doing all those years? Ought not shame to cover my face?[20]

John Wesley (1703–1791)

No man can be a theologian who is not first a philologian. He who is no grammarian is no divine.[21]

A. M. Fairbairn (1838–1912)

---

[19] Cited by Scott Hafemann, as part of "The SBJT Forum: Profiles in Expository Preaching" *SBJT* 3, no. 2 (Summer 1999): 89, quoting Melanchthon's inaugural address on "The Reform of the Education of Youth" (1518), cited in Hans Joachin Hillerbrand, ed., *The Reformation: A Narrative History Related by Contemporary Observers and Participants*, new ed. (Grand Rapids: Baker, 1987), 59–60.

[20] John Wesley, *The Works of the Rev. John Wesley: With the Last Corrections of the Author*, vol. 10 (London: Wesleyan Conference Office, 1872), 491. Minor changes were made to the spelling and punctuation of this quote.

[21] Address before the Baptist Theological College at Glasgow, reported in *The British Weekly*, April 26, 1906, as cited by A. T. Robertson, x.

"At the Classroom Door" (a poem)

Lord, at Thy word opens yon door, inviting
Teacher and taught to feast this hour with Thee;
Opens a Book where God in human writing
Thinks His deep thoughts, and dead tongues live for me.
Too dread the task, too great the duty calling,
Too heavy far the weight is laid on me!
O if mine own thought should on Thy words falling
Mar the great message, and men hear not Thee!
Give me Thy voice to speak, Thine ear to listen,
Give me Thy mind to grasp Thy mystery;
So shall my heart throb, and my glad eyes glisten,
Rapt with the wonders Thou dost show to me.[22]

J. H. Moulton (1863–1917)

I have never looked into the Greek New Testament five minutes without
finding something I never saw before.[23]

A. T. Robertson (1863–1934)

The more a theologian detaches himself from the basic Hebrew and
Greek text of Holy Scripture, the more he detaches himself from the
source of real theology! And real theology is the foundation of a fruitful
and blessed ministry.[24]

Heinrich Bitzer (1900–1980)

---

[22] Poem printed on unnumbered front page of the first separately published fascicle of Moulton, *A Grammar of New Testament Greek*, vol. 2, part 1, "General Introduction: Sounds and Writing," ed. Wilbert Francis Howard (Edinburgh: T&T Clark, 1919). The poem, written in Bangalore, India (where Moulton was serving as a missionary) is dated February 21, 1917.

[23] Everett Gill, *A. T. Robertson: A Biography* (New York: Macmillan, 1943), 189.

[24] Bitzer, *Light on the Path*, 10.

APPENDIX 1:

//////////////

FREQUENT NEW TESTAMENT VOCABULARY

(WORDS OCCURRING MORE THAN 50X IN THE NT IN ORDER OF FREQUENCY = 310 WORDS)

ὁ, ἡ, τό	the (19,864)
καί	and, even, also, but (8,998)
αὐτός, ή, ό	he, she, it; self, same (5,597)
σύ, ὑμεῖς	you (sg); you (pl) (2,900)
δέ	but, and, rather, now (2,788)
ἐν	in, on, at, to, by, among, with (2,752)
ἐγώ, ἡμεῖς	I; we (2,570)
εἰμί	I am, exist (2,463)
λέγω	I say, speak, call (2,353)
εἰς	into, in, to, for (1,768)
οὐ	not (with ind verbs and positive answer questions) (1,621)
ὅς, ἥ, ὅ	who, which, what, that (1,407)
οὗτος, αὕτη, τοῦτο	this; he, she it (1,384)
θεός, ὁ	God, god (1,317)
ὅτι	that, because, for (1,296)
πᾶς, πᾶσα, πᾶν	every, all; everyone, everything (1,243)
μή	not (with non-ind verbs and negative answer questions) (1,042)

513

γάρ	for, because, so, then (1,041)
Ἰησοῦς, ὁ	Jesus, Joshua (918)
ἐκ	from, (out) of, away from (914)
ἐπί	on (gen); on, at in (dat); on, to, for (acc) (890)
κύριος, ὁ	lord, master, sir, Lord (716)
ἔχω	I have, possess, hold (708)
πρός	for (gen); at (dat); to, for, against, with, at, by (acc) (700)
γίνομαι	I become, come, exist, am born (669)
διά	through, during, with, at, by (gen); because of (acc) (667)
ἵνα	That, in order that, so that (663)
ἀπό	(away) from, with, for (646)
ἀλλά	but, yet, rather, nevertheless (638)
ἔρχομαι	I come, go (631)
ποιέω	I do, practice, make (568)
τίς, τί	who? which? what? why? (554)
ἄνθρωπος, ὁ	man, human being, husband (550)
τις, τι	someone, anyone, certain one, something (533)
Χριστός, ὁ	Messiah, Christ, Anointed One (529)
ὡς	as, like, that, about (504)
εἰ	if, since, whether (502)
οὖν	so, then, therefore, consequently (498)
κατά	down, against (gen); according to, along (acc) (473)
μετά	with, among, against (gen); after (acc) (469)
ὁράω	I see, perceive (452)
ἀκούω	I hear, listen, obey (428)
πολύς, πολλή, πολύ	much, many, large, great (416)
δίδωμι	I give, grant (415)
πατήρ, πατρός, ὁ	father, Father, ancestor, forefather (413)
ἡμέρα, ἡ	day, time (389)
πνεῦμα, -ατος, τό	spirit, Spirit, wind, breath (379)
υἱός, ὁ	son, Son, descendent, child (377)
εἷς, μία, ἕν	one, single (345)
ἀδελφός, ὁ	brother, fellow believer (343)
ἤ	or, than (343)
ἐάν	if, when (333)
περί	about, concerning (gen); around, near (acc) (333)
λόγος, ὁ	word, Word, message, statement, account (330)
ἑαυτοῦ	(of) himself, herself, itself (319)
οἶδα	I know, am acquainted with, understand (318)

λαλέω	I speak, say (296)
οὐρανός, ὁ	heaven, sky (273)
μαθητής, ὁ	disciple, follower (261)
λαμβάνω	I take, receive, seize (258)
γῆ, ἡ	earth, land, ground (250)
μέγας, μεγάλη, μέγα	large, great, important (243)
πίστις, -εως, ἡ	faith, belief, trust, faithfulness, doctrine (243)
πιστεύω	I believe (in), have faith (in), trust, entrust (241)
ἐκεῖνος	that (person) (240)
οὐδείς, οὐδεμία, οὐδέν	no one, nothing, no (234)
ἅγιος	holy, saints (pl) (233)
ἀποκρίνομαι	I answer, reply (231)
ὄνομα, -ατος, τό	name, title, reputation (228)
γινώσκω	I know, understand, perceive, acknowledge (222)
ὑπό	by (gen); under, below (acc) (220)
ἐξέρχομαι	I go out, come out (218)
ἀνήρ, ἀνδρός, ὁ	man, husband (216)
γυνή, -αικός, ἡ	woman, wife, bride (215)
τέ	and, so (215)
δύναμαι	I can, am able (210)
θέλω	I will, want, desire, wish (208)
οὕτως	in this manner, thus, so (208)
ἰδού	see! behold! look! (200)
Ἰουδαῖος	Jewish; a Jew (195)
εἰσέρχομαι	I come in, go in, enter (194)
νόμος, ὁ	law, rule, principle (194)
παρά	from (gen); with, beside (dat); at, on (acc) (194)
γράφω	I write, record (191)
κόσμος, ὁ	world, earth, universe; adornment (186)
καθώς	as, just as, even as (182)
μέν	on the one hand, indeed (179)
χείρ, χειρός, ἡ	hand, power (177)
εὑρίσκω	I find, discover; obtain (mid) (176)
ἄγγελος, ὁ	angel, messenger (175)
ὄχλος, ὁ	crowd, multitude (175)
ἁμαρτία, ἡ	sin, sinfulness (173)
ἔργον, τό	work, deed, action (169)
ἄν	(conditional particle used with sub) (166)
δόξα, ἡ	glory, majesty, splendor (166)
βασιλεία, ἡ	kingdom, reign, rule (162)

ἔθνος, -ους, τό	nation, gentiles, people (162)
πόλις, -εως, ἡ	city, town (162)
τότε	then (160)
ἐσθίω	I eat, consume (158)
Παῦλος, ὁ	Paul (158)
καρδία, ἡ	heart, mind (156)
Πέτρος, ὁ	Peter (156)
ἄλλος	other, another, different (155)
ἵστημι	I stand, set (155)
πρῶτος	first, earlier, foremost (155)
χάρις, -ιτος, ἡ	grace, favor, thanks (155)
πορεύομαι	I go, travel (153)
ὑπέρ	for, on behalf of, about (gen); above, beyond (acc) (150)
καλέω	I call, address, invite (148)
νῦν	now, the present (147)
σάρξ, σαρκός, ἡ	flesh, body, sinful nature (147)
ἕως	until, while (146)
ἐγείρω	I raise up, restore, awaken (144)
ὅστις, ἥτις, ὅ τι	who, whoever (144)
προφήτης, -ου, ὁ	prophet (144)
ἀγαπάω	I love (143)
ἀφίημι	I leave, forgive, divorce (143)
οὐδέ	and not, neither, nor (143)
λαός, ὁ	people, crowd (142)
σῶμα, -ατος, τό	body, corpse (142)
πάλιν	again, furthermore (141)
ζάω	I live, recover (140)
φωνή, ἡ	voice, sound, call (139)
δύο	two (135)
ζωή, ἡ	life (135)
Ἰωάννης, -ου, ὁ	John (135)
ἀποστέλλω	I send (out/away) (132)
βλέπω	I see, look at, watch (132)
ἀμήν	amen, truly, so be it (129)
νεκρός	dead, useless (128)
σύν	(together) with, accompany, besides (128)
δοῦλος, ὁ	slave (124)
ὅταν	whenever, when (123)
αἰών, -ῶνος, ὁ	eternity, age, world (122)

ἀρχιερεύς, -έως, ὁ	high priest (122)
βάλλω	I throw, cast, put (122)
θάνατος, ὁ	death (120)
δύναμις, -εως, ἡ	power, ability, miracle (119)
παραδίδωμι	I hand over, betray, entrust (119)
μένω	I remain, stay, abide, live (118)
ἀπέρχομαι	I go away, depart, pass by (117)
ζητέω	I seek, look for (117)
ἀγάπη, ἡ	love (116)
βασιλεύς, -έως, ὁ	king (115)
ἐκκλησία, ἡ	congregation, assembly, church (114)
ἴδιος	one's own, home, individually (114)
κρίνω	I judge, decide, condemn (114)
μόνος	only, alone, deserted (114)
οἶκος, ὁ	house(hold), home, family, temple (114)
ἀποθνήσκω	I die (111)
ὅσος	as much as, as many as, as great as (110)
ἀλήθεια, ἡ	truth, truthfulness (109)
μέλλω	I am about to, am going to, intend (109)
ὅλος	whole, all, entire (109)
παρακαλέω	I exhort, comfort, urge (109)
ἀνίστημι	I stand up, arise, raise, bring to life (108)
σῴζω	I save, preserve, heal, deliver (106)
ὥρα, ἡ	hour, moment, time (106)
ὅτε	when, while (103)
πῶς	how? in what way? (103)
ψυχή, ἡ	soul, life, living being (103)
ἀγαθός	good, useful (102)
ἐξουσία, ἡ	authority, right, power (102)
αἴρω	I take (up/away), raise (101)
δεῖ	it is necessary, one must (101)
ὁδός, -οῦ, ἡ	road, way, journey (101)
ἀλλήλων	one another, each other (100)
καλός	good, beautiful, useful (100)
ὀφθαλμός, ὁ	eye, sight (100)
τίθημι	I put, place, appoint (100)
ἕτερος	other, another, different (98)
τέκνον, τό	child, son, descendent (98)
Φαρισαῖος, ὁ	Pharisee (98)
αἷμα, -ατος, τό	blood, death (97)

ἄρτος, ὁ	bread, loaf, food (97)
γεννάω	I beget, give birth to (97)
διδάσκω	I teach (97)
ἐκεῖ	there, in that place (95)
περιπατέω	I walk, live, conduct myself (95)
φοβέω	I fear, am afraid, reverence (95)
ἐνώπιον	before, in the presence of (94)
τόπος, ὁ	place, location (94)
ἔτι	still, yet (93)
οἰκία, ἡ	house(hold), home, family (93)
πούς, ποδός, ὁ	foot (93)
δικαιοσύνη, ἡ	righteousness, justice (92)
εἰρήνη, ἡ	peace (92)
θάλασσα, ἡ	sea, lake (91)
κάθημαι	I sit (down), stay, live (91)
ἀκολουθέω	I follow, accompany (90)
ἀπόλλυμι	I destroy, ruin, lose (90)
μηδείς, μηδεμία, μηδέν	no; no one (90)
πίπτω	I fall (down), perish (90)
ἑπτά	seven (88)
οὔτε	neither, nor, and not (87)
ἄρχω	I rule; begin (mid) (86)
πληρόω	I (ful)fill, complete (86)
προσέρχομαι	I come/go to, approach (86)
καιρός, ὁ	time, season, age (85)
προσεύχομαι	I pray (85)
κἀγώ	and I, but I, I also (84)
μήτηρ, -τρός, ἡ	mother (83)
ὥστε	so that, in order that (83)
ἀναβαίνω	I go up, ascend (82)
ἕκαστος	each, every (82)
ὅπου	where, since (82)
ἐκβάλλω	I cast out, drive out, lead out (81)
καταβαίνω	I go down, descend (81)
μᾶλλον	more, rather (81)
ἀπόστολος, ὁ	apostle, messenger (80)
Μωϋσῆς, -έως, ὁ	Moses (80)
δίκαιος	righteous, just, right (79)
πέμπω	I send, appoint (79)
ὑπάγω	I go away, depart (79)

πονηρός	evil, bad, wicked, sick (78)
στόμα, -ατος, τό	mouth, speech (78)
ἀνοίγω	I open (77)
βαπτίζω	I immerse, dip, baptize (77)
Ἰερουσαλήμ, ἡ	Jerusalem (77)
σημεῖον, τό	sign, miracle, wonder (77)
ἐμός	my, mine (76)
εὐαγγέλιον, τό	good news, gospel (76)
μαρτυρέω	I bear witness, testify, approve (76)
πρόσωπον, τό	face, appearance, person (76)
ὕδωρ, -ατος, τό	water (76)
δώδεκα	twelve (75)
κεφαλή, ἡ	head, authority, source (75)
Σίμων, -ωνος, ὁ	Simon (75)
ἀποκτείνω	I kill, put to death (74)
χαίρω	I rejoice, am glad; greetings (74)
Ἀβραάμ, ὁ	Abraham (73)
πίνω	I drink (73)
φῶς, φωτός, τό	light (73)
αἰώνιος	eternal (71)
πῦρ, -ός, τό	fire (71)
αἰτέω	I ask (for), demand (70)
ἱερόν, τό	temple, sanctuary (70)
τηρέω	I keep, guard, obey (70)
ἄγω	I lead, bring (68)
Ἰσραήλ, ὁ	Israel (68)
ῥῆμα, -ατος, τό	word, saying, object (68)
σάββατον, τό	Sabbath, week (68)
τρεῖς, τρία	three (68)
ἐντολή, ἡ	commandment, command, law (67)
πιστός	faithful, reliable, believing, trusting (67)
πλοῖον, τό	boat, ship (67)
ἀπολύω	I release, dismiss, divorce (66)
καρπός, ὁ	fruit, crop, result (66)
πρεσβύτερος, ὁ	older, elder, presbyter (66)
φέρω	I bear, carry, endure (66)
φημί	I say, affirm (66)
εἴτε	if, whether (65)
γραμματεύς, -έως, ὁ	scribe, scholar, expert in the law (63)
δαιμόνιον, τό	demon, evil spirit (63)

ἔξω	outside, outer, out (63)
ἐρωτάω	I ask, request (63)
ὄρος, -ους, τό	mountain, hill (63)
δοκέω	I think, suppose, seem (62)
θέλημα, -ατος, τό	will, wish, desire (62)
θρόνος, ὁ	throne (62)
Ἱεροσόλυμα, ἡ/τά	Jerusalem (62)
ἀγαπητός	beloved, dear (61)
Γαλιλαία, ἡ	Galilee (61)
δοξάζω	I glorify, praise, honor (61)
ἤδη	now, already (61)
κηρύσσω	I proclaim, announce, preach (61)
νύξ, νυκτός, ἡ	night (61)
ὧδε	here, in this place (61)
ἱμάτιον, τό	garment, coat, robe (60)
προσκυνέω	I worship (60)
ὑπάρχω	I am, exist, am present (60)
ἀσπάζομαι	I greet, welcome (60)
Δαυὶδ, ὁ	David (59)
διδάσκαλος, ὁ	teacher (59)
λίθος, ὁ	stone (59)
συνάγω	I gather, bring together (59)
χαρά, ἡ	joy (59)
θεωρέω	I look at, perceive, see (58)
μέσος	middle (58)
τοιοῦτος, -αύτη, -οῦτον	of such a kind, such (57)
δέχομαι	I take, receive, welcome (56)
ἐπερωτάω	I ask (for) (56)
μηδέ	and not, but not, nor (56)
συναγωγή, ἡ	synagogue, assembly (56)
τρίτος	third (56)
ἀρχή, ἡ	beginning, origin, ruler (55)
κράζω	I cry out, call out (55)
λοιπός	remaining, rest, other (55)
Πιλᾶτος, ὁ	Pilate (55)
δεξιός	right (hand/side) (54)
εὐαγγελίζω	I announce good news, proclaim, preach (54)
οὐχί	not, no (used with positive answer questions) (54)
χρόνος, ὁ	time (54)
διό	therefore, for this reason (53)

ἐλπίς, -ίδος, ἡ	hope (53)
ὅπως	in order that, that, how (53)
παιδίον, τό	child, infant (53)
ἐπαγγελία, ἡ	promise, pledge (52)
ἔσχατος	last, end (52)
πείθω	I persuade, convince (52)
σπείρω	I sow (52)
εὐθύς	immediately, at once (51)
σοφία, ἡ	wisdom, insight (51)
γλῶσσα, ἡ	tongue, language (50)
γραφή, ἡ	writing, scripture (50)
κακός	bad, evil (50)
μακάριος	blessed, fortunate (50)
παραβολή, ἡ	parable, comparison, symbol (50)
τυφλός	blind (50)

APPENDIX 2:

/////////////////

NOUN AND ARTICLE CHARTS: A SURVEY OF 12 GRAMMARS

Some grammarians only discuss more unusual uses of the cases. The lack of a syntactical category under a particular author's name does not necessarily indicate the author's denial of that grammatical function. Category titles that are bold and underlined reflect the same nomenclature as those used in the present volume. Category titles that are bold indicate that the category is covered in the present volume but with different nomenclature. This only applies for the case categories chart, however (i.e., it does not apply to the article chart).

NOMINATIVE CASE CATEGORIES

ROBERTSON (1934)	DANA & MANTEY (1927)	MOULE (1953)	BDF (1961)	TURNER (1963)	ZERWICK (1963)
Predicate Nom.	The Subject Nom.	In Reference to a Person or Thing Which Is in Fact not the Subject of the Sentence	Nom. Used to Introduce Names	The Nom. "ad sensum"	Pendent Nom.
Unaltered in apposition	The Predicate Nom.		Parenthetical Nom.	Proper Nouns without Syntax	Nominative for Vocative
Nom. Absolute	Nom. of Appellation	In a Context Where an Acc. of Duration Would be Natural	Predicate Nom.	Nom. Is found in Parenthesis	
Parenthetic Nom.	The Independent Nom.			The Nom. with Time-designation	
In Exclamations	Nom. of Exclamation	Used for the Vocative			
Used as Vocative					

BROOKS & WINBERY (1979)	PORTER (1994)	YOUNG (1994)	WALLACE (1996)	BLACK (1998)	KÖSTENBERGER, MERKLE & PLUMMER
Subject Nom.	Subject	Subject Nom.	PRIMARY USES OF THE NOM.	Subject Nom.	MAJOR USES
Predicate Nom.	Predicate	Predicate Nom.	Subject	Predicate Nom.	Subject
Nom. of Appellation	Apposition	Nom. of Apposition	Predicate Nom.	Nom. of Address	Predicate Nom.
Independent Nom.	Nominal Clause (Absolute)	Nom. of Address	Nom. in Simple Apposition	Nom. Absolute	Apposition
Apposition	Independent Clause (Hanging)	Nom. of Appellation	GRAMMATICALLY INDEPENDENT USE OF THE NOM.	Nom. of Appellation	OTHER USES
	Direct Address and Names	Nom. Absolute	Nom. Absolute		Address
	Time	Adverbial Nom.	Nominativus Pendens (Pendent Nom.)		Appellation
			Parenthetic Nom.		Absolute
			Nom. in Proverbial Expressions		Hanging Nom.
			Nom. for Vocative		
			Nom. of Exclamation		
			NOMS. IN PLACE OF OBLIQUE CASES		
			Nom. of Appellation		
			Nom. in Apposition to Oblique Cases		
			Nom. after a Preposition		
			Nom. for Time		

GENITIVE CASE CATEGORIES

ROBERTSON (1934)	DANA & MANTEY (1927)	MOULE (1953)	BDF (1961)	TURNER (1963)	ZERWICK (1963)
GEN. (PROPER)	**GENITIVE CASE (PURE GEN.)**	**GEN. OF DEFINITION**	**THE ADNOMINAL GEN.**	**TRUE GEN.**	**GENERAL GEN.**
Local Use	Gen. of **Description**	Gen. of Time, Place, and Quantity	• **Gen. of Origin** and **Relationship**	Possessive Gen.	• <u>Subjective</u>
Temporal Use	Gen. of **Possession**	Subjective/Objective Gen.	• **Objective Gen.**	With Verbs and Verbal Adjectives	• <u>Objective</u>
With Substantives	Gen. of **Relationship**	Gen. of Separation	• The **Partitive** Gen.	Local and Temporal Ablatival Gen.	**Hebrew Gen.**
• **Possessive Gen.**	The Adverbial Gen.	Partitive Gen.	• **The Gen. of Quality**		**A Certain Intimate Relation**
• **Attributive** Gen.	Of Time	Gen. Absolute	• Gen. of Direction or Purpose		**Epexegetic Gen.**
• Predicate Gen.	Of Place		• **Gen. of Content and Appositive Gen.**		Multiplicity of Gens.
• **Apposition** or Definition	Of Reference		**The Adverbial Gen.**		Gen. Absolute
• **Subjective Gen.**	Gen. with Nouns of Action		**The Gen. with Adjectives and Adverbs**		
• **Objective Gen.**	Subjective Gen.		<u>**The Gen. of Comparison**</u>		
• Gen. of **Relationship**	Objective Gen.		The Gen. of **<u>Place and Time</u>**		
• **Partitive** Gen.	Gen. of Apposition				
With Adjectives	Partitive Gen.				
With Adverbs and Prepositions	Gen. Absolute				
With Verbs	**ABLATIVE CASE (ABLATIVE GEN.)**				
Gen. of the Infinitive	Abl. of Separation				
The Gen. Absolute	Abl. of Source				
ABLATIVE	Abl. of Means				
Rare w/ Substantives	Abl. of Comparison				
With Adjectives					
With Prepositions					
With Verbs					

GENITIVE CASE CATEGORIES (CONTINUED)

BROOKS & WINBERY (1979)

THE GENITIVE
Gen. of **Description**
Gen. of **Possession**
Gen. of Relationship
The Adverbial Gen.
- Of **Time**
- Of **Measure**
- Of Place
- Of Reference

Gen. with Nouns of Action
- **Subjective Gen.**
- **Objective Gen.**

Gen. of Apposition
Gen. Absolute
Gen. of Advantage
Gen. of Association
Gen. of Attendant Circumstances
Gen. of Oaths
Gen. of Root Idea or
Gen. of Direct Object

THE ABLATIVE
Abl. of **Separation**
Abl. of **Source**
Abl. of **Agency**
Abl. of **Means**
Abl. of **Comparison**
Abl. of Cause

PORTER (1994)

Quality, Definition or **Description**
Partitive Use
Possession, Ownership, Origin or **Source**
Apposition
Objective Gen.
Subjective Gen.
Comparison
Value or **Price**
Time or **Space**
Object

YOUNG (1994)

GENS. FUNCTIONING AS ADJECTIVAL PHRASES
Gen. of **Description**
Attributive Gen.
Gen. of **Possession**
Gen. of **Relationship**
Gen. of **Content**
Gen. of **Material**
Partitive Gen.

GENS. FUNCTIONING IN DEEP STRUCTURE EVENT CLAUSES
Subjective Gen.
Objective Gen.
Verbal Gen.
Compound Verbal Gen.

GENS. FUNCTIONING AS ADVERBIAL PHRASES
Gen. of **Time**
Gen. of Space
Gen. of Disassociation
Gen. of Manner
Gen. of **Comparison**
Gen. of **Price**
Gen. of Reason
Gen. of Purpose
Gen. of **Means**
Gen. of Reference

WALLACE (1996)

ADJECTIVAL GEN.
Descriptive Gen. ("Aporetic Gen.")
Possessive Gen.
Gen. of **Relationship**
Partitive Gen. ("**Wholative**")
Attributive Gen. (Hebrew Gen., Gen. of Quality)
Attributed Gen.
Gen. of **Material**
Gen. of **Content**
Gen. in Simple **Apposition**
Gen. of **Apposition** (Epexegetical Gen., Gen. of Definition)
Gen. of Destination (a.k.a. Direction) or Purpose
Predicate Gen.
Gen. of Subordination
Gen. of Production/Producer
Gen. of Product

ABLATIVAL GEN.
Gen. of **Separation**
Gen. of **Source** (or Origin)
Gen. of **Comparison**

BLACK (1998)

Gen. of **Possession**
Gen. of **Relationship**
Partitive Gen.
Subjective Gen.
Objective Gen.
Gen. Absolute
Gen. of Direct Object
Gen. of **Material or Contents**
Descriptive Gen.
Gen. of Apposition (epexegetical gen.)
Gen. of **Comparison**
Gen. of **Time**
Gen. of Measure
Gen. of **Source**

KÖSTENBERGER, MERKLE, & PLUMMER

ADJECTIVAL USES
Description
Attributive
Possession
Relationship
Source
Material or Content
Partitive

VERBAL USES
Subjective
Objective

ADVERBIAL USES
Time or Place
Separation
Means or Agency
Comparison
Price

OTHER USES
Gen. of Apposition
Gen. of Direct Object

GENITIVE CASE CATEGORIES (CONTINUED)

BROOKS & WINBERY (1979)	PORTER (1994)	YOUNG (1994)	WALLACE (1996)	BLACK (1998)	KÖSTENBERGER, MERKLE, & PLUMMER
Abl. of Rank Abl. of Opposition Abl. of Purpose Abl. of Exchange Partitive Abl.	Quality, Definition or **Description** **Partitive** Use **Possession**, Ownership, Origin or **Source** **Apposition** **Objective Gen.** **Subjective Gen.** **Comparison** Value or **Price** **Time** or **Space** Object	**GENS. FUNCTIONING AS NOUN PHRASES** Gen. Subject Gen. of **Apposition** Gen. **Direct Object**	**VERBAL GEN. (I.E., GEN. RELATED TO A VERBAL NOUN)** **Subjective Gen.** **Objective Gen.** Plenary Gen. **ADVERBIAL GEN.** Gen. of **Price** or Value or Quantity Gen. of **Time** (within which or during which) Gen. of **Place** (where or within which) Gen. of **Means** Gen. of **Agency** Gen. Absolute Gen. of Reference Gen. of Association **AFTER CERTAIN WORDS** Gen. after Certain Verbs (as a Direct Object) Gen. after Certain Adjectives (and Adverbs) Gen. after Certain Nouns Gen. after Certain Prepositions		

DATIVE CASE CATEGORIES

ROBERTSON (1934)

LOCATIVE CASE

Place

Time
- Loc. with Adjectives
- Loc. with Verbs
- Loc. with Substantives
- Loc. with Prepositions

INSTRUMENTAL CASE

Place

Time

Associative Idea
- With Words of Likeness and Identity

Manner
- Degree of Difference

Cause

Means
- With Prepositions

THE DAT. (TRUE) CASE
- With Substantives
- With Adjectives
- With Adverbs and Prepositions
- With Verbs
- **Indirect Object**
- **Dativus Commodi vel Incommodi**
- **Direct Object**
- With Intransitive Verbs
- **Possession**
- Infinitive as Final Dat.
- **Dat. of the Agent**
- Dat. because of Prepositions

DANA & MANTEY (1927)

THE DAT. CASE (PURE DAT.)
- Dat. of **Indirect Obj.**
- **Dat. of Advantage or Disadvantage**
- **Dat. of Possession**
- Dat. of **Reference**

THE LOCATIVE CASE (LOCAL DAT.)
- Loc. of **Place**
- Loc. of **Time**
- Loc. of **Sphere**

THE INSTRUMENTAL CASE (INSTRUMENTAL DAT.)
- Instr. of **Means**
- Instr. of **Cause**
- Instr. of **Manner**
- Instr. of Measure
- Instr. of **Association**
- Instr. of **Agency**

MOULE (1953)

ABLATIVAL USES
- **Temporal Uses**
- Metaphorically **Local**
- **Instrumental** Uses
- Of **Measure**
- An Absolute Use

HARD TO CLASS
- **Content**
- **Accompaniment**
- **Causal**

NATURAL TO A LATINIST
- With Certain Verbs
- *Dativus Commodi*

BDF (1961)

THE DAT. PROPER
- The Dat. as a Necessary Complement
- **Dat. of Advantage and Disadvantage**
- Dat. of **Possession**
- Εἶναι with the Dat. and Predicate Nouns
- **Dat. of Agent**
- The Ethical Dat.

THE INSTRUMENTAL-ASSOCIATIVE DAT.
- **The Associative Dat. with Verbs**
- **The Associative Dat. with Adjectives and Adverbs**
- In the Genuinely *Instrumental* Sense
- The Dat. of **Cause**
- The Dat. of **Respect**
- **The Associative Dat.**

THE LOCATIVE DAT.
- **The Dat. of Place**
- **The Temporal Dat. (When?)**
- **The Temporal Dat. (How long?)**

THE DAT. WITH COMPOUND VERBS AND THEIR DERIVATIVES

TURNER (1963)

- As **Indirect Object**
- **The Dat. of Advantage and Disadvantage**
- **Reference**
- *"Davitus Relationis"*
- Ethical Dat.
- Use with Εἶναι
- **Dat. of Possession**
- Use with Εἰμί
- **Dat. of Agent**
- **Instrumental** Dat.
- **Associative Dat.**
- **Cognate Dat.**
- **Cause**
- With Compound Verbs
- **Locative**
- **Temporal**

ZERWICK (1963)

- With Verbs
- **The Dat. of Respect**
- **The Dat. of Time**
- **The Dat. of Interest**
- **The Dat. of Place**
- **The Dat. of Cause**
- **The Dat. of Agent**
- **The Dat. of Manner**
- **Cognate Dat.**
- Accompanied by the Preposition ἐν
- Parables

DATIVE CASE CATEGORIES (CONTINUED)

BROOKS & WINBERY (1979)	PORTER (1994)	YOUNG (1994)	WALLACE (1996)	BLACK (1998)	KÖSTENBERGER, MERKLE, & PLUMMER
The Dat.	Respect (**Association, Possession, Sphere**)	Dats. Functioning as Noun Phrases	**Pure Dat.**	Dat. of **Indirect Object**	Pure Dat.
Dat. of **Indirect Object**		Dat. of **Indirect Object**	Dat. of **Indirect** Object	**Instrumental Dat.**	**Indirect Object**
Dat. of Advantage and Disadvantage	**Advantage or Disadvantage**	Dat. of **Direct Object**	Dat. of **Interest** (Including Advantage and Disadvantage)	**Locative Dat.**	**Personal Interest**
Dat. of **Possession**	Instrument, Agent, **Cause, Means or Manner**	Dat. Subject	Dat. of **Reference/Respect**	Dat. of **Time**	**Reference or Respect**
Dat. of **Reference** or Dat. of **Respect**		Dat. of **Apposition**	Ethical Dat. (Dat. of Feeling)	Dat. of **Possession**	**Possession**
Dat. of Root Idea or Dat. of Direct Object	**Time** or **Space** (Locative)		**Dat. of Destination**	Dat. of **Direct Object**	LOCATIVE DAT.
	Object	**DATS. FUNCTIONING AS ADVERBIAL PHRASES**	Dat. of Recipient	Dat. of **Reference**	**Place**
THE LOCATIVE		Dat. of **Reference**	Dat. of **Possession**	DAT. OF ADVANTAGE OR DISADVANTAGE	**Sphere**
Loc. of **Place**		Dat. of **Sphere**	Dat. of Thing Possessed		**Time**
Loc. of **Time**		Dat. of **Time**	Predictive Dat.	Dat. of **Manner**	INSTRUMENTAL DAT.
Loc. of **Sphere**		Dat. of **Means**	Dat. in Simple **Apposition**	Dat. of **Association**	**Means**
		Dat. of **Agency**		Dat. of **Agency**	**Agency**
THE INSTRUMENTAL		Dat. of **Manner**	LOCAL DAT. USES		**Association**
Instr. of **Means**		**Dat. of Degree**	Dat. of **Place**		**Manner**
Instr. of **Cause**		Dat. of **Association**	Dat. of **Sphere**		**Material or Content**
Instr. of **Manner**		**Dat. of Reason**	Dat. of **Time** (When)		OTHER USES
Instr. of Measure			Dat. of Rule		**Cause**
Instr. of **Association**		**DATS. FUNCTIONING AS ADJECTIVAL PHRASES**	INSTRUMENTAL DAT. USES		**Cognate Dat.**
Instr. of **Agency**		Dat. of **Possession**	Dat. of **Association** (Accompaniment, Comitative)		**Apposition**
		Dat. of Relationship	Dat. of **Manner** (or Adverbial Dative)		**Direct Object**
		Dat. of Identification	Dat. of **Means**/Instrument		
			Dat. of **Agency**		
			Dat. of Measure/Degree of Difference		
			Dat. of **Cause**		
			Cognate Dat.		
			Dat. of **Material**		
			Dat. of **Content**		
			THE USE OF THE DAT. AFTER CERTAIN WORDS		
			Dat. **Direct Object**		
			Dat. after Certain Nouns		
			Dat. after Certain Adjectives		
			Dat. after Certain Prepositions		

ACCUSATIVE CASE CATEGORIES

ROBERTSON (1934)	DANA & MANTEY (1927)	MOULE (1953)	BDF (1961)	TURNER (1963)	ZERWICK (1963)
With Verbs of Motion	The Acc. of **Dir. Obj.**	**Cognate Acc.**	**Simple Acc. of the Object**	**The Simple Acc.**	**With Transitive Verbs**
Extent of Space	The Adverbial Acc.	**Double Acc:**	**Simple Acc. of Content**	Content, or internal object	With Intransitive Verbs used Transitively
Extent of Time	• Of **Measure**	Acc. of **Respect** or Reference	**(Cognate Acc.)**	(" **cognate acc.** ")	Acc. with the Passive
With Transitive Verbs	• Of **Manner**	• Extent of Space	**The Double Acc:**	**Double Acc:**	**Acc. of Respect**
Cognate Acc:	• Of Reference	• Extent of Time	The Acc. with the Passive	Acc. with Passive	**Adverbial Use**
Double Acc:	**Cognate Acc:**	Acc. Used Predicatively	Acc. of **Respect** and Adverbial Acc.	Adverbial Acc.	
• the Predicate Acc.	**Double Acc:**	Acc. in **Apposition** to a Sentence	**Acc. of Extent**	(1) **Manner**	
• the Acc. of the Person and of the Thing	• Personal and Imper-sonal Object	Anticipatory Acc.		(2) **Extent**	
With Passive Verbs	• Direct and Predicate Object			(3) Point of Time	
The Adverbial Acc. [General Reference]	Acc. Absolute				
The Acc. by Antiptosis	Acc. with Oaths				
The Acc. by Inverse Attraction					
Acc. with the Infinitive					
Acc. Absolute					
Acc. with Prepositions					

ACCUSATIVE CASE CATEGORIES (CONTINUED)

BROOKS & WINBERY (1979)	PORTER (1994)	YOUNG (1994)	WALLACE (1996)	BLACK (1998)	KÖSTENBERGER, MERKLE, & PLUMMER
Acc. of **Direct Object**	**Object**	Acc. of **Direct Object**	**SUBSTANTIVAL USES OF THE ACC.**	Acc. of **Direct Object**	**SUBSTANTIVAL USES**
Cognate Acc.	**Double**	**Double Acc.**	Acc. **Direct Object**	**Double Acc.**	**Direct Object**
Double Acc.	**Respect (manner,** adverbial)	**Cognate Acc.**	**Double Accs.:**	**Acc. of Time**	**Cognate Acc.**
• Personal and Impersonal Objects	Time or Space	Acc. of Oaths	• Double Acc. of the Person and Thing	Adverbial Acc.	**Double Acc.**
• Primary and Secondary Objects	**Apposition** (independent)	Acc. **Subject of Infinitive**	• Double Acc. of Object-Complement		**Subject of Infinitive**
Adverbial Acc. of Measure	Absolute	Adverbial Accs.	**Cognate Acc.** (or Acc. of the Inner Object)		**Apposition**
Adverbial Acc. of Manner		(1) **Manner**	Predicate Acc.		**ADVERBIAL USES**
Adverbial Acc. of Reference or Adverbial Acc. of Respect		(2) **Reference**	**Acc. Subj. of the Infinitve**		**Measure**
Acc. with Oaths		(3) **Space**	Acc. of Retained Object		**Manner**
Acc. Absolute		(4) **Time**	Pendent Acc. (*Accusativum Pendens*)		**Respect**
Acc. of Purpose		Acc. of **Apposition**	Acc. in Simple **Apposition**		
Acc. of Result		Acc. Absolutes	**ADVERBIAL USES OF THE ACC.**		
Acc. of Cause			Adverbial Acc. (Acc. of **Manner**)		
Acc. of Possession			Acc. of **Measure** (or Extent of Time or Space)		
Acc. of Comparison			Acc. of **Respect** or (General) Reference		
Acc. of Relationship			Acc. in Oaths		
Predicate Acc.			Acc. after Certain Prepositions		

VOCATIVE CASE CATEGORIES

ROBERTSON (1934)	DANA & MANTEY (1927)	MOULE (1953)	BDF (1961)	TURNER (1963)	ZERWICK (1963)
The Use of ὦ with the Voc. Adjectives Used with the Voc. Apposition to the Voc. Voc. in Predicate The Article with the Voc.	**Direct Address**	**The True Voc.** The True Voc. Being Supplanted by the Nom.	**The Use of ὦ (ὤ)** Nom. Instead of Voc.	**The Use of ὦ** Nom. Form Instead of Voc.	Voc. with ὦ

BROOKS & WINBERY (1979)	PORTER (1994)	YOUNG (1994)	WALLACE (1996)	BLACK (1998)	KÖSTENBERGER, MERKLE, & PLUMMER
Person or Thing Being **Addressed** Sometimes Appears in What Appears to Be a Nom. Form	**Direct Address**	**Direct Address**	**Direct Address** Exclamation Apposition	**Direct Address**	**Direct Address**

ARTICLE CATEGORIES

ROBERTSON (1934)	DANA & MANTEY (1927)	MOULE (1953)	BDF (1961)	TURNER (1963)	ZERWICK (1963)
Varied Usages of the Art. With Substantives • Proper Names • Second Mention (anaphoric) With Adjectives With Participles With the Infinitive With Adverbs With Prepositional Phrases With Single Words or Whole Sentences With Genitive Alone Nouns in the Predicate Distributive Nominative with the Art. = Vocative As the Equivalent of a Possessive Pron. With Possessive Pronouns With Αὐτός With Demonstratives With Ὅλος, Πᾶς (Ἅπας) With Πολύς Ἄκρος, Ἥμισυς, Ἔσχατος, Μέσος With Ἄλλος and Ἕτερος Μόνος **POSITION WITH ATTRIBUTIVES** With Adjectives With Genitives	The Regular Use of the Art. To Denote Individuals To Denote Previous Reference With Abstract Nouns With Proper Names The Generic Use With Pronouns With Other Parts of Speech The Special Uses of the Art. With Nouns Connected by καί As a Pronoun • Demonstrative Pronoun • Alternative Pronoun • Possessive Pronoun • Relative Pronoun With the Subject in a Copulative Sentence The Absence of the Art. The Position of the Art. Attributive Position Predicate Position Repeated with Adjective With the Participle Demonstrative Pronouns in the Predicate Position	Simple Definition With Participles and Adjectives in Place of a Relative Clause To Turn Words and Phrases into Virtual Nouns The Art. with Multiple Substantives To Treat a Whole Clause as a Single Entity Practically Equivalent to a Demonstrative Pronoun The Use or Non-use of the Art. Apollonius's Canon Colwell's Rule Renewed Mention Semitic Idiom	Ὁ ἡ τό as a Pronoun The Art. with a Substantive • With Appellatives The Art. with Abstract Nouns The Art. with Nouns Governing a Genitive The Art. with Proper Names The Art. with Adjectives Used as Substantives The Substantivizing Art. with Numerals, Adverbs, etc. • The Art. with Numerals • With Substantivized Adverbs and Prepositional Expressions • The Art. with Quotations and Indirect Questions. The Art. with Appositives The Art. with Two or More Attributives The Art. and the Position of Attributive • Attributive and Predicate Adjective • The Art. with an Attributive Genitive • With Prepositional Attributives The Art. with Predicate Nouns The Art. with Pronouns and Pronominal Adjectives • With Pronouns • With πᾶς, ὅλος, etc. The Art. with Two or More Substantives Connected by καί	The Art. with Adjectives • Individual Sense • Generic Sense • Abstract Ideas The Art. with Attributive Adverbs The Art. with Prepositional Phrases The Art. with Genitives of Nouns The Ellipse of Various Nouns Substantival Art.	The Function of the Art. The Omission of the Art. The Repetition of the Art. The Distinction between the Attributive and Predicative Use of Adjectives

ARTICLE CATEGORIES (CONTINUED)

BROOKS & WINBERY (1979)	PORTER (1994)	YOUNG (1994)	WALLACE (1996)	BLACK (1998)	KÖSTENBERGER, MERKLE, & PLUMMER

To Identify or Denote Persons or Things and to Distinguish Them from All Others
 	
To Indicate that a Substantive Is Monadic
 	
To Denote Previous Reference
 	
To Distinguish One Quality from Another
 	
To Call Special Attention to a Proper Name
 	
To Distinguish One Class or Group from Another, to Indicate that a Substantive is Typical or Representative of Its Class or Group
 	
To Indicate the Relationship of Substantives Connected by καί
 	
To Express the Idea of a Pronoun:
• A Demonstrative Pronoun
• An Alternative Pronoun
• A Possessive Pronoun
• A Relative Pronoun
 	
To Distinguish the Subject Nominative from the Predicate Nominative in a Sentence Containing a Linking Verb
	A SCHEME FOR THE ART.
	
	Usage with the Art. (Articular or Arthrous)
	• 'Particular' use of the Art.
	• 'Categorical' use of the Art.
	
	Usage without the Art. (Anarthrous)
	• 'Non-particular' (Qualitative) Use without the Art.
	• 'Individual' Use without the Art.
	
	Distinctive Uses of the Art.
	
	Anaphoric Usage
	
	Usage with Names of Places and People
	
	Usage with Abstract Substantives
	
	Usage with Adjectives, Participles and Phrases
	
	Usage with Linking Verbs
	
	The Granville Sharp Rule
	
	Apollonius's Canon
		FUNCTIONS OF THE ART.
		
		The Art. Used to Make a Noun Definite
		• Distinguishing Persons or Things
		• Distinguishing Classes
		• Particularizing an Abstract Quality
		
		The Art. Used to Refer to a Previous Reference
		
		The Art. Used as a Pronoun:
		• Possessive Pronoun
		• Alternative Pronoun
		• Personal Pronoun
		• Demonstrative Pronoun
		• Relative Pronoun
		
		The Art. Used to Construct a Noun Phrase
		• Preceding an Adverb
		• Preceding a Genitive
		• Preceding a Prepositional Phrase
		• Preceding a Clause
		• Preceding Other Elements
		
		The Art. Used with Monadic Nouns and Proper Names
		• Monadic Nouns
		• Proper Nouns
		
		The Article with Nouns Connected with καί
		
		Arts. Used in Copulative Sentences
			**PART I
			REGULAR USES**
			
			As a Pronoun ([partially] Independent Use)
			• Personal Pronoun
			• Alternative Personal Pronoun
			• Relative Pronoun
			• Possessive Pronoun
			
			With Substantives (Dependent or Modifying Use)
			• Individualizing Art.
			  » Simple Identification
			  » Anaphoric (Previous Reference)
			  » Kataphoric (Following Reference)
			  » Deictic ("Pointing" Art.)
			  » Par Excellence
			  » Monadic ("One of a Kind" or "Unique" Art.)
			  » Well-Known ("Celebrity" or "Familiar" Art.)
			  » Abstract (i.e., the Art. with Abstract Nouns)
			• Generic Art. (Categorical Art.)
			
			As a Substantiver
			
			(With Certain Parts of Speech)
			
			As a Function Marker
			
			ABSENCE OF THE ART.
			
			Indefinite
			
			Qualitative
				GENERAL USES OF THE ART.
				
				To Make a Substantive Particular
				
				Anaphoric Use
				
				Proper Names
				
				Abstract Nouns
				
				Make a Substantive Representative of a Category of Items
				
				As a Possessive Pronoun
				
				To Identify the Case of Indeclinable Nouns
				
				As a Personal Pronoun
				
				As a Mild Relative Pronoun
				
				SPECIAL RULES FOR THE ART.
				
				Colwell's Rule
				
				The Granville Sharp Rule
					WITH SUBSTANTIVES
					
					Identification
					
					Par Excellence
					
					Monadic
					
					With Abstract Nouns
					
					Previous Reference
					
					Generic
					
					AS A PRONOUN
					
					As Personal Pronoun
					
					As Relative Pronoun
					
					As Possessive Pronoun
					
					As Demonstrative Pronoun
					
					As Alternative Pronoun
					
					ABSENCE OF ART.
					
					Indefinite
					
					Qualitative
					
					Definite
					
					SPECIAL RULES
					
					Granville Sharp Rule
					
					Colwell's Rule
					
					Apollonius's Canon

ARTICLE CATEGORIES (CONTINUED)

BROOKS & WINBERY (1979)	PORTER (1994)	YOUNG (1994)	WALLACE (1996)	BLACK (1998)	KÖSTENBERGER, MERKLE, & PLUMMER
To Indicate that a Nominative is Being Used as a Vocative To Indicate Grammatical Relationships To Take the Place of a Noun	Special Constructions • Art. Functioning Pronominally • Μέν . . . δέ • Ambiguous Constructions • Omission of the Art. in Prepositional Phrases	REASONS FOR ANARTHROUS CONSTRUCTIONS Abstract Nouns Monadic and Proper Nouns Nouns in Genitive Constructions Objects of Prepositions Technical Expressions To Make a Noun Non-differentiated To Focus on the Quality of the Noun	Definite • Proper Names • Object of a Preposition • With Ordinal Numbers • Predicate Nominative • Complement in Object-Complement Construction • Monadic Nouns • Abstract Nouns • A Genitive Construction (Apollonius's Corollary) • With a Pronominal Adjective • Generic Nouns PART II SPECIAL USES AND NON-USES OF THE ART. Anarthrous Pre-Verbal Predicate Nominatives (Involving Colwell's Rule) The Art. with Multiple Substantives Connected by Καί (Granville Sharp Rule and Related Constructions)		

NAME INDEX

////////////////////

537

SUBJECT INDEX

////////////////

SCRIPTURE INDEX

////////////////